OCTAVIA HILL'S
LETTERS TO
FELLOW-WORKERS
1872–1911

OCTAVIA HILL'S

LETTERS TO FELLOW-WORKERS 1872–1911

TOGETHER WITH AN ACCOUNT OF THE WALMER STREET INDUSTRIAL EXPERIMENT

EDITED BY
Robert Whelan

ASSOCIATE EDITOR
Anne Hoole Anderson

CONTRIBUTING EDITORS
Ian Ginsberg, Laura Probert,
Gavin Tucker, Skye Wheeler, Emma Wilson

FOREWORD BY
Jane Lewis

KYRLE
BOOKS

First published January 2005
KYRLE BOOKS
77 Great Peter Street
London SW1P 2EZ

© Kyrle Books 2005

ISBN 0 9548914 0 6

Typeset by Catherine Green and Richard Kelly
Book designed by Richard Kelly

Printed in Great Britain by
The Cromwell Press
Trowbridge, Wiltshire

Now, how shall I thank you all who have helped during the past year... in all our work, in houses, for open spaces, with our poor; with all our writing and accounts, our entertainments? How can I thank you all who make our work what it is, so full of helpfulness, so thorough, so full of love and life? This poor little letter, sent once a year, and necessarily so brief and general, seems utterly unsatisfactory, and I would so gladly write to each, individually, some little word of thanks about what I, as we all, owe to him or her. But it cannot be; and I hope each will read between the lines something of the thought that goes with the letter—so various, so living, so individual—as I write my name on the cover, and think just how this or that friend has helped, and what I should like to say in sympathy with the life of each one of my friends and fellow-workers.

LETTER TO MY FELLOW-WORKERS, 1901

In memory of my mother

Violet Whelan
1914–2003

*I have to record that she has left us, that no more on this earth
we can carry to her our completed work for her approval,
nor turn to her for sympathy in its progress.*

LETTER TO MY FELLOW-WORKERS, 1902

Contents

LETTERS TO FELLOW-WORKERS

APPENDICES

List of illustrations

Acknowledgements

One of the rites of publication is the list, affixed to the front of most non-fiction titles, of all those people without whom the book would not have been possible. In this case, however, it is more than a formality, because a book such as this one could no more be the product of one person than was Dr Johnson's dictionary. The range of Octavia's interests and the sheer volume of her activities have required a small army of researchers to piece together the extraordinary jigsaw of 'work among the poor' covered by these letters. First and foremost my thanks are due to Anne Anderson, my associate editor, who has brought to the project her encyclopaedic knowledge of nineteenth-century art and culture. Her appendix to this volume represents one of the first extended assessments of the work and significance of the Kyrle Society, so influential in its day and now almost completely forgotten. Dr Anderson is also the author of many of the more extensive footnotes covering the lives and work of the artists associated with Octavia Hill, as well as the complex, interlocking world of the Victorian aristocracy. Ian Ginsberg and Gavin Tucker spent many hours in the library of Lambeth Palace studying the archive material relating to Octavia Hill's involvement with the Ecclesiastical Commissioners. Once again, the appendix, coupled with their numerous footnotes, represents one of the first attempts to paint a detailed picture of this extremely important collaboration, the fruits of which remain one of Octavia Hill's most tangible legacies. Laura Probert has supplied invaluable material on Octavia Hill's involvement with the saving of open spaces in London, especially through the Kyrle Society. Skye Wheeler performed the same service for the early acquisitions of the National Trust. Emma Hunt unravelled the history of the cadet corps. Chris and Penny Harvey checked all of the accounts, and found some errors in the addition. Catherine Green was as patient and meticulous as ever in typesetting what has turned into a very big book, and Richard Kelly, who grew up in one of Octavia Hill's Notting Hill properties, has made the design of the volume into a labour of love. My thanks are also due to Helen Baker, Sarah Blizzard, Kieron Boyle, Andrew Brown, Susan Cash, James Cave, Norman Dennis, Joan Dils, Luke Geoghegan, Monica Harkin,

Olive Jones, Sacha Kumaria, Richard Lines, Colin Mason, Allen and Elizabeth Mills, Ben Mitchell, David Preiskel, Tom Rafferty, Valerie Riches, Eleanor Rogerson, Mark Scrase-Dickins, Colin Stone, Anthony Tricot, Norman Wells and Christine Wagg. The research would not have been possible without the assistance of the staff at the London Library, the Women's Library, the Theatre Museum and the Lambeth Palace Library. Special thanks are due to Sarah Duffield at the Church of England Archive and Alison Kenney at the Westminster City Archive. Finally, everyone who studies Octavia Hill owes an unpayable debt to Peter Clayton, the chairman of the Octavia Hill Society, who did more than anyone else to rescue Octavia from the undeserved oblivion into which she had fallen during the twentieth century, and Gillian Darley, whose *Life* of Octavia Hill is a masterpiece of the biographer's art.

Authors

Robert Whelan is the deputy director of Civitas. He was educated at the John Fisher School, Purley, and Trinity College, Cambridge, where he read English. His books include *Choices in Childbearing*, Committee on Population and the Economy (1992); *Broken Homes and Battered Children* and *Teaching Sex in Schools*, Family Education Trust (1994 and 1995); *The Cross and the Rainforest* (with Joseph Kirwan and Paul Haffner), Acton Institute and Eerdmans (1996); and, for the Institute of Economic Affairs, *Mounting Greenery* (1988), *Making a Lottery of Good Causes* (with Roger Cummins) (1995), *The Corrosion of Charity* (1996), *Octavia Hill and the Social Housing Debate* (ed.) (1998), *Wild In Woods: The Myth of the Noble Eco-Savage* (1999) and *Involuntary Action: How Voluntary is the 'Voluntary' Sector?* (1999). *Helping the Poor: Friendly Visiting, Dole Charities and Dole Queues* was published by Civitas in 2001.

Anne Hoole Anderson trained as an art historian and archaeologist and worked as an archaeologist for eight years. In 1993 she became a lecturer in fine arts valuation at Southampton Institute, where she specializes in Victorian fine and decorative arts, architecture and interior design. As a senior lecturer, she now concentrates on research and publications. She was awarded a PhD in English in 2001. Her research interests include the aesthetic movement, especially art pottery, and the arts and crafts movement. She has published in leading commercial and academic journals, including the *Antique Dealer and Collector*, the *Victorian*, *Garden History* and *Women's History Review*. Books include *Interpreting Pottery* (1984) and *The Cube Teapot* (1999). Anne is a Trustee of the Victorian Society and a fellow of the Society of Antiquaries. Television credits include BBC's *Going for a Song* and *Flog It!* She is a descendant of Elijah Hoole, Octavia Hill's favourite architect.

Ian Ginsberg studied languages at Trinity Hall, Cambridge, where he graduated with a first and studied as a postgraduate. He now works as a researcher. His particular interests include nineteenth-century history and thought and he has researched and written on *fin-de-siècle* Germany and national identity in Germany.

Emma Hunt read history at St Catharine's College, Cambridge, specialising in the modern history of the developing world, and graduated with a double first class honours. She entered the civil service through a Faststream appointment. She is a keen traveller and has visited many countries in Asia, Africa and Europe.

Jane Lewis is Professor of Social Policy at the London School of Economics. Prior to that she was Barnett Professor of Social Policy at the University of Oxford and Professor of Social Policy at Nottingham. Her books include: *The End of Marriage? Individualism and Intimate Relations* (2001), with Kathleen Kiernan and Hilary Land, *Lone Motherhood in Twentieth Century Britain* (1998), *The Voluntary Sector, the State and Social Work in Britain: The Charity Organisation Society/ Family Welfare Association since 1869* (1995); and *Women and Social Action in Victorian and Edwardian England* (1991).

Laura Probert studied for degrees in European studies (with German) and librarianship as a mature student. She now works as a librarian in South East London. She has been researching nineteenth-century women achievers in London and Berlin for some years. One of her heroines is Emma Cons, founder of the Old Vic and Morley College, and trusted fellow-worker of Octavia Hill. Laura's other interests include art nouveau architecture and design, especially the more angular styles from Glasgow and Vienna. She particularly admires the work of Charles Rennie Mackintosh, Charles Harrison Townsend and Voysey. She also enjoys visiting museums and steam railways.

Gavin Tucker holds a bachelor's degree in archaeology from University College, London and a master's degree in international and European politics from Edinburgh University. He now works in the field of social care.

Skye Wheeler is a philosophy graduate. She is currently living and writing in South London.

Foreword

THE SHEER VOLUME of these letters written by Octavia Hill, mainly about her 'practical' work with poor people, is testimony to her extraordinary commitment. For most of the twentieth century the kind of work she did—above all in managing what might be termed today 'bad estates'—failed to find favour. However, pendulums have a habit of swinging and one of the challenges that has emerged for those facing the task of urban regeneration is how to acknowledge and address very similar kinds of problems to those familiar to Hill. Octavia Hill's letters are not going to provide us with any ready answers, but a better understanding of her approach helps us to interrogate our own, and to highlight issues that were not addressed for much of the post-war period.

Hill devoted herself to the 'quiet' and 'detailed' work of 'personal service'. This might today be termed 'social work', but Hill's canvas was considerably broader than that of modern social work. She was convinced that only by working alongside and with poor tenants could real and lasting social change be achieved. Furthermore, such work was a matter of Christian duty, which ideally should be carried out on a voluntary basis. Hill's 'fellow-workers', to whom she addressed her letters, were in the main middle-class, female volunteers. Under Hill's leadership, they offered practical help in budgeting, in finding temporary casual work for an unemployed tenant and in tackling bad landlords—while in return the tenant had to pay rent regularly and stop anti-social behaviour. Hill did not face drugs and guns, but there was plenty of drunkenness, dirt and domestic violence.

There was, of course, a conviction on the part of Hill and her rent collectors that is disturbing for the modern reader living in a profoundly pluralist society: they thought that they knew best. But the relationship between worker and tenant was not purely and simply one of paternalism and deference. Hill's main inspiration was her Christian duty to serve, and in her view everyone had to do his or her duty. The main duty of the tenant was to pay (his) rent and provide for his family, while his wife cared for home and children. The better-off had to be prepared to become active citizens, and give time, rather than money, to helping those less fortunate than themselves.

Many of Hill's contemporaries, as well as those who came after, could see problems with this relentlessly individualist approach, even if the final goal was the building of more trusting and self-sufficient communities. There was no room for structural or collective reform involving state intervention in Octavia Hill's mindset. She enjoyed considerable success in the vast majority of her projects, not least because of her hard work day-in day-out, and year-in year-out. But her projects were inevitably small-scale and she also suffered defeats. 'Poor Deptford' proved too much for her and she withdrew. Short leases and high population turnover made it infertile ground for her methods.

Indeed, there seems to be little here for a profoundly secular society, in a country preoccupied with the all too pressing problems of long-standing neglect of its infrastructure, and where women have gained hard-fought-for access to the public sphere and more attractive work opportunities than the 'womanly work' Octavia Hill offered. However, Hill's insistence on living with the poor, on gaining a close knowledge of their problems, on gaining their trust, on respecting their point of view, on sorting out the day-to-day problems that beset them (the nineteenth-century equivalents of overflowing rubbish bins and broken lifts), and also on fighting for a better environment via her campaigns for open spaces, was forgotten for too long in the post-war decades, when too many in central and local government thought that 'system change' would suffice. Octavia Hill's way of building community cannot work today: there has to be more democratic participation as well as wise leadership. But nor can we neglect the responsibilities of the rich as well as those of the poor, and Hill's engagement with the nitty-gritty of social administration remains a valuable example.

Jane Lewis
Professor of Social Policy
London School of Economics

Editor's Introduction

It is helpful ... to me to be called on to survey the year
with its many hopes and labours.

LETTER TO MY FELLOW-WORKERS, 1908

OCTAVIA HILL WAS one of those rare people who try their hands at many things and succeed in all of them. She was a pioneer of what we now call social housing, devising her own system for making decent accommodation available to low-income tenants. She was regarded as one of the most important leaders of social reform movements of her generation, and was consulted by ministers and official bodies. She was a member of Royal Commission on the Poor Law from 1905–9, which was the first to allow women to be commissioners.[1] She was a pioneer of the open spaces movement and became one of the founders of the National Trust. She was a pioneer of what is now described as cultural philanthropy, which was based on the conviction that art and beauty can raise the quality of life, and that such things should not be the preserve of the rich. She was effectively the founder of the cadet corps.

Such was the esteem in which she was held by her contemporaries that she was one of only three women invited in their own right to attend the 1897 service in Westminster Abbey marking Queen Victoria's Diamond Jubilee. (The other two were Florence Nightingale and Josephine Butler.) After her death her family were offered the honour of burial in the Abbey—an offer which they were obliged to decline as Octavia had wanted to be buried in Kent.

However, her posthumous reputation went into decline. This was partly owing to the fact that Octavia had steadfastly resisted an enlarged

---

1   She would have been a member of the Royal Commission on Housing in 1884 had the home secretary not objected to the absolute impropriety of a female commissioner.

role—or indeed almost any role at all—for the state in the provision of welfare services. She objected to local authority housing, to state pensions and to free health care. She maintained the hard line against state welfarism that was identified with the Charity Organisation Society, of which she had been a founder member in 1869, long after most of her contemporaries had softened it. As a result, her views came to be seen as outmoded, if not downright objectionable, as the welfare state entered what many regarded as its golden age in the two decades following the Second World War. The series of post-war acts of parliament that created the rights-based, cradle-to-grave welfare state violated Octavia's most deeply held principles. Octavia had described the public provision to the working classes of any 'necessary of life' like housing as a 'disastrous policy'.[2] The welfare state provided not only housing, but health care, unemployment benefit, pensions, education and every conceivable 'necessary of life', 'free at the point of delivery', not only to the poor but—even more strangely, Octavia would have thought—to the rich as well.

It is because Octavia maintained the sternest line against any form of subsidy or state provision to the end of her life—to the exasperation of colleagues like Beatrice Webb and the Barnetts who felt that she was failing to read the signs of the times—that she came in for so much unfavourable comment in the last part of the twentieth century. Social policy analysts, who tend to come from the political left, either ignored her completely or heaped abuse on her head. According to one:

> 'The legacy she left to housing managers has been baneful. She founded a tradition which is inconsistent with the rights of tenants and destructive of their welfare.'[3]

Even David Owen, in his magisterial history of English philanthropy, can scarcely conceal his exasperation with 'the inexorably moralistic individualism of Octavia Hill':

---

2   Hill, Octavia, 'Improvements Now Practicable', part of a symposium that appeared in *The Nineteenth Century*, 14 December 1883, under the heading 'Common Sense and the Dwellings of the Poor'.

---

3   Spicker, P., 'Legacy of Octavia Hill', *Housing*, June 1985, p.39, quoted in Brion, Marion, *Women in the Housing Service*, London: Routledge, 1995, p.16. Chapter Two of Marion Brion's book gives a good account of the changing responses to Octavia's work.

'Though her contemporaries regarded her as an oracle on working-class housing and her accomplishments in the field were, in fact, staggering, they no longer command unquestioning admiration... they were... expressions of a social outlook that today is almost incomprehensible.'[4]

However, David Owen was writing in 1965, and in some ways we are further from the *zeitgeist* of his world than we are from that of the Victorians. The golden age or classic era of the welfare state is now at an end. Its problems are now everywhere apparent. Not only are the services provided by the state seen as being slow, wasteful, unresponsive and of low quality, but the recognition of the morally corrupting effects of welfare dependency has long since ceased to be the exclusive concern of the political right. There is a greater interest now than at any time for several decades in the extent to which a mixture of voluntary and statutory bodies can supply the services that, until recently, were thought to be within the exclusive domain of the state. When my collection of Octavia Hill's writings on housing was published in 1998, the response of the housing and social work media was an indication of this changing climate.[5]

Octavia as an author

A contributing factor to Octavia's rehabilitation has been the emergence of women's studies as an academic discipline. The achievements of women who struggled in a male-dominated environment are now appreciated, and Octavia achieved more than most. Not only did she create housing management as a profession for trained women, but she insisted that her ladies should be regarded by property owners in the same way that they regarded their solicitors, surveyors and architects

---

4   Owen, 1965, p.387.

---

5   'This extremely useful book is well worth reading... Many of Octavia Hill's ideas have important implications, particularly in terms of the current debate about anti-social behaviour, and would repay being widely discussed and thought about.' *Housing* (June 1998). 'Octavia Hill wrote with the confidence of the autonomous voluntary worker who knew what she was talking about... The relevance of her example to the dilemma we now face is immediately apparent.' *Community Care* (2-8 July 1998). 'Ironically, in view of the criticisms which have been levied at her, she seems more relevant than ever in the modern welfare debate.' *Housing Agenda* (April 1998).

(1900, p.450; 1904, p.519). In other words, her women deserved the respect afforded to professional status as much as the men.

One problem for academics and scholars who feel that it is time for a re-assessment of Octavia Hill is that her writings are so hard to come by. From 1866 onwards, she wrote pamphlets and articles for magazines, as well as contributing a chapter towards Charles Booth's great study *Life and Labour of the London Poor*, but these published efforts did not amount to forty in all, and are in any case difficult to access now. Seven of her articles were collected together for publication in book form in 1875 as *Homes of the London Poor*. As this enjoyed some success the publisher, Macmillan, brought out a second collection in 1877 called *Our Common Land*, which was not a success. There was a reprint of *Homes of the London Poor* in 1883, and a modern edition in 1970,[6] but *Our Common Land* has never been reprinted, and the high prices which both command on the second-hand book market reflect their scarcity. Apart from some short collections of Octavia's writings,[7] she is, for most readers, almost inaccessible.

The letters to fellow-workers

As the scope of Octavia's work grew, from managing a few run-down properties in Marylebone to managing hundreds of properties on large estates, from trying to create a playground in Drury Lane to buying up huge swathes of the Lake District, so she found it increasingly difficult to keep in touch with her many supporters and helpers by means of personal correspondence. Although, like many Victorians, she was a prolific letter-writer, she came to the realisation, early in the 1870s, that there were just never going to be enough hours in the day. As a result, she started producing small, printed newsletters to send to the network of volunteers, donors, well-wishers and co-workers, past and present, in Britain and overseas, whom she called her fellow-workers. The first letter to fellow-workers appeared in 1872, and they

---

6   It was published by Frank Cass and Co, together with Andrew Mearns's *The Bitter Cry of Outcast London*.

---

7   Whelan, Robert, (ed.) *Octavia Hill and the Social Housing Debate*, London: Institute of Economic Affairs, 1998; Payne, James L. (ed.), *The Befriending Leader: Social Assistance Without Dependency, Essays by Octavia Hill*, Sandpoint, Idaho: Lytton Publishing Company, 1997.

appeared at yearly intervals thereafter, with the exception of 1884, until 1911. However, the letters were printed 'For Private Circulation Only', and Octavia resisted all attempts to persuade her to publish them. She wanted to be free to write about her failures as well as her successes in a way that would have been difficult in a more public forum. The print run for the letters was necessarily small—we know she had 500 copies of the 1886 letter printed[8]—and most of these copies probably shared the fate common to voluntary sector ephemera: the recipients read them then threw them away. As a result, letters to fellow-workers are extremely rare and most of the extant copies are, in booksellers' terminology, in captivity—i.e. in libraries. However, even the British Library does not have a complete set,[9] and most of those libraries that hold any letters have far fewer. Apart from some brief collections of extracts,[10] this is the first time they have ever been published.

The fact that the letters are so difficult to access, even for scholars, makes a full appreciation of Octavia's life and work very difficult. This is partly because of their sheer bulk: at 130,000 words combined, they exceed in length all of her other printed writings put together. More importantly, however, it is only in the letters that you can follow the concurrent development of all of her interests—housing, open spaces, cultural philanthropy—and see how they all fit together, like pieces of a jigsaw. They cover the full panoramic scope of Octavia's concerns—

---

8   Letter from Octavia to Sydney Cockerell, 17 March 1887, in the collection of the Westminster Central Archive (D Misc 84/2).

---

9   It is missing the letter for 1892.

---

10   In 1933 Elinor Southwood Ouvry, Octavia's niece, published a short book entitled *Extracts from Octavia Hill's 'Letters to Fellow-Workers', 1864 to 1911*. The intention was to provide an account, in Octavia's own words, of her work in housing from the very beginning in Paradise Place. However, as the first of the letters to fellow-workers covered 1872, the preceding years had to be dealt with by means of private correspondence—most of which had been taken from the Edmund Maurice biography—and some of Octavia's magazine articles. The selections from the letters are interesting, but brief and fragmentary. It had been preceded in 1921 by a slender volume edited by Miss Jeffery and Miss Neville called *House Property & Its Management* which contained some very brief extracts from the letters. Both of these titles are rarer than Octavia's own books. Amongst more recent publications, *The Befriending Leader* (Payne,1997) and *Octavia Hill and the Social Housing Debate* (Whelan, 1998) contain some extracts.

from rehabilitating slums to buying the Cheddar Gorge—and show how all of these things are linked. Every letter is described as an account of her 'work among the poor', and everything springs from her central concern to improve the quality of life of those living without the advantages of wealth, education or social position.

Octavia began by making decent, healthy accommodation available to poor people; she knew that if they didn't have work they wouldn't be able to pay the rent, so she created employment opportunities for her tenants; she realised they had educational and cultural needs to be met; that poor people living in crowded tenements needed somewhere to escape into the fresh air; that idle teenage boys would get into trouble, and needed organised activities; and so on. One thing leads to another, and it is both impossible and undesirable to regard Octavia as 'just' a housing reformer, or 'just' a founder of the National Trust. She made no distinction between these things in her own mind, and neither did her fellow-workers.

The letters to fellow-workers are important for another reason. Unlike many of the great nineteenth-century philanthropists, Octavia was an extremely private person who had no wish for personal publicity. Whereas William Booth and Thomas Barnardo had a thirst for celebrity that would have put them completely at ease with the culture of the modern mass media, Octavia always tried to keep herself in the background, even when she was the key player in a campaign.[11] While she was willing to participate in existing organisations, like the Charity Organisation Society, and was one of the founders of the National Trust, she refused to found an organisation to handle her own work. She had neither treasurer nor secretary, no minutes and no AGMs.[12] Had she not begun to print these brief accounts of her year's work, we would have only a very incomplete idea of what she actually got up to. The letters to fellow-workers are effectively the annual reports of

---

11 'I would rather work in the unsought-after, out-of-sight places, side by side with my fellow workers, face to face with tenants, than in the conspicuous forefront of any great movement.' (1882, p.156.)

---

12 Octavia emphasised the deliberate informality of her arrangements in the conclusion to the second letter: '… we are bound by no laws… enrolled in no book, our members take different parts in the work which is various and not easily defined, we are placed in very different circumstances, some of us are widely separated in place, but we form a large company united in a common work, we have entered into fellowship one with another, and are bound together by a common hope for blessing on all we have in hand.' (1873, p.23.)

Octavia Hill charitable enterprises, but written in the informal style of personal correspondence. They are a sort of professional autobiography.

The beginning of the letters

The letters to fellow-workers grew out of two brief accounts for the parish annual report of what Octavia referred to rather grandly as her Walmer Street Industrial Experiment. Octavia's vicar, the Rev. Fremantle, was a dynamic and innovative character. He was determined to sort out the muddle of the various agencies for the relief of poverty in his parish of St Mary's, Bryanston Square, in Marylebone and he was happy to enlist the help of a forceful young woman who was already making a name for herself in the parish with her system of working-class housing. Octavia had taken over Paradise Place in 1865 and Freshwater Place in 1866. In 1869 she began her involvement with Barrett's Court, off Oxford Street, the slummiest and most threatening of them all. In the same year the Charity Organisation Society was formed to bring a more systematic and scientific approach to the relief of poverty, and Rev. Fremantle formed the first of its district committees in Marylebone. He asked Octavia to join it, and she was delighted to do so, as the COS views on the right and wrong ways to administer relief chimed exactly with her own. She persuaded Rev. Fremantle to let her conduct an experiment in Walmer Street and Walmer Place— the worst slums in the parish—which involved setting up workshops to provide work for any able-bodied person who needed it, but refusing to give anything at all to those who declined to work. She was asked to write up the experiment for the parish annual report in 1870, and her account was subsequently published as a pamphlet. The same thing happened in 1871, except that there was an interesting addition to the pamphlet version: whereas the 1870 pamphlet had only included accounts for the industrial experiment itself, in 1871 Octavia included a list of 'donations received for various purposes'. As Octavia had established a reputation for herself as someone who was genuinely concerned for the welfare of the poor, who could also be trusted not to waste money, so people began giving her funds to administer on their behalf. Somehow or other, she had to account for these funds, but it was clearly impractical for her to enter into correspondence with everyone who donated ten shillings: 'As it is difficult to me always to find time to render an account of these sums to the separate donors, I must ask their permission to insert one here'. (Appendix 1, p.693.)

It was at this point that Octavia conceived the idea of an annual circular that would contain the accounts for her donation fund, with a few words about how the money had been spent. She makes her intention clear in the opening words of the first letter:

'In sending to those who have kindly placed money at my disposal for distribution during the past year some account of the ways in which it has been used, it is not necessary that I should add much to what the balance sheet will tell them.' (1872, p.3.)

As the years went by, and the letters became longer, Octavia still maintained the position that the letters themselves were no more than little appendages to the accounts—'nothing but a little summary of account of donations received' (1883, p.169); 'I must print and circulate an audited account of money sent to my donation fund; and I could not send it without a word' (1897, p.399). She makes it clear that she dislikes the idea of a printed letter altogether: 'I do not want to make this a public letter, I wish I could write with my own hand to you all, for I want to say much more individually than I can in a circular letter' (1873, p.23). However, it was better than the alternative, which would have been to fail to render an adequate account to her donors of how their money had been used, and to lose touch with the increasingly large group of people on whom the success of her ever-expanding work depended.

'How shall I thank you? How can my voice reach you? How can I even write to you with my own hand? Only this poor, general, printed letter can come to you; but read between its lines, and reach each of you, if you can, that separate distinct word of heartiest thanks I would so gladly write to each, and believe that memory is stronger than time and space, and as the several gifts are seen or remembered, thoughts of you each come to me with a rush of thankfulness which if I could I would send in written letter, or utter in spoken word.' (1888, p.247-8.)

The style of the letters

The letters were, in Octavia's view, very definitely second-best. This makes it all the more surprising that they are so good. The best of the letters blend narratives of current campaigns with philosophical and spiritual reflections, spiced up with anecdotes, in a way that makes them, in purely literary terms, a very good read. And yet Octavia did not hit her stride immediately. The early letters betray their origin in parish annual reports. They tend to be dry and impersonal, containing exhortations to adopt the methods of the Charity Organisation Society in the relief of poverty, without the 'human interest' stories that made much of Octavia's journalism around this time so rivetting. For the letters to fellow-workers were far from being Octavia's first attempts at writing for print. She had realised, early on in her career in housing management, the value of journalism in spreading the word, and had begun to write accounts of her approach to the housing of the working classes almost as soon as she put it into effect. She took over Paradise Place in Marylebone in 1865, and wrote 'Cottage Property in London' to be published by the *Fortnightly Review* in November 1866. She took over Freshwater Place in 1866 and wrote 'Four Years' Management of a London Court' to be published by *Macmillan's Magazine* in July 1869 (the 'four years' dates from Octavia's takeover of Paradise Place, although most of the article is about Freshwater Place). She began work in Barrett's Court in 1869 and wrote about it as 'Blank Court; or Landlords and Tenants' for *Macmillan's Magazine* in October 1871. These articles, which blend practical advice on housing management with fascinating 'real-life' stories, were the best things Octavia ever wrote, and they formed the first three chapters of *Homes of the London Poor* in 1875.[13]

When Octavia sat down to write the first of the letters to fellow-workers, in December 1872, these articles were behind her, as were the major developments in her approach to housing management. What was she to write about? The first letters, with their somewhat dry and theoretical tone, suggest a problem that Octavia herself would recognise later in the series:[14] when work is going on steadily, on established lines, with no major setbacks or leaps forward, it is not very 'newsy'. The letters at the end of the 1870s suffer from another problem: in 1877 Octavia experienced a complete breakdown that took her away from her work for four years, most of which she spent travelling. She continued to write the letters, presumably because she felt it was

---

13 They are reproduced in *Octavia Hill and the Social Housing Debate*, Whelan (ed.) 1998.

---

14 'Continuous work, which is in many ways the most valuable form of help, necessitates a certain monotony in an annual letter.' (1897, p.399.)

important to hold the body of fellow-workers together in her absence, but she is for the most part reporting second hand on things she has not dealt with herself. However, having returned to work in the early 1880s, she began to manage housing for the Ecclesiastical Commissioners, who also agreed to lease a plot of land for a garden in Southwark. This was the beginning of the Red Cross project—garden, cottages and Hall—which gave Octavia the opportunity to create her model urban community. Octavia's excitement about the whole thing is obvious from 1886 onwards, and it is from this point that she seemed to find the right pitch for her circular letters. It would be going too far to describe them as gossipy, but Octavia was able to speak to her readers almost as warmly as she would have done in an individual letter, certain that they would share her enthusiasms. However, the printed format allowed her to be rather more philosophical, as well as more exhortatory, than she could easily have been in private correspondence. It is easier to ask people for money when you are not asking them personally.

There is one important aspect of the letters that it is easy to miss, perhaps because it carries less weight with us than it would have done with Octavia's original readers: they contain frequent religious observations, and a number of passages of spiritual reflection.[15] In Octavia's published writings there are references to transcendental things, but not with anything like the degree of intensity we find here. It was still not considered entirely proper for women to speak of such matters, and so, when writing for *Macmillan's* or *The Nineteenth Century*, Octavia kept it in check. She was under no such restrictions when writing 'For Private Circulation Only', and it is from the letters to fellow-workers that we can appreciate the extent to which Octavia's religious faith was central to everything she did, especially when the going got rough: 'one seems the more thrown back on the certainty that the Lord is King'. (1909, p.617.)

'… have confidence that this world, being God's and not the devil's, there is a course of action which shall meet the individual need and the common and future welfare of the people.' (1876, p.73.)

---

15 'There is much work done thoroughly, and in God's sight, which will stand the fire and be proved as good pure gold. Wherever it exists, it tells in a quite marvellous way. One true-hearted clergyman, one conscientious mistress of a house, one firm mother who teaches her boy what duty means, one faithful workman, one human soul who looks day by day through earthly things clearly to the Lord of them, one

Writing and printing the letters

Octavia wrote the letter at the end of the year she was covering, or in the first months of the following year. There are 39 letters to fellow-workers, of which 32 can be dated, either from the printed text or on the basis of internal evidence. Seventeen of them—just over half—were written in December and ten in January. Four were written in February, and one—1886—in March. They varied considerably in length, from 2,022 words in 1872 to 5,256 words in 1876. As Figure 1 shows, it was by no means the case that they got longer as the years went by and Octavia had more to report on. Rather, the length of the letter seems simply to reflect the amount of time Octavia had to write it in.

Of the 31 letters for which we have printers' details, 24 were printed by Waterlows, the firm owned by Octavia's friend and fellow pioneer of social housing Sir Sydney Waterlow.[16] Three were printed by George Pulman, who had also printed the 1871 account of the Walmer Street experiment, and whose printworks were in Marylebone, close to Octavia's home. One was printed by Provost and Co., one by the Hampstead Record Printing Works, one by Hunt, Barnard and Co., and one (1879) by the House-Boy Brigade Printers, who were also printing rent books and other stationery items for Octavia in that year.

The print-run of the letters is difficult to determine. The only one for which we have a quantity is 1886, when 500 were printed. Presumably the numbers printed must have risen as the work expanded and drew in more people,[17] and certainly it is the first letters, from the early 1870s, that are the rarest,[18] but there is no simple linear

---

statesman who is careless whether any follow or applaud, but who makes straight on for what is right, all of these prepare the way of the Lord, and do something to make England what we all wish her to be.' (1884/5, p.186.)

---

16 Sydney Waterlow made his fortune by turning the small stationery business he inherited from his father into one of the biggest print operations in Victorian England. He founded the Improved Industrial Dwellings Company in 1863 to provide good accommodation for working-class tenants whilst showing a five per cent return on capital for investors.

---

17 'Each year I find that I have to address a larger number of you...' (1873, p.17); 'You who year by year increase in number...' (1905, p.535).

---

18 The 1874 letter seems to have been a rarity almost as soon as it appeared. In November 1876 Princess Alice of Hesse-Darmstadt, Queen Victoria's second daughter

Figure 1: Word count of the letters to fellow-workers, 1872–1911

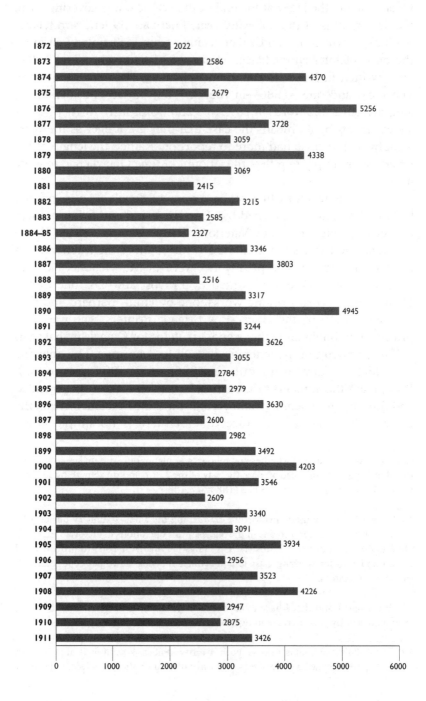

progression. From 1881 onwards Octavia was in the habit of recording in her accounts the expenses involved in producing and circulating the letters, and these amounts are shown in Table 1. We know that in 1886 she spent £3 15s 6d on a print-run of 500 letters, but the amounts spent in each year vary so much, from £3 10s 11d in 1882 to £9 8s 7½d in 1909, with no discernible pattern, that we can only say that the quantity must have fluctuated from year to year in response to factors we know nothing of.

The content of the letters: housing first

The letters paint a panoramic picture of a woman who was involved with many different things, from smoke abatement to boarding out orphans, and from flower shows to buying up large chunks of the Lake District. It is the housing work, however, that has pride of place in almost every letter. Typically, Octavia begins with a brief account of the housing projects already in hand, followed by the new ones in prospect. However, in the years covered by the early letters, there were no major breakthroughs in housing management. With the reclamation of Barrett's Court, which was already well under way by 1872, Octavia had perfected her system. In the early letters we find her encouraging the ladies to become, in so far as it was possible, independent of her— queens in their own domain (1874, p.38)—and this policy proved invaluable when, following her breakdown in 1877, Octavia had to leave everything in the hands of her fellow-workers. However, the first major new development to the housing work came in 1884, when the Ecclesiastical Commissioners asked her to take over the management of certain courts in Southwark. This was to have the most momentous consequences for Octavia, the Commissioners and the history of social housing. At first, they gave her the most run-down courts to manage, many of which were due for demolition. She complained that it was impossible to do her work, which was as much to do with improving the tenants as the tenements, on such a short-term basis, and she asked

---

and a great admirer of Octavia's work, asked Octavia to send her a copy, and Octavia replied that she would look for one—implying that she had none 'in stock'. (She eventually sent a copy in the New Year of 1877.) The letter for 1873 is not included in the Octavia Hill Birthplace Museum's bound collection of the letters, which contains every other letter, and in 1896 Octavia describes the 1879 letter as being 'out of print' (1896, p.387).

Table 1: Expenditure on printing and postage of the letters to fellow-workers, 1881–1911

Year	£	s	d
1881	4	0	4
1882	3	10	11
1883	3	11	1 ½
1884	3	9	11
1886*	3	15	6
1887	3	19	11
1888	5	15	4
1889	4	10	6 ½
1890	5	7	1 ½
1891	6	6	5 ½
1892	6	4	4
1893	8	2	4 ½
1894	7	4	6
1895	4	3	0
1896	3	18	6
1897	4	13	0
1898	4	18	1 ½
1899	3	16	0
1900	3	16	0
1901	3	16	0
1902	3	16	0
1903	3	12	6
1904	4	9	6
1905	3	12	6
1906	4	14	6
1907	5	7	0 ½
1908	5	19	11
1909	9	8	7 ½
1910	6	10	0
1911	6	18	1 ½

* 500 copies of the 1886 letter were printed

for properties that were not about to be swept away. She also asked for a 999-year lease on a plot of land in Red Cross Street, Southwark, to turn into a garden for the local people. Red Cross garden was soon overlooked by Red Cross cottages and Red Cross Hall. Octavia became the squiress of this little village in South London, looking after the needs of the tenants with open-air festivals, a flower show, indoor entertainments, educational activities, a library, clubs, a cadet corps for the young men and an annual performance of *The Messiah*. The Ecclesiastical Commissioners were impressed, and the relationship of Octavia to the Commissioners changed into something more like residential property consultant than rent collector. As Ian Ginsberg shows in his appendix to this volume, they fell in with everything she wanted them to do, often against their own initial expressed intentions. Instead of demolishing all the old cottages to replace them with tenement blocks, they not only restored some of them, but began building new cottages, and leasing land to Octavia's friends to do likewise. Then came the two big redevelopments: the Lambeth estate in 1901 and Walworth in 1903. These were massive undertakings, involving the demolition of houses covering many acres and the creation of new roads, recreation grounds and community facilities. These projects, on which Octavia was the manager in all but name, took her work to a new level. She was able to command the considerable resources of the Ecclesiastical Commissioners, with their legal and financial advisers and construction experts,[19] instead of having to do all the donkey work herself, or try to persuade her friends to do it for nothing. In Walworth, especially, she was able to put into practice all of her ideals of urban community living which she had been developing on a smaller scale at Red Cross in Southwark. And yet, there seems to have been a nagging doubt at the back of Octavia's mind as to whether this was really the right way for her to be going about things. 'The fashion of clearing away, which makes a grand show, has, in my estimation, gone quite far enough',[20] she wrote in 1902—the year before she became involved with clearing 22 acres in Walworth. She justified the demolition of the old houses on the Lambeth and Walworth estates by saying that they

---

19 'I should like here to record how much I owe to the unwearied, kind and efficient co-operation of the officers of the Ecclesiastical Commissioners, who have advised and supported us ably and promptly about all technical matters.' (1902, pp.485-6.)

---

20 p.485.

were beyond the point of repair,[21] but she had always opposed large-scale demolition in favour of building up communities bit by bit, working with the sitting tenants in old houses.[22] The Commissioners' new-builds 'meet the wants of a superior class of tenants' (1908, p.591)—but these were not the sort of tenants Octavia had originally sought to work with. As if to compensate, she took on Notting Hill.

In 1899 Rev. Charles Robers, the vicar of St Clement's, Notting Dale, asked Octavia to take over the management of five houses in St Katherine's Road. This was one of the worst streets in one of the worst slums left in central London, and represented just the sort of challenge Octavia relished. The old slums in Marylebone had long since become respectable, so here was the chance to start the whole process over again. Octavia realised that she couldn't do much to change the tone of the area with only five houses under her management, so she started drafting in her supporters to acquire control of more. She spread out bit by bit until she controlled 100 houses by 1910. As of old, she threw herself into training 'the more forlorn of our tenants' (1909, p.620) as odd-job men, to tide them over slack periods. There were tenants' outings, a children's choir and another branch of the cadet corps. It was Barrett's Court and Red Cross cottages all over again. 'The work at Notting Hill', Octavia wrote in 1906, 'is one after my own heart, and I feel that there we are meeting, so far as in us lies, with the most difficult of all the housing problems, and doing good in ways which no new building schemes can achieve.' (1906, p.556.)

---

21 '... my mind could not but revert to the day in October of 1903, when the [Walworth] estate reverted to the owners; of the rotten and leaking roofs; of the falling plaster; of the dangerous staircases; of the forlorn dirt and over-crowding. I thought of the far-sighted wisdom which had led the Ecclesiastical Commissioners to resolve to rebuild the area...' (1905, p.536.)

---

22 'If a court is taken over full of its old inhabitants, there are some among them who have the opportunity of being raised in and with it, who never could have such an opportunity in any new buildings. In letting to new tenants one must ask for good references... the poor may indeed be received, but not those whose character is doubtful: the preference is fairly and rightly given to the sober, industrious and clean. But buy up, or take over, a court full of the less hopeful tenants, and it becomes your duty to try them; some of them always respond to the better influences, and are permanently raised ... With that class we, if anyone, must deal, and I would earnestly ask those who are working with me not to lose sight of that fact, not to be led away by tempting plans for rebuilding.' (1883, pp.175-76.)

The content of the letters: open spaces, cultural philanthropy, social activities

Octavia begins the 1896 letter with an explanation of how all of the various activities with which she was associated grew out of her initial interest in the housing of the poor:

> 'It is from the narrow space in rooms and crowded alley that I first learned how the small garden near the narrow court or huge block was the necessary complement of the home... it was in their colourlessness and unloveliness that I learnt how the colour and music brought by the Kyrle Society were needed... it was in watching the lives of the poor in long-ago days that I learnt the need of amusements for them... and the importance of companionship in these; it was watching in near relation to our people how much what they did themselves interested and developed them, that led to the training of the tenants' children to act little plays, and of the tenants themselves to sing, to act, to cultivate flowers... In fact, whatever we have found to do has been suggested by the need as we saw it affecting the homes, and members of the homes, with which charge of the houses brought us in contact.' (1896, p.385.)

We know from Octavia's accounts of her early housing ventures that these concerns had always been integral to her approach to housing. She was never interested in just putting a roof over people's heads: housing management had to involve other things that would improve the whole quality of life of poor people (which everyone is now in favour of) and which would make them into better people[23] (which makes us a bit uneasy). It was for this reason that Octavia would never allow her ladies to be referred to as rent collectors. Anyone could collect the rent. Most slum landlords were interested in nothing else. Octavia and her ladies had a wider vision, which involved improving people's

---

23 'Surely there must be many volunteers who would care to take charge of some group of tenants ... with the sort of quiet continuous control which may slowly mould the place and people to conformity with a better standard than prevails in poor courts in general.' (1881, p.148.) '... we hope our poor friends there [Notting Hill] — though many of them broken by difficulty, temptation and physical infirmity—may be braced to better things by wise rule in the houses, and by the constant presence among them of those who are set on helping them to do better.' (1901, p.465.)

behaviour, raising their expectations and broadening their horizons. It was grand vision for a bunch of not-very-influential women who started off with a few decrepit houses in Marylebone.

As soon as Octavia got control of the first houses, she set about turning an outhouse at the bottom of her garden in Nottingham Place into a room that could be used for educational and social activities. Because of the significance of Octavia's work on the grand scale—creating estates for the Ecclesiastical Commissioners, buying up swathes of the Lake District for the National Trust, sitting on a royal commission—it is easy to overlook the small-scale work to which she herself attached enormous significance, especially encouraging rich and poor to meet on a basis of friendship and mutual respect. Octavia's aim was to bring together the owners of central London courts with their tenants on the same basis as a country squire would relate to his people.[24] 'Manly friendship' between rich and poor was her goal, and she tried to bring this about by organising entertainments and outings for her tenants. These social activities feature in almost every single letter. In fact, with the exception of the housing work itself, they feature more frequently than any of Octavia's other concerns. Year after year we hear about these outings. Sometimes they were grand affairs, like the Archbishop of Canterbury's tea parties in the garden of Lambeth Palace, or the Countess of Selborne's outing to Hatfield, her ancestral home. For the most part, however, they were modest events, hosted by middle-class people whose houses were no doubt comfortable but not magnificent. They were certainly a faithful crowd: the Misses Johnston in Hampstead, Sir Frederick Pollock in Haslemere, Dr Longstaff in Putney; they crop up year after year. Octavia's step-brother Arthur lived in the admittedly rather grand Erleigh Court in Reading, but he persuaded his son, who was rector of Shere, to entertain groups of tenants on a regular basis in the parish. Rev. Hill's parish magazine contains some fascinating descriptions of these outings, involving up to 200 tenants from Marylebone who had to be transported to the middle of Surrey, with wagons to take the elderly and infirm, for a day of festivities on the recreation ground. As anyone who has organised outings for even a small group of people will know, such events take up a great deal of time, and yet for Octavia this outing to Shere was just

---

24 '... a part of my own special work has been to connect individuals possessed of education, conscience and means, with particular courts in London. In this way has been established the relation between landlord and tenant, with all its mutual attachments and duties, as it exists in many country places.' (1883, pp.176-77.)

one of a series throughout the summer months.[25] The social events must have consumed a great deal of Octavia's time, and yet, far from resenting this, she expresses regret when for some reason the programme has been less busy than usual. In view of the fact that Octavia has sometimes been caricatured as a woman who was against giving anything to the poor, it is worth mentioning that these outings, as well as many of the entertainments she organised for the tenants, were free. She realised that it would be easier to expand the social programme if charges were levied, but she also realised that this would alter the relationship between those organising the events and those attending: 'directly we cease to be hosts and hostesses, we cease in a great measure to set the tone of the performances'. (1874, p.35.)

It is because the letters demonstrate the relative importance that Octavia attached to the different parts of her work that they are so important. They put everything into perspective—her perspective. She always insisted that grand schemes—'specious theories of reform *en masse*, and plans for relieving misery by the million' (1891, p.304)— would come to nothing if they were not based on meticulous work with individual men and women. She wanted to know poor people one by one, family by family, not as statistics in the blue books that Beatrice and Sidney Webb were so fond of consulting. She refused to allow her growing status and celebrity to get in the way of this fundamental principle. Thus, in 1909, Sir Moses Montefiore asked her to take on a street of run-down cottages in Hoxton. Octavia gives an enthusiastic account of the way in which she and her lady manager put in hand the repair of the gutters and the stripping of 12 or 13 layers of dirty wallpaper. (1909, p.618.) She came to this from a three-year stint on the Royal Commission on the Poor Law, which represented the most important review of the country's welfare policy since 1834, and which she had been personally invited to join by the prime minister. How many women, in Octavia's position, would have worried about wallpaper-stripping in Hoxton?

Of all the activities that grew out of her involvement with housing, her pioneering work in the open spaces movement would provide by far the most lasting legacy. Octavia's strictness as a landlady, starting

---

25 The donation fund accounts show that the number of excursions tailed off in the 1890s, and more markedly in the 1900s, by which time Octavia was in her sixties. However the social programme of parties, concerts, plays and lectures continued, centred around the Red Cross Hall in Southwark and St Christopher's Hall in Marylebone.

eviction proceedings against tenants as soon as the second week's rent went unpaid, and her steadfast opposition to state-provided welfare, have made her unpopular with many social policy professionals from the middle of the twentieth century onwards. However, in the field of open spaces, or what we would now call environmentalism, she was one of the early leaders of a movement that now carries all before it as an unquestioned force for good. No one would now dispute the need to preserve access to common lands for the benefit of the community, but this was not the case in the middle of the nineteenth century when private property rights and minimal public expenditure were regarded as the hubs around which policy had to revolve. If it is now taken for granted that everyone should have access to fresh air and the pleasures of the countryside, it is because Octavia's forceful campaigning turned what had been regarded as an eccentric point of view into an orthodoxy.

Octavia had been concerned about getting plots of land cleared to provide somewhere for tenants to relax ever since her earliest days in housing. Wherever she could, she tried to create a space, no matter how modest, to which tenants could escape from overcrowded rooms, and where children could play as an alternative to the pavement. When she created the Kyrle Society, with her sister Miranda, in 1876, it put the campaign on a more formal basis. One of the original aims of the Kyrle was to get churchyards opened to the public and laid out as gardens. London churchyards had been closed to new interments since 1852,[26] when severe overcrowding under the ground made them not only unpleasant but an extremely serious health hazard.[27] They were locked up and allowed to become rubbish-strewn and overgrown. The sight of these wasted plots was a source of great frustration to Octavia and her ladies, working in densely populated areas like Drury Lane

---

26 In 1850 the Metropolitan Interments Act was passed forcing local parishes to make 'better provision for the interment of the dead in or near the Metropolis'. Subsequent acts in 1852 and 1853 forced London churchyards to close for new burials. These Acts also empowered the metropolitan parishes to set up burial boards. These boards had to choose between opening their own municipal cemeteries or purchasing plots in other cemeteries such as Finchley or Brookwood. St George's Bloomsbury, St Giles-in-the-Fields, St Nicholas Deptford and St Anne's Soho all used Brookwood cemetery. Even as late as 1902, however, the church of St Mary in Upper Street, Islington, had to be temporarily closed down by the medical officer of health because of the smells coming from the crypt. The coffins were removed to Finchley cemetery.

---

27 'The soil had become saturated with human putrescence and bones, and the remains of coffins were often seen lying on the surface of the graves.' Walter E. Brown, 'St Pancras Open Spaces and Disused Burial Grounds', London, 1902, p.4.

where the poor had absolutely nowhere to escape from the noise and the smell of their tenements.[28] The Kyrle campaign was almost immediately successful, getting the churchyards in Drury Lane and Waterloo opened, soon to be followed by Bloomsbury and Bethnal Green. Other spaces were commandeered for the poor, including the site of Horsemonger Lane Gaol and the Poors' Land in Bethnal Green.[29] However, Octavia was only finding her feet with these little ventures. The scope increased dramatically with the campaigns to create Vauxhall Park and to add Parliament Hill Fields to Hampstead Heath. Now that it is almost taken for granted that the costs of environmental amenities will be met by public authorities, it is salutary to be reminded that, in these early campaigns, most of the costs, and in some cases all of them, had to be met by people who put their hands in their pockets to prevent a site from being built upon and lost as an open space forever. As the campaigns got larger, and the amounts of money needed increased, so the public funding element became more important,[30] but the big question, in the last part of the nineteenth century, was: who was to own and manage these open spaces once they had been saved?

---

28 The closure of burial grounds in the centre of the metropolis came at a time when the different railway companies were competing for prime sites for their London termini. The St Pancras vestry met in May 1874 to consider an offer by the Midland Railway Company to purchase St Giles and St Pancras burial grounds. The vestry decided to oppose the Midland Railway Bill by a petition in the House of Lords, but they had to act quickly to ensure the preservation of the burial grounds as open spaces. By July 1874 the General Purposes Committee had obtained a plan and estimate for the laying out of the burial ground, at an approximate cost of £2,000, and had given instructions for the plans to be lithographed, and a copy sent out with a circular inviting subscriptions to help towards the purchase of the grounds for the people. St Pancras churchyard was finally purchased in 1890.

---

29 A list of 'public urban parks and recreation grounds in the United Kingdom' drawn up in 1883 included no fewer than 62 London burial grounds turned into public gardens. In addition, 53 'small enclosures' had been opened to the public. (Brabazon, 1886, pp.213-15.) Clearly, the Kyrle Society had been pushing at an open door. In 1885 the *Charity Organisation Review* was able to express the hope that 'soon it will only be in the pages of Dickens that the dreary London burial grounds depicted in *Bleak House* will be found.' (*Charity Organisation Review*, December 1885, p.506)

---

30 In the case of really enormous campaigns, like the one to save Parliament Hill Fields, Octavia accepted that public funding was vital, but she never wavered in her conviction that voluntary offerings were better. She opposed seeking government funds for the purchase of the site of Horsemonger Lane Gaol in 1879, asking: 'Is it to be all compulsory taxes, and no free-will offering?'(Maurice, 1914, p.393.)

Octavia's involvement with open spaces in these years was mainly through the Kyrle Society, but the Kyrle was only one of several organisations in the field, including the Commons Preservation Society and the Metropolitan Public Gardens Association. None of these organisations was constituted to receive and manage land. Once the sites were saved they had to be passed on to public bodies, originally the vestries, sometimes the Corporation of London and, after 1888, the London County Council. However, it was by no means taken for granted that public funds should be spent on maintaining open spaces, and some of these public bodies were reluctant to add to the costs being borne by their ratepayers.[31] By the end of the 1880s the Metropolitan Public Gardens Association was in a financial hole, because the Metropolitan Board of Works was refusing to take on churchyards and other sites that the MPGA had acquired. The situation was saved only when the London County Council replaced the Board of Works and turned out to be more sympathetic to providing such amenities. As late as 1907 the levying of a two-pence-in-the-pound rate to acquire Purley Beeches was so controversial that a poll of the whole parish had to be taken, and 40 per cent of the ratepayers voted against it. (1904, pp.524-25.)

With her deep mistrust of public bodies in general, and the LCC in particular, Octavia would, in any case, have had reservations about handing over to the state sector an asset acquired by the generosity of individuals. In the 1880s she and Robert Hunter began to formulate a plan for a new type of organisation, set up by the private sector to

---

31 It is one of the ironies of the letters that, as the years go by, Octavia becomes more and more concerned by the 'alarming extravagance on the part of local authorities' (1907, p.572), piling costs onto ratepayers. She was objecting to their ventures into the field of housing, which she felt were totally unnecessary, whilst she was at the same time adding considerably to the burden on ratepayers by acquiring one open space after another and passing it on to public bodies, prior to the creation of the National Trust.

---

32 As the National Trust is now one of our largest voluntary bodies, with the status of a major national institution, it is inevitable that the references to its early acquisitions will be of special interest to the modern reader. The Kyrle Society, on the other hand, through which Octavia conducted most of her open spaces work for twenty years, and a good deal even after the formation of the Trust, closed within five years of her death. It is now almost completely unknown, which makes it difficult to assess its relative importance at the time. However, it was famous and influential in its day, and Octavia allocates more space in the letters to the Kyrle Society than to the National Trust. Nobody could have foreseen at the time the extent to which the Trust would eclipse

receive and administer land in the public interest. In 1894 this bore fruit with the foundation of the National Trust.[32]

From that point onwards, there is a shift in Octavia's accounts of her open spaces work. First of all, it moves outside of London and its suburbs to cover the whole country. Second, the spaces involved get much bigger. Instead of six acres in Bethnal Green, eight acres in Vauxhall or 45 acres of Hilly Fields, Octavia was after 108 acres of Derwentwater and 700 acres of Ullswater. The only open space campaign on this scale in the pre-National Trust days was Parliament Hill Fields at 310 acres, but that was so large and so expensive that even Octavia had taken it for granted that the bulk of the money would have to come from public sources. The National Trust properties, on the other hand, were privately funded[33] and privately managed. The extraordinary aspect of Octavia's account of the early days of the Trust is the speed with which the sites were acquired. With scarcely any staff and minimal resources at its disposal, the Trust acquired, in the 18 years described by Octavia, the most important of its now enormous landholdings in the Lake District, together with very substantial areas in Kent and Surrey, Morte Point in Devon, the Cheddar Gorge and other properties spread around the country. It was as if a barrier had been broken through, and people suddenly found the sort of organisation they had been looking for 'to keep for her people for ever, in their beauty and accessible to all, some of England's fairest and most memorable places' (1896, p.393).

The formation of the National Trust marks another important development in Octavia's treatment of environmental issues in the letters to fellow-workers. In the earlier campaigns for open spaces in London, she had argued on the basis of health. People in crowded tenements needed some open space to sit in, to breathe some fresh air, to get

---

all of the other open spaces organisations of the time. 'Of course, it might grow, but then it might not', Octavia had written to Sydney Cockerell in 1896 (Maurice, 1914, p.538). For an assessment of the importance of the Kyrle Society in Octavia's work, see Appendix 2.

---

33 'Most of us are in no way urging that such purchases should lose their grace and spring and spontaneity by being made compulsory, nor, by being embodied in the nation's expenditure, press hardly on those who are struggling for absolute subsistence. We are not asking that such areas should be acquired by rate or tax, but that, by the voluntary combination of many, great and permanent possessions should be acquired for the people.' Octavia Hill, 'National beauty as a national asset', *The Nineteenth Century and After*, vol. 58, 1905, p.938.

away from the noise of the children, to rest after a long day at work. However, Octavia also regarded open spaces as having a moral and spiritual value. They could bring people, poor as well as rich, into a frame of mind that made them open to transcendental reflections. Although Octavia had always held this view,[34] it comes to the fore in discussions of National Trust properties. She makes it explicit in her confidence that Gowbarrow will be 'consecrated to the nation':

> 'There are too many who know that man does not live by bread alone; that when all material wants have been duly recognised and attended to, there does remain in England enough wealth for her to set aside a few areas where man may contemplate the beauty of nature, may rest, may find quiet, may commune with his God in the mighty presence of mountain, sky and water, and may find that peace, so difficult to realise in the throng of populous cities.' (1904, p.527.)

The accounts

As we have seen, the letters to fellow-workers have been difficult to access ever since they were circulated, being made available only in very brief extracts. The accounts, however, have never been republished at all. They are unknown quantities. This is unfortunate, because the letters were originally conceived as appendages to the accounts. Without the need to render accounts to donors, there would have been no letters to fellow-workers at all. So what do they tell us?

The first and most obvious thing to say is that they show how meticulous Octavia was about accounting for every penny she received. Indeed, it was said she made her ladies balance their accounts to the halfpenny, and would accept no excuses. A failure to balance accounts was, in Octavia's eyes, a flaw of the most serious nature which could vitiate the whole work. Whilst preparing this volume, the accounts were all checked, and some errors found in the totals. These must derive

---

34 In 1877 she had argued for open access to common land as a means of encouraging patriotism and improving character: '... the love of being connected with the land is innate; it deepens a man's attachment to his native country, and adds dignity and simplicity to his character... It will be a link between the many and through the ages, binding with holy happy recollections those who together have entered into the joys its beauty gives... into one solemn joyful fellowship.' (*Our Common Land*, pp.205-06.)

from errors in typesetting, when compositors read a 3 for an 8 or something of that nature. (1899, p.440.) Octavia had her accounts audited from the early days, and it is inconceivable that either she or her auditor would have approved a set of accounts that failed to balance.

The other thing the accounts tell us is how Octavia was prepared to make her life more difficult than it need have been by insisting on opening separate accounts for various projects, in order to make sure that money given by the donors was spent exactly as they would have wished. She frequently insists, by means of asterisked comments to the donation fund accounts, that a particular item of expenditure reflected a donor's exact, stated preference. Indeed, she admits that she spent a good deal of time in matching donors' wishes to requests for assistance.[35] But she went further than that, publishing separate accounts for the workroom in Walmer Street, the fund for improving houses, and the Red Cross Hall and garden. From 1907 onwards, the Red Cross splits into sub-divisions: the main Hall and garden account, the flower show account, and a separate fund for the balcony appeal in 1907. In truth, most of the people who sent Octavia money were probably interested in her work as a whole. Like her, they could see the connection between housing, the environment, social activities, and so on,[36] and it is not surprising that we find the same names cropping up in different lists. Nevertheless, Octavia felt it important to make it clear that people who gave money for the flower show were not supporting orphans, and vice versa.

It is important to realise that the accounts do not present us with a full picture of all of Octavia's interests. They contain nothing at all about her activities in housing management, for example. Octavia rendered accounts for that directly to the owners of the properties, and as far as she was concerned they were none of anybody else's

---

35 'I will ask my kind donors to believe me, that to the very best of my power the spirit of their trust has been fulfilled in each case, and that the kind of object which they would desire to aid has been assisted.' (1876, p.70.)

---

36 Octavia liked to boast of how she had led them on: 'donors began to realise that the gift of joy, and personal intercourse with those who work among them might be as much needed by the poor as gifts of coals and bread, and money was sent to me for our summer and winter parties; then the need of beauty in the surroundings of our people became clear to some of my kind friends and donors, and money was sent for carriage of flowers and such things as that.' (1876, p.69.)

---

37 Octavia made an exception in the letter for 1891, when she printed details of rents collected from Ossington Buildings in the last three quarters during which it

business.[37] She also makes it clear that, although she is constantly appealing for funds for organisations that she supported like the Kyrle Society and the National Trust, anything sent as a result to those organisations would appear in their own accounts and not in hers.[38] There was, however, one significant exception.

In 1907 Octavia appealed for funds to add a bit of land to Mariner's Hill, which had been acquired for the National Trust in 1903. In the 1908 letter she triumphantly announces the purchase, which she had accurately predicted would cost £1,500, and prints a separate account to show how the money had been raised. She had transferred £188 from the donation fund, which was £40 more than the fund had received in 1908, and she attaches a list of donations via the National Trust, including £150 from the Trust's own meagre assets. (1908, p.600, n.14 and 608-9.) As Octavia was a committee member of the Trust, and her companion Miss Yorke was the treasurer, this shows how useful it was to Octavia, at critical moments, to have a finger in several pies.[39]

On the whole, however, the donation fund accounts tell us nothing of the extent to which Octavia was fundraising for projects managed by other bodies, and for that reason they give us only a very imperfect picture of her activities. As Figure 2 shows, there was considerable fluctuation in the fund's income, with no perceptible pattern. The poor performance of the fund in some years post-1900 (falling below Octavia's minimum required figure of £150 for educating orphans

---

had been under her management. She was clearly annoyed by the removal of the property from her control. (1891, p.302.)

---

38 The Red Cross project was in an anomalous position. The land for the Hall, cottages and garden was leased by the Ecclesiastical Commissioners to a board of trustees, so, strictly speaking, it was not under Octavia's direct control, and there was no more justification for adding its accounts to the letters than there would have been for the Kyrle Society and the National Trust. In reality, Red Cross was Octavia's pet project, mentioned in every letter from 1886 onwards, and she assumes that her supporters would want to know about 'so integral a part of my work as that carried on in the Red Cross Hall and garden' (1888, p.242). She attaches the Red Cross accounts to the letters for 1887 and 1889 to 1894 inclusive. In 1895 she announces that the Red Cross accounts are printed in its own report (1895 p.375), and they do not appear again until 1901. Thereafter they appear every year until 1906, when, once again, Octavia directs her readers to the Red Cross report, but from 1907 onwards Octavia re-jigs the donations page to give Red Cross a permanent status as part of her work that she expects the fellow-workers to fund.

---

39 For a similarly useful rotation of her several hats in the purchase of Postman's Park, see 1900, pp.455-56, n.16.

Figure 2: Contributions to the donation fund 1872–1911, excluding interest, loans repaid and balances carried forward

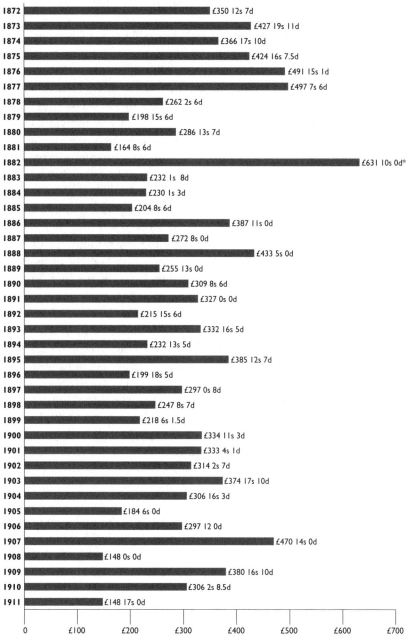

1872	£350 12s 7d
1873	£427 19s 11d
1874	£366 17s 10d
1875	£424 16s 7.5d
1876	£491 15s 1d
1877	£497 7s 6d
1878	£262 2s 6d
1879	£198 15s 6d
1880	£286 13s 7d
1881	£164 8s 6d
1882	£631 10s 0d*
1883	£232 1s 8d
1884	£230 1s 3d
1885	£204 8s 6d
1886	£387 11s 0d
1887	£272 8s 0d
1888	£433 5s 0d
1889	£255 13s 0d
1890	£309 8s 6d
1891	£327 0s 0d
1892	£215 15s 6d
1893	£332 16s 5d
1894	£232 13s 5d
1895	£385 12s 7d
1896	£199 18s 5d
1897	£297 0s 8d
1898	£247 8s 7d
1899	£218 6s 1.5d
1900	£334 11s 3d
1901	£333 4s 1d
1902	£314 2s 7d
1903	£374 17s 10d
1904	£306 16s 3d
1905	£184 6s 0d
1906	£297 12 0d
1907	£470 14s 0d
1908	£148 0s 0d
1909	£380 16s 10d
1910	£306 2s 8.5d
1911	£148 17s 0d

* Includes an anonymous donation of £500, the largest ever made to the donation fund. (1881, p.147.)

and other long-term commitments in 1908 and 1911) could suggest a withering of the support network, except that we know she was raising enormous sums in this period for the purchase of open spaces, mainly for the National Trust.[40]

The donation fund covers all the charitable acts of comfort and support that Octavia undertook when she was responsible to no one but herself. 'I only acknowledge here the money sent to me for disposal privately' (1891, p.301). When explaining the purpose of the donation fund in the letters, Octavia always makes it clear that it had two purposes. The first was to provide assistance to various needy individuals she had come across in the course of her work: 'there are boys to get to sea, girls to put to service, bread winners to send to the country, the patients to send to hospitals, the little pensions to provide if the club breaks' (1886, p.208). In most years, the largest grants from the donation fund would go to pensions, the training and boarding-out of children and medical care. However, the second and more interesting role of the fund was to provide support for fledgling movements at critical moments, for example the Charity Organisation Society in its early years, the Barnetts' work in Whitechapel, the Kent and Surrey committee of the Commons Preservation Society, the smoke abatement movement and the cadet corps. When Octavia had her breakdown and went abroad for several years, she left the donation fund in the hands of her sister Emily (Mrs Edmund Maurice). In the 1878 letter she tells her fellow-workers, with a frankness that must have taken Emily aback somewhat, that while she had every confidence in her sister being able to carry out the first part of the fund's function, she lacked the contacts to fulfil the second. Octavia therefore urges her donors to think twice about sending her money at all. (1878, pp.105-06.) Octavia was depressed when she wrote this, and she seems to have had second thoughts about this somewhat blunt observation on her sister's lack of social standing because she makes a point of praising Emily's handling of the donation fund in subsequent letters, but the damage was done. Contributions fell off dramatically for a few years, although never below the £150 per annum that Octavia calculated was her bare minimum for meeting standing commitments (1878, p.105). As Figure 2 shows, donations picked up when Octavia was back in the driving seat.

---

40 £6,500 for Brandelhow in 1902; £12,800 for Gowbarrow in 1906. 'The donation accounts... show not a tithe of what has been sent.' (1891, p.301.)

It is tempting to scan the list of donors for people whose names we still recognise a hundred years later. As we would expect, a number of the fellow-workers turn up: the Barnetts, Edward Bond, G.F. Watts, Miss Tait, Elijah Hoole, Ellen Chase, Margaret Sewell and Ralph Clutton, the Ecclesiastical Commissioners' agent. John Ruskin gave 80 guineas in 1877 and £80 in 1878, no doubt as guilt-offerings for his part in Octavia's breakdown. Several donations, some of them quite large,[41] are credited to 'Miss Octavia Hill's Fellow-Workers'. These sums represented money that had accrued as a result of many of Octavia's housing managers being volunteers, and thus not taking the normal five per cent commission on the rents collected. However, Octavia would not imperil the integrity of her business arrangements by allowing landlords to escape this normal business outgoing:

'I have always charged the owners the ordinary commission on rents collected, because I hold that such property should be managed on a sound financial basis. The fact that we have volunteers secures to the tenants a far larger amount of personal care than would be possible without them, but it also diminishes the cost, and I should like here heartily to thank all who have helped, both in the courts and with the accounts, and to ask them to realise that it is practically they who have made this large gift to the Ullswater fund.'[42] (1904, p.525.)

Then there is a handful of celebrities amongst the donors: Florence Nightingale, Gertrude Jekyll, Baroness Burdett-Coutts, Baroness de Rothschild, Sir Charles Trevelyan. Lord Ronald Gower and Campbell Dodgson[43] provide unexpected links to Oscar Wilde's circle. Some of these people gave only once, or a few times. What is more impressive is

---

41 The largest was £250 for the extension to Mariner's Hill in 1908.

---

42 In 1904 Octavia gave £100, on behalf of her fellow-workers, to the appeal to purchase Ullswater for the National Trust.

---

43 Lord Ronald Gower (1845–1916) (donated £20 in 1875) was a sculptor whose most famous work is the Shakespeare Memorial in Stratford. He was a somewhat predatory homosexual, supposedly the model for Lord Henry Wotton in *The Picture of Dorian Gray*, who actually adopted one of his young men, a character by the name of Frank Hird. This led Wilde to observe that 'Gower may be seen but not Hird'. At the time of Wilde's prosecution on charges of gross indecency, Gower left the country, fearful for his own situation. He was a committee member of the Kyrle Society for

the way in which several members of the same family, sometimes across generations, became regular donors: the Cockerells, the Martineaus, the Schusters. Stella Duckworth inherited the mantle from her mother, Mrs Leslie Stephen. Mrs Bannerman took on the responsibility from her deceased daughter (1901, p.472, n.8).We see some names appearing, year after year, until death cuts short the record. Some of these 'regulars' were people of substance, like the Duchess of Cleveland, who gave £25 in 1893, then £50 every year after that until 1901, when she appears in the donor list as 'Cleveland, Duchess of (the late)'. Others are identifiable. Mrs Macaulay, who appears as a donor in the first and last letters, and every letter in between except for nine, was presumably the mother of Mary Macaulay, who was a schoolgirl when she met Octavia in 1862 and went on to marry Charles Booth. However, some were people of whom we know nothing. Who, exactly, was Miss Mary Wells, who donated in 31 years? Or Miss J. Forman (donated in 30 years)? Or Mr and Mrs Gillson (28 years)? Or Miss Frankau (26 years)? Or Rev. Plummer (25 years)? Of these, and of many other donors, we will probably never know anything more than that they were charitable souls, who felt sure that Octavia could be trusted to do something useful with their money.

Editing the letters

Octavia was a woman with an enormous workload, and the letters to fellow-workers were written under pressure. Furthermore, they were printed 'For Private Circulation Only', which meant that they did not go through the normal processes of commercial publishing, like copy-editing and proof-reading. Presumably Octavia sent her copy direct to the printer, after having it read through by whoever else was around at the time.

As a result, there are numerous small errors. Octavia clearly did not stop to check things, so there are mistakes in the spelling of people's names[44] and in many dates, even the dates of her published articles

---

many years. Campbell Dodgson (donated £5 to the Mariner's Hill appeal in 1908) was engaged in 1893 as a private tutor for Lord Alfred Douglas after Douglas had failed his exams at Oxford. Douglas took Dodgson to spend a few days with Oscar Wilde at Babbacombe Cliff near Torquay. Not much studying was done, and Dodgson wrote to a friend that: 'I shall probably leave what remains of my religion and my morals behind me'.

and key events in her own career. Her quotations of verses of poetry and scripture were done from memory, with the result that very few of them are completely accurate. This poses problems for an editor who is bringing these letters to publication in their entirety for the first time since they were written. Given the impossibility of consulting with the author, to what extent should they be tidied up?

The intention has been to reproduce the letters exactly as they were written and circulated. No attempt has been made to re-write or improve the text, except to correct obvious typographical errors and spelling mistakes. The directness with which Octavia speaks to her fellow-workers, without the intermediary of editing, adds to the forcefulness of the letters. The tortured syntax of the 1877 letter reflects Octavia's state of mind following her breakdown; and it would, in any case, be difficult to unscramble the metaphors of a sentence like: 'Walworth and Notting Hill ... are in the radius to which the tide is setting' (1907, p.574). Following convention, I have eliminated the heavy use of capitalisation and double punctuation, of which the Victorians were so fond, but which now constitutes a distraction to the reader. Where there are errors in Octavia's quotations from poetry or scripture, I have noted them in the case of wrong words, but silently corrected punctuation and italicisation.

The accounts required more work to make them easily intelligible to a modern reader. Because each letter was produced individually, and often, one suspects, in a great hurry, there was no attempt to establish a house style. For example, Octavia sometimes heads her columns Cr and Dr for credit and debit, and sometimes receipts and expenditure. The latter is obviously the right form for charitable accounts, and has been adopted throughout. For some reason, Octavia always describes the donation fund as an 'account' and the Red Cross fund as a 'balance sheet', when it is no more a balance sheet than the donation fund. The pages have been headed accordingly. She sometimes refers to the Red Cross accounts as representing the Red Cross Hall, and sometimes Red Cross Hall and garden. As they almost all include

---

44 Anna Scrase-Dickins, the founder of the Horace Street Trust and consequently one of Octavia's most important donors, appears as Mrs Scrase-Dickins, Scrase Dickins and Scrase Dickens. (Her descendant Mark Scrase-Dickins tells me that family still suffers from the same problem.) Mrs Macaulay, the only person who appears as a donor in the accounts for the first and last letters, appears as Macaulay and Macauley, sometimes in the same set of accounts. These mistakes have been silently corrected in the present edition.

items such as pigeon food and maypoles, which clearly relate to the garden, the latter form has been adopted from 1889 onwards.[45].

Every attempt has been made to track down and footnote the individuals, places and events mentioned in the letters. In spite of the incalculable hours of research carried out by my own fellow-workers, there are still some gaps. I would be pleased to hear from anyone who knows where the East End boulevard was projected, or what the Popular Municipal Alliance actually did. It would also be good to have more information on the fellow-workers themselves. As social historians have been observing for many years, history tends to be written by and about rich people; the poor are more difficult to track down. So, we were able to find out a good deal about the Countess of Selborne and the Countess of Ducie, less about Miss Lumsden and Miss Covington. And yet without these persevering women of modest means, going week after week to visit the tenants, chasing up arrears and putting in hand repairs, there would have been nothing for Octavia to write letters about.

Octavia's two accounts of the Walmer Street Industrial Experiment are reproduced as an appendix. They are the immediate predecessors of the letters to fellow-workers, and resemble them in some ways, but they were written for publication. Anne Anderson's essay on the Kyrle Society, and Ian Ginsberg's on the Ecclesiastical Commissioners, also appear as appendices. With the chronology and bibliography of Octavia Hill's writings, they help to put in context this extraordinary series of letters, neither public nor private, which give us the insider's view of an interlocking cluster of social reform movements at the end of the nineteenth century and the beginning of the twentieth.

ROBERT WHELAN

---

45 The 1887 Red Cross account was specific to the appeal for the Hall, and the 1888 account, which appears at the end of the 1889 letter, is also exclusively concerned with the Hall.

Chronology

1838   Octavia Hill born 3 December, the third child of James, banker, corn merchant and campaigner for radical reform, and Caroline, educationalist and daughter of Thomas Southwood Smith, pioneer of sanitary reform.

1840   James Hill is declared bankrupt.

1843   James Hill experiences a severe nervous breakdown. He will never live with his family again.

1843–52 Octavia lives with her mother and sisters in Finchley.

1852   Caroline Hill is appointed manager of the newly founded Ladies Guild, a Christian Socialist venture to teach craft skills to women and girls. Caroline and her daughters move to Russell Place in Bloomsbury, giving Octavia her first experience of London life. Octavia is put in charge of a workshop of girls from a ragged school who are being taught to make dolls-house furniture. The venture brings the Hill women into contact with the leaders of the Christian Socialist movement, including F.D. Maurice, who will become a mentor to Octavia.

1853   John Ruskin visits the Ladies Guild and meets Octavia. He will become the second great influence on her life.

1855   Caroline Hill is dismissed as manager of the Ladies Guild for refusing to withdraw an invitation to F.D. Maurice, who had been accused of heresy, to teach a bible class to the children. John Ruskin offers to train Octavia as a copyist of paintings.

1856   The Ladies Guild closes, but Octavia keeps the toymakers' workshop going. She is offered the position of secretary to the women's classes at the Working Men's College in Red Lion Square.

1857   Toymakers' workshop closes.

1859   The Hills move from Russell Place to Francis Street in Westminster, then Milton Street (now Balcombe Street) in Marylebone.

1860   The Hills move to 14 Nottingham Place, Marylebone, which will be their home for the next 31 years.

1861   Octavia asks her close friend Sophia Jex-Blake to leave the Nottingham Place household, following clashes with her mother.

1862   Octavia and her sister Emily open a small school for girls, taking both boarders and day-pupils, in the house in Nottingham Place.

1864   Octavia begins teaching at the Working Women's College in Queen Square.

1865   John Ruskin pays £750 for a 56-year lease on three run-down houses in Paradise Place (now Garbutt Place), Marylebone for Octavia to manage. Octavia ceases to work for Ruskin as a copyist. Octavia's sister Gertrude marries Charles Lewes, the son of George Henry Lewes and stepson of Marian Evans (George Eliot).

1866   John Ruskin pays £2,880 for the freehold of five houses in Freshwater Place, Marylebone and one on the Marylebone Road (now Old Marylebone Road) and places them under Octavia's management. Miranda gives up her teaching job to help with the Nottingham Place school.

1869   Octavia is invited by Rev. Fremantle to join the Marylebone district committee of the newly formed Charity Organisation Society. Her involvement with Barrett's Court (now St Christopher's Place), Marylebone, begins when 11 houses come on the market and are purchased by Lady Ducie and Mrs Stopford Brooke.

1870   Octavia devises her Walmer Street Industrial Experiment, offering work to all unemployed men and women in the poorest part of Rev. Fremantle's parish, but refusing to give handouts. Her account of the scheme is published as a pamphlet.

1871   Two sisters, Hester and Julia Sterling, purchase the houses in Walmer Street and Walmer Place for Octavia to manage. Octavia's second account of the scheme is published as a pamphlet, accompanied by a list of donations. Octavia's father, James Hill, dies.

1872   Octavia's sister Emily marries Edmund Maurice, son of F.D. Maurice. Octavia writes the first Letter to Fellow-Workers.

1873   Lady Ducie has numbers two to five Barrett's Court demolished and replaced with Sarsden Buildings.

1874   A group of Octavia's friends, including George Eliot, collect £3,000 to invest on her behalf, thus freeing her from the necessity of supporting herself financially.

1875   Octavia's first open spaces campaign, to save Swiss Cottage Fields, is a failure. *Homes of the London Poor*, a collection of Octavia's magazine articles, is published by Macmillan.

1876   Princess Alice of Hesse-Darmstadt, Queen Victoria's second daughter, visits some of Octavia's properties, and arranges to have *Homes of the London Poor* translated into German. The Kyrle Society is formed by Octavia and her sister Miranda.

1877   *Our Common Land*, a collection of articles and talks by Octavia, is published by Macmillan. Octavia becomes engaged to Edward Bond, then the engagement is broken off. John Ruskin attacks her publicly in *Fors Clavigera*. Jane Nassau Senior and Sydney Cockerell die. Octavia experiences a severe nervous breakdown, withdraws from her work and spends most of the next three years travelling with Harriot Yorke, who will remain her companion for the rest of her life.

1880   Octavia returns to campaigning by involving herself, through the Kyrle Society, with smoke abatement.

1881   Ruskin decides to dispose of his courts. Octavia buys Paradise Place herself. William Shaen buys Freshwater Place. The Smoke Abatement Exhibition opens in South Kensington.

1882   Octavia returns to active involvement with housing management after her breakdown. St Christopher's Hall is built in Barrett's Court by Harriot Yorke.

1884   Octavia gives evidence to the Royal Commission on Housing. She undertakes the management of properties in Deptford for a private landlord, and in Southwark for the Ecclesiastical Commissioners. Harriot Yorke moves into 14 Nottingham Place and the girls' school closes. Harriot Yorke pays for a house to be built at Crockham Hill in Kent as a country retreat for herself and Octavia.

1886   Ecclesiastical Commissioners grant 999-year lease on a plot of land on Red Cross Street (now Redcross Way) in Southwark to be laid out as a garden. Anna Scrase-Dickins gives Octavia three houses in Horace Street, Marylebone. Octavia forms the Horace Street Trust to hold them.

1887   Red Cross garden laid out at the expense of Lady Ducie. Ecclesiastical Commissioners agree to let to the trustees of the garden an adjacent site for the construction of Red Cross Hall and cottages. Octavia is one of only three women (the other two being Florence Nightingale and Josephine Butler) invited in their own right to attend the celebration of Queen Victoria's Golden Jubilee in Westminster Abbey.

1888   Red Cross Hall and garden opened by the Archbishop of Canterbury.

1889   Ecclesiastical Commissioners make land available for White Cross cottages, behind Red Cross cottages. Octavia joins the committee of the Women's University Settlement in Southwark. Cadet corps formed in Red Cross Hall. Parliament Hill Fields and Vauxhall Park saved for the people.

1890   Through the Kyrle Society, Octavia organises the official opening of Vauxhall Park by the Prince and Princess of Wales. Walter Crane's panel of Alice Ayres is unveiled in Red Cross Hall.

1891   Octavia, Miranda and Harriot Yorke move out of 14 Nottingham Place and into 190 Marylebone Road, where Octavia will live until her death. Octavia forms the Kent and Surrey committee of the Commons Preservation Society. Octavia's contribution to Charles Booth's survey *Life and Labour of the People in London* is published.

1893   Hilly Fields in Lewisham is saved. On Octavia's suggestion, the Ecclesiastical Commissioners begin to build new cottages to let, instead of demolishing old cottages to replace them with blocks. The Commissioners offer 999-year leases on Red Cross Hall and cottages to bring them into line with the garden. First flower show held at Red Cross Hall. Training courses for social work introduced at Women's University Settlement. Emilia Russell Gurney gives Octavia her tenement block in Paddington, which is added to the Horace Street Trust. Octavia gives evidence to the Royal Commission for the Aged Poor. She begins the process of rebuilding Charles Street (now Ranston Street), Lisson Grove, site by site.

1894   First meeting of National Trust for Places of Historic Interest and Natural Beauty takes place on 16 July.

1895   Dinas Oleu at Barmouth becomes the first National Trust property, accepted at the first meeting of the executive committee in February. Lady Ducie dies and leaves Sarsden Buildings to Octavia.

1896   Barras Head in Cornwall becomes the first National Trust property to be acquired by public subscription.

1897   Lady Jane Dundas dies and leaves Octavia £1,000 for work among the poor.

1898   Octavia's portrait is painted by John Singer Sargent. First part of Postman's Park saved. G.F. Watts creates a 'cloister' there to commemorate deeds of working-class heroism.

1899   Octavia's involvement with housing in Notting Hill begins. Octavia receives a large donation in memory of a deceased supporter—probably Lady Ducie—which she calls the In Memoriam fund.

1900   John Ruskin dies. Second part of Postman's Park saved.

1901   Ecclesiastical Commissioners put Octavia in charge of houses on the Lambeth Estate that will be cleared as part of a seven-acre redevelopment, carried out with Octavia's close involvement.

1902   HRH Princess Louise opens the Brandelhow Park in the Lake district for the National Trust. Octavia's mother, Caroline Southwood Hill, dies.

1903   Ecclesiastical Commissioners announce that they intend to demolish, and rebuild, housing covering 22 acres at Walworth. Octavia becomes, effectively, the project manager. It will be the biggest estate she will ever manage, and reflects her mature view of an urban community.

1905   Octavia is asked to become a member of the Royal Commission on the Poor Law.

1906   Gowbarrow purchased for the National Trust and dedicated to the public.

1909   Octavia signs the majority report of Royal Commission on the Poor Law, but enters reservations on two points: the extension of free health care and the creation of artificial work in periods of recession.

1910   Miranda Hill dies.

1911   Octavia writes the last Letter to Fellow-Workers in December.

1912   Octavia dies in August.

LETTER

ACCOMPANYING THE

ACCOUNT OF DONATIONS RECEIVED

FOR

WORK AMONGST THE POOR

DURING 1872

৽৽৽৵৽৽

BY

OCTAVIA HILL

LONDON:
JAMES MARTIN, PRINTER, 9 LISSON GROVE, N.W.
1873

SUMMARY

The success of housing work: offers of capital received faster than managers can be trained... entertainment of the tenants... district visitors... help for the unemployed... Samuel and Henrietta Barnett depart for Whitechapel.

EDITOR'S NOTE

The first of the letters is also the shortest—at 2,022 words it is less than half the length of the longest (1876: 5,256 words). It contains very little about Octavia's work in housing, although she devotes space to the outings and entertainments for tenants which would remain one of the regular themes of the letters until her death. This letter continues in the vein of the two accounts of the 'Walmer Street Experiment' (see Appendix 1), explaining Octavia's elaborate scheme for the relief of poverty in the parish of St Mary's, Bryanston Square, Marylebone. This involved the co-operation of the parish visitors with the guardians of the poor law, the school board, the Charity Organisation Society, and, of course, Octavia's workroom for which the accounts are included at the end of the letter. She would include the workroom accounts in the letters for 1873, 1874 and 1875, but not thereafter. The 'human interest' in this letter comes from the news of the departure of Samuel and Henrietta Barnett for Whitechapel. Octavia describes this as 'the founding of our first colony', as she and the Barnetts were so much of one mind that she felt sure they would carry her approach to the relief of poverty to 'that terrible East End, where the thickest of the battle must be waged'. Octavia kept her promise to 'strengthen their hands in every possible way': the accounts for the rest of the 1870s show substantial grants to Whitechapel projects.

14, Nottingham Place, W.
December 31st, 1872

In sending to those who have kindly placed money at my disposal for distribution during the past year some account of the ways in which it has been used, it is not necessary that I should add much to what the Balance Sheet will tell them. But they may be glad to know something of the directions in which the work we are engaged in is growing and spreading.

They may be glad to hear that not only are all the sets of houses sub-let to the poor going on satisfactorily, and paying, as they have done all through, a minimum dividend of five per cent, but that offers of additional capital for investment are continually pouring in. These offers come much faster than we can train suitable superintendents for the management of such property. It is extremely important not to advance beyond the sphere which can be managed by trained and tried workers, which naturally contracts our own operations; but I may mention that one spirited lady proposes giving not only money but time also to the work, and has invested £7,000 in a block of buildings which she intends to superintend herself with the aid of a trained worker supplied by us and paid by the rents of her houses.[1] The accounts of the properties under my charge do not appear here, but are sent to the various owners

---

1   The 'spirited lady' was the Countess of Ducie. According to an article that Octavia wrote for *Macmillan's Magazine* in October 1871, her involvement with Barrett's Court, a notorious alleyway of slum properties between Oxford Street and Wigmore Street, began at the end of 1869 when she heard that a large number of houses were on the market. The Countess of Ducie bought six ten-roomed houses, then Mrs Stopford Brooke bought another five. (Whelan, 1998, p.67.) However, Octavia's name does not appear in the ratebook for Barrett's Court until 1871, so either the transactions were delayed, or the ratebook was not updated fast enough. In 1871 Octavia was recorded as paying the rates on ten properties, and by 1872 it was eleven. Within a few years she was managing almost all of the properties on both sides of the Court. Lady Ducie's original purchases included numbers three, four and five. She then acquired number two, and in 1873 pulled down two, three, four and five to replace them with Sarsden Buildings, a block named after the place of her birth in Oxfordshire (1873, p.17). Lady Ducie left Sarsden Buildings to Octavia after her death in 1895. They now belong to Octavia Housing and Care, and are the only part of Octavia's Barrett's Court (now St Christopher's Place) still in use as social housing.

of the houses; but I shall be happy to show them to any one to whom it may be of use to see them.

When the interest that has come from them has exceeded five per cent, it has invariably been left in my hands for purposes of permanent improvement, such as paving places hitherto unpaved, making additional windows, heightening rooms, laying on gas, etc.[2]

Besides these solid advantages conferred upon their tenants, a large number of the owners of the sets of houses have given summer excursions or winter entertainments to them, thus not only giving pleasure, but deepening the sense of personal relation and responsibility. And where this has not been the case, the same old friends have often come forward to help the group they helped in years before, so that former links of sympathy have been kept up. This division of the burden of expense has lightened its pressure on my donation fund wonderfully. Our population is now so large, however, that though we give only one evening entertainment in winter, and one day in the country in summer to each person, the sums so spent are considerable; but as I have often repeated, I consider them to be an integral portion of the work. Whilst on this subject of entertainments, I cannot refrain from mentioning Mr Fremantle's spirited and most successful scheme of entertaining his whole parish street by street.[3] I suppose no London parish was ever

---

2   The social housing movement traces its origins to the housing societies of the nineteenth century, set up to provide decent housing for working-class tenants at affordable rents. As it was considered demeaning to provide anyone with a 'necessary of life' like housing at a subsidised price, the rents had to show a real return on the capital invested; hence the phrase 'philanthropy and five per cent'. Since her earliest venture in housing in 1865, Octavia had always promised her investors a five per cent return on capital, and she more than succeeded in achieving it. On 28 February 1872 the Council of the Charity Organisation Society adopted a report on the management of Octavia's properties in the four areas of Marylebone where she was working: Paradise Place, Freshwater Place, Barrett's Court and Bell Street. In the five years that Octavia had been managing Freshwater Place, she had achieved the five per cent return, 'with a surplus which is represented by the cash in hand [£26 on an expenditure of £1,152]. For the future, it may be expected to pay... 6¼ per cent'. Paradise Place was paying eight per cent. Considering that Octavia was dealing with the lowest class of tenants, and providing a far better service than most landlords, it is a testimony to the efficiency of her system that she was able to show such returns. The report contains some valuable information about the number of tenants Octavia was responsible for—a subject on which she was always very cagey. (Whelan, 1998, p.10.) 'The total number of rooms in all the houses managed by Miss Hill is 432. The number of separate tenements is 274. The rent of single rooms varies from 2s. to 4s.; the rent of two rooms varies from 4s. to 5s. 6d.; and there are some tenements over shops in the Bell Street property the rents of which are as much as 7s. 6d.' (Charity Organisation Society, 1872, p.2.)

so brought together before. Such a gathering once a year of the district to meet the district visitors and their friends, would do much to bring us into happier and healthier relations to one another.

As regards the work carried on by visitors, I have this year much progress to record. We have still further carried out our plan of making every district visitor the agent in her own district for all the various work carried out there. We are sure that these different works help each other, and that the knowledge of the action of one body is most valuable in executing that of another. The school board work we hope will introduce the visitor into definite duties with regard to a higher class of people than that she would otherwise meet with in her business connection with her district, while the information from the guardians throws light on the lower portion of the population under her care, so that the school board and the guardian work take her both higher and lower in the social scale than she would otherwise go. It may be interesting to the visitors to know that by an arrangement with the guardians, which will come into force almost immediately, they will have notice each week of every case from their district which comes before the Board, and an opportunity will be given them of bringing any information they may have bearing on the case, to the notice of the guardians. I shall, of course, communicate with them saying how this is to be done when the details are arranged.

Next with regard to the providing of employment for those who are out of work; it may be satisfactory to know that in no former year has anything like the amount of employment passed through our hands. The greater part of this help—bridging over as it often does, the hard time which might be a family's ruin, or introducing the members of a family to permanent employment, does not appear in these accounts. Being given, as it is, to the able-bodied and independent, it could not well appear in an account of 'donations', and yet it represents most real and efficient aid. I still, however, manage the workroom, and with the workroom account I have incorporated a small amount paid for

3   William Fremantle (1831–1916), rector of St Mary's Bryanston Square in Marylebone and later dean of Ripon, was a clergyman of remarkable vision and abilities. His determination to sort out the chaotic system for the relief of poverty in the parish gave Octavia the opportunity to devise new approaches and carry them out. Octavia described these efforts in her account of the Walmer Street Industrial Experiment (see Appendix 1). Rev. Fremantle formed one of the first district committees of the Charity Organisation Society in Marylebone and, at the suggestion of his friend Lady Ducie, asked Octavia to be a member of it. After Ruskin and F.D. Maurice, he has a good claim to being one of the most important formative influences on Octavia's life.

messages and to little girls for scrubbing, although the workroom also is, to a certain extent, self supporting. I much value this power of employment for aged women, and for those incapable of more independent work, and also as a test for the lazy.

The donation account, therefore, represents a very small amount of the work done by us amongst the poor, since in every instance where it is possible we avoid making gifts. But it represents stored-up power to aid on those rare occasions when a gift seems desirable—in cases of deep distress when no other assistance is possible, or when a gift now, seems a stepping stone to independence hereafter. Let me again return my warmest thanks to all who have placed this power in my hands by their liberal gifts. It has been the greatest support and help to me.

I cannot conclude without telling those who are interested in this work one thing more which is at present occupying much of my thoughts.

It has for some time been evident to me that if workers and money continue to come to me, it must be intended that the strength should be directed to some much poorer and more desolate district than St Mary's. That though the sorrow and the joy and the work of past years had attached me personally to it, though the far-sighted wisdom and hearty co-operation of the rector, the guardians and the committee of the Charity Organisation Society, made it specially suitable ground for trying a model system of help, which might be adapted to other districts in various ways, yet the devotion of out-lying people, whether of time or money, should not be turned to this—a West End parish—where the inhabitants could, and should do their own work, and bear their own burdens. The question was, how to train and keep together my volunteers in any field so far removed from my other work; how to secure the wise expenditure of money entrusted to me, where I had no personal knowledge of the wisdom of donors, and no such excellent machinery was in existence as that in St Mary's. Another, and to my mind an even greater difficulty lay before me. It had always seemed to me that one charm of our work, and one cause of the depth of our power, lay in the way the work had grouped itself round my own home. Even if I had been prepared to devote ample time to work in the East, if the work begun here had been established well enough to spare me, I could not uproot and transfer the home with its associations for us all, poor and rich. But the difficulty has been met; two are going from amongst us—going from us, only to be more deeply united to us— who will found such a home in that terrible East End, where the thickest of the battle must be waged.[4] It is for us to strengthen their hands in every possible way. The living of St Jude's, Whitechapel, has just been given to one of the clergymen of St Mary's, who has gone side by side with us through all our work and experience here. He takes with him as his wife, one known to nearly all of you, loved by all who know her.[5] It is not for me to say a word in praise of either of them; they seem, after all we have gone through together, to stand almost too near. The

---

4   The East End of London was to the Victorians what Africa has become to us: the place where you go to do charitable and missionary work. The activities of the various charities and churches were so numerous that it was said, without much exaggeration, that you could find a mission on every street. The view that the East End and West End were splitting into separate tribes, which would never meet except on hostile terms, affected both the sociological literature of the day and its popular fiction. Writers such as Conan Doyle and Oscar Wilde depicted the East End as a place of unimaginable vice—especially after the Jack the Ripper murders—although the crime rate was a fraction of what it is today. Cosmo Lang, Archbishop of Canterbury, who as a young man had helped the Barnetts to establish Toynbee Hall in Whitechapel, wrote in his memoirs of an evangelical lady who told him of her 'nephew, such a noble young man, a clergyman who works in that dreadful East End of London; and he tells me of the dreadful things the people say about the aristocracy and Our Lord'. (Lockhart, 1949, p.46.)

---

5   Rev. Samuel Barnett (1844–1913) had become a curate at St Mary's, Bryanston Square following his ordination in 1867. He was put in charge of parish relief, and thus became involved with Rev. Fremantle's overhaul of the system. This brought him into contact with Octavia, for whom he conceived a degree of veneration bordering on hero worship. It was at Octavia's 32nd birthday party, on 3 December 1870, that Samuel Barnett met, and fell in love with, Henrietta Rowland (1851–1936), then only 19 and one of Octavia's parish visitors. On 4 February 1872 he proposed marriage to her, much to her surprise, as she had believed him to be taking no more than a kindly interest in the social work of a young parishioner. She was inclined to say no, but realised that, were she to do so, one or other of them would have had to withdraw from 'Miss Hill's social experiment'. Henrietta was convinced that Octavia's new approach to the relief of poverty in Marylebone, which was already being copied in other parishes, was of such importance that nothing must be allowed to jeopardise it, so she told Samuel that he would have his answer in six months, and that he was not to mention the matter in the meantime. He ignored the second condition and bombarded her with love letters until, before the expiry of the six months, she accepted his proposal. They decided that they were called to work in the East End, and through Octavia's influence Samuel Barnett received the offer of St Jude's in Whitechapel, although the bishop warned him that 'it is the worst parish in my diocese, inhabited mainly by a criminal population, and one which has, I fear, been much corrupted by doles'. St Jude's was on Commercial Street, next to the site on which Toynbee Hall would be built in 1884. It was demolished in 1924 and an office block now occupies the site. Samuel and Henrietta were married on 28 January 1873, fours weeks after the date of this letter, and moved to Whitechapel in March. (Barnett, 1918, i, pp.13-71.)

entire confidence I have in them, must be expressed in deeds, not in words. But I may tell you one ground of my hope for their success in their work; it is that they are going out in their full strength, yet determined to remember that it is not enough for them to spend that in the work, but many labourers are needed for the harvest, and that, for the sake of workers, as well as those worked for, they must enrol the strength of heart, of intellect, of wealth, and of time from the West.

I shall, please God, myself labour on in the old scenes, among the old faces and in the home round which my people have gathered, so long as I may have strength and time given me, but the work in the East will be sadder, lonelier, more urgent, if that were possible, and whatever of fresh workers come to offer themselves, whatever donations are entrusted to me, will be freely shared with that East End parish.

Mr E. Hollond, whose long residence in the East, and whose intimate friendship with Edward Denison,[6] make his words of value, writes to me from Dresden:

'I heard yesterday by a letter from my brother, that Mr Barnett had been appointed to St Jude's, Whitechapel. I know that parish well—almost every stone in it—having been for two years almoner

---

6   Edward Denison (1840–1870) was the son of the Bishop of Salisbury and the nephew of the speaker of the House of Commons, who arranged for him to become MP for Newark in 1868. As a result of working as an almoner for the Society for the Relief of Distress, he decided to go and live among the poor. In August 1867 he moved into a house in Philpot Street, off the Commercial Road, in Stepney, where he remained for eight months as a sort of one-man mission. He built and endowed a school, in which he taught, as well as giving a series of lectures to working men on the meaning of the bible. Passionately interested in the relief of poverty, his belief in the need for scientific methods, patient, detailed work among the poor and the extirpation of doles put him on Octavia's wavelength. He was involved with some of the preliminary meetings to set up the Charity Organisation Society (COS), but towards the end of 1869 he was obliged to travel to Australia for the sake of his health, where he died shortly after landing. He was described by David Owen as the John the Baptist of the COS (Owen, 1965, p.219), and the COS office in Vauxhall Bridge Road was named after him. His letters and writings on poverty were collected together and published in 1872, the year of this letter. Edmund Hollond had followed his example and gone to live in Stepney. On 1 November 1869 Denison had written to a friend: 'H [Hollond] has taken a lodging in Philpot Street, and I am sure he and R will get through some wholesome work this winter. It is a great comfort to me to feel that things are not at a standstill in that quarter.' (Leighton, 1872, p.165.) According to a pamphlet published by the Religious Tract Society in 1896, 'by the year 1874 it had become the custom for a few Oxford graduates to spend part of their vacation in the neighbourhood of St Jude's, Whitechapel, and to join in some of the work of the parish. Among them was

for the Society for the Relief of Distress in it. I cannot tell you how interested I feel about the matter, and how almost impelled I feel to go straight back to England and break through my medically imposed bonds and set to work with him and help him with the knowledge I possess of the parish. But do you know, it is about the worst, if not *the very* worst, in the East End to work. Not that the population is excessive, 8,000 about, of which 1,500 or more are Jews, I should think, and about the same number Irish of a very low stamp. For the rest, there are innumerable lodging houses: the very lowest—full of thieves and some prostitutes. New Court and George Yard are specially criminal portions. Oh, I tremble for Mr Barnett, if he looks for success there. The houses of the Whitechapel Road that bound the south side of the parish are full of publics. There are sometimes three together, next each other. Well, I do fear for Mr Barnett, that he will come out of that with terribly broken feelings if he looks to succeed there—all is so dark and miserable.'

Those who have helped me hitherto, will I think agree with me, that the sending forth from amongst us of such friends as those who are now leaving us, to found as it were a small centre of help in the midst of this mass of wretchedness, is the great event of the working year with us. They will feel it as our first contribution of help towards those heroic efforts which a few earnest workers have been carrying on in the East End for years past—as the founding of our first colony; and they will feel anxious, with me, to strengthen it to the utmost of their power.

OCTAVIA HILL

Arnold Toynbee. The intensity which Denison and Toynbee threw into their teaching and example made a great impression on public opinion, and the settlement at Toynbee Hall took an organised and permanent form in the year 1884.' (Henry Walker, *East London: Sketches of Christian work and workers*, Religious Tract Society, 1896.)

DONATION ACCOUNT, 1872

RECEIPTS

	£	s	d
Cash in hand	8	6	7
Loans repaid	2	15	0
Miss Wickens	1	0	0
Mrs Gillson	10	0	0
Mrs Macaulay	2	0	0
F.D. Mocatta, Esq	3	0	0
Rev. R Boyle	1	0	0
Miss Meredith	1	0	0
Mrs Grove	2	0	0
Miss Sterling (for her tenants' entertainment)	20	0	0
Miss Sterling	2	2	0
Mrs Scaramanga	2	2	0
Miss Waggett	0	5	0
Interest and Capital No 24 Henrietta Street	5	10	0
Alfred Hill, Esq	5	0	0
Mrs Sheffield Neave (for excursion)	0	12	0
Edward Spender, Esq	5	0	0
Sir George Phillips	5	0	0
The Countess of Camperdown	23	0	0
Mrs Watson	0	5	0
H.G. (for boy in industrial school)	5	10	0
Lady Caroline Charteris	3	0	6
Miss White	1	0	0
Mrs Arthur Mills (for pleasure vans)	3	10	0
Mrs Gouger	2	0	0
Collected by Miss Lukin (for Orphan Home)	2	16	1
Mrs Whittaker	1	0	0
Mrs Stopford Brooke (for entertainment)	5	0	0
Mrs Arthur Whately (for St Mary's entertainment)	1	0	0
Hornsby Wright, Esq	1	0	0
Lady Thompson (for two special cases)	1	0	0
Miss Wickenden (per Miss R. Hill)	1	0	0
Charity Organisation (for Mrs T.)	0	15	0
Miss Manning (for entertainment)	1	0	0
Miss Pipe (emigration of a family)	20	0	0
Miss Pipe	4	0	0
Lady Dilke	1	6	6
Mr and Mrs Lewes	10	0	0
Miss Cock	1	0	0
Mrs Lindesay	7	0	0
Francis Fox, Esq	1	1	0
Miss Pyne (for playground festival)	0	8	0
Mrs Stephen Ralli	1	0	0
Miss Trevelyan	1	0	0
Mrs Herbert Duckworth	5	0	0
The Honorable Esther Pomeroy	0	5	0
Mrs Kincaid	5	0	0
Miss Dawson	0	2	0
Berkeley Hill, Esq (for T. in hospital)	0	2	6
	£186	14	2

Received for specific objects requiring larger sums

	£	s	d
S.B.	100	0	0
Julian Sturgis, Esq	50	0	0
A Friend	25	0	0
	£175	0	0

DONATION ACCOUNT, 1872

EXPENDITURE

	£	s	d
S.T. Fare to Dover	0	4	9
E.L.'s Rent (per Miss Holland)	1	10	0
Boys' Excursion (Walmer Street)	3	11	10
Charity Organisation (for C.)	1	0	0
Cab with Invalid	0	2	0
Industrial School (J.W.)	3	15	0
Excursion (Bell Street Tenants)	6	0	11

Excursion, Walmer Street:

	£	s	d			
Hire of Steamer	8	8	0			
Food	15	8	4			
				23	16	4

	£	s	d
Gate Keeper, and Labels for Flower Show	0	6	7
Excursion (Spicer Street Children)	0	5	6
Convalescent Home (Mrs S.)	2	1	8
Excursion (Freshwater & Paradise Pl. Tenants) (Vans)	3	10	9
Stock for Shop (C.)	2	0	0
Journey, to Ben Rydding, and clothes (Loan to P.)	2	0	0
Rent (Mrs C.)	1	0	0
Cupboard for stock of clothes	3	10	0
Miss Sharman's Orphan Home	2	16	1
Charity Organisation (for Emigrant)	1	10	0
For Convalescent at a Home	1	10	0
Boots for child's attendance at school	0	9	6
Old Pensioner	1	0	0
Charity Organisation (Lady Thompson's case)	0	10	0
Poor seamstress, for Mrs C.'s dress	0	4	4
Mrs T's clothes	0	5	3
Travelling (D. and F.)	0	2	10
Children's Board (Father in Hospital)	0	4	6
Entertainment (Freshwater and Paradise Places)	1	4	10 1/2
Concert for Blind (Tea etc, for 500 people)★	3	0	4
Entertainment (Lady Ducie's tenants)	4	13	6
Binding books for Library	0	4	9
Employment of children half a year	2	5	0
Entertainment (Mrs B.'s Tenants)	2	18	0 1/2
K.H. in Hospital	2	2	0
Rev. W.H. Fremantle (for St Mary's parties)	6	0	0
Clothing Club, Lisson Grove	5	0	0
Baked Potato Can (M.)	3	0	0
Boys' Home	10	0	0
Entertainment (Walmer Street children)	2	9	8
Widow of D.	1	0	0
Charity Organisation (for Madame W.)	5	0	0
Christmas Tree (Barrett's Court)	1	19	10
Mrs C.	2	0	0
Treat for Choir children	0	10	0
May Festival	2	5	4
Rocking Horse	0	1	0
Board of Children (Mother in Hospital)	1	16	0
Excursion (Barrett's Court)	12	0	9
Emigration (W.S.)	6	8	0 1/2
Loan (W.)	0	13	0
Pensions T. and K. and N.	1	18	8
Starting Co-operative Store	2	14	0
W.R.	2	12	0
Framing pictures, Workroom and Club	0	4	0
Printing, Postage, Account Books, and Expenses for School Board Work	2	3	9
Cash in hand	37	1	9 1/2
	£186	14	2

★ The hire of Piano, Printing of Programmes, and all other expenses were paid by Mr Harry Taylor and his Friends.

WORK-ROOM ACCOUNT, 1872

RECEIPTS

	£	s	d
Cash in hand	15	13	3 ¼
Sale of Work	70	6	2 ½
Grants from St Mary's Relief Committee (wages of workers)	10	8	11
	£96	8	4 ¾

PLAYGROUND ACCOUNT, 1872

RECEIPTS

	£	s	d
Balance brought forward from 1871	18	11	11 ½
Miss Bell	0	5	0
	£18	16	11 ½

WORK-ROOM ACCOUNT, 1872

EXPENDITURE

	£	s	d
Superintendent	27	19	6
Wages:			
Women ... ... 29 1 9 ½			
Men 1 17 9			
	30	19	6 ½
Materials	29	16	7 ¼
Gas, Coals, Wood etc	4	3	10
Printing, Postage etc	2	3	9
Furniture and Repairs	0	12	6
Cash in hand	0	12	8
	£96	8	4 ¾

PLAYGROUND ACCOUNT, 1872

EXPENDITURE

	£	s	d
Salary of Superintendent	10	8	0
Chain and Lock	0	3	6
Balance	8	5	5 ½
	£18	16	11 ½

LETTER

ACCOMPANYING THE

ACCOUNT OF DONATIONS RECEIVED

FOR

WORK AMONGST THE POOR

DURING 1873

BY

OCTAVIA HILL

LONDON:

WATERLOW AND SONS, PRINTERS, GREAT WINCHESTER STREET, E.C.

1874

SUMMARY

Housing: Edward's Place, four houses in Barrett's Court demolished to make way for Sarsden Buildings, St Pancras, Lambeth, Whitechapel... the relief of poverty... the club in Barrett's Court... an inscription in Freshwater Place... the donation fund... entertainments for the tenants... support for Charity Organisation Society in Whitechapel and Marylebone... an anonymous donation... support for Samuel Barnett in Whitechapel.

EDITOR'S NOTE

After giving an account of the development of the housing work, Octavia returns to her scheme for bringing together the various agencies working for the relief of poverty in Marylebone. She once again emphasises the great importance she attaches to outings and entertainments for tenants, particularly when these are paid for by their landlords, as a means of breaking through class barriers. Octavia reveals that she still has reservations about printing a circular letter at all, as she feels she should really be writing individually to her supporters—an option by now impractical owing to the scale of her work. She speaks of her willingness to support the Barnetts in their work in Whitechapel, and this is borne out by the accounts, which show the largest single donation going to St Jude's (Samuel Barnett's church) with further grants to the Charity Organisation Society in Whitechapel and to the project to build baths and wash-houses there.

14, Nottingham Place, W.,
December 1873

My Dear Friends,

Each year I find that I have to address a larger number of you, and to speak with added gratitude of all that you are doing. But besides this, I have to speak of better work, and of new fields of work opening before us.

Among the triumphs we have this year to note is the purchase of a house in the worst court in South Marylebone. I think no one would say I was wrong in so describing Edward's Place, or in saying that some of our courts have been as bad, but are so no longer. Though we have only one house there, yet we usually find that the possession of one leads on to more. Even one gives us a footing from which to extend our influence, and I can see that it is gaining a hold of the people day by day.

We have also bought six more houses in Barrett's Court, and are rebuilding four of the old ones.[1] Each tenement will be approached by an outside balcony, the staircase will be lighted by gas, and the arrangements for water, drainage, and dust, will be admirable. When these houses are completed we shall have really good rooms there to offer to those of the tenants in the court who strive to live quietly, and to keep their homes clean and orderly. You all know why I shall rejoice to have such rooms to offer to good and careful tenants, you all know why, until the inhabitants had been trained to some degree of care, we

---

1   The four 'old' houses were numbers two, three, four and five. Number two had been acquired during 1873, and as Lady Ducie already owned the other three, she was able to demolish them all to create Sarsden Buildings, named after her birthplace in Oxfordshire, which she helped to manage herself. She left the block to Octavia, who in turn left it to her nieces Elinor Lewes and Maud Hopwood. It now belongs to Octavia Housing and Care and is still used for social housing. Amongst the houses acquired in 1873 were numbers 17, 18 and 19, between 15, 16 and 20 which Mrs Stopford Brooke already owned. They would all be demolished to make way for St Christopher's Buildings in 1877, but, unlike Sarsden Buildings, that redevelopment would be forced upon Octavia by the medical officer for the Marylebone vestry (1877, p.84-6).

could not have trusted them in new houses, and therefore, if we had rebuilt, we must have turned them out in favour of a higher class, thus compelling them to crowd in courts as bad as Barrett's Court itself was when we bought it.

We have purchased two houses in St Pancras, which are being managed by those who have local influence, and interest in the people, and I earnestly trust that this may form a new centre of work.

A block of model buildings in Lambeth, which had been a failure commercially, and, as it appears to me, a failure in its effect on the tenants also, has been put in our hands to manage. We at once put the management on a sounder footing, and have now let all the rooms. I do not know how far it may be burdened with responsibilities incurred previously. I am only answerable for the current accounts of rental and repairs, and for the arrangements with respect to the inmates, but I have the data of its annual accounts, and judging from these I cannot help hoping that we may transform it into a commercial success. In order that the undertaking may prove beneficial to the tenants, I must try to secure some earnest volunteer near the spot who will devote time to them.

Besides these buildings already under our control I earnestly hope that we may ere long secure a block of houses in St Jude's, Whitechapel. I have seen one that makes me long to take possession of it, with power to redeem it. In St Jude's there is, as you know, such personal power as will make the undertaking sure to accomplish whatever good it is capable of. Perhaps, before I am again writing this yearly letter to you, that block of houses may be ours.

The scheme of co-operation with the guardians alluded to in my last letter has come into full operation this year, the machinery appears to me to be admirable, and to offer all the advantages of the Elberfeld system of out-door relief. I will not here enter into any particulars about the plan adopted in Marylebone, as I have already given a full account of it in a report to the local government board. Mr Stansfeld has kindly promised that after this report has been laid on the table of the House it shall be reprinted separately. But though I do not write again of the machinery I wish to point out to those of you who are visitors, that the system has two great objects. First, to secure that out-relief shall be confined to the sober and respectable only. Secondly, to endeavour that it shall be so limited as to stir up the people to raise and keep themselves far above the pauper level. The first object you can achieve far better than the relieving officer, only because you have fewer cases to deal with and have opportunities of learning facts about them which are difficult for him to discover. But the second is a special work which you, and you alone, can do, for it is a question mainly of the spirit and temper which you, as friends of the poor, will stimulate in them, and of habits acquired before the day of trial comes, and you alone can encourage these habits. For instance, two men are struck down by illness, one of them has fourteen shillings weekly from a club because he paid seven pence a week during health. Who taught him to do so? The other is penniless. Who left him in ignorance of how and why to belong to a club, and neglected to call up the manly spirit in him which would have prompted him to do it? Try for the higher aim long before misfortune comes, and you may have every year fewer and fewer spiritless paupers in your districts.

I am glad to record that St Luke's district is now co-operating with us as to the work for the guardians and the school board, this enables us to give information to the relieving officer and school board visitor concerning nearly the whole of their district.

So much for new work. Of our old work I need not say much. It goes on silently progressing in the best way, I think. Certainly the club in Barrett's Court has gained in vigour very remarkably. It now numbers 88 members. They have formed a band, and paid upwards of £16 for their own instruments. They have a strong sense of corporate life, which is a healthy and ennobling thing. It shows itself in their pride in all their club property, their desire to make the club self-supporting, but above all, in their evident feeling that a good turn done to one member is a kindness to all. When we remember what life in that court was, and look at these men now, bound to order by rules of their own making, keeping their Christmas Eve sober and happy in the room they themselves decorated, or marching out with their band to oblige other societies, one can only be deeply thankful for the progress made.

Some of us have resolved to put up an inscription in beautifully coloured tiles on the houses in Mr Ruskin's freehold court where we have been so long at work.[2] The letters are all promised now, each is

---

2   Mr Ruskin's freehold court was Freshwater Place in Marylebone. John Ruskin (1819-1900) was a major influence on the culture of Victorian England. He was a connoisseur in the original sense of the word, imbued with a profound love and appreciation of art. His writings on art turned him into a critic of social and economic conditions, as he became convinced that good art can only be created by people living the good life in a good society. He believed the good life to be unachievable for the masses in a capitalist, industrial society, and consequently advocated radical reform of economic and political structures. His grand vision, which allowed him no time for attention to detail, combined with his idealistic view of human nature, doomed every

given by one of my fellow-workers, and in many cases a family has given a word, so that the inscription will be memorial as well as beautiful.[3]

---

practical project he devised to failure. When he met Octavia as a teenage girl, her intensity of feeling, combined with an abundance of common sense and a patient grasp of detail, must have suggested her to him as the obvious agent to carry out his plans for human betterment. When his father died, Ruskin inherited a considerable fortune. He was inclined to allow Octavia to carry out her plans for the management of working-class housing, and in 1865 paid £750 for the 56 years remaining on the lease of three slum tenements in the inappropriately named Paradise Place in Marylebone. In the following year he paid £2,880 for the freeholds of five houses in nearby Freshwater Place, together with a house in Old Marylebone Road that backed onto them. Because he owned the freeholds, Octavia was able to demolish the outbuildings and clear the yards to create her first open space. The houses in Paradise Place (now Garbutt Place) are still standing, but Freshwater Place was demolished to make way for Homer Row, which is still used for social housing. A rift occurred between Octavia and Ruskin over her refusal to support publicly his St George's Guild, a utopian scheme to recreate Merrie England, especially when she realised that his fiscal imprudence could imperil the properties she was managing so carefully on his behalf to show an annual return on capital of five per cent. Ruskin attacked her in *Fors Clavigera*, his monthly letter to the working men of Britain, and this helped to bring about Octavia's nervous breakdown in 1877. She retired from housing work for four years, and just when she was getting back to it, Ruskin made further difficulties by insisting on disposing of Paradise Place and Freshwater Place. Octavia managed to acquire Paradise Place herself, and Freshwater Place was bought by the Shaens, in order to keep it under her management (1881, pp.143-4).

---

3   Two months before writing the 1873 letter, Octavia had written an extra letter to the fellow-workers asking them to sponsor the inscription in Freshwater Place: 'Every house is builded by some man; but He that built all things is God' (Hebrews 3:4). 'There are 56 letters; if each letter is a foot square, the inscription will occupy the full length of the four houses; each letter will cost nearly eight shillings. If any of you will give a letter, you may feel that you have helped to write a sentence that will speak when you are far away, and after you are dead.' Octavia ended her letter with two long quotations from John Ruskin, and the comment: 'They, no doubt, taught me to care for permanent decoration, which should endear houses to men, for external decoration should be a common joy.' Octavia raised the money, letter by letter, as she had planned: amongst a long list of donors, the Hill family paid for 'builded', the Barnetts for 'by', and John Ruskin for the 'H' of He and the 'G' of God. Octavia demonstrated her advanced aesthetic taste by commissioning the tiles from William De Morgan, the artist-potter who was busy reviving the ancient traditions associated with Islamic ceramics at his pottery in Orange House, Cheyne Row, Chelsea. De Morgan had set up his pottery only a year before, and was not well-known. His work was both advanced in taste and very expensive, being all hand-made. Octavia had probably been directed to him by either Ruskin or William Morris, to both of whom he was well known. Octavia recognised that not everyone would appreciate his 'dim subdued solemn colour, and blurred uncertain suggestive outline' but she was determined to go for this rather

I have not yet said a word about the donations, and yet this letter is intended specially to accompany the balance sheet explaining them. Yes, but can I render a better account to the donors than by telling them what we have been and are doing—what kind of work it is that they are directly or indirectly helping? For though the houses are self-supporting and pay a good dividend, though the school board and guardians' work cost little, but postage and office expenses, yet all we do for them brings us face to face with people who at times want help, and abundant help, too, if they are to be well dealt with. I think our hearts would have failed—though somehow hearts never do fail that are bent on doing right—but I am sure their burden would have been far heavier, if we had not all felt, that, however sparingly we might use it, there was a fund strong to meet every demand which could be made upon it rightly. If we have used it sparingly it has always been for the sake of the spirit of the poor, not of the pockets of the rich, and so when the moment for wise abundant giving came, we have always been ready, thanks to the splendid liberality of the donors. Looking back to the feeble and solitary beginning of work some years ago, I cannot but contrast with awe my position then and now. I can hardly realise how difficult it once was to get money for the poor. Now I am always well supplied with it. Something of this is no doubt due to the confidence felt in the success of the work, but more, I believe, is owing to the desire to give full measure of help to the poor, which has deepened and extended rapidly in the last ten years.

As to the donation account it speaks very much for itself, but I would again draw attention to the considerable amount spent in entertainments, and to the fact that the owners of the houses have contributed very largely to provide these for their own tenants. I repeat that these entertainments appear to me more and more important, that I

---

than the 'clearly defined edge and crude but gay colour of some other tiles... We must prepare other people to be disappointed.' De Morgan wanted to use a mixture of colours including 'a lovely copper lustre which gleams like a fish's back', but Octavia was determined to have it all in shades of blue. She had probably seen De Morgan's Isnik pallette of peacock blue, which would later be used in his most famous commission: Lord Leighton's gorgeous Arab Hall in his house in Holland Park. Unfortunately, De Morgan's tiles in Freshwater Place were soon loosened by the frost, fell off the wall and shattered. He eventually refined his technique to cope with these problems, and the results can be seen in the entrance to the Debenham House in Addison Road, Holland Park, which have survived the London pollution. Although some have crazed, they have kept their colour and are still firmly attached to the wall.(Maurice, 1914, pp.293-97; Darley, 1990, pp.144-45).

personally feel every farthing spent on them, well spent, for they meet a great need, that of healthy amusement, and they bring us all nearer to one another in a really satisfactory way.

I have it very much on my mind, if ever time permit and I secure efficient help, to see what can be done to set on foot self-supporting and more public entertainments. The question is a different and much more difficult one, but perhaps we may be able to grapple with it. Our small club concerts are leading the way.

It will be observed that several rather large sums have been given to institutions, the baths and wash-houses in Whitechapel, and the Charity Organisation committees in Whitechapel and Marylebone. I hope those who kindly send me funds consider this within the limits of the trust committed to me. I have often seen that it would accomplish very important good. I never do it without intimate personal knowledge of the exact position of affairs, and distinct perception of need. The baths and wash-houses when once set free from debt will be self-supporting, they are situated in the midst of a densely populated and poor district, and will be of great value. I knew the leaders on the committee and felt sure that they would collect the rest of the money, but it was terribly up-hill work while so very little had been given. The event has proved as I expected, the amount is now so far made up that the vestry can and will do the rest. The Whitechapel Charity Organisation committee was nearly penniless when I sent the donations, they had not had time to prove their value to the district, now local subscriptions are beginning to come in. In Marylebone I gave the donation to assist the committee to engage a second agent in order to expedite enquiries, this I knew would be a gain to the poor, though few people care as yet to pay for machinery, it is, when well directed, one of the best forms of help.

Here I may acknowledge a large sum from an unknown donor, which reaches me through a friend, and of which no account is to be entered in the balance-sheet. It is sent to lighten my work in whatever way seems best to me. It has, in the first place, enabled me to engage an additional assistant, this is not only a great help to me, but a means of training one more capable leader of volunteer help among the poor. The remainder of the money I spend in various ways which facilitate work for which no one is exactly responsible, and yet which are truly helpful. When an undertaking is first started expenses often arise which naturally no one is willing to meet until the plan is proved useful. I have, heretofore, had to bear the main burden of such myself. Now I feel quite free to appropriate this fund to them. I hope the unknown donor will accept here the thanks I cannot give in person, and will be able to realise something of the strength and relief the sum gives me.

Lastly, it will be seen that I have sent something to St Jude's, Whitechapel. It should have been more, and I trust will be more. But Mr Barnett has wished very wisely to develop the resources of his own parish, poor though it be. The needs there, however, will grow as the work does, and I hope that whenever he sees further than his supporters in the parish, whenever a scheme of good opens before him for which he has not money, he may know that funds are in my hands on which he can draw freely for whatever may be necessary. The work there is awful in its character and extent, it is no small sacrifice voluntarily to live in such a district. May we with money and personal service strengthen the hands of all workers there to the extent of our power.

I do not want to make this a public letter, I wish I could write with my own hand to you all, for I want to say much more individually than I can in a circular letter, much more warmly than I like to do in print, how very deeply I feel the kindness of your help. I have perhaps hardly any right to thank you for it as if it were a personal help, I know very well that it is all for the poor, and is a sign of that deepening sympathy and sense of duty of which I spoke above, but the fact that it is for them only deepens the gratitude I feel, while somehow nearly all the help I receive has about it something of trust, of kindness, of individual response to hope or plan of mine, so that I cannot help feeling as if I should like to write to thank each of you, instead of all. But it cannot be; and something we gain as we always do by obeying the trumpet call, if it is the Master's: He has led us on to a large work, bidding us sacrifice old attachment to details, and enlarge our hearts and minds to wider fields. So though we miss now the individual reply to individual gift, we gain perhaps the sense of being a company, we are bound by no laws indeed, enrolled in no book, our members take different parts in the work which is various and not easily defined, we are placed in very different circumstances, some of us are widely separated in place, but we form a large company united in a common work, we have entered into fellowship one with another, and are bound together by a common hope for blessing on all we have in hand.

I am,
Yours always faithfully,
Octavia Hill

DONATION ACCOUNT, 1873

RECEIPTS

		£	s	d
1873	Balance from Work-room Account*	0	12	8
	Balance from Playground	8	5	5 ½
	Balance from Donation Account	37	1	9 ½
	Balance from Large sums for specified objects	175	0	0
Jan 12	Mrs Herbert Duckworth	5	0	0
	Mrs Stopford Brooke	3	0	0
Feb 2	Sir G. Phillips, Bart (for St Olave's)	5	0	0
	Mrs Cortauld	1	0	0
8	G.	7	3	10
	Sir G. Phillips, Bart	5	0	0
15	Miss Trevelyan (for St Barnabas)	2	0	0
	Loan returned (Pierman)	0	13	0
	Lady Thompson (for child's travelling,&c.)	0	6	6
Mar 1	Mrs Scaramanga	1	1	0
	Mrs Ernest Hart (Mrs Norman)	1	6	0
8	Edward Spender, Esq	5	0	0
	A Friend	100	0	0
	Lady Harrington	1	0	0
15	Mrs Lindesay	3	0	0
	H. James, Esq, M.P.	1	0	0
	Lady Grove	1	0	0
	Sir G. Phillips, Bart	5	0	0
	Hornsby Wright, Esq	1	0	0
	Mrs Western	1	0	0
22	Sir Edward Ryan	1	0	0
	Mrs Gouger	2	2	0
	Mrs Martineau	1	0	0
29	Sir Richard Wallace	20	0	0
	Miss Clover	1	0	0
April 5	Gen. Black	0	10	0
	Edward Bond, Esq	4	0	0
	Mrs Gillson	5	0	0
19	Mrs Nassau Senior	1	0	0
26	Loan repaid (Pierman)	0	5	0
May 17	Mrs Stopford Brooke	5	0	0
24	F.R. Statham, Esq	1	0	0
	Miss Harrison	0	3	0
31	Mrs Stephan Ralli (for Band)	5	0	0
June 21	Ernest Hart, Esq (for chairs for clubroom)	1	1	0
	James Cropper, Esq	5	0	0
30	Miss Manning	0	10	0
July 12	Miss Harrison	1	0	0
19	Charity Organisation (for V.)	0	11	0
Aug 2	A Friend	10	0	0
	Rev. W.H. Channing	1	0	0
9	Miss Sterling (for Excursion)	30	0	0
	Lady Florence Herbert	2	0	0
Sept 13	Mrs Arthur Mills	3	10	0
27	Mrs Maurice	1	0	0
Oct 11	Miss Barker	3	0	0
	Julian Sturgis, Esq	11	6	2
	Mrs Whittaker	1	0	0
	Mrs Gillson	5	0	0
	Lady Thompson	0	2	6
Nov 15	Henry Arkwright, Esq	102	3	9
29	Hornsby Wright, Esq	1	1	0
	Miss Malkin	50	0	0
Dec 13	Miss Pipe	1	10	0
	Miss Manning	1	0	0
	Miss Humphreys	0	12	0
		£649	17	8

* Miss L. Tagart having most kindly undertaken the entire supervision of the work-room, all the accounts relating to it except these items, which refer to an earlier date, will be found on page 12. (*Editor's note:* Pages 26-7 in this edition.)

DONATION ACCOUNT, 1873

EXPENDITURE

	£	s	d
St Jude's, Whitechapel	108	0	0
Two years Rent of Club and all other expenses for it	59	14	1
Baths and Wash-houses, Whitechapel	40	0	0
Excursion (Walmer Street Tenants)	38	0	10 ½
Additional Agent's Fund (Marylebone Charity Organisation Committee)	25	0	0
Excursion (for Tenants from Barrett's Court, Bell Street, Henrietta Street)	27	6	4
Emigration of Large Family	24	0	0
School and Clothes for Orphan (W.L.)	18	6	7
French Pasteur	16	0	0
School, Industrial, C.S.	13	0	0
Migration of family, Mrs S.	12	0	0
Playground- Salary of Superintendent	10	16	0
Employment of necessitous persons	7	7	8
Sewing machine for Widow, Mrs L.	6	15	2
Coals, Gas and other workroom expenses not included in Balance Sheet*	8	18	10 ½
Interest on Savings	6	11	1
Printing, Postage, Account Books, and expenses for School Board work	5	13	6
Clothes and support at Convalescent Home, F.M.	5	11	6
Surgical appliances	5	5	0
St Olaves Charity Organisation Committee (sent by Sir G. Phillips Bart)	5	0	0
Band for Whit-Monday Excursion	5	0	0
Whitechapel Charity Organisation Committee	5	0	0
Excursion (Parochial Mission Women)	4	14	3
Emigration, G.	4	14	2
Entertainment for Tenants, Paradise Place and Freshwater Place	4	9	2
Expenses for Night School, &c.	3	18	0
Vans, Excursion (Freshwater and Paradise Place tenants)	3	10	0
Employment of Children	3	16	0
Entertainment (Walmer Street Children)	3	10	11
Emigration K.O.	3	0	0
Poor Seamstress at Hoxton	2	19	0
May Festival	2	18	0
Mangle H.M.	2	10	0
Excursion (Children from playground)	2	17	6
Entertainment (Bell Street Tenants)	2	6	9
Gifts of Clothes	2	4	0
Flower Show	2	0	0
Mission Room, St Barnabas	2	0	0
Various patients at Convalescent Homes	1	15	9
Board of child (Mother in Hospital)	1	10	0
Knitting	1	6	5
Pension (Mrs N.)	1	6	0
Hire of Pianos	1	5	6
Tea party for Families in the North	1	3	4
Cups, Saucers &c. for parties	1	3	4
Entertainment (Freshwater and Paradise Place children)	1	0	2
Gift (per Miss Hesse)	1	0	0
Gift (by Mrs Maurice's desire)	1	0	0
Parochial Mission Women	1	0	0
Entertainment (Drury Lane Tenants)	0	16	5
Rent for Mrs G. (per Mrs Wodehouse)	0	15	0
Boots for V.	0	11	0
Child in Hospital	0	10	4
Woman in Hospital (Mrs C.)	0	9	0
Rowing Expeditions	0	4	6
Fare to Hendon (Lady Thompson's case)	0	1	3 ½
School fees (M.D.)	0	3	0
Cash in hand (including large sums for specified objects)	128	2	2 ½
	£649	17	8

WORK-ROOM ACCOUNT, 1873

RECEIPTS

	£	s	d
Sundry Accounts of Work Sold and done to Order … … … … … … … … …	26	2	9
Sale of Old Clothes …	9	6	7
Sale of New Clothes …	2	0	9
Grants from St Mary's Relief Committee (wages of workers) … … … … … …	8	3	11
Donation of clothing for Orphan Homes, Mrs Gillson … … … … … … … …	5	0	0
Donation of Calico and Materials … … … … … … … … … … … … … … … …	6	3	2
Deficit paid by Miss O. Hill … … … … … … … … … … … … … … … … … …	1	16	11
	£58	14	1

The thanks of the managers are due to those who have kindly sent presents of old and new clothing.

WORK-ROOM ACCOUNT, 1873

EXPENDITURE

	£	s	d
Superintendence …	26	10	0
Wages:			
Women … … … … … … … … … … … … … … … 9 0 11			
Man, Cobbler … … … … … … … … … … … … 0 8 2			
	9	9	1
Materials …	17	17	10
Coals, Wood, &c. …	0	17	8
Cleaning …	2	3	4
Soap, Soda, &c. Washing … … … … … … … … … … … … … … … … …	0	6	1 ½
Sundries, Carriage of Parcels, Tape, Cotton, &c. … … … … … … … …	1	10	0 ½
	£58	14	1

LETTER

ACCOMPANYING THE

ACCOUNT OF DONATIONS RECEIVED

FOR

WORK AMONGST THE POOR

DURING 1874

BY

OCTAVIA HILL

LONDON:

WATERLOW AND SONS, PRINTERS,

GREAT WINCHESTER STREET, E.C.

SUMMARY

Housing: Octavia's system of management... the role of the district visitor... the Charity Organisation Society and the relief of poverty... entertainment of tenants... Drury Lane and Whitechapel... the need for more detailed work... fellow-workers as queens in their own domain.

EDITOR'S NOTE

Octavia begins by describing the work of her housing managers, then goes on to describe the system of district visiting which she has established in her own parish in Marylebone. These visitors were not responsible for managing property, but they liaised between the parish relief committee, the COS, the school board and the poor law authorities to find the best way of responding to requests for assistance. Octavia describes her work at this time as consisting of four main elements: housing management, visiting, working with relief committees and supporting the COS, but the last three were all tied together. The exhortation to her fellow-workers to seize the initiative and not rely on her so much shows why Octavia wanted the letters to be 'for private circulation only': she wanted to be free to discuss 'the imperfections which still remain in our organisation' as well as the successes of the work.

14, Nottingham Place, W.
(December 1874)[1]

My Dear Friends,

In printing once more a letter at the close of the year to all of you whom my voice cannot otherwise reach, about our work here, it appears to me that it would be well to make it serve three purposes:

First. That of bringing you all a message of my deep and ever-deepening gratitude to you for the various help you are giving.

Secondly. Of setting down for those who are not so closely bound up with our work, and for those who see only one little bit of it, a short sketch of each undertaking we have in hand.

Thirdly. I should like to note in it how far I think we have now attained; where, I think, we still fail; and what progress I hope for in the near future.

With regard to the thanks, all words are so poor; but I do just want to point out that your help is now so considerable, so very valuable, that it is no longer to be called *help* of my work; it *is* the work now, and I am but a centre round which it has pleased God that it should all gather; and when it seems well to Him to call me away, the work, whether it gathers round some other centre, round many, or round none, will go on so long as there is need for it, and so long as you, and all whom you may hereafter influence, are governed by the spirit which has hitherto guided you. You will readily feel how thankful and how rested such a sight makes me; partly like one whose deepest desire is accomplished, and partly like a soldier whose watch is over because others have come to relieve guard.[2]

The sketch of the work in hand, though but in outline, cannot be very short. First in order of history, first perhaps in my mind in order

---

1 Dates given in brackets are conjectural. Octavia refers to 'the close of the year' in the first sentence.

---

2 This is the earliest of several passages in the letters in which Octavia contemplates the fate of her work after her own demise (see also 1876, 1880, 1906, 1908). That Octavia can feel 'like a soldier whose watch is over' at the age of 36 suggests that she was always a very old young person.

of importance, first certainly in having pre-eminently engrossed my attention during the past year, is the management of houses let to the poor. We have now 15 blocks of buildings under our care; they contain between two and three thousand tenants. Each block belongs to a separate person or company, who entrusts me with the collection of rents and management of the houses. Each block is placed by me under a separate volunteer worker, who has the duty of collecting rents, superintending cleaning, keeping accounts, advising as to repairs and improvements, and choice of tenants, and who renders all personal help that can be given to the tenants without destroying their independence, such as helping them to find work, telling them of good trades to which to bring up their children, collecting their savings, supplying them with flowers, teaching them to grow plants, telling them of provident dispensaries, of good schools, arranging happy amusements for them, and in every way helping them to help themselves. Of course the weekly visit to every family to collect rent gives a capital opening for all this work; and the control of the house itself, judiciously used, gives power for good much greater than that possessed by the ordinary district visitor. My assistants and I are ever ready and at hand to assist, advise, and relieve guard in the various houses, and of course the responsibility of so large an amount of property having been entrusted to me, the supervision of all and the passing of accounts rests with me; but my ideal is the utmost possible independence of the lady in charge of the houses, an ideal to which, as mentioned hereafter, we are more and more approximating. Every owner who entrusts the care of his houses to me receives five per cent on the purchase-money, and, in the case of leasehold, a yearly instalment of capital sufficient to repay the whole during the time the lease lasts. All the profit beyond this is expended in steady improvement of the houses year by year, a separate sum being set aside for each house, so that careful households benefit by their own care. The gradual improvement of the buildings thus managed, definite, tangible and easily marked, is a source of the greatest satisfaction to me, and I feel ever more strongly convinced that this intimate personal care and friendship of those who know them well, combined with the stimulus afforded by the clearly marked advantage they gain by taking care of what is around them in their houses, is the only way of educating the lowest classes of the poor to be fit for the better houses which one hopes Londoners will soon insist on providing.

The next great scheme we have in hand to which I shall allude is that of the system of district visiting, now for some time established in

St Mary's, Bryanston Square, and of which an account will be found in *Macmillan's Magazine* for July, 1869.[3] But I may here recapitulate a little, and also bring the sketch up to date. Every visitor has a court or street assigned to her. Her personal work, with the exception of rent-collecting, keeping accounts, supervising cleaning and repairs, is exactly the same as that which I have described above as belonging to the head of one of our own blocks. The district visitor is the agent in her court for the relief committee, the school board, and the board of guardians. As soon as any one applies for relief to the mission house of the parish, the name of the applicant ought to be sent to the visitor, and she reports on the case to the relief committee; she has no voice, however, in voting relief, but, if granted, she takes it to the applicant. She pays the church pensions to the sick and old; she is expected to keep a book respecting applicants in prescribed form, and to make the entries in it monthly. From the school board officer she receives weekly the names of all absentees or irregular attendants at schools, except such as require prosecution; these the school board officer attends to himself. She is also expected weekly to report to him all children coming to reside in her district, and such facts about them as will enable him to learn definitely if they are at school, and to fill up in his books the returns required by the school board.

For the poor law authorities, her duties are to give, on a form provided, such information respecting applicants resident in her district as may be valuable to the guardians in deciding rightly the question of the amount and form of relief.

The visitor also gives notice throughout her district of all flower-shows, lectures, &c.; and she takes the lead in the entertainments given yearly in St Mary's to her district, and in every way serves as the personal head of her flock. This sounds as if it implies a great deal of work, but the very beauty of the plan is, that it can be undertaken on a small scale, that, though the work is important and responsible, it can be handed back to us here, or to the paid officials, at any moment, if necessary; that, therefore, it renders available all that multitude of workers whose home duties prevent their volunteer work from having the first claim upon them. Also it must be remembered that the number

---

3 'Four Years' Management of a London Court', *Macmillan's Magazine*, July 1869, was not, in fact, about district visiting, but about the management of Freshwater Place, Octavia's second court in Marylebone, bought for her by John Ruskin. Octavia was probably thinking of 'The Work of Volunteers in the Organisation of Charity' which appeared in *Macmillan's* in October 1872. Both articles were included in *Homes of the London Poor*, Octavia's first book, which was published in 1875, also by Macmillan.

of cases in a given district is so small that it secures for each that careful personal thought and watchfulness on which alone wise action can be based, and which has proved so valuable at Elberfeld. This scheme for district visiting is partially adopted now in several districts, and is rapidly gaining ground. I should like to point out to anyone establishing it, that it is very important to secure a good centre of visitors who shall be a link with the official bodies concerned.

The reform of the relief, by which I mean planning it on such principles as makes it really helpful to the poor, in various parishes is really a work which depends primarily on the clergy, but I mention it as one in which we are here engaged, because the form requires that many should at once rally round any clergyman who is willing to adopt a wise system—people who will act on his relief committee form a link with the Charity Organisation committee, and enlist and keep up communication with good visitors. I am satisfied that the experience gained on such committees is invaluable as teaching wise ways of dealing with special difficulties, and that no knowledge gained at a Charity Organisation committee is complete without it; the mere fact that all applicants attend is a great help. Wise and thoughtful men are urgently needed for this part of the work, and I feel that those who are kindly attending such committees are doing valuable service, and preparing themselves for taking the lead under the clergy in other districts. Some of the Charity Organisation Society's committees in poor districts appear to be sadly in need of earnest leaders or supporters, and a part of our strength has been turned to finding such. I hope that this part of our work, too, may be extended, and that quickly. The Charity Organisation Society is by no means anxious to stop charity, but only to make it really helpful to the poor: this is distinctly understood in those districts where the clergy and relief agencies co-operate, but, where they do not, the Charity Organisation has to steer between two evils: it must either become a new relieving agency itself, which is unadvisable, or it must leave good cases without help. Either course creates evil and misapprehension. What we want then in recruits for the Charity Organisation Society's committees is men who themselves know what wise relief and good investigation mean, and who will promote them in the various relief societies of the district.

These four—the management of houses, the district visiting, the assistance at reformed relief committees, and the reinforcement of charity organisation committees in outlying districts—may be considered our main works at present, and I may add that the second is for the moment the one in which I most need fresh workers. But besides these four I must enumerate several other schemes we have in hand.

There are our winter entertainments and summer parties. I have again and again described how much good these appear to me to do. We take the tenants from each block of houses once a year to spend a good long day in the country. This involves 15 excursions at the least; no small tax on strength and time and money, yet giving the people a bright glimpse of fair and still places, not yet blackened or built over— one day's holiday in the company of those who would gladly teach those of them who need it that a holiday may be a really glad day, free from pollutions by drunkenness or low riot. It is a very great help if anyone can invite us to their grounds. Several people did this for our parties last year, and not only did it save us heavy expenses, but it gave that beautiful sense of personal hospitality which sustains the tone of the people, and gives them the gracious sense of being cared for which nothing else can. It is also a great help to those of us who conduct the expedition thus to be reinforced on our arrival. In short, it is one of the best ways of helping us.

Our winter parties are not such difficult things to manage; and I am anxious in these, as in the summer parties, to associate with our people, first, those who have really worked among them, who know them well, and to whom the meeting is a real meeting of friend with friend; but the help of decorators, singers, and actors is most valuable too. In connection with this question, I may mention a most interesting experiment now being made among us by Mrs Ernest Hart, as to the provision of more abundant recreation for the people. The subject has long been much on my mind. I give one evening every week from October till March, and yet I barely provide one evening's amusement for each of our people. That enables us to meet them at least once face to face, but it does not supply enough happy, healthy amusement for the young people. Now, I don't think it would be well to provide much more amusement quite free; certainly it would be very difficult. Yet directly we cease to be hosts and hostesses, we cease in a great measure to set the tone of the performances. How to make amusements self-supporting and yet pure and good is the problem. Mrs Ernest Hart thought she could solve it by establishing them where she had a nucleus of girls under her own influence, and where the experiment might be tried on a very small scale. Accordingly every Saturday night we now have an entertainment held in Barrett's Court, in the room where the Institute for Women and Girls is, and to these the members are admitted free. Other people pay 1*d*. The place is tiny and the work in its infancy, but those singers, actors, conjurors, or people having curiosities or magic lanterns to show, who do not despise the day of small things, might help us very much by banding themselves in small groups and conducting an entertainment one Saturday. Teachers, too, for the classes there would be of great use. We have organised little parties for rowing in the Regent's Park, going to the British Museum and other places on Saturday afternoons, and should be very glad of more helpers here. The balance-sheet shows an expenditure for flowers; many more have been sent us this year, thanks partly to Miss Stanley and the flower mission; but we are always glad of any number.[4]

Lastly, there is one large court at the back of Drury Lane lately put under our care by the society to which it belongs, who are ready to help in every way, where we would gladly organise, if we had but fellow workers enough, all that has been so powerful for good in Barrett's Court—a good working men's club, a teetotal society, night classes for girls and boys, and collection of savings on Saturday night.

---

4 Alice Marion Hart, *née* Rowland, (1848–1931) was Henrietta Barnett's sister and the second wife of Ernest Hart. She studied medicine in London and Paris, and was no less interested than her husband in philanthropic reform. She studied medicine for six years in Paris and London, working as a dresser and a clinical clerk in London's Royal Free Hospital. (See 'Interview with Alice Hart' in *Women's Penny Paper*, 14 September 1889, pp.1-2.) Alice was honorary secretary and treasurer of the Institute for Women and Girls in Barrett's Court, and the first Annual Report for 1874–75 gives a good indication of the full privileges which could be had for one penny a week. 'Classes were held every night, including Sunday; twice weekly in reading, writing and arithmetic, once a week each in singing and needlework… They had lessons in cutting out and making dresses, in mending, trimming and use of the sewing machine… Four lectures had been held during the year. Mrs Buckmaster had spoken on "Cheap cooking with practical illustrations", Miss Frith on the management of babies, Mrs Johnstone on infectious diseases, and, breaking new ground, Revd Mr Geary on the Arctic, with magic lantern illustrations. Mrs Lankester [secretary of the National Health Society] had promised lectures to working women on homes, health and children for next summer. Evenings devoted to amusements had been given over to games, reading, singing or dancing, whilst winter Saturday evenings were for set entertainments—of which there had been twenty. Among the plays produced was *The Winter's Tale* and two works by George MacDonald. At Christmas the MacDonalds laid on a carol concert… Later on Mrs Baylis, Emma Cons's sister, provided operettas. In summer the club members were offered outings: they went to the South Kensington Museum, Hampton Court, the Zoological Gardens, Hampstead Heath and the other London Parks… The first Report appealed for presents to improve the rooms; chairs, a carpet, a bookcase or shelves, a second-hand piano. Books were needed for a small lending library of "readable books". Miss Dunlop was thanked for her loan of watercolours, Mrs George Lewis (*sic*)—in fact George Eliot—had given a Wilcox & Gibbs sewing machine.' (Darley, 1990, pp.139-40.)

I spoke last year of the hope that I had that, before I wrote to you again, part of a court in St Jude's, Whitechapel, might be under our care. This hope has been realised. But we have not bought the larger part of that court, which had since been offered to us, nor have we bought a very tempting one in the neighbourhood of Lisson Grove, partly because the price asked was high, but more, because of the imperfections which still remain in our organisation. This brings me to the third subject of my letter.

No one could be more deeply grateful than I for the wonderful help which people have given. I am more and more impressed with the number of those who come forward, with their kindness and their earnestness; and though I speak of wanting additional help, this is really not because our workers fail us, for more and more come, till, as I say, I am quite astonished, but because our area and the population have so rapidly increased. But what we want now, before we dare further enlarge our area is—and now I write to my near fellow-workers only—that they should seriously consider with themselves and me the possibility of the still further subdivision of the work, with the distinct aim of making it far better in its details. This is very true of the district visiting, which needs much more thoughtful realisation of the relations and objects of the different bodies concerned, whether school board, guardians, or Charity Organisation Society, so that the reports to them should be written with distinct comprehension of the work in hand, and above all that the visitor should feel her responsibility for doing infinitely more in the way of radical reform than any of these bodies can effect. For instance, if the relief committee refuse help because a man has not saved, it is for the visitor to make this clear to him, to show him how it is the farther-sighted kindness, to get him heartily to value the decision, and to tell him or to get him to learn where he can save when he gets into work again. If the guardians want a report, it is for the visitor not only to give account of the respectability and ages of the family, but to think out for the young widow the means by which she can free herself from the necessity of parish pay, to suggest the plan to the relief committee and get it carried out, and so to bring all the accurate and abundant knowledge she has of the case to bear for permanent good. But though this applies to the district visitors, I care most to urge it here in relation to the management of the houses.

There is in each block of houses a great deal of actual business to be done, and a great deal of personal work to be done. I am satisfied that they ought to be in the same hands as far as possible, and I want all those at work to think, each with regard to her own block, how far that is possible. There is an immense amount of detail which ought to be swiftly, and yet really well, decided. How far can each qualify herself to decide it? We from here can keep the business going, and must under any circumstances be finally responsible for it, but we can never carry any of the buildings to a high state of perfection, nor can we ever deeply influence the life and habits of the people, from this central position. We may be, and are delighted to be, at the service of the visitors in each property, but they must take the position of *queens*, as well as *friends*, each in her own domain. As to the kindness of their help I cannot write too warmly, and I think they are interested in the work. I think it must be partly my own fault for not explaining matters better, and partly the difficulty of getting details re-arranged, that has hitherto prevented them from entirely fulfilling all we hope for from them. I will try my best about re-arrangement of details, and shall be thankful for any suggestions. As to the object to be obtained, I may say briefly that, as a rule, they have not taken high enough ground to satisfy me. I want them all to feel as I said 'queens': of course they must keep within definite bounds as to expenditure, for the sake of the owners, but those bounds they ought intelligently to master, and, treating them as a designer would the limiting lines of his field, make them bring out the perfection of their skill. But except for this distinct sense of responsibility to the owner, whose claims I can always define accurately, I should like them to take the complete control of the houses under their charge, as they would of their own house, garden or field; to take them as bits of God's earth, which He has entrusted to them to make of them the best possible; to take the people in the same way under their wing, and, carefully respecting their independent right as tenants, to make them the best possible. All questions should be decided by the visitor as to new and old tenants, over-crowding, and arrears of rent; as to whether long-suffering or rigid rule is the best way of dealing with any evil in the life they lead, as to quarrels among them, and the attendance of children at school. Then as regards the houses—those parts which are common to the tenants, and, consequently under the charge of the landlady, ought to be made models of cleanliness, order, and even of beauty, if it may be. All portions of each house for which the tenants are themselves responsible, but which others are concerned with, ought to be kept up to the mark; all repairs should be promptly, thoroughly and economically executed; and finally, the permanent, brooding thought as to all radical improvement of the place or people should haunt the mind of the visitor till it bears good fruit. 'Easy to write', I daresay you all think, 'but how difficult to do'. Perhaps; but was any work which is worth doing ever *quite* easy? And you are ready most of you, too, for difficulty, I know, if it will bear good fruit. But besides that, I am not talking just now of whether it can be perfectly done, but of whether it can be well comprehended, and persistently aimed at. I think you have few of you realised that this is what I mean when I ask you if you will take charge of the houses; you think of it as collecting and then rendering an account to me here; you think the responsibility of action lies here. Will you all try in future to believe that though I am quite ready to resume the charge of any district when you are unable to carry on the work there, though the responsibility to the owners is mine, and gives me distinct duties with regard to your action, all the kingdom is your own while you hold it, to make of it what good thing you can. And do not be afraid: whatever knowledge, whatever power, whatever time, I and my assistants have, is wholly at your service; you can lean upon us to any extent you may deem advisable; but take the initiative yourselves, manage the details yourselves, think out your problems yourselves, for you alone can; and when you have made yourselves tolerably independent of us, then you or we may extend the work, but not till then can it be done.

Some of you have playfully called me 'General', and so I will be, if you like, in directing you to the most important places in the great field of work, for one sees them very clearly from the centre; but if I am to be general, let the officers be such as Mr Frederick Maurice[5] describes in his essay on army organisation. I know nothing of course about army organisation, but it was deeply interesting to me to learn that modern warfare, with its vast machinery, did but bring out more fully the need for what seems to be the principle of modern life in free countries, that we are not directed from above like mere tools, but have to think out what it is best to do each in his own sphere. My friends, our sphere is but a tiny place compared with London, but it is already too large for any high perfection to be reached by central guidance;

---

5   John Frederick Maurice (1841–1912) was the brother of Edmund Maurice, who married Octavia's sister Emily in 1872. Edmund and Frederick were the sons of F. D. Maurice (1805–1872) who exerted such a great influence on Octavia's ideas. Frederick Maurice would help Octavia to set up the cadet corps in 1889, and it was he who persuaded Lord Wolseley to preside at the inaugural meeting. Maurice had been Wolseley's private secretary during the famous Ashanti campaign in 1873–74. The essay Octavia refers to here was *The System of Field Manoeuvres Best Adapted for Enabling Our Troops To Meet a Continental Army* by Lieut F. Maurice, Royal Artillery, Instructor of Tactics and Organisation, Royal Military College, Sandhurst, published by William Blackwood and Sons, 1872.

take up then strongly, each your own work, for you only can bring to bear upon it that individual knowledge and love which alone can advance it. If any action or regulation of mine ever thwarts or hinders you, please come straight to me and talk it over, for believe me, I do want you to be free. I do not expect just now to get right down among the poor myself for much individual work; if I ever did, it would be in a smaller sphere than at present; what is my great desire—what, as far as I have been able to carry them with me, is the great desire of my assistants—is to be entirely at your service, that we may secure if possible, more life in the various portions of the work, and that you, each for yourselves, may realise the joy of feeling that you have a little spot which you can try to put to rights, and where you will be surrounded by those you care for.

I have delayed writing my report that it might not be written under the shadow of an anxiety of which some of you have heard, but which, heavily as it clouded me, I knew, even at its worst, would only be temporary. Anxiety, storm, and pain had certainly not been characteristic of the year which was drawing to its close, and temporary or permanent, had no right to cloud a report of 1874 with all its glad progress. I waited for the cloud to pass that I might not mention it, and yet write what I was most thinking of; and now that I begin to hope it is past, somehow it seems quite impossible to omit mention of it, because it brought out a depth of sympathy, of trust, and a magnificence of helpfulness, the existence of which I had no idea. This, and other help of which some of you know, has made me feel, this year, drawn far closer to many of you, made me surer than ever of the abundance of care for the poor, and sympathy with those who are trying to serve them, made me conscious, too, of how you would all gather round in any time of need, and given me a strange new sense of rest in the great generosity of your help. It might have made me very proud, if it did not make me so very humble; I feel so small a thing among you all in whom the gathering sense of responsibility is growing day by day, but a small thing which is allowed to take part in a very large work, the influence of which shall last long after the memory of individual workers has been forgotten.

I am,
Yours always faithfully,
OCTAVIA HILL

DONATION ACCOUNT, 1874

RECEIPTS

	£	s	d
Cash in hand, Jan 3rd ...	128	2	2½
Mrs Herbert Duckworth, Jan 24th	10	0	0
Miss Behrens, Feb 7th ...	20	0	0
Miss Marten, Feb 21st	0	10	0
Miss Pipe, Feb 28th	2	14	0
Mrs Martineau, Mar 7th ...	3	0	0
A.G. Crowder, Esq	10	10	0
F.D. Mocatta, Esq, Mar 14th	10	0	0
Mrs Pollard, Mar 21st	5	0	0
Rev. Brooke Lambert, Mar 21st	5	0	0
Miss Pipe, Mar 21st	10	0	0
G. Clover, Esq, Mar 21st	10	0	0
Alfred Hill, Esq, Mar 21st ...	5	0	0
Edward Spender, Esq, Mar 21st	11	0	0
Mrs Scaramanga	2	0	0
Miss Trevelyan	2	0	0
Mrs Owen, April 4th	0	10	0
C.B.P. Bosanquet, Esq, April 11th	1	0	0
Miss Wilson	3	0	0
Mrs Greaves	10	0	0
Lionel Fletcher, Esq, May 2nd	5	0	0
Mrs Gascoigne, May 9th ...	5	0	0
Philip Holland, Esq	5	5	0
J.B.Smith, Esq (Provident Dispensary)	5	0	0
Miss Martineau, May 16th	2	0	0
Mrs Ernest Hart	5	0	0
Mrs Wilkins, May 23rd	0	4	0
The late Herbert Mayo, Esq, May 30th	6	0	0
H.Parnell, Esq, June 6th ...	1	0	0
Mrs Macaulay	1	0	0
Edward Bond, Esq, June 13th	5	0	0
Robert W. Monroe, Esq ...	0	10	0
Mrs W. Shaen	1	10	0
Mrs Gillson, June 27th ...	15	0	0
Mrs H. Blair, July 2nd	7	2	0
Mrs Whately	5	0	0
Hornsby Wright, Esq, July 11th	1	1	0
Baroness Meyer de Rothschild	30	0	0
Miss Rothschild	10	0	0
Sir Charles Trevelyan, July 18th	2	0	0
Lady Caroline Charteris ...	2	0	0
Per C.B.P. Bosanquet, Esq	2	0	0
Miss F. Hill, July 25th	0	10	0
Robert W Monroe, Esq ...	0	10	0
Lady Camperdown (Provident Dispensary) Aug 1st	3	0	0
R.D. Wilson, Esq	3	3	0
Miss J.Sterling, Sept 5th	30	0	0
Miss Meredith	25	0	0
Mrs Whittaker	1	0	0
Miss Mayo, Sept 12th	1	1	0
Mrs Macdonald	5	0	0
Mrs Allen, Sept 26th	1	0	0
Small Donations	0	4	6
Carriage of Flowers	0	13	6
Callaghan's Loan	0	4	0
Balance of Donation, S.B. ...	6	10	0
Capital and Interest of Henrietta Street	4	2	9
Hon. Augusta Barrington, Oct 17th	1	0	0
Directors of Central London Dwellings Company	2	0	0
Edward Spender, Esq, Oct 31st	4	5	0
Loan repaid (Goddard) ...	1	0	0
Mrs Maurice (for Kirby), Oct 24th	0	3	0
C.K.W.	3	16	0
Miss F. Baldwin	1	0	0
Mrs Ernest Hart, Nov 14th	5	0	0
A.G. Crowder, Esq, Nov 14th	10	10	0
Rev. S. and Mrs Barnett, Nov 28th	5	0	0
For Palings round Trees H.A.F.	0	5	0
Mrs Sheffield Neave, Dec 5th	2	0	0
Miss Tagart	0	4	1
Sir G. Phillips	5	0	0
Miss Manning, Dec 26th ...	2	0	0
Miss Chamberlain	5	0	0
	£496	0	0½

The following ladies and gentlemen were so very kind as to entertain parties of our tenants in their grounds last summer:

Mrs Bond	George Macdonald, Esq
— Buxton, Esq	Miss Pipe
Mrs Gwyn Jeffreys	Miss Temple
Andrew Johnston, Esq	

DONATION ACCOUNT, 1874

EXPENDITURE

	£	s	d
St Jude's, Whitechapel	50	0	0
Barrett's Court Club, Rent and other Expenses	38	15	4
Tenants' Excursion:			
Barrett's Court and Henrietta Street	37	0	0
Walmer Street	25	11	0
Parker Street	6	0	0
Freshwater and Paradise Place	7	7	5
Bell Street	10	19	0
New Court, Whitechapel	1	2	6
Children's Excursion Gt. York Mews	3	9	11
Railing and New Swings, Playground Freshwater Place	17	7	0
Superintendence of Playground Freshwater Place	10	4	6
New Swings and Planting Trees, Playground, Lambeth	5	15	0
Provident Dispensary, Special Donations	36	0	0
School and Clothes for Orphan (W.L.)	25	8	10
Industrial School (C.S.)	9	15	0
French Pasteur	16	0	0
Printing, Postage, Account Books, and Expenses for School Board			
and Guardians' Work	12	15	6
Printing, Rev. Brooke Lambert's Lecture (special donation)	5	0	0
Two Winter Parties:			
Tenants of Drury Lane	10	2	4 $\frac{1}{2}$
Lady Ducie's Tenants	5	16	5
Children from Walmer Street	5	7	0 $\frac{1}{2}$
Mr Somerset Beaumont's Tenants	5	15	9
Children from Barrett's Court	2	2	2
Winter Party:			
Tenants of Bell Street	3	2	0 $\frac{1}{2}$
Albert's Building, Lambeth	2	17	5
Freshwater Place	2	14	6 $\frac{1}{2}$
Concert for the Blind	4	18	7 $\frac{1}{2}$
Employment for various poor People	5	7	1
Interest on Savings	5	17	10 $\frac{1}{2}$
Expenses of Flowers	2	15	3 $\frac{1}{2}$
Working Men's College	5	0	0
Board of Child (Mother in Hospital)	5	8	0
May Festival	2	16	7 $\frac{1}{2}$
Children's Festival. Lincoln's Inn Square	2	17	0 $\frac{1}{2}$
Balance returned to Miss Sterling	6	1	6
Fare (Special Donation)	5	0	0
Rent for Workroom	1	16	11
	2	9	9
Pension, Mrs J.	2	14	0
Pension, Mrs K.	2	3	0
Employment of Children	3	17	6
Expenses for Nightschool and Service	5	7	1
Eastbourne Letter, special donation	1	1	0
Child at School (F.M.)	21	19	9
Work Tickets, St Mary's	1	1	0
Tea-pots, Jugs &c. for Parties	2	0	9 $\frac{1}{2}$
Various Patients at Convalescent Homes	2	18	0 $\frac{1}{2}$
Hire of Piano for Concert	0	7	0
Medicine for Prevention of Cholera	0	15	0
Rowing Expeditions	0	7	6
Loan (Goddard)	1	0	0
Cash in Hand	43	10	11
	£496	0	0 $\frac{1}{2}$

WORK-ROOM ACCOUNT, 1874

RECEIPTS

	£	s	d
Sundry Accounts of Work sold and done to Order	32	12	8 ½
Sale of Old Clothes	7	13	0 ½
Sale of New Clothes	2	4	6
Grants from St Mary's Relief Committee (wages of workers)	8	3	0 ½
Grants from St. Luke's (wages of workers)	0	2	0
Miss Kinder, Miss M.E. Martineau, and Miss Scott (wages of workers)	0	17	0
Clothes sold in New Zealand, sent out in 1871	16	7	2
Donation of Calico and Materials	1	15	3 ½
	£69	14	9

WORK-ROOM ACCOUNT, 1874

EXPENDITURE

	£	s	d	£	s	d
Superintendence				26	0	0
Wages:						
Women	17	16	2 ½			
Man, Cobbler	0	4	1			
				*18	0	3 ¼
Materials				12	18	8 ¼
Coals and Wood				2	14	5
Cleaning				2	6	0
Washing, Soap, Soda, &c.				0	15	6
Stationery				0	2	10
Painting, Papering, and Repairs				5	12	0
Carriage of Parcels, and Messenger				1	5	0 ½
				£69	14	9

* This figure should be £18 0s 3½d, which means that the column total should be £69 14s 9¼d.

LETTER TO MY FELLOW-WORKERS

TO WHICH IS ADDED

ACCOUNT OF DONATIONS RECEIVED

FOR

WORK AMONG THE POOR

DURING 1875

BY

OCTAVIA HILL

LONDON
WATERLOW AND SONS, PRINTERS,
GREAT WINCHESTER STREET, LONDON, E.C.

SUMMARY

The formation of the housing managers… the need for district visitors to liaise with other bodies… more workers needed for the Charity Organisation Society… greater importance attached to perfecting the work than extending it.

EDITOR'S NOTE

This short letter (2,679 words) lacks the human interest stories that enliven others in the series. It is mainly concerned with methods of assistance, and Octavia uses the letter to urge her fellow-workers to refine their work before thinking about expanding it. She emphasises the need for detailed reports to the poor law guardians and the Charity Organisation Society, and appeals to what she sees as the increasing idealism of the age to find more committed helpers for the latter. This letter is, however, most remarkable for what it omits. First, there is no mention of the publication by Macmillan of Homes of the London Poor, *a collection of Octavia's magazine articles which enjoyed some success. Second, 1875 had seen Octavia's first major campaign to save an open space, and it had failed. Swiss Cottage Fields, which provided the nearest open space to Marylebone and Paddington, were threatened with development. Octavia undertook to raise the £10,000 that the owners demanded in order to save them from being built over. It was a remarkably brave attempt, as such a thing had never been done before, and within three weeks Octavia had raised £8,150. Then, in mid-August, the owners withdrew their offer. The land was built over and Fitzjohn's Avenue now stands on the site. As a result of this bitter disappointment, Octavia learned a valuable lesson. As Sir Robert Hunter wrote in* The Times *after Octavia's death: 'In all subsequent projects of the kind… a definite option of purchase for a specific time was obtained before public support was solicited'. (Darley, 1990, pp.175-78.) In view of the fact that Octavia had always intended to use the letters to share her failures as well as her successes, it is surprising that she has nothing to say to the fellow-workers about this.*

My Dear Friends and Fellow-Workers,

Another year has passed over us unmarked by any great changes, and yet I think it has been one characterised by steady progress.

I need not sketch again the various undertakings we have in hand, as I did so last year. I propose only to mention—1st, the points in which advance has been made in the objects then set before you; 2nd, where I think we shall still trace the same defects in our work; and lastly, I shall briefly notice any new developments of our duties.

I feel specially that progress has been made in the subdivision of our work. I pointed out last year that the tenants in each block of houses could not be cared for, nor the houses themselves dealt with as they ought to be, unless more concentrated thought were devoted to them by those who had power and will to act without referring questions back here for decision. Decidedly progress has been made in this direction.

The most notable improvement has been due to those ladies who are so kind as to act as my regular assistants. I find them almost daily better able—they have been, from the first, most kindly willing—to take up, and efficiently carry through, the business connected with each block of houses, to comprehend what should be aimed at, and to do it. Some of the volunteer collectors have certainly improved wonderfully, all of them a great deal, but my assistants have made most progress. Now this is certainly very satisfactory, for they seem to me to have just the position which will enable them to carry forward the work admirably. They have three or four courts each, just enough for them to look after thoroughly as to general arrangements, and yet they must feel that their domain is too large for them to attend to the details of personal work or of business themselves, therefore they will naturally seek to develop all the power of those ladies who each take one block only, and to delegate as much to them as possible, being always ready to advise, to relieve guard, or to form a medium of communication

---

1   Octavia refers to 'this dawning year' on p.54.

between those ladies and myself. I trust that when they have themselves gained experience, they will see that the noblest, because the most useful thing, is to slip gradually away from place after place as it can be filled by others, looking out always for the power they can develop in their fellow-workers. The old law 'He that will be greatest among you let him be as him that serves',[2] is eternally binding; and if they can realise that the best service is to develop the power of work in many, so that they shall help others to bring to bear on the poor all that concentrated thought, all that bright influence and refreshment which people can give who deal only with a few, and who come out from homes full of varied interests and life, they will be doing a better work than if they threw themselves, however heroically, into any breach and spent their strength devotedly, but hopelessly, in trying to deal with hundreds—nay, thousands of the poor. They will find that though it costs them something to retreat from the delight of carrying through to completion much interesting work, which they must plan and leave to others; though it costs them something to break links that were forming, and go to whichever of their courts needs them most, instead of staying where the fruit of their work begins to rejoice them—they will not lose their reward. For they will begin to feel how much better a thing it is to help others to excel than to excel oneself; they will feel how good it is to see work they care for planted so that it no longer depends on them, and to know that they are so planning their lives that all which they think beneficial in the fifteen courts we now have may, through others whom they shall teach, be carried out for hundreds of the poor they never saw. When I can feel that I have three or four friends side by side with me day after day, set with me on accomplishing this one object, I shall feel my strength multiplied many fold. I am myself taking their work in one block of buildings, and that of the volunteer collectors in another, that I may be face to face with the same difficulties, and may make out if I can the best way to meet them. I am satisfied that my assistants have not yet found out the best way of communicating with the collectors, or getting the full benefit of their help. The assignment of particular courts to individual assistants has worked well, what I still wish to see is that the volunteers should take the lead, each in their own block of buildings.

I am very anxious to urge upon my fellow-workers who are district visitors in St Mary's, St Luke's, or St Thomas', and who are good enough to undertake to report on cases to us for the guardians and

---

2   Matthew 23:11.

school board the extreme importance, now that we have a capital machinery, of using it thoughtfully for important ends. For instance, I do not hear of much information voluntarily contributed to the school board officer. Yet it is the visitor who should be the first to know of the arrival of a new little flock in her street. Perhaps the parents may be fresh from the country, and may not know the schools near; perhaps they may have been in a neighbouring street, and have removed to escape prosecution and to keep their children idle, dirty, and untaught; almost certainly particulars about the children ought to be entered in the school board officer's books, that his returns may be accurate, and that he may have his district well in hand.

Again, the visitor's reports to the guardians are coming in much more regularly and promptly, and I am quite sure it must be a help to the visitors to trace accurately the action of the poor-law authorities in their district, and that information as to the actual items of help reaching applicants from charitable sources, and the various clues furnished about their circumstances must be of value to the guardians, but many reports reach me which I cannot but feel might have been much fuller. Valuable they are, but more valuable they might have been. Has it ever occurred to the visitors to think out any ways by which these reports might be improved? First of all, might it not be well for the visitor to call sometimes at the Charity Organisation committee in Marylebone Road, and ask to look at papers relating to a case about which she knows little. Without making it a rule, which might be difficult, it might be done now and then. Any visitor can call there, and if the case is on the books much valuable information would be obtained in a minute or two. There are some two or three thousand Marylebone cases recorded there now, I believe, so that there is really a chance of finding the one needed. In St Mary's parish the papers relating to cases which have been dealt with during the month are borrowed from the Charity Organisation committee, on a given day, for the use of the visitors, that they may make an abstract in their district books, but I fear little use is made of this opportunity. If it were, the books themselves would be far more valuable to present to future visitors, and ample reports could be made to the guardians when asked for, without the trouble of calling at the Charity Organisation committee. Again, the return of income of applicants for poor law relief is often manifestly impossibly small. Every St Mary's pensioner must have in all 7s weekly, yet I get many a report which does not contain the items of this 7s. I am not saying that every report should be exhaustive; this could not be achieved without great labour, and is not needed, and the shortest report may be of value, but

I do think reports might often be fuller without much trouble, and that it might sometimes be worth while to give really exhaustive reports on the points which bear on the question of whether or not any given form of relief would be beneficial.

And now, having completed the task of pointing out in what direction I think improvement is needed in our present work, let me dwell on what newer work lies before us. We have been very happy in securing a great many fresh workers, who have come in most heartily to join in what we are doing. I think it is splendid to find so many and such earnest ones. Of course we want more. I suppose we always shall, for fresh work is ever opening out before us. Perhaps the place where I most feel workers needed now is for the Charity Organisation Society in the South of London. It is of the deepest importance that the Charity Organisation Society should not become a fresh relieving society, for added societies are an evil, and besides it can never investigate cases, and organise charities as it ought if it becomes a relief society. But the Charity Organisation Society must secure abundant and wise relief where needed, and it must stop that which is injurious. To accomplish these two ends it must win the confidence of private donors and relief agencies. Besides this if its investigations are to be trustworthy and effectual, and gently conducted, they must be watched over by people of education, and with deep sympathy with the poor. You cannot learn how to help a man, nor even get him to tell you what ails him till you care for him. For these reasons volunteers must rally round the Charity Organisation Society, and prevent it from becoming a dry, and because dry, an ineffectual machinery for enquiring about the people; volunteers must themselves take up the cases from the committees, must win the co-operation of local clergy, and support them in the reform of their charities, must themselves superintend the agents, and conduct the correspondence, and for all this work we want gentlemen, specially for the poorer districts. Do you know what people tell me? That they don't expect to find honorary secretaries for the 37 district committees willing to work steadily and who have time to spare! I know how many people there are busy all day, and I am thankful to think of it, for work is a happy, good thing, and when such people give of their not abundant leisure generously to the poor it is valuable in kind, for they bring to bear the power of trained workers, and the fervour of those who have sacrificed something to make their gift. But do you mean to tell me that among the hundreds who have no professional work, young men of rank or fortune, older men who have retired from active work, there are not 37 in all this vast rich city who care enough for their poor neighbours to feel it a privilege to give a few hours twice or thrice weekly or even daily to serve them? My friends, I am sure that there are. The sense of the solemnity of life and its high responsibility is increasing among men, and the form it is taking is that of desiring to serve the poor. The same spirit which prompted men in another age to free the Holy Land, to found monasteries, to enter our own church, now bids them work for men as men; for the poor first, as having nothing but their manhood to commend them to notice. 'Oh, yes', I am told, 'you will find gentlemen of leisure attend committees in the West, but the poor districts are too far out of the way'. Out of the way! Yes, so out of the way that we must set the need very distinctly before rich volunteers, or they will never come across it now that the poor and rich are so sadly divided into different neighbourhoods. But show them the need, and never fear the distance. What, a paltry three or four miles which they would walk before they began a day's shooting, and never count it in the day's work! What, the trouble of a short railway journey, and the annoyance of dirt and noise separate their poorer fellow citizens from those who, if there were a war and a cause they believed in, would meet danger and death in hideous forms without shrinking! The need is not before their bodily eyes, their imaginations are dim and indistinct, but let anyone they trust take them quietly for a few days face to face with the want, without exaggerating it, simply and silently, and if there are not 37 men of leisure who will come forward, and work too, yes twice or thrice 37, then I don't know English hearts at all.[3]

---

3   This is the first of three extended appeals in the letters (see also 1876 and 1877) for the Charity Organisation Society (COS), with which Octavia was closely involved from its foundation in 1869 until her breakdown in 1877. The Victorian voluntary sector was enormous, and the COS had been formed to co-ordinate the activities of the various charities in order to prevent 'overlapping'—the practice amongst applicants for assistance of going from one charity to another telling the same hard-luck story for multiple handouts. The original intention was that the COS would not become another 'relieving' society: in other words, it would not make grants in its own right, but would steer applicants towards whichever existing charities were best suited to meet their needs. In order to function effectively, the COS needed to have the fullest possible information about each applicant. This entailed not only carrying out interviews and taking up references with employers, landlords and others, but 'visiting'—a key component which entailed going to see the applicant in his or her home, getting to know the person and befriending them, so that help could be given as efficiently and delicately as it would be given to a friend, without 'pauperising' or, as we would put it, causing welfare dependency. This was an extremely labour-intensive method to use for the relief of distress, and it relied upon being able to call upon a large body of voluntary helpers to take on the many 'cases'. The intention was to have a district committee of the COS covering each of the London poor law districts, so that the

Whether they will find the problems very easy to deal with when they come face to face with them is another matter. But they must have patience, and realise that problems must be well looked into before they can be solved, and are not solved except by men resolved to grapple with difficulties one by one as they arise. How many of the 37 will be wise enough or great enough to make themselves the centre of other workers I don't feel sure; but of their going, and of their working when once they see the want, I have no doubt.

Our own work this year has been rather perfecting itself than extending, which, you will remember, we determined last year would be the best thing to aim at. I hardly know whether the increased hope of making places beautiful should count as an extension or perfection, but distinct advance has been made in this direction. My sister's small society, of which most of you will have heard, will be a great help to all this in the future.[4] I hope before this dawning year passes away to

---

COS could liaise, not only between the various charities, but between the charities and the poor law guardians, to make sure that people were not deriving funds from both charitable and state welfare agencies, telling lies to both. By 1870 there were COS offices in 12 of the poor law districts, by 1872 there were 38 and the number afterwards settled at just over 40. The position of secretary to a COS district committee was an arduous one, involving a great deal of detailed work to co-ordinate the activities of the paid agents and the teams of volunteer visitors, to say nothing of keeping in touch with the poor law guardians, the local clergy, and the various charities and friendly societies operating in the district. It was, if properly carried out, a full-time job, but, without an effective secretary, the whole work was compromised. Hence Octavia's concern, expressed in this passage. It was difficult enough to fill the position in areas where rich and poor households could be found in proximity, but in poor areas, with no leisured people in sight, it meant that COS volunteers had to travel in from other districts. Even if it were possible to find visitors on this basis, it was doubtful if anyone was going to take on the position of secretary for a committee on the other side of London. The question inevitably arose as to whether paid staff should be used, in spite of the COS ideal of voluntary service. In 1881, by which time Octavia was no longer a member of the central council of the COS, the decision was taken to employ paid secretaries, the first of whom were appointed to Hackney and Poplar. The move was controversial amongst COS members, and Rose Dunn-Gardner, the author of an important paper on training volunteers, resigned in protest when a paid secretary was appointed for Lambeth. She felt that, with the right training, volunteers could have handled the work. In spite of Octavia's reservations, expressed here and elsewhere, about the COS becoming 'a fresh relieving society', the COS soon found it necessary to raise and disburse its own funds, as it was impossible to deal with all needs at second hand by co-opting other charities. (Whelan, 2001, pp.9-23.)

---

4   This was the Kyrle Society, of which Octavia reports the formal institution in the next letter (p.70). Miranda Hill had read a paper to the girls in the Nottingham Place

count at least one open space preserved among a waste of houses to be made fair and free for the people. I hope our own tiny plots of ground, back yards and small forecourts, may be fuller of trees or grass, or creepers. I hope that at least our club and institute rooms, which are the common sitting-rooms of our courts, may be furnished with brighter colour. I hope that we may have a more organised body of singers, led by a conductor whom they know, and ready to sing in out-of-the-way places.

I am thankful for much progress already made in all these ways; thankful, very thankful, to all you my fellow-workers, who seem nearer and dearer year by year; thankful to the many generous donors who have trusted me so largely with their help, of which I herewith render what small account figures will give; thankful for life which is so full of rich blessings, memories and hopes, and precious possessions; thankful for the great patience all my fellow-workers have had with my many sins, negligences, and ignorances; thankful for the certainty that they will not be allowed to retard whatever God will have accomplished; thankful, above all, for His love, which bestows all human love and fellowship to enrich and ennoble life, and which binds us all together, rich and poor, learned and unlearned, old and young, joyous and sad, into one great company, able to help and bless each other, and each individually and together to look up to Him as our King.

OCTAVIA HILL

---

school on the need to bring beauty into the lives of the poor, for highly moral reasons: 'Beautiful pictures, music, architecture, do more than merely delight us, I believe they make us better.' Octavia was so impressed, she arranged for Miranda to give the same talk to the National Health Society, then had it printed and circulated in December 1875. 'Though it is only a week old, it is meeting with the warmest response, so that I fancy we shall have to let it become something larger and more public. I want our clubs, institutes, school-rooms, when we have our parties there, and the outsides of our churches and houses, to be brighter.' (Letter from Octavia to Florence Davenport Hill, 12 December 1875, Maurice, 1914, p.340.)

DONATION ACCOUNT, 1875

RECEIPTS

	£	s	d		£	s	d
Cash in hand	43	10	11	Miss Nevinson, for E.M.	0	5	0
Mrs Duckworth	10	0	0	Mr and Mrs Ernest Hart	1	0	0
Mrs Allen Jan 9th, April 10th,				Countess of Ducie	5	0	0
May 29th and July 10th	3	12	6	A.G. Crowder, Esq, June			
Mrs Pollard, Jan and Oct	15	0	0	and July	20	10	0
Mrs Lindesay	1	0	0	K. Brock, Esq, June and Nov	1	0	0
Mrs L, returned	0	7	3	Hornsby Wright, Esq	1	1	0
Mrs Scaramanga	1	0	0	Mrs Cookson	1	1	0
General Stuart	0	5	0	Miss Manning	5	0	0
Lady Thompson	5	0	0	Central Dwellings Company			
Miss Alice Fletcher	0	7	0	Shareholders	3	3	0
The Honourable Mrs Liddle	2	0	0	Mrs Wilkins	0	10	0
Lady Grove	1	1	0	Miss Robarts	1	0	0
Mrs Gascoigne	1	0	0	Edward Spender, Esq,			
H.A. Forman, Esq	1	0	0	July and Oct	9	5	0
James Cropper, Esq	5	0	0	Miss Coates	1	0	0
Mrs Gillson	10	0	0	Miss L, Tagart, July and Oct	5	10	0
Mrs Spender	2	0	0	Mr and Mrs Pooley	1	1	0
The Misses Martineau, March				Miss Hooper	1	0	0
and November	3	13	6½	R.W. Monro, Esq	0	10	0
W.S. Seton-Kerr, Esq	1	0	0	— Phillips, Esq	0	10	0
Charity Organisation Society,				J.W. Hales, Esq	1	1	0
for Miss W.	2	0	0	Charles E. Seth Smith, Esq	3	0	0
Returned for C.W.	1	0	0	Mrs Macaulay	1	0	0
Miss Baldwin	1	2	4	C. Critchett, Esq	1	0	0
Mrs E. Sumner	0	10	0	R.D. Wilson, Esq, July and			
Miss Tatham	1	0	0	August	5	10	0
The Rev. Basil K. Wood				Sir C. Trevelyan	2	0	0
(for flowers)	0	3	0	Hon. and Rev. Augustus			
Mrs Shaen	2	0	0	Legge	5	0	0
Edward Bond, Esq	5	0	0	Mrs Robert Bruce	25	0	0
Mrs Wright	25	0	0	Phillip Holland, Esq	10	0	0
Miss S.J. Harris	1	0	0	R.P. Harris, Esq	2	0	0
Mrs Ralli, May and October				Miss Sellar	1	0	0
(for May Festival)	2	0	0	Miss Schuyler	5	0	0
Miss Edwards				Lady Mary Hamilton	10	0	0
(for May Festival)	0	5	0	G.F. Watts, Esq	50	0	0
Lord Ronald Gower	20	0	0	Miss Burnaby	1	0	0
Miss Forman				For Gas at Girls' Institute	0	16	9
(for May Festival)	0	5	0	Miss Armitage	3	0	0
Mrs Fitch	2	0	0	The Misses Sterling	37	10	0
Mrs Cornwall	2	0	0	Mrs Lipscombe	5	0	0
Mrs Strong (for May Festival)	0	5	0	Charity Organisation Society	0	10	0
Miss Taylor	1	0	0	Mrs Whately	5	0	0
For May Festival	1	0	0	Mrs Mallet (for railway fares)	0	7	6
Miss Wells	1	0	0	St Mary's (for R.)	2	0	0
Per Miss Meredith	25	0	0	Printing	0	8	0
Mrs Bond	2	0	0	Miss Trevelyan	1	0	0
H. Parnell, Esq	1	1	0	Miss Bell	0	5	0
The Rev. H.R. Haweis	3	3	0	Returned W.L.	0	4	3
Sir George Phillips, June and				Interest on Savings	0	3	2
Nov	15	10	0	Carriage of Flowers	0	9	9
Countess of Camperdown	5	5	0	Miss Armitage	1	0	0
Honourable Augusta				Parcel, returned for	0	1	2
Barrington, June and Nov	3	0	0		£468	19	1½

We have also to thank the following ladies and gentlemen who were so good as to entertain some of the Tenants at the Summer Excursions:

Mr and Mrs Andrew Johnston	Mr and Mrs Paddock	Mrs Pollard
Mr and Mrs Lake	Miss Coates and Miss James	
Mr and Mrs Gwyn Jeffreys	Miss Hill and Miss F. Hill	

This form of help is of very great value to us, as the arrangements for the summer parties are complicated, and we should be glad if any ladies or gentlemen who propose to entertain the tenants would give us notice as soon after Easter as is convenient to them.

DONATION ACCOUNT, 1875

EXPENDITURE

	£	s	d
St Jude's, Whitechapel	16	0	0
St Jude's, Whitechapel for Convalescents	4	4	0
Barrett's Court Club, Rent and Repairs	53	12	6
Tenants' Excursion:			
Walmer Street	38	15	0
Barrett's Court and Henrietta Street	26	0	0
Granby Place and Parker Street	16	14	0
Freshwater Place	12	12	4 ½
Bell Street	4	14	0
Albert Buildings	11	4	1
Paradise Place	2	13	3
New Court, Whitechapel	1	0	8
Little Edward Street	1	7	0
May Festival	3	7	7 ½
Lincoln's Inn Festival	2	11	2
Winter Party:			
Freshwater Place	2	8	5 ½
Granby Place and Parker Street	2	3	2
Mr Somerset Beaumont's Tenants	0	19	0
Bell Street (two years)	3	13	6 ½
Albert Buildings (two years)	5	19	1
Children	0	16	4
Concert for the Blind	3	12	10
Playground, Freshwater Place	11	5	8 ½
Playground, Albert Buildings	2	6	6
Child at School (W.M.)	4	0	0
Child at School (W.L.)	15	5	10
Child at School (Pasteur)	13	0	0
Outfit for C.W. to go to service	2	0	0
Donation to Reformatory at Hampstead	5	0	0
Payment for Patients at Convalescent Houses:			
R.B.	2	14	0
J.R.	2	0	6
P.D.	0	15	6
Lady Camperdown's protégé	1	16	0
Expenses for School Board and Guardians' Work and Printing, Postage,			
and Account Books	12	9	1 ½
Interest on Savings	0	17	9 ½
Employment of various poor people	3	7	3
Employment of various poor children	3	15	0
Lambeth Work Society	1	1	0
Migration of family to Yorkshire	5	17	8 ½
Provident Dispensary	10	0	0
Council of Charity Organisation Society	5	5	0
Miss W.	2	0	0
Expenses for Teetotal Society Service and Band	27	19	7
Expenses for Room for class, New Court, Whitechapel	0	8	0
Expenses for Women's Institute, Barrett's Court	6	3	6
Pensions, Mrs K. and Mrs J.	2	16	0
Galvanic Machine	1	10	0
Expenses for Library	0	6	9
Oil Paints for decoration	0	5	11
Fares for tenants to party	0	5	9
Carriage of things to party	0	1	6
Carriage of Flowers	3	17	10
Food, Clothes and Furniture	1	16	5
Gas for Girls' Institute	0	16	9
Coals for Workroom and various small items	1	16	1 ½
Cash in hand	101	10	0
	£468	19	1 ½

WORK-ROOM ACCOUNT, 1875

RECEIPTS

	£	s	d
Sundry Accounts of Work sold and done to Order … … … … … … … … … …	29	8	0
Sale of Old Clothes …	9	9	8
Sale of New Clothes …	1	8	2
St Mary's Relief Committee (wages of workers) … … … … … … … … … … …	1	2	3
Received for 'Free Registry of Girls', April 17th to August 17th at 2/6d a week	3	5	0
Miss M.E. Martineau and Miss O. Hill (wages of workers) … … … … … … …	0	12	6
Miss Tagart (advanced in cash and materials) … … … … … … … … … … … …	8	18	1
Debts Uncollected …	4	6	10
	£58	10	6

As the work-room is not supported by subscription as other needlework societies are, orders for work to be executed, either of fine or coarse description, are very welcome.

WORK-ROOM ACCOUNT, 1875

EXPENDITURE

	£	s	d
Superintendence …	26	0	0
Wages (29 women employed) … … … … … … … … … … … … … … …	9	11	5
Materials:			
by Cash … … … … … … … … … … … … … … … … 5 12 6½			
by Cheques … … … … … … … … … … … … … 9 19 3½			
	15	11	10
Firing, Coals, &c. …	1	2	4
Cleaning …	2	16	8
Messenger and Parcels … … … … … … … … … … … … … … … … … …	1	9	5
Stationery …	0	3	4
Washing, Soap, Soda, &c. … … … … … … … … … … … … … … … … …	1	1	10
Suit of Clothes Supplied for Boarding-out Case … … … … … … … …	0	13	8
	£58	10	6

LETTER

ACCOMPANYING THE

ACCOUNT OF DONATIONS RECEIVED

FOR

WORK AMONGST THE POOR

DURING 1876

BY

OCTAVIA HILL

LONDON:
WATERLOW AND SONS LIMITED, PRINTERS,
GREAT WINCHESTER ST, E.C.

SUMMARY

Criticism of the fellow-workers and praise for Emma Cons... expansion of housing work... the purposes of the donation fund... the formation of the Kyrle Society... the importance of visiting and need to co-operate with the Charity Organisation Society... how to deal with failure... open spaces: the Quaker burial ground and the failure to obtain 'out-door sitting rooms'.

EDITOR'S NOTE

At 5,256 words, this is the longest of the letters. Like the 1875 letter, it is somewhat dry and theoretical, being mainly concerned with methods of charity organisation. There are few references to current projects and the letter concludes with a list of failures—some of which later turned into successes. The severe criticism that Octavia felt able to direct towards her fellow-workers in this letter shows how devoted they must have been to her, to be willing to be thus corrected. In spite of the exhortations in previous letters, Octavia still accuses some of the fellow-workers of lack of attention to detail. Emma Cons, on the other hand, is held up as exemplary and, by this time, almost totally independent of Octavia. Octavia follows her criticism of the fellow-workers with criticism of the clergy for failing to co-operate with the Charity Organisation Society in the relief of poverty. Ironically, Octavia was writing at the time when clergy involvement with the COS was approaching its peak. It would decline in years to come as the position of the COS central council in public policy debates and welfare issues became increasingly politicised.

My Dear Friends,

Christmas is here and the old year will quickly be gone, and we begin to count up what we have given and what gained during the time. Individually, collectively, nationally, all men are asking themselves these questions. We want to know, and we ought to want to know, whether we have lived up to the knowledge we have had, whether we have striven to increase that knowledge, whether we have nobly used all powers entrusted to us, whether we have entered into, and been thankful for, all the joys sent to us, whether we have met all difficulty with resolution, and all pain with endurance. We want to know, too, what has been meant by the events which have occurred; what they were intended to teach us; this as the old year's bells ring him out we ask as we ponder over the past. The future we are content to leave in His hands, who ordered all the past for us, only solemnly as we dwell on what its mysteries may be, we ask to have our understandings enlightened, our hearts inspired with noble desires, and fortified with abundant courage, that whatever come we may be ready to meet it in a spirit which no evil can contaminate, no pain embitter, no loss crush, and no prosperity corrupt.

I look back over my year in its relation to you all, and I feel that the old song of thankfulness may rightly be taken up again like a Christmas carol. We have many successes to record, much bright promise for the future. Let me set down some of them for the sake of those among you who have not known of them as they occurred.

I have written to you so frequently about the sub-division of our work that I hardly like to do so again, and yet it is the object I have most deeply at heart. For you see if we cannot sub-divide we must deal with our tenants collectively, not individually, by routine instead of by living government; and moreover we cannot extend our work further and bring to other courts the blessings we have secured for our own. So I long for signs of success in sub-division. Well, I think we have them. We have certainly secured sub-division without fatal collapse. I fear that is all we can at present say of many of our blocks of buildings

63

and groups of tenants; our volunteer workers and assistants do *just* make the undertakings remunerative, and keep the tenants *passably* sober, peaceful and contented. Not more in many cases. I do *not* yet see in most of our courts a high standard of perfection, a distinct progress towards it, or a powerful rule and will at work among them. It is something, indeed it is much, that the schemes go on at all under inexperienced collectors, but it is not all we want. I would earnestly ask all my collectors to think well over what could be done to bring each court under their care more into the condition in which they would wish to see it, to ask themselves why that something is not done, and how it can be done. In nearly every case, I should be inclined to say, closer and above all much prompter attention to detail was needed; and the habitual examination of themselves as to what should be done in every case in which things are not satisfactory. This sounds very vague, but I cannot help thinking the recollection of this fact really would be helpful to the collectors. We too readily sit down under imperfect or bad conditions, instead of setting ourselves to think out what may be done to alter them. So far for the stagnant courts, of which I regret to say we have several. But there are some which are by no means stagnant, but magnificently progressive. I may refer to a group of them which shows the most considerable success we have achieved in the way of sub-division. I refer, of course, to the courts near Drury Lane which Miss Cons has taken entirely under her charge.[1] She has undertaken them wholly, makes her own centre quite

---

1 Emma Cons (1838–1912) was one of Octavia's earliest and most faithful fellow-workers. The two women were exact contemporaries (dying in the same year) and first met as teenagers when they worked at the Ladies' Guild in Fitzroy Square, a self-governing co-operative set up by the Christian Socialists and run by Caroline Southwood Hill, Octavia Hill's mother. Octavia was in charge of a class of girls who made dolls' furniture. Miss Emmie and Miss Ockey, who were both destined to become important social reformers, had much in common, including the fact that they both came from families with several unmarried girls who could no longer rely on the male breadwinner. It was at the Guild in 1853 that the girls first met John Ruskin. When in 1864 Octavia began her long career as a provider of working-class housing, Emma Cons was one of those who enrolled as a housing manager. She helped Octavia with the first of her courts, Paradise Place, and with Barrett's Court. The Sterling sisters, Hester and Julia, purchased Walmer Street and Walmer Place in Marylebone, which Emma managed whilst living on the site. She became an independent manager of working-class dwellings at Surrey Buildings in Lambeth in 1879, designed by Elijah Hoole for the South London Dwellings Company. Unlike Octavia, Emma Cons was an ardent teetotaller and opened her first coffee tavern in Skelton Street off Drury Lane. The Walmer Castle public house, on the corner of Walmer Street and Seymour Place, also became a temperance club. In 1879 the Coffee Music Halls Co. was formed

independent of this house except as to funds, enrols her own volunteer workers, founds her own classes, clubs, savings' banks, keeps her own accounts, supervises all the business and all the personal work, and reports to the owners of the courts direct. I asked her to adopt this plan, because I saw that she was quite able to take the lead in any group of courts entrusted to her, that she might grow to be a centre of workers, and so be able to extend the plan to more courts than we could while she was only my lieutenant, and while all decisions came from me. I knew she would manage courts differently from me. I thought this rather a gain than otherwise; you cannot get the full benefit of heart and head, and active will, unless you give those who serve you active responsibility, freedom of action, the opportunity of forming, and striving to realise their own ideal. Miss Cons had an ideal; left to herself she would gladly have sacrificed it to mine in a moment, and dwarfed her own nature, power and work. That could not be. I set her free to work towards her own standard; I knew we should each learn from the other. I must say I have been astonished how little her work is different from mine; still it *is* her very own, and I hope will be a joy and blessing to her. To me what is it? a joy such as words can hardly speak. I see several courts full of people watched over, saved, cared for, all without me. I see a group of volunteers working with full energy, with deep devotion, some of whom I never knew. I hear of classes, clubs and entertainments, I hear of repairs and improvements contemplated, to which no thought of mine has been devoted; and I feel with a kind of joy no words will convey, that it is *not* true that this reformatory work in the homes of the people, or the gentle and just rule which improves

---

by Emma to provide music halls in London 'at which a purified entertainment shall be given and no intoxicant drinks be sold'. In January 1881 Emma Cons signed the lease for the old Royal Coburg Theatre near Waterloo Station, renamed the Royal Victoria on the accession of Queen Victoria and now known as the Old Vic. In 1891 she bought the freehold of the theatre, having raised £17,500. Emma introduced weekly penny lectures on science subjects on Tuesday evenings, open to both men and women, and persuaded many eminent scientists of the day to speak. After one lecture, two teenage boys asked Emma how they could pursue their education. In response, she knocked together several of the dressing rooms to make two classrooms and formed a part-time educational institution for both men and women. This officially opened in 1889, and eventually developed into Morley College. Emma Cons became an Alderman of the newly created London County Council in 1889, and was immediately challenged, with two other women, in a bitter dispute over the capacity of women to act as councillors. As a result of her experiences at the LCC, Emma became one of the vice-presidents, along with Dr Elizabeth Garrett Anderson and Henrietta Barnett, of the London Society for Women's Suffrage.

them and their houses together, depends the least on this frail life, or feeble body of mine; that when it shall please God that it shall rest at last, or wherever the influence of the spirit which dwells in it cannot reach, then and there nevertheless, however flatterers may chatter, or friends exaggerate, that which I have striven to do will be done by others, perhaps in ways better than I have ever dreamed. Of course I knew this in a sense always, but it is good for others to know it, and I myself know it in a completer way than ever, when I see what is being done in those Drury Lane courts. But there are other courts under volunteer guidance which are progressing admirably quite independent of me. This is most satisfactory; it enables me to see my way very distinctly to extending our work, as soon as ever suitable sites or blocks of buildings are found near any of the places where we are at work in Whitechapel, St Giles's, Marylebone, or even Westminster, but not at present in Lambeth or St Pancras. We have promises of money and workers, but we are always glad of more, of the latter especially; but money itself may be needed in large amounts if we find it practicable to carry out by arrangement with the Board of Works any of the schemes under the Artisans' Dwellings Bill.[2] In view of extended work, and

---

2   The Artisans' Dwellings Bill was introduced in the early part of 1875 and became law, as the Artisans' and Labourers' Dwellings Improvement Act, later in the year. It became known as the Cross Act, after R.A. Cross, Disraeli's Home Secretary, who introduced it. Unlike the Torrens Act of 1868, which empowered local authorities to demand the demolition and rebuilding of individual slum properties, the Cross Act was aimed at clearing whole areas and selling them on for rebuilding. Although the Act applied to all large cities, its principal application was in central London, where it was administered by the Metropolitan Board of Works and the City Commissioners of Sewers. It was partly the result of lobbying by the Charity Organisation Society, which had set up a special committee on working-class housing, with Octavia as one of the members. This committee reported in 1873, and in 1874 Octavia wrote an article for *Macmillan's Magazine* called 'Why the Artisans' Dwelling Bill Was Wanted'. (The use of the past tense was odd, as it wasn't passed until the following year.) She argued that the Torrens Act was ineffective, because the problem of the slum related to the way in which a set of badly planned and maintained properties created an undesirable living environment for which no individual landlord would accept responsibility. The members of the COS committee had been influenced by the success of an 1866 act that enabled the city authorities in Glasgow to purchase large areas of slums, clear them and sell them on for rebuilding by commercial interests. (Octavia claimed there were no philanthropic housing societies in Glasgow at all at the time.) The COS used the success of Glasgow to lobby for similar legislation in London and other cities. The Cross Act, however, did not perform as well as expected. The procedure for putting compulsory purchase orders on groups of properties was time-consuming. Compensation had to be paid to landlords at the full commercial value, without taking

feeling that trained workers are essential to it, I have engaged two more assistants. Applications are coming to me also from several of the large towns for help in starting similar undertakings to our own, which I am unable to meet, for want of trained workers. I also feel sadly, and daily tell myself that what we most need is *better* work in many of the courts we have. It is easy to cover large surfaces, very difficult to do really well on those we have, but let us all try.

Before leaving the subject of the houses I ought to mention that owing to an interview with the owner of the land in one of the courts in which we hold the leases, and which for many years we have desired to rebuild, the rebuilding has been arranged and is in progress. I was glad to find that once appealed to, the sense of duty as landlord was so strong and deep, and led to prompt and generous action. By co-operation of the freeholder and leaseholder that court is now being put thoroughly to rights, which it was impossible should be done by either of them singly.

I myself resumed this time last year the collecting and detailed work in one court, and I hope to continue there face to face with my people in continual intercourse with them as of old. This is a great delight to me, bringing me to such human work among them as is only possible when intercourse is pretty frequent. I am content to resign detailed work in other courts, even those I love most and have most memories of, even those where my dearest friends are at work. I shall still for many years, I trust, be able to help them if large questions arise about purchase, rebuilding, or such like, but I am sure it is best for them that I should stand aside and let the local or appointed workers make some

---

into account the dilapidated state of the property. This meant that the sites, when cleared, were too expensive to sell on to building companies and societies. Also, the Metropolitan Board could still interfere to a considerable extent with what was done on the sites, insisting that the same number of people had to be accommodated who had been displaced—a peculiar requirement, when overcrowding was clearly one of the contributory factors to slum creation. By 1879, the Board found itself with a number of large, expensive and unsaleable cleared sites on its hands. The Peabody trustees offered to take on a batch of them at a price that was so low it represented a massive loss to the ratepayers, but the Board had no alternative but to accept. In the same year, the Cross Act was revised to try to deal with some of the more obvious problems. Between the passing of the Cross Act in 1875 and the dissolution of the Metropolitan Board of Works in 1888, the Board had carried out 16 schemes, and started a further six which were taken on by its successor, the London County Council. The 16 sites covered 42 acres. In order to meet the requirements of the Act, the Board had to rehouse 23,188 people. In fact, they accommodated 27,780 people on the sites, actually raising the population density considerably. (Tarn, 1973, pp.77-83.)

good thing of the work without my meddling. I am sure that when a course of action is *best*, clearly best, one need not fear that in following it, any good thing, large or small, which God meant for us will be lost, that which He means to take away we must ask for grace to resign to Him trustfully, sure that He knows best. We think of Abt Vogler and the words, 'There shall never be *one* lost good',[3] or of Mrs Browning's saying, that though God break our idols to our faces we shall behold them raised and glorified, new Memnons singing in the great God-light,[4] and as we think, all regret seems temporary, short-sighted, small, and we are content to wait till it shall be taken away in fuller sight.

The area over which we have control has been increased during the past year. We have completed the additional building at Bell Street. The Central London Dwellings Improvement Company,[5] for which we were previously managing a few courts, has now put three more courts under our care; this comprises all the property which they own. Mr Ruskin has handed over to me another house in my own immediate neighbourhood. Besides these, a block of buildings erected by Mr Crowder in a court in Whitechapel in which we had charge of three houses, has been completed and filled; four houses adjoining these have been bought and are worked on our system. A block of buildings is nearly completed on the ground of what was once the worst court in Hampstead, chiefly by the instrumentality of one of our friends; and the sister of our architect, who had bought and was herself managing some houses in a court in St Pancras, has lately purchased additional ones. These latter, the indirect outcome of our work, are, as you will readily understand from what I have said of the value of sub-division, more satisfactory than any undertakings for which we here are responsible, because they make us know that in numbers of places where we are powerless the same work may and will be done.

In rendering my annual balance-sheet of money sent to me to be expended for the poor, I ought perhaps to mention a change which is coming over the character of the fund thus entrusted to me. Long ago

---

3   From 'Abt Vogler', ix, by Robert Browning. Octavia uses the same quotation in 1903, p.499.

---

4   'New Memnons singing in the great God-light' is the last line of 'Futurity' by Elizabeth Barett Browning.

---

5   Formed in the 1860s by a group of gentlemen in Lincoln's Inn to renovate and let nearby property for the very poor. Emma Cons was appointed as manager in 1870. From 1874 to 1882 the directors made regular contributions to the donation fund.

it used to be sent almost exclusively for persons coming under my own observation specially needing necessaries of life; then donors began to realise that the gift of joy, and personal intercourse with those who work among them might be as much needed by the poor as gifts of coals and bread, and money was sent to me for our summer and winter parties; then the need of beauty in the surroundings of our people became clear to some of my kind friends and donors, and money was sent for carriage of flowers and such things as that. But this year a still greater change has arisen in regard to this my donation fund. Persons write to me asking my opinion as to their larger gifts, consult me as to fitting institutions to which to subscribe. It often happens that after thus consulting me they send their gift straight to the societies I mention, in which case no record of course appears in my balance-sheet, but if they send it asking me to forward it to any given institution, or if they send me a sum asking me to divide it between those societies I named, the item must necessarily be included in my accounts. Again, I have seen fit three or four times during the year, publicly or privately, to call the attention of those who have money to give to causes or societies urgently needing liberal support, such for instance as the Commons Preservation Society,[6] or the Society for Befriending Young Servants.[7]

---

6   The accounts show a donation of £10 6s. The Commons Preservation Society had been founded by a young barrister, George Shaw-Lefevre, on 19 July 1865 at a meeting convened at his chambers in the Inner Temple. Shaw-Lefevre attracted the support of, amongst others, Thomas Huxley, the eminent scientist and defender of Darwin, John Stuart Mill, then at the peak of his reputation as a writer on social and economic issues, and, from the world of letters, Thomas Hughes and Leslie Stephen. Within a few months £1,400 had been raised for the new society, and on 24 January 1866 the Lord Mayor of London chaired a meeting at the Mansion House for the public launch of the CPS, which by this time had attracted the support of the Bishop of London, the Deans of Westminster and St Paul's, members of parliament, fellows of learned societies and Henry Fawcett, whose garden in Lambeth would later become the basis of Vauxhall Park. The CPS was Britain's first national conservation body. It was enormously successful in its campaigns to preserve public access to open spaces by insisting on the upholding of ancient common rights. The CPS was involved with high-profile campaigns in Berkhamsted, Wimbledon, Wandsworth, Tooting, Coulsdon and Banstead. It profited from the appointment of Robert Hunter as its solicitor in 1867, who waged spectacular legal battles to save Epping Forest and the New Forest. In 1899 the Commons Preservation Society merged with the National Footpaths Preservation Society to become the Commons and Footpaths Preservation Society. It still exists as the Open Spaces Society.

---

7   The accounts show a donation of £33 13s. The Metropolitan Association for Befriending Young Servants had been founded by Octavia's friend Jane Nassau Senior

After my letters in *The Times* and *Daily News* about the latter I received several sums to hand over. These must be entered in my accounts. But I hope the fact of their appearing will not confuse the mind of those donors who have been accustomed to entrust me with money for those individuals whom I and my fellow-workers meet, and whom the donors could not otherwise reach. I always devote to these primarily the money sent to me to be expended for the poor. Indeed, I will ask my kind donors to believe me, that to the very best of my power the spirit of their trust has been fulfilled in each case, and that the kind of object which they would desire to aid has been assisted. As a rule the small sums have been sent for carriage of flowers, gifts of food or clothes, and the larger ones were for institutions or great causes. I hold it to be an important part of my duty to enlist help for these latter. Times of crisis occur when it is of the greatest consequence to secure such aid, my position often enables me to know swiftly where the need is, and I am very thankful for the confidence and generosity of those friends who have enabled me to meet it.

I send herewith to all my fellow-workers and donors the report and balance-sheet of the Kyrle Society, because in the earlier part of the year, before the Society was formally constituted, the money was sent to me. The accounts are made up to the end of the year, and include all that has been sent to me or to the Society. It is a great satisfaction to me to see that it has become an independent body, with, I trust, an important function in the future, and I am very glad to be its treasurer and one of its members.[8]

Now, as to the visiting. Here too we have made progress, but rather in extending our field of operations than in perfecting the work in the area over which we had influence. A not satisfactory kind of progress, but for special reasons, which I shall explain, it seemed to me that extension must be aimed at this year and must be also in the year

---

(1828–1877), the daughter-in-law of the economist and sister of Tom Hughes. 'This institution could boast 25 branch registry offices, 17 associated homes, and over 800 women visitors by the mid-1880s, by which time it was placing over 5,000 pauper girls in domestic employment each year, about 25 per cent of them coming out of the London poor-law schools.' (Prochaska, 1980, p.150.)

---

8 'The letter of my sister, which inaugurated the Kyrle Society, can be had (price 2*d*) from the hon. secretary Miss Picton—14 Nottingham Place, W.' (*Editor's note:* These words appear to have been written in Octavia's hand on all copies of the 1876 letter.)

which is to come. It happens that at this time there are a certain number of persons who have devoted time and thought to the study of questions affecting the permanent welfare of the poor. They have noticed what forms of gifts are harmful, what forms beneficial in their influence; they have amassed a quantity of knowledge and may be generally described as enlightened workers. But they are few and far between, they are for the most part unconnected with the old-established charities, they are some of them a little hard and dry in their manner of urging their views, and but few of them have real, living, personal intercourse with the poor. On the other hand, there exists a large body of kindly, liberal, devoted workers among the poor, who *never* look beyond the immediate result of the special gift, who are injuring them irreparably by ill-considered doles, but are linked to them by many a memory of kind offices. Now, these two sets of people must be brought together and learn to understand one another, and that quickly. Each is the complement of the other, neither can really help the people without the other; if either drives the other from the field, nay, if both do not heartily and fully co-operate, catastrophe will be the result. Our problem this year was, as it must be in the coming year, how to bring them together. 'Bring them together', did not the very words used in their spiritual meaning suggest, taken in their physical meaning, the solution of the difficulty? It seems so to me. If you want two people to understand one another you bring them together, you let each see what the other is doing. If the problem was, as it seemed to me, how to get such men as formed the Charity Organisation Society to understand such visitors as form the district visiting societies, the only chance was to bring the daily work of each under the notice of the other. What I wished to see done was that one visitor should be chosen as secretary to every group of visitors, whose special function it should be to study questions affecting the temporal condition of the poor, to consult with all new and less experienced visitors, to attend the Charity Organisation district committee, to be a medium of communication between all bodies dealing with the poor of her district, and to enlist for them the services of her fellow visitors. I think all that is needed will follow from the understanding that would then be secured, of the aim, function, and practice of all who are at work. I gladly, therefore, accepted the kind proposal of the Bishop of Gloucester and Bristol that I should meet at his house chosen visitors and clergy from many districts of London, and talk over with them plans of co-operation with those who had given time to study systems of relief. Note, please carefully, that it is the clergy and visitors that are ignorant of their need of the Charity

Organisation Society men. The latter are eagerly anxious for co-operation from the visitors and have always been so. We met at the Bishop's and I read a paper, which was subsequently reprinted in the July number of *Good Words*,[9] setting forth what seemed to me a very simple, practical plan of co-operation, and one which could be adopted by any single ecclesiastical district or group of workers which cared to come forward. That meeting was in May. During June and July and since the autumn holiday, I have received invitations from clergy and others representing groups of visitors asking me to meet their workers and further discuss changes of the system. In various degrees and ways important reforms are being adopted in many places. To this work my main strength must be directed in the opening year so far as I can foresee. For I look upon the crisis as a very serious one, and I would urgently entreat all who are connected with our charities to ponder over it, and that in time. Specially, if my voice could reach them, would I ask this of the clergy, for they could help as no other men could, and they by special training ought to be the first to see the need. They have that deep, personal, near knowledge of the poor which gives them individual influence; they know practically the value of the gentle care of visitors, yet they have dealt with such numbers of poor that, if they had time to pause and think they *must* see the evil effect of the present relief and feel the need of a better. Yet they have hardly time to amass quantities of detailed information about the labour market in various places, poor-law reforms, safe clubs and investments, machinery for savings, improved sanitary laws, loans, and all the manifold subjects on which wise dealing with the poor depends. Will they not then heartily and thankfully meet and recognise the group of men who in every poor-law district now meet at the Charity Organisation committee to apply the results of their knowledge on these and other such subjects to the poor who are clustered under every clergyman's charge? If they find some of them dry and a little apt to be cold and generalising, will they not remember that, in spite of reserve in speaking, there must be *some* devotion in the spirit of young officers, merchants, noblemen, lawyers, bankers, who work hard and continuously in out-of-the-way

---

9   Octavia Hill, 'District Visiting', *Good Words*, July 1876, vol. 17, pp. 488-93, reprinted as a pamphlet by Longmans, Green and Co. and the Charity Organisation Society, 15 Buckingham Street, Adelphi, W.C., price 3*d*, and included in *Our Common Land*. 'This paper has been slightly altered from one which was read on the 4th May last to a meeting of district visitors and clergy at the Bishop of Gloucester and Bristol's house in London.'

poor neighbourhoods for their fellow citizens; will they not at least consent to use the knowledge to be thus so easily obtained? Will they not, too, place at their service, so far as in them lies, the help of those district visitors who *have* the individual care for the people, and are not likely certainly to generalise too much, or to look *too* carefully into future results of impulsive liberality? It fills me with awe when I see the ill-considered tide of injurious almsgiving flowing on nearly unchecked, and watch the isolation of the few in each district who are lifting up their voices against it. I feel inclined to say to the clergy, 'Oh, for God's sake! join them while you may; bring them all they need of individual knowledge of poor man, woman, or child, as you and your visitors see them in that home-life which they hardly know; do not lose for yourselves the help of that grave, calm outlook which the students of great questions gain; test their principles by the application to life—let them stand or fall by that; test your action by what they show you of its result: do not, like ostriches, hide your heads in sand, and think because you *will* not see that danger is not near. Study together what the poor need; have confidence that this world, being God's and not the devil's, there is a course of action which shall meet the individual need and the common and future welfare of the people. Join the students while you may, for the day may come when one of two results may overwhelm you. Either the organisations, too feeble to stand longer waiting for the co-operation of you and your visitors, who ought to have been from the first an integral part of their body, may be extinguished when you learn at last that you want them; or possibly they, representing science, and attracting daily more and more of the earnest young blood of England, which *will* not flow in the old channels, and finds humanity in science, and generalises and looks on, will suddenly alter their course, and tired of entreating you to use them, will find themselves strong without you, organise systems of relief and bodies of visitors which will either compete with or supersede your own, Theirs, yours, it matters not so that they be God's. But why risk warfare where there might be peace; you, too, who are messengers of peace. I do not dream of threatening you. I am sure some of you are far too great men, and some too pre-occupied to notice a threat. I do not even believe the idea as yet occurs to our committees to act independently of you. But I, a churchwoman, see that it may come to that, to your discomfort. Again and again in the course of her history has the church missed her moment for seeing the great truths which were gathering strength in the hearts of her people, and, instead of accepting them, instead of being the first to herald them in, she has tried to ignore them, and they have been too strong for her. Clergymen, yes ministers of all denominations, yes, governors of charities which of old bore witness to men of Christian lovingkindness and care, be among the first rank of those who see the deeper lovingkindness of wiser action in the changed times. The wealth, the organisation, the leadership of hundreds of men and women is yours now. Use them with deepest thought, that so you may not let the wisdom and much of the earnest effort of the age slip by you to conclusions which must prevail, and without the hallowing teaching of much you know. The day is yours now. Use it nobly as leaders of an advancing church, as attentive watchmen who see the daylight coming and rejoice in it.'[10]

Before I end my letter for the year, let me recall to you, my dear fellow-workers, my failures as well as my successes. For, first, it is more honest to do so; secondly, there is a peculiar tenderness in the thought of those who have stood beside us in a hope and an effort into which the world did *not* enter. It is easy to join the triumphant army as it marches along conquering, and everyone can then be proud of his place in it; but there is a nearer link between those who stood side by side in a fight when the order came to advance to the breach and comrades were few and hope not very bright, and the advance slow and difficult, and if the repulse came and was inevitable, the sense that it *was* inevitable, that the best effort was made, and ought to have been

---

10 The tone of this passionate piece of invective against the church for refusing to co-operate with the Charity Organisation Society (COS) has a menacing air, in spite of Octavia's assurance that she would not dream of threatening the clergy. She implies that it will be curtains for the Church of England, unless its ministers wake up to the new scientific methods for the relief of poverty offered by the COS. The tone of Octavia's talk at the Bishop of Gloucester and Bristol's house, reproduced in *Our Common Land*, had not been quite so blunt. (As the accounts show, the Bishop gave her ten shillings for it.) The passage in quotation marks here is not taken from it, but was written for this letter. Certainly, the COS had always gone out of its way to involve the clergy, since the earliest days of the Marylebone committee, which Octavia was invited to join by the Revd Fremantle. In some COS districts, all local clergy were considered *ex officio* members of the COS—although whether they responded to the invitation was another matter. Ironically, Octavia was making her plea when clerical support for the COS was at its height: it would tail off drastically after 1880, as the COS Central Council became increasingly politicised in its attitude towards such welfare issues as old-age pensions, which it resolutely opposed. The clergy may have been unwilling to identify themselves with an organisation seen to be hard-hearted. An analysis of the membership of the COS committee in Fulham and Hammersmith shows clergy participation falling from a high of 59 per cent in 1878 to only five per cent in 1900, and remaining low thereafter. (Whelan, 2001, p.36.)

made, is clear to those who advanced together there in darkness. Nay, the very indifference of the world, the absence of its hurrahs, which can but come when palpable success follows effort, makes the sense of friendship deeper between those who remember together in silence all the struggle, all the hope which flashed with sudden gleams like lightning, to be lost as instantaneously in the darkness of disappointment. So we, who have sometimes laboured in vain, will not fail to recall the repulses we have shared together. Thirdly, we will recall our failures because in one sense we dare to recall them because we *dis*believe in them; because we think that it is only what *should* fail which *does* fail: because we believe the words:

> Not all who seem to fail have failed indeed;
> Not all who fail have, therefore, worked in vain;
> For all our acts to many issues lead,
> And out of earnest purpose pure and plain,
> Enforced by honest toil of hand or brain,
> The Lord will fashion, in His own good time,
> Be this the labourer's proudly humble creed,
> Such ends as to His purpose fitliest chime
> With His vast love's eternal harmonies.
> There is no failure for the good and wise.
> What though thy seed should fall by the wayside,
> And the birds snatch it, yet the birds are fed,
> Or they may bear it far across the tide,
> To yield rich harvests after thou art dead.[11]

We have tried earnestly this year to secure small open spaces for outdoor sitting-rooms for the people in various parts of London—hitherto without one atom of success. I think I never spent so much heart, time, and thought on anything so utterly without apparent result. We tried for an East End boulevard, with an avenue, and wider spaces of green

---

11 Octavia probably found this verse in Samuel Smiles' *Character* (1871). In Chapter 12: 'The Discipline of Experience', Smiles praises men who have suffered for the sake of religion, science and truth. 'They perished, but their truth survived. They seemed to fail, and yet they eventually succeeded.' Smiles uses the poem as a footnote to this statement, and attributes it to a book called *Politics for the People* (1848). This is a collection of unsigned political pamphlets which uses the poem as an epigraph. It has been attributed by some critics to Archbishop Richard Chenevix Trench (1807–1886). In transcribing the verse Octavia omitted the line beginning 'Be this the labourer's...'.

and flowers—an East End embankment, as it were, where the people might have strolled on summer evenings, and sat out of doors, and we failed. We tried to get a church-yard planted and opened in Drury Lane, and the matter has not progressed very far yet. We tried to get trustees to act themselves in regard to other spaces, and we hear little from them. We tried to get leave from one nobleman to plant trees along an East End road, where he is lord of the manor, and he postpones the question. We tried to get the board school playgrounds open, and so far without success.[12] We tried—Oh! how we tried—to get the Quakers to devote to the service of the poor their disused burial grounds, and they, even they, have decided to build over by far the more precious of the two, a spot which might have been a perpetual joy and rest to the people, and now is gone, I suppose, for ever.[13] They have one space left —the vicar, the guardians, we ourselves, are asking for it for the people, but their past action does not form much ground for hope.

Next year, this time next year, if I am here writing you once more, will there be any spot saved from the waste of bricks and mortar or the hideousness of neglect to be devoted to the people? I cannot help believing there may. You and I will not achieve much, for we are few and weak; but there is a gathering sense of the heart-hunger in the spirits of people for more beauty and more quiet; and when England realises a need, there is much liberality among us which rejoices in meeting it; many love to dedicate what they have to the service of the people. Let us then hope, not in your strength, still less in mine, but in His Who, though He has sent to many of us for our purification much personal pain, has guarded and guided our work to triumphant successes more than we can count, as if in the main it had in very deed been in harmony with His own ends, which if it be we may leave it all to Him, He will retard, He will hasten it; we may watch to try and see what He means by all He does with it and us; wonderful glimpses of meaning and mercy may at times be revealed to us; when they are all hidden we need not fear for ourselves or for it. If now sometimes when

---

12 See 1877 pp.90-91 for the successful conclusion to the Drury Lane churchyard scheme, and a more hopeful prospect for the playgrounds.

---

13 Octavia was particularly upset by the determination of the Quakers to sell their large burial ground in Bunhill Fields for development, in spite of representations from herself, and she expressed herself forcefully about it in *Our Common Land* in the following year. (*Our Common Land*, 1877, pp.123-30.)

things are puzzling we can only, with the old poet, say in strong patience,

> Only do Thou lend me a hand,
> Since Thou hast both mine eyes,[14]

we look on with a hope which carries patience before it as with a flood to the day when we shall each of us hear the words, 'Well done, good and faithful servant, enter thou into the joy of thy Lord!'[15] Shall not that joy be the fullest sight of what our Father meant and means for us and all we love?

---

14 The concluding lines of 'Submission' by George Herbert (1593–1633). Octavia was fond of one of Herbert's mottos, which she used to describe her relationship with the fellow-workers: 'A dwarf, on a giant's shoulders, sees further of the two'. (Maurice, 1914, p.339.) See 1883 pp.173-74 for Octavia's scheme to inscribe one of Herbert's verses on the wall of St John's Church, Waterloo.

---

15 Matthew 25:21.

DONATION ACCOUNT, 1876

RECEIPTS

	£	s	d
Cash in hand	101	10	0½
Mrs Pollard	13	0	0
A.G. Crowder, Esq	20	0	0
Mrs H. Duckworth	10	0	0
Mrs H. Duckworth (Orphan family)	27	0	0
Baron Amphlett	1	10	0
Sir G. Phillips	60	0	0
Mrs Martineau	10	0	0
Mrs Hart	0	14	0
K. Brock, Esq	2	2	6
Lord Dunsany	30	0	0
Miss Cave Brown	5	0	0
The Bishop of Gloucester and Bristol	0	10	0
Mrs Scaramanga	2	0	0
R.W. Monro, Esq	7	0	0
The late Miss Monro	5	5	0
Mrs W. Shaen	2	0	0
Mrs S. Winkworth	30	0	0
Mrs Llewellyn	10	0	0
Mrs Wright	25	0	0
Miss S.J. Harris	1	0	0
Miss Buchanan (May festival)	0	10	0
Mrs Lindesay	1	0	0
Mr and Mrs J.W. Blundell (Playground festival)	0	10	0
Mrs Stone (Playground festival)	1	0	0
Mr and Mrs J.W. Blundell	0	10	0
For General Purposes	3	0	0
Miss Alice Fletcher	2	0	0
Miss Meek	1	0	0
Elm	5	0	0
Miss Stone	0	1	0
J. Hornsby Wright, Esq	1	0	0
N.C. Curzon, Esq	25	0	0
Mrs H. Mallet	0	10	0
Patrick Anderson, Esq	1	0	0
Sir Charles Trevelyan	2	0	0
Hamilton Hornby, Esq	0	10	0
Mrs Whateley (District Committee Aid)	5	10	0
Mrs Allen (Charity Organisation Society)	2	0	0
Mrs Allen (Charity Organisation Society)	0	2	6
Lady Thompson	3	10	0
Miss H. Gurney	0	8	0
Miss Bessie Holland	1	0	0
George Brightwen, Esq	10	0	0
Mrs F. Hill (for toys)	0	2	0
Mrs Joshua	1	1	0
Mrs Arthur Mills	2	10	0
Mrs Strong	0	5	0
Mrs Smith, Muswell Hill	1	0	0
W. Bousfield, Esq	0	10	0
R.D. Wilson, Esq	5	0	0
Mrs Flowers	5	0	0
Rev. John Bond	0	10	0
W. Matheson, Esq (for drivers)	0	10	0
F.D. Mocatta, Esq	5	0	0
Percy Bigland, Esq	1	0	0
Ernest Hart, Esq	1	7	6
Miss Sterling (Walmer Street excursion)	25	8	8
Miss Hart	0	5	0
Miss Harrison	0	2	6
Miss Tatham	1	1	0
Mrs H. Gillson	0	5	0
Miss Curtis-Hayward	0	7	6
Edward Bond, Esq	15	0	0
W.S. Seton-Kerr, Esq (For tenants' party)	0	10	0
Miss Stephen (for A)	8	13	0
Miss Thackeray	3	0	0
Miss Bragg	1	10	0
Miss E. Manning	3	0	0
Hamilton Hill, Esq	0	10	0
John Fletcher, Esq	10	0	0
Miss C. Williams	1	1	0
S.J. Cockerell, Esq	0	5	0
Alfred Hill, Esq	10	0	0
Miss Roleston	1	1	0
W. Ford, Esq	10	0	0
Three Shareholders, Central London Dwellings	3	0	0
Sale of food remaining after a party	0	15	0
Returned by mother of W.L. for clothes	0	4	11
Club room rent from Teetotallers	2	1	0
Per Miss O. Hill	1	10	9
Band, rent from	0	9	0

CARRIAGE OF FLOWERS

	£	s	d
Miss F. Baldwin	0	5	3
Rev. R.W. Vidal	0	2	0
Rev. Basil Wood	0	2	6
Miss Gibson	0	0	6
Misses Williams and Sumner	0	10	0
Miss C. White	0	3	0
Mrs Reiss	5	0	0

SOCIETY FOR BEFRIENDING YOUNG SERVANTS

	£	s	d
Miss Greaves	5	0	0
J. Cropper, Esq	5	0	0
Anon.	20	0	0
Mrs Eiloart	0	10	0
Miss Erle	1	1	0
W. Edwards, Esq	1	1	0
Mrs Dowling	1	1	0
£594	**594**	**0**	**1½**

DONATION ACCOUNT, 1876

EXPENDITURE

	£	s	d
Pensions (Mrs K.)	2	12	0
Pensions (To various persons at the East-end)	8	5	0
Playgrounds	12	12	2
Rent, Coal, Gas, Cleansing and Furniture for various Clubs and Institutes and Classes	82	4	11
Employment of various Poor People	2	10	11
Child at School (W.L.)	4	12	10
Child at School (W.M.)	12	15	0
Carriage of Flowers	8	10	8
Miss Nicholls, Reformatory, Hampstead	10	0	0
St Jude's Whitechapel	54	0	0
Expenses for School Board and Guardian's Work and Printing Stationery and Postage	11	12	7
Winter Party:			
Lady Ducie's Tenants	9	1	1
Mr Somerset Beaumont's Tenants	1	0	6
Institute	0	3	6 1/2
Tenants of Freshwater Place	1	0	10
Tenants of Albert's Buildings	2	11	4 1/2
Tenants of Granby Place and Parker Street	16	1	1
Walmer Street Children	3	3	8 1/2
Charity Organisation Society	20	10	0
Boy's Home, Church Farm, Barnet	20	0	0
Gifts of Clothes and Money, Cabs to Hospitals, &c.	2	15	4
Society for Befriending Young Servants	33	13	0
Commons Preservation Society	10	6	0
Tenants' Excursions:			
Granby Place and Parker Street	16	3	7
Little Edward Street	0	12	5
Mr S. Beaumont's	4	19	0
Paradise Place	1	5	0
Bell Street	6	0	0
Lady Ducie's	5	13	6
New Buildings	3	0	0
Albert's Buildings	8	17	1
Walmer Street	25	7	8
New Court	3	0	0
Freshwater Place	2	10	0
Open Air Festivals at Lambeth, Lincoln's Inn, and Freshwater Place	7	6	5
Various Patients at Convalescent Homes	8	18	6
Education of Two Orphans	39	0	0
Miscellaneous	1	1	0
Interest on Savings' Bank Deposits	5	6	4 1/2
Loans (J.W.)	2	0	0
Fittings for Shop, Stock, &c. (A.)	8	19	6
Cash in hand*	113	17	6 1/2
	£594	0	1 1/2

* N.B.— Of this balance £105 has to be retained for special objects mentioned by the donors, and to which I have myself promised help. This leaves me a very small available balance in hand.

I have to acknowledge so very much help, assuming such various forms, that it becomes impossible to enumerate either the donors or their gifts, but I must just mention the following ladies and gentlemen who were so very kind as to entertain some of our people in their parks or gardens, a form of help which is most valuable to us:

Mr and Mrs George MacDonald	Mr and Mrs Marshall
Mr and Mrs George Brightwen	Mr and Mrs Masters
Mr and Mrs Andrew Johnston	Mr and Mrs Ernest Hart
The Misses Hill	Mrs Pollard
Mr and Mrs Fawcett	Miss Townshend, who received us
Mr and Mrs Harvey	several times at Wimbledon

LETTER TO MY FELLOW-WORKERS

TO WHICH IS ADDED

ACCOUNT OF DONATIONS RECEIVED

FOR

WORK AMONG THE POOR

DURING 1877

BY

OCTAVIA HILL
(FOR PRIVATE CIRCULATION ONLY)

LONDON:
PRINTED BY GEO PULMAN,
24, THAYER STREET, MANCHESTER SQUARE, W.

SUMMARY

Five orphans fostered... Barrett's Court and the club: death of Sydney Cockerell... Lady Pembroke's houses in Whitechapel... other housing work: Westminster and Kensington... the need for the clergy to work with the Charity Organisation Society... the need for more workers in South London... open air sitting-rooms for the poor: Drury Lane; Waterloo; St Giles... open spaces: the reservoir at Thirlmere... Octavia's work takes on a more campaigning tone: the need for gentleness.

EDITOR'S NOTE

The gloomy tone of this letter is not entirely due to the death in December of Octavia's old friend Sydney Cockerell, who ran the club at Barrett's Court. 1877 was Octavia's annus horribilis. *John Ruskin attacked her in print in* Fors Clavigera *for refusing to support his utopian schemes, and her engagement to Edward Bond, a handsome barrister and 'the beloved of the philanthropic set' according to Beatrice Webb, was announced, then unannounced the next day after objections from his mother (Darley, 1990, 188–90). As a result of these two setbacks, Octavia suffered a physical and mental collapse. She withdrew from her work for several years, leaving it the hands of the fellow-workers while she travelled in Europe. The rambling and morbid first page, with its shaky syntax, is an indicator of Octavia's state of mind. Unusually, instead of starting with an account of the housing work, Octavia describes a project of the donation fund—the placing of five orphans 'in memory of the dead'. As Octavia does not mention Sydney Cockerell's death for several pages, her readers must have wondered what was going on. One of the orphans was boarded out in memory of Jane Nassau Senior, the first woman poor law inspector and another faithful friend and supporter who had passed away during the year. (Maurice, 1914, p.352.) The uncharacteristically sour remarks about the people of Manchester (p.92) are also indicative of Octavia's disturbed state of mind. This is the first letter to bear the words 'For Private Circulation Only' on its title page. They were printed on every subsequent letter except 1880, when Octavia forgot to add them and had to write them by hand on every copy. The accounts show a donation of 80 guineas from Ruskin, and those for 1878 another donation of £80. These were Ruskin's only contributions to the donation fund, and no doubt represented guilt-offerings for his part in Octavia's breakdown.*

Once more, dear friends, I sit in the shadow of the closing year, and ask you to look back with me on what it has brought. Of what has been lost in it some of you will need nothing to remind you, the great gaps which death has left among us are clear enough. But we must look across them, the holy and good spirits which cannot actively help, or audibly teach us, must not be far from any of us who knew them. We must live in the memory of what they were, in the consciousness of their continuous life, we must be sure to live worthy of the honour of having been allowed here to call them friends. The separation between us and them, while we so live, is but an outward thing, we long to see their faces, to hear their voices, to receive their thoughts, to rest upon their kindness or their love, the sense of pain or loss no time takes away, but we *know* that we are near them while we live in distinct memory of their teaching, and harmony with their lives.

We must also try to remember that though they sleep, or have passed into some world of mightier action, or yet deeper feeling, we here have distinct duties among the men and women to whom their death is nothing, duties to fulfil with regard to the tangible things of this world, of which a strict account will be asked us; that One who knows us set us this work, called us to this struggle, and leaves us still here to fight it. The trumpet-call of duty summons us, the sense of high and important work must inspire us, the tenderest love of God protects us while we stay, and appoints the length of our days. No little task He sets us is beneath His care, can it be beneath ours? Busy, obedient, patient, hopeful, listening intently for His command above the stormy sounds of passion, pain or struggle, let us be sure the still small voice will reach us, and following its guidance can it lead us anywhere but straight to our Father? What then have we, as a group of workers done in the busy outside world since the year began?

One thing, though not first in date, I may mention first. It was done for the living, but in memory of the dead. We have taken charge of five little orphans. We have placed them in families where they will grow up as members of households. We felt that just as pauper children growing up in large schools under abnormal conditions failed to find and fill their places in life as happy, useful citizens, so it was with orphans of a higher class, and that we might take these little friendless creatures and instead of placing them in orphanages, where even after the drawbacks of election were passed, no home-life opened to the children, we would look out for happy country homes where child-life was a clear gain to foster-parents, and there we would plant the young things. Orphanages and industrial schools seemed to us to fill a want as mere schools when children had widowed mothers to watch over them, bestow individual love, and provide a home in holidays or after life, but for children wholly orphaned it seemed to us different. We take destitute children needing homes, not being paupers; mere poverty is not sufficient claim on us. Our funds are not large, we had no wish for a strong permanent association with funded property. We thought our work should live, shrink, or increase, naturally, according to its value, that the donors should know and remember the special children taken, should give again for them in the years to come if they cared to keep them in the homes, and under the influence we had selected for them; that the villages where they are, the people who watch over them, the small committee which chooses and places the children should be under the eye of those who trust us with funds. Some of course *cannot* watch the work in detail, all ought to know enough of its value to give or withhold with intelligence. In charitable work above all let us remember and enter into the spirit of the words, 'I will not offer unto the Lord that which costs me nothing'. The easy complacency which hands over the cheque and thinks no more of it, quiets for a moment the conscience of the donor who doesn't want to do *very* selfishly, but who has never realised that the limit of his duty is that of the power given him by his Father. We, who were working in memory of a human generosity which gave its utmost, under the influence of a divine love which gave itself, asked to give ourselves, our thoughts, our money, our heart, our time; we are bound together afresh by the united work, and the small children we have taken become henceforward part of our charge in life.[1]

The buildings in Barrett's Court have been during the past year finished and all filled. They are called St Christopher's Buildings, in memory of the old saint who found after he had learned to serve the poor and helpless, that good was in reality the strongest power.[2]

---

1 The confused syntax, which makes this sentence unintelligible, reveals Octavia's inner turmoil.

---

2 This brief reference to the demolition of 15-20 Barrett's Court and their

replacement with St Christopher's Buildings gives little indication of the struggle between Octavia and the local authority—the vestry—which left her with a life-long hatred of officialdom. In 1871 Octavia had written an article for *Macmillan's Magazine* describing her work in Barrett's Court. It was a powerful piece of writing, painting a vivid picture of the slum she was turning around. However, it turned out to be a bit too graphic for her own good, as complaints were made to the medical officer of health of the Marylebone vestry about the existence of such a slum in the heart of the West End. As a result, the medical officer, Dr Walker, started inspecting the houses with threats of closure notices. Octavia was furious, as she was working in her usual manner to gradually improve both the physical environment of the Court and the behaviour of the tenants. She opposed large-scale demolition and rebuilding because it would force out the 'less hopeful tenants', the type who would get drunk on a Saturday night and make a bonfire of the banisters. This sort of behaviour, which could be handled in a run-down building, would become impossible to tolerate in a new 'model dwelling' (1883, p.175). Octavia's supporters swung into action. The Charity Organisation Society set up a sub-committee on 20 November 1871 'to inquire into the sanitary and financial success of Miss Octavia Hill's plan for improving the condition of the poor... in consequence of some strictures passed on Miss Hill's houses by the medical officer of health of St Marylebone'. The sub-committee reported in February 1872 that: 'With respect to Barrett's Court, this property has only been two years under Miss Hill's care, and some of the houses are not in quite as good a condition as those on the other properties. Everything, however, which is required to put them into proper sanitary condition is done... The fact that though small-pox has visited the court, no case of it has occurred in Miss Hill's houses, bears witness to the thoroughness of the sanitary arrangements.' (Charity Organisation Society, 1872, p.3.) Dr Walker pressed ahead, and submitted his report to the Marylebone vestry in November 1874. On the night before the meeting Octavia's friend Ernest Hart went to see him. Hart was the chairman of the National Health Society and a specialist in sanitary legislation for the British Medical Association. He told Dr Walker that his position was 'utterly untenable' and that 'he would only get into difficulties' if he persisted. (Maurice, 1914, pp.311-12.) Walker was alarmed and backed off. The vestry accepted his report but left the decision as to what to do to be worked out between Octavia and Dr Walker. This was not the end of the matter. According to E. Moberly Bell: 'the medical officer did not readily forgive the exposure of his incompetence; his position made it possible for him to hamper Octavia's work, his *amour-propre* made it delightful to him to do so. She had to submit to perpetual pinpicks; he would issue a sheaf of orders about trifles, would announce in the local newspaper that he was about to submit another report on Barrett's Court, would threaten to shut this or that house.' (Moberly Bell, 1942, p.138.) We do not know when the axe finally fell, but in 1877 a row of Mrs Stopford Brooke's houses was demolished and replaced with a block of model dwellings designed by Elijah Hoole. In spite of the fact that it had been forced upon her, Octavia was pleased with the result. However, the Hon. Mrs Maclagan, who managed Mrs Stopford Brooke's houses and who left an account of her time in Barrett's Court, said that the tenants bitterly regretted losing their old properties, and that the model dwellings were unpopular: 'the staircase, the laundry and the water-tap served for six or eight houses, and the "privacy", such as it was, of the tenements was deeply regretted'. (Darley, 1990, p.136.) It was Octavia who decided on the name for the new block and asked the Kyrle Society to arrange for the carved

It is well to remember what once stood where those buildings stand, how sun and light and air have purified the ground there, and clean, fresh, wholesome work now replaces the decayed and rotten work. If we ever rebuild the rest of the court it may be well to try to rebuild it as separate houses, not as a block, it is not good to concentrate too large a population on a small area, and we have now two large blocks containing a considerable number of tenants; it would, I think be well not to increase the population on the remaining space, but whether this is financially possible remains to be seen; I am in no hurry to rebuild.

The club in Barrett's Court has sustained so heavy a loss in the death of Mr Cockerell that it will be difficult for it to survive.[3] His deep perception of right, and sympathy with it wherever found, so that it always increased where he was, combined with the entirely liberal view that discussion, self-government, and freedom, were essential to the healthy education of man, this rare combination of qualities which taught him to leave the management to the Club itself, and yet ensured a steady improvement, will be hard to find again. Still I believe that work such as his in Barrett's Court will not die, and I do trust that in

---

copy of Dürer's engraving of St Christopher to be set into its wall (1879, pp.120-22). When Harriot Yorke built a 500-seat hall for the tenants it was called St Christopher's Hall (1882, p.159) and in 1885 Barrett's Court was renamed St Christopher's Place. St Christopher's Buildings is now called Greengarden House. In July 2004 serviced apartments were being advertised at rates of up to £2,240 per week. *See ills. 20 and 21.*

---

3   Octavia had met Sydney Cockerell, of George Cockerell & Company, coal merchants, in 1871 at Ben Rhydding, a health spa near Leeds. He had written to his sister at the time: 'First and foremost of all the guests… comes Miss Octavia Hill; an unobtrusive, plainly dressed little lady… of great force and energy, with a wide, open and well-stored brain, but, withal, as gentle and womanly as a woman can be… Miss Hill has done great things among the poor, in her own district of Marylebone.' Sydney Cockerell took over the running of the working men's club in Barrett's Court in 1873, and, in addition to that, was one of Octavia's most trusted advisers in her various projects. Following his death in 1877, Octavia wrote to his widow to tell her 'how much I miss him now, and shall miss him on through whatever years are to come, and how largely that was due to that exquisite sympathy and goodness which all of us felt in some measure'. In 1898, when Octavia was presented with John Singer Sargent's portrait of herself (1898, pp.420-01), she recalled the fellow-workers who had passed away, especially Sydney Cockerell, Mrs Nassau Senior (who also died in 1877), Mrs Russell Gurney, F.D. Maurice and William Shaen. (Darley, 1990, pp.110, 196, 268.) Sydney Cockerell's son, also Sydney, would become secretary of the Red Cross Hall at the age of 19, ten years after his father's death, and would eventually heal the rift between Octavia and Ruskin (1892, p.321, n.5).

some way or other the Club may recover its shaken footing. The problems before us in this court seem to me in some ways more serious than ever they were, the place is full of vigorous life, apt to run into terrible sin, but trembling too in the balance; if we could but win the hearts and lead the spirits there, the vigour would be powerful for so much good. We ought to be a great deal there; for conviction, reverence, refinement, and gentleness, such as we ought to have acquired in our homes, does impart itself insensibly where intercourse is frequent, and friendships naturally grow up.

Lady Pembroke[4] has purchased fifteen houses in St Jude's,[5] they are old houses likely to be very troublesome, but affording a power of control in a part of the parish where it was sorely needed, this ought to be a great cause of thankfulness to us. What interests me very much in the place is that there exists at the back of the houses a capital bit of ground which I greatly hope Lady Pembroke will make, or let us make into a garden for the tenants, it is really quite a good sized bit of ground

---

4 The Countess of Pembroke, Lady Gertrude Frances Talbot (1840–1906), was the daughter of the Earl of Shrewsbury. She married George Robert Charles, thirteenth Earl (1850–1895), in 1874. The family home was Wilton, just outside Salisbury. Her other sisters were Lady Adelaide Talbot, Countess Brownlow (1844–1917), wife of the third Earl Brownlow, whose family homes were Belton House, Lincs and Ashridge Park, Surrey, and Lady Constance Harriett Talbot, Marchionness of Lothian (1836–1901), chatelaine of Blickling, Norfolk, who married her first cousin, the noted book collector. Together with Katrine, Countess Cowper they made up the 'Aunts' and constituted the older generation of the Souls, the privileged group of élite men and women who dominated late Victorian Society. The Aunts were persons of legendary magnificence and beauty.

---

5 These houses cost £6,000 and were in Angel Alley, which still exists as a much truncated cul de sac off Whitechapel High Street. In November 1876 Octavia had been visited by Princess Alice of Hesse-Darmstadt, Queen Victoria's second daughter, who was deeply interested in Octavia's work among the poor. Octavia took her to Whitechapel to see the very worst the East End could offer, and they visited 'a horrid lodging house' full of dark rooms and disreputable people. In February 1877 Octavia was able to write to Princess Alice to tell her of the purchase of the 15 houses 'which are many of them let to the immoral poor and of which we are most anxious to obtain control. Among them... is that last common lodging house you saw, the one in Angel Alley, where there was the poor wizened little old-looking baby, and the degraded woman. We hope to have a model common lodging house there, where they may sing, and where young Oxford men and other gentlemen may go in and have a chat, or a discussion, and reach perhaps many a wild, undisciplined young man, or a broken down old one... Mr Barnett is so very happy in the thought...' (Darley, 1990, pp.168-69.) This vision would eventually materialise with the foundation by the Barnetts of Toynbee Hall in Whitechapel in 1884.

for London. We think of asking her too about building there a parish room specially planned for entertainments, concerts, or parties, much prettier than the school-rooms and free from heavy desks and school-furniture. This will be the first building where I have not had to consider the independence of the tenants, and how to make the scheme pay. It will be purely an uncommercial speculation, depending on gifts, so we hope to be able to build a really beautiful, though of course very simple room. Several of Lady Pembroke's houses have been used as common lodging-houses, these will most of them be turned into dwellings for families, one will I hope be kept as a really good common lodging-house for men, under responsible managers, and where I hope gentlemen will help us by spending the evenings sometimes with the unsettled and somewhat wild frequenters of such places.

We have lately undertaken to manage a small block of houses in Westminster, and are in treaty for one in Kensington, but the main extension of the work (which has been considerable) has been by purchase made by private people quite independent of us here, which is of course much more satisfactory. I am ready to purchase in Lambeth now, as a lady is going to reside there to manage houses, but I have not met with suitable courts. I have a capital list of persons who will give money, more than I shall need a great deal, unless the Artisans' Dwellings Bill comes into swift force in Whitechapel.[6]

In referring to last year's report I see that I brought before you strongly the need of getting the managers of old fashioned charities, the clergy, and the district visitors, to study wiser ways of helping the poor, which I thought they would do best by co-operating with the Charity Organisation Society. This I feel even more strongly now. I

---

6   Whitechapel was the very first area to be targeted under the new slum-clearance legislation of the Artisans' and Labourers' Dwellings Improvement Act, known as the Cross Act, when Dr John Liddle made the first official representation to the Metropolitan Board of Works on 27 July 1875. However, there was no 'swift force' about the way in which the system was cranked up into action. Disputes over compensation to the owners dragged on until July 1878, and it was only in December of that year that the cleared sites were advertised for sale. There were no bidders, owing to the strings attached. Eventually, the Peabody trustees offered a knock-down price, well below what the Board had already spent, and obtained a large area to the west of John Fisher Street and east of the Royal Mint. Other sections were taken by the East End Dwellings Company and by the Rothschilds. The final sections of this, the very first area to be tackled under the Cross Act, were not disposed of until 1890. (Tarn, 1973, pp.79-87.) Octavia would never, in fact, be involved with any of the slum-clearance schemes under the Act, probably because they all required operations on a larger scale than she cared to engage in, and because of the amount of red tape.

had an unexpected opportunity of bringing the matter before the Archbishop of Canterbury, who entered into it and gave most kind co-operation. He arranged a meeting of all the Metropolitan clergy at Lambeth Palace. I worked hard to make it meet the want, very hard; one never knows what anything may have silently done, but it seems as if the conference only illustrated instead of meeting the need. The clergy in general did not come forward as leaders; those who did were not welcomed by the meeting; few seemed to realise that they were only asked to consider how best to meet the growing thoughts of the age, or that they had anything to learn from social reformers. I cannot say that I date any change from that meeting. Nor can I see any marked improvement in this direction from other causes in other places in London. The two sets of workers seem to be going further apart; the wise thinkers appear to me to be hardening themselves, and going farther away from the gentle doers, but the fault is, it appears to me, almost wholly with the latter: the Charity Organisation Society in every district in which it works, in every paper it issues urges, entreats, the clergy and their workers to come forward, and yet they hold aloof.[7]

The Charity Organisation Society gets stronger by the infusion of young blood; all the young thinkers join it, and on the committees where it seems to me they ought to meet the leaders of all gentle thought (the clergy, the givers) there are few to be found. The Charity Organisation Society itself is suffering grievously at the centre; the tone gets harder, the alienation deeper. They ought to be brought into close contact with the workers among the poor. But the fault is with the workers amongst the poor who will not join them. It often makes me anxious to see this. I can only watch with awe, raise my voice of warning or pleading with both parties here and there, tell each how much it appears to me to need the other, and leave the issues to the great Commander of all things, who certainly has not forgotten us here below, however much we forget Him.

I am convinced the South of London needs more help than any part, and that it is specially difficult to send workers of the kind I think

---

7   The fact that Archbishop Tait had invited Octavia to Lambeth Palace to repeat the harangue she had delivered at the Bishop of Gloucester and Bristol's house the year before is a sign of the seriousness with which she was taken. Her gloomy assessment of the meeting was no doubt influenced by her depressed state when she was writing this letter. However, clerical support for the COS would fall away, as it came to be perceived as taking a hard-line approach to old-age pensions and other anti-poverty measures. The Archbishop's daughter Lucy would later introduce Octavia to the Ecclesiastical Commissioners (p.738).

it wants because we have no good leaders or centres there. The East is far richer in them. I therefore no longer attend regularly in my own place on the Marylebone Charity Organisation committee, though they are kind enough still to let me be a member. I am busy at work in Lambeth. We have a capital group of workers there now, so that the work goes really well, but we sorely want more of the Lambeth, or at any rate South London, residents, on the committee. I hope they will rally round us soon. We want more gentlemen on the evening committee: as we are sending our three best lady-workers to other districts we may want more ladies on the morning committee; they need not necessarily be residents. The lady of whom I spoke who is going to live in Lambeth in order to work among the poor may make a good link with the Lambeth people.

In my last report I referred to the need of spaces as open air sitting rooms for the poor. The subject belongs perhaps properly to the Kyrle Society, but as it is one so very near my heart, and as I mentioned it last year, I may be allowed to return to it. The question had made far greater progress than I dared to hope it could in so short a time. Drury Lane churchyard has been planted and opened,[8] so has St John's Waterloo Road.[9] Canon Nisbet[10] has been in communication with me about the

---

8   The Drury Lane churchyard, also known as the Tavistock burial-ground, was planted by the Kyrle Society, and opened to the public by Rev. G.M. Humphreys on 1 May 1877 at a cost of £160. It was almost immediately closed again, as the crowds of people had trampled the ivy and the yuccas. However, Octavia would never allow failure of crowd management or accusations of vandalism to thwart her schemes, and she insisted that Emma Cons had investigated thoroughly and found no evidence of deliberate destruction. She suggested that, if the population of the area were too large for such a small garden, it might be advisable to restrict admission by tickets issued to local workers, a least initially. Failing that, Octavia offered to take over the management of the garden for a year, until things settled down. (*Our Common Land*, 1887, pp.118-21.)

---

9   'The large churchyard in the Waterloo Road is in process of being turned into a garden. The Rev. Arthur Robinson has collected £290, and is laying it out more like a country garden, and less like a place planned by a Board of Works, than any other I have seen. He has stumps prepared for ferns to grow on (and wants some, by the way, which some of you might send him); he has a nice bank, winding walks between the turf, knows which side of the church his wisteria will grow, spoke with hope of getting the large blue clematis to flower, wants numberless creepers to cover the church walls, and to wreathe around and make beautiful the few tombs which he leaves unmoved because relatives are still living and care to retain them. I understand he purposes applying for the vestry to help, and in view of the many churchyards there are to deal with, this would seem the right thing to do in general. At the same time, I can see we

St Giles' churchyard, a capital bit of ground running down to Seven Dials, its wilderness of tall rank grass, and shivering leafy trees would, even if untouched be something green for the people to look at, if the great wall which hides them were but down, and should the untidy neglected looking graves, and green damp paving stones be put in order, and bright beds of flowers made in the grass, and some of the trees given a chance of larger life, than their fellows allow them at present, should the great gates be opened, and a look of care and brightness given, what a possession the place would be to the residents near! This I trust may be done; for on every side the subject seems awakening attention, and churchyard after churchyard is spoken of as likely to be planted and opened. The school board has considered a scheme for opening its playgrounds to the children on Saturdays and after school on week-days. A memorial is being sent to the attorney general asking him to consider the advisability of devoting some money from the city charities to laying out such gardens. A meeting was held by the National Health Society last May at which the Duke of Westminster presided,[11] where I read a paper on the subject,[12] and the best of it all is, that

---

should get a more country-like garden, the more the planning of it could be left in the hands of a man of culture, who loves plants and colour.' (From a talk written by Octavia and read to the National Health Society, 9 May 1877, reproduced in *Our Common Land*, 1877, pp.121-22. Arthur Robinson was vicar of St John's from 1874 to 1881.) In 1883 the Metropolitan Public Gardens Association erected some gymnastic apparatus and playground equipment. The church received a direct hit during a bombing raid in 1940, but was rebuilt and became the official Festival of Britain church in 1951. The garden survives, without its banks and winding walks, and the flowerbeds contain evergreen shrubs now. There is still a small, fenced children's playground towards the back of the garden.

---

10 John Nisbet was rector of St Giles in the Fields from 1867 to 1892.

---

11 Hugh Lupus Grosvenor (1825–1899) third marquis, later first Duke of Westminster (created 1874) was one of Octavia's stalwarts. He represented Chester in parliament from 1847 to 1868, and was ADC to Queen Victoria. The family owned about 30,000 acres in Cheshire and Flintshire and 600 acres in London. He succeeded his father in 1869. The Duke, whose generosity financed many of Octavia's projects, was roped into the Kyrle Society as chairman, and on 2 November 1884 the Society's public meeting was held in the Rubens Room of his London home, the sumptuous Grosvenor House, on Park Lane. Westminster accepted the presidency of the Joint Committee (Kyrle and National Health Society) of the Smoke Abatement Exhibition in 1881 (1881, p.145, n.3). The Duke went on to become a founder member of the Coal Smoke Abatement Society in 1898.

---

12 The paper, 'Open Spaces', was included in *Our Common Land*, Octavia's second

though friends of mine are active here and there about it, the movement does not owe its strength to us or depend on us, but the longing to forward it seems general and widely diffused.

I will not here mention the commons; many of you will learn from my new book how very deeply anxious I am that the 37 schemes for inclosure which will probably be before the House this year should not be passed without careful consideration of the value of such beautiful rural spaces to England in the future.

The scheme for using Thirlmere as a reservoir is occupying my earnest attention, and I hope all of you who can, will help to prevent the Manchester Bill's passing into law without careful consideration by Parliament of the possibility of supplying the needs of South Lancashire in some effectual way without destroying the Lake scenery. It is confidently asserted by men of scientific knowledge and experience that the problem is by no means a difficult one, but the facts are not likely to come out unless public opinion is brought to bear. We ought not as a nation, to bow to the greed of Manchester, and her dense incapacity for seeing or caring for beauty, but before we trust one of our loveliest lakes, and three valleys to her keeping, should know whether indeed there are not wells and collecting grounds in which she may build reservoirs without using one of the few peaceful and unspoiled spots in England, and monopolising water to sell for profit to a whole county, without restrictions as to the way in which she mars the scenery. If sadly we find that in spite of her new red sandstone and its wonderful resources for well-digging, in spite of her untouched miles of moorland between the Ribble and the Lune stretching far up into Yorkshire, Lancashire must resort to the lake district for water, at least let it be first distinctly proved to Parliament, or before a disinterested committee composed partly of men who do care for the beauty so far that they would not consider the price of a reservoir out-weighed it, exactly what is necessary. If the Lake district must be invaded by engineers and water companies, at least let them be under proper restrictions imposed by Parliament, and let the water, when obtained, be distributed cheaply

---

collection of essays, published towards the end of 1877. In her talk, delivered on 9 May, she had reported that 'the London School Board... have in all 57 acres of playground, which they entirely close on the children's one holiday, Saturday, and during the summer evenings'. However, she had a meeting with the Board scheduled for 30 May, which must have been successful because, by the time *Our Common Land* was published, she was able to add a footnote announcing the 18 of the playgrounds were to be opened. (*Our Common Land*, 1877, pp.75, 130-31.)

over all Lancashire, not all given to Manchester for her to trade in without restriction, else there will be great temptations to other towns to take other lakes, and we shall have the maximum of destruction and the minimum of good.

Help to get Parliament to look into it, help to bring out the thought of the men who prize the peace and beauty of the valleys of England, all of you who can.

Perhaps we may not succeed, though I have good hope. But I told you last year what I think about success. Our failures may bear fruit in time to come, long after we are gone. Such an agitation as this is distinctly educational for the nation, and it may help to save other places. We cannot tell what may not grow out of our failures, they bear direct fruit in training us to fortitude, and to the habit of looking on to magnificent completion of our feeble beginnings, and indirectly it is marvellous how surely after many days bread cast on the waters is found.[13]

---

13 For once Octavia's pessimism was justified. Thirlmere was turned into a reservoir, with its water piped to Manchester, but the campaign surrounding it was so controversial that it divided the three future founders of the National Trust. The Thirlmere debate pitted against each other two movements that had hitherto been almost indistinguishable: sanitary reform and open spaces. Both sought to improve the lives of the poor, the first by fresh water and sewers to prevent cholera and typhoid, the second by giving access to fresh air and sites of natural beauty. But what if the first aim clashed with the second? As the grand-daughter of Thomas Southwood Smith, a pioneer of sanitary reform, Octavia was well aware of the dilemma, but she took the view that alternatives to Thirlmere had not been sufficiently explored. Robert Hunter became involved with the anti-reservoir campaign but then backed off. Hardwicke Rawnsley, who as founder of the Lake District Preservation Society had led every other campaign to preserve the beauty of the Lakes, steered clear of this one. His experience in the slums of Bristol and Drury Lane had convinced him that poor people needed clean water. On 1 October 1894, when the water was turned on to flow to Manchester, Hardwicke opened the proceedings with a prayer and was later called upon to propose a toast to the waterworks committee. He took a more generous view of Manchester than Octavia: 'There was a time when every Manchester man was looked upon as a vandal or worse, but those who have been brought into communion with the tender kindness of Manchester is this particular part of England would remember not only how generous and unselfish and considerate she has been, but how they could trust her in the future to help in the battle for preserving the beauty of this land of the lakes.' He had meanwhile laboured to save the 'Rock of Names', on which Wordsworth, Coleridge and others had cut their names. He obtained permission from the Manchester Corporation to move the rock, but it proved impossible to shift. A year later, hearing that the rock had been dynamited, Hardwicke and his wife went back and collected the fragments containing the names, which were re-assembled beside the road, at a higher level than the original rock, but almost exactly above its site. (Rawnsley, 1923, pp.79-81; Murphy, 1987, p.81.) In 1984 the 'Rock of Names'

You will notice, or at least I notice, very sadly, how year by year this little letter has to do with larger and more public questions. In one way I ought to be thankful, but I cannot be wholly so. My work becomes less home-like, more struggling; there is in it necessarily more of opposition; it brings me into contest with people further off, whom I do not know well, nor care for at all. I accept the responsibilities of the position, it has been clearly sent me, I never sought it. Also I know that a smooth life when all men are friendly is not wholly healthy for us, and that the church and her members have had to be militant at all times, for there are the world, the flesh, and the devil still to fight. We may not enter into peace yet in one sense, but in another we may. The peace in the midst of war we can always win for ourselves.

The more of opposition I have myself had to do, the more it has been necessary to me to dwell on the duty not only of patience but of gentleness. When I cast my bread on the waters, I have had to make sure that it was bread—not a hard stone cast at a brother—but bread to feed him, which he may one day find and feed on, though he does not see it now. Let us be gentle. The might and endurance of gentle things is very great; the earthquake shatters the rocks and hurls them violently down, and we notice what it is doing and think it forcible, but the little cyclamen winds up and up, its thread-like stem penetrating between the stones that form the gigantic heap that marks the Syrian murder, and its frail flower blossoms above all the stones; kings declare war, and statesmen struggle, but the child's voice penetrates to the heart of a man and alters it; the ways of the Lord are slow and gentle, destruction is sometimes swift, but even that is often led up to by the unnoticed slight actions of years, and the building up is usually gradual. And then, let us be gentle because we know so little. Even when most indignant against wrong and bound to put down or fight against it to the death, let us separate the thought of it from the wrong doer; there are depths in all the people we have to attack we never dream of, mysteries we never fathom, least of all when we are ungentle; we strike wildly at something we see, really see, but what may there not be we never saw? With bowed heads in reverence for every human being let us be so gentle; where we know and love deeply in some slight measure we may dare to be stern, but we must take care; it is only the Father

---

was moved again to the more accessible site of the Wordsworth Museum at Grasmere. Initials scratched into the rock include those of two sisters, Mary and Sara Hutchinson. The first sister was to marry Wordsworth, and the second was the one with whom Coleridge, already married, so inconveniently fell in love.

who can rightly pierce with fiery dart through and through a human being, for He never wounds what is good in him, nor by seeming ignorant of it rouses the self-justifying spirit. His action is ever just; He alone in giving pain can bring His own love home to the heart of His child; we all know it. There is something in the touch of His hand when He touches our life before which we yield in trust. We *know*, however little we *see*, that it is the powerful hand of Love.

DONATION ACCOUNT, 1877

RECEIPTS

	£	s	d
Cash in hand	113	17	6 ½
Mrs Allen	2	10	0
Miss Baldwin	3	0	0
S.B.	100	0	0
Edward Bond, Esq	10	0	0
C.B.P. Bosanquet, Esq	3	0	0
Miss Burnaby	1	0	0
Miss Chamberlain	10	0	0
Mrs C.	5	0	0
C. Critchett, Esq	1	0	0
A.G. Crowder, Esq	20	0	0
Mrs Duckworth	10	10	0
Mrs Durrant	0	10	0
Miss Fletcher	5	0	0
Mrs Gillson	10	0	0
Miss S.J. Harris	1	0	0
Miss F. Hill	0	8	0
A.J.	5	0	0
Miss Jackson	3	3	0
R.B. Litchfield, Esq	5	0	0
Miss Lidgett	0	10	0
Miss Lakin	1	0	0
Mrs Llewellyn	10	0	0
Mrs Lyell	20	0	0
Miss Lyell	10	0	0
Mrs Mallett (per)	1	0	0
Miss Martineau	5	0	0
Mrs Merivale	5	0	0
A. Miles, Esq	2	0	0
R.W. Monro, Esq	5	0	0
Captain Moseley	5	0	0
Miss Oldham	5	0	0
Miss H.J. Ormeron	0	10	0
Mrs Pollard (the late)	10	0	0
Mr and Mrs Fooley	1	1	0
Mrs Rawlinson	0	15	0
Mrs Reiss	5	0	0
John Ruskin, Esq	84	0	0
Mrs Scaramanga	2	0	0
W. Shaen, Esq	2	0	0
Edward Spender, Esq	10	0	0
Miss Sterling	30	0	0
Chas. Stewart, Esq	2	0	0
Miss L. Sumner	0	10	0
Miss Helen Taylor	2	0	0
Lady Thompson	2	0	0
Sir C. Trevelyan	2	0	0
Lady Trevelyan	1	0	0
Miss Wells	2	0	0
Miss M. Wells	1	0	0
R.D. Wilson, Esq	8	0	0
Mrs Winkworth	30	0	0
Mr and Mrs Whately	5	0	0
Mrs Wright	25	0	0
Miss Yorke	5	0	0
Anonymous	0	2	6
Charity Organisation Society (for Mrs S.)	0	8	0
	£610	15	0 ½

I have specially to thank Mrs Arthur Cohen for her gift of a piano, and also the following Ladies and Gentlemen who were kind enough to entertain the tenants in the country.

Mr and Mrs George MacDonald	Colonel & Mrs Gillum
Mr and Mrs Andrew Johnston	Mr and Mrs Müller
Wilbraham Taylor, Esq	Mrs. Arkwright

DONATION ACCOUNT, 1877

EXPENDITURE

	£	s	d
Pensions (Mrs K.)	0	18	0
Pensions (Mrs W.)	7	16	0
Pensions (various poor persons in the East End)	10	0	0
Playgrounds	55	19	0
Rent, &c., &c. for Clubs	61	3	0
Employment for poor people	4	2	10 ½
Keeping H.M. at a home	5	0	0
Keeping W M.	9	15	0
Keeping E.W.	5	0	0
St Jude's Whitechapel	42	0	0
St Thomas'*	10	0	0
Charity Organization Society*	15	0	0
Commons Preservation Society*	.24	0	0
Kyrle Society for Commons Preservation Society*	50	0	0
Society for hefriendimmg Young Servants*	6	2	6
Expenses of Printing, Stationery, &c.	10	19	0
Tenants' Excursion Bell Street	7	0	7
Tenants' Excursion Freshwater Place	2	10	0
Tenants' Excursion Lambeth	6	15	0
Tenants' Excursion Drapers' Place	0	10	0
Tenants' Excursion Drury Lane	35	14	2
Tenants' Excursion Walmer Street	26	18	2
Tenants' Excursion New Buildings	6	0	0
Parties (New Buildings Bell Street, &c.)	5	14	4
Open Air Festivals, (Freshwater Place, Lambeth, and Lincoln's Inn)	9	9	10 ½
Providing Hospital aind other relief to the Sick	2	17	2
Clothes for Children	0	17	2 ½
Carriage of Flowers	0	2	8
Gift to Mrs D.	1	10	0
Gift to Mrs O.	2	10	0
Gift to Mrs S.	0	8	0
Gift to Miss Cons, for Drury Lane	2	0	0
Balance in hand	182	2	6
	£610	15	0 ½

* These sums were given by special desire, or from the known sympathies of the donors.

N.B. — The balance in hand seems large but it is all appropiated for special objects except £35

LETTER TO MY FELLOW-WORKERS

TO WHICH IS ADDED

ACCOUNT OF DONATIONS RECEIVED

FOR

WORK AMONG THE POOR

DURING 1878

❦

BY

OCTAVIA HILL
(FOR PRIVATE CIRCULATION ONLY)

LONDON:
PRINTED BY GEO PULMAN,
24, THAYER STREET, MANCHESTER SQUARE, W.

SUMMARY

The growing independence of the fellow-workers... losses as well as gains from de-centralisation... the club at Barrett's Court following Sydney Cockerell's death... a playground in Whitechapel... problems with the Commons Preservation Society... the donation fund as managed by Mrs Edmund Maurice; supporters urged to give money locally for work under their own supervision.

EDITOR'S NOTE

Octavia spent this year travelling in France, Austria and Italy with her faithful companion Harriot Yorke, recovering from the effects of her breakdown. Her knowledge of events in England was, therefore, second-hand. Once again, we have to admire the patience with which Octavia's fellow-workers endured criticism in the semi-public forum of these letters. Octavia was so unsure of the ability of her sister Emily—Mrs Edmund Maurice— to manage the donation fund in her absence that she actually urges people not to give to it. As the accounts for the next few years show, donations fell (although never below the £150 that Octavia calculated was the bare minimum to meet ongoing commitments like the education of orphans), perhaps because Octavia's supporters shared the pessimistic view expressed in this letter that she might never be well enough to re-enter the fray of public campaigns.

It is well, my friends, that we should fix our eyes very resolutely on all that has been gained during the past year. At the end of last year, 20 courts which had been bought by various gentlemen and ladies interested in the improvement of the tenants and their houses, still, in greater or less degree, depended on me for supervision. I had tried, as you all know, to render them independent of me, and had succeeded very imperfectly. But when I left England the volunteers who were collecting consented most kindly to accept more responsibility than of old. Several gentlemen were good enough to undertake to audit and supervise the accounts. My assistants, who used to work in a little company under my direction, were placed in direct communication with the volunteers and auditors, and these latter were asked to report direct to the owners of the courts, and obtain their decisions on all important matters. The work is thus entirely decentralised. The place I once filled—the place it was well for me to fill while the attempts were in their infancy, need be no longer filled.

The advantage of the change must be clear to anyone who thinks

---

1   This is the only one of the letters to carry an address other than Octavia's home. Octavia was staying with Mary Harris, a member of the Society of Friends and one of Octavia's closest friends from the time they met in 1854, when Octavia was only 16. According to Octavia's brother-in-law Edmund Maurice, 'from the time they first met till 1893, when Miss Harris died, Octavia poured out more of her secret thoughts to her than to anyone else, and when they were away from each other wrote to her constantly'. (Maurice, 1914, p.19.) In 1928, 14 years after Edmund Maurice's edition of Octavia's correspondence, Emily Southwood Ouvry, Octavia's niece, brought out a further edition of letters, of which half were addressed to Mary Harris. The closeness of the relationship no doubt accounts for the fact that Octavia went to stay with her when she was at her lowest ebb, and was, for the most part, keeping herself out of England. Mary had gone to live at Derwent Bank in Broughton, Cumbria, a handsome mansion erected in 1846, in order to look after her five nieces following the death of their mother. In 1861 Octavia had written to her sister Miranda about a blissful summer spent there with Mary: 'If I raise my eyes I see the mountains, perhaps crowned and veiled in a lighted cloud; if I walk round the garden, the long sprays of rose, or delicate green ferns, delight me; if, in the night... I come into this room which adjoins mine, I see the moonlight lying over the river, field and hills.' (Maurice, 1914, p.195.)

about the work. Every collector knows that the court under her care depends on her for any progress it is to make; she cannot fancy that I am any longer thinking how to light a dark staircase, where to clear a yard blocked up with building; she knows that she alone is watching over her people. She must decide whom to keep, whom to dismiss, whom to employ, how to gladden the tenants, how to purify the houses. She can act swiftly and securely, for she is certain that no decision of hers can possibly clash with any plan or thought of mine. Any capacity for constructive ingenuity that is in her has free scope; all the sense of protecting pity that she has will be called out, for her people must look to her alone for it.

The auditors are gentlemen accustomed to business, and the management of money. They do easily accounts which many ladies find difficult, they see clearly the safe and wise thing to do about money. Each has one, two, or three courts only to think of, and can think out the small financial problems, bearing on them with care. Their experience is brought to bear without excessive calls on their valuable time, and these calls, such as they are, come at hours they can manage. It may be of wide-spreading importance to any future development of the plan on a large scale that several men of business should understand the management and accounts connected with the houses of the people, even though the scale on which they learn it is now still a small one.

The owners who had always so very kindly seconded me and trusted me about the conduct of their properties—so kindly and fully that perhaps I hardly referred to them all the questions I might have done —now know as they never knew before, that the courts are in very deed their own, that I was but a vicar with semblance of power, and that it is their will, and their will alone, on which the progress in these courts finally depends. Several of them have been looking into things, caring for them, deciding on them, as they never did before; they know far more of those who are working in the courts; and, though most of them reside out of London, or are for other reasons not able, or not prepared to enter into details of business, I hear of them now and again in their courts, and feel that my old dream of landlords of towns coming into a near relation to their tenants and estates as they do in the country, is more sure to be realised than if I had been still at work.

Of course the change is not *all* gain, and no one knows so well as I just where it is loss, and how, and the thought of it cuts me like a knife, and of course it was not quite my own idea of how things would go. I fancied that new courts would be bought in London by new landlords, as they are now being bought there, and in provincial towns, and that I might to the end, perhaps for a long life, have kept my old place among the owners, and fellow-workers, and tenants I had lived among so long, and it is no use calling loss and collapse, gain and vigour. We must face the fact of pain, and even loss. But when God appoints our course, our little plans and imaginings all pale and fade, and, even trembling, we go out to do His will, and know that somehow it is better than ours, though the pain never dies away, and the loss abides. And I know that it is not given to many to see in their life-time the thing which they have worked for grow to vigorous independence of them, and show its own life and power of further growth, like a tree planted by the water-side, drawing vigour from earth, and water, and sun, and which shall live when the hand that helped to plant it is cold. And whenever I think of my trees, I never fail to thank my Father that He has made the streams by which they are planted so full of water, and that they do not any longer depend on my watering morning and evening.

The club at Barrett's Court seems to have survived its day of difficulty. It has been revived by the energy of those who have most conscience in the court. I trust they will not make it exclusive. I am delighted it should be in the hands of those who really have a strong feeling of what is right and wrong. The distinction sorely needs enforcing in the court, there is a great tendency to think that good nature is the only good. It is refreshing to think of the club re-organised, re-ordered, numerous, well-attended, commercially sound, and in all ways a living influence for good. The men have put up the memorial to Mr Cockerell there.

I mentioned last year a piece of ground in Whitechapel, which was attached to Lady Pembroke's newly bought houses, and which I hoped would be made into a playground, or garden for the people. The ground, I hear, looks even more valuable now it is cleared. But it will cost a good deal to fence it, and keep it well managed till the people have learnt to keep order there themselves. Money is very much needed for this, I hope any of you that can help, will do so. It would be a pity to lose the ground, and, as it is proposed to use it for the whole neighbourhood, its expenses cannot be charged on the houses which it adjoins, and which will indeed require every farthing of their income spent to improve them.

I have told you in what way I feel that the houses for which I was responsible have really gained by my absence, but, the Commons Preservation Society, to which I had hoped to be useful has certainly suffered. The committee is composed mainly of members of parliament, very busy men, who are doing the parliamentary work thoroughly;

indeed some of them think they have successfully got through the worst part of *that*. But then the Society had functions, distinct from this parliamentary work, in which I hoped to help. It has to help those who oppose in the law-courts the numerous illegal enclosures which take place in England; for this it needs large funds. These funds ought to be drawn from hundreds of annual subscriptions, not necessarily large sums, we can hardly expect the people who are *very* rich and have large sums to give, and probably own land, to care so much for what remains of the common land as professional men, and working men, whose only link with the land is the share they have in its open spaces. It is we, it is they, who should come forward with our guinea or our five shillings, year by year, till the work be done of preserving what commons are left, *and that before it is too late.* I had hoped to interest these people, to make them want to give their money, to help them to bring the weight of public opinion to bear on the preservation of open spaces. To be a link between those members of parliament, the busy men giving their legal experience and advice on the committee, and the large unthinking public, losing their commons while they hardly knew it, seemed my special place. It is empty now, and the time is passing, and I am afraid my last book, *Our Common Land,* which I hoped would speak while I was silent, does not speak quite as powerfully as the living voice would.[2] And I should often be sad if I did not know God cared for England and its people and its commons.

My sisters say they will gladly take charge of money, or names of annual subscribers, for the Commons Preservation Society, as they do of money for my other work, if any of you care to send it, and that is for the moment all I can do.

This brings me to the question of my own donation fund. I am bound to give you, the donors who have so kindly trusted me, and strengthened my hands for work, some account of the way in which, during absence, I have fulfilled the trust committed to me by you. My letter was printed last year, before I knew I was going, or I would have spoken to you then, but I felt sure you would know that I saw my way

---

2   Octavia's second book did not enjoy the same degree of success as *Homes of the London Poor*. It shows every sign of having been rushed out by Macmillan to capitalise on the success of its predecessor, being composed of articles and speeches put together over only two years and containing a good deal of repetition. *Homes of the London Poor*, on the other hand, drew on material produced over eight years and contained, in its three opening essays, Octavia's most powerful and comprehensive statement of her methods of housing management.

to spend your money as I believed you would wish it spent, or I would not in silence have retained the charge of it. Indeed I did; the money has been spent entirely to my satisfaction, and what I am sure would be to yours. My sister, Mrs Edmund Maurice, took charge of it for me: I gave her notes of the various regular expenses such as those for maintenance of orphans, help of clubs, supervision of playgrounds, &c. These permanent expenses, all of which I had planned myself, amount to a little more than £150 a year. I also gave her a list of all sums which had been sent me for any special purpose. After providing for these, I asked her to spend the balance according to her own discretion.

Now I would ask you to note that my donation fund has for some years, though entered as one account, practically fulfilled two perfectly different objects. It has given me the money to meet the needs of those individuals whom my life, so very near the poor and the workers among the poor, taught me to know well, so that I could help them when the great times of trouble came; some of them I knew really as friends, many of them with that watchfulness which enabled me to discover permanently helpful ways of re-establishing them. I had done this, but Mrs Maurice can do it far better than I. I have *entire* confidence in her judgement about it; and partly her greater leisure, and her utter sympathy, and quiet, and the fact that she is not dealing with quite such large things as I latterly did, made me extremely happy in the knowledge that she would make the fund *more* useful than I could in this way. The number of people she has saved with it, and watched over, giving time with the money, would be a delight to you all if you could know it. It is not therefore want of entire reliance on her judgement that makes me write what follows, but, my friends, you know the fund you sent me was large, and it had another function which my sister's place and life haven't called her to fulfil. I was myself in the midst of the leaders of great works, I knew of them before they were great, when they had only the capacity of growing great, I knew when the time of crisis came; and what is true of the work was also true of the workers, I knew many of them in the days of their beginning, before the world did and they grew strong, and when the world misunderstood them, or had not large enough hope to see as they saw, and they faltered for want of encouragement and help. You had trusted me with sums to cherish the early sparks of life in a great work, to support it at the moment of crisis, to cheer lonely workers and to encourage them in difficulty, and I could do it with large sums, and over a wide field, because you trusted me, and I was on the spot. These larger grants my sister has made this year, for I could direct her about them from far off—but—to be honest as I must be the more carefully because many of you will trust me—the power of doing this will inevitably decrease with longer absence, and my sister is not, as I say, placed precisely where she could *continuously* do it. I ought to say to you all then (hard as it is not to cling on to the hope that whatever life is before me might be such as to bring me back to the old places to work in the old ways, and that in time not to lose my clue to the great works I cared for) that I believe you would be wiser if you entirely review, as from the beginning, the wisdom of sending money to me in the opening year.

There are however several things I had in hand, the wisdom of which cannot change for many a year; training of little orphans, support of my own clubs, and keeping open of little playgrounds, and other things, all which I have looked into myself years ago, and where near and dear friends are at work from whom I hear regularly and whom I know and trust. These undertakings cost about £150 a year, and the balance which appears in the annexed account is nearly all of it appropriated, so we may be said to have nothing in hand. If these friends were straitened, or if the things I care for fell through for want of money I should be sadder than I am.

If any of you, or rather if all of you altogether, for any memory, or in any trust, will send me that £150 I shall be glad. Every penny you send beyond it, my sister will spend in wise ways, and she knows much of old friends and fellow-workers, whom I trust, and who are working in out of sight places.

But it seems natural, it seems right, that my donation fund should not be much larger than these needs require, the great grants from it seem a little unnatural any longer, and the hope of making them could only be kept up by one who was clinging on to dead things. Let us be brave, you and I, and accept the changed conditions. Will you not each of you consider whether in your own neighbourhood, or some place where you can come really near the people, you can yourselves spend on and for the poor the sums which you used to send to me, or whether you yourselves know any younger workers among the poor whose discretion is as great as their hearts are kind, to whom you should send it? Watch over your gift, learn what it does, and how it does it, and never think I shall misunderstand the blank in the list of my donors. Indeed, if it brings you nearer yourselves to the poor, to those out of the way, you will be nearer to me too, though there be no outward link. How could my donation fund die better, and die we know it must some day any way, than by bringing all you who helped me to yet nearer ways of serving the poor? Do not fear for me, I could not fear for myself. I think some of you will carry on, or through to their end, the things I leave in my sister's hands, and will find her a faithful, thoughtful, wise, and sympathetic distributor of all you care to send her; but if you can get nearer still to the poor anyhow else, take my absence as a message reminding you that that is always best, better than trusting me, or any one. And, believe for me, as I steadfastly believe for myself, that if it be God's will to bring me back to any of the old places, the old work, and the old friends, He will not leave my hand without any power which He wants me to have, whether of money or anything else. Money would come, or the want of it would be best. He would order that, as He has ordered all. Does He not create both souls and tangible things? Whomsoever He wants He will strengthen to fulfil His purpose, we may await His command to come or to go, to labour or to pause, and without one little fear for *His* England which He has made *our* England, nor for out little places in it, where we once had influence; it was all from Him.

> God doth not need
> Either man's work or his own gifts; who best
> Bear his mild yoke, they serve him best, his state
> Is kingly. Thousands at his bidding speed
> And post o'er land and ocean without rest:
> They also serve who only stand and wait.[3]

---

3   From Milton's sonnet 'On His Blindness', 1655.

DONATION ACCOUNT, 1878

RECEIPTS

	£	s	d
Cash in hand	182	2	6
Miss Aitken	0	2	6
Mrs Bond	5	0	0
K. Brock, Esq	1	0	0
Mrs Browne	3	0	0
Miss E.M. Bush	3	0	0
Miss Campbell	1	0	0
Miss Chalmers	1	0	0
Mrs S.E. Clark	0	5	0
Nathaniel Curzon, Esq	25	0	0
Mrs Duckworth	15	0	0
Lord Dunsany	10	0	0
Mrs Durrant	0	10	0
Mrs Faunthorpe	5	0	0
Miss Fletcher	5	0	0
A Friend	5	5	0
A Friend	10	0	0
Miss E. Harrison	0	10	0
Miss Jekyll	10	0	0
The Misses Kennedy	1	0	0
Mrs Lyell	1	0	0
Miss Lyell	0	10	0
Miss F. Martineau	5	0	0
Miss Martineau	1	0	0
Miss C. Martineau	1	0	0
Miss Meek	1	1	0
J.T. Nicholetts	1	0	0
Mrs Pooley	1	1	0
J. Ruskin, Esq	80	0	0
Mrs Rawlinson	0	5	0
Mrs Shaen	5	0	0
Mrs Scaramanga	2	0	0
Mrs William Sheen	2	0	0
Colonel Smith	1	1	0
Mrs Stallybrass	0	1	0
Miss Willington	2	0	0
Mrs S. Winckworth	30	0	0
Miss King	0	10	0
Mrs Wright	25	0	0
Four Young Servants	0	1	0
Miss Sparling	1	0	0
	£444	5	0

DONATION ACCOUNT, 1878

EXPENDITURE

	£	s	d
Books and Furniture*	9	18	10
Orphans (boarded out)*	23	0	0
Girls' classes and Library (rent and fuel)	15	17	1
Clubs (rent and fuel)	34	10	9
Keeping E. at a School	6	10	0
Keeping W.M. at a School	13	0	0
St Thomas' Poor Fund*	10	0	0
Playgrounds	11	8	6
Employment for poor people	6	11	2 ½
Lambeth Charity Organisation Society*	1	1	0
Lambeth Mrs C. and Mrs S.*	3	0	0
Commons Preservation Society*	20	0	0
Free Library, Whitechapel*	10	0	0
East End Pension Fund*	10	0	0
Expenses of Printing, Stationery, &c.	6	15	0
Country Excursion:			
Barrett's Court Girls	0	7	1
Lambeth	6	0	0
Little Edward Street	1	3	11
Bell Street	2	0	0
Whitechapel	12	10	0
Laying out Gardens and other spaces*	37	2	2
Carriage of Parcels received	0	7	9
Clothes for Children	0	14	0
Providing Hospital and other relief to the Sick	8	7	8
Parties for Tenants:			
Drury Lane	6	4	8
Lambeth	2	19	6
Barrett's Court	2	0	0
Freshwater Place	0	10	0
May festivals, Lambeth	3	18	7
May festivals, Marylebone	4	3	6
Society for Befriending Young Servants*	0	11	0
Ornamental Tiles, Freshwater Place*	1	11	6
Cash in hand	172	1	3 ½
	£444	5	0

* These sums were given by special desire; or from the known sympathies of the donors.

N.B.— The balance in hand seems large; but it is all appropriated for special objects, except £9 8s 3½d.

LETTER TO MY FELLOW-WORKERS

TO WHICH IS ADDED

ACCOUNT OF DONATIONS RECEIVED

FOR

WORK AMONG THE POOR

DURING 1879

BY

OCTAVIA HILL.

(FOR PRIVATE CIRCULATION ONLY)

LONDON:

HOUSE-BOY BRIGADE PRINTERS,

146 MARYLEBONE ROAD

1879

SUMMARY

The progress of housing work and the superiority of housing management to district visiting and other forms of charitable work... the need for trained workers... the US edition of Homes of the London Poor... *the Kyrle Society: open spaces, Burnham Beeches, Lincoln's Inn Fields, St Anne's, Soho, Horsemonger Lane Gaol... the need for volunteers in playgrounds... Dürer's St Christopher in St Christopher's Place... £150 needed annually for the donation fund.*

EDITOR'S NOTE

This had been another year of travelling, in France and Italy, and in Britain. The letter is more hopeful in tone than the last. Although 'the work near to the people is still shut from me by illness', Octavia has been busy with some schemes of 'cultural philanthropy' that she can arrange from a distance, and she can foresee a time when she will return fully to her old position. She must have had second thoughts about discouraging her supporters from giving to the donation fund in the last letter, because she goes out of her way here to praise the work her sister Emily—Mrs Edmund Maurice—was doing in her absence, and to ask for more resources. As usual, Octavia is still insisting on the need for detailed, sustained, thoughtful work by her fellow-workers, and this letter contains one of her few aphorisms: 'Beware of well-meant failures'.

My Friends,

It is well in the opening year to pause and look how we stand with regard to our work.

First let us consider the houses. Of all the 20 courts formerly under my care, and now under yours, it may certainly be said that they are being managed thoughtfully with a view to the interests of the tenants, and at least on a self-supporting footing. Your presence in them warrants the expectation that the more you gain experience, and, with experience, power and hope, the more practice gives you facility in dealing with technical matters, the more life you will be able to infuse into your work, and the easier and the happier it will become to you. I cannot tell you how much I have felt for those of you on whom since I went away has fallen the burthen of all the accidents, troubles, and responsibilities which, arising from the tenants' misfortune, carelessness, or ignorance, affect the property in the courts. The questions you have had to settle were new to many of you, were difficult, and I cannot help thinking they must often have seemed to some of you who cared much for the people hardly worth your time. On the other hand there was danger that those of you who took up these definite questions of business might become engrossed in them. Am I wrong in thinking that some of you are finding gradually by experience what you gain by the technical work which no mere district visiting can give you?—that others are obtaining such mastery and facility with the mere business that they will soon find strength and time to develop all the better work which should grow out of it?

I should like to note down what it appears to me you are all feeling as to the difference between the charge of a court where the people are your tenants and much other visiting among the poor. I do not deny that all work should possess some of these characteristics; but I do not think that other kinds gain them so easily. The care of tenants calls out a sense of duty founded on relationship; the work is permanent; and the definite character of much of it makes its progress marked. Have you ever asked yourselves why you have chosen the charge of courts,

113

with all its difficulties and ties, rather than other benevolent undertakings which are more easily taken up and thrown down? The burthen of the problems before you has been heavy, and the regularity of the occupation has often demanded of you great sacrifices. Why have you not chosen transitory connection with hundreds of receivers of soup, or pleasant intercourse with little Sunday scholars, or visiting among the aged and bed-ridden, who were sure to greet you with a smile when you went to them, and had no right to say a word of reproach to you about your long absences in the country? Why did you not take up district visiting, where, if any family did not welcome you, you could just stay away? Because you preferred a work where duty was continuous and distinct, and where it was mutual. And then all the petty annoyances brought before you at such awkward moments, with so little discretion or good temper—all the smoky chimneys, broken water-pipes, tiresome neighbours, drunken husbands, death, disease, poverty, sin—call not only for your sympathy, but for your action. From the greatest to the least the problems have implied some duty on your part. 'What ought I, in my relation to the tenants, to do for them in this difficulty?' you have each had to ask yourself. From the merest trifle of a cupboard key broken in a lock, to the future of some family desolated by death, or sunk into misery from drink, all has asked for your sympathy, much has demanded your action. Nor have you chosen for whom these duties shall be undertaken: the family are tenants, that fact implies your relation to them. Thus you have not felt the duty a self-chosen one; the tie has been closer, more like that in your own homes—deep, real, lasting, not always easy—often involving management of trifles, giving no sense of self-congratulating pride as in a work of supererogation. It has implied a share in the people's pain— as we bear one another's burthens at home; but bringing, I know you have all felt by this time, something of the same quiet sense of indestructible connection, a solemn blessing in fulfilment of simple duty. It has brought to you also, I feel sure, a real attachment to your people. You know they are yours; they know it; and as the years go on this sense of attachment will deepen and grow. Sometimes, when the difficulty of dealing with the manifold technical matters is very heavy upon you, you will all remember that these grow *much* lighter the more experience you gain, that the power among your little flocks increases tenfold after a time, above all, that the burthen of absolutely right action in this, as in all positions of life, is not with you, only the duty of trying to see and do right. If you keep this steadily before you, your Father will be continually bringing out of all your feeble efforts and clumsy mistakes all manner of great joy, and help, and wonderful results you never thought of; and a great sense of supporting help will be with you, a sort of cloud to shelter you by day, and fire to light you by night; you will feel that this is He who gave you the relation to your tenants, is helping you in it, as He helps us each in whatever duty He calls us to, never giving the command without the power.

The charge of tenants has been valued by you too, because the duty is mutual: it implies your determination, not simply to do kindness with liberal hand, popular as that would be, but to meet the poor on grounds where they too have duties to you. The fulfilment of these takes away the glamour of almsgiving: it substitutes the power of meeting the people as they are, on simple human ground, as fellow-citizens, not mere receivers of your alms. You have all felt the effort of trying to keep them up to the mark; the effort, I know, will be less and less to you each as time goes on; the love that springs from the duty will be more and more. The day will come to each of you, who are happy enough to go on working long, when the business will seem easy routine, and the tenants will be to you like a large family of friends or of children, with many memories in common; when even the places—those ugly London courts—will be to you so dear; for you will remember how and where you made them lighter, cleaner, better: the rooms, the yards, the streets will be associated with the faces that brighten when they see you, and with victories over evil which you helped to achieve by your presence, or which you had the great privilege of seeing achieved—you hardly know which it was—you felt so one with the spirit that conquered the wrong.

I am glad to record the considerable extension of the work, not only in London, where houses have been purchased in various places (two new blocks in Marylebone), but steps are, I understand, being taken to set it on foot in Liverpool, Manchester, and Paris, and it has been begun successfully in Dublin this year. It is very important that all measures should be taken that should ensure its being well done wherever it is begun, and I would advise all who are thinking of purchasing houses to put themselves into communication with my fellow-workers before buying any court, in order that they may have the full benefit of the experience already gained. At Leeds they were wise enough to find a lady who was willing to come up to London and work side by side with us five or six weeks, and so gain an insight into much which it is difficult to learn except practically;[1] and in Dublin

---

1   This was Miss Martin, who had stayed in the Hill household in Nottingham Place during the spring of 1875. (Darley, 1990, p.221.)

the work has been begun under the direction of a lady who had managed a court here. I am sure my fellow-workers would gladly show and help any one thinking of undertaking houses. Indeed, if the plan is to extend safely and well—extend somehow it evidently *will*—I would earnestly commend to every one concerned the absolute necessity of training future collectors. Let those of you who have the charge of courts introduce, side by side with yourselves, promising fellow-workers, who may see and learn now what is being done, and may, in the future, be ready to fill vacant places. Everybody is building and buying, but I was appalled to find, on my return, how few were doing anything towards training volunteers. And yet, if you think of it, *all* the technical work is new to the very ladies whose spirit is needed for the conduct of these houses when built and bought; and IT IS NO USE to have the right spirit if the technical matters, all the sanitary and financial arrangements, are in a mess. Beware of well-meant failures. Have your drainage, and your clean stairs, and your distempering, and your accounts, all as perfect as possible, and to do that you need trained workers.

For the information of those who have the conduct of houses, I ought to mention that I have arranged with Mr C. H. Chevens, manager of the House-Boys' Printing Brigade, 146, Marylebone Road, that he should print and keep in stock the various collecting books, rent books, order books, and forms which we use, so that any one can purchase them.[2] I have also placed with him a few copies of the one shilling American edition of *Homes of the London Poor*, which contains all the book except the article on the Hampstead Fields.[3] Macmillan's edition is out of print. He has nothing now of mine except *Our Common Land*, which does not treat of the houses, but of charity and of the commons.

When I last wrote to you I was a little downcast about the commons. I suppose one never ought to be downcast. I had hardly left England before the Kyrle Society took up the subject with the greatest zeal, and formed a sub-committee, which I do think has done as much as it was possible to do for the cause in the present state of public feeling. The acquisitions of land for the people cannot be *very* many in a single year

---

2   The Brigade was also the printer of this letter—the only one they were entrusted with.

---

3   'Space for the people' had originally appeared in *Macmillan's Magazine* in August 1875. It described, in hopeful terms, the campaign to save Swiss Cottage Fields. Presumably the chapter was dropped from the cheap American edition of the book as the campaign had been a failure. The owner of the Fields withdrew his offer when most of the money had been raised, and the site was built on.

till the general interest in the subject has spread and deepened very considerably; but I do not think a small band of earnest persons *could* have worked more zealously or achieved more, and that by the sheer might of work, than that sub-committee has done. They have been daunted, too, by no fear of failure, however large and impossible the object to be obtained might look. They seem just to have said they would do as much as in them lay, and leave the issue with others. The consequence is that they have done much to cultivate public interest; they have let nothing fail through their own fault; they have had some failures, but at least one splendid success. Of course you will know I mean the purchase of Burnham Beeches for the people. I don't under-rate what others did. We all know the Corporation paid the money,[4] and the Commons Preservation Society helped greatly in the conduct of the matter; but neither one nor the other would have brought the thing to pass without the quiet persevering labour of members of the sub-committee I speak of, or the high, confident, sustained hope they had throughout, that however large the thing might look, there was a chance that *some one* would *give* this great gift to the people if once the way were made quite clear and the business done, and the scheme got into workable form. In this hope, in spite of the discouragements and almost scorn of those who didn't believe in success, steadily was the work carried on, till it was ready for acceptance or refusal; and only those who have carried on a work in its early days, in spite of disbelief, know how much that means. Other smaller successes, too, that sub-committee has had, and several schemes they have prepared in the same way, doing all their part: these now await the decision of others. The sub-committee has offered to find money for due supervision of Lincoln's Inn Fields,[5] and of St Anne's Churchyard, Soho,[6] if the

---

4   Although Octavia writes of the open spaces movement as a fragile new development from which not much can be expected, its real strength can be guaged from the way in which the Corporation of the City of London could be persuaded to acquire 540 acres of ancient woodland in Buckinghamshire, where it would have had no obvious connection.

---

5   This is the only reference in the letters to the long-running campaign to open Lincoln's Inn Fields, the largest square garden in central London, to the public. The land had originally been common land but, in 1734, an act of parliament had vested it in trustees drawn from the neighbouring houses who closed it to the public and maintained it as a private garden, with very limited access to non-residents. In 1877 Octavia had recorded that: 'The trustees of Lincoln's Inn Fields have for the last two or three years, kindly granted me leave to take in a company of children of our tenants one afternoon each summer. It is a pleasant sight. The square is larger, I believe, than

trustees of the one, and the vicar of the other, will but allow them to be opened to the public. Will they? At any rate the sub-committee has done its part, and must now leave the next step to others. One still more critical question is being decided probably while I write—that of whether the site of Horsemonger Lane Gaol shall be used as a garden, or playground, for the poor inhabitants of the crowded neighbourhood of Southwark.[7] The sub-committee has had enormous labour in

any in London, and the trees are quite beautiful. They have also just given permission to the boys from the refuge in Great Queen Street to exercise there two mornings a week from seven to nine o'clock. But this is a small amount of use to make of one of the largest, and most beautiful, and most central spaces of the metropolis.' (*Our Common Land*, 1877, pp.132-33.) The trustees were unwilling to grant any general open access, and in 1880 the Kyrle Society's open spaces committee submitted a memorial to the Metropolitan Board of Works, asking them to take over the land under powers conferred upon them by the Metropolitan Open Spaces Act 1877. The Kyrle Society had offered to reimburse the trustees for any losses, in terms of fees paid by residents and the need for increased supervision if the garden were open to the public, but the answer was still no. The Metropolitan Board of Works was equally unenthusiastic, and nothing happened until this body was replaced by the London County Council (LCC). In 1894 the trustees finally agreed to surrender their rights by leasing the garden to the LCC for a term of 661½ years. The gardens were opened on Saturday 23 February 1895 by Sir John Hutton, chairman of the LCC.

6   St Anne's Church was the centrepiece of the urban development of Soho that began in the 1670s. In 1853 all churchyards in London were closed to further interments, and in 1891 the Metropolitan Public Gardens Association arranged for St Anne's churchyard to be laid out as a public garden. On 27 June 1892 it was officially opened by Lady Hobhouse. Responsibility for the garden passed to the City of Westminster in 1903. The garden continues to provide a welcome open space in this crowded part of central London.

7   The prison, still a site of popular executions in the first part of the nineteenth century, was demolished in 1880. Newington Gardens, covering one-and-a-half acres of the former stoneyards at the eastern end of the site, was laid out by the Metropolitan Public Gardens Association (MPGA) at a cost of £356, and opened by Mrs Gladstone, the prime minister's wife, on 5 May 1884. The MPGA had taken a lease on the site at a nominal rent from the Surrey magistrates. In 1886 it was taken over by the vestry. A census of children visiting the park on four days in May and June 1885 found that, on average, 2,839 children came every day. It cost about £100 a year to maintain. (Brabazon, 1886, pp.32-37.) The area was known locally as Gaol Park for many years. The prison walls and gatehouse were later demolished when the site was extended and an area was fitted with 'gymnastic apparatus'. The extension was officially opened by the chairman of the LCC's Parks and Open Spaces Committee, Mr J. W. Cleland, on 7 September 1903. The grounds were re-furbished in 1997. Half of the site is now a basketball court, and the rest consists of a paved area with mature trees. There is still a fenced children's playground at the lower end of the site.

bringing that question well before the magistrates, on whom the decision now depends. If they consent to give the ground, will you help them to plant and lay it out? The vestries have promised their share, and others will, I fancy, help; but a good deal will be wanted.[8]

I am very anxious to bring before any possible future workers the great need of volunteer help in the various gardens and playgrounds already gained for the poor. We find the superintendents sometimes a little inclined to think more of the flowers than of those for whom they were planted; and we want a little hospitable-heartedness poured into them by the presence of those who are not tired by work, or continuous intercourse with the people. It is less trouble to have playgrounds empty than full, but they hardly fulfil their purpose so! The board school playgrounds are announced as at last opened in compliance with our request, but is it hard on the care-takers to imagine that they can keep the playgrounds full of life and order without help, especially till the children have learned to play. The same thing holds good of our own playgrounds in Freshwater Place, Lambeth, and Whitechapel. We pay some one to open the door at proper hours, and to see that no gross abuse is made of privilege of the ground being open; but we can hardly expect the door-keeper to see that the swings are not monopolised by two or three children, that the see-saw is not made utterly useless by too many children sitting resolutely on it; nor can we expect them to teach the children games. If there were any, especially strong young people, who could and would devote one afternoon a week to going to some of these playgrounds or gardens, at any rate till the children learn to play, it would be an immense help, and they would find a sphere of great usefulness open to them. In the hot summer, flowers, or beads, or pictures, or seaweeds, or needlework, might make groups of little children very happy in the gardens; children who else would be either shut up in the one close room, in which the whole family live and sleep, or else exposed to the dangers and demoralisation which meet them playing in the streets. In the playgrounds, the loan of skipping-ropes, instruction in games like terza or puss-in-the-corner, or the use of songs with movement used in kindergarten schools, would make elder children happy, good, and active. Young gentlemen, too, might gather together the lads who are too old for the little playgrounds, and take them to

---

8   In September Octavia had written to her sister Emily objecting to the idea of applying for government funding for this project, 'After all, even if the government *did* give it, that only means all being taxed;... Is it to be all compulsory taxes, and no free-will offering?' (Maurice, 1914, p.393).

Battersea or Victoria Parks, where there is room for cricket or prisoner's base, and thus much healthy out-of-door life might be promoted, and the high spirits and animal energy which often lead such lads into mischief find its due exercise and vent. A drilling-master has kindly promised to give a course of six drilling lessons, during the Easter holidays, to some of the elder girls, in one of our playgrounds, which will show volunteers how to carry this on in various places. It has been found that the girls in work-houses delight in being drilled, and it has done them much good. Mr Edmund Maurice, who is secretary of the sub-committee for open spaces, will gladly tell any one where and how they may be present at these lessons, or where and when they can best help in the gardens and playgrounds. We have a few MOST valuable workers, but they are not training nearly enough people to extend the work, and it is much needed EVERYWHERE.

I want to thank those who so kindly helped with the money for the Whitechapel playground. It is now laid out very nicely. It, as well as other such, needs, I think, now the life I have spoken of above.

While I am on the subject of money spent on beautiful things, I may add that I spent during the past year some, given me specially for such objects, on laying out a little garden in Mile End, and also in carving a large figure of St Christopher, soon to be placed outside St Christopher's Buildings in Barrett's Court.[9] The figure is one which I began enlarging long ago, from Albert Dürer; friends have most kindly finished it, and are getting it carved. The confidence, to which service brings St Christopher, that God is the strongest of all powers, had always made him a saint I liked to remember in Barrett's Court, and accidental associations made me very fond of him; but it was quite startling to me in the Tyrol to learn, as I did, for the first time, when I saw his great figure on the churches where pilgrims used to be received, that he was the special protector of travellers, and I used to have a strange sense of his being there to teach me a message needed there among the beauty by a wanderer far from home, quite as much as ever it was in Barrett's

---

9   See ill. 20. On 26 March 1880, three months after writing this letter, Octavia would write from Athens, to her sister Miranda: 'I shall be glad if anything is managed in the way of a little ceremony in Barrett's Court for St Christopher... I had thought of little medals with date and motto to be given to the eldest and youngest child in each family resident there at a given time, and their marching in procession through St Christopher's room to receive them, with music and flowers and flags... I think these common memories good for tenants and workers.' (Maurice, 1914, p.413). The accounts for this letter reveal that the carving cost £13 10s, and a further £2 was spent on the ceremony in 1880 (p.139).

Court. So I liked to think I had asked to have the buildings named after him, and I used to think that, if ever I came back, I should like to put up his figure there, that others, perhaps, might learn about him more than they else would know, and hear him tell the same old message of how he found the devil not the strongest after all.

But I didn't only put him up for my own pleasure, nor for his history. I was much stuck while I was abroad, as every one must be, with the beauty of the outside of the houses, and old words, by an author we all know, read long ago,[10] as to the generosity of *external* decoration, haunted me, and I kept thinking what we could do if I lived to come back again, to make the outside of the houses of the poor beautiful. First I thought of Albert Dürer's St Christopher, and I determined on that first of all. But then, in North Italy, I was impressed with the beauty and simplicity of the brick architecture of the town-halls and houses, and, in the Tyrol, by the quaint irregularity of the home-like oriel windows, set on at the corner of the tiny houses in the village streets, with pretty little separate conical roofs, and I seemed to see that this home-like irregularity, this prominence of roof, this simplicity of brick ornament, could be at once applied to our people's houses, whenever and wherever there was money to do it.[11] That any of us might make a gift of a window here, or a cornice there, or a balcony in the other place. I saw that the possession of many groups of houses, by those who had cared to buy them for the good of the poor, and put them under our care, would enable us to have the rare privilege of giving these additional structures to those who deserved to have them, that they would be a delight to all who passed down the street in proportion

---

10 The author was John Ruskin. In 1853 he delivered a series of lectures at Edinburgh on art and architecture, which were published the following year. On 8 August 1853 he had written to the secretary of the Philosophical Union in Edinburgh, in reply to a request for an outline of the lectures, saying that his first lecture would be on the topic of 'General construction of domestic buildings', and he included amongst his sub-headings 'the generosity of external rather than internal decoration'. However, the lecture did not follow his outline, and the phrase was not used, either here or in any of his other published works. When Cook and Wedderburn produced their edition of Ruskin's complete works, the letter containing the phrase was reproduced in the relevant volume, (vol. 12, p.xxix), but that was in 1904. The question remains, how did Octavia know it in 1879? It is quite possible that Ruskin was in the habit of using it in conversation or correspondence. It is certainly a very Ruskinian idea, expounded in *The Seven Lamps of Architecture* (1849), especially 'The Lamp of Beauty'.

---

11 This Tyrolean influence would make itself felt in Elijah Hoole's designs for the Red Cross cottages in 1887.

as they grew to like what was home-like, quaint, and pretty. So I have arranged, if the owners like it, to devote some money specially given me for beautiful things, to putting a little oriel window at one corner of the new houses for the poor in Lambeth.[12] I paid this sum, and that for carving St Christopher, through the Kyrle Society, as they can see to the building while I am away, and one hopes their subscribers may care to do more of the same kind.

I have been able to arrange a thing or two of this sort, but the work near to the people is still shut from me by illness. Only I have to ask you once again whether you will strengthen our hands that the old work I left going on, and still know ought to go on, may not fall through. We ought to have for it in the coming year nearly £150 to render it efficient. For though one or two things I set on foot long ago are well carried through and done, yet on the other hand one of my fellow-workers in the South of London needs strong support in money, that her own great power among the people may be effectual. Where there is personal power, wisdom, devotion, labour, no particle of energy ought to be crippled for want of money, if it be possible to avoid it. My sister, Mrs Edmund Maurice, too, is now in such connection with a district in the East of London that she has considerably extended her knowledge of individuals to whom help is really important. She spends marvellously little in proportion to the good done, for she gives thought, and gets others to give thought, but the money she does want is wanted much. I always used to help in such cases long ago from my donation fund; I want still to do it if it be possible.

She heard some time ago of a poor girl sleeping on door-steps and in the street, willing to go to a place, but with no clothes fit to go in. 'Send her to me', she said, though half-doubting if the girl meant work. The girl, an orphan, came at the appointed time, with very ragged clothes, and a large white apron over her torn jacket. After a little talk, my sister got her into a home and, later, to service. Mrs Maurice only had to pay 7s 6d to save that girl, for part of the money for the clothes was repayable from her wages, and part was supplied by a clergyman; but to have such a 7s 6d ready, to have the power of becoming responsible for much more, if the call for action is sudden, is very important.

Again, my sister said to me, the other day, 'What do you THINK about your donation fund next year? Will your old friends send to you though you are still away? I ask because there is a carpenter struck blind at 27

---

12 The accounts show that the oriel window cost £30.

years old; he wants to learn a trade, and has walked all over London and found the Institution in Berners Street. It will cost £10 to teach him. His wife will support him and the child meantime.' What should I answer? My friends, I said, I thought you would send help as of old. I don't retract a word of what I said to you last year about its being better for you yourselves to know and help the girls sleeping on door-steps, and the men struck down by sudden calamity. But it needs experience to know how to do this wisely, and circumstances prevent some people from even knowing the poor: and to those of you who do not require all your available money for those under your own care, I should like to say that I advise you to send me as help long ago. So far from my work dying with my absence, it has grown—not in my hands, but in the hands of those whom I know to be doing valiantly and well. Strengthen them, not only to complete or support what I planned (this in itself will cost still a large part of £150, what with all the valuable classes, and playgrounds, and clubs, and finishing the education of some orphans), but strengthen them still more; strengthen them for their own work, which is growing, for all the gentle, separate help they are giving, day after day, to the poor and the outcast.

I do not know if I shall be back among you to be of any use, it looks more like it than it did, but whether I am here or not, my sister will use well any money you send her.

Now, may I thank you all for all you have done, I will not say for me, but for my people, which is so much more. I wish I could do, or be, more which would be helpful to you all, and could at all express the sense I have of your goodness and your kindnesses. All through the long silences, believe me, I think of you all.

OCTAVIA HILL

DONATION ACCOUNT, 1879

RECEIPTS

	£	d	s
Cash in hand	172	1	3 ½
Miss Barrett	1	0	0
C.B.P. Bosanquet, Esq	4	10	0
Lady Cadogan (Cobbling Class)	5	0	0
A.G. Crowder, Esq	5	0	0
Miss Fletcher	5	0	0
Mr and Mrs Gillson (Pension. A) annual	2	12	0
Mrs Henley	25	0	0
F. Hill, Esq (Whitechapel Playground)	0	10	0
Miss E. Harrison (Ornamental Tiles)	0	10	6
Miss Jekyll	16	0	0
Mrs Lewes	5	0	0
Mrs Lyell	8	0	0
Mrs Lyell (Commons' Preservation Society)	5	0	0
Mrs Lyell (Whitechapel Playground)	5	0	0
Miss Lyell	5	0	0
Miss Meek	2	2	0
Mrs Oldham	5	0	0
Mr and Mrs Pooley	1	1	0
A Servant	2	0	0
W. Shaen, Esq, per (Whitechapel Playground)	5	0	0
Mrs W. Shaen	2	0	0
Mrs L. Stephen	10	0	0
Miss Helen Taylor	1	0	0
Mrs Arthur Whateley	2	0	0
S. Winkworth, Esq (Pension A, up to Lady Day)	6	10	0
Mrs S. Winkworth	10	0	0
Mrs S. Winkworth 2nd Donation	5	0	0
Mrs Wright	25	0	0
Hornsby Wright, Esq	3	0	0
Miss Wilson	1	0	0
Miss Yorke	25	0	0
	£370	16	9 ½

DONATION ACCOUNT, 1879

EXPENDITURE

	£	s	d
Books and Shelves (Barrett's Court Library)	2	10	0
W. (boarded out)	5	14	0
Clubs (Rent and Fuel)	52	0	0
Keeping W.M. at School	13	0	0
Keeping R.W. and E. at Homes	11	5	0
Excursions to the Country and Museums	3	0	6
Commons Preservation Society*	5	0	0
Care of Playgrounds and Mending See-saw	11	18	0
Laying out Whitechapel Playground and Mile End Garden*	65	10	0
Providing Hospital and other Relief to the Sick	8	19	0
Employment for Poor People, Outfits, &c.	2	13	2 ½
Ornamental Tiles*	0	10	6
May Festival	2	10	7
Oriel Window, per Kyrle Society*	30	0	0
Carving Figure of St Christopher, per Kyrle Society*	13	10	0
Clothes and School fees for Poor Children boarded out	2	0	11
Mission Woman for Dust Sifters (Lambeth)	31	4	0
Teacher and Leather for Cobbling Class	2	6	11
Rent, Fuel, and Light for three Girl's Classes Bank Library and Mother's meeting	18	17	9
Printing, Stationery, &c.	5	13	10
Cash in hand†	82	12	7
	£370	16	9 ½

* These sums were given by special desire; or from the known sympathies of the donors.
† This balance is nearly all appropriated.

Examined and found correct, A. P. Fletcher, December 22nd 1879

LETTER TO MY FELLOW-WORKERS

TO WHICH IS ADDED

ACCOUNT OF DONATIONS RECEIVED

FOR

WORK AMONG THE POOR

DURING 1880

BY

OCTAVIA HILL
(FOR PRIVATE CIRCULATION ONLY)

LONDON:
WATERLOW AND SONS LIMITED, PRINTERS,
GREAT WINCHESTER STREET, E.C.

SUMMARY

Direct assistance to poor families... the work of Mrs Edmund Maurice... smoke abatement, the Kyrle Society and the exhibition in South Kensington... Octavia's acceptance of her illness and possible changes to her life in future.

EDITOR'S NOTE

Octavia was still recovering from her breakdown, and the first part of the year had been spent travelling with Harriot Yorke to Rome, Corfu, Athens, Constantinople and Nuremberg, returning to Britain in the summer. Although Octavia writes of 'this broken year' and her 'sudden collapse from an active life', the tone of this letter indicates a return of strength. While she is still not actively involved in housing or work among the poor, she has thrown herself with the old enthusiasm into a completely new cause: smoke abatement. The prominence which Octavia gives to her sister Emily's work, to the extent of reproducing Emily's accounts of it, probably indicates a continuing feeling that she needs to make amends for the doubts expressed about Emily's stewardship of the donation fund in the 1878 letter.

My Friends,

I have not been long back in England, and there does not seem much which I need say to you as to work, but I do not like to omit sending you a few words of thanks and of New Year's greeting, now that I am rendering you an account of the money with which you have entrusted me during the past year.

You will see that we begin with a balance for our regular work, of which I am very glad; it relieves me of a great sense of responsibility, and I am very glad to know that any money you are good enough to send me will be available if fresh important need arises, for I am seeing very few of you, and shall have little opportunity of telling you what is wanted.

A great part of the work during this past year has been the direct assistance of separate poor families. I know this will interest some of you more than anything else. It certainly is satisfactory in several ways. It brings the giver into such close relation with the recipient that the real effect of the gift is clearly seen. The gift is associated with the gracious human sympathy which is so sadly lost in much of the *large* charity which comes from afar and occupies itself with masses of people. Even the charity which deals with the eradication of evil, though it be grounded on human sympathy, is often not seen to be so by those whom it benefits; for it is sympathy guided by memory and penetrative imagination, and it is often invisible for long years to those whom it serves; action prompted by it often causes temporary pain, and rouses bitterness even among those whom finally it will help. Such work has indeed its own peculiar blessing, that which follows self-sacrifice, and constancy tested by pain; there falls a special sense of communion with God on those who, in order to help His children, accept misinterpretation and loneliness. If such duties lie straight before us, we must fulfil them cheerfully; but we may, on the other hand, be thankful, when life leads us face to face with the few, and those really cared for; when smile, and look, and voice, and thoughtful kindly act, translate into life, to the people for whom we live, the care and sympathy we feel. We may be thankful for ourselves, we may be much more thankful for them, for we are able to carry them much further with us in any reforming, or educating, work we want to do for them. We win and carry with us their hearts, and our discipline is felt to be gentle, and their efforts are lightened by our encouragement, and cheered by our hope. It is, I believe, *only* by such individual work, lightened by love, and softening pain by near sympathy, that those who have fallen out of the way by ignorance, by sorrow, or by sin, can be led back, and by it alone can natural human intercourse be restored between the rich and poor inhabitants of our great city.

I never talk with Mrs Edmund Maurice over her plans for the people she is helping with your money without feeling how real and how good is such personal work. During part of the past year she has been deprived of the help of a paid worker, who used to assist her in this sort of work, and enabled her to extend it to the people in a very poor East End district. But lately, through the liberality of a great friend, I am able to give Mrs Maurice this added power again, and we begin the New Year with it. I cannot here tell you of the number of people cured by country air, established in self-supporting positions, helped through sickness and trained to work, all by the fund you supplied to us. There has been a very large number, one which, in proportion to the expenditure, has been surprising and delightful to me. But I will not write of these now. Mrs Maurice asks me to tell you about the money sent specially for the blind man and the cripple, as circumstances led her to change somewhat the plans she had in view when I wrote to you of them. She writes:

'In regard to the blind man mentioned in last year's letter, it was found that his health was too bad for him to learn a trade. The money given for him, therefore, was used for employing his wife till she could find work. She made for me some clothes for children boarded out, and for girls going to service. After a time she procured regular work at a warehouse, by which she earns 18*s.* a week. This winter, however, she has been out of work again, and was laid up with rheumatism for a time, so the rest of the money was used in supplying her with flannels and coals.

A cripple's carriage was bought with the money in my hands, with some little help from other societies, for the boy of fourteen, who has a mechanical turn, mentioned last year. It was hoped that he could go backwards and forwards in this carriage to a shop to learn watchmaking, as that is a trade in which cripples are often employed. This, however, failed, partly owing to the boy's delicacy, partly to slackness of trade, but the carriage has been a great blessing to the lad, as it enables him to go out in the fresh air, and move himself about, the doctor said this would keep his limbs from being paralysed. He went into the country this year, and took his carriage with him, so that he was able really to enjoy the change.'

Mrs Edmund Maurice has done one fresh thing this year, of which I am very glad. She has arranged periodically for some far quieter excursions into the country than can be secured when large numbers go together. The large parties are jolly, and sociable, and bright, and may give to a large group of tenants a sense of corporate life, happy memories in common, and promote neighbourly feelings among them, but the quiet influence of beauty and country stillness *they* cannot give. Small parties occupy much time, but they seemed well worth arranging, and some of the money given for country excursions has been used for these fortnightly parties, a different group going every fortnight. Mrs Edmund Maurice says:

'I arranged last summer to bring little parties of six or eight very poor women, most of them widows, from the East End to Hampstead. They came to tea at a little cottage and then took a long country walk. Journey and tea only cost 1s. each. Many of them were people who had not seen the country for years, and their delight in the beauty and quiet was very touching. It was also a great rest to the women to escape from the sound of the children's voices; but they always went home loaded with wild flowers 'to surprise the children when they wake in the morning'. One widow who had supported her bedridden husband for a long time, till his death, had gathered a large bunch of daisies. When one of the women laughed at her for not gathering some of the rarer flowers, she said, 'I always love daisies because they were such a pleasure to my poor husband. He liked to have a saucer-full of them by his bed, and watch them open in the morning. He used to offer the children a farthing a-piece for the daisies.' Another woman was so delighted to hear the cuckoo, she had not heard it since she was a child in the country. One wished she could but take some of the good air back, she always had a headache at home.'

I have, I think, in previous letters, told you that the money sent to me comes from two distinctly marked sets of people, the one deeply interested in personal work among the sick and poor, and sad, whom they know that I have always sought and loved; the second, who believe me to be—not so much in the centre of important work—as trained to be swift to see opportunities for beginning it, to know work which will be far-reaching in its helpfulness in time to come, and which needs strong support in its early stages.

A little of this latter work I have been able to do even in this broken year. I have done it in connection with our Kyrle Society, the workers of which still gather round us in this house, and make us strong to carry through anything which seems to us good, which falls within the scope of the society.

Some of you will, I know, be interested to hear about this larger work. I must tell you, then, that I was much impressed while abroad with the better out-door life of the people in towns. I saw that this was not wholly due to the greater amount of fine weather, but in some measure to the prettier public gardens. If I lived to come back, I told myself, I would see if the Kyrle Society could not get rid of the smoke. We had indeed enumerated the abatement of smoke as one of our objects, when the society was formed, but up to that time nothing had been done, members were all busy with other parts of the work. It was time we should grapple with this evil, too. It appeared a natural sequel to what we had tried to do to secure open spaces, when once the world seemed wakening to the necessity of obtaining those, to endeavour to make them such as trees and flowers and grass would grow in, and show their natural colour and brightness. Immediately on my return I proposed to the Kyrle Society to appoint a sub-committee to deal with the prevention of smoke. They at once consented, and asked the National Health Society for their co-operation.[1] This was cordially given,

---

1   The National Health Society was founded in 1871 by Dr Elizabeth Blackwell, an Englishwoman who gained her degree at Geneva Medical College, New York and became Europe's first modern woman doctor. The society offered lectures on health education. Miranda read her famous essay, 'A suggestion to those who love beautiful things', to the NHS in 1875, where it was received with stunned silence—not an auspicious start for the Kyrle Society! Octavia represented the Kyrle Society on the joint committee set up with the NHS to organise the smoke abatement exhibition, and her opposite number from the NHS was Ernest Hart, Henrietta Barnett's brother-in-law and chairman of the National Health Society. Ernest Abraham Hart (1835–1898) was a surgeon specialising in diseases of the eye, being appointed ophthalmic surgeon at St Mary's hospital at the age of 28. His main work, however, was as a medical journalist, starting with the *Lancet* in 1857 as sub-editor. When Hart was offered the editorship of the *British Medical Journal* in 1866, his resignation sparked

and a joint sub-committee was at once appointed. It was too late in the season to do more than name our committee and fix the date of meeting in the autumn. A sudden general public interest began to show itself in the autumn, and we were all ready to use it and to increase it.

Our committee found, what I certainly had hardly realised before, that there were smokeless fuels, and smokeless grates in plenty, that the fuel must be cheaper, the grates simpler before they would meet with general approval, but that a very little would just turn the scale in favour of their adoption. As I was mainly interested in the question of household fires as likely to affect London air most powerfully, it was evident that what was needed was to examine and report on the cheapest and simplest of smokeless grates and fuels. This our committee is now prepared to do. Through the kindness of the Commissioners of the Exhibition of 1851,[2] buildings at South Kensington have been lent to our committee, that they may hold an exhibition of various inventions for preventing smoke. Professor Frankland,[3] Professor Abel,[4] and many

---

the '30 years' war' between the two journals. There were threats of libel and even physical violence. During Hart's editorship, the *British Medical Journal* grew from 20 to 64 pages. His work on behalf of the British Medical Association is demonstrated by the increase from 2,000 to 19,000 members. From 1872 to 1897 he was chairman of the Association's Parliamentary Bills Committee. His public work covered virtually every aspect of sanitary legislation, including the notification of infectious diseases and vaccination. He took a leading part in the exposures which led to the inquiry into the state of London workhouse infirmaries. In 1874 he had come to Octavia's aid in her battle with the medical officer of health for Marylebone who wanted to issue a closure order on Barrett's Court (1877, p.85). In 1882 Hart was a co-founder, with Lord Brabazon, of the Metropolitan Public Gardens Association, becoming its first vice-chairman. His second wife Alice had set up the Institute for Women and Girls in Barrett's Court (1874 pp.35-6).

---

2   The Great Exhibition of 1851 had been the responsibility of a Royal Commission, chaired by Prince Albert. The six months of admissions to the Crystal Palace in Hyde Park had generated profits of £186,000, which were used to buy the stretch of land from Kensington Gore to Cromwell Road on which were erected the clutch of cultural institutions now known as Albertopolis.

---

3   Sir Edward Frankland (1825–1899) was a chemist and member of the Royal Society, which awarded him a medal in 1857. He was also chair of the Royal Institution and, at the time of this letter, professor of the Royal School of Mines. He was appointed to a number of royal commissions investigating ways of improving metropolitan drinking water.

---

4   Frederick Augustus Abel (1827–1902) was a member of the Royal Institute of

other scientific men have joined our committee, and promise to report on the various inventions. The exhibition will assuredly stimulate inventors still further, already many exhibitors have sent in their names, and numbers of improved grates and fuels have been brought to our notice. The buildings will require to be put in order, and the exhibition will involve expense which at present the committee has not funds to meet. But I earnestly hope so beneficial a movement may not fail for want of money to carry it through. When once we are able to pronounce on the best stoves and fuels for various domestic purposes, we shall try to make the facts well known, and I have no doubt there will at once be a great number of people ready and glad to use them.

The saving ought to be enormous, as the smoke all consists of unconsumed fuel. Some scientific men say that as much as three million out of five million tons annually used in London flies away in smoke, and so does harm and no good. Be the proportion what it may, the waste in mere fuel is considerable, to say nothing of the cost of extra washing, caused by the destruction of all kinds of material by dirt, and the artificial light required in the day-time. But, independently of any question of saving, many of us would, I believe, be ready to make an effort to diminish smoke, were it only for the beauty and comfort and cleanliness, and for the life of the flowers we might then preserve round us.[5]

It was interesting to me to learn that the law does forbid smoke, so far as it can be prevented, issuing from factories, large and small, from steamers, and from all chimneys other than those of private houses. I was glad to learn the machinery of the law, and that it is entrusted by the Sanitary Act of 1866 to vestries, as well as by that of 1853 to the police, so that we can each of us, in our capacity of ratepayers, bring it prominently before those who are bound to put it in force. So far as

---

Chemistry. He was a prominent adviser to the government on scientific matters, and was instrumental in developing military technologies such as mustard gas.

---

5   It is strange that Octavia mentions economic and aesthetic reasons for smoke abatement, but not the health reasons which made it a life-and-death issue for many people until the middle of the twentieth century. The London smog (a term coined in 1905 by Dr Harold des Voeux, treasurer of the Coal Smoke Abatement Society) was almost the signature of the capital. It resulted from the combination of large quantities of pollutants such as sulphur dioxide, produced by burning coal, with fog, and was most likely to occur in calm weather. These 'pea-soupers' could last for days and proved fatal to many people with respiratory problems. The smog of the winter of 1879-80—just before the period covered by this letter—was blamed for 2,400 deaths.

regards steamers it rests with the Conservators of the Thames to carry out the law. I have no doubt that, owing to the general interest now awakened, all the bodies entrusted with powers under the law will be roused to fresh energy.

As to my own future work I am afraid I can tell you nothing at present. I am not well enough, even if it were my first duty now, to take up any public work. I am sure you all know my desire to serve the poor is not slighter than in old days, but I come back to find many things changed, and the changes imply different duties.

Were I inclined to regret this I should remind myself that various kinds of life may all be equally helpful, and I have always maintained that a life given wholly to the poor was one-sided, that our work among them should be less engrossing, and grow more naturally out of our home life. I think sometimes I feel this now more than ever, because so very many people are throwing themselves almost restlessly into work exclusively for the poor, and seeming to think that *that* only is good. I feel as if anyone who has entered fully into public work, and has strength, when duties change, to step quietly back into an out-of-sight ordinary household, and be thankful and quiet there, and to look upon her position there as just as distinctly an appointed one, might almost do more good than if she hurried back to large undertakings.

I am *sure* this would be so if it were not for those terrible wildernesses of poor, and only poor, which cover large tracts of our city, wildernesses with the dwellers in which, except by deliberate purpose, no educated person would naturally be brought into contact. These do seem to demand that we should not all be satisfied with our home, and the poor naturally near to us and it. I have not forgotten, I never could forget, those tracts of London. I am not in them now; whether I ever shall be again will depend, not on what I decide to be intrinsically—or even in the present age—the noblest life, but on what degree of strength may be mine in the years I still have to live, and on what may be the nearest, simplest duties which open out before me. Once my way was clearly out among the poor; now it is equally clearly not there. Where it may lie in the future who can say?

One thing more let me add. Whether my life henceforward be amongst rich or poor, in a quiet house or in the great world, there is one service you, my friends, have rendered me, which will make me specially bound to live whatever remains to me of life not *un*worthily. The sudden collapse from an active life, where every act brings result, is apt to lead one to a great sense of valuelessness. This is a temptation. You helped me to resist it. Your confidence, your help, your affection taught me, when I had to be most completely inactive, that, useless as I seemed, there must be a strange value in my life; the memory of you all goes on whispering to me still that message, which all human trust and love is for ever bearing to human creatures when they are tempted to despise themselves—that message, which you and I, whenever our work was worth anything, were carrying to the poor, in old days, which was the root and strength of whatever we were able to do—that they must never despise, never despair of, themselves; that God in His love, and man in his, had put great honour on them. 'Remember', it seemed to say, 'be reminded by our abiding care for you, of what you were meant for. It isn't wholly a question of action; you may fail in action again and again, but by all the Divine, by all the human love which ever gathered round you, you are bound to remember that you were meant to live among the angels, meant to hold communion with great souls, living and dead, present and absent. You are greatly honoured. See, however small and faulty you are, God has entrusted you with *some* power to serve or cheer your fellows.' Love waits patiently for our full growth, for it sees what we are meant to be; it always tells us that we are worthy, meant to be worthy of that full love and magnificent trust which is the sunlight in which human spirits grow.

DONATION ACCOUNT, 1879–1880†

RECEIPTS

	£	s	d
Cash in hand	82	12	7
Anon.	40	0	0
Mrs Atkinson	1	10	0
Mrs Bates	1	0	0
Mrs Bond	5	0	0
K. Brock, Esq	5	0	0
W. S. Browne, Esq	2	2	0
Miss Cave Browne	3	0	0
Rev. E. Carpenter	5	14	0
A.G. Crowder, Esq	5	0	0
Miss L. Denison	2	0	0
Miss M. Duer	0	10	0
Miss S. K. Duer	0	10	0
Mrs Fawcett	0	10	0
A.P. Fletcher, Esq	2	2	0
Miss A. Fletcher	5	0	0
Miss Forman	1	0	0
C.E. Flower, Esq	2	0	0
Miss F.	1	0	0
Miss Gander	5	5	0
Mrs Greaves	1	1	0
Miss H. Gurney	1	1	0
W. Bullock Hall, Esq	1	0	0
Rev. Canon Harrison (Pension A. to Xmas)	2	12	0
Rev. S. Hill	0	2	6
Mrs Hughes	2	0	0
Miss Jackson	3	0	0
The Misses Johnston	25	0	0
J.K.	0	6	0
Mrs Lyell	8	0	0
Mrs Macaulay	0	10	0
Miss Lucy Martineau	10	0	0
Mrs Oldham	5	0	0
Mr and Mrs Pooley	1	1	0
Shareholders of Central London Dwellings Company	3	0	0
Mrs Stephen Ralli	5	0	0
A Servant	2	0	0
Mrs E. Spender	2	2	0
Mrs L. Stephen	10	0	0
S.R.D.	1	0	0
Sir U. Kay-Shuttleworth	5	0	0
Miss A. Shuttleworth	0	4	1
Mrs Taylor	10	0	0
W. Tendron, Esq	5	0	0
F.T.	1	0	0
Mrs Whately	1	0	0
Miss Mary Wells	1	1	0
S. Winkworth, Esq (Pension A. up to Lady Day)	6	10	0
Mrs S. Winkworth	24	0	0
Miss Wing	5	0	0
Miss White	5	0	0
Miss M. White	5	0	0
Mrs Wright	25	0	0
Wm. Wynyard, Esq	1	0	0
Miss Yorke	20	0	0
	£369	6	2

DONATION ACCOUNT, 1879–1880†

EXPENDITURE

	£	s	d
Boarding out Two Children (School-fees, clothes, &c., for Six others)	29	10	7 ½
W.M. at Industrial School	13	0	0
Industrial School for B.R., and W.J. and K.	18	12	6
Excursions to the Country and other Entertainments	14	4	9
Negotiations about Recreation Ground 3	3	0
Care of Playgrounds	10	13	0
Providing Hospital and other Relief to the Sick	21	18	1 ½
Employment for Poor People, Outfits, &c. 9	16	7
Mangle 4	0	0
May Festival 3	17	2
Unveiling St Christopher's Statue 2	0	0
Mission Women for Dust Sifters (Lambeth)	15	12	0
Rent, Fuel and Light, for Three Girl's Classes, Bank, Library, and			
Mothers' Meeting	21	13	10
Club, Rent and Fuel	41	12	0
Cripple's Carriage 9	10	0
Kyrle Society (to set on foot the Smoke Committee)	10	0	0
Pension (A.)	20	0	0
East End Pension Fund 5	0	0
Printing and Postage 4	5	0
Cash in hand*	110	17	7
	£369	6	2

* This balance is all appropriated.

N.B.—The funds entrusted to me come from two very clearly marked classes of donors. The one anxious that their money should be devoted to the direct help of the sick and poor. The other class wishing to strengthen my hands that I may help forward in its difficult stages any great movement. My sister and I recognise this distinction, and in deciding about every grant, carefully consider *whose* money it is that is used, and follow the wish of the donors faithfully.

Examined and found correct, A.P. Fletcher, January 12th 1881.

† *Editor's note:* This is the only set of accounts to cover more than one calendar year. It is not clear why Octavia departed from her usual practice. The heading may simply be a mistake, as the auditor did not sign off the accounts until 12 January, and there is nothing to indicate that they cover April to April.

LETTER TO MY FELLOW-WORKERS

TO WHICH IS ADDED

ACCOUNT OF DONATIONS RECEIVED

FOR

WORK AMONG THE POOR

DURING 1881

BY

OCTAVIA HILL
(FOR PRIVATE CIRCULATION ONLY)

LONDON

PRINTED BY WATERLOW AND SONS LIMITED,

GREAT WINCHESTER STREET, LONDON E.C.

SUMMARY

Paradise Place and Freshwater Place acquired from Ruskin… smoke abatement exhibition… work of the Kyrle Society… work among the poor… the need for more trained housing managers.

EDITOR'S NOTE

Although still too weak for any of the face-to-face work among the poor, Octavia is back in London and can be seen hitting her stride again with the organisation of the smoke abatement exhibition in South Kensington. She is also back in charge of the donation fund. Octavia manages that part of it that supports new movements in social reform, while her sister Emily takes charge of 'members of individual poor'—although Octavia is now involved with that side of the work as well. She still regards herself as the donors' 'representative among the poor, however broken I have become during the late years'. The letter ends with one of Octavia's most moving appeals for more labourers in the vineyard.

14 Nottingham Place, W.
January, 1882

Once more, my dear friends, I am sending you an account of what I have been able to do with the money with which you have entrusted me. I am sorry that I have so little to add of any work done by myself. There is very little which my strength and my home duties now allow of my undertaking for the poor. At the same time, looking back on the year which has just closed, I cannot but feel that the things I have been able to achieve, as it were, by the way, simply from being at home among my old friends and fellow-workers, have been neither few nor inconsiderable. The fact is, that though, just now, I am not, and cannot be, responsible for any work among the poor, I am in such close and constant communication with those who are, and the years of work in the courts have given me such a radical knowledge of them all, that I am really able to be of use in 50 small ways without feeling the fatigue, and now and again I am called in about great matters where my experience is useful. All this I say to remind myself, and to assure you, that, very deliberately, I have satisfied myself that I do not feel wrong in asking you still to trust me as of old, and to look upon me as representing the poor, though I have still so little definite work with them.

If this little letter is to contain a record of the most important facts affecting the work among the poor for which I have laboured and thought, I ought here to record the repurchase from Mr Ruskin, during the past year, of the two courts which were the earliest entrusted to my care. Last spring I learned that he wished to sell them. I knew that the determination was a wise one; he had proved to many others able to give personal attention to the courts that the scheme was practicable and beneficial, many were willing to undertake such work, and there seemed no reason why he should continue it. But you will realise that I wanted to keep the tenants who for years had been my neighbours and friends still in near relation to ourselves, and to secure that they should be thoroughly well cared for. Mr Ruskin entered most kindly and heartily into my wish, and sold to me the court which I had had longest under my charge, a little group of three houses, within a stone's throw of my own house. That is now my very own; and I am thankful that the fact of ownership implies a continuous duty towards the people there, which must always claim due fulfilment even when home duties are many.

The second court which Mr Ruskin had bought, and which contains the playground and the first trees I was instrumental in planting in London, was too expensive for me to purchase back, yet in some ways I was more attached to it than to the other, and saw even greater danger for it if it passed away to ordinary landlords. For to anyone not trained to think first for the people, and temperately to accept five per cent only, and let the balance be spent, or renounced, for their good, there would certainly be an overpowering temptation to build on the playground and cut down my trees. It was rather a sad time when I thought it might all pass out of our hands; yet I thought Mr Ruskin wise to sell it, and he was very cordial about me trying to find a friend of my own as a purchaser. When they heard about it, my old friends Mr and Mrs Shaen said they would like to buy it. There seemed a singular appropriateness in the arrangement; they had known its history, and some of the many thoughts bound up with it, and the hopes and plans for it from the first. It was Mr Shaen who, in the early days, had expressed confidence in the plan when no one else, except Mr Ruskin, had believed in it, and steadily on through the advancing years I had owed to him all strong support and valuable help in business for all the courts. Mrs Shaen had been one of my earliest friends in London, to them both I was linked by memories which make their possession of the place I had loved a great satisfaction to me. I was, you may readily believe, thankful indeed to help them to purchase the court, which they had done, and I feel the strongest hope that in their hands it may prosper better than it ever has done, for I am sure that on every side they enter into the purpose of the work, and will bring that knowledge to bear strongly on this one court. If, in return for all their trouble, they ever love the place and the people half as much as I do they will be well recompensed. Meantime, I feel it doubly mine in being theirs.[1]

So much of my other work this year has been bound up with other

---

1   On 16 April 1881 Octavia wrote to her sister Miranda to say that Ruskin had accepted the offer for Paradise Place (now Garbutt Place), and on 25 April she wrote to Mr Shaen about purchasing Freshwater Place (now demolished, although social housing still occupies the site on Homer Row, and there is still a garden). The next day Octavia wrote to Mrs Shaen: 'It is only when one feels what the *narrow* courts are, and how the people get maddened with the heat of them in summer, and how the children have *nowhere* to play, and how their noise hurts their mothers' nerves, that one feels what these few square yards of ugly space are'. (Maurice, 1914, p.444.)

people and other societies, it becomes difficult to write of it. You will all have seen in the public papers how our smoke abatement movement has grown and thriven. There may not be to be found in the present exhibition the simple, cheap, cheerful smoke-consuming grate suitable for all our own rooms at once, which would meet our needs instantly; but a large and important step has been made this year in forwarding the cause we have at heart. The object is well and prominently, not only before the public, but before inventors and manufacturers; and I think the invention of such a grate as is wanted for domestic use in sitting-rooms will not long be found beyond the reach of British skill and science. Meantime, every *improved* grate (and there are numbers in the exhibition) is both cheaper and better, mainly because it ensures more complete combustion—that is, it more thoroughly burns up coal, and consequently emits less smoke. Of these improved grates numbers are being bought, and more will be bought, continually.[2] The improvements for manufacturing purposes are, I hear, considerable. The immense gathering at the opening of the Exhibition was, to my mind, very cheering; for when many Englishmen really *want* to do a practical thing, they usually find a way to do it, and I cannot help thinking that the effort to abate smoke will steadily grow, bringing with it a gradual success.[3]

---

2 'Manchester is considering the advisability of at once opening a Smoke Abatement Exhibition. A deputation from that City has been up to see the London Exhibition, and correspondence is now going on between our own Committee and the Manchester authorities.' [*Octavia Hill's note.*] *Editor's note:* In 1946 Manchester Corporation established the first smokeless zone, ten years before the Clean Air Act 1956 gave statutory support to smokeless zones.

---

3 The Smoke Abatement Exhibition opened in a building beside the Royal Albert Hall on 30 November 1881 and ran for 11 weeks, so it was still running when Octavia wrote this letter. Attendances numbered 116,000, of whom 70,000 were admitted free as members of invited groups, such as engineers, architects and builders. Receipts totalled £1,522, and expenses came to £2,476. It contained displays of smokeless coal-fired grates, stoves and ranges; gas appliances for cooking and heating; hot-air and hot-water diffusion services; heavy industrial heating equipment; and displays of different types of coal, including smokeless anthracite. As a result of the exhibition, George Shaw-Lefevre, First Commissioner of Works, ordered samples of the best devices for installation in government buildings, and the Duke of Westminster, president of the organising committee, instructed his agent to consult with tenants on the Grosvenor Estate about the use of smokeless stoves. Smoke abatement had levered Octavia back into campaigning, after her years of recuperation, but she did not stay with the cause, and does not mention it again. The National Smoke Abatement Society was formed to carry forward the work, but this lasted only a few years. It was succeeded

Of the scheme for establishing classes for teaching working people to sing, in all parts of London, in which I am deeply interested, and in promoting which I have been engaged, I will not write here, because it is the work of the Kyrle Society and will be duly noticed in their reports—this is true also of the smoke question, but as I mentioned it in my last letter to you and as I am to a large degree responsible to our Kyrle Society for that branch of its work, I felt that you would be interested to hear of it. Moreover, it was a vote from the fund with which you entrusted me, that enabled the Kyrle Society to unite with the National Health Society in establishing the fund with which the joint committee began the good work it has since done.

With regard to the fund with which you have again so kindly trusted me, I can only once more assure you of my gratitude for it, and tell you what a help and strength it has been. Money like this, on the spot, in the hands of one who is in the centre of workers, has a manifold use: it is, as it were, spent many times over, for it enables me often to go on strongly and independently and with a care-free heart in many a good thing for which I do not know that anyone is ready to give money. Often, after all, others do come in to take the expense themselves, and your money is not spent on that undertaking at all, but is carried on to some future one. It is curious how often this happens.

My sister, Mrs Edmund Maurice, is still taking charge for me of numbers of individual poor with all the old wisdom and care. The very large sum you will see in the balance-sheet set down as spent in providing hospital and other relief to the sick, and for employment for poor people, outfits, &c., means, as I have seen often and often, a very great deal of help given, just in the most helpful way, with separate thought and care and economy. I am doing a little of the same kind myself now with some of my other fellow-workers, but nothing to be compared with the amount Mrs Maurice is doing for me. Her assistant, for whom one friend so kindly pays, links her with a large, poor, outlying district, where no other ladies are at work. She mentions to me with special satisfaction, among the people helped by this fund, two tiny children who were never expected to walk, but whom she boarded out

---

by the Coal Smoke Abatement Society in 1898, with Princess Louise as vice-president. Legislation to achieve its aims was a long time in coming. Following the great London smog of 1952, which was blamed for 4,000 deaths, the 1956 Clean Air Act sought to control domestic sources of smoke pollution by introducing smokeless zones, and in 1963 coal fires were banned in London. There have been no smogs since 1962, and in 1971 it was reported that winter sunshine in London had increased by more than 50 per cent. (Marsh, 1962; Ranlett, 1981.)

in the country for some months, and who are now plump healthy little things.

I have received, but just after my accounts were closed and ready for auditing, a very munificent donation, the account of which will appear in next year's letter.[4] It opens before me larger vistas of possible money help to my friends hard at work among the poor than I ever began any year with before. While the thought of its administration fills me with joy, it fills me, too, with a sort of awe—for who am I that such power should be given me?—and I can only hope that I may be made humble and gentle, for in such a temper alone can the needs of the poor be made visible. The trust is like a call to me to tell me that you, my friends, those whom I know well and those I have never seen, look to me with confidence that I shall still be able to be your representative among the poor, however broken I have become during the late years, and your hope sometimes is a lesson to me to keep my own high, where no earthly mists can dim it. I think it right to mention this large gift, but I hope it will not make any of you, my old friends, think I do not need your help this year. I think I shall want it as much as ever, for this sum, being a large one, will probably be best spent on large objects, and the work I have had on hand for years should not suffer. Moreover, the mere fact of administering it will bring me face to face with much want, and for that I may need greater resources than are at my disposal. Send money then to me as of old, if you easily can, only remember *never* send it if it prevents your giving to any person or things you yourselves know and watch, and for which you are certain your gifts are helpful, for those gifts are best of all and thrice blessed.

In conclusion, I have but one subject more to refer to, and that is our great need of additional workers in our courts. The courts are numerous, the funds for their purchase are practically unlimited, but the quiet, steady, permanent workers, whom it is worth while to train, and who afterwards exercise an abiding influence in our courts, though they are increasing in number and very greatly in efficiency, are not by any means as numerous as they should be. During my absence every one has been buying courts, and so few, comparatively, have been training workers. I have now taken one to train myself, and one of my best friends, who is in daily communication with me, is ready to train another,

---

4   This donation of £500 appears in the accounts for 1882 (p.164), attributed to 'anonymous'. Octavia appears to have spent most of it on open spaces (1882, p.165). The sums of £280 for open spaces and £46 for a recreation ground and gymnasium at Lambeth probably come from this source.

and I would at all times be thankful to tell workers where they could serve a sort of apprenticeship. Surely there must be many volunteers who would care to take charge of some group of tenants, large or small, near their own quiet homes, or in some dreadful district of poverty, with the sort of quiet continuous control which may slowly mould the place and people to conformity with a better standard than prevails in poor courts in general. Surely there are some who would prefer the simple and natural relation to the poor which springs from mutual duties steadily fulfilled, to the ordinary intercourse between uncertain donors, and successive recipients of chance gifts. If any one should read this who would care to learn how to take a court and its occupants quietly in hand and establish such rule there as should be beneficial, if they come not with high hopes of gushing gratitude, of large, swift, visible result, but remembering the patience of the great husbandman content to sow good seed and trust that in time it will bear fruit somehow, if they come ready to establish gradually such arrangements as must tell on the lives of their poorer neighbours, if they come with reverent spirits prepared to honour all that is honourable in the families they have charge of, and gradually to let the ties of real friendship grow up so that poor and rich may be friends as in a country parish, let them come to me and I will shew them work that I think they will feel opens to them a sphere of unnoticed usefulness such as few others can equal. Let them come quickly, for the need is great.

DONATION ACCOUNT, 1881

RECEIPTS

	£	s	d
Cash in hand	110	17	7
Mrs Astley	2	0	0
Miss Benecke	0	5	0
Rev. and Mrs E. Carpenter	0	10	0
Mrs S.E. Clark	0	5	0
A.G. Crowder, Esq	5	0	0
C.E. Flower, Esq	3	0	0
Miss Forman	1	1	0
Mrs Gillson (Pension, A.)	5	12	0
Mrs Gillson (general purposes)	5	0	0
Rev. T. Hill	0	2	6
Alfred Hill, Esq	10	0	0
Mrs Fredk. Hill	0	10	0
Miss Howitt	1	0	0
C. James, Esq	2	2	0
Mrs Keightly	20	0	0
Mrs Macaulay	0	5	0
Mrs Richd. Martineau	1	0	0
Miss Monro	3	0	0
Mrs Oldham	5	0	0
Mr and Mrs Pooley	1	1	0
Mrs W. Shaen	2	0	0
Miss Amy Smith	0	10	0
Mrs Leslie Stephen	10	0	0
Miss Stephens	0	5	0
F.T.	1	0	0
S. Winkworth, Esq (Pension, A)	13	0	0
Mrs S. Winkworth	20	0	0
Mrs S. Winkworth. Second Donation (work for Mr S.)	5	0	0
Mrs S. Winkworth. Third Donation	10	0	0
Mrs Wright	25	0	0
Miss Mary Wells	1	0	0
Miss Yorke	10	0	0
	£275	6	1

DONATION ACCOUNT, 1881

EXPENDITURE

	£	s	d
Boarding out (Clothes, Schooling and Partial Board for 10 Children)	17	17	9 1/2
W.M. Industrial School	13	0	0
Excursion to the Country and other Entertainments	20	0	0
Care of Playground	10	8	0
Providing Hospital and other relief to the sick	26	11	7
Employment for Poor People, Outfits, &c.	15	0	8
May festival	4	3	7
Mission Woman for Dust Sifters (Lambeth)	15	12	0
Rent, Fuel and Light for Club and Girls' Classes, Barrett's Court and			
Freshwater Place	27	7	1
Kyrle Society (Open Spaces)	30	8	0
Pension, A.	20	0	0
Working Men's College	10	0	0
Furniture for starting Temperance Hall 3	10	0	
Books for Library 0	19	5	
Salary for Assistant	10	0	0
Printing and Postage of Letter to Fellow-workers 4	0	4	
Cash in hand	46	7	7 1/2

£275   6   1

N.B.—The funds entrusted to me come from two very clearly marked classes of donors. The one anxious that their money should be devoted to the direct help of the sick and poor. The other class wishing to strengthen my hands that I may help forward in its difficult stages any great movement. My sister and I recognise this distinction, and in decidng about every grant, carefully consider *whose* money it is that is used, and follow the wish of the donors faithfully.

Examined and found correct, A.P. Fletcher, January 2nd 1882.

LETTER TO MY FELLOW-WORKERS

TO WHICH IS ADDED

ACCOUNT OF DONATIONS RECEIVED

FOR

WORK AMONG THE POOR

DURING 1882

BY

OCTAVIA HILL

(FOR PRIVATE CIRCULATION ONLY)

LONDON:
PRINTED BY WATERLOW AND SONS LIMITED,
GREAT WINCHESTER STREET, E.C.

SUMMARY

Detailed, private work, close to home... housing: Chelsea; Paradise Place; Freshwater Place; Barrett's Court and the building of St Christopher's Hall... donation fund... rooms for labourers rather than mechanics... the need for more fellow-workers.

EDITOR'S NOTE

Although Octavia describes this year as 'one more of private than of public work', she is now back in harness 'after a long unavoidable break', dealing with tenants, taking advice on the trees in Freshwater Place and rejoicing over the creation of St Christopher's Hall in Barrett's Court. She hopes that 'the same citizen spirit which of old led men to make gifts to their city, or to obey its call, burns in me as strongly at least as in earlier days'. The letter begins with an important statement of Octavia's preference for small-scale personal work: 'if one works on a large scale one often works for systems'. Octavia would 'rather work in the unsought-after, out-of-sight places... than in the conspicuous forefront of any great movement'.

14 Nottingham Place, W.

(January 1883)[1]

My friends,

I think some of you may like to know what I have been able to do in the past year, though it has been one more of private than of public work. It has not been, in my estimation, any worse for that. I hope the same citizen spirit which of old led men to make gifts to their city, or to obey its call, burns in me as strongly at least as in earlier days, nor do I feel as if my ear had lost its attentive habit of listening for the call, and the day may come when great undertakings may again occupy my time, but, in an age when a restless activity is abroad, and public action appears to have a strange fascination for many, it often seems to me as if the fulfilment of detailed duty, in and near home, in the very best way possible to me, was far more helpful than the excited response to the eager calls which come pouring in day after day. After a long unavoidable break had occurred in all my public work, I accepted the voice speaking by that break, as telling me I was right in believing that on my return home *my* duty, at any rate, lay in making *sure* of all thoroughness in the work near me, and seeing that it was, as far as I could make it so, very good. On my return therefore, partly from want of strength, but much more, as believing it best, I took up my home duties and those in a few courts which had the nearest claim on me, and, to the utmost extent of my power also, the thorough training of fellow-workers. The old courts were well started, I had little temptation to touch them; the open spaces question, which had seemed unrecognised in past years, and sorely needing attention, I returned to find recognised as important in the minds of hundreds, and to the offers of public work which have reached me since my return I have replied with an invariable and unhesitating 'No'. I *know* there is good and important work to be done on a large scale and in public, but somehow it seems to me as if it were better, in all quietness, to see that the things near at hand were done thoroughly, and as in God's sight, so far as one may. The spirit seems so much

---

1   The auditor signed off the accounts on 30 January 1883, which was unusually late.

more, too, than the form of the work, and if one works on a large scale one often works for systems. Now systems are bad or good, to a great extent, according to the spirit which animates them, and in public work contentions are many, and the spirit of it is often questionable. Moreover, much work in large schemes is necessarily delegated, so that the spirit of the leader is not in direct contact with those for whom the work is set on foot. I would rather work in the unsought-after, out-of-sight places, side by side with my fellow workers, face to face with tenants, than in the conspicuous forefront of any great movement. If a great movement need a forlorn hope let us be proud to lead if we can, but the forlorn hopes in English philanthropic work are fewer now than they were a few years back, thanks to awakened English sympathy and principle, and what seems to me our danger is that we shall many of us rush out to lead, and that near us, in neglected places and hours, weeds shall grow up in our vineyards. Therefore for the present I am quietly weeding my vineyard, side by side with future workers, and hearing the old words I have for years been so fond of, and which I fancy I must have quoted to you before:

Let others miss me! never miss me, God![2]

They always seem to me a sort of warning not to leave the out-of-sight work undone, and when old friends and new leaders write and tell me of any public things they want done, I always seem to hear these words as I put the letters from me, and write my variously worded but uniform 'No'.

What then have I been at with the past twelve whole months given for labour? Many a little thing it wouldn't interest any of you to hear, but of public work, mainly the following.

A friend whose health has failed, built a block of buildings near her own house in Chelsea; she had hoped to be a 'neighbour' to the tenants in the Bible sense of the word, but it wasn't to be. The people and the building were much on her mind, and I bought them,[3] in conjunction

---

2   Spoken by Marian Erle, a character in Elizabeth Barrett Browning's poem 'Aurora Leigh', published in 1856. Marian walks out on her job as a seamstress, which she desperately needs, to nurse a dying friend. Octavia had not used this quotation in earlier letters.

---

3   This block was Hereford Buildings on Church Street, Chelsea, designed by Elijah Hoole for Caroline Stephen, the younger sister of Leslie Stephen and consequently the aunt of Virginia Woolf, who depicted her as 'Aunt Lucy' in *The Voyage Out*. It

with a friend of mine, partly out of love for the builder, and not to let her work and hope fall fruitless, and partly because, pondering on it, I felt that it would be well if houses for the people in that part of London could be entrusted to some kind-hearted lady who would be a 'neighbour' to the tenants, and who could not work in far off east or south London, but might be glad of a little group of friends near her. The old courts were, moreover, most of them well started and independent of me, and therefore, I wanted more space to train new workers, of whom there is great need.

The financial problem about these houses is, however, a difficult one, and to train others, one must know one's tenants and houses well, so I have been, up to now, more or less obliged myself to keep these buildings in my own hands, and I only wish it were to go on, so happy has even my very slight intercourse with the tenants made me. Taking it up again after some years, I am more than ever impressed with the delightfulness of the work, the great power given by the relation to the tenants, and the vista of good work that opens before one in the courts.

At Paradise Place too, I have been in and out, more or less, not nearly enough, not enough to plan several improvements as to appliances, nor to raise the standard of cleanliness, but long enough to try a rather interesting scheme. I found the rents had been raised during my absence—rents in Marylebone have risen everywhere: I was sorry, as we could have made the old rents pay, and I was about to lower them, but I determined instead to return a bonus at the end of the quarter to those who paid every Monday before 1 o'clock without failing once. I am able to return discount thus to each tenant. The plan has worked admirably.

In Freshwater Place, I have been very anxious about my trees, but we have followed the advice of Mr Downs,[4] who planted them for Mr

---

consisted of 28 flats on three floors, grouped around a courtyard. Octavia does not name the friend who assisted her with the purchase, but Hereford Buildings cost £4,000 and must have come into Octavia's sole possession, because she bequeathed it to her niece Blanche Lewes. 'Hereford Buildings was governed by a number of rules: occupants had to hang lace curtains at their windows and look after the geraniums by their front doors. There was a wash-house in the roof and an iron gate which was closed every night. Over the entrance were inscribed the stirring words: "Unto the upright there ariseth light in darkness". In 1879 Caroline Stephen joined the Society of Friends... and went to live in Dorking.' (Darley, 1990, pp.153 and 333.) Hereford Buildings still stands in Old Church Street, Chelsea.

---

4   David Downs was John Ruskin's gardener. He had come from Scotland to work for Ruskin's father in the household at Denmark Hill in South London. When the

Ruskin, and I hope they may do well: we are looking anxiously to see. My friends Mr and Mrs Shaen are in one heart with me, as to all that should be aimed at there, and they have, as their representative there, one who has known and worked with us for years, so though I am little there, these and many other reasons make it seem one of my *special* courts.

In Barrett's Court, however, one of the greatest achievements of our year has been accomplished. One of my friends has rebuilt another large part of the court, making now three quarters of it rebuilt. The new buildings are very satisfactory, and sometimes when I go down there and just think of what the court was in 1865 or 1866,[5] when I

Denmark Hill household was broken up, Downs went to Ruskin's Lake District property Brantwood, where he laid out the garden. He travelled extensively with Ruskin and became involved with many of his projects, such as the road-building at Hinksey. He worked for Ruskin until his death in June 1888.

---

5 Octavia was surprisingly careless about dates, probably because she was writing the letters to fellow-workers under pressure of time. Her career in housing management began in 1865 with Paradise Place, and grew in 1866 with Freshwater Place. Her first contact with Barrett's Court did not occur until the end of 1869 when she heard that a large number of houses were for sale, and she persuaded the Countess of Ducie to buy six of them. (1872, p.1.) The block Octavia is referring to here was the third major re-build, after the replacement of 2-5 in 1873 with Sarsden Buildings and of 15-20 in 1877 with St Christopher's Buildings. The new block, which was known as St Christopher's Buildings South and is now called St Christopher's House, covered the sites of 21-27. The ratebooks show us how Octavia's fellow-workers acquired one property after another until the site could be redeveloped. In 1871 Octavia was paying the rates on 24 and 25, which must have been amongst the first six houses Lady Ducie acquired; in 1872, 22 was added and, in 1874, 23. Between 1880 and 1882, when Octavia was travelling after her breakdown, Lady Ducie was paying the rates on these properties herself, then in 1883 Harriot Yorke appears as the ratepayer for 21-27. However, 21 and 27 must have changed hands in the previous year, as they form part of the new block. Harriot Yorke appears thereafter as the ratepayer on St Christopher's Buildings South, so either she took over the management of Lady Ducie's properties after Octavia's return, or she bought them herself. This is not improbable, as she was a woman of independent means and, as Octavia reveals in the next paragraph, she had built St Christopher's Hall in the new block. As the Hall 'belongs' to Harriot, she must have owned at least some of the properties to be able to construct such a large auditorium. St Christopher's Buildings, North and South, still survive as privately rented serviced appartments, known as Greengarden House and advertised in August 2004 at rents of up to £2,240 a week. No trace of the Hall survives. Sarsden Buildings was left by Lady Ducie to Octavia, and is still used for social housing. The only one of Octavia's properties in Barrett's Court to survive in its original form is number one - now (2004) number one St Christopher's Place and a jeweler's shop.

first drew a map of it, with all the old houses and buildings over the backyards, I can hardly believe that our little band of workers can by gradual steps have wrought so great a change of form and of spirit.

One of our main causes of thankful delight is St Christopher's Hall, which forms part of the last block built; it is a large red brick hall, with platform, separate entrances, and is capable of holding about 500 people. It is just such a room as for 20 years I have dreamed of having, but never thought to have. I believe that in the time to come we shall do much there. It has already made our winter parties much happier and easier. I talk about having it. It isn't really mine in any sense, but belongs to a friend so much one with me that it is to me as if it were in very deed my own.[6]

With Barrett's Court my links are almost as close as in the old days. I am in and out continually, and the friends working there are with me so much that I follow the histories of the tenants, and plan and discuss the improvements and decisions as if I were really collecting there.

But I must not write of the other courts or I shall never have done.

As to the donations, of which an account is attached, no words will tell you what they've done for us. That strong sense that the power is ours to act and support at critical times, nerves and enables us for numerous undertakings of which no record is given. The individual care which we are able to secure for so many of those who need help, constitutes a reforming power of singular force. It seems often as if applicants for money help obtained in addition strong and faithful friends and sympathisers for life, and were transported into an atmosphere of love and holiness in which evil died. I mustn't tell the

6   This is the first reference in the letters to Harriot Yorke, who became Octavia's companion for her travels abroad in 1877, and retained the role for the rest of Octavia's life. She moved into the Hill household in 1884, and in the same year she paid for Larksfield, the house designed by Elijah Hoole for Octavia and herself in Crockham Hill, Kent. Harriot was the eldest daughter of Rev. Isaac Yorke, vicar of Shenfield in Essex. She was independently wealthy and supported Octavia's work both practically and financially. Harriot was honorary treasurer of the National Trust from 1896 until 1925, and she remained on its executive committee until her death in 1930. She kept a tight control of finances, and threatened to resign in 1898 if the Trust acquired more house property. Although she did not carry out her threat, it is inconceivable that the Trust's programme of acquiring stately homes, begun in the 1930s, could have occurred during Harriot's lifetime. Harriot possessed considerable organisational abilities, including the tact that Octavia notoriously lacked. She was known as the 'keeper' to Octavia's 'lion', and Octavia's biographer Gillian Darley credits her for 'thirty-five years of [Octavia's] almost unbroken good health'. (Darley, 1990, p.335.)

details of this work, but the impression of it is increasingly strong on me, and if any of you ever have occasion to appeal for aid for your protegées, instead of so generously helping us to help those unknown to you, something of its blessing will be clear to you.

In connection with the donation fund, I should mention a special donation sent for the benefit of little children's health. It has been very valuable in several ways; with part of it two children have been sent into a little home near Flitwick where there are some mineral waters that seem to be particularly beneficial to London children. The home has a garden and field attached to it, and is superintended by a very kind matron, herself an excellent nurse. My sister writes to me: 'The two children I have sent there have been perfectly cured. One, a boy who had suffered for a long time with a bad throat and general debility, the other, a child of two-and-a-half years who had always been ailing, could not stand and all its teeth decayed as they came. It now, after eight weeks, begins to run about, is *quite* well and no more of its teeth have decayed.'

It is very satisfactory to see in how many cases the help given is radically helpful, starting something which hereafter lives of itself. Mrs Maurice writes: 'I paid the first quarter for H.P. at the school, that his mother, a widow with several children, might get a start with the payments which have to be made in advance: *she has kept up the payments herself since then.*' And again: 'The machine supplied to the wife of that blind man at Hoxton has raised the family out of want. She is now getting plenty of work.' These are only two instances; but this note of self-supporting success runs through the whole of this branch of the work to a delightful and surprising extent.

The £2 mentioned as contributed towards the purchase of a harmonium, is for a service got up by the people themselves in one of the courts first purchased. The superintendent lends her own room for it, and she and her husband suggested the plan themselves, invited all the people who went nowhere else to worship, made the room pretty and comfortable, got their own daughter to play the hymns, and organised a simple short service every Sunday evening. Many come in who are shy of going elsewhere, many who have been in no place of worship since they left the country in their youth. The superintendent and her husband went freely to live in the court nine years ago to help; since then much has been done to make the place cleaner, healthier, more respectable, flowers and creepers have been introduced, and many have taken and kept the pledge, numbers of social gatherings have been held; at last they felt that the time had come when they might ask

1. Octavia Hill, photographed at some time in the first decade of the twentieth century.

Reproduced by permission of the City of Westminster Archives Centre, D Misc 84/2.

2. Red Cross cottages and garden, Southwark, 1894.

'Looking out upon the public garden in Red Cross Street, Southwark, six four-roomed cottages have been built on land belonging to the Ecclesiastical Commissioners at a cost of £220 each. The fronts are in red brick partly rough-cast and tile-hung, and a bay window has been introduced in the first floor. They adjoin Red Cross Hall, which has been decorated by Walter Crane, and though among the lofty Southwark warehouses, are most pleasantly situated. Each cottage has its own yard with detached wash-house etc in rear. In White Cross Street, which is parallel to Red Cross Street, six more four-roomed cottages of somewhat larger dimensions have been placed. The tenants greatly prefer these cottages to the sets of rooms in the blocks adjoining. Each cottage is self-contained, and has its own yard with washing and sanitary appliances. The cost of the White Cross cottages was £200 each.'

Text and photograph from: 'The Dwellings of the Poor: Report of the Mansion House Council for the year ending December 31st, 1894', London: Cassell. Reproduced by permission of the British Library.

3. Good Shepherd mosaic, Red Cross garden, Southwark.

'A present from Venice, a mosaic of lovely colours, has been sent to me, and it is to light with its brilliant beauty a space on our garden wall at Southwark…The Shepherd lays His hand quietly on the head of the lambs which feed around Him, and the words are those which tell of His love. Into that love may we enter; then neither life nor death can separate us from Him, nor storm nor change can shake our perfect peace.'

LETTER TO MY FELLOW-WORKERS, 1887

Photograph from the 'Red Cross Hall and Garden Report, 1906'. Reproduced by permission of the Church Commissioners.

4. Red Cross cottages, Southwark, 2003.

5. Mosaic of the Sower, Red Cross garden, Southwark.

This mosaic roundel, by James Powell after a sketch by Lady Waterford, has been re-sited, and is the only one of the garden features and ornaments described by Octavia to survive. It was the gift of Miss Minet, who also donated a sundial inscribed with the legend: 'As hour follows hour, God's mercies on us shower'.

> 'The panel… has been executed at Messrs Powell's by the same workmen who did the mosaic at St Paul's.'
>
> LETTER TO MY FELLOW-WORKERS, 1896

6. Study for the Alice Ayres panel in the Red Cross Hall, Southwark, by Walter Crane, c.1889 (*opposite*).

Reproduced by permission of the Royal Borough of Kensington and Chelsea Libraries and Arts Service.

7. Alice Ayres panel, Red Cross Hall, Southwark

'The first of the series of panels illustrative of heroic deeds which Mr Walter Crane has so generously designed, has been this winter completed, and now forms part of the wall of the Hall. It is that of Alice Ayres, the young servant who saved two children from fire at the cost of her own life. The incident took place in Southwark within a stone's throw of the Hall, and many of those who frequent it saw the fire and remember Alice Ayres. The interest shewn in the beautiful painting has been deepened by this personal memory.'

LETTER TO MY FELLOW-WORKERS, 1890

This photograph of the panel, from the 'Red Cross Hall and Garden Report, 1906', shows how the design changed after Walter Crane's sketch, reproduced opposite, particularly in respect of the pose and draperies of Alice Ayres herself.

Photograph reproduced by permission of the Church Commissioners.

8. Railway navvies panel, Red Cross Hall, Southwark.

'The panel is most beautiful, the whole story being told wonderfully in the navvies' faces and action, and the steady advance of the fatal train along the curved line of rails giving a feeling of what is coming. We do very earnestly thank Mr Crane for the great gift he has made to us. There must be some who feel the teaching which lies in the memory of deeds like this, and the help which beautiful and powerful art offers in districts like Southwark.'

LETTER TO MY FELLOW-WORKERS, 1892

Photograph reproduced from the 'Red Cross Hall and Garden Report, 1906' by permission of the Church Commissioners.

9. Letter from Octavia Hill to Sydney Cockerell, 10 September 1887.

This letter about the arrangements for partitioning off the club room in the Red Cross Hall give some idea of the detailed and time-consuming work in which Octavia involved her fellow-workers. She wants Sydney Cockerell to discuss with the builder, Mr Goulding, three possible ways of dealing with the pitched roof-space of the building to allow a private space to be created for the club, which can at other times be thrown in with the main hall.

Reproduced by permission of the City of Westminster Archives Centre, D Misc 84/2.

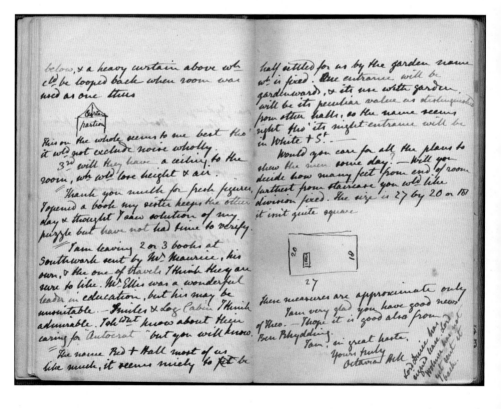

14 Not. Pl. W
Sep. 10th /87

Dear Sydney,

I saw Mr Hoole about the plans yesterday & came to satisfactory arrangements about everything except the divisions of the club room. — The room you will remember has no ceiling but is open to the roof. Mr H does not see his way to a moveable partition closing this arched portion of the room in any easy way.

Will you consult your men, & if he is easily get-at-able Mr Goulding & ask them, under the circumstances what they wd choose about it.

1st will they have the upper portion permanently divided, & a moveable partition below. Thus

That wd look ugly when room is used in one whole.

2nd will they have moveable partition below, & a heavy curtain above wh cld be looped back when room was used as one thus

This on the whole seems to me best tho' it wd not exclude noise wholly.

3rd will they have a ceiling to the room, wh wd lose height & air.

Thank you much for fresh figures. I opened a book my sister keeps the other day & thought I saw solution of my puzzle but have not had time to verify.

I am leaving 2 or 3 books at Southwark sent by Mr Maurice, his own, & the one of travels I think they are sure to like. Mr Ellis was a wonderful leader in education, but his may be unsuitable. — Smiles & Log Cabin I think admirable. I don't know about their caring for "Autocrat" but you will know.

The name Red + Hall most of us like much, it seems nicely to fit be half settled for us by the garden name wh is fixed. The entrance will be gardenward, & its use with garden will be its peculiar value as distinguished from other halls, so the name seems right tho' its night entrance will be in White + St. —

Would you care for all the plans to shew the men some day? — Will you decide how many feet from end of room furthest from staircase you wd like division fixed. The size is 27 by 20 or is it not quite square

27

These measures are approximate only.

I am very glad you have good news of Theo. — I hope it is good also from Ben Rhydding.

I am, in great haste,
Yours truly
Octavia Hill

10. Red Cross Hall, Southwark, interior.

This rather magnificent representation of Elijah Hoole's Hall, which makes it look much larger than it really was, shows the positioning of the Alice Ayres panel on the left. The image was conjectural, because this illustration appeared in *The Builder* on 9 November 1889, but the panel was not put into place until the following year. It was taken from Walter Crane's sketch, which was exhibited in 1889, and shows Alice sitting on the window sill rather than standing, as she did in the finished panel. The official unveiling took place in December 1890.

SKETCHES FROM THE HOME ARTS AND INDUSTRIES EXHIBITION

FROM NEWTON

FROM COMPTON

FROM CHISWICK

FROM ICKLEFORD

FROM RED CROSS

11. Red Cross Home Arts branch.

'The girls' club, boys' club, and men's club have continued their work throughout the year. Attached to the latter is a very successful carving class. I believe the men have been deeply interested in their work, and have furnished good exhibits for the Home Arts Exhibition; indeed they have quite distinguished themselves there.'

LETTER TO MY FELLOW-WORKERS, 1889

The bellows, decorated with an owl, were entered by the Red Cross Hall branch of the Home Arts and Industries Association in the annual exhibition for 1901.

Reproduced from 'The House: its furnishing, decoration, social functions, sanitation, amateur work, cuisine and general comfort', vol. IX, 1901, p.171.

their neighbours to meet them on yet higher, deeper, better ground—those of them at least who felt they could—and the services were accordingly begun. They felt it a very solemn responsibility for they feel the meaning of their faith and its reality will be tested by life and deed, but trusting in God's grace and helping power they are not afraid, but feel that all of us can ask for power to make our prayers real by our effort to walk rightly, and our daily work good, by the memory of our daily prayer. They know that when our lives have done their utmost, though they fail, God takes up the teaching of those we love, and carries it farther than we had ever dreamed. It has been a pleasure to me that, especially as I am so seldom with them, this little contribution from the fund should speak to them of my deep sympathy and my confidence that they are right.

Some of the large sum anonymously contributed last year is still, I am thankful to say, in hand. I have been able with it to do some most valuable things, especially with regard to some open spaces, of which two are in exceptionally poor neighbourhoods, and are now frequented by numbers of the very poor.

I usually find, in writing this letter, that there is some important new work opening out, with which I may, or may not, be myself connected, but to which I am anxious to draw the attention of my friends, that they may watch it, and see whether they care to help it forward. This year I feel this specially strongly with regard to a scheme just being undertaken by a few gentlemen. They have it in contemplation to apply for one of the sites cleared under the Artisans' Dwellings Act, and to build on it expressly for labourers, in contradistinction to mechanics. The fact that the unskilled labourers displaced by the Act are not accommodated in the rebuilt houses is patent to all.[7] These gentlemen

---

7   It was always Octavia's proud boast that, while other housing societies concentrated on the meeting the needs of the artisans, or respectable working poor, she dealt with those lower down the social scale. In order to accommodate them 'on a thoroughly sound commercial principle' and show a five per cent return on the capital invested, it was necessary to be extremely careful about the amenities provided. To keep the rents affordable might mean not taking the water supply to each floor, and certainly not to each household, and having communal laundries. In her 1874 article 'Why the Artisans' Dwellings Bill Was Wanted', she had warned against the tendency of housing reformers to tear down slums and replace them with model dwelling in which the amenities put the rents beyond the reach of the slum-dwellers who had been displaced. 'It is far better to prove that you can provide a tolerable tenement which will pay, than a perfect one which will not. The one plan will be adopted, and will lead to great results; the other will remain an isolated and unfruitful experiment, a warning to all who cannot or will not lose money.' Octavia failed to foresee the other possibility: that

have determined, I understand, to meet the difficulty of replacing the poorer people by adopting a simpler plan of building. I hope they will secure that their arrangements for water and drainage shall be much simpler than they are in the buildings, which, by the help of companies, have done so much to meet the need of mechanics' dwellings. In building for labourers the arrangements should be less expensive, though equally healthy: this they can easily be, and I hear that the very simple plan, which has been used in much smaller blocks, for securing separate access to each room will probably be adopted, so that the rooms will be separable, and a man need not immediately, whatever the size of his family, or their ages, hire a suite of rooms.

If the promoters of this scheme keep these two points in view, and plan well as to the all important question of management, and take advice in all their building arrangements of those who have watched the small points on which depend the comfort of a room to a working man's family, and consider the value of every atom of expenditure to the minutest point of detail, so as to keep down their rents, this undertaking of theirs appears to me as if it might almost be the most important in its effect on the life of the poor of London of any I am now watching. A great deal of capital will be required, as the sites are large, and the need of cheaper houses great, but I hope it will be forthcoming. The scheme is intended to be remunerative, and to show that well-planned homes for unskilled labourers *can* be made to pay. Houses which will be light, clean, airy, well drained, well supplied with water, though cheaper, because not providing so many appliances as those built specially for mechanics, and not necessitating the hire of three or four rooms. I shall be very glad when the time comes to hear from any of you who may feel inclined to consider the advisability of taking shares, and to give you any advice I can on the point, or information as to my opinion of the prospect the scheme has of being successful and beneficial.

Before ending this letter, I must return to an old subject again. I have spoken often, but must speak again, of the need of workers. In the houses, we are wanting trained workers sadly. The work grows, and the workers, though they are increasing, do not keep pace with it. The need is, it is true, greatest of those who can take the lead among the tenants, bear responsibility, think and judge wisely, and devote regular

---

as the accepted minimum standard for working-class accommodation rose, the objection that the cost of the 'appliances' could not be met from the rent would be countered by a demand for large-scale public subsidy of housing.

time. But these leaders grow out of the ranks of the helpers, so we want people to come forward to be trained. None are of use who have not set their minds to working for the real good of the poor, not to please them—still less to please themselves—but to be helpful. Women ready to be serviceable, courteous, patient, observant, firm and punctual— women, who looking round upon their group of tenants, feel to them as a little group of friends to whom they have duties, and who have duties to them, a sort of enlarged household to be made, as they would make their own at home, orderly, happy, self-respecting, helpful and good, and who will look at the houses, as at their own, where all should be in order, and well kept up. And I would ask those already training, to keep this idea before them, to think with all their might for, and of, the tenants and the houses, to imagine what, if I were not there, they would try to make of both, so the sooner will they be fit queens in the domain where we have set them now as hand-maidens, so will the work in their hands be able to be extended to some of the many courts to take which I receive such heart-stirring appeals, so shall they leave me free to train those who should be following them. So finally shall they need me, and such as I, no more.

OCTAVIA HILL

DONATION ACCOUNT, 1882

RECEIPTS

	£	s	d
Cash in hand	46	7	7 ½
Anon.	500	2	0
Miss Astley	5	0	0
Miss Maud Berry	0	10	0
Shareholders of Central London Dwellings Co.	3	2	0
Mrs Bond	10	0	0
Miss Meta Bradley	0	5	0
J. Cropper, Esq, M.P.	1	0	0
A.G. Crowder, Esq	5	5	0
Rev. Estlin and Mrs Carpenter	5	0	0
Chas. Flower, Esq	2	2	0
Miss Forman	1	1	0
W.H. Hall, Esq	1	0	0
Rev. T. Hill	0	2	6
Mrs Macaulay	1	0	0
Mrs C. Mitchell	1	1	0
F. Nettlefold, Esq	20	0	0
Mrs Oldham	5	0	0
Miss Constance Oldham	4	0	0
Miss Pipe	1	1	0
Mr and Mrs Pooley	1	1	0
Mrs Sargant	0	2	6
Mrs Wm. Shaen	2	0	0
Mrs Leslie Stephen	10	10	0
Miss Stephen	0	5	0
Mrs Wright	25	0	0
Hornsby Wright, Esq	3	0	0
Stephen Winkworth, Esq	13	0	0
Miss Yorke	10	0	0
	£677	17	7 ½

DONATION ACCOUNT, 1882

EXPENDITURE

	£	s	d
Open Spaces*	280	0	0
Recreation Ground & Gymnasium, Lambeth*	46	0	0
Temperance Hall and Coffee Room*	55	0	0
Pension A.*	20	0	0
Pension G.	5	0	0
Providing Hospital and other relief to the Sick	22	13	9
Boarding out (Clothes, Schooling, and partial Board for 14 children)	21	7	8
Industrial Schools, W.M., G.S., H.P.	19	7	11
Employment for Poor People, Outfits, &c.	12	7	5 1/2
Care of Playground	10	8	0
Mission Woman to dust sifters (Lambeth)	15	12	0
Salary for Assistant*	10	0	0
Rent, &c., Classes	6	10	0
Excursions to the country and other Entertainments	2	0	7
Creepers for poor people's gardens	1	8	0
Harmonium	2	0	0
Protestant Mission Abroad*	1	1	0
Printing, and Postage of Letters to Fellow-Workers	3	10	11
Cash in Hand	143	10	4

£677   17   7 1/2

* Special donations.

N.B.—The funds entrusted to me come from two very clearly marked classes of donors. The one anxious that their money should be devoted to the direct help of the sick and poor; the other class wishing to strengthen my hands that I may help forward in its difficult stages any great movement. My sister and I recognise this distinction, and in deciding about every grant, carefully consider *whose* money it is that is used, and follow the known wish of the donors faithfully.

Examined and found correct, A.P. Fletcher, January 30th 1883.

LETTER TO MY FELLOW-WORKERS

TO WHICH ARE ADDED

ACCOUNTS OF DONATIONS RECEIVED

FOR

WORK AMONG THE POOR

DURING 1883

BY

OCTAVIA HILL

(FOR PRIVATE CIRCULATION ONLY)

LONDON

PRINTED BY WATERLOW AND SONS LIMITED,

GREAT WINCHESTER STREET, E.C.

SUMMARY

The Kyrle Society, the Commons Preservation Society and open spaces: Mile End, St George's Gardens, Bethnal Green... the need to protect burial grounds... inscription on St John's, Waterloo... preference for old houses in poor areas... Octavia's aim to connect landlords with their tenants.

EDITOR'S NOTE

After a short discussion of open spaces work (including a rebuke to the wealthy for their meanness), and the attempt to set an inscription on St John's church, Waterloo, Octavia devotes the rest of this short letter to housing. (The donation fund receives only the most perfunctory mention at the end.) It contains one of the most important statements of the principles on which she operated: the refusal to form a company because she believed in connecting one landlord with a particular set of tenants; the belief that women make the best housing managers; the underlying principle of connecting 'individuals possessed of education, conscience and means with particular courts in London'; the importance of helping the disreputable members of the poor rather than concentrating on the respectable ones; the conviction that this could only be achieved by face-to-face contact and not by grand schemes; the preference for taking over old buildings rather than putting up new ones, since the tenants, including 'the less hopeful tenants', would then challenge the housing manager to work with them with a view to raising both tenants and property to a higher level; the use of improvements in the property as a reward for good behaviour by the tenants; and the opposition to subsidy—'I am firmly convinced that the people should pay for their houses'. The reference to Christ's parable of the Good Shepherd (p.176) shows the high ideals that lay behind Octavia's practical work.

14 Nottingham Place, W.

My friends,

Those of you who have been in the habit of receiving this letter, will realise that it is nothing but a little summary of account of donations received, and of thanks to the kind donors, which gives an opportunity for my saying more quickly and better than I could easily write it, anything that concerns our own little body of fellow-workers, or any remark, or news, as to public questions which may interest you.

In the first place, I am desirous to bring before you a few facts respecting open spaces. My work regarding them has been done mainly as a member of the Kyrle Society, so that I am obliged here to treat of some of the same subjects which are to be found in the Kyrle Report.

The Kyrle Society has this year been able to carry to a satisfactory conclusion the negotiations for handing over to the vestries three gardens in poor districts. It has arranged plans and secured money for laying them out. One of these gardens is in Spicer Street, Mile End, one near Gray's Inn Road,[1] and one in Bethnal Green.[2] The donations

---

1   This was the old burial ground at the rear of the Foundling Hospital, just off Gray's Inn Road. Two churches, St George's, Hanover Square and St George the Martyr in Bloomsbury, had their burial grounds side by side on the site. The grounds had closed to burials in 1855 and both parishes agreed to grant a long lease on the grounds on condition that the St Pancras vestry would maintain them as a public garden. The Kyrle Society was, however, obliged to confine its attentions to the burial ground of St George's, Hanover Square since there was, in the other section, a temporary structure, erected by permission of the rector, which was the only private dissecting room in London. According to *The Times* (2 July 1884): 'it yields a rent of some £20 a year, and affords an income to the gentleman who there gathers around him a class of medical students. This strange source of profit proved an insuperable obstacle to the reclamation of the graveyard of St George the Martyr'. The graveyard of St George's, Hanover Square was formally opened as a garden, still under the management of the Kyrle Society, by its president Princess Louise, Marchioness of Lorne, on 1 July 1884. Some way of surmounting the 'insuperable obstacle' of the dissecting room must have been found, because, on 12 August 1889, the graveyard of St George the Martyr was finally declared open as an addition to the garden. However, it was not until over a year later that 'the vestry of St Pancras have expressed themselves satisfied with the work done, and have definitely taken over the ground and relieved

for these gardens, amounting in all to about £600, were mainly received by me, but as they came to me as treasurer of the Kyrle Society in answer to letters in the papers, an account of them does not appear here, but in the report of that Society. I refer to them here, because many of them came from old friends, and fellow-workers, and with kind letters; also, because much of our strength this year has been thrown into the provision of open spaces. The increasing appreciation of the value of open spaces is most satisfactory, but much has still to be done now public interest in the matter is aroused. Not only ought all our metropolitan burial grounds that are closed to be preserved as gardens for the people, and some general law passed which should prevent their being built over, but larger hope, and greater liberality and sense of citizen duty should surely, before long, provide for securing larger areas, in suburban districts within easy reach of the poor of London. The hills, especially, that are still unbuilt over, in the near neighbourhood of town, are of paramount importance. The view, the air, the pleasure of going up and down, all render hilly parks, or recreation grounds, of peculiar value. Yet we have not an inch of ground saved for the public at Highgate; and Traitor's Hill (from which the view extends as far as to the Crystal Palace,[3] and where there is always a breeze), looks doomed

---

the [Kyrle] Society from further responsibility. The two burial grounds form together a charming garden of nearly three acres'. (Kyrle Society report 1890, p.20.) By this stage the involvement of the Kyrle Society had lasted for seven years, during which it had assumed financial and organisational responsibility for a complicated and unspectacular project. It provides a good example of the level of commitment of Kyrle Society members to providing small open spaces in the heart of London. The site is now known as St George's Gardens.

---

2   A tiny garden, one-quarter of an acre in extent, was planted by the Kyrle Society at St Peter's, Bethnal Green and opened on 15 July 1884 by the Bishop of Bedford who 'expressed his gratification at the amount of pleasure which the [Kyrle] society had been able to afford to the poor in varius parts of the metropolis, by laying out and opening for their use churchyards and disused burial grounds... The Rev. C.E. Roberts presented the keys of the grounds to the bishop, who thereupon, amid the cheers of the assembly, unlocked the gates and opened the churchyard, which was at once entered by the children and others who had been waiting during the speeches.' (*The Times*, 16 July 1884.) The church stands on a square site surrounded by roads. The garden still has a formal layout with shrubs, but the part behind the church has been asphalted and is used as a car park.

---

3   The Crystal Palace, designed by Joseph Paxton and built to house the Great Exhibition of 1851, had been dismantled at the end of the Exhibition in Hyde Park in October 1851 and re-erected, on a much larger scale, as a commercial attraction in

to be covered with buildings; this is the more to be regretted, as it is accessible to all the poor and increasingly crowded district of Kentish Town, and enables all North Londoners to reach the Heath through fields, instead of by weary streets.[4] An effort on the part of some small shopkeepers at New Cross, to save a hill near there which belongs to the Haberdashers' Company, does not seem likely to succeed.[5] In fact,

Sydenham, South East London. It was never a financial success and in 1911 the company was declared bankrupt and the building and site put up for auction via Knight, Frank and Rutley on 28 November. The land was by now extremely attractive for house-building, but Lord Plymouth intervened to save it as an open space. He bought it for £230,000, and, according to the Kyrle Society, 'will hold his purchase for a limited time in order to give the public and local authorities an opportunity of acquiring it. The chief stumbling block seems to be the question of future upkeep and management. This is a serious difficulty, but one capable of being surmounted, and the committee would view with deep concern the handing over of grounds of 200 acres in extent to the builder and the failure of Lord Plymouth's generous action.' (Kyrle Society report, 1911, p.9.) Fortunately it did not come to this: the Lord Mayor of London set up a fund to relieve him of financial responsibility and, in 1913, the whole site was purchased for the nation and vested in the London County Council, later to become the Greater London Council. In 1986, upon the dissolution of the GLC, it passed to the London Borough of Bromley, which still maintains it as an open space. In 1936, to the relief of all concerned with its management, the Crystal Palace itself was burnt to the ground in one of the most spectacular conflagrations to be seen in the capital since 1666.

4   'I am glad to hear that a movement is just set on foot to endeavour to save this ground if possible' [*Octavia Hill's note*]. Traitor's Hill is now known (and was known in Octavia's time) as Parliament Hill. It was not 'doomed to be covered with buildings'— see letters for 1884/5, 1887 and (triumphantly) 1889, when it was handed over to the London County Council.

5   As usual, Octavia takes the most pessimistic view. Telegraph Hill Park, which belonged to the Haberdashers' Company, was saved as an open space for the public in 1895 thanks to a generous donation by Sir George Livesey. The *Lewisham Gazette* of 22 May 1895 commented that 'in no way could Mr Livesey have more fitfully or gracefully disposed of the money given him as a testimonial for his action during the great gas strike'. In 1889, as manager of the South Metropolitan Gas Company, George Livesey had broken a strike by workers who opposed his plan for a profit-sharing scheme. Despite the formation of a Gas Workers and General Union, led by Will Thorne in East London, Livesey managed to maintain the gas supply throughout the strike. J.J. Sexby designed the layout of the new park. The bandstand has gone but the ornamental pond with weeping willows is still there. The site is in two parts on either side of Kitto Road. In Napoleonic times a semaphore station, consisting of wooden shutters, was erected on Plow Garlic Hill, as it was then known. News of the victory at the Battle of Waterloo was relayed to Westminster from here in 1815, and the hill has been known as Telegraph Hill ever since. The view from the top of the site looking

it is strange to notice that, though other towns have had parks given to them, the thousands of rich people who owe their wealth to London, or who avail themselves of its advantages, have not, so far as I know, given one single acre of ground, that could have been sold for building use, to Londoners, for recreation ground, or park, if we except Leicester Square.[6]

The revelations made in the report of the Medical Officer of Health for Bethnal Green, as to the prospect of dwellings for working people being erected on the Peel Grove burial ground, which is a mass of graves, and the uncertainty as to whether the law can stop their erection, will surely lead Parliament, next session, to introduce some clause into the Buildings Acts forbidding the use of burial grounds as building sites. The Commons Preservation Society will, I believe, take action in the matter, and all public support ought to be given to them. How necessary some such general law is, and how difficult it is to defeat separate schemes, may be seen from the history of the bill by which the London and North Western Railway Co. proposed to take the burial

---

westwards towards Westminster, and towards the Isle of Dogs to the north, is still spectacular, but has changed almost beyond recognition in the last hundred years. In 2003 the Heritage Lottery Fund granted £1.1 million for the restoration of the park and new railings.

---

6 Leicester Square dates from 1635 when the first houses were built there by Robert Sydney, Earl of Leicester. Leicester House, on the north side, was for some time a royal residence, home to George II when Prince of Wales. The Square has always attracted an artistic and bohemian community, including Sir Joshuah Reynolds and William Hogarth. The patch of land in the middle, known as Leicester Fields, was for many years a favourite site for duels, then became so overgrown and neglected that it was not much better than a rubbish dump. It was bought, landscaped and presented to the nation by Albert 'Baron' Grant MP, for £50,000 in 1873. He paid for the replica of William Kent's Westminster Abbey statue of Shakespeare which stands in the middle of the Square, carrying on its base an inscription recording his own generosity. Grant, whose real name was Albert Gottheimer, was a fraudster who was credited with being the first to discover how easy it was to milk gullible investors for non-existent schemes, whilst sheltering behind the new legislation for setting up limited liability companies. He floated companies to a total market value of £24 million, of which £20 million was lost by the subscribers. He is widely regarded as the original for the appalling Augustus Melmotte in Trollope's *The Way We Live Now* (1875), and was perhaps an unfortunate example of civic responsibility for Octavia to use. When presenting Leicester Square to the people he was asked if he included the sub-soil rights in his gift and replied magnanimously 'Yes, yes, I give it all'. After his exposure as a fraud he realised that, thanks to the building of the London underground system, the sub-soil rights had become extremely valuable and he sought compensation, but without success. He died penniless in Bognor in 1899.

ground of St James's, near Tottenham Court Road. The graves would have been disturbed in order to build, on part of the ground, stables for omnibus horses, and an open space would have been lost, which was situated in a populous neighbourhood, and which was overlooked by a row of poor houses, a hospital, and a factory; yet the bill passed the House of Commons and the second reading in the Lords, and was only saved by the spirited action of the St Pancras vestry, which opposed the bill at every stage, and was finally victorious before a committee of the House of Lords.

The Commons Preservation Society intends this year to take up the preservation of public rights in connection with the Thames, examining and vindicating rights to walk along the towing paths, to row on the backwaters, &c. They will need funds and public support, which it is hoped may be forthcoming for this new and important branch of the work.

The importance of the smaller central open spaces, as an adjunct to the houses of the poor, appears to me not generally recognised. House-room is so costly in London, that, at best, the poor can have but limited accommodation indoors; and open spaces, such as churchyards, or board-school playgrounds form nurseries, play rooms, gymnasia, outdoor sitting rooms, and often, for the men, dining rooms, when they are working far from home. All the funds in the hands of the Kyrle Society which are available for these gardens are now appropriated, and they expect, almost at once, to be asked to lay out a disused burial ground in Bermondsey. The laying out is costly, as the local vestries which take over, maintain, and manage these gardens, will not do so unless they are well-drained, and unless strong, permanent, wide paths are provided.

I feel, myself, very strongly, the importance of rendering such gardens very beautiful, and had hoped to have received contributions to have paid for carrying out a scheme for placing an inscription in a Lambeth garden. The design was most kindly drawn and given to the Kyrle Society by Mr Statham.[7] It was planned to be executed in permanent colour, that is, in glass mosaic. The words were George Herbert's:

---

7   Henry Heathcote Statham (1839–1924), editor of *The Builder* for 25 years, was an architect who exhibited architectural views and designs at the Royal Academy from c.1872–1904, including 'West Front, Tewkesbury Abbey' and 'St Paul's Cathedral'. He was largely resident in Liverpool and was involved in the first annual meeting of the National Association for the Advancement of Art held in Liverpool in 1888. The president of the Association was none other than Sir Frederick Leighton. H.H. Statham

All may have, if they dare try, a glorious life or grave.[8]

I liked to think of the words being there, they were to run the whole length of the blank outside wall of the church, which bounds the garden. I believed the words might go home to many a man as he hurries along the crowded thoroughfare near, if he caught sight of them between the trees, their colour attracting his notice, perhaps, first, in its contrast with the dreary dinginess all round. I liked to think some busy man might renounce a profitable bargain, or might even dream, for a minute or two, of renouncing it, for the sake of some good deed. Or I have sometimes liked to fancy a working man, from among the men who sit in that public garden, might be reminded, as he read the words, that though his life was out of men's sight and seemed occupied with little things, seemed perhaps somewhat broken and wasted, there was the possibility of nobleness in it, if bravely and unselfishly carried on. But to whatever heart it might or might not go, the words seemed fit to be spoken to each one of the multitude, hurrying in and out, or pausing there, and worthy to be set , with some care, in lovely colour, to last for years. However, I got little answer to my appeal, and it seems that few care to help about it.[9]

To come now to the question of the houses. I need touch on nothing here except the personal work. We have a larger number of workers in

---

sat on the central committee, alongside Eustace Balfour, Edmund Gosse, George Howard (Earl of Carlisle), Rev. Loftie and T. Humphrey Ward. In 1889 the National Association met in Edinburgh, with the section for architecture headed by R. Rowan Anderson as president and Statham as honorary secretary.

---

8   From stanza 15 of 'The Church Porch' by George Herbert, a series of poems in *The Temple*, 1633. These words may not have been Octavia's first choice for the wall. Moberly Bell records that she 'suggested that Kingsley's words "Do noble deeds" should be put up on a wall near Waterloo Station'. (Moberly Bell, 1942, p.152.) Octavia may have switched from Kingsley to Herbert in order to have enough words to run the whole length of the wall.

---

9   'May I here express, as I have no other way of thanking the kind donor, my great delight, on returning home a few days after that letter was circulated, to find on my table £30 in notes, accompanied by a few words from an anonymous friend to say that the gift was for this inscription? This donation so nearly completed the amount required that the mosaic is now being executed.' ('Colour, Space and Music for the People', Octavia Hill, *The Nineteenth Century*, 15 May 1884.) The inscription was set into the side-wall of St John's Church, Waterloo, overlooking the former burial ground which had been laid out as a garden in 1877 (1877, p.90). It is still there. *See ill. 16.*

training for management of houses than I have had for some years. Some of them shew promise of being soon capable of taking the lead in more responsible positions than they now occupy.[10] I am consequently ready with their kind and increasing help, to take over two, or possibly three, more poor courts or blocks of buildings to manage for any owners caring for the people, who may wish to place them under my charge. I should prefer to take old houses, and should like them to be in a decidedly poor neighbourhood. I am sure old houses form much the best training ground for workers among the poor, besides which in them, inevitably, one can meet and help a lower class of people than in any new buildings, however cheaply they may be let. If a court is taken over full of its old inhabitants, there are some among them who have the opportunity of being raised in and with it, who never could have such an opportunity in any new buildings. In letting to new tenants one must ask for good references; the drunkard, the dirty thriftless woman, is rarely accepted, cannot be accepted; the poor may indeed be received, but not those whose character is doubtful: the preference is fairly and rightly given to the sober, industrious and clean. But buy up, or take over, a court full of the less hopeful tenants, and it becomes your duty to try them; some of them always respond to the better influences, and are permanently raised. In old houses, moreover, unsatisfactory tenants can be tested much more easily, there is no risk of their destroying expensive appliances, they can be encouraged by the gradual improvement in proportion to their own care of the places they are in. In new houses nothing is to be gained by tenants by their care, for nothing is to be added, while much may be lost by their carelessness. In old houses the reverse is the case, the fresh distemper, the mended grate, the new cupboard, can be offered as a reward for care, while one or two more banisters broken or burnt are not a very serious loss to the landlord. Now though all classes of the poor want help of one kind or another, and the encouragement of the striving is perhaps *more* lost sight of just now than reform of the thriftless, yet the former is work which many are fitted to carry on; the latter must be done, if it is to be done at all, by some such agency as our own. Ladies must do it, for it is detailed work; ladies must do it, for it is household work; it needs, moreover, persistent patience, gentleness, hope. There

---

10 Octavia was probably thinking of Elisabeth Haldane (1862–1933), a member of a family of distinguished Scottish intellectuals, who started work with Octavia at the age of 20, and who, with Patrick Geddes, set up the Edinburgh Social Union in 1885 (1902, p.489, n.18).

is great need that someone should build quite simply for the very poor; it requires special experience to plan and manage such houses, still I do not purpose in the opening year to enter upon this work. The more personal one, I am satisfied, is even more pressing, it cannot be done except by some such group of workers as our own. The need of it is not clearly before the public yet; in all the late stir the cry has been as to the dreadfulness of the houses and the landlords. If all that is true under this head were remedied tomorrow, the public would see—clear sighted workers face to face with the poor *do* see—that a large class would remain, which could not, without education, be drafted into better houses. With that class we, if anyone, must deal, and I would earnestly ask those who are working with me not to lose sight of that fact, not to be led away by tempting plans for rebuilding, but to remember that singly the people must be dealt with, that face to face only can their education be carried on, that it will take years to accomplish, and many workers will be needed for it, and for the sake of London and our country time should not be lost; and that we, like our Master, must set ourselves to seek and save that which is lost.[11]

I should wish our fresh courts then to be in a poor district, we have so much strength now that we ought to be face to face with a larger body of the poor once more. Two or three of my friends, who will themselves manage them, are willing to buy courts. I hope they will buy old ones rather than build new. For myself I feel rather doubtful as to whether, in the uncertainty as to public action, buying at all, just now, can be safely recommended to anyone who depends on receiving a fair interest for their capital; and so, having now a pretty strong band of workers, I would rather manage for those who now own than recommend purchase to my friends; still, much might depend on the price, the neighbourhood, and the state of the houses.

A few words of thanks are due to those who have so kindly and generously helped me with money. Taking into account the money sent me for open spaces, I never received so much in any year before. I have, besides, had a very great number of offers of money for houses. I have not been able to accept these as gifts, for I am firmly convinced that the people should pay for their houses. I have not been able to accept them either as shares, for a part of my own special work has been to connect individuals possessed of education, conscience and means, with particular courts in London. In this way has been established the relation between landlord and tenant, with all its mutual

---

11 Luke 19:10.

attachments and duties, as it exists in many country places. I have never, therefore, formed a joint-stock company for purchasing courts, but have got some one person to buy each group of houses. Some of the kind donors have allowed me to use their offered contributions for other purposes, to some I have replied that if a company is formed by men of practical experience to build simple houses for the very poor, I shall be delighted to put them into communication with the directors; at present, however, so far as I have heard, there is no company which is managed by those who have a full knowledge of the subject, and which has adopted sufficiently simple plans to suit the requirements of the very poor.

With the money sent straight to the donation fund a great deal of good has been effected. All the personal power, all the gentle watchfulness, all the thoughtful wisdom which have helped us in past years have been again ready for those who have been assisted from this fund. I have been, and am, very happy about this part of our work.

I am, my friends, with always deeper gratitude,
Yours faithfully,

OCTAVIA HILL

DONATION ACCOUNT, 1883

RECEIPTS

	£	s	d
Cash in hand	143	10	4
Miss Astley	5	0	0
Miss Ball	0	10	0
per Rev. H.R. Collum	4	11	4
A.G. Crowder, Esq	5	5	0
C.L.	2	12	0
Miss Forman	1	1	0
— Fothergill, Esq	0	8	4
C. Flower, Esq	3	3	0
Mr and Mrs Gillson (Pension, A.)	5	4	0
Mr and Mrs Gillson (General purposes)	5	0	0
Miss Gosset	1	0	0
Alfred Hill, Esq	10	0	0
Rev. T. Hill	0	5	0
Mrs Lynch	10	0	0
W. Matheson, Esq	1	1	0
Mrs Macaulay	1	0	0
Hon. Mrs Maclagan	3	0	0
F. Nettlefold, Esq	20	0	0
Miss Oldham·	3	0	0
Sutton Palmer, Esq	10	0	0
Miss Pipe	10	0	0
Mr and Mrs Pooley	1	1	0
Mrs Stephen Ralli	3	0	0
Mrs Southwood Smith	0	10	0
Mrs Leslie Stephen	10	10	0
Mrs Wm. Shaen	2	0	0
Stephen Winkworth, Esq (Pension, A.)	13	0	0
Mrs S. Winkworth	20	0	0
Mrs S. Winkworth (special for education)	50	0	0
Mrs Wright	10	0	0
Miss Yorke	20	0	0
	£375	12	0

DONATION ACCOUNT, 1883

EXPENDITURE

	£	s	d
Industrial School for F.B., G.S. and M.K.	37	6	8
Boarding out (Clothes, Schooling and Partial Board for 4 Children)	6	7	2
Providing Hospital and other Relief to the Sick	8	18	6
Pensions for Mrs E., and Mrs H. and M.G.	7	18	6
Employment for Poor People: Outfits, &c.	2	11	10 ½
Excursions to the Country and other Entertainments	5	19	3
Miss Poole's Orphanage*	10	0	0
Miss Poole's Orphanage*	5	0	0
Education*	31	8	0
Rent for Classes, &c.	8	6	6
Pension, A.*	20	19	6
Care of Playground	16	8	0
Care of Garden	16	0	0
Salary of Assistant*	10	0	0
Printing and Postage of Letter to Fellow-Workers	3	11	1 ½
Cash in Hand	186	16	11

	£375	12	0

* Special donations.

N.B.—The funds entrusted to me come from two very clearly marked classes of donors. The one anxious that their money should be devoted to the direct help of the sick and poor. The other class wishing to strengthen my hands that I may help forward in its difficult stages any great movement. My sister and I recognise this distinction, and in decidng about every grant, carefully consider *whose* money it is that is used, and follow the wish of the donors faithfully.

Examined and found correct, A.P. Fletcher.

LETTER TO MY FELLOW-WORKERS

TO WHICH IS ADDED

ACCOUNTS OF DONATIONS RECEIVED

FOR

WORK AMONG THE POOR

DURING 1884 & 1885

BY

OCTAVIA HILL
(FOR PRIVATE CIRCULATION ONLY)

LONDON
PRINTED BY WATERLOW AND SONS LIMITED,
GREAT WINCHESTER STREET, E.C.

SUMMARY

Housing: Deptford; Southwark and the commencement of the work for the Ecclesiastical Commissioners; a greater sense of responsibility among landlords... the Kyrle Society and open spaces: Parliament Hill Fields... the uses to which individual donations have been put.

EDITOR'S NOTE

1884 was the only year between 1872 and 1911 that Octavia did not describe in its own letter. The reason for this unique gap which Octavia gives—that there had been so much talk about work for the poor that she felt silence to be preferable for the time being—is unconvincing. The letters were not for public consumption, but 'For Private Circulation Only'. In the depths of her depression Octavia had managed to produce a letter each year, so important had she felt it to be to keep up the spirits of her fellow-workers, so why should she miss a year in 1884, by which time she had become, in the words of her biographer Gillian Darley, 'a figure of national and international standing'? (Darley, 1990, p. 221.) Her methods of housing management were being imitated in schemes across the British Isles, in the USA, in Germany, Holland and elsewhere. She was recognised as an expert on work among the poor, and was called to give evidence to the 1884 Royal Commission on Housing. (She would have been a member of the Commission herself had the Home Secretary not objected to a female commissioner.) Astonishingly, she does not mention in the letter either the Royal Commission or the resulting legislation: the 1885 Housing of the Working Classes Act. But then the letter is sketchy compared with other letters. Apart from some very brief facts about Parliament Hill Fields (a major open-spaces campaign of the time) there is a lack of detail. The work of the donation fund is glossed over briefly, as in the 1883 letter; there is no mention of the opening of Toynbee Hall in Whitechapel in 1884 by Samuel and Henrietta Barnett, former protégés who figure so largely in the early letters; and the opening page-and-a-half, as well as subsequent passages, consist of generalisations which look like 'padding'. In spite of the fact that it covers two years, at 2,327 words it is the shortest letter apart from 1872. It is difficult to avoid the conclusion that it was written in a great hurry when Octavia realised that she could not let another year go by without at least rendering accounts to her donors. (The 1884 accounts had actually been signed off by the auditor on 14 January 1885, even though they were not circulated.) This letter is chiefly significant

182

for containing the first reference to Octavia's work for the Ecclesiastical Commissioners, which would achieve great importance in the years to come.

14 Nottingham Place, W.
(February 1886)[1]

My friends,

It is two years since I have written to you, and I can no longer delay
rendering an account of my stewardship, at least so far as the printing
of my balance-sheets is concerned. I assure you they have been carefully
and duly audited by my kind friend Mr Fletcher, though I did not
think it well to print a letter last year. The truth is, I have been under a
very strong conviction that silence was better in these days than any
words. There seems such a rush of talk about work for the poor, so
much self-consciousness forced on the doers of it, so ruthless a dragging
to the light of all simple, neighbourly, quiet acts that would fain be
done in silence as a natural and simple duty, that I felt as if it were
really better not to write anything even privately to you, my old friends
and fellow-workers. But I must print my balance-sheets in common
duty of treasurer, and it seems unnatural to send them without a few
words of thanks to all who have so generously and kindly helped me
with money. Then, if I acknowledge the money, how can I be silent
about the even greater help of faithful and continuous work? And then,
how ungracious not to tell those of you who are far away in country
places a little of the progress of the work with which you have helped!
Besides, times change, and there may be things to say neither gossiping
nor popular, which are hard to utter, and are not sure to bring any
clamour of talk, being truths that the world would like to turn from,
but which a low voice within says to me, 'Write or say, for those that
will hear, who may not be so near the facts of life in a great city as you,
and who will accept Truth though her beautiful face is veiled, and she
looks sad and stern, but who know her as the daughter of God, and
desire to see her, and ask for her guidance even if she leads them through
ways they would not choose, but who trust, that where she leads, the
paths are firm, if stony, and, though they are dark at first, must lead out
into the sunlight and presence of God.' And the truth, so far as I see it,

---

1   The 1885 accounts were not signed off by the auditor until 1 February 1886,
which was later than usual.

185

is, that the days are full of difficulty; the temper of the poor is difficult, the old submissive patience is passing away, and no sense of duty has taken its place; the talk is of rights, not right. The ideal the poor form for themselves is low, and the rich support them in it. The rich, on the other hand, while they are continually coming forward more and more to help the poor, are thoroughly cowardly about telling them any truth that is unpalatable, and know too little of them to meet them really as friends, and learn to be natural and brave with them. We have great relief funds[2] and little manly friendship, idleness above and below, and an admiration for what is pleasant which degrades all life. This temper makes work difficult, and sometimes fills one with wondering awe about the future of rich and poor.

But, my friends, let us take heart. There is much work done thoroughly, and in God's sight, which will stand the fire and be proved as good pure gold. Wherever it exists, it tells in a quite marvellous way. One true-hearted clergyman, one conscientious mistress of a house, one firm mother who teaches her boy what duty means, one faithful workman, one human soul who looks day by day through earthly things clearly to the Lord of them, one statesman who is careless whether any follow or applaud, but who makes straight on for what is right, all of these prepare the way of the Lord, and do something to make England what we all wish her to be.

Now as to my own small undertakings. I have, since I last wrote to

---

2   The 1884/5 letter is not dated, but as it shows signs of having been put together in a hurry (see editor's note) it is reasonable to assume that Octavia was writing it later than usual, perhaps in February 1886. On 11 February 1886 *The Times* announced the first meeting of 'the Mansion House committee of the fund now being raised by the Lord Mayor, on the appeal of the working men, for the relief of the deserving unemployed in the metropolis'. £3,300 had already been raised, going up to £10,000 the next day, and £20,000 the day after that. It would raise £78,629 by the time it closed in July, by which time it had become notorious for its profligacy and chaotic administration. Instead of working through existing organisations, like the Metropolitan Visiting and Relief Association or the Charity Organisation Society, the Mansion House Fund set up its own ad hoc committees which, sometimes acting under the threat of civil disorder and initially without any rules or procedures, gave out vast sums of money without proper checks. Many fraudulent claims were met and those who had been doing careful, steady work in poor areas saw their efforts undermined. 'The Mansion House Fund, its terrible mistakes and failures, have occupied us a great deal', Octavia wrote to her sister Emily on 28 February 1886: 'The City Missionary at Deptford says that, if the money had been thrown into the sea, it would have been better.' (Whelan, 2001, pp.59–85.) Although the 1886 Fund had been only the latest in a long series of such appeals, there would be no more like it as a result of the controversy.

you, been successful in establishing my work in South London, according to the long-cherished wish of my heart. In March of 1884, I was put in charge by the owner of 48 houses in Deptford.[3] In May of the same year, I undertook the care of several of the courts in Southwark for the Ecclesiastical Commissioners.[4] In November of the same year, the Commissioners handed over to me an additional group of courts.[5]

---

3 The juxtaposition of two sentences about Deptford with references to the Ecclesiastical Commissioners has led some readers to assume that the houses in Deptford belonged to the Ecclesiastical Commissioners. In fact, the houses, in Queen Street, Deptford, belonged to a speculator who had acquired them on an 18-year lease, expecting that a tram-line would be cut through them and that he would be compensated. When the tram failed to materialise, he handed the properties over to Octavia to manage. They were in poor condition and the tenants proved resistant to Octavia's methods of improvement. The problems associated with 'poor Deptford, our black sheep' (1892, p. 318) became a *leitmotif* of the letters until 1894, when Octavia withdrew from their management. Queen Street was eventually demolished as part of a road-building scheme. See Appendix 3, pp.755-56, for Lucy Tait's recommendation of Octavia to the Archbishop of Canterbury, in which she mentions the Deptford houses as if they represented Octavia's first housing venture. In fact, Octavia had by this time nearly twenty years of experience in housing management, which makes it curious that Lucy Tait should have singled out Deptford for special mention.

---

4 A letter from Cluttons to the Ecclesiastical Commissioners confirming Octavia's appointment refers to 'Blocks A and B on the plan attached to the Report of the Special Commitee.' (Letter from Cluttons to the EC, 20 March 1884.) On the plan is a handwritten note stating that these are 'Parvey Place, Union Court, Worcester Place, a block South from Adams Place and Henry's Place'. It is fair to presume that these are the properties referred to. It is also most likely that these earliest buildings were also those gradually demolished in the course of the rebuilding of the Southwark Estate (Henry's Place, for example, was later to become the site of the Red Cross garden). EC 65065.

---

5 It is likely that this refers to the following properties: 20-22 Essex St, 1-9 Farnham Place, 1-15 Thornton Grove, 23-31 Gravel Lane, 8-34 Dyers Buildings, 2-9 Williams Place (Letter from Cluttons to the EC, 12 January 1885, confirming Octavia's application for further cottages). There is scant knowledge of the precise locations of many of the old properties later given over to Octavia by the Commissioners. This is probably because, after 1885—the Commissioners having agreed in principle to give all old property over to Octavia—property was transferred on the basis of agreements made directly between Octavia and Cluttons, without reference to the Commissioners. We do know from scraps in the archive that Octavia collected in 146 holdings for the Commissioners, in Great Guildford Street and other unnamed streets. There are mentions of old properties being handed over in the 1892, 1896, 1901 and 1907 letters. Those in Great Guildford Street probably belong to the earliest batch.

In January of 1885, I accepted the management of 78 more houses in Deptford. A friend is just arranging to take 41 houses in Southwark,[6] on lease from the Commissioners, and one lady has bought the freehold of another house in a court where we have long been at work. On the other hand, the Commissioners have decided to pull down some of the houses in Southwark, new buildings having been erected by a company on land belonging to the Commissioners.[7] But I hope to retain the trained workers and a portion of the tenants, who will be thus displaced, if I am able to find suitable houses to be bought in the neighbourhood, for which purpose I have a promise of money. The staff of my fellow-workers has largely increased, and so has their efficiency. There are now many more about whom I know that, if a court is committed to them, they think out what will be for the welfare of the tenants in a considerate and responsible way, which is quite independent of me or my advice. I ought, however, to repeat here once more that there is much which is technical and which must be thoroughly learnt, and that unless intending workers set aside time to learn their business thoroughly with us or others who have experience, they will do more harm than good by undertaking to manage houses.

One distinct advance that is noticeable since I last wrote is the readiness shown by men of business and companies to place their houses under our care. A deeper sense of responsibility as to the conduct of them, a perception of how much in their management is done better by women, and, I hope, a confidence that we try faithfully, and succeed tolerably, in the effort to make them prosperous, have led to this result. This method of extending the area over which we have control has been a great help. It has occurred at a time when, owing to the altered condition of letting in London, I could no longer, with confidence,

---

6   25-58 Zoar St and 1-22 Russel Place. Octavia applied for a 21-year lease on these properties on behalf of Miss Janet Johnson (Letter from Cluttons to the EC, 25 October 1885). By 1932 Russel Place was known as Hopetown Place and was under the management of Miss L.C. Mitchell (Letter from Cluttons to the EC, 8 October 1932).

---

7   These are Stanhope and Mowbray Buildings on Red Cross Street, erected in 1884/5. Although Octavia refers to a single company, this was probably a syndicate represented by a Miss Vernon. A report by the Ecclesiastical Commissioners, published in 1904, attributes ownership of Stanhope Buildings to the Victoria Dwellings Association and Mowbray Buildings to the Metropolitan Industrial Dwellings Company respectively. Soon after they were built Octavia began collecting there. They represented the EC's first serious attempt to deal with slum housing on their lands (Appendix 3, p.738).

have recommended to those who are unacquainted with business, and who depend on receiving a fair return for their capital, to undertake now the responsibility of purchasing houses.

When we began in Southwark, we secured an almost entirely new group of volunteers, who learnt there under one or two leaders, and who now form a valued nucleus from which to expand yet further.

In Deptford, I was obliged at first to take with me helpers from some distance, as we had none near there; but gradually, I am delighted to say, we have found many living in Blackheath and its neighbourhood who are co-operating with us, and we hope they as the years roll on will be quite independent of us.

Of the success of our work? Well! I am thankful and hopeful. Of course it has varied with the nature and constancy of our workers, and with the response our tenants give us. The new places always tax our strength, and we have had difficulties in them, but we seem to make steady progress; I feel all must go well in proportion as we love our people and aim at securing their real good, and base our action on wise and far-sighted principles. There is not a court where I do not mark distinct advance, but none know better than I how much more might have been done in each of them, and how much lies before us still to do.

May I here say what an intense joy it is to my sister Miranda and to me to see some of our former pupils entering the ranks of workers both in the houses and in the neighbourhood of their own homes. It is specially delightful when they are associated with us in this new relation.

The Kyrle Society, which takes up now what I always felt to be an integral and important part of my duty, has steadily grown, and has certainly been successful in calling attention to the need of the people for what is beautiful. The importance of securing open spaces in London, for which it was the first Society that laboured, is now fully recognised. The importance of larger spaces, such as Parliament Hill, was brought prominently before the public at a meeting at the Duke of Westminster's, in May of 1884, at which I had the honour of reading a paper.[8] Whether that particular scheme will be carried through or not

---

8 'N.B. "Colour, Space, and Music for the People", Price 3*d*, Kegan Paul.' (*Octavia Hill's note.*) This was published in *The Nineteenth Century*, 15 May 1884, pp.741-52. 'Adapted from a paper read before the Kyrle Society at Grosvenor House on 24th March last.' Octavia was confusing the date of the meeting with the date of publication. The Duke of Westminster agreed to become chairman of the Hampstead Heath Extension Committee, formed by Octavia, Shaw-Lefevre and Baroness Burdett-Coutts.

will be decided by a Bill now before Parliament. I was very anxious myself that a certain portion of the land should be secured by private donors, that they should contribute, for instance, the lovely nine acres known as the Elms, supposing that the vestries and Metropolitan Board and the parochial charities contributed a large enough grant for purchasing the rest of the land. We have understood that the Metropolitan Board would only carry out the scheme if contributions were forthcoming, and I cannot but think that in this metropolis, where rates press so heavily on the poor, there should be many a rich and generous hearted man who would like to contribute something, above his bare share of the rate, to give to his fellow townsmen some few acres more of sloping grass, with stately trees, a place where the noise of carriages is not heard, and the toil and rush of life pauses for a while. I should like myself nothing better, if I had the money, than to make so great and lasting a gift to the people—and I rather hope, when the bill is in a more advanced stage, that the Kyrle Society may be the medium of securing some such gift, from those whose labours have been abundantly blessed by resultant wealth, or who inherit much from their ancestors. If all fails, it may be possible to the Kyrle Society to rescue, at least, a few acres where the hill top enables the Londoner to rise above the smoke, to feel a refreshing air for a little time and to see the sun setting in coloured glory which abounds so in the earth God made, but of which so small a share remains visible to the inhabitants of our huge town. One great gift of a generous man, a whole £1,000, I am keeping to secure what I can there. I often wonder it is not met by many another. The time will surely come when regret will be deep if those slopes are lost to the public, which is slow to realise its opportunities in time.

In 1884 a huge tract of land had come on the market, encompassing 250 acres of Lord Mansfield's Kenwood estate and 60 acres belong to Sir Thomas Maryon Wilson, and abutting onto Hampstead Heath. The importance of acquiring the land as an extension to the Heath, which at that time included only a narrow strip of land to the east of Spaniards Road, known as the Vale of Health, was immediately recognised, but the price of £305,000 meant that it would be necessary to secure the support of public bodies. Robert Hunter and Shaw-Lefevre drafted an enabling bill for parliament to authorise its purchase by local authorities. The vestries involved, St Pancras, Marylebone and Hampstead, could not raise the sum on their own, and the Metropolitan Board of Works was unenthusiastic—hence Octavia's pessimism about the prospects. The eventual success of the project was partly owing to the fact that in 1888 the Metropolitan Board of Works was replaced by the London County Council, which was much more enthusiastic about open spaces (1889, pp.258-60).

Now, as to gifts of money you have sent me, you cannot think how grateful and glad I have been for them. They have met needs without number, and there are such histories lying behind the bare figures which appear in the balance sheet as would move you, too, to glad thankfulness that you have been able to charge them with such power of blessing, if only you could know about it all. But the veil of reverent and tender sympathy makes me prefer to say nothing further here.

One new balance sheet appears here; it marks a new departure. It records the gifts of those who wished their donations spent in houses. I explained to them that the houses under our care were self-supporting, and did not need gifts. But I asked leave to accept the gifts in order to form a permanent fund, from which advances might be made to be used in courts when first they came under our care to effect the repairs which should have been gradually done in years long before we managed them, more quickly than the rent allowed, and also to enable me now and again to risk in a justifiable way some purchase of a house or substantial improvement of it, or to supply some addition for the tenant's good which the landlord could not be expected to provide. In this way we underpinned and rendered quite dry and healthy two small houses which have now nearly repaid the whole sum advanced. We re-arranged all the water supply in one street in time for a hot summer when we expected cholera; we have also many a time put work in hand for some poor man out of work, which else must have waited. It has been a most helpful part of the donation fund, and kept as a loan fund, so as not to interfere with the substantial independence of the courts, is most useful.

Now, good bye, my friends. I wish I could see you oftener, and tell you more of all the joy that there is in the trying to do even this little which you are all in various ways strengthening and helping me to do. But I know that you are ready, as we all must be, to put our little seed into the ground invisible, and to believe that God will bring out of it, in His own good time, fruit a hundred fold.

OCTAVIA HILL

DONATION ACCOUNT, 1884

RECEIPTS

	£	s	d
Cash in hand, January 1884	184	16	11
Anon.	5	0	0
A Friend, per Mrs W. Shaen	5	0	0
A Well-Wisher at Torquay	20	0	0
Miss Brand	5	0	0
Per Rev. H. Bulkley	2	16	6
A.G. Crowder, Esq	5	5	0
Dalewood Parishioners, per Rev. C. L. James	1	7	7
Miss Forman	1	1	0
Charles Flower, Esq	3	3	0
General Lynedoch Gardiner	2	0	0
Miss Gossett	2	0	0
Mr and Mrs Gillson	12	12	0
Miss Glanville	20	0	0
Canon Harrison	2	12	0
G.M. Hicks, Esq	10	0	0
Mrs Hailston	1	0	0
Per Miss Johnson	1	10	0
Miss Lushington	1	0	0
Rev. Dr Littledale	7	7	2
Mrs Julian Marshall	16	0	0
Wm. Moore, Esq	0	10	0
Mrs Macaulay	1	0	0
Mrs James Macdonell	0	10	0
Miss Monro	4	0	0
Mrs Gower McCrea	1	1	0
Mrs Oldham	5	5	0
Mr and Mrs Pooley	1	1	0
Rev. Charles Plummer	5	0	0
Miss Pipe	2	2	0
Mrs Leslie Stephen	10	10	0
Miss Stephens	0	5	0
Mrs Wm. Shaen	2	0	0
Mrs Scott	1	1	0
Miss Tait	3	0	0
R.P. Tebb, Esq	3	0	0
Stephen Winkworth, Esq	14	0	0
Mrs Stephen Winkworth	20	0	0
The Misses Waters	2	2	0
Miss Mary Wells	2	0	0
Miss Wansey	2	0	0
Mrs Wright	10	0	0
Miss Webb	5	0	0
Miss Yorke	10	0	0
	£414	18	2

DONATION ACCOUNT, 1884

EXPENDITURE

	£	s.	d.
Boarding Out (clothes, schooling, and partial board for seven children) ...	10	9	7 ½
Industrial School for M.K., T., E.H., L.H., G.S.	34	7	6
Excursions to the Country and other Entertainments	22	7	8 ½
Care of Playground	10	8	0
Providing Hospital and other Relief to the Sick (chiefly Children)	40	0	0
Rent of Rooms for Classes	11	12	0
Pensions: A., G., B., E., T.H., M., Br.	54	7	7
Employment and Apprenticing	30	1	0
Miss Poole's Orphanage 2	2	0
May Festival 2	5	5
Education: K.	45	4	6
Salary of Assistant	10	0	0
Printing and Postage of Letter to Fellow-Workers 3	9	11
Transferred to Houses Account	20	0	0
Cash in hand	118	2	1

	£414	18	2

N.B.—The funds entrusted to me come from two very clearly marked classes of donors. The one anxious that the money should be devoted to the direct help of the sick and poor. The other class wishing to strengthen my hands, that I may help forward in its difficult stages, any great movement. My sister and I recognise this distinction, and in deciding about every grant, carefully consider *whose* money it is that is used, and follow the wish of the donors faithfully.

Certified to be correct, A. P. Fletcher, January 14th 1885.

DONATION ACCOUNT, 1885

RECEIPTS

	£	s	d
Cash in hand, January 1885	118	2	1
Miss Ball	0	7	6
Per Miss Ball	0	2	6
Mrs Charles Buxton	10	0	0
The late Miss Fullagar	1	0	0
Charles Flower, Esq	2	2	0
Miss Forman	1	1	0
Mrs Gillson (Pension A.)	2	12	0
Miss Hardcastle	0	6	0
Canon Harrison (Pension A.)	2	10	0
Rev. Thomas Hill	0	10	0
Miss Johnson	1	0	0
Mrs Lewes	1	12	6
Dr Littledale	5	5	0
Mrs Macaulay	1	0	0
Miss McNair	5	0	0
Mrs Julian Marshall	5	0	0
Mrs Mason	2	0	0
Miss Meek	2	0	0
Miss Middleton (Parochial Mission)	20	0	0
Miss Constance Oldham	2	10	0
Rev. Charles Plummer	5	0	0
Mrs William Shaen	2	0	0
Mrs Leslie Stephen	10	0	0
Miss Wells	2	0	0
Miss Jane Wells	1	0	0
Mrs Stephen Winkworth	40	0	0
Mrs Stephen Winkworth (for K.'s Education)	50	0	0
Stephen Winkworth, Esq (Pension A.)	6	10	0
Miss Wordsworth	2	0	0
Mrs Wright	10	0	0
Miss Yorke	10	0	0
Loan returned	1	0	0
Materials returned	0	0	4 ½
	£323	10	11 ½

DONATION ACCOUNT, 1885

EXPENDITURE

	£	s	d
Boarding Out (clothes, school, and partial board for six children)	14	14	1 ½
Industrial School for F.B., L. and E.H.	39	0	0
Hospital and other Relief to the Sick	4	19	10
Pensions: A., G. and B.	22	10	0
Employment and Apprenticing	11	9	6
Excursions to the Country and Entertainments	35	5	6
May Festival: Plants, Flowers, &c., during the Year	8	0	0
Care of Playground	7	16	0
Rent of Rooms for Classes	10	1	6
Education: K.	44	18	6
Salary of Assistant	7	10	0
Materials for Mounting Pictures	0	8	1 ½
Cheques	0	0	7
Parochial Mission, Deptford	20	0	0
Transferred to Houses Account	12	2	0
Tower Hamlets Pension Fund	2	0	0
Cash in hand, December 1885	82	15	3 ½

£323 10 11 ½

Examined and found correct, A.P. Fletcher, February 1st 1886.

195

DONATIONS FORMING FUND FOR IMPROVING HOUSES

From December 1883 to December 1885

RECEIPTS

		£	s	d
1883				
	The Marchioness of Salisbury	20	0	0
	Mrs Pryor	25	0	0
	Mrs Cook	5	0	0
1884				
Oct	Miss E. Fisher	1	0	0
Nov	Caritas	5	0	0
Dec	Rev. C. Plummer	5	0	0
	Transferred from Donation Account	20	0	0
1885				
Feb	Mrs Charles Buxton	10	0	0
	Miss Gossett	1	0	0
	D. Cruikshank, Esq	5	0	0
April	C. Dodswell, Esq	1	1	0
Sept	Mrs Gillson	5	0	0
Oct	Miss Fisher	1	0	0
Dec	Repaid by Property A.	6	0	0
	Transferred from Donation Account	12	2	0
		£122	3	0

DONATIONS FORMING FUND FOR IMPROVING HOUSES

From December 1883 to December 1885 (continued)

EXPENDITURE

		£	s	d
1883				
	Survey Fees … … … … … … … … … … … … … … … … … … …	1	1	0
	Training Worker (specially given for) … … … … … … … … …	15	0	0
	Advance to Property A. … … … … … … … … … … … … … …	20	0	0
	Advance to Property B. … … … … … … … … … … … … … …	14	0	0
1884				
Sept	Advance to Property B. … … … … … … … … … … … … … …	25	5	0
Dec	Advance to Property B. … … … … … … … … … … … … … …	14	16	3
1885				
Mar	Advance to Property B. … … … … … … … … … … … … … …	3	17	6
June	Advance to Property B. … … … … … … … … … … … … … …	3	10	3
Sept	Advance to Property B. … … … … … … … … … … … … … …	6	17	0
Dec	Advance to Property B. … … … … … … … … … … … … … …	5	14	0
	Advance to Property B. … … … … … … … … … … … … … …	10	0	0
	Advance to Property B. … … … … … … … … … … … … … …	2	2	0
		£122	**3**	**0**

LETTER TO MY FELLOW-WORKERS

TO WHICH ARE ADDED

ACCOUNTS OF DONATIONS RECEIVED

FOR

WORK AMONG THE POOR

DURING 1886

BY

OCTAVIA HILL
(FOR PRIVATE CIRCULATION ONLY)

LONDON

PRINTED BY WATERLOW AND SONS LIMITED,

GREAT WINCHESTER STREET, E.C.

SUMMARY

Problems with blocks and advantages of cottages... Ecclesiastical Commissioners make available land for Red Cross garden... an appeal to build Red Cross Hall... plans for Red Cross cottages... management of 240 tenements in Southwark taken on... uses of the donation fund: a £1,000 donation for suburban open spaces from Lady Jane Dundas... Parliament Hill Fields... death of William Shaen.

EDITOR'S NOTE

This letter begins with an important and detailed statement of Octavia's preference for cottages over blocks of flats, coupled with her realisation that the escalating value of land in central London meant that most of the new dwellings constructed for the working classes would be in blocks. This leads to an announcement, in terms of excitement which are rare in the letters, of what was to become Octavia's most cherished scheme: the construction of the Red Cross cottages, Hall and garden. The creation of this village-like community, which still exists, in the heart of South London, was the realisation of a dream for Octavia, and the manifestation of her most deeply held beliefs concerning community living.

My friends,

It is a beautiful spring morning when I sit down to write to you, a great contrast to the wintry and dark days when I usually prepare my report. I have been waiting to do this because of a great success, and a great hope of possible further advance, for which I desire to ask the co-operation of any of those who trust me, and feel they can help.

I mentioned in my last letter to you that the Ecclesiastical Commissioners were pulling down many of the old cottages in Southwark. I had been much impressed by the way in which the tenants cared for small cottages, and had noticed many reasons which amply justified their choice. I am aware that there are many well-managed blocks in London, but the arrangements for management in others are defective. In too many instances where numerous families reside, and the staircases, laundries and yards are used in common, they are under the supervision of one man, who is exposed to great temptation to overlook disorder. Even with the best will in the world, he is often powerless to enforce order, and to secure a good tone among the families in a large block. There is no organised system of government, except through him. The consequence is that if anything goes wrong, the quiet, steady tenants have no redress, they therefore leave, the rampant ones grow more unruly, good tenants avoid the place, which moreover through mismanagement has become insanitary. Empty places are tenfold more difficult to keep in order than those that are let, directors are in despair, the block stands half empty, while the neighbouring houses are over-crowded and there are ten or twelve applicants for any of them that fall vacant, but none for tenements in the block. Think what living in such close quarters must be, if there is no one to provide

---

1 William Shaen, whose death Octavia refers to in the P.S. to this letter, had passed away on 2 March 1887. On 17 March she wrote to Sydney Cockerell asking him to chase Waterlows for the delivery of the letter and giving the quantity as 500—the only such reference we have. She was therefore presumably writing the letter at the beginning of March, which would make it the latest of those letters we can date.

for the protection of the weak, or to consider and meet their wants. You get a family where the man works by night, he wants to sleep by day, the family in the next room are noisy and vigorous, there is no one to move him to the quiet corner of the block. Or there is a timid widow with little girls, she does not dare let them come up the noisy, ill-kept staircase, she wants to bring them up well, and the neighbours' children all use bad language. Think of the roughness and insolence of the drunken woman in the common laundry, of the dirt on the stairs when the tidy friend, or particular employer, comes to visit, of the drunken revel at night, echoing through the large building, and compare it with the quiet, separate little home in the cottage.

Then picture to yourself the utter impossibility in the block building of getting any kind of individual taste developed, such as the little separate yard allowed. Go down one of the courts of cottages which still linger in parts of London, pass through one of the passages and glance along the small back yards; in one you will see plants and creepers carefully trained, in another rabbits, in a third a little shed for wood, in a fourth all the laundry arrangements well provided, in a fifth the little delicate child sits out unmolested, in nearly all some evidence that the man has something to work at and improve when he comes home. The place has the capacity of being a home, not a couple of barrack-like rooms. If the court is well managed, the flags in front form a safe playground for the children living there among a small group of neighbours whom they know.

'Well!' you say, 'but is not the day for all this gone by? Land is too valuable in London for us to build cottages, we must have blocks.' Let that be granted for the moment, but that does not preclude those who own such cottages from keeping them where they are built. And I wish that any words of mine might avail with even one such owner, to induce him to pause and consider, very seriously, whether, at any rate for a time, he might not manage to drain, and improve water supply and roofs, and thoroughly clean such old buildings, instead of sweeping them away. As to cost, the cottages are far more valuable than the cleared space; as to health, they may be made, at a small cost, far more healthy than any but the very best constructed and best managed blocks. As to the life possible in them—of which the charitable and reforming and legislating bodies know so little—it is incomparably happier and better. Let us keep them while we can.

And suppose we grant that London is coming to block buildings, and must come to them; the preservation of the cottages gives time for the question of management to be studied and perfected. The improvement may come from the training and subsequent employment of ladies like my own fellow-workers, under the directors of large companies, and in conjunction with good resident superintendents. Or it may come by the steady improvement of the main body of the roughest tenants, making them gradually better fitted to use things in common. But, seeing in all classes how difficult it is to get anything cared for which is used in common, unless there be some machinery for its management, I think this latter remedy should rather be counted on as making the work easier, than as sufficient in itself.

While I am on this subject, may I remark that it would be well if those who build blocks would consider, in settling their plans, what machinery they are mainly trusting to for securing good order. If they depend on getting a small group of families with self-respect and self-control, who will take a pride in their separate staircase, they will build those staircases up straight from the street; but, if they are hoping to take in the rougher working people, let them plan the position and out-look of their superintendent's rooms, and bring the staircases down, say, to a common yard, the entrance to which their superintendent's rooms command.

In a rough neighbourhood this precaution may be needed, even if the tenants themselves are tidy, careful and trustworthy, for the police are not bound to watch private staircases, which, being used by many families, are apt to be open at night, and frequented by strangers with the worst results. Much trouble and expense may be saved by well considering these points before building. One advantage of bringing the staircases down into a large yard or playground is that the grown-up people, passing and repassing, are a protection to, and restraint upon, the children playing there.

Noticing all this, I asked the Ecclesiastical Commissioners if they would see me, and talk over the whole question, as it affected their Southwark Estate where they have had large, good, new blocks built, and where they had also cottages standing. They were very kind about seeing me, and we had a long talk, with the result that, I believe, they will, by preference, leave cottages standing, instead of clearing them away, so long as they are not interfering with plans for new streets or rebuilding.[2]

Also I asked them whether—as they had already cleared away so

---

2 For details of this encounter see Appendix 3, pp.741-42. Given the strength of Octavia's personality, the Commissioners probably felt they had little choice about seeing her. The meeting took place on 25 November 1886.

many cottages, thus depriving the children of a number of small play-spaces; and as their new blocks had, quite unintentionally, failed to secure garden or playground, even for the tenants who lived there, while the high blocks of tenements and warehouses had shut out more and more light and air from all the dwellers in the district—they would see their way to give a plot of land for garden and playground for the public. They said there were grave difficulties about it, but, on consideration, especially as the land suggested was immediately opposite their own tenants' residences, they decided to lease to responsible trustees, at a nominal rent, for 999 years,[3] a space of land, on my undertaking to get it laid out, and kept up as a garden and playground.

I hardly could believe so great a benefit would have been secured. There it is, in the very heart of Southwark,[4] just opposite high buildings, where five hundred families live;[5] near to numerous small courts, which are reached under arches and by narrow passages, where hundreds live; close to large Peabody and Industrial Dwellings; an outdoor sitting room, a third of an acre in extent,[6] where, in time to come, the trees may grow, and crocuses flower, and where tired men may sit and smoke on summer evenings, and women, weary of the noise indoors, may just cross the road with their work, and breathe cooler air; a playground where children too small to go to park or gymnasium, may run about freely. We are to have a small portion of the playground covered, where, on wet days, they may play battledore and shuttlecock; and we are to have a tiny pond with fish, and a drinking fountain, and what not, in the days to come.[7]

---

3   This was originally 600 years but Octavia argued for an extension.

---

4   'To the south of Union Street lay the once notorious Mint Rookery, with Marshalsea Road as its main thoroughfare. It was outside the city jurisdiction; a paradise for criminals and prostitutes, and consequently entirely rebuilt from the later nineteenth century awards.' (Pevsner, 1983, p.588.)

---

5   The land was opposite Mowbray and Stanhope Buildings (1884/5, p.188) of which, as Octavia reveals a few pages further on, she had only recently undertaken the management at the time of her meeting with the Commissioners. She used her experience in these blocks to argue for the garden. In particular, she claimed that the noise made by children playing in the internal courts of large blocks was intolerable, and made the rooms difficult to let—hence the advantage of a garden on the other side of the road. (Darley, 1990, p.271.)

---

6   This was Henry's Place, originally a block in which Octavia collected. It was 124 feet by 120 feet.

One friend[8] is undertaking the whole cost of this for us, through the Kyrle Society. I have asked this Society to lay out the ground, and they are superintending the work, and managing the general arrangements.

But now, it is to complete this scheme that I am asking your help this year, and if you are able to give it to me it will be the very greatest delight to me, and I cannot but think it will be useful in time to come. Finding that I had not to collect the large sum needed for laying out the garden, I at once entertained the hope of carrying out my long-cherished wish of having a hall in connection with a garden. We have no place at all where we can meet groups of our tenants in Southwark; those under my care now number 1,600.

I have sixteen ladies working regularly with me there, and a large group of others who help occasionally. We want space for carving and mosaic classes, for musical drill, for winter parties, and lectures and concerts, for dances and acting. We have a good workmen's club there, and a hall will be an important adjunct to it. But, independent of our own needs, in my opinion, a hall in connection with a garden has a special value. We are to have a band-stand in the garden, and hope to have a band there on a Saturday afternoon. Suppose it rains; ought we not to be able to adjourn to the neighbouring hall? If we have a flower-show of the window plants, does not the same hold good? Moreover, might not a hall have newspapers, magazines and books; so forming a reading room and public library in connection with our garden?

Moreover, this special site has high warehouses on two sides, and a street with the many-storeyed tenement houses on the third. What is to come on the fourth? 'Not high warehouses, if it be possible to avoid them', I said to myself. So I set to work to make my plans, and I think I may say that I feel pretty sure that I have the refusal from the Ecclesiastical Commissioners of the lease of the adjacent land on the fourth side. If I obtain help, I shall erect on it six small four-roomed cottages with yards.[9] These cottages will be most tempting and happy

---

7   On 12 February 1887 Miranda Hill had written to a friend: 'I went with Octavia yesterday to see the piece of ground that the Ecclesiastical Commissioners have given for the garden... At present it is in a deplorable state... Lord Ducie told his wife he thought it "the most unpromising piece of ground he had ever seen".' (Maurice, 1914, pp.470-71.)

---

8   Lady Ducie.

---

9   The first cottages were named Red Cross cottages.

little homes, I hope. They will overlook the garden, and will enable us to bound it, not with a ten-foot wall as arranged, but with an iron railing, through which the tenants will look, and those in the garden will see a row of little cottages, I hope rather pretty, and certainly only two stories high. At one end of the garden, and communicating with it by large doors, would be the hall. It would have an entrance from the opposite end from a street, so as to be used by night and day. I hope, if the scheme is carried out, to place in one cottage some family who would have permission to sell refreshments, and I should provide accommodation for their doing so. We shall have a flat roof forming a sort of terrace over the children's covered playground, where there will be tables and chairs, so that, if people like, they could have tea and coffee out of doors.

I propose to make the cottages a separate and, if possible, a remunerative investment, but low cottages on valuable land will make this very difficult, and I could only accept the money of those to whom possible loss of interest would not be serious. I estimate the cost of these at £1,300.

For the hall I propose to ask you all for gifts, pure and simple. As it is only leasehold, I want to invest enough to pay ground-rent, as I think without this provision trustees might hesitate to accept the trust, and certainly its usefulness would be crippled if it were not handed over to them free of ground-rent. Altogether I think we ought to have for the building and the ground rent about £2,000. The scheme is one very near my heart, and if you can help me I shall be very glad, but if you cannot—and I know how many claims most of you have—I shall drop the scheme, feeling sure that, had I been meant to do it, the power would have been forthcoming, and that He who loves His earth, down to the last clod of it in Southwark, and His people, down to the feeblest and forlornest there, has some better thing in store for them, of which I have not even thought.[10]

You will ask me of our year's work. I think on the whole it has been very good, this garden and the great gift for laying it out being by far the largest real gifts for the people I ever had, or dreamed of.

Our work has grown. In July, the directors of the company which owns the blocks referred to above in Southwark, asked me somewhat

---

10 This paragraph is an excellent example of Octavia's technique for direct mail fundraising, long before the term had been coined. She puts pressure on her donors whilst appearing to let them off the hook.

suddenly to take charge of 240 tenements.[11] Thanks to the help of my experienced and most zealous workers, Miss Ironside and Miss Johnson,[12] I was able to do this, and steady progress has been made there. But it was a strain on our machinery, and I had to spare Miss Ironside from Deptford, which has been a difficulty to us there. Still, I am satisfied that the only permanent success will depend on developing the local help, and, therefore, I am not wholly sorry that we were thus forced to depend more on it. Deptford is certainly the part of our work which lags most behind us in success, but I do think that we have made progress even there this year.

We want more workers, but they ought to be first-rate to be of much use; we want people prepared for sacrifice, for steady and for quiet out-of-sight work, and we want people in full vigour, neither too young nor too old, and ready to give a good deal of time. These are not easy to find, but we have found some, and we hope for more. Specially should I be glad of co-operation from Blackheath, St John's, Chislehurst, Beckenham, or any of the South-eastern places from which Deptford is easily accessible. Also, I specially need the help of gentlemen—one who has been with us while preparing to enter the church will be leaving us soon, and we shall miss his help sadly. For some of the work in the houses, for our clubs, gymnastics, cricket, and for some kinds of

---

11 Octavia is referring to the recently constructed Mowbray and Stanhope Buildings, situated on Red Cross Street opposite to the site of Red Cross Hall, garden and cottages. Although the buildings were owned by two separate companies—the Metropolitan Industrial Dwellings Company and the Victoria Dwellings Association —in practice they operated as a syndicate. (1884–5, p.188.) Having provided the land for these buildings on advantageous terms, it appears that the Ecclesiastical Commissioners took the view that they had done their bit for social housing. Octavia, of course, had other ideas.

---

12 Janet Johnson (1858–1955) was one of Octavia's most faithful fellow-workers. She had lived for a while as a member of the Hill household in Nottingham Place, and in 1885 had taken a 21-year lease from the Ecclesiastical Commissioners on 41 houses in Southwark, to manage herself (1884–5, p.188). She joined the five original trustees of Red Cross Hall, together with Miss Ironside, in 1888 (1888, p.244) and was one of the original trustees of the Horace Street Trust, together with Lord Wolmer and Octavia (1892, p.318). According to Gillian Darley: 'Her father, Manuel Johnson, Radcliffe Observer, was closely associated with the Oxford movement. In 1888 she became the first woman guardian in Southwark. Her obituary mentions her delight in travel, with holidays in "the form of complicated bicycle tours, having the dual object of looking up boys [from workhouses] in country situations and visiting properties of the National Trust of which she had become a trustee in succession to Miss Octavia Hill".' (Darley, 1990, p.363.)

business, we cannot get on without more gentlemen now our work is so large.

The donation fund has been of increased value during the past year. As my leading fellow-workers grow in experience and power, much becomes possible to them as to devising really wise ways of helping individuals among the poor, and I am able, as I never did before, to trust their judgement in such matters, while, as our area of work increases, more such claims arise. It is of the greatest moment to us that our hands should be well strengthened for any such when they come before us. There are boys to get to sea, girls to put to service, bread winners to send to the country, the patients to send to hospitals, the little pensions to provide if the club breaks; all this, and more, wants doing, and is being wisely done in various centres from the fund. Also some of the classes and entertainments are now more numerous as the work extends, so that more money is wanted for them—and I find Mrs Maurice, besides the personal work she can herself see to, is a sort of banker to my other responsible fellow-workers, though I fear they often meet more of these expenses themselves than they should do with all their hard work and many claims.

May I mention one gift specially remarkable, not only for its size, but for the object to which it is destined. That of £1,000 for some *beautiful* suburban open space.[13] I have a special object in view for it, and till matters can be arranged about it, the money is invested in consols, in the joint names of myself and Miss Harriot Yorke. The interest will be expended in the same object. This gift, the first, I trust, of many which the rich will one day learn to give, is all the more precious because it comes among those first which mark the clear eye that sees the beginning of important movements, and which herald the fuller sight. It is in the early days that the seer is tested, and has an opportunity of obedience to the call which reaches the listening ear. No help given in the full flood of public approval ever comes with such a sense of blessing.

Will Parliament Hill Fields go to the builders, and neither representatives of ratepayers, nor great donors, realise their opportunity till it is lost?

OCTAVIA HILL

---

13 The donor was Lady Jane Dundas (1887, p.227) and the beautiful space was Parliament Hill Fields.

PS—Since writing this I have heard of the sudden death of Mr William Shaen. He and Mrs Shaen were almost the first friends I had in London. For more than 25 years he has been my adviser in all the work I have undertaken and much of the difficulty which I have encountered. From the early days when first Mr Ruskin purchased the houses, to the very week of his death, when I was consulting him about my Southwark Hall, there was no plan about which I had not his sympathy and help. From the time when each scheme was only a vision of what might one day be, up to the time when the deeds came to be drawn, he followed its history, and helped me at every stage.

He never gave me any advice that I regretted having followed, his counsel proved right both as to worldly wisdom and as to that higher wisdom which outlasts all worlds. Gifted with a tenderness that found expression in the gentle reception and ever ready help of the poorest and most out-of-the-way, with a justice that perceived the claims of all concerned in any business, with a magnificent intellect that grasped the essential point of all questions he dealt with, and a truth that could not swerve, he will be missed by hundreds whom his silent help has blessed, and by none more than myself. I hardly know how much my work has owed to his advice, and it needs all the courage I have to take it up again without him.[14]

---

14 'William Shaen... had helped Octavia search out the original premises, Paradise Place, and from then on had acted as her solicitor and business adviser. When Barrett's Court was causing her the most worry, Octavia wrote to Emily [11 November 1873]: "We owe more to him than to almost anyone else who has helped us."' (Darley, 1990, p.147.) William Shaen was probably the driving force behind a collection taken up by Octavia's friends to provide her with sufficient investment income to enable her not to have to worry about supporting herself at the same time as managing all of her philanthropic projects, for which she took no payment at all. In 1874 Shaen wrote to her from his office at Shaen, Roscoe and Massey to inform Octavia that £3,000 had been invested in American and Russian bonds on her behalf. See the 1900 letter (pp.453-54) for a later, retrospective, assessment by Octavia of the foresight displayed by William Shaen in his work for her.

DONATION ACCOUNT, 1886

RECEIPTS

	£	s	d
Cash in hand	82	15	3 ½
Mrs Allen	0	12	0
Miss M. Ball	0	10	0
Mrs Bird	0	10	0
Miss Buckin	0	10	0
Mrs Coxhead	15	0	0
A.G. Crowder, Esq	5	5	0
G.E. Elliot, Esq	5	0	0
Miss E. Fisher	1	1	0
Chas. Flower, Esq	5	5	0
Miss Forman	1	1	0
Miss Frankau	3	0	0
Mrs Gillson	2	12	0
Lady Goldsmid	50	0	0
Miss Gosset	1	10	0
Mrs Graham	2	0	0
Miss Glanville	5	0	0
Per F. Hill	0	5	0
Miss L. Harris	10	0	0
Mrs Hart	0	10	0
Arthur Heathcote, Esq	3	3	0
Miss Head	1	10	0
A. Hill, Esq	10	0	0
Miss Hogg	1	1	0
Miss B. Holland	1	1	0
Mrs Hollist	5	0	0
Miss Humphreys	5	0	0
Miss Hunter	0	10	0
Miss Johnson	1	1	0
Miss Amy Johnson	0	10	0
Rev. Dr Littledale	3	3	0
Mrs Macaulay	1	0	0
Mrs Malkin	4	0	0
Rev. H.F. Mallet	5	0	0
Mrs Julian Marshall	13	0	0
Miss Meek	2	0	0
F. Nettlefold, Esq	20	0	0
O. Nettlefold, Esq	5	0	0
Miss Florence Nightingale	2	2	0
Mrs Oldham	10	10	0
Mrs Leslie Stephen	10	0	0
Miss Lucy Stone	1	1	0
H. Stephen, Esq	3	3	0
Miss Tait	3	0	0
Mrs Tarratt	10	0	0
Miss Thompson	2	0	0
Miss M. Wells	1	0	0
The late Stephen Winkworth, Esq	6	10	0
Mrs Stephen Winkworth	126	10	0
Lord and Lady Wolmer	5	0	0
Mrs Wright	10	0	0
Mrs Wilde	0	5	0
Loans returned	1	5	0
Mrs Walker	5	0	0
	£471	11	3 ½

DONATION ACCOUNT, 1886

EXPENDITURE

	£	s	d
Industrial School for F.B., A.B., L.H. and E.H.	38	16	0
Boarding out (clothes, schooling, and partial board) four children	8	10	11 ½
Providing Hospital and other Relief to the Sick	11	18	0
Pensions for A., M., B. and S.	36	5	0
Employment for poor people, tools, &c.	7	9	6 ½
Excursions to the Country and other Entertainments	59	12	3
Girls' Home, Charlotte Street	10	0	0
Education: K.*	46	13	6
Tower Hamlets	11	0	0
Furniture for a Hospital	0	8	0
Rent for Classes, &c.	23	19	2
Care of Playground	13	0	0
Plants and Flowers for Tenants	1	13	3 ½
May Festival	2	9	0
Home Art Class for Tenants	1	8	0
Salary of Assistant*	7	10	0
Printing and Postage of Letter to Fellow-Workers	4	15	6
Loans	4	2	0
Cash in hand, December 1886	182	1	1
	£471	11	3 ½

* Special donations.

Examined and found correct, A.P. Fletcher, January 15th 1887.

DONATIONS FORMING FUND
FOR IMPROVING HOUSES, 1886

RECEIPTS

	£	s	d
Hon. Edith Johnstone … … … … … … … … … … … … … … … … … … …	50	0	0
Property A. repaid …	3	0	0
Miss Baiss …	5	0	0
	£58	0	0

DONATIONS FORMING FUND
FOR IMPROVING HOUSES, 1886

EXPENDITURE

		£	s	d
Mar	Property B.	4	4	3
Oct	Property B.	6	6	10
Nov	Property B.	0	5	0
Dec	Property B.	11	14	5 ½
	Range	0	13	6
	Balance in hand	34	15	11 ½
		£58	0	0

LETTER TO MY FELLOW-WORKERS

TO WHICH ARE ADDED

ACCOUNTS OF DONATIONS RECEIVED

FOR

WORK AMONG THE POOR

DURING 1887

෴

BY

OCTAVIA HILL
(FOR PRIVATE CIRCULATION ONLY)

LONDON
PRINTED BY WATERLOW AND SONS LIMITED,
GREAT WINCHESTER STREET, E.C.

SUMMARY

Red Cross garden... Red Cross Hall and cottages... housing: Deptford... working men's club, boys' club and girls' club in Southwark... donation fund... August Bank holiday party at Lambeth Palace and other outings for the tenants... open spaces: Parliament Hill Fields... fellow-workers: new arrivals and a death... Red Cross garden: the Good Shepherd mosaic.

EDITOR'S NOTE

In this, one of the most upbeat of all the letters, Octavia records her progress with the cherished Red Cross scheme in Southwark. She has clearly been throwing herself with all the old vigour into arranging every detail of the cottages, the Hall and the garden. It is hard to believe that, less than ten years earlier, Octavia had been wondering if she would ever return to work at all (1879, p.123; 1880, p.135). The other cause for rejoicing in 'so glad and triumphant a year' was the possibility of saving Parliament Hill Fields, with only £7,000 still to raise of the £52,500 required from private donors.

14 Nottingham Place, W.
(December 1887)[1]

My friends,

I write to you at the close of the year with a very happy sense of good and successful work accomplished. It has been a year strangely full of building and laying out, of dealing with tangible things, with regard to which progress is often easier than it is in spiritual ones, but which are very valuable in their own way, and lead up to the spiritual, very distinctly, wherever they are ordered and carried out and used by honest and right workers.

First among these great successes stands our Southwark garden. Many of you know that it was given for 999 years by the Ecclesiastical Commissioners, who felt that by destroying so many small cottages with tiny yards, and courts which were not thoroughfares, they had deprived the children of play places and the women of space for sitting out of doors. The blocks erected, though they might have advantages, were wanting in open space. The Commissioners therefore gave me a plot of land for a garden, opposite blocks of improved dwellings containing about five hundred families. This land has been vested in trustees for the use of the public. Lord Ducie,[2] Lord Wolmer,[3] Mr

---

1   Octavia refers to 'the close of the year' in the opening sentence, and the auditor signed off the accounts on 31 December 1887.

---

2   Henry John Reynolds-Moreton, third Earl of Ducie (1827–1921), MP for Stroud 1852-53, succeeded his father as earl in 1853. He was a serious establishment figure: lord lieutenant of Gloucestershire, lord warden of the Stannaries in Cornwall, and rider and main forester of Dartmoor. A fellow of the Linnean Society, Ducie established a notable arboretum at Tortworth House, Falfield, Gloucestershire. Tortworth, where Octavia was often a guest, was designed by Teulon, an architect of the Gothic Revival, in 1849 and completed in 1851.

---

3   Lord Wolmer (1859–1942) was born William Waldegrave Palmer, and became second Earl of Selborne on the death of his father in 1895. His family was at the heart of the Victorian political establishment. When he married Lady Maud Cecil in 1883 the bride was given away by her father, the leader of the opposition, and the toast was proposed by Gladstone, then Prime Minister. He became First Lord of the Admiralty

Hunter,[4] Mr Praed[5] and I are the first trustees.

Lady Ducie,[6] directly she heard of the garden, undertook the entire cost of laying it out, and has followed the record of its progress with sympathy and much interest. It was, when handed over to me, a waste, desolate place. There had been a paper factory on one-half of it, which had been burnt down. Four or five feet of unburnt paper lay in irregular heaps, blackened by fire, saturated with rain, and smelling most unpleasantly. It had lain there for five years and much rubbish had been thrown in. A warehouse some stories high fronted the street on the other half of the ground, with no forecourt or area to remove its dull height further from the rooms in the model dwellings which faced it. Our first work was to set bonfires alight gradually to burn the mass of paper. This took about six weeks to do, though the fires were kept alight day and night. The ashes were good for the soil in the garden, and we were saved the whole cost of carting the paper away. Our next

---

(1900–05) then governor of the Transvaal and High Commissioner for South Africa (1905–10).

---

4   Robert Hunter (1844–1913) was by this time a leading light in the open spaces movement. In 1867 he had become solicitor to the Commons Preservation Society and had run brilliant campaigns to preserve Wimbledon Common, Wandsworth Common and Putney Heath as open spaces. His most spectacular success had been the court battle, lasting from 1871–74, in conjunction with the Corporation of London, to declare illegal the enclosure of 3,000 acres of Epping Forest. After a hearing of 23 days, Sir George Jessel declared all enclosures made in the forest in the previous 20 years illegal. In 1878 an act of parliament vested control and maintenance of the forest in the Corporation. His work for the CPS brought him into contact with Henry Fawcett MP, the Postmaster General, and in 1882 Hunter became solicitor to the Post Office. He had to relinquish his position with the CPS, but he remained actively involved with all major campaigns for open spaces for the rest of his life, including Vauxhall Park, Hilly Fields and Parliament Hill Fields. As his *Times* obituary put it: 'Few of those who enjoy the great stretches of common land throughout England are conscious of the debt they owe to the group of able men whose action 40 years ago saved them for the nation.' (*The Times*, 7 November 1913.) Hunter became chairman of Octavia's Kent and Surrey Committee of the CPS, and co-founder, with Octavia and Hardwicke Rawnsley, of the National Trust. Henry Fawcett once said that he had never known a professional man to do so much professional work for nothing.

---

5   Herbert Praed (1841–1921) was born Herbert Mackworth. Although he styled himself Mackworth-Praed, he did not assume the name by licence until 1905, when he was created a baronet. He was a founder member and treasurer of both the Charity Organisation Society and the Working Men's Club and Institute Union. He was chairman of the Victoria Dwellings Association (1900, p.451, n.5) which built Stanhope Buildings in Redcross Way, opposite Red Cross Hall and garden. He was Conservative

task was to pull down the warehouse, and let a little sun in on our garden, and additional light, air, and a sight of sky to numerous tenants in the blocks in Red Cross Street.[7]

The next work was to have a low wall and substantial iron railings placed on the side bounded by the street, so that the garden could be seen and the light and air be unimpeded.

Then came the erection of a covered playground for children; it runs the whole length of a huge warehouse which bounds the garden on one side; it is roofed with timber from the warehouse we pulled

---

MP for Colchester from 1874–80, and in later years a partner in the bank of Praed and Co.

---

6   Julia Reynolds-Moreton, Lady Ducie (1827–1895) was the daughter of James Haughton Langston of Sarsden, Oxfordshire. She married her first cousin, Henry John Reynolds-Moreton, third Earl of Ducie, in 1849. They lived at Tortworth Court in Gloucestershire and Wimbeldon. Octavia enjoyed a long and close friendship with Lady Ducie, sharing philanthropic and artistic interests. Their relationship began when Octavia gave her daughter and niece drawing lessons. In the autumn of 1866, Octavia was invited to stay at the Ducie's home, Tortworth Court, to continue the lessons. Visits to Tortworth became a regular event in Octavia's year, and, according to Darley, 'her only close contact with the world of the aristocracy'. (Darley, 1990, p.112.) Octavia sought refuge with the Ducies during her crisis year of 1877, when Lady Ducie stood by with constant support, hospitality and friendship, offering 'magnificent silent sympathy, and that exquisite depth of tenderness of hers'. (Darley, 1990, p.190.) Octavia and Lady Ducie also enjoyed foreign excursions, Octavia joining Lady Ducie in Menton and Nice in 1885, where her old friend had been recovering from an illness. According to Lady Amberly, Bertrand Russell's mother: 'Lady Ducie is such a wonderfully energetic woman in good for the poor and all so very sensibly and not from the pauperising and charitable point of view. She has now started a Co-operative store and it answers wonderfully though the place is purely agricultural and the houses very scattered. Lady Ducie lent books about it and talked and urged etc. and then there was a meeting about it and they elected a Committee, Lord and Lady Ducie keeping quite out of it then that it might be worked entirely by the people.' (Darley, 1990, p.112.) Lady Ducie invested £7,000 in 1872 to buy houses in Barrett's Court, intending to superintend the properties herself with a trained worker paid from the rents—Henrietta Rowland, later the wife of Canon Barnett, who described herself as Lady Ducie's 'volunteer and inefficient rent-collector'. (Darley, 1990, p.126). Lady Ducie was certainly 'hands-on' when it came to the tenants. Groups were taken on visits to her house in Wimbledon, whereas Octavia's other aristocratic patrons rarely let the poor into their homes. Lady Ducie's other ventures included a convalescent hospital and a scheme of training midwives. It was probably Lady Ducie who first recommended Octavia to Revd Fremantle, when he was putting together the Marylebone district committee of the Charity Organisation Society in 1869.

---

7   Now Redcross Way.

down, and the roof is supported on massive wooden pillars. The space is paved with red bricks set diagonally so as to make a pretty pattern. At one end of this arcade is a drinking fountain of plain grey granite.

The roof of this covered playground is flat, and forms a long terrace 12 feet 6 inches wide, which is approached by a flight of wide, low stairs. The terrace has warehouse walls at the end and at the back, and on the garden side a balustrade of wood designed very successfully for us by Mr Hoole,[8] and formed out of the smaller pieces of wood from the warehouse. This woodwork is painted white and looks very nice. Outside on a wide ledge boxes for creepers or bright flowers can be placed, and we hope to get creepers, too, up the pillars.

Immediately in front of this terrace is a space of gravel, which will form a playground for children on ordinary days, but in the centre of which an octagonal band-stand, with balustrade like the terrace, is being

---

8   Elijah Hoole (1837–1912) was the architect of choice for Octavia and her fellow-workers. From the time that she came into contact with him, Octavia gave him every commission over which she had control, including her tombstone. (Although Hoole predeceased her by four months, the stone was erected over Miranda's grave in 1910, and Octavia's name was added to it.) He designed Larksfield, the house in Kent which Harriot Yorke had built for Octavia and herself. Hoole, like Octavia, was from a socially conscious family. His father, born and educated in Manchester, and also called Elijah Hoole (1798–1872), was a pioneer missionary appointed by the Wesleyan Methodist Missionary Society (WMMS). He married Elizabeth (d. 1880) daughter of the lockmaker Charles Chubb in 1835. Elijah junior, born in 1837, was later to build Messrs. Chubb and Son's lock and safe factory off the Old Kent Road in 1869. Elijah senior was WMMS general secretary from 1836–72, with his son acting as a Wesleyan architect. He built many mission churches in, amongst other places, Newfoundland, Naples, Cannstatt, Belize, and Kandy. His favourite Wesleyan chapel was Holly Park Chapel, Crouch Hill. He restored the churches of St James-the-Less, Bethnal Green, and St Martin, Haverstock Hill and many others, including Wesley's chapel and house in the City Road. The Bermondsey Wesleyan Settlement, Farncombe Street was another of his major projects. He was commissioned by Emma Cons to remodel the Old Vic. Hoole was a pupil of James Simpson, at one time president of the Institute of Civil Engineers, whom he assisted in the design and construction of engineering buildings for the Chelsea, Lambeth, Cardiff and other waterworks companies. Hoole commenced practice as an architect in London in 1864. He was primarily an industrial architect, in effect more of a builder and an engineer, his work practical and solid, but he carved out a reputation for constructing workmen's industrial dwellings, for which he won medals at the Health, Inventions and Paris Exhibitions. His workmen's housing went up in Whitechapel, Lambeth (Surrey Buildings), St Pancras, Marylebone, Chelsea, Westminster, Peckham, Southwark, Bristol and Oxford. In Bristol he constructed a rugged group of tenements on Jacob Wells Road for the Bristol Industrial Dwellings Company Limited. He become an acknowledged expert on model housing and several of his projects were illustrated in the *Builder*.

erected. On high-days and holidays we hope parents and children will enjoy music heard from both ground and terrace.

This playground melts off irregularly into the garden proper, which forms, as I have often said, an open-air summer sitting room; walks wind about between small lawns and flower-beds set with flowering trees and shrubs. Two plane trees are planted on the larger spaces of gravel, which are to have circular seats round them, and where we hope working women will sit and rest and do needlework, and tired men sit and smoke on summer evenings. A small pond has been made in the garden, and a jet of water forms a fountain in it. The narrowest part of the pond will be crossed by a little bridge, with railing like the terrace balustrade.

There are two gates opening on the street which are opposite to the entrances of the model dwellings, and there will be a thoroughfare through the garden to a narrow passage leading to another street.

There are huge warehouse walls on two sides of the garden; we have planted creepers, which we hope in time will, in the main, cover these.

We have planted bulbs in plenty, a thousand yellow crocuses, which thrive better than most flowers in London, and we hope when these are in bloom, if our bridge and band-stand are finished, and our playground quite cleared, to have the gravel brought, the last coats of paint put on iron and wood, and open the ground to the public. For the whole of these expenses Lady Ducie has paid, and the work has been done by the Kyrle Society.

I mentioned in my last letter to you my desire to secure a hall to use with the garden, and the hope that I might obtain the land adjacent for this purpose and for building some small cottages. My request for help to do this was responded to most generously, as the subjoined account shews. £2,695 was at once entrusted to me for the land and hall, and by the great kindness of Lady Jane Dundas the money for the cottages, which I hope may be financially independent, but which being kept low for the sake partly of the garden, form a very anxious financial enterprise, is being lent to us at only three per cent. We could not buy the freehold, which belonged to the Ecclesiastical Commissioners, but I thought it best to pay a premium which frees the site of the hall from ground rent for 80 years.[9] The legal and other arrangements took long to settle, but at last the building was begun; an old and dilapidated skin

---

9   The estimated value of the land was £2,174. The premium was £1,424. The land for the cottages was let at £30 per annum, and the land for the Hall at a nominal rent of £1 per annum.

factory, by no means a pleasant adjunct to a garden, was pulled down, and the walls of my hall begin to rise, and three of my cottages are getting their roofs on. They have pretty gables, and one has a little bay window; they are to have red hanging tiles and a little red brick foot-way in front. All their front windows will look straight over the garden.[10]

The hall has two wide doors, at one end, opening on to garden, at the other end is a committee room, two rooms for caretaker, and an approach from a street, so that it can be used by night without crossing the garden. Before the plans were approved, our working men's club sent to me and asked whether I could build for them a more suitable room than the one they were occupying in our blocks. We decided to do so, and the initial cost of this additional room, which occupies the first floor over the caretaker's and committee rooms, brings the estimate above the sum for which I appealed. I hope that help to complete it, and to furnish the hall, may be given. For the decoration of the hall we have received the most welcome offer from Mr Walter Crane[11] to design panels for us, some of our artist friends will paint them under his

---

10 In the South London volume of the great Buildings of England series, Nikolaus Pevsner and Bridget Cherry describe the Red Cross development as 'a specially interesting group... embodying [Octavia Hill's] belief that the working classes deserved a civilised environment instead of the tenements common at the time... The architect was Elijah Hoole. The earlier cottages have a picturesque variety of different-sized gables and upper bay-windows, the later ones are tile-hung with an end gable. The style is more enjoyable than that of Hoole's socially progressive institutional buildings (Toynbee Hall).' (Pevsner, 1983, pp.588-89.) Considering that Pevsner had a reputation—partly due to John Betjeman's hostile criticism—for being a doctrinaire modernist, this is high praise for a small-scale, traditionalist development.

---

11 Follower of John Ruskin and friend of William Morris, Crane (1845–1915) was an important 'art-socialist'. Named 'the artist of socialism' by H.M. Hyndman, founder of the Social Democratic Party, Crane produced propaganda, reprinted in *Cartoons for the Cause* (1896), and designs for union banners. Essays and lectures include *Why Socialism Appeals to Artists* and *The Socialist Ideal as an Inspiration in Art*. Crane credited Morris with his conversion to socialism in 1884. A painter, decorative artist, art theorist and educator, Crane was an associate of Frederic Leighton, Edward Poynter, G.F. Watts and Edward Burne-Jones. Crane was a major player in the late Victorian art establishment, with links to the aesthetic avant-garde. Born in Liverpool, Crane had a practical education, coming up through the print trade and apprenticed in 1859 to William Linton, a radical London wood engraver. His father, who made a living as a portrait painter, encouraged Crane's interest in the arts. This practical background, and much self-education, conditioned his later theories on art education. As a black-and-white illustrator in the 1860s, Crane was influenced by the work of the Pre-Raphaelites, especially Rossetti and Millais, but it is important to remember that he never trained at the Royal Academy. Under the aegis of the printer Edmund Evans

supervision on panels of fibrous plaster, which our builder will leave spaces for and will build into the wall. Mr Hoole, who has designed and is supervising all our building,[12] is arranging with Mr Crane as to these decorations. In this, too, I hope for help from the Kyrle society.

We are anxious, especially as the hall ought to be used in connection

---

(1826–1906), Crane developed illustrated children's books, like *One, Two, Buckle My Shoe* (1868), influenced by the craze for all things Japanese and the designs of E.W. Godwin, the architect employed by Whistler and Wilde. In other words, Crane became a participant in the Aesthetic movement, which preached interior decorating and the House Beautiful. Under the influence of Morris, Crane believed that art would improve society, elevated taste leading to gentility and the high moral ground, and that art could only be created by those who enjoyed beautiful surroundings. Beautiful children's books were a manifestation of this belief. From 1873 to 1876 Routledge produced a series of 13 six-penny books on the back of Crane's reputation, which displayed a virtuoso range of antiquarian knowledge and stylistic wit. Their wide circulation helped to popularise the decorative language of the Pre-Raphaelites and the so-called 'Queen Anne' style. Crane was a diverse commercial designer, producing designs for ceramics and wallpapers. By 1871 Crane was in the arts and crafts clique, a friend of William De Morgan, the famous potter, Philip Webb, the architect, Hungerford Pollen, William Morris and Burne-Jones, whose *Cupid and Psyche* series, which he helped to complete, introduced him to mural decoration. He illustrated Morris's books for the Kelmscott Press in the 1890s. From 1882 Crane attended meetings of The Fifteen, of which Lewis F. Day was the secretary, and from this 'think-tank' the Art Workers Guild emerged in 1884. Crane became its third master in 1888-89. In 1888 he led the splinter group that initiated the Arts and Crafts Exhibition Society. Most importantly, he emerged as an educator, a role that Morris failed to grasp, being appointed Director of Design at the Manchester School of Art and then Principal of the newly constituted Royal College of Art. Although he only held this position for one year, failing to cope with its entrenched views, Crane initiated the introduction of Arts and Crafts practices into the Schools of Art. His books became the basis of design teaching for many years: *The Bases of Design* (1898) and *Line and Form* (1900). Politically speaking, Crane was the most devoted of Morris's followers, and his social concerns were reflected in his artistic practice. He took up cultural philanthropy as he saw art as a form of moral education. He served on the council of the South London Fine Art Gallery, later the Arts and Crafts School of Camberwell, which, in the Peckham Road, was a counterpart to Canon and Henrietta Barnett's art exhibitions in the East End. By 1890 he was on the general committee and the decorative branch sub-committee of the Kyrle. He was still a member of the council in 1910.

---

12 *See ill. 10.* Four years earlier Elijah Hoole had adopted the 'Queen Anne' style when designing Toynbee Hall for the Barnetts in Whitechapel. With its mullioned windows, tall brick chimneys and picturesque roofline, it looks like an English manor house. However, for Red Cross Hall he returned to the Gothic idiom he was happiest with. The Hall resembles Westminster Hall or the Great Hall at Christchurch College, Oxford, built by Cardinal Wolsey, and brings to mind the communal living of medieval colleges. It was to be a meeting place to improve the body and the mind.

with the garden, not to hand it over to the local authorities, at any rate at present. We want to have flower-shows there, and to use it in other ways which it would be difficult for a vestry to manage. But if I and my co-trustees are to keep it to be used thus to its utmost capacity, we must get money for caretaker, cost of water, and keeping up, to say nothing of music and other such expenses. The hall, too, if it is to be fully used, will be a cause of expense beyond any charges we may recover. For all these objects I would ask your aid.

The building and laying out has been a great and increasing interest to us and all our Southwark neighbours and friends, and we look forward to much useful and happy time there. I have been specially touched by the consideration of the people, and feel sure we may trust them all to help preserve the garden and keep order there. The local authorities have shewn us much kind co-operation. They have just put up another lamp at the corner of the garden, where it will be very helpful.

With regard to my other work, I feel that many parts of it have become quite independent of me—or at any rate of any ordinary help of mine. Miss Ironside, Miss Johnson, Miss Sturge[13] and many others are really the managers of the houses under them, have their own standard of excellence, are themselves the leaders and friends of the tenants, and if they look to me at all it is only from time to time as old friends and fellow-workers talk over things together. This is as it should be, and is a great delight and rest to me to think of. Southwark has progressed well this year.

My poor Deptford, in spite of gallant and most capable and devoted help, still lags far, far behind; one seems to pour work upon it, and yet all is so sad there. Sometimes I fancy it is a little better, and often and often I remind myself that such work as is given to it, and the presence

---

13 Elizabeth Sturge was a member of a Quaker family from Bristol who in 1886, at the age of 37, came to live as a member of the Hill household in Nottingham Place and be trained in housing management. She was put in charge of 'a court at Southwark in which were a number of little houses, and of the tenants who lived on one of the staircases of a large block of buildings near the Borough'. She was unpaid and survived on a 'competency'—an annuity of £104 per annum from an uncle. In her privately printed volume of *Reminiscences*, Elizabeth Sturge wrote of the 'indescribable aroma of refinement that pervaded the whole household and circle', with its connections by the marriages of sisters Emily and Gertrude to F.D. Maurice and George Eliot, and George MacDonald giving a lecture on Dante in the drawing room. The Kyrle Society was run from a room at the back of the house, while Charity Organisation Society business and open spaces campaigns were also managed from the premises. Understandably, the aroma of refinement became a bit much, and Miss Sturge moved out after 18 months. (Sturge, 1928, pp.45-51.)

of such workers as it has up and down among its people, must tell, but it seems really hardly to move. Still I am sure it will, and God grant me and those who are with me spirit to hope and wait, and to be sure that all loving and careful work will be accepted and used by God in His own time.

In Southwark the business is so far started that it has become possible to the workers there to turn their attention to the formation of clubs and classes. The workings men's club has been in existence about a year and a half, and seems very thriving. A library has been added to it this year, and eight shillings was paid by the members themselves, in a very short time, for books taken out to read. As only one halfpenny a volume is charged, this means much reading. Lectures have been given in the club, which have been listened to with great attention. But the larger room we are to build is much needed, and will stimulate the club to fresh development. A boys' club has just been opened in a workshop we have rented and put in order. Many boys have joined. It is proposed to form classes for the boys in singing and in the new Swedish carpentering, which seems so suitable for the object in view. A girls' club was opened on December 30th, which will use the same room on alternate nights; they are to having singing, needlework, musical drill, &c. We are thankful to have, at any rate, a nucleus of workers to make these clubs a really happy place of friendly meeting.

My donation fund has proved itself as valuable as ever during the past year. A good deal of it is devoted to children whose health, poverty, or surroundings, make it almost essential for them to be well trained for future life away from home. For instance, one little girl of four, whose father died of consumption, and whose mother supports three other children on very low wages, has been sent to the country to careful and affectionate people. The child is very delicate, and her mother necessarily at work all day, when she was sent home in hopes that she might stay there; within a fortnight she had bronchitis and nearly died. Her life seems to depend on the care and country air. Again a little girl, one of seven children of a widowed mother, who seemed really almost starving, has been placed in an Industrial School. £10 was paid on entrance, and she will now be educated till old enough to be placed at service. Some—indeed a good large sum—has been spent in our delightful August Bank Holiday party at Lambeth Palace; it is the means of enjoyment to some 700 people, and keeps the day a good and healthy one for them, besides being a great time for us and them, and former fellow-workers among them, to meet. Nothing can exceed the Archbishop's kindness in welcoming us, and we feel that the party is well worth the very small sum which each person's pleasure costs, though as a total it seems large. To various other friends who have invited our tenants in the summer our warmest thanks are due. Many such parties are gathered up in our memories with separate thought, though they are lumped in our balance sheet in one item. The sums spent for the sick and old imply much help of quite vital importance to many a sorrowful or forlorn human being. The amounts given me this year for special objects so largely exceed all that I had ever imagined could be sent me in one year, that it is not wonderful that these huge extra donations should have affected, as they seem to have done, my ordinary donation fund, and that the balance we have in hand should be too small for us to see our way to retain at school or country home the little children we have so far rescued and seen to; but my sister and I believe that, quarter by quarter as the year goes on, we may receive enough not to let one of these children return till the object we hoped to attain is accomplished, and that our other individual work will not be cramped. We are quite sure that all of you have given most abundantly; we foresee no such great appeals as the two we have had to make this year; and as our work grows, so our helpful friends have grown, and we believe they will; and, though our balance is small, we look forward without any fear to the opening year.

I spoke of two great special appeals; you will find in this letter the account relating only to one, that for the Southwark Hall[14] and cottages; but you realise that I could not complete my yearly letter without some reference to Parliament Hill. I have spoken of it in previous letters as of a hope too great, too vague, too utterly distant for me even to dare to ask for it; a vision to be set before us, a thing to be struggled for, worked for, steadily advanced towards, but gained! Dare one, might one think of it? I write this letter in the near view of the consummation, not exactly of the scheme, but of getting the money for it; for I need not anticipate that the £7,000 still wanting will fail us now so much is obtained. Nine short weeks ago a yeoman's £1,000, which was promised

---

14 Red Cross Hall had not yet definitely assumed its name. On 10 September 1887 Octavia wrote to Sydney Cockerell: 'The name Red + Hall [sic] most of us like much, it seems nicely to be half settled for us by the garden name which is fixed... so the name seems right tho' its night entrance will be in White + St.' White Cross Street is now Ayres Street, Red Cross Street is now Redcross Way. Curiously, while Red Cross cottages and garden retain their name, the Ministry of War requested in 1934 that the name of the Hall should be changed, and it has been known as Bishop's Hall ever since. The Ministry may have been concerned, in the face of imminent hostilities, that Red Cross Hall could have been mistaken for a first-aid centre.

after the Grosvenor House meeting in May of 1884, and Lady Jane Dundas's £1,000, which I mentioned in my last letter, were the only nucleus of the £52,500 which had to be raised by private subscription. How large is the sympathy with the poor, how intelligent the knowledge of their wants, which has led donors to devote, in unprosperous times, and so swiftly, so large a gift as to procure this land! I do not know how the remaining £7,000 will be secured. I hope, by more such donations, the rates, take it all in all, will bear a large share of the burden; the City Companies can be approached for more difficult schemes than this now is. I should like to see the rich of London proud to share the remaining part of a gift which will be, so far as we can see, a great, a lasting and a visible blessing to thousands.[15]

The whole of this Hampstead Heath movement and many others this year have shewn how much public interest on the subject of open spaces has increased. I am writing for the February number of the *Nineteenth Century*,[16] and need not repeat here, an account of the

---

15 According to the Kyrle Society report for 1887: 'the Metropolitan Board of Works have decided to contribute one half of the £305,000 required by the present owners of the land... the Charity Commissioners have been directed by an Act of Parliament to contribute £50,000, and the vestries of Hampstead, St Pancras and Marylebone have promised £20,000, £30,000, and £5,000 respectively, leaving £47,500 to be raised by public subscription. Since the time when the first general appeal was issued, more than £41,200 has been subscribed, but £6,300 is still required.' Clearly, the money was pouring in, and the total still needed had been reduced by £700 in the weeks that elapsed between Octavia's writing of the letter to fellow-workers and the writing of the Kyrle report for the same year. However it is difficult to account for the difference between the figures given for the amount required from the public: £52,500 according to Octavia and £47,500 according to the Kyrle. The confusion may have been caused by the Marylebone vestry coming late to the table with its £5,000.

---

16 Octavia Hill, 'More Air For London', *The Nineteenth Century*, 23 February 1888, pp. 181-88. The memorial related to the expenditure of funds under the City of London Parochial Charities Act of 1883. Under this act, the ancient and lavish endowments of the various city churches, many of which had by this time only tiny congregations, had been brought together into one great fund for the benefit of Londoners. Octavia and her colleagues took the view that some of the £50,000 a year which was available should go on providing open spaces. 'Sometimes I think that God has ordered that this great gift from the generous men of old should become available just when the people have wakened up to the need of space.' To make her point, Octavia had used a map of London to divide the city into quadrants. She calculated the population of each quadrant, and the amount of open space available to the people. She reached the startling conclusion that, in the two western quadrants, there was one acre of open space for every 682 people, while in the east it was one acre for 7,481 people. Moreover, within a four-mile radius of Charing Cross, there were only two sites remaining that

memorial to the Charity Commissioners on the subject of open spaces, prepared by the Kyrle Society and presented in conjunction with the Commons Preservation Society and the Metropolitan Public Gardens Association.[17] I was occupied for a good part of the autumn in getting

---

could be saved: Parliament Hill Fields and Clissold Park. (They both were.) In this article Octavia asks: 'Might it not be possible to secure sometimes a green belt to a road newly cut across the country, plant it with trees, and make of it a walking and riding way?' This is one of the first uses, if not the first, of the term 'green belt'.

---

17 The joint deputation, led by James Bryce MP, vice-president of the CPS, met the Charity Commissioners on Wednesday 14 Decemeber 1887. The Metropolitan Public Gardens Association (MPGA) was founded in 1882 in response to the passing of the Metropolitan Open Spaces Act of 1881, which simplified the transfer of gardens and burial grounds to public authorities. This act was the result of several years of lobbying by open spaces activists, including Octavia Hill, Robert Hunter and the Commons Preservation Society. The passing of the act appears to have galvanised the activists who were agitating for metropolitan amenities, including Lord Brabazon, later Earl of Meath and chairman of the MPGA, and Ernest Hart, Henrietta Barnett's brother-in-law, the first vice-chairman, who was willing to merge his open spaces sub-committee of the National Health Society with the new association. The MPGA advocated the physical regeneration of the people as a necessary prior condition for mental and moral improvement. The public garden would assist not only in the purification of the urban atmosphere but would help to reform habits and morals as well by 'encouraging country tastes'. In his desire to return the slum-dweller to the countryside, Brabazon would be a keen advocate of state-directed emigration to the colonies, but for the vast majority the country had to come to the city. The Association had clear links with the sanitary reform movement, working in conjunction with the National Health Society, and medical officers of health lent their support to appeals. This was more than simply 'parks for the people', as the MPGA envisioned playgrounds and recreation fields with gymnastic and games equipment, plus free instruction, all publicly funded. The Association was determined to use its influence to obtain the erection of baths, wash-houses, and swimming baths. Initially the Association had a formal standing executive committee of about 20 people, but this was dispensed with in 1883 and replaced with a council that was in effect controlled by Brabazon, Hart and 12 officers: Rev. Sidney Vatcher, Viscount de Vesci, Lord Mount-Temple, Lord Dorchester, Sir Henry Peek, Bt., Sir William Vincent, Bt., Sir George Hodgkinson, J.T. Bedford, Y.H. Burges, Capt. G. Ivan Thompson, Miss Isabelle M. Gladstone and Miss Fanny Wilkinson, the Association's landscape gardener, who also acted in this capacity for the Kyrle. In 1883 the membership included Catherine Gladstone, Henry Fawcett, James Bryce, the Bishop of Rochester and the Marquis of Salisbury, the future prime minister. Tennyson and HRH Princess Louise joined a little later, while Walter Besant, author of *All Sorts and Conditions of Men*, was an early supporter. By the end of 1887, after five years work, the Association had disbursed over £22,000 and completed about 130 projects. However, many of these still had to be maintained by the MPGA, as local authorities often refused to accept responsibility for a garden or recreation ground following its completion. The foundation of the London County Council in

facts for the memorial, and, the more I looked into the matter, the more I was impressed with the fact that unless some very much larger view of the quantity of open space needed should be taken by the authorities, and some really great scheme be adopted for purchasing important land at once, the time would go past very rapidly when it would be possible to save what in the future would be felt to be almost essential to the health and well-being of Londoners. To secure the support of the public in pressing forward large schemes, and that at once, I must use all ways open to me in the coming year.

Among the gifts brought us by the year which has just closed may I record that of many valued fresh workers. I would note first a small group of gentlemen who have come to help in Southwark, one or more of whom are about to live there in order to join in night classes; their assistance has been very useful and promises to be even more so. Among the ladies who have come forward to help, besides the old friends, and new ones from various English and Irish homes, I should like specially to record the presence among us of help from the New World; one young Bostonian, who has come to study what we are doing here, and who has while staying among us thrown herself so generously, so heartily, and so helpfully into all we have at heart, as to cement yet closer the bonds between the workers in the old country and the new.

Then may I mention one loss—a great one. Mr Henry Cowper, whom I had never seen, sent me, on reading my letter about the Southwark Hall, £2,000 towards it.[18] We exchanged many letters, in which he shewed the greatest interest in the scheme, and several times last summer we tried to arrange a day on which he might meet me to see the place, for I wanted him to see it in all its confusion and dinginess, that he might realise afterwards what renovation his great gift had achieved. It never happened that when he was free I was, and I have no memory of him, but of his gift and his hearty, beautiful letters. I was waiting till he returned to town to propose another day to shew him

---

the following year resolved the dilemma, as the LCC was from the start enthusiastic about open spaces.

---

18 There is a copy of Octavia's letter to *The Times* (14 March 1883) preserved in the collection of her letters to Sydney Cockerell now held in the Westminster City Archives (D-Misc 84/2). It is annotated in Sydney Cockerell's hand: '£2,105 subscribed same day (£2,000 from Hon. Henry Cowper) by the end of March the total was over £2,500. I saw Octavia Hill in the evening of 14th March and started work as secretary of the Red Cross Hall fund.' He was still only 19 and would last for five years in the job (1892, p.321).

the place. I took up a newspaper to learn that I should never see him or hear him speak.[19] I thought it sad that those whom he had so served should know so little of him, but I told my Southwark friends what I had hoped to have told them gladly when he came down to opening or festival, and we have agreed to put up on our wall a memorial which will have the words,

TO THE HON[BLE] HENRY FREDERICK COWPER,

WHOM WE NEVER SAW,

WHOM WE HOPED TO SEE,

BUT WHOM GOD TOOK TO HIMSELF

BEFORE WE HAD TIME TO REJOICE HIM BY OUR JOY HERE,

OR THANK HIM WITH AUDIBLE WORDS.

Perhaps children may ask, 'What did he do, that we should thank him, Mother?' and the record, as well as the result, of his great gift, live after we who first knew of it are gone.

The thought of loss strikes a key of sadness with which I must not close a letter about so glad and triumphant a year as 1887 has been, but must turn to the great hope for England and London which all its success teaches me to trust more and more is well founded; for what are all the successes in my small circle but the result of the larger sympathy and deeper sense of duty which are, so far as my memory serves, growing yearly among all classes in England, and which, whatever the chances and changes of the future may be, cannot but knit her children together in closer and closer union so that neither chance nor change can harm them? For what can injure those in whom love is strong? It makes radiant the darkest night, and no pain can be so great that it will not conquer it.

A present from Venice, a mosaic of lovely colours, has been sent to me, and it is to light with its brilliant beauty a space on our garden wall

---

19 Henry Cowper's death had been announced in *The Times* on Saturday 12 November 1887. He had died at the age of 51 on the previous Thursday at Panshanger near Hertford, the seat of his brother, the seventh Earl Cowper. Henry Cowper had been born in 1836, was educated at Harrow and Christ Church, Oxford, and served as MP for Hertford from 1865 to 1885. As well as being the brother of the Earl, Henry was the heir to the title, as his brother had produced no male offspring despite being married to Katrine Compton, daughter of the Marquess of Northampton and a famous beauty (see 1877, p.87, n.4). The earldom became extinct on the death of the seventh earl in 1906.

at Southwark.[20] It is the Good Shepherd, and even our memorial will look less sad in His presence. The Shepherd lays His hand quietly on the head of the lambs which feed around Him, and the words are those which tell of His love. Into that love may we enter; then neither life nor death can separate us from Him, nor storm nor change can shake our perfect peace.

OCTAVIA HILL

---

20 *See ill. 3.* It was the gift of Mrs Lynch and Miss Gregg. The mosaic was by Antonio Salviati, and 19 years later Octavia was able to report that 'it has preserved its freshness of colour perfectly'. (*Red Cross Hall and Garden Report*, 1906.) Antonio Salviati was a lawyer who became convinced that the traditional Venetian skills of glass-making and mosaic were dying out. He collaborated with a workman called Radi to bring back into use techniques of enamel mosaic which had been abandoned for more than a century. He exhibited at the Great Exhibition of 1862 at the Crystal Palace, where his work so impressed Queen Victoria that she commissioned him to execute the roof and walls of the Wolsey Chapel at Windsor and, later, the spandrels and pediments of the Albert Memorial. He was also commissioned to execute the reredos of Westminster Abbey. However, Salviati had neither the capital nor the organisation to carry out commissions on this scale. Fortunately he came into contact with Henry Layard, the archaeologist whose discoveries of the magnificent base-reliefs in Assyria formed the nucleus of the British Museum's Assyrian collections and whose books on Nineveh and Babylon led to his being dubbed 'the man who made the Bible true'. In 1852 Layard was elected MP for Aylesbury and had an equally successful career in politics. Layard had a passion for Italian art in general and for Venice in particular. In 1867 he teamed up with Salviati to found the firm of Salviati and Co., which in 1868 became the Venice and Murano Glass and Mosaic Co. Ltd. Layard was able to use his contacts with British art lovers to capitalise Salviati's enterprise at a different level. Unfortunately, Layard was Chief Commissioner of Works and Buildings when the firm was commissioned to supply mosaics for the decoration of the Central Hall of the Palace of Westminster. Questions were raised about conflict of interest and Layard was obliged to dispose of his interest in Salviati's venture in 1869. (Norwich, 2003, pp.198-200.) The Good Shepherd mosaic was originally fixed to the wall of Red Cross Hall. (*Charity Organisation Review*, August 1888, p.369.) It has long since disappeared.

DONATION ACCOUNT, 1887

RECEIPTS

	£	s	d
Cash in hand	182	1	1
Miss Bonham Carter	2	0	0
Miss Chase	14	0	0
A.G. Crowder, Esq	5	5	0
Miss Cruikshank	5	0	0
Miss Erle	20	0	0
Mrs Evans	1	0	0
Mr Charles Flower	5	5	0
Miss Forman	1	1	0
Miss Frankau	3	3	0
Mrs Gillson	2	12	0
Mr Alfred Hill	10	0	0
Rev. Thos. Hill	0	2	6
Lieut-Colonel Hollist	5	0	0
Per Rev. Charles James	1	2	6
Returned Loans	1	5	0
Miss Lawrance	5	0	0
Rev. Dr Littledale	2	2	0
Miss Meek	2	0	0
Miss Orgill	1	0	0
Mrs Peile	1	0	0
Rev. Charles Plummer	5	0	0
Mrs Rolfe	5	0	0
Miss Emily Simpson	2	0	0
Mrs Leslie Stephen	10	0	0
Miss L.A. Shaen	1	0	0
Miss Tait	3	0	0
Mrs J.P. Thompson	2	0	0
Mrs Tufnell	5	5	0
Mrs Leonard Waterhouse (for Tower Hamlets Pension Fund)	50	0	0
Miss Jane Wells	1	0	0
Miss Mary Wells	2	0	0
Mrs S. Winkworth	78	0	0
Lady Maud Wolmer	1	0	0
Mrs Wright	10	0	0
Chas. Vaughan, Esq	10	0	0
	£455	14	1

DONATION ACCOUNT, 1887

EXPENDITURE

	£	s	d
Industrial School, F.B. and A.B., S.	44	17	6
Boarding out (clothes, schooling, and partial board for children)	39	4	9 ½
Providing Hospital and other Relief to the Sick	20	11	3
Pensions, A.M.B.	33	0	0
Employment for poor people	12	15	6
Excursions to the Country and other Entertainments	69	19	4 ½
Education: K.*	64	15	7
Tower Hamlets Pension Fund*	50	0	0
Rent: Fires and Books for Classes and Clubs	14	6	2
Care of Playground	10	8	0
Plants and Flowers for Tenants 1	16	8	
Printing and Postage of Letter to Fellow-Workers 3	19	11	
Open Spaces 1	7	0	
Cash in hand, December 1887	88	2	4

| | £455 | 4 | 1 |

*Special donations.

Examined and found correct, A.P. Fletcher, December 31st 1887.

DONATIONS FORMING FUND
FOR IMPROVING HOUSES, 1887

RECEIPTS

	£	s	d
Balance from 1886	34	15	11 ½
Miss Edith Fisher	1	1	0
	£35	16	11 ½

DONATIONS FORMING FUND
FOR IMPROVING HOUSES, 1887

EXPENDITURE

	£	s	d
Expenses in improving court	10	3	0
Balance in hand	25	13	11 ½
	£35	16	11 ½

DONATIONS TO THE RED CROSS HALL FUND, 1887

	£	s	d
Hon. Henry F. Cowper (the late)	2,000	0	0
Mrs Evans	100	0	0
Mrs Holland	100	0	0
Mrs Winkworth	50	0	0
Mr J. P. Thomasson	50	0	0
S.B.	50	0	0
M.R.	50	0	0
The Baroness Burdett-Coutts	20	0	0
Mrs Charles Buxton ...	20	0	0
B.	20	0	0
Miss Mayo	20	0	0
Mr G.T. Clark	10	0	0
Miss Courtenay	10	0	0
Miss D'Oyly	10	0	0
Mr Rogers Field	10	0	0
Lady Goldsmid	10	0	0
Mr E.A. Goulding	10	0	0
Miss Prance	10	0	0
Mrs Hamilton Yatman ...	10	0	0
Miss M. Arkwright	5	0	0
Mrs Bevan	5	0	0
Miss Chase	5	0	0
Mrs Deane	5	0	0
Mrs R.H. Ellis	5	0	0
Miss E. Erle	5	0	0
Mrs Gandar	5	0	0
Miss Haddon	5	0	0
Miss R.S. Henderson	5	0	0
Mrs Macaulay	5	0	0
Prof. and Mrs Marshall ...	5	0	0
Miss Miles	5	0	0
Mrs Pilcher	5	0	0
Mr F. Pollock	5	0	0
Mrs Stephen Ralli	5	0	0
Rev. Edward Stone	5	0	0
A.S.	5	0	0
Rev. E.S. Dewick	3	3	0
Rev. Dr Paget	3	3	0
Carried forward	2,651	6	0

	£	s	d
Brought forward	2,651	6	0
Mrs Watson	3	3	0
Mrs Shaen	3	0	0
Mrs and Miss Simpson ...	3	0	0
Mrs M. R. Brown	2	2	0
Mrs Denny Urlin	2	2	0
Mr H.G. Hart	2	0	0
Mrs A.G. Smith	2	0	0
Mr G. Smith and Mrs Smith	2	0	0
G.G.	2	0	0
Playtime	2	0	0
Mr A.C. Allen	1	1	0
The Misses Du Bois	1	1	0
Mrs Faunthorpe	1	1	0
Miss Hogg	1	1	0
Mrs F. Sheffield	1	1	0
Rev. W. Thompson	1	1	0
Mrs Wise	1	1	0
F.B.E.	1	1	0
Mrs Britten	1	0	0
Rev. J.F. Cornish	1	0	0
Miss Frankau	1	0	0
Miss Gosset	1	0	0
Mrs Hutchins	1	0	0
Mr A.T. Malkin	1	0	0
Miss Temple	1	0	0
M.G.G.	1	0	0
Miss Bell	0	10	0
Miss Blandford	0	10	0
Miss Edith S. Fisher	0	10	0
Miss Goodenough	0	10	0
Mrs Mills	0	10	0
Miss Catharine Punch	0	10	0
Miss Tabor	0	10	0
L.L.	0	10	0
Miss Laura Bird	0	5	0
Mrs Bleckley	0	5	0
Mrs Richardson	0	5	0
£2,695		16	0

RED CROSS HALL AND COTTAGES ACCOUNT, 1887

RECEIPTS

	£	s	d
Donations	2,695	16	0
Interest on Money invested by Miss O. Hill	3	0	10
Rent for Cottages	17	12	9
	£2,716	9	7

RED CROSS HALL AND COTTAGES ACCOUNT, 1887

EXPENDITURE

	£	s	d
Hall:			
Premium	1,424	0	0
Invested for Dilapidations	50	0	0
Commissioners' Solicitor's Costs	19	10	2
Printing 0	0	18	2
Postage 0	0	12	0
Telegrams, Tracing Paper, &c. 0	0	8	6
Account Books 0	0	1	5
Cottages:			
Macfarlane Bros, on account for building cottages	200	0	0
Architects Commission	10	0	0
Repairs to Cottages 3	3	0	9
Balance of Rent in Miss Hill's hands	14	12	0
Balance at Bank	834	11	8
Invested by Miss O. Hill	154	1	6
Cash in Secretary's hands 4	4	13	5
	£2,716	9	7

Sydney C. Cockerell

LETTER TO MY FELLOW-WORKERS

TO WHICH ARE ADDED

ACCOUNTS OF DONATIONS RECEIVED

FOR

WORK AMONG THE POOR

DURING 1888

BY

OCTAVIA HILL

LONDON
PRINTED BY WATERLOW AND SONS LIMITED,
GREAT WINCHESTER STREET, E.C.

SUMMARY

The need for thoughtful giving… opening of the Red Cross Hall and garden by the Archbishop of Canterbury… activities in the Red Cross Hall… hopes for a cadet corps… erection of Gable cottages… the printed letter must stand for personal thanks.

EDITOR'S NOTE

This surprisingly brief letter commemorates a triumphant year for Octavia in which the beloved Red Cross project in Southwark was opened by no less a figure than the Archbishop of Canterbury. Red Cross dominates Octavia's thoughts to such an extent that she says almost nothing about any other housing or open spaces work except for the reference to Gable cottages, which Octavia sees as a 'spin-off' from Red Cross cottages. Apart from a few opening generalisations about the need for careful giving, which can scarcely have seemed original to any except the newest recipients of Octavia's 'poor, general, printed letter', this is really the Red Cross letter.

14, Nottingham Place, W.

My friends,

I am late in writing my annual letter to you,[1] yet I do not seem to have anything special to say beyond recording quiet steady work for the year, and rendering an account of the money with which you have entrusted me. Even this latter duty, as work grows larger and larger by the year, is apt to be taken off me. For more and more the money you send me is for large, important work, which has public committees, and reports therefore publicly. This year, for example, you have sent me some £7,400 for The Lawn, but then it was as one of the treasurers of the Kyrle Society that I received it, and it is in the report of that body that the acknowledgment of it will be found.[2] Again, the balance of £7,000 needed for Parliament Hill when I wrote to you last was all given, and much of it was sent to me with private letters, which I prized much; but it is in the Parliament Hill report, which will be issued when

---

1   But we don't know how late as there is no means of dating this letter. The accounts were signed off by the auditor on 10 January 1889.

---

2   In 1887 a number of public meetings were held in Vauxhall led by Slingsby Tanner, Honorary Secretary of the Kyrle Society, Mark Beaufoy, MP for Kennington, and William Morris. They asked all 'Working Men and Women' to come and express their opinions about securing land for the People's Park. The park, which would become known as Vauxhall Park, was to consist of two sites put together, those of the Lawn and Carroun House. The Lawn was a row of eight houses with large grounds, facing onto South Lambeth Road. No.8 had been the home of Henry Fawcett, a popular and public spirited MP who has made a great success of his position as Postmaster General, in spite of the fact that he was blind. He had been an ardent supporter of the open spaces movement, and wanted his grounds to be laid out for the pleasure of the working people. Following his death in 1884, his widow Millicent Fawcett strove to carry out his wishes, working closely with Octavia and the Kyrle Society. In 1886/7 a speculative developer called John Cobeldick from Stockwell Green bought the whole site between Fentiman Road and what is now Lawn Lane, including the Lawn and Carroun or Caron House next door. Cobeldick intended to build streets of houses on the site, but he was persuaded to sell eight-and-a-half acres to the Metropolitan Board of Works. The Board was replaced by the London County Council before the transaction was complete.

the last of the deeds securing the land are signed, that the account of all these moneys will be found. I do not propose even, this year, to include in this my private letter to you, my friends, the account of the funds for so integral a part of my work as that carried on in the Red Cross Hall and garden because a responsible committee will from time to time render an account to the donors. I shall write only of the work there. I also hold in trust two large donations—one of £200, and one the balance of which is £158, given for special objects, about which I shall report direct to the donors. Here I only write as it were straight to you who have helped me, and worked with me, of all which during the past year has occupied us, and interested us, and join with that letter an account, duly audited, of the sums which have come to me to be expended entirely on my own responsibility, which are available either in great want for some important work which I happen to know might else collapse, or which stands in need of sudden reinforcement; or for those numberless cases of people we ourselves know, men, women, or children, who are in real want, and for whom strong, kind, efficient help is required. Such are the cases summed up under those dull general words 'Pensions', 'Hospital and other relief to Sick', 'Boarding out', 'Industrial Schools', 'Emigration.' Many a heavy heart has been cheered, many a worn body rested, many a wavering conscience fortified for life, by the sums represented by the figures standing against these general headings. They cannot be multiplied tenfold unless those who know, and watch, and love, and think for and with them, can also be multiplied; therefore they stand there not only in their dumb way, to try to tell you what your gifts have done, but they stand there too to urge those of you who can come forward as workers and friends to the poor; and to train yourselves to be wise as well as kindly. When we have ourselves made friends among the poor we can more easily realise what forms of help are safest and most helpful to those of them whom we do not know; and I am sometimes quite astonished to see how, with all the apparent longing to give daily necessaries to individual poor people, how with the vivid appreciation that food and fuel are, after all, the primary wants of life, a society for giving these to the aged, and even to the provident aged, those whose little savings have been lost in fraudulent club, or spent in protracted age, languishes for want of funds, and may even have to diminish the number of those old people who have best deserved to be kept from the workhouse, and who live in that very East End about which there is such immense profession of sympathy, and into which such a quantity of money is poured, devoted to schemes which are, to say the least, questionable in their effect on the best of our poor. It is very curious to me, I say, to learn that such a body as the Tower Hamlets Pension Society is obliged to consider the cutting off of some of their little pensions to the old, for want of about £200 a year in subscriptions; while money for free meals for hundreds who should support themselves flows in freely. Keep together in old age the couple who have lived simply and saved self-denyingly; send the lady who knows them with her little weekly sum, just enough to eke out the hardly won savings, and leave, oh, in true pity leave, the stalwart singer in the street; do not support the drunkard's home, during his idleness, by your wretched, inefficient help.[3]

This does not come exactly into a report of the year's work, but it is what has been necessarily much in my mind in watching all that has been passing near my people during the past year. Still I cannot help being hopeful that whatever of real sympathy, and sense of human duty, prompts the present foolish gifts, may, with that true instinct which accompanies all right purpose, lead on to wiser courses of action those who are quite single-minded in their desire to help.

And now to the report of our own work.

Red Cross Hall and garden were opened last June by the Archbishop of Canterbury.[4] We were particularly glad that he should open the garden, because he represents the Ecclesiastical Commissioners, who

---

3   The Tower Hamlets Pension Fund was one of Octavia's favourite causes, and a regular beneficiary of the donation fund, no doubt because of its close association with the Charity Organisation Society (COS). It was founded as the East End Pension Fund in 1877 with the object of providing pensions for poor persons who seemed worthy of assistance outside the workhouse. Applicants had to be resident in East End poor law unions where out-relief had been abolished. Cases for assistance were investigated initially by the district committees of the COS. In June 1923 the Charity Commission approved a scheme whereby the allocation and management of the Tower Hamlets Pension Fund was handed over to the COS.

---

4   On Saturday 2 June 1888. This was Archbishop Edward White Benson. Hardwicke Rawnsley sent Octavia a sonnet to mark the occasion, which ended:

> And shall your Southwark heart not faster beat
> Shall Hope and Love not more eternal seem
> And Life beneath your Red Cross banner rise,
> Where in the midst of woe and weary feet
> You set the Hall and Garden of your dream
> To bless the poor with thoughts of Paradise?

(Sent by Octavia to Sidney Cockerell, 9 June 1888, City of Westminster Archive, D-Misc 84/2)

had devoted the ground as a garden. We were also very thankful that Lady Ducie, who had laid it all out so generously and thoughtfully, was able to be among us that day, and to see something of the pleasure she had given, and was preparing for people in the years to come. Lord Ducie took the chair for us. On the day of the opening too, Lady Jane Dundas most kindly made the trustees a present of the £1,200 she had advanced for building the six cottages which overlook the garden. This gift of hers is of quite untold value, for the interest on the £1,200 gives the trustees an endowment sufficient to very nearly pay the caretaker's salary for the public garden and hall. The day of the opening was a lovely one, could not have been more beautiful; kind friends from far off sent us the most lovely flowers and green boughs in plenty; a group of friends undertook the decorating, under Miss Astley's direction, and they put on one of the great bare warehouse walls, not yet overgrown by the young creepers, which we hope will one day clothe them, a large inscription, red letters on white ground, framed with garlands 'The wilderness shall rejoice and blossom as the rose'; the Kyrle Choir came and sang for us, my mother was able to be present and watch all from a quiet little room overlooking the garden; we many of us had a sense that perhaps the spirit of him who had given so much to help, might be near us and rejoicing; all gave a solemn sense of gladness to the great gathering of fellow-workers, rich and poor, which will long live in our memories as crowning a time of very full blessing.

The garden has been a great success; the behaviour of the people in the neighbourhood has really astonished me, for though there are many respectable working people living near, who one knew would be careful and helpful, there are also many very rough characters and boisterous boys; yet the order has been excellent, and there has been hardly a flower plucked or a foot on the grass. We had a band in the garden several times last summer, and spent very happy Sunday afternoons, sitting out listening to music. If a shower came, we opened the doors and all went into the Hall. As autumn and winter drew on, the Hall became a more important feature in our work there. My friends, and tried fellow-workers, Miss Ironside and Miss Johnson, had kindly consented to become joint-trustees with the five of us who were first named.[5] The trustees appointed a small managing committee, with power to add to their number. We determined to endeavour to secure a

---

5   The original trustees were Lord Ducie, Lord Wolmer, Robert Hunter, Herbert Praed and Octavia herself (1887, pp.217–18).

small number of working men as members of the managing committee. One was elected to represent the Working Men's Club, and three were elected by the neighbourhood. In this latter election a difficulty arose owing to the fact that so few of the residents knew one another; but we hope, as common work brings us together, that this difficulty may diminish, and at the next annual election we may have several candidates to choose from.

The committee thus formed proceeded to organise various lectures, entertainments, and gatherings, in the Hall. These have been very successful and well attended. We have had magic lanterns, concerts, lectures, and plays provided for us by various kind friends.[6] On Sunday afternoons we have opened the Hall free to all grown-up people who like to come; by the great kindness of friends we have been able to provide really beautiful music, Sunday after Sunday; also they have brought microscopes, shells, water-colour sketches, photographs, books and vases. Always we have been supplied with flowers, and the Hall looks really lovely, all lighted up, and with its three great cheerful fires, which are a great attraction, especially when one turns in from the mud, fog, and general dinginess of a London winter afternoon in Southwark; tea, coffee, warm drinks, cakes and oranges are sold, and the Hall becomes a bright winter drawing-room for the neighbourhood, and pleasant little groups of friends congregate at various tables in the Hall, looking at the *Graphic* and illustrated books. We have had a splendid contribution of books for our library sent by the kindness of Messrs Cassell. We have secured a certain number of movable gymnastic apparatus, and a sergeant capable of seeing to the learners; this is put up on a Thursday in the Hall, and is used by the men's club, the boys' club, and the public on three succeeding evenings, and on Saturday afternoon. We have let our small committee room to a teetotal lodge, and they and the men's club have given entertainments in the Hall from time to time. There was a soirée for 200 persons on New Year's Eve, in the Hall, organised by the working men's club. So the Hall has been well used. We shall consider the winter session at an end on March 31st, but hope to take up the same things strongly next winter, with perhaps the addition of some classes and more lectures.

---

6   It is strange that Octavia does not mention here that the first evening performance in the Hall was the MacDonald family's production of *The Pilgrim's Progress* on Saturday 22 September, although she refers back to it in the letter for 1905 (1905, p.537). Octavia wrote to her mother on 23 September 1888: 'It is *most* beautiful. The working men, I hear, felt the play most. I fancy they followed the sense best.' (Maurice, 1914, p.483.)

We are hoping to organise a cadet corps of volunteers, composed of the boys under eighteen. An officer has most kindly undertaken the charge of it; we hope to secure a place for outdoor drill, free, and we shall certainly use our Hall for indoor drill. In Whitechapel such a corps has been the making of many a lad, and I heard Mr Barnett say, the other day, that he thought there was *nothing* which would so gather in some of the most difficult, rough boys, and do them so much good, as such a corps. The War Office has met us very kindly, and I quite hope the scheme may be set on foot. But we shall have considerable expenses, especially at starting; uniforms, sergeant's pay, &c., will be needed; to begin with we shall not organise a band, but arrange, we hope, to march out with another such corps. Later we shall hope for a band. We estimate that we want £100 to start with.

All this work among the men and boys has been possible because of the presence among us, as a resident in Southwark, of my friend, Mr Brooke,[7] who has given his life to work there, and round whom I trust

---

7 Although Octavia Hill is regarded by many as the founder of the cadet movement, the Southwark cadet corps, which would come into existence as a result of this initiative, was not the first to be formed. The movement can trace its origins to 1859, when most of the British army was serving in India to suppress the Indian Mutiny, and there was a threat of invasion from France. The Volunteers, ancestors of the Territorial Army, were formed, and in many cases boys' companies were formed alongside the battalions of Volunteers. Several public schools, including Eton, Harrow, Winchester and Rugby, had cadet corps, formed of boys and masters, but, needless to say, these did not involve working-class boys. However, Eton College supported a mission at Hackney Wick, in East London, where a cadet corps was formed. Then Samuel Barnett, the warden of Toynbee Hall, formed a corps in Whitechapel under the command of Henry Nevinson. This corps was connected with the Whittington Club and is variously referred to as the Whitechapel corps, the Toynbee Hall corps and the St George's-in-the-East company. William Ingham Brooke was a resident at Toynbee Hall at the time and had the opportunity to see how much good could be achieved by giving working-class lads a sense of discipline and purpose. He then moved to Southwark, where he lived at 60 Stanhope Buildings, opposite Red Cross cottages, and, in 1888, set up a boys' club in two small rooms over a forge in Red Cross Street. His location and activities (he was also the secretary of the Charity Organisation Society in Southwark) brought him into contact with Octavia, and he persuaded her to establish a corps for Southwark lads, based at Red Cross Hall. Whilst the Southwark corps was not, therefore, the first, the way in which the cadet corps developed as an important and still-existing youth movement was owing to Octavia's personal influence. 'The prestige of that remarkable woman's name', wrote Henry Nevinson in his memoirs, 'gained large numbers of supporters.' (Nevinson, 1923, p.93.) At a meeting held on 30 May 1899 to commemorate the tenth anniversary of the meeting held in Red Cross Hall at which the Southwark corps was formed (1889, pp.262-63), the Lord Chancellor claimed that 'the originator of the movement was Miss Octavia Hill—a

others may gather. So far as the men and boys are concerned, we could have done nothing but for him.

Red Cross cottages have been a great success, forming comfortable homes for families.[8] The demand there was for them encouraged me to recommend the repetition of the experiment to a gentleman who consulted me about the best and most safely remunerative use of a bit of ground in the neighbourhood. He has just completed the erection of 20 more four-roomed cottages, designed by Mr Hoole,[9] and I trust next year to be able to report that the result is financially successful. If so, it will be a great pleasure to many, for working men appreciate the privacy and comfort of these small separate dwellings.

And now my friends, I have only once more to thank you for help, without which all my efforts would be as nothing, for they are built up on the foundation of your strong support. It is because those of you who are working with me are what you are, and do what you do, keeping the spirit of all round you, so far as may be, gentle and duty doing; reducing the tangible things under your care so far as is possible into order, cleanliness, and beauty; it is because those who are further off answer with so responsive, so faithful, so generous, so prompt a help, whenever I tell of great and urgent need, that any of the things I have to report as done are done, that my home here is a centre of helpfulness, that the old work in the much-loved courts is carried on with quiet, steady growth, that eight acres of land in the quarter of London which most needs space, have been, within as many weeks, saved for the people for ever, and set apart as a breathing space among the high houses, for the poor to rest and be refreshed. How shall I thank you? How can my voice reach you? How can I even write to you with my own hand?

name associated with every good work.' (*The Times*, 31 May 1899.) The companies at Whitechapel and Hackney Wick were later absorbed into the Southwark battalion. Unlike the Volunteers, which were associated with public schools and the upper and middle classes, the cadet corps would cater for 'only genuine working boys... for to allow grown-up sons of comparatively well-to-do people in the ranks would be to miss the object of the existence of the corps'. ('History of the Senior Cadet Battalion', *The Volunteer Services Gazette*, 24 March 1899.)

8   The six cottages were let for, in total, £2 11s 6d per week, later reduced to £2 5s 6d.

9   *See ill. 14.* These were the Gable cottages on Little Suffolk Street, now Sudry Street. The 'gentleman' was Rev. Thomas Bastow, vicar of Peatling Parva in Leicestershire from 1885–1912.

Only this poor, general, printed letter can come to you; but read between its lines, and reach each of you, if you can, that separate distinct word of heartiest thanks I would so gladly write to each, and believe that memory is stronger than time and space, and as the several gifts are seen or remembered, thoughts of you each come to me with a rush of thankfulness which if I could I would send in written letter, or utter in spoken word. Not only then to all, but to each, let me be felt to be,

Yours gratefully,
OCTAVIA HILL

DONATION ACCOUNT, 1888

RECEIPTS

	£	s	d
Cash in hand	88	2	4
Anon.	100	0	0
Miss Ball	1	0	0
Mr F. Braby	10	0	0
Miss Braby	2	0	0
Mrs Brander	1	0	0
Miss Burrage	20	0	0
Miss Chase	5	7	6
Miss Darwin	3	0	0
Miss L.M. Dixon	1	0	0
Mrs Dowling	30	0	0
Miss E. Erle	10	0	0
Miss Edith Fisher	1	1	0
Miss Forman	1	1	0
Miss Frankau	3	3	0
Mrs Gillson	2	12	0
Mr Evans Gordon	5	0	0
Miss Gossett	1	0	0
Miss Harrison	1	0	0
Miss Head	1	10	0
Mr Alfred Hill	5	0	0
Miss Johnston	2	0	0
Mr Luxmoore	15	0	0
Miss Meek	5	0	0
Mr F. Nettlefold	20	0	0
Miss Orgill	1	1	0
Mrs Peile	1	0	0
Mrs Plummer	5	0	0
Sir F. Pollock	10	0	0
Mr C.A. Reiss	2	0	0
Hon. Mrs Robarts	10	0	0
Mr W.F. Robinson	1	1	0
Miss Lily Shaen	1	0	0
Mrs Southwood Smith	5	0	0
Mrs Leslie Stephen	10	10	0
Miss Stephen	0	5	0
Mrs Tufnell	1	1	0
Miss M. Wells	2	0	0
Mr W. Westgarth	5	0	0
Miss Wilde	0	2	6
Mrs Stephen Winkworth	116	10	0
Lady Maud Wolmer	5	0	0
Mrs Wright	10	0	0
Loan returned	1	10	0
	£522	17	4

DONATION ACCOUNT, 1888

EXPENDITURE

	£	s	d
Industrial Schools, A.B., W.B., E.	23	17	0
Boarding out (clothes, schooling, and partial board for ten children)	48	2	0
Providing Hospital and other Relief to the Sick	13	7	1 ½
Pensions, A., M., B.	30	2	6
Employment for poor people	1	17	5 ½
Excursions to the Country, Garden Parties	14	0	2
Education: K. and B.*	79	7	4
Tower Hamlets Pension Fund	5	0	0
Indoor Entertainments	27	16	1
Rent: Fires and Books for Classes and Clubs	17	19	6
Bank Holiday Party, Lambeth	43	5	8
Gymnastic Apparatus for Southwark Hall	27	0	0
May Festival	5	15	5
Care of playground	9	6	0
Emigration*	3	0	0
Open Spaces (The Lawn, N. Woolwich, Latrigg, Footpaths)	62	14	0
Printing and Postage of Letter to Fellow-Workers	5	15	4
Cash in hand, December 1888†	104	11	9
	£522	17	4

* Special donations.

† Of this, £95 10s is appropiated.

Examined and found correct, A. P. Fletcher, January 10th 1889.

DONATIONS FORMING FUND
FOR IMPROVING HOUSES, 1888

RECEIPTS

	£	s	d
Balance from 1887	25	13	11 ½
Mrs Clarke	2	2	0
	£27	15	11 ½

DONATIONS FORMING FUND
FOR IMPROVING HOUSES, 1888

EXPENDITURE

	£	s	d
Property B., various improvements … … … … … … … … … … … … … … … … …	20	19	10
Property A. ……	0	7	6
Cash in hand ……	6	8	7 ½
	£27	15	11 ½

LETTER TO MY FELLOW-WORKERS

TO WHICH ARE ADDED

ACCOUNTS OF DONATIONS RECEIVED

FOR

WORK AMONG THE POOR

DURING 1889

BY

OCTAVIA HILL

(FOR PRIVATE CIRCULATION ONLY)

LONDON
PRINTED BY PROVOST AND CO., PRINTERS
HOLLY MOUNT, HAMPSTEAD

SUMMARY

The need to help those who will never be independent... open spaces: Vauxhall Park; Parliament Hill Fields saved and handed over to the London County Council... housing: Ossington Buildings; Marylebone; Barrett's Court; land for White Cross cottages; Deptford; difficulties in the rental market... events in Red Cross Hall: cadet corps, library and clubs... outings and entertainments for the tenants... Women's University Settlement, South-wark... public questions: 'free' welfare services.

EDITOR'S NOTE

This letter contains news on a number of fronts, the familiar ones of housing, open spaces and entertainments for the tenants, and the important new developments of the cadet corps in Red Cross Hall and the founding of the Women's University Settlement in Southwark. However, it is topped and tailed by an important exposition of Octavia's views on the right and wrong ways of giving assistance. In the opening paragraph Octavia complains of the follies of unwise private giving, which has 'eaten out the heart of the independent, bolstered up the drunkard in his indulgence... discouraged thrift' and so on. At the end of the letter Octavia says that she has no intention of discussing the great public questions of free school meals and free education—and then does just that. She points out that these things are not 'free': they 'cost someone, somehow, just as much, probably a great deal more, than if provided otherhow'. With typical candour, she admits that people who hold opposing views to her own may very well do good, as long as they are sincere and remain open to new information which 'may modify all systems' (a favourite Octavia theme). However, the concluding exhortation to 'hold [Truth] very fast' leaves little doubt as to which side Octavia felt that allegorical lady would be on.

My friends,

Once more I am writing to thank you for all your kind help so generously given during the year that has just closed. The balance sheet, rendering account of the donations in money, you will find at the end. It shews that the largest sums have been given for education, emigration, boarding out and other such schemes, which have for their object the preparation of the young and vigorous for the battle of life. But I am glad to be able to point, too, to other entries such as letters for hospitals and relief in sickness; and to know that even the more radical help has been given for those who were forlorn and out of the way. We have made many mistakes with our alms; eaten out the heart of the independent, bolstered up the drunkard in his indulgence, subsidised wages, discouraged thrift, assumed that many of the most ordinary wants of a working man's family must be met by our wretched and intermittent doles, till we have almost confused ourselves about gifts at all, and we reorganise all the old bequests that have come down to us, applying them for the clever, the vigorous, the well trained, and the richer classes. In spite of all our mistakes, however, there remain among us the poor, the maimed, the old and the sickly—those whom we can never prepare for breadwinners, and for whom our help should be ready. Let us see that we know them. Take, for instance, a man following the unhealthy trade of baker; he has been our tenant fourteen years; he and all his family have behaved well; he belongs to a club which supports him some months after he becomes ill, he falls out of benefit. We get him a letter for Brompton Hospital; he has to wait his turn. That man will never earn again; there is no way of setting him up, no way out of the long illness but death. Of course his children will need help to prepare them for successful work; but also, is there no need to care for the man himself? And for his widow when he dies, until her children can support her? We rush from one extreme to another, and this in

---

1   The letter cannot have been circulated before the end of February, as the accounts were not signed off by the auditor until 17 February 1890.

large measure because we do not watch over the people we know. Our public charities are more difficult to organise; and though I am awed to see how they are passing one after another in prizes for the capable, instead of help for those who have met with real misfortune; I know well how difficult any great system of relief is to organise wisely. I think it at once unjust and cowardly of those who have it to do to divert the funds because of the difficulty; but I fully see the difficulty. But for our own private charity surely there is no such difficulty. We know, or we may know many an incurable lonely woman, many a widow with little children, many an old woman or woman whose savings are lost. It is with these we should share the blessings we have received. Let us indeed prepare the widow's children for life, strengthen the convalescent for work, teach the young man a trade and handicraft, so removing him from the keen competition of the unskilled workers for his and their good; and in doing such things rejoice that our money bears much fruit. But is there none of our money we would gladly, as it were, sink, let it just go, feeling that it is given to ease the last days of one who will never work again, to support, through perhaps long years, some young person suffering from disease? Why should we want all our money to do so very *much*; we have received it very liberally; let us be content for some of it at least to produce, not strong workers henceforward independent of us, but that peace in the heart of those who are roughly pushed out of the highway of life, and who are so apt to be out of sight in pain, or want, or loneliness.

The open space movement has made great advance this year, and we have had our own particular successes. The Lawn at Lambeth (eight acres in a central and poor district of London) has been saved, and is being laid out by the Kyrle Society. The time for collecting the £9,000 needed from donations was very short; and the help sent me by my friends and by strangers came most wonderfully. I could hardly have believed in such a success.[2] Parliament Hill and the rest of the land

---

2   On 21 January 1889 a meeting was held at Willis's Rooms, attended by HRH the Princess Louise, vice-president of the Kyrle Society, which sought funding to buy the Lawn, eight houses fronting onto the South Lambeth Road, of which number eight had been the home of the late Henry Fawcett MP, and Carroun House next door, in order to create a park 'in the interests of the moral and physical health of the neighbourhood', according to a handbill produced at the time. With Princess Louise on the platform were Octavia Hill, Emma Cons, Mrs Millicent Fawcett, Mark Beaufoy MP, and Lieut-Gen Keatinge, the chairman of the Kyrle Society. Other members of the Vauxhall Park Committee included Robert Hunter, George Shaw-Lefevre, Walter Derham and F.D. Mocatta, a wealthy Jewish philanthropist. A letter from the

bought with it, will all come into possession of the London County Council this year.[3] We are trying to get them to preserve the rural character of the ground. Certainly that is what the people who use it and they who bought it would wish; but it needs those in touch with the people to interpret their wish to the authorities.

During the past year the number of houses under our care has increased. Ossington Buildings, a group of new dwellings recently erected within a stone's throw of this house, and consisting of nine blocks, has been placed by the directors under my charge. It is inhabited by a very respectable body of tenants, who, I hope, will grow to be our real friends as time goes on. It was a great interest to me to take up the references of the applicants; and it is a real pleasure to see homes so tidy, so happy, and so independent. The place is of easy access; and I

Archbishop of Canterbury, who lived nearby at Lambeth Palace, was read out by the honorary secretary of the committee, Mr Slingsby Tanner. The Archbishop described the population of Vauxhall as: 'working men and women who labour on the Middlesex side of the Thames, but sleep "over the water". The condition of these dense areas is, as far as any material grace or brightness is concerned, perhaps as low as that of any population in the metropolis, or even in the kingdom. The streets are the playground of the children, the promenade of the young and the meeting place of the aged. Within the last few weeks out of 76 cases of scarlet fever in the parish of Lambeth, 22 came from the Vauxhall ward, which is one of only eight wards in the parish. To save the Lawn and Carroun House grounds from the builder, would greatly enhance the health of the neighbourhood, and secure to future generations of children a reasonable chance of growing up under favourable conditions of existence.' The Lambeth vestry and the LCC each agreed to contribute an initial £11,746 towards the purchase of the land, and the Charity Commissioners promised £12,500 Mark Beaufoy, the MP for Kennington who owned the vinegar factory to the south of the site, guaranteed to pay the £600 maintenance of the park for the first three years, and to pay the interest on a loan used to purchase the land. Spurred on by the efforts of a local working men's committee, the public subscribed a further £9,400 of the total cost of £43,500. The Duke of Bedford and the Bishop of Rochester donated £500 each. The Act 'to authorise the acquisition of the Lawn and Carroun House, Lambeth, and its utilisation for public purposes', or the Vauxhall Park Act, received Royal Assent in August 1888 and the ownership of the land passed to the Lambeth vestry in May 1889. All houses on the site were demolished with the exception of number eight, which became known as Fawcett House. It was originally intended to use this as a museum, but it was demolished in 1891 and a statue of Henry Fawcett erected on the site.

---

3   The London County Council had only just come into existence under the 1888 Local Government Act, with its first elections being held on 17 January 1889. It replaced the old Metropolitan Board of Works which had ended its long existence in disgrace after an investigation had revealed corruption amongst its staff, particularly the architects. The old Board had been distinctly unenthusiastic about the appeal for

trust that it will be possible to make it a valuable training ground for more difficult work.[4]

My friend Miss Yorke has also been requested to take over the management of another set of buildings in Marylebone, and has consented to do so.

We have succeeded at last in obtaining possession, through the generous kindness of two friends, of a house at the corner of a court where we have been at work for many years, where the character and condition of the houses under our management has steadily progressed, and where the existence of other property held by those who had different objects was a constant difficulty. This particular house was owned by a publican who did not live on the spot; it was the haunt of the roughs from far and near, and a perpetual annoyance to quiet neighbours. The other day in taking possession and going up and down the dirty stairs and into neglected corners, the times long ago came vividly to my mind; and I felt proudly thankful to reflect how different the other houses in the court now were from what I remembered them long ago.

I have, by the kind and liberal co-operation of the Ecclesiastical Commissioners, obtained the lease, on favourable terms, of a small plot of land adjoining Red Cross Hall,[5] on which this spring I hope to

---

Parliament Hill Fields, or any other open spaces for that matter, which had been one of the reasons for Octavia's low expectations of success. However, the LCC was to be a much more pro-active body than the Board of Works, not only in acquiring open spaces, of which Octavia approved, but in providing social housing, of which she strongly disapproved.

---

4   Ossington Buildings could scarcely have been more convenient for Octavia. It was beside her first houses in Paradise Place, which John Ruskin had bought for her in 1864, and a few yards from her own home in Marylebone. The original nine blocks lie to the north of Moxon Street (formerly Paradise Street), which runs west off Marylebone High Street. They are dated 1888 and 1889, and bear the intertwined initials PID, for Portland Industrial Dwellings Company. The company was connected with the Portland (now Howard de Walden) Estate, on which they stand. The blocks are named after Lady Ossington, the sister of the Duke of Portland, who was a leading light in the temperance coffee-house movement. Each of the blocks is of four storeys above a basement, faced in yellow London stock brick, with red brick detailing. Although they were supplied with water and gas, the dwellings were 'associated', with only two lavatories per floor. The former communal steam laundry building still survives.

---

5   Rent £30 per annum.

erect six more small cottages for working people.[6] About half the money for building them has been given to me; so that the interest on that part of the capital will form a fund to meet the expenses of the garden and Hall, in the same way that Lady Jane Dundas's gift does. This will be most helpful to the work in garden and Hall. Provision of funds for all the work there is a constant responsibility to me, and a further small regular income would be a great help. The cottages will be vested in the same trustees: Lord Ducie, Lord Wolmer, Mr Robert Hunter, Mr Herbert Praed, Miss Ironside, Miss Johnson[7] and myself. These cottages will be a great pleasure to tenants, who much appreciate having separate little houses like these. They will be in near proximity to the garden and Hall, so that the tenants will benefit by all that goes on there. Moreover the cottages will occupy space which we had much feared might have been covered by high warehouses, which would have prevented the passage of air, and kept off the sunlight from our little garden. We shall be able when building, slightly to widen the approach to the garden and to the Red Cross cottages on one side, and to keep the passage to them clean and orderly by erecting a gate, over which we shall have control. Besides this, White Cross Street, in which the new cottages will be, and which forms our only access to the Hall at night when the garden is closed, is a dark, ill-paved miserable street. We have, it is true, induced the vestry to put up one additional lamp there, and have ourselves put a very large one over the Hall door, which we light so far as funds allow; but nothing will at once protect, improve, and even light the street, so well as a little group of cottages inhabited by such tenants as usually occupy any four-roomed cottages which we have let. So, on many grounds, I am looking forward joyfully to the building there this spring.

Poor Deptford continues the great difficulty to us. The conditions of letting in London have become more and more difficult as years have gone on. The great supply of tenements—though much to be rejoiced in, on many grounds—has this of drawback, that it makes the rampant and disorderly tenant tenfold more headstrong; and it becomes almost impossible to exercise any just and wise rule, or to secure any order. Good tenants can be made comfortable, but as to improving the bad, except by strong personal influence, it seems much more difficult

---

6   These were to be the White Cross cottages on what is now Ayres Street.

---

7   Miss Ironside and Miss Johnson had joined the board of trustees after its formation in 1887 (see 1888, p.244).

than of old. They can cheat you of tenfold more than you can give them as reward for care, and with those who have neither conscience nor honour, the law gives practically no help now that the demand for rooms is so much diminished. Our task is difficult. But the more difficult it is the more I feel bound, so long as God gives me strength, myself to see how the difficulties are to be met; there are few who do not yield to patience, to work, to quiet watchings, to the ever wakeful thought and invention of one who knows and loves those concerned. I must say I feel now, more than ever, that improvement among such tenants depends on personal influence always. The outside helps were not very effectual without personal power; now they seem wholly ineffectual. Certain distinct progress, even in Deptford, I see. Perhaps by next year there may be more.

The committee of management of Red Cross Hall and garden agreed with me that it would be well to attach their balance sheet to this letter. So large a part of our work has been there; so very many of my friends have helped us there this year, in all sorts of ways difficult to catalogue, but vividly present to our memories that I thought many of my fellow-workers ought to see the balance sheet. They have enabled us to give a really capital set of entertainments during all last winter and this winter, which have been open free to the whole neighbourhood, and which have given very great pleasure to many somewhat cheerless lives, as well as beginning to cultivate in the younger members of the community a taste for better music, simpler acting, merrier and purer fun. There have been some really beautiful plays, first-rate music, and a few lectures. The Hall has been open during the winter months on Sunday afternoons with music, flowers, pictures, microscopes. The bright fires and the talk among friends makes the Hall like a parish drawing room. Tea and coffee and cakes are sold to those who wish for them; and really we have most enjoyable times there.

The Hall has also been much used for various athletic exercises; as there seemed little provision for such in the neighbourhood. The gymnastic apparatus is used weekly on one evening by the men's club, and on another by lads. Musical drill is held on Saturday afternoons for pupil teachers.

On two nights weekly the Hall is lent to the cadet corps, which is making great progress. Lord Wolseley[8] was so very kind as to preside

---

8 It was an immense coup, and a sign of the seriousness with which people took Octavia's various projects, that Colonel Frederick Maurice, son of Octavia's mentor F.D.Maurice, had been able to get so distinguished a figure as Lord Wolseley (1833–

on May 30th at a meeting to inaugurate the formation of the corps; and to his presence and support it is due that the corps was formed. 160 lads have joined, and a large number have continued steadily drilling. Sixty are now in uniform having completed the requisite number of drills. They are hoping to march out, and perhaps camp out, when the summer comes; we ought to get a band this year, which means expenditure for instruments and band-master. The influence of the corps has been very helpful; and we are heartily glad to have been successful so far with it.

One part of the work which has deeply interested us this year has been the library and reading room. It was founded first with the books so kindly sent by Messrs Cassell; but since then several valuable donations have been received from Dr Williams's trustees and other friends. The Hall is open for about two hours daily as a reading room. In summer, with the doors to the garden wide open, it forms a very pleasant place for men in dinner hour, or children between morning and afternoon school. We are not able yet to lend many books, as the library is still so small; but a limited number of tickets for books on loan are placed in the hands of members of the committee of management.

The girls' club, boys' club, and men's club have continued their work throughout the year. Attached to the latter is a very successful carving class. I believe the men have been deeply interested in their work, and have furnished good exhibits for the Home Arts Exhibition;[9] indeed they have quite distinguished themselves there.

1913) to preside at her meeting (see 1874, p.39, n.5) He was one of the most famous and popular military men of the last part of the nineteenth century, described by the *Encyclopaedia Britannica* (1999 online edition) as 'chief troubleshooter of the British Empire'. He led expeditions against the Ashanti and the Zulu in Africa in the 1870s, seized the Suez Canal and defeated the Pasha in 1882, and led the expedition to save General Gordon in 1884. He arrived in Khartoum on 28 January 1885, two days after the fall of the city and Gordon's death. He was created a viscount on his return for his efforts. He was joined on the platform at the meeting in Red Cross Hall by the Earl of Ducie, Lady Jane Dundas and Albert Salmond. Salmond was a solicitor by profession and a captain in the Derby Militia. He had been approached by Octavia in January to help with the formation of a cadet corps, and had applied to the War Office for permission to raise two companies in Southwark. This permission was granted on 23 May—a week before the meeting—and he began enrolling cadets on 31 May as the commanding officer. The Southwark cadet corps was attached to the Queen's Royal West Surrey Regiment.

---

9   The Home Arts Exhibition was an annual event organised by the Home Arts and Industries Association (HAIA). This was a confederation of arts and crafts classes

All this means, I need hardly say, the co-operation and steady kind help of many friends much too numerous to mention or to thank here, but the memory of whose help can never pass away.

Our ordinary summer parties for groups of tenants in other parts of London have gone on much as in previous years. The Archbishop of Canterbury again granted us the use of the Lambeth Palace grounds on Bank Holiday. We had delightful days at Haslemere, at Woodford, at Hampstead, and at Erleigh; thanks to the hospitality of Sir Frederick Pollock, Mrs Smith Harrison, Mrs Cash, Miss Johnston, Mr Edmund Maurice, and Mr Arthur Hill.[10]

Besides this, I have been much pleased that we have had several

---

inaugurated in 1884, initially promoting art as a recreational hobby, although in several cases important rural industries developed. The supporters of the HAIA were primarily aristocrats and gentry, like Lord Brownlow, its first president, who directed the Ashridge and Belton classes, and Lady Lovelace, who was still its champion in the 1930s. Alexandra, Princess of Wales, would found her own class at Sandringham and become the HAIA's president. The HAIA has been seen as part of the 'back to the land' movement and the regeneration of the countryside, but its main remit was 'rational recreation', keeping the working classes away from the music hall and the pub, and 'learning by doing', using practical crafts to develop moral character as well as learning new skills. The organisation grew very quickly once Earl Brownlow became its president. By 1886 there were 116 classes, of which 14 were in London. The exhibition for 1888 was held at the Albert Hall, South Kensington, which was to become the permanent home of the HAIA. At the close of 1887 there were 291 classes in England alone, and some 346 worldwide, with classes in Ireland and the colonies. A Home Arts class appears to have been initiated in Southwark in 1887, before the Red Cross Hall was completed. In 1889—the year covered by this letter—George Kimberley won a prize 'for his diapered oak blotting-book cover, carved at the Red Cross class, Southwark'. (*Building News*, 7 June 1889, p.790.) The Southwark class was 'under the skilled superintendence' of Miss Seawell, and in 1898 *The House* commented that 'the nine years Miss Seawell has spent on this labour of love have not been in vain... a collection of which both workers and teachers were justly proud'. (*The House*, vol.III, 1898, p.163.) 'Miss Seawell' was, in fact, Margaret Sewell, the head worker at the Women's University settlement in Nelson Square. In 1901 *The House* reported that Red Cross, Southwark, had submitted carvings and embroidery, and illustrated a set of bellows. See ill.11. (*The House*, vol.9, 1901, p.171.)

---

10 Arthur Hill, Octavia's half-brother, was nine years her senior and the son of James Hill's second wife Eliza. Arthur began his working life in railway construction, but then became involved with organising programmes of emigration to Australia for the government. It was said that he was responsible for 250,000 departures from Plymouth. He acquired a coal-dealing business in Reading in 1851 which proved to be the basis of his fortune, although he is described by Alan Alexander as 'a manufacturer of rubber goods'. He was elected to Reading Council in 1876 on the promise of 'a jealous regard for the practice of every economy... consistent with our true interests',

entertainments in which the tenants themselves have taken part. Several short plays, written purposely by my sister, have been most successfully acted by the children of the tenants in Marylebone to the great delight of their parents and friends. I am sure the learning, the discipline, and the working together under the kind and watchful care of Miss Hamer and the other ladies, who have got up the plays, has been wholly beneficial, and that the pleasure has been ten-fold greater because of the preparation. We have not got to this point in Southwark yet; but one gentleman is kindly beginning a boys' singing class, and we have tried some choruses on Sunday afternoons. It will be well if in time, by means of singing or music classes, by acting arranged among the people, and by a good band for the cadet corps, the performances in the Hall and garden should be gradually more often given by residents in the neighbourhood.

In addition to all the old work, I have this year been asked to join the committee of the Women's University Settlement in Southwark.[11] I

---

and he is credited with reforming the corporation's finances, issuing stock to pay off old debts, and then reducing the rates. He became mayor of Reading in 1883, a position he retained for four years, during which he extended the boundaries of the borough. He was asked to stand for parliament, but to Octavia's relief he refused. He lived for a number of years in Elm Lodge, Oxford Road, Reading, then moved to Erleigh Court, built in the time of Henry VIII but largely altered in the eighteenth century. The chapel was said to pre-date the Norman conquest. Previous owners included Sir Owen Buckingham, MP for Reading in the time of William III, who was killed in a duel for making advances to another man's wife, and Lord Sidmouth when he was prime minister. (Alexander, 1985, pp.75-78, 102; Dormer, 1911; 'Reading's Prominent Men: No. 6, Alderman Arthur Hill Esq, J.P', *Reading Standard*, 23 February 1907.)

---

11 The Women's University Settlement was the first settlement house to be dependent on women volunteers. It was formed as the result of a series of meetings on social issues organised by a group of ladies in Cambridge. Although the ladies were living in the town rather than members of the university, meetings were open to students at Girton and Newnham. In February 1887 Henrietta Barnett, who, together with her husband Samuel, had founded Toynbee Hall in Whitechapel in 1884, addressed the ladies on settlements. As a result of the meeting the University Women's Association was formed, involving ladies from Somerville and Lady Margaret colleges at Oxford as well as Bedford and Royal Holloway colleges in London. Its draft constitution gave as its aim: 'to promote the welfare of the poorer districts of London, more especially the women and children, by devising and advancing schemes which tend to elevate them, and by giving them additional opportunities for education and recreation'. The first executive committee meeting was held in June 1887, and the settlement commenced operations on 12 September in 44 Nelson Square, Southwark. At the first AGM, chaired by Mrs Alfred Marshall in June 1888, it was agreed to change the

have complied with the request not because I have very much confidence in the beneficial result of large, or many settlements of workers bound together by no family ties, and with no natural connection with a district; but because the settlement is the practical outcome and centre of a very large association (I believe some 580 of the young, highly educated, and thoughtful ladies of England) and because a small group of these, settled in the heart of the South London poor, may be of the greatest use. These residents may themselves be of those who can and should devote their main time to work for the poor, and may form a link between their poor fellow associates in many scattered homes and the poor of South London. The house, too, may be a meeting place, a resting-place, and a place of training for many non-resident workers. And the Settlement members may suggest, and organise, and hand on work, and bind the changeful groups of successive workers one with another. The past year has been little more than one of transition, as there has been a change of head workers with an interval between them; but this year I hope the place will develop and that much good may come of it.

I will not, in this, which is my one letter of the year to you, my friends and fellow-workers, enter on the great public questions which are attracting an ever increasing degree of interest. Whatever be done about free meals, free education (why do we call them free instead of paid for by charity, by rates, or by tax, do you think?), whatever may happen about strikes, or immigration from the country, for you and me there remain much the same great eternal duties, love, thought, justice, liberality, simplicity, hope, industry, for ever, still human heart depends on human heart for sympathy, and still the old duties of neighbourliness continue. Let us see that we fulfil them, each in our own circle, large or small; perhaps we may find the fulfilment of them answer more social problems than we quite expected. Perhaps we may find changes of system effect little reform unless courageous and honest men carry them out with singlemindedness and thought for others.

If the free meal, free education, subsidised house accommodation, attract you, will you pause and remember, first, that they are by no means free, but cost someone, somehow, just as much, probably a great deal more, than if provided otherhow? The question, if you get rid of

---

name to the Women's University Settlement, and that the main aim should be 'to raise character rather than diminish suffering'. In December 1888 Miss Gruner, the first head worker, resigned, but worked out her notice and left in March 1889. It was at this point that Octavia joined the committee. The AGM that year, and for many years to come, was held at the Red Cross Hall.

the word 'free' which is deceptive, clears up a little, and becomes 'Is this the best way of, 1st, providing, and 2nd, paying for, these necessities?' And then, having answered this for yourselves, see to it that you are wholly singleminded if you advocate this sort of subsidy for the poor. Be sure you do so neither from cowardice, nor from ambition. If indeed it be pity, genuine kindness, and a sense of justice that moves you, then the feeling is so good that in some way I believe it will lead you right; besides you will keep your power to watch and see and alter as you come face to face with facts, and may modify all systems, and keep the desire to do justice and help in whatever way is seen finally to be really helpful.

But, if you let one touch of terror dim your sight, and flinch before the most terrible upheaval of rampant force, or threat; if, for popular favour, or seat at board, or success on platform, you hesitate to speak what you know to be true, then shall your cowardice and your ambition be indeed answerable for consequences which you little dream of. They may come now, or they may come later, but come they will; for only Truth abides and will stand the test of time. Let us see that we hold her very fast. Only those who are loyal to her can.

OCTAVIA HILL

DONATION ACCOUNT, 1889

RECEIPTS

	£	s	d
Cash in hand	104	11	9
Anon.	5	0	0
Miss M. Arkwright	10	0	0
Mrs W.R. Biggs	1	0	0
Miss Bonham Carter	1	1	0
Mrs Bridgeman	2	0	0
Rev. H. Bulkeley	2	0	0
Miss Chase	5	0	0
Mrs Dowling	30	0	0
Miss E. Erle	10	0	0
Miss Frankau	3	3	0
Mrs Gillson	2	12	0
Miss Gosset	1	0	0
Alfred Hill, Esq	10	0	0
Miss Head	4	0	0
Miss Head (second subscription)	2	0	0
Miss Florence Davenport-Hill	2	0	0
R.B. Litchfield, Esq	5	0	0
Mrs Laycock	5	0	0
Mrs Mason	1	0	0
Mrs Meek	2	0	0
F. Nettlefold, Esq	20	0	0
Mrs Newbury	5	0	0
Mrs Peile	1	0	0
Rev. Charles Plummer	5	0	0
Mrs Ramsden Roe	1	0	0
E. Robins, Esq	5	0	0
Miss Lily Shaen	1	0	0
Mrs Leslie Stephen	10	10	0
Miss Stephens	0	5	0
Mrs Thompson	2	0	0
Mrs Tufnell	1	1	0
Mrs Tufnell: Subscription for 1890	1	1	0
Mrs Stephen Winkworth	20	0	0
Mrs Stephen Winkworth (Education K.)	54	0	0
Mrs Stephen Winkworth (A.'s Pension)	18	0	0
Mrs Wright	5	0	0
Miss Yorke	2	0	0
Transferred from Employment Fund	3	4	0
	£363	8	9

DONATION ACCOUNT, 1889

EXPENDITURE

	£	s	d
Pensions, A., N., V.	33	17	0
Emigration	21	2	2 ½
Boarding out (clothes, schooling, travelling and partial board for 5 children)	55	11	2 ½
Providing Hospital and other Relief to the Sick	19	18	10
Education, K. and B.*	43	11	1 ½
Reading Free Library for Children*	2	0	0
Care of Playground	11	1	0
Industrial Schools, B., A., L.	13	12	6
Cripples' training	8	0	0
Mrs Watts Hughes' Home for Boys	2	0	0
Tower Hamlets Pension Fund*	2	10	0
Red Cross Hall (Furniture, Books, Gymnasium)	24	12	6
Boys' Club	10	0	0
Country Excursions, May Festival and Tenants' parties	53	6	10 ½
Employment for Poor People	3	4	0
Printing and Postage of Letter to Fellow-Workers	4	10	6 ½
Cash in hand, December 1889	54	10	11 ½
	£363	8	9

* Special Donations.

Examined and found correct, A. P. Fletcher, February 17th 1890.

RED CROSS HALL ACCOUNT, 1888

January 1st to October 23rd

RECEIPTS

	£	s	d
Balance at Bank	834	11	8
Balance transferred to bank by Miss O. Hill	154	1	6
Balance in Miss Hill's hands for Cottages	14	12	0
Balance in Secretary's hands	4	13	5
Miss Miles	5	0	0
F. Rickett	5	5	0
H.B. Praed	10	0	0
A.M. Heathcote	3	0	0
Miss Paine	1	0	0
J.P. Thomasson	24	5	5
Mrs Scrase-Dickins	110	0	0
Mrs Lyell	20	0	0
Miss Laura Bird	0	10	0
G.M. Hicks	2	2	0
Miss Roget	10	0	0
Miss Temple	1	0	0
W.S. Seton Kerr	2	0	0
Mrs Evans	50	0	0
Mrs G.R. Cockerell	1	1	0
G.B. Gregory	2	0	0
Per Mrs Barrington, for panels	35	0	0
Interest, Red Cross Cottages	33	18	7
Rent of Club, three months	6	0	0
Rent of Rooms, three months	2	18	6
Sale of Programmes	0	10	7
	£1,333	9	8

RED CROSS HALL ACCOUNT, 1888

January 1st to October 23rd

EXPENDITURE

	£	s	d
Building Expenses	1,064	4	6
Architect's Commission	53	4	3
Legal expenses	49	11	0
Land Tax	5	0	6
Fire Insurance	1	5	0
Water	1	3	9
Furniture for Hall	40	9	8
Panels in Hall	35	0	0
Stationery	0	18	6
Postage	2	3	10
Draft Stamps	0	5	0
Printing	3	8	3
Woodwork for acting	1	7	5
Festival Expenses, June 2nd	11	9	9
Sundry small items	3	13	3
Caretaker, May 21st to October 23rd	23	0	0
Transferred to Cottage a/c	17	12	10
Balance at Bank	16	0	9
Cash in hand	3	11	5
	£1,333	9	8

RED CROSS HALL AND GARDEN ACCOUNT

October 23rd 1888 to December 31st 1889

RECEIPTS

	£	s	d
Balance at Bank	16	0	9
Cash in hand	3	11	5
Lady F. Mitchell	1	0	0
Miss Eve	5	0	0
Anon.	2	10	0
W.F. Drew	2	2	0
Mrs R.S. Henderson	5	0	0
Mrs Temple	1	1	0
Miss Ethel Smith	0	5	0
Per Miss Octavia Hill	10	0	0
Mrs Urlin	1	0	0
Mrs Laycock	10	0	0
F. Braby	5	0	0
Professor Tyndall	10	0	0
Miss Edith Fisher	1	1	0
Ecclesiastical Commissioners (for legal expenses)	10	0	0
White, Borett & Co (for legal expenses)	5	5	0
Miss Tabor (programmes)	0	4	0
Miss Rucker (work in Hall, March 29th 1889)	1	5	10
Lady Nicholson (for fixing panels in Working Men's Club)	2	0	0
Miss Yorke (for bands)	1	16	0
Kyrle Society (for bands)	4	0	0
Per Miss Octavia Hill (for entertainment expenses)	10	0	0
Per Miss Octavia Hill (for work in hall)	4	10	10
Per Miss Octavia Hill (for cleaning)	6	18	9
Per Miss Octavia Hill (for gymnasium)	34	2	0
W. Ingham Brooke (for gymnasium)	3	3	6
Mrs Randall Webb (for books)	0	10	0
Miss L.H. Stone (for books)	0	10	0
Mrs Stone (for books)	2	0	0
Red Cross Cottages interest	48	0	0
Victoria Dwellings Association Dividend	2	10	0
Collections and Sale of Programmes	12	0	0
Gymnasium receipts	6	15	2
Working Men's Club:			
Rent	28	5	6
Committee room	0	5	0
Hire of Piano	0	5	0
Purchase of Piano	2	0	0
Sons of the Phoenix, rent	2	0	0
Rent of rooms under Men's Club	14	12	6
Letting of Hall	4	19	0
	£281	9	3

RED CROSS HALL AND GARDEN ACCOUNT

October 23rd 1888 to December 31st 1889

EXPENDITURE

	£	s	d
Caretaker:			
Wages October 26th 1888 to December 30th 1889 … … … … … …	62	0	0
Overtime and odd jobs … … … … … … … … … … … … … … … … …	2	9	0
Cleaning …	9	1	2
Water …	11	1	6
Gas, Carbon, and footlights … … … … … … … … … … … … … … …	10	3	8
Fuel …	3	17	7
Hire, removal and tuning of piano … … … … … … … … … … … …	7	10	0
Music stool …	0	2	0
Refreshments for performers … … … … … … … … … … … … … …	2	12	0
Making and repairing curtains … … … … … … … … … … … … … …	2	9	3
Lamp over door in Whitecross Street … … … … … … … … … … …	14	0	0
Printing and Bill posting … … … … … … … … … … … … … … … …	32	9	6
Postage …	1	18	10
Limelight at lectures … … … … … … … … … … … … … … … … … …	3	15	0
Carriage of Pictures … … … … … … … … … … … … … … … … … … …	1	8	4
Carpentry and other work in Hall … … … … … … … … … … … …	8	16	2
Collecting box …	0	10	9
Notice board …	0	0	10
Cap for Caretaker … … … … … … … … … … … … … … … … … … …	0	6	6
Sundry small expenses at entertainment … … … … … … … … … …	0	10	8
Architect's commission … … … … … … … … … … … … … … … … …	0	3	6
Cheque book …	0	2	6
Stationery …	0	1	7
Legal expenses (for lease) … … … … … … … … … … … … … … …	15	5	0
Insurance …	1	8	5
Ecclesiastical Commissioners, ground rent … … … … … … … … …	0	10	0
Taxes …	4	14	4
Gymnasium, plant … … … … … … … … … … … … … … … … … … …	39	11	0
Gymnasium, Serjeant's wages and expenses … … … … … … … …	7	19	8
Library:			
Bookcase …	3	17	6
Books and binding … … … … … … … … … … … … … … … …	1	3	6
Garden:			
Soil …	0	8	0
Plants and work … … … … … … … … … … … … … … … … …	7	0	8
Pigeons' and fishes' food … … … … … … … … … … … … …	1	14	8
Door to Whitecross Street Entrance … … … … … … … … …	1	6	0
Mending seats … … … … … … … … … … … … … … … … … …	0	8	0
License of Balcony … … … … … … … … … … … … … … …	0	5	0
Paint, brushes, &c. … … … … … … … … … … … … … … … …	2	14	0
Sundry tools and small items … … … … … … … … … … …	2	15	4
Bands in Garden …	3	16	0
Balance at Bank …	4	2	11
Cash in hand …	6	18	11
	£281	9	3

Compared with books and vouchers and found correct, Ernest Jukes, January 17th 1890.

LETTER TO MY FELLOW-WORKERS

TO WHICH ARE ADDED

ACCOUNTS OF DONATIONS RECEIVED

FOR

WORK AMONG THE POOR

DURING 1890

∾⌣⚹⌣∾

BY

OCTAVIA HILL
(FOR PRIVATE CIRCULATION ONLY)

LONDON
PRINTED AT HAMPSTEAD RECORD PRINTING WORKS, HOLLY MOUNT

SUMMARY

Uses of the donation fund and the dangers of irresponsible giving... housing work: Ossington Buildings; White Cross cottages Southwark let before they were finished; housing problems in Deptford... Red Cross garden and Hall: Walter Crane's panel of Alice Ayres... cadet corps: camp at Churn; Southwark corps becomes 1ˢᵗ cadet battalion in London... outings for the tenants and a play performed by the Southwark tenants' children... open spaces: opening of Vauxhall Park by the Prince and Princess of Wales; Bethnal Green... Women's University Settlement: a new scheme of district visiting... the Hill family to move from Nottingham Place.

EDITOR'S NOTE

At 4,945 words, this is the second longest letter. Octavia opens with a stern warning against the perils of donating money to 'any huge, general, far-away scheme' which would disburse funds in a way likely to demoralise the poor, 'creating a body of thriftless, ungracious mendicants, living always on the brink of starvation'. The letter contains important news of the growth of the cadet corps, and of the opening of Vauxhall Park by the Prince and Princess of Wales—the Kyrle Society's greatest triumph. However, Octavia regards as 'the most important part of my letter' the announcement of a scheme of district visiting to be carried out by members of the Women's University Settlement in Southwark. This is surprising in view of the somewhat disparaging picture Octavia painted of district visiting in the letter for 1879—in a passage of which she thought so highly that she reproduced it in the letter for 1896—criticising it on the basis that the visitors lacked the specific, detailed relationship of a housing manager to the tenants under her charge. The visitors in this 'new departure' are to begin by taking up the collection of savings, but after that the duties appear to be vague. Although Octavia presents the scheme as uniting 'the human sympathy of the old-fashioned district visitor with the wise methods of action now better understood', it is difficult to see it as the breakthrough she presents it as. The real value of Octavia's association with the Women's University Settlement lay in the opportunity it gave her to formalise her training programmes for women going into social work (see 1892, 1893, 1894).

My friends,

Another year is ended, and the record which I lay before you will be partly an account of the steady progress of those efforts of our own of which you have previously heard, and partly of those which I have worked in concert with other bodies who will render their own report. I will briefly chronicle the progress in the various branches of our own work, taking up *seriatim* the subjects dealt with in my last letter to you. I will then touch on those efforts in which we have been associated with other organisations, for you may not be uninterested in a few words from me, in addition to the official reports which you will read in due course.

I dealt last year with that portion of our donation fund which had been devoted to the sick, the old, the dying, or the helpless; not that spent in putting men or women into self-supporting positions, or in training the young for the battle of life, but that spent on the alleviation of pain, the comfort of those who will never work again. I said, and I feel it always, that this kind of help should have the very first place of honour in any scheme of Christian charity. It is greatly to be impressed on almsgivers that the best way of helping the destitute is to find, if possible, some radical remedy for their destitution, such as training a widow's children: but that does not alter the great law that it is the helpless who are to be aided. Let us be clear therefore a certain portion of what we give should be just spent on the aged, the dying, and the disabled, not as if it were invested in preparation for life, but spent as in merciful help. But, oh! my friends, do not let us deceive ourselves. We may not enter into the blessing of thus sharing with the stricken-down people what God has given us of money, by subscribing to any huge, general, far-away scheme; we cannot delegate the duty, nor depute the responsibility on a large scale and without thought. If we are not prepared to give ourselves, at least to some extent, at least to the extent of choosing thoughtfully, watchfully, whom we will depute; and if those, who have not much time, but whose wealth claims from them large gifts, are not ready to choose large objects, so that the thought demanded may be possible to them; if they will not give in individual charity regularly and quietly, undertaking definite duty to groups of pensioners among the aged, or incurable, or to costly cases of training; and if they will not see that the personal care they cannot give is at least rendered by those whom they know and trust; then, believe me, their gifts are in terrible danger of doing harm. If we want to ease our consciences by giving money and yet will not take trouble about it; if we want to make a great effect with a little money; if we want to do what is popular; assuredly our alms will bring curses. The more I watch, the more the action of the public puzzles me. By rashly pouring vast sums into new largely advertised, wholesale schemes, their feverish excitability is creating a body of thriftless, ungracious mendicants, living always on the brink of starvation, because taught to look to what may turn up. And those who love and know the people have to stand sadly aside, feeling that all giving is fatal till such rushes be over; that growth of independence and thrift is impossible, while such wild action is frequent, and all the time they know that the blessing of quiet well thought-out gifts to their friends among the poor is a reality; and that there are old men and old women who have saved, but whose club has failed; bread winners stricken down with sudden accident; incurable invalids, whom to know is a privilege, and to whom if we know and watch and adequately help them we are doing unmixed good. Neither the remedial, nor the incurable evils can ever be rightly met *en masse*. It is singly and by those who know the sufferers, that the right methods of starting them afresh, or the only safe granting of pensions, can be arranged. So we would ask for full, real, and due honour for the part of our work which is pure gift, and request help for it as being an undoubted blessing, bringing messages of peace and hope to many hearts. At the same time we would add that these gifts are only possible to us, because the members of our group of workers are in touch with hundreds of self-supporting homes, and know people before the time of loss or trial comes, or stand, as it were, beside them, sometimes for years, while it lasts. In our courts what we dread most for our people is the lavish and sudden rush of ill-considered gifts; and yet we would say there is a steady, quiet opportune gift which is the crown of all friendship and has a life-bringing blessing.

I noticed four new groups of houses last year as either taken over by us, or about to be so.

Ossington Buildings continues to do well. It is a great pleasure to us to be in communication with so many happy respectable homes. The place is easy of access for our workers, and we have a large group of kind helpers there.

The block of buildings which Miss Yorke took over has quite marvellously improved under her care and that of my friend Miss Sim, to whom I owe so very much for her ever constant and most wise and able help in many ways during the past year. The block is now quite full, though it was nearly half empty when we took it, and the improvement in cleanliness and order is very much marked.

The house at the corner of one of our courts which we obtained possession of last year, so rescuing it from the hands of those who had rendered it a place of disorder and misrule, has not been a financial success. A great deal had to be spent on it, and then it was difficult to let. We earnestly hope for better financial results when the bad name of the place is forgotten. The rooms are large, light, and nice; and the place is now orderly and very clean. But in spite of the pecuniary loss we cannot but rejoice in the purchase which was made by a lady and gentleman heartily willing to risk, or if it must be to lose money in the purification of a place where evil had been rampant, and in a neighbourhood where many tidy families were trying to make happy homes and bring up their children in decent surroundings.

The third scheme I mentioned last year was that for building six more cottages immediately adjoining the Hall and garden at Red Cross. This has been most successfully accomplished during the year. The new cottages are called White Cross cottages. They were let before they were finished, being eagerly sought by many.[1] The sum of £690 was most generously given towards the cost of erection. The interest on this portion of the capital forms an additional fund towards the annual expenses of the garden and Hall. We trustees are very thankful indeed for this addition to Lady Jane Dundas's previous gift of the same kind; as the regular outlay for keeping up the garden, for caretaking, water, taxes, fires and cleaning in the Hall, to say nothing of concerts, library, and all the expenditure for making garden and Hall useful, are a heavy tax. The remainder of the money for building White Cross cottages has been lent at four per cent, and could be replaced by donations, should these be forthcoming at a future time.

Deptford remains a source to me, not only of anxiety but of pain. In spite of the splendid help I have had from my fellow-workers there, it has been hitherto impossible so to call out the sense of responsibility and care on the part of the tenants, as to render the houses anything

---

1   Let for £3 per week in total, later reduced to £2 11s.

like what they ought to be. And this, in spite of the fact that money for repairs has been poured upon them. No one not in and out of them continually would believe how much real, thorough, good work has been done there, and how much is weekly done. With even a moderate amount of care on the part of the tenants (shall I even say if the tenants were not positively destructive?) these ought to be, with the amount of repairs done in them, the prettiest, most comfortable little houses. It is true that they are badly built; the brick-work and plaster are shocking, and the roofs too low pitched, the sculleries have such bad foundations that settlements are frequent; but with all this the houses are nearly all of them well planned, comfortable little places, smaller than the houses now being built in Deptford, and therefore much prized by the people, as more often giving them the chance which they so greatly desire of keeping a house themselves. In spite of the above named drawbacks, with the amount and kind of repairs done there, if the houses were in the occupation of tenants, such as those we meet with in Southwark, they would be the most comfortable little homes. Certain things we have been able to do since we have been there. The drainage has been satisfactorily dealt with; the water has been all altered so that it is drawn from the main, instead of, as of old, from large open cisterns, not clear cut off from drainage; the walls, which we found with eight or even 12 papers on them, have been continually and thoroughly cleansed, many more cooking ranges have been placed, and all dilapidations and destructions are noted three times weekly, and so far as possible, at once put to rights. But in spite of this, the street is disgraceful. What more to do I do not know, I don't want to throw all the blame on the tenants of whom I am fond, whom we have failed to help to be better. I have had good workers there, better couldn't be, but of course it is a *great* drawback that we work from such a distance, and also that we have had changes in our staff. Whatever be the cause (I am quite willing to think it is my own fault, only I do wish I could see how, and set to work to remedy it) I am bound to record this street as a failure up to now, as far as human eyes can see. Only, and be this specially addressed to my fellow-workers there, I don't doubt for a moment that the spirit in which their work has been done has told, must have told, in ways which we can never estimate. Even the ordinary duties of honesty, truth, punctuality, exactness in business, and care in over-looking repairs, are an inestimable blessing, and a great example in such a street. When to these are added, self forgetfulness, humility, gentleness, patience, utter indifference to what is popular, thought concentrated only on the people and what is good for them, I do not believe that it can be without effect, far reaching and deep-seated, though we may never see it. The presence in the houses day after day, and month after month, of workers whose only desire is to be about their Father's business, has its weight somehow, we may be sure.

The Red Cross garden and Hall balance sheet is appended as last year. We have had, and are having most successful winter seasons there. The Sunday afternoon gatherings, and the Thursday entertainments are a great success. They appear to fill a want in the neighbourhood. I have most heartily to thank all those ladies and gentlemen who have at various times come down so kindly to help us. The music they have given, the plays they have acted, the flowers they have sent, the microscopes they have shewn, the kindly help they have rendered in so many ways have enabled us to arrange for a continual succession of the most enjoyable evenings, and provided for the people in the district the possibility of spending happy afternoons on Sundays with their friends in the Hall, which has formed as it were a bright, cheery, large drawing room for many men, young and old, and many women too. The workmen's club has this winter arranged to provide and sell the tea. I think we owe much to their skilful management.

The first of the series of panels illustrative of heroic deeds which Mr Walter Crane has so generously designed, has been this winter completed, and now forms part of the wall of the Hall.[2] It is that of Alice Ayres, the young servant who saved two children from fire at the cost of her own life. The incident took place in Southwark within a stone's throw of the Hall, and many of those who frequent it saw the fire and remember Alice Ayres. The interest shewn in the beautiful

---

2   *See ills. 6 and 7.* Mrs Russell Barrington described the opening ceremony, on a sunny Sunday afternoon in December 1890, in an article in *The English Illustrated Magazine* (June 1893): 'More than half of those who were present in the Hall that Sunday afternoon had witnessed the real fire and the real heroism of Alice Ayres, when the little oil shop was burnt to the ground in April 1885... Music began and we all settled down to listen. Something very beautiful was played. I think it was by Haydn, and while listening we looked up at the beautiful design which so nobly illustrates the brave girl's self-sacrifice: a worthy record of a splendid deed; and we all, I am sure, felt a very satisfying contentment as we realised the fact that the courage and heroism of Alice Ayres will ever find a record and acknowledgment on the walls of the Red Cross Hall for so long as those walls shall stand.' Unfortunately, although the walls are still standing, Walter Crane's panels have long since disappeared, damaged by the gas lamps. However, Alice's memory was honoured by the renaming of White Cross Street, behind the Hall, as Ayres Street. For another account by Octavia of the effect which the Alice Ayres panel had on visitors to the Hall, see 1893, p.344.

painting has been deepened by this personal memory. Mrs Russell Barrington,[3] to whose faithful kindness we owe the initiation and progress of the scheme, is very anxious for donations towards the cost of the other panels on which Mr Crane is now engaged.

The Hall has been much more used this winter, having been in great demand by the local clergy, local organisations, and by the Women's Settlement. It is a pleasant room, and so planned that it is much in request for social gatherings and performances. We are very glad that it should thus become a kind of parish parlour.

One night each week it has been used for gymnastics; but we much want some gentleman who would help, on the night the Hall is thus open for athletic exercise.

The garden has been looking very pretty and forms a nice breathing space and out-door sitting room. But owing to the illness of the valued fellow-worker whom we hoped would have been the centre of work there, we did not attempt last summer to organise any special festivals there. The garden was just used for the everyday play of the children, and for the rest of the grown-up people. One of my great hopes is to get the residents near to care for, and share in, the gardening. I am so sure it would be a refreshment and an interest to them; but the

---

3   Mrs Russell Barrington (*née* Emilie Isabel Wilson) (1841–1933) was the daughter of James Wilson, founder of *The Economist*. She had been drawn into the circle of the Pre-Raphaelites at an early age, when she paid a visit to Rossetti's studio in 1866. In 1868 she married Russell Barrington, a grandson of the fifth Viscount Barrington. She chose well, as he was rich, amiable and 'putty in her hands'. She herself was cultured, intelligent, well-read and an accomplished artist. She formed a close association with G.F. Watts and in 1876 he asked her to buy the house adjoining his in Melbury Road. Watts was used to women looking after him, and as a married woman Mrs Barrington was highly convenient. A gate was made between the two properties and a regular routine was established. His alleged shyness made him hate all money transactions where his pictures were concerned and Mrs Barrington came to his rescue, acting as a go-between for artist and prospective purchaser. Mrs Barrington was on both the general committee and the decorative branch sub-committee of the Kyrle Society. Acting on a suggestion from Watts to commemorate the 'Heroic Deeds of the Poor', Mrs Barrington initiated the decoration the Red Cross Hall, albeit with Walter Crane as the chosen artist. The 1888 Red Cross accounts show that she gave £35— a substantial sum—towards the cost of the panels. She was a keen publicist for the Kyrle and its activities: articles were placed in *Good Words*, the *Spectator* and the *English Illustrated Magazine*. Later Mrs Barrington proposed giving Octavia's portrait to Red Cross Hall but Octavia was against such aggrandisement and opposed the gift: 'Now I can't have this done... the committee should respect my wish about it and back me up in saying it cannot be'. (Moberly Bell, 1942, p.241.) Octavia had an almost pathological longing for 'silent obscurity'.

arrangement for them to help would need thought, and special workers to see to it. I hope something may be managed next summer. All we have been able to do was to get a few children to help plant the crocuses which we hope will make the place gay in the spring. At present the slides they can make across the playground without danger to passers-by are their main pleasure.

The lending library continues to be a great success, and we have to thank many kind donors of books.

On two nights a week the Hall is used for drilling the cadet corps, which has been extremely successful during the year. The numbers enrolled, since the corps was started in May 1889, is 398.

The numbers of lads who desired to be enrolled was so great that we were obliged once or twice to suspend the admission of candidates, until we saw our way to secure funds for the uniforms to which the fresh volunteers would be entitled after performing a certain number of drills. Happily the extreme and prompt generosity of our friends enabled us soon to begin enrolling again, to the great satisfaction of the new recruits. The corps has taken part during the year in important ceremonies. They went to the Military Exhibition[4] and did very well there. They formed part of the guard of honour from the 4th West Surrey Regiment which attended on the occasion of the visit of the Prince and Princess of Wales to Vauxhall to open the Lawn as a public garden. The boys were stationed all down the approach by which the Royal Party walked to the platform, and their young faces beamed with interest and pleasure. I hear that they felt much pride in having taken part in the ceremony, and felt like public men who had done something for their country, especially those who had sacrificed half-a-day's wages to attend. I feel, myself, that this corporate action, and the way in which it enables them to take part in national, or municipal, ceremonies, in which life of nation or city finds expression, is one good feature of this movement; and I was therefore particularly glad that the Lord Mayor acceded to our request that the corps should take part in his annual procession.

One most delightful feature of the cadet corps life during the past year was their camping out with their officers at Churn, for a week in July. One hundred and ten of them were able to go. It gave them a quite new, and wholly healthy experience, and they returned as brown as

---

4   On 31 May 1890. The Military Exhibition later became the Naval and Military Tournament, then the Royal Tournament.

berries. A charming account of their time at Churn appeared in the *Charity Organisation Review* for October.[5]

The band attached to the cadet corps has been taught by Mr Fletcher, and has progressed very well indeed, I believe. There is nothing which tells so much on the physical and moral training of a London boy such as a corps, and the association, in all its works and festivals, with the gentlemen who are its officers. But the uniforms, the rent of orderly room, the instruments, the necessary supplement of what working boys can afford to pay for expenses of camping out, are so high, that unless some special body of annual subscribers can be found, we cannot hope to keep the corps up as has been done heretofore. A few friends have this year given largely; but such donations could not be looked for in the future. I have myself a very great desire to see the corps taken up by some of the large boys' schools. Many of them are now supporting missions, and other works, in which boys, as boys, would not feel naturally so intelligent an interest as they might in the love of exercise and country felt by a small London boy, who has few opportunities of enjoying cricket, football, or fives. My friend, Mr Edward Stone, has interested some of his pupils at Stonehouse who have therefore subscribed to the corps; and I earnestly wish other school masters could

---

5   'Our Camp at Churn', *Charity Organisation Review*, October 1890, No. 70, pp.396-98. 'Our corps of boys between the ages of 13 and 18 is recruited from all the working-classes; the artisan and the labourer, the architect's boy and the cat's-meat boy, fall in side by side... Prudence urged that we could not possibly join the Home Counties Brigade at Churn. "It is all very well for the public schools, but you cannot afford it."... But we felt that it would be impossible to expect the boys to go on week after week, coming long distances, often straight from their work, without time for tea, only to march through the dusty streets for drill in an asphalted square.' The boys were all given a letter which had to be signed by their employers, giving them a week off, and they were charged 3s 6d—'a sum which the poorest could afford'. A battalion of 110 went to Churn for camp under the command of Lord Wantage, a distinguished military man and an enthusiastic supporter of the volunteer movement in the army who had been appointed Brigadier-General for the Home Counties in 1888. The boys arrived on Wednesday of one week and departed on Wednesday of the next. On the Tuesday, Lord Wantage entertained the cadets at his magnificent estate of Lockinge, which he had made a model of advanced agricultural methods and improved model dwellings for labourers. According to Octavia's biographer and descendant William Thompson Hill: 'Boys' camps were a new thing in 1890... this poor boys' camp in Berkshire was as significant as Baden-Powell's first summer, years afterwards, with his boys on Brownsea Island'. (William Hill, 1956, p.140.) Octavia had, in fact, anticipated Baden-Powell by more than 20 years in instigating cadet corps as a means of bringing discipline and purpose into the lives of working-class boys.

do the same.[6] The Southwark corps is now the 1st cadet battalion in London.[7]

The summer parties were a great success this year. Various groups of tenants were entertained at Haslemere, Chiselhurst, Hampstead and Erleigh by the great kindness of Sir Frederick and Lady Pollock, Mrs Ward, Mrs Allen, Miss Davenport Hill, Miss Johnston and Mr Arthur Hill.

The Southwark tenants' children will this year, for the first time, follow the example set by the Marylebone ones, who for eight years now have performed an annual play. My sister has again written one for their use; and Miss Hamer and her friends have trained the little actors and managed the performance. Miss G. Barter has painted, for use at St Christopher's Hall, a very pretty out-door scene. This adds greatly to the effect, and will be of permanent service.

---

6   Edward Stone's daughter Mary had been a pupil at the school run by Octavia and Miranda Hill in their home in Nottingham Place. When Mary became seriously ill, her mother came to stay in the Hill household to nurse her. She and Octavia became close friends, and it was probably Mrs Stone's influence which led to her husband's scheme to link his pupils with the working-class lads in Octavia's cadet corps. Moberly Bell places him at Eton rather than Stonehouse, where he was headmaster (Moberly Bell, 1942, p.197), and it may be this mistake which led to the apocryphal story that the boys at Eton paid for the scarlet uniforms of the Southwark corps. Eton College was already meeting the full costs of the Hackney Wick corps, and Octavia wrote a letter to *The Times* on 30 April 1891 urging other public schools to do likewise. Haileybury, Sherborne and Westminster were amongst the schools which responded. Although the War Office had provided the Southwark corps with rifles, all other expenses—uniforms, band instruments and the costs of going to camp—had to be met from private sources.

---

7   Four cadet corps were required to form a battalion. Albert Salmond had originally undertaken to form two companies in Southwark, but the rush of applicants soon caused this to grow to three, then four. In October 1890 the War Office recognised the Southwark corps as the first cadet battalion in London and the senior in the country. Major Salmond remained the commanding officer, with William Ingham Brooke, Lancelot and Cyril Bennett and Benton Fletcher as his four captains. In March 1891 Salmond amalgamated the Whitechapel and Hackney Wick (Eton Mission) companies, which actually pre-dated the founding of the Southwark corps, to create the first six-company cadet battalion. He subsequently raised companies in Paddington, North Kensington, Marylebone, St Andrew's (Westminster), St Peter's (Westminster), Bethnal Green and Stepney, all of which became part of the 1st Cadet Battalion Queen's Royal West Surrey Regiment. (*The Regiment*, 8 October 1898, Lieut. Colonel Albert Salmond, letter to the editor.) The national cadet movement developed out of this battalion. A short history of the battalion, *Sixty Years a Cadet*, published in 1949, claimed that 6,000 boys had been enrolled in Southwark alone since the first member was accepted in 1889. (William Hill, 1956, p.137.)

I think this ends the principal catalogue of progress in our ordinary regular work, except that I have said nothing of the steady management of our older groups of houses by the friends of so long standing, and of the gradual training of the ever fresh band of willing workers who come in each year to learn how to manage courts and blocks. They who are with me regularly, and thus helping in the main body of our serious duties, seem almost too near to be thanked; while their work, bound up as it is with the lives and homes of the tenants who are their friends and ours, seems best left in the silence of its own deep course. They need no word from me; they know what I feel of the help they render, for they and I are very near, and in our difficulties and rejoicing are one.

To touch now on the more public work in which I have been associated not only with groups of friends and fellow-workers, but with organised bodies rendering their own reports, let me just touch first on the great joy of remembering that the Lawn, or as they like it called, Vauxhall Park, is saved and handed over to the public. Those only who were working with us at the time know the immense difficulties and anxieties through which we had to make our way towards this result, and how the responsibility of a large public ceremony at which the Prince and Princess of Wales were to preside, had to be undertaken pretty suddenly by the Kyrle Society.[8] Never shall I forget the devotion, or the power, of some of the men and women who came in then to

---

8   *See ill. 12.* On Monday 7 July 1890 'in fulfilment of a promise most kindly made at the interview with working men at Lambeth Palace in the previous winter, HRH the Prince of Wales, accompanied by HRH the Princess of Wales and TRH the Princesses Victoria and Maude, declared the park open to the people… A feature of the ceremony was the presence and co-operation of working men. The drives and paths in the Park were lined with the members of the various friendly societies of Lambeth, and an address written by the Working Men's Committee was presented to the Prince, who responded most graciously and cordially.' (Kyrle Society report 1890, p.16.) The Archbishop of Canterbury also attended, as did the Duke of Edinburgh and Princess Louise, as president and vice-president of the Kyrle Society respectively. Although Octavia was, understandably, so enthusiastic about this enormously prestigious ceremony that she devotes most of the space in this letter allocated to Vauxhall Park to it, the involvement of the Kyrle had been much more than a merely social one. The Kyrle had acted as a focus for the many groups and individuals involved with the campaign, and had raised £6,710 for the scheme in 1889. (Kyrle Society report 1889, p.31.) This was in addition to the £7,400 that Octavia had raised in 1888 (1888, p.241). Out of this, the Kyrle paid £2,000 for draining, fencing and laying out the park. They commissioned Fanny Rollo Wilkinson, one of the few women landscape gardeners and a member of the Kyrle's open spaces sub-committee, to design the

help; never shall I forget the extreme and most willing and gracious kindness shewn by the Prince and Princess of Wales. It was to me a very solemn scene, because all classes were so entirely gathered in, each to do what in them lay to accomplish the good work. And now it is done; and for long years, as long as our people need it, and wish for it, flowers will grow there, and sunlight have leave to penetrate, and no wheels will make dust or noise there; but, near their homes, the old may rest, and the young play; and spring after spring the golden crocuses shall teach how bright life comes out of the dark earth, and after the winter chill.[9]

One more open space I believe we may amongst us claim the honour

---

park for them. Unfortunately, 'the work of laying out the ground has been considerably hampered by the action taken by the vestry of Lambeth in insisting upon a personal guarantee from the officers of the Society, that the grounds should be laid out in accordance with a plan deposited at the vestry hall beforehand. Such action, fortunately an isolated instance, tied the sub-committee's hands to a great extent, as it was impossible for the officers to undertake more than a limited pecuniary responsibility beyond the funds in the committee's hands and the scheme suffered in consequence.' (Kyrle Society report 1889, p.19.) Fanny Wilkinson's design was informal and picturesque. It consisted of two main paths meeting at a right angle at Fawcett House, off-centre of the layout, together with other winding paths and banks of shrubs and flowers. 'His Royal Highness also planted a tree in Mr Fawcett's old garden, and expressed his pleasure not only in the preservation of the Park, but in the retention intact of Mr Fawcett's house... Fawcett House is now historical as the home of Henry Fawcett during the last ten years of his life. It was here that he pondered scheme after scheme for the bettering of the condition of the poor.' (Kyrle Society report 1890, p.16.) Unfortunately, even the warm sentiments of the Prince of Wales were not sufficient to preserve Fawcett House, which the Lambeth vestry demolished in 1891, despite protests from the Kyrle Society. However, in 1892, the open spaces sub-committee of the Kyrle had the pleasure of announcing 'that Sir Henry Doulton has made a colossal terra cotta memorial statue [of Henry Fawcett] from designs by Mr Tinworth', and this was erected on the site of the house. (Kyrle Society report 1892, p.17.) The present whereabouts of the statue, sculpted by George Tinworth and adorned with panels representing Justice, Good and Bad News, Sympathy, Courage, Truth, India and the Post Office, is unknown. When the contents of Fawcett House were auctioned they raised £75 10s, which was accepted by Henry Doulton as payment for a very fine fountain of Doulton Ware, made at his nearby factory in Lambeth and erected on the east side of the park. The architect Charles Harrison Townsend, a member of the Kyrle Society, designed the entrance gates and railings, most of which are no longer there. His later work included the Horniman Museum in Forest Hill (1901), the Whitechapel Art Gallery (1901) and the Bishopsgate Institute.

---

9   Visiting Vauxhall Park, while researching her book *London Parks and Gardens*, the Hon. Mrs Evelyn Cecil noted that 'what gives most pleasure is the sand-garden for little children. For hours and hours these small mites are happily occupied digging

of having saved this year. I mean the Poors' Land at Bethnal Green, about which I wrote a letter in *The Times* of November 9th.[10] Since then we have learnt that the Charity Commissioners feel that the trust deed, which has for two hundred years preserved the land from being built over, cannot be set aside if building be opposed. Therefore as the Kyrle and Commons Preservation Societies certainly would feel it their duty to oppose the building over six-and-a-half acres of land in Bethnal

---

and making clean mud pies, while their elders sit by and work. It is touching to see the miniature castles and carefully patted puddings at the close of a busy baby's day.' (Cecil, 1907, p.163.)

---

10 The letter was actually published on 6 November 1890. Octavia reported on a meeting she had attended during the summer 'composed of the poorest working people in Bethnal Green…One speaker said that: "It wasn't much of the land in which they were born they seemed to have much say in, but this bit did seem to belong to them, and it did seem hard the gentlemen at the West End wanted to decide about it". Another said: "One gentleman at Whitehall told us it was 16 years since he had been at Bethnal Green. Now I was born and bred there, and I do think I ought to know best what we want down here for the missus and the little ones". A third said "he had been born in Bethnal Green, and he could remember flying his kite in this place and how it was open fields there…and now every space is covered with buildings, every little front garden, every back yard is covered with buildings, the model lodging houses go up to the sky, and where are the children to play?"' There were proposals to sell off some of the Poors' Land in Bethnal Green for a town hall, a hospital and a library. The land had been held in trust since 1677 when the property owners surrounding the green bought the land to prevent it being built on. Some land had already been sold in 1872 to accommodate the new Bethnal Green Museum of Childhood. The trustees voted in favour of the sale but the Metropolitan Public Gardens Association, the Kyrle Society, the Commons Preservation Society and the London County Council vigorously opposed the scheme. The Charity Commissioners initially supported the proposal, intending the 'resettle the trust' by applying the funds to technical and art schools. In the face of the protest, they intervened in February to devise a new scheme for a permanently maintained public recreation ground 'accessible to the inhabitants of the said parish'. This was eventually agreed after several years of legal wrangling and the land was transferred to the London County Council. The gardens were opened to the public on Whit Monday, 3 June 1895, the first time for over 200 years that the public were allowed to walk there. It was known locally as Barmy Park because of the lunatic asylum nearby. £6,000 was paid for the larger 6.5 acre southern section, and £2,000 for the northern half. According to J.J. Sexby, the LCC's chief officer of parks, 'the principal works of laying-out comprised the erection of an ornamental wrought-iron enclosing fence' parts of which can still be seen, and 'the formation of broad walks and shrubberies—a sunk garden with a central fountain flanked by an extensive rockery for the display of alpine and other suitable plants' and a gymnasium for the children 'together with other necessary buildings'. (Sexby, 1898, pp.225-54.) In 1969 the gardens became part of a conservation area.

Green, left under trust not to be built over, the land will, I understand, undoubtedly be preserved and thrown open, and the Charity Commissioners are directing that this should be done. The details only remain to be settled.

I have received during the past year, not only a great many generous donations for open spaces now secured, but from one friend the very large gift of £1,000 as a trust for future use. It is placed in the names of General Innes and myself, as we are joint treasurers of the Kyrle Society; and it will be devoted to certain pioneer work for open spaces which I have it in my mind to carry through if it be possible in the coming year.

I come now to what is perhaps the most important part of my letter, because it relates, not to steady continuance and development of the old work, but to a description of what is, in some measure, a new departure.

I refer to the work which I am just planning to start in Southwark. The scheme has been drawn up at the request of the Women's University Settlement committee, of which I am a member; and it will be worked by them.[11] The paper sketching the scheme was read at a meeting of members of the WUA; which was held here, in November last. It will not be published, as I am anxious the work should begin quietly; but I think it may interest some of you to hear a little about it. We propose to enrol as district visitors, under an experienced leader, those ladies who would like to be permanently connected with a small group of families in Southwark, with whom, as time goes on, they may become real friends. But we propose immediately to give these district visitors definite work to do, so as to obtain for them something like the relations we secure for those ladies who manage houses for us. Necessarily the duties will be different, because the houses in which these new visitors will be will not be under our charge as the others are, so that neither the landlord's duties nor his powers can be delegated to them. But, to make up, so far as may be, for this, we shall ask them to take up collection of savings from room to room; and we shall gradually add to that, so far as each visitor may desire, such work for the various legal and

---

11 A sub-committee was formed consisting of Octavia, Miss Argles and Miss Sewell, the head worker at the Settlement. Although Octavia 'talks up' the visiting in the next letter, 'the all-purpose district visiting scheme never became very widespread, being confined to only one parish in Southwark'. Its real value to the Settlement lay in the way in which it provided a focus for activities. The newsletter of Newnham College, Cambridge in that year reported that: 'It is generally hoped that on these lines the rather loose ends of present Settlement work may be gathered together and a unity and definiteness given to it which it at present lacks'. (Judge, 1994, pp. 12 and 15.)

voluntary bodies as may concern the residents in their several districts. Definite work for the school board, the guardians, the Charity Organisation Society, the Mabys,[12] the Country Holidays,[13] and many other agencies, will be reported to, or committed to them through a trained secretary, who will act as secretary to the group of visitors, and will be attached to the settlement. I will not here go into detail. I will only add that the effect of the whole scheme will be, that a visitor will have a small and permanent group of families to watch over; and that she will, so far as her time and power allows, be able to do among them all the various things which are needed to be done by the organised and thoughtfully planned agencies, bringing to these plans that individual knowledge, affection and continuous watchfulness, which will enable her to apply intelligently and sympathetically, as from friend to friend, those systems which may be wise on the whole, but which, unless they are individually applied, lack the life and the affectionateness which render them really helpful. This week we are to settle in a few of our new visitors; and I hope they will link the inmates of some courts in Southwark with happy West End homes, in a really human way. I shall be delighted to see, by appointment, any possible new workers who would like to unite the human sympathy of the old-fashioned district-visitor with the wise methods of action now better understood, and who would like to do a little of many things for her own people, in a small area, rather than much of one thing for a large mass of scattered strangers.

This, my friends, is the last letter I shall write to you from the home of 30 years.[14] We are to leave the old home in March. It is so crowded

---

12 Metropolitan Association for Befriending Young Servants, founded by Octavia's friend Mrs Nassau Senior (1876, pp.69-70).

---

13 The Children's Country Holiday Fund had been founded by Samuel and Henrietta Barnett as a means of giving poor and sickly children a recuperative holiday in a country cottage, where they would be the guests of philanthropic couples. As a result of a letter from Samuel Barnett to the *Guardian* towards the end of 1877, nine children were given holidays. The next year it was 33, and the next year 173. In 1881 the arrangement was formalised as The Children's Holiday Committee, changing its name to The Children's Country Holiday Fund in 1884. By 1918 Henrietta Barnett estimated that 956,253 London children had been sent 'to gain health and gladness among fields and flowers and on sea-shores'. (Barnett, 1918, i, pp.177-79.)

---

14 Nottingham Place has been re-numbered since Octavia's day. Her number 14 became number 42 and was demolished to make way for the Princess Grace Hospital. The new home at 190 Marylebone Road—which has also been demolished—was

with memories, that it seems quite alive with them; and there isn't a sound of a latch or bell, an echo or a footfall, that has not associations which wake the years that are past. Past! How then is it that I feel now more than ever, as the time to leave the familiar rooms draws so close, that I shall carry all with me? The little tree that is now three feet high, which has grown outside my window from the acorn I planted there long ago, and which for so many years gladdened me with its fresh green in spring, is going to Crockham, and is to be set free from London gloom, having near it the words from my mother's fairy tale for children which I remember since my own childhood.

> Oh! I would live again!
> Then plant me in the plain,
> And let the sun and rain,
> My pleasant life sustain,
> Oh! I would live again!

And as its life is, we hope, to be continuous, though all around it is changed, shall ours, the greater human life, fail to be so? Surely that spiritual continuity which has made us each what we are, which makes the home, the work, what they are, and which links us with such eternal

---

only a stone's throw away. 'It is smaller than this, with much smaller rooms', Miranda Hill wrote to a friend, 'but... it has a garden in front—and a yard behind—to our great delight; a little light, space and *quiet* being our chief requirements. There will be room for Octavia and me with Miss Yorke and two of the friends now living with us, Miss Pearson and Miss Sim. It would be a great sorrow to part with them; so we are grateful to get a house large enough for us all. The Marylebone Road used to be noisy, but now it has a wooden pavement, a great boon.' (12 November 1890, Maurice, 1914, pp.514-15 and Moberly Bell, 1942, pp.217-18.) Octavia mentions Miss Sim earlier in this letter as helping Harriot Yorke to manage a block of buildings in Marylebone. She had originally been employed as Octavia's secretary and housekeeper. 'Miss Pearson did accounts but was not involved in the housing work. She was an aunt of Robin Barrington-Ward, editor of *The Times*.' (Darley, 1990, p.373.) Harriot Yorke, who had been Octavia's constant companion since 1877, had moved into the household in 1884, when the small girls' school that Octavia and her sisters had been running in the Nottingham Place house closed. Octavia's mother and her youngest sister Florence had already moved out, first to Pinner and then to Tunbridge Wells. Marathon House, which occupies the block between Balcombe Street and Gloucester Place, and is now 200 Marylebone Road, has a plaque in its foyer stating that: 'On the site of this building at 190 Marylebone Road/ Octavia Hill/ Co-founder of the National Trust/ Pioneer of housing reform/ Lived and worked from/ 1890 until her death in 1912.' The move actually took place in March 1891.

links to the friends who are left to us now, and to those who have gone before us into the world of light, can be sundered by no change even in the beloved house which has been our home for so long. Shall the oak put out its spring leaves in the sunlight at Crockham shewing how its little roots are penetrating into the earth and taking hold? And shall we have no sunlight on our faces in the new home that is to be, shewing that we too are able to cling, again and again, with ever fresh strength, and with roots that will draw life, while life be ours, from whatever earthly things our Father gives us? Change may come, but not in our memory, not in our love, and while they hold, what matters any outward change? So surely I may sign myself in the new days as in the old, in the new home as in the old,

Faithfully yours
OCTAVIA HILL

DONATION ACCOUNT, 1890

RECEIPTS

	£	s.	d.
Cash in hand Dec 1889	54	10	11 ½
A.C. Allen, Esq	2	2	0
Mrs Bleckley	1	0	0
Miss S. Burgess	0	5	0
Christmas Gift	20	0	0
Mrs Dowling	25	0	0
Lady Jane Dundas*	50	0	0
Miss E. ErIe	10	0	0
Mrs G.H. Ellis	5	0	0
Chas. E. Flower, Esq	3	3	0
Miss Forman	1	1	0
Miss Frankau	2	2	0
Mrs Gillson	5	4	0
Miss Gosset	1	0	0
Miss Head	5	0	0
Interest on Mrs Scrase-Dickins's Gift	1	16	7
Miss Bessie Holland	6	6	0
E. Howard, Esq	5	0	0
Miss Meyrick Jones	0	7	6
Miss Johnston	10	0	0
Miss Johnson	1	0	0
Mrs James Macdonell	0	10	0
Miss Meek	2	0	0
Howard Morley, Esq	25	0	0
Frank Morris, Esq	1	1	0
Mrs Oldham	5	0	0
Rev. C. Plummer	10	5	0
Per Mrs Powell	2	2	0
Mrs Ramsden Roe	1	0	0
Mrs Leslie Stephen	10	0	0
Mrs Thompson	2	0	0
Miss M. Wells	2	0	0
Mrs S. Winkworth (Education)	50	0	0
Mrs S. Winkworth (Pensions)	25	0	0
Mrs S. Winkworth (General Fund)	20	0	0
	£365	16	0 ½

* Balance of Gift of £300 distributed to Kyrle, cadet corps, and garden.

DONATION ACCOUNT, 1890

EXPENDITURE

	£	s.	d.
Boarding out (clothes, school, & partial board for 6 children)	64	12	2
Industrial School	2	7	4 ½
Hospital and other relief to the sick	3	0	3
Pensions for 5 persons A., R., T., N. & G.	37	11	0
Employment	1	8	3 ½
Excursions to the country & other entertainments	51	14	5
Care of Playground	13	0	0
Education	89	13	11 ½
Open Spaces	10	6	0
Carriage of Flowers	0	5	6 ½
Printing & Postage of letters to fellow-workers	5	7	1 ½
Cash in hand, (balance of Lady Jane Dundas's Gift)	50	0	0
General Fund*	36	9	11

	£365	16	0 ½

* The small pensions to the old, and payments for orphans, fatherless, or destitute children at schools or boarded out, whom we have under our charge, amount to £50 a year. The balance, therefore, of £36 is quite too small to meet even these fixed expenses.

Examined and found correct, A.P. Fletcher, January 11th 1891.

RED CROSS HALL AND GARDEN ACCOUNT, 1890

RECEIPTS

	£	s.	d.
Balance at Bank	4	2	11
Cash in hand	6	18	11
Mrs Temple	1	1	0
Miss Chase	10	0	0
Miss Harris	1	0	0
G.B. Gregory	2	10	0
Highfield Benevolent Society	5	5	0
Miss Lee Warner	1	0	0
Women's University Settlement (subscription)	2	2	0
Women's University Settlement (for fires, Nov 20th)	0	1	0
Miss M.M. Eve	5	0	0
Thomas Hare	5	0	0
E. Jukes	0	10	0
Per Miss Octavia Hill (for cleaning)	3	15	0
Per Miss Octavia Hill (for garden)	10	0	0
Red Cross Cottages: Interest	48	0	0
White Cross Cottages: Interest	6	10	8
Collections and Sale of Programmes	5	14	10
Gymnasium receipts	1	5	2
Working Men's Club:			
Rent	22	3	3
Arrears	1	17	9
Gymnasium	0	7	0
Rent of rooms under Club	11	14	0
Hatters', Furriers' Investment Society: Use of room	2	11	0
Marshalsea Entertainment Club: Use of room	2	7	6
Olde Tabarde Musical Society: Use of room	1	7	0
Letting of Hall	15	3	6
Sale of pigeons	0	1	9
	*£177	9	0

* *Editor's note:* The total should be £177 9s 3d. Error in original.

RED CROSS HALL AND GARDEN ACCOUNT, 1890

EXPENDITURE

	£	s.	d.
Caretaker:			
Wages	52	0	0
Overtime and odd jobs	2	3	0
Help	0	16	6
Cleaning	7	5	7
Water	10	13	6
Gas, carbon, and footlights	12	12	2
Fuel	2	15	11
Hire of piano	3	10	0
Tuning piano	0	15	0
Cover for piano	0	17	9 ½
Repairs to lock	0	8	0
Refreshments for performers	0	19	1
Printing	7	12	0
Postage	1	19	10
Carpentry and other work in hall	11	2	4
Stopping gas escape	0	18	9
Wire protection for Mr Crane's panel	1	6	6
Cap for Caretaker	0	6	6
Sundry small items	0	14	3
Insurance of Hall	1	3	9
Insurance of lamp	0	4	6
Insurance of panel	0	7	0
Rates and taxes	4	14	3
Gymnasium, eyes and staple	0	5	2
Gymnasium, attendance	2	5	0
Books for library and calico for binding	2	2	3 ½
Garden:			
Plants and work	11	10	6
Pigeons' and fishes' food	1	7	8
Paint, brushes, etc	2	2	3
Small items	0	16	2
Cheque books	0	5	0
Balance at Bank	26	15	6
Cash in hand	4	13	3
	£177	9	0

Examined with vouchers and found correct, Ernest Jukes.

LETTER TO MY FELLOW-WORKERS

TO WHICH IS ADDED

ACCOUNT OF DONATIONS RECEIVED

FOR

WORK AMONG THE POOR

DURING 1891

❧

BY

OCTAVIA HILL
(FOR PRIVATE CIRCULATION ONLY)

LONDON:
PRINTED BY HUNT, BARNARD AND CO.,
BLANDFORD STREET, W.

SUMMARY

Housing work: the loss of Ossington Buildings... programme of events at Red Cross Hall and garden... outings for the tenants... the Women's University Settlement and the need for detailed work... open spaces: West Wickham; Hilly Fields; the formation of the Kent and Surrey Committee of the Commons Preservation Society... problems with the approach to Freshwater Place.

EDITOR'S NOTE

After several pages of what seems like a rather routine account of the progress of different projects, Octavia breaks out—as she always does—into a more expansive view of the fundamental principles underlying the work. She inveighs against 'specious theories of reform en masse, and plans for relieving misery by the million', advocating instead 'sound, steady work'. (For Octavia, 'en masse' was always a pejorative term.) The mistrust of 'any gigantic scheme' was characteristic of Octavia, and on this occasion it was sparked off by the sensational success of General Booth's Darkest England scheme for the Salvation Army. Like other leading lights of the Charity Organisation Society, Octavia feared that it would lead to indiscriminate charity. These fears were not realised, because General Booth was no more inclined to 'pension in a life of license every drunkard of [the] parish' than Octavia would have been. The passage also contains an important statement of Octavia's objection to a universal state pension: by attempting to 'get rid of charity, and to substitute a rate distributed as a right' it would turn out to be 'the most gigantic scheme of inadequate relief ever dreamed of by men', because the sums available per capita under such a scheme would be too small for the relief of real distress.

190, Marylebone Road, N.W.
February, 1892[1]

My friends,

I am very late in writing to you. Here is February nearly over before I send to you all heartiest thanks for last year's help. It has not been, believe me, for want of thought about you, and desire to write, and as to the donation accounts they have been closed and audited and waiting to be printed for weeks. I suppose I have been specially busy; it has seemed to me that I have. But accept now, please, though they come so late, my sincerest thanks for all the powerful, ready, and affectionate help which has carried through so large an amount of useful work during the past year.

I am more deeply impressed than ever with the amount of thoughtful sympathy with all good work that exists now in England, and with the readiness on the part of many to make great sacrifices for whatever gift they believe to be of real value. Certainly I come in for a very full share of such help. I never make known any need without receiving assistance from a large number of new fellow-workers, as well as from the tried friends of old-standing. With regard to money help, the donation accounts printed herewith show not a tithe of what has been sent. In general my large appeals are issued in connection with some public body which renders its own accounts, and I only acknowledge here the money sent to me for disposal privately. With regard to workers who give, not money, but themselves, we are always enrolling more, and we are always needing more; not only because our work is always increasing, but because, as our workers grow, they are continually becoming leaders able to be the centre of fresh groups of younger workers, either near us still, or in the districts far away that may need them even more.

Most of the management of houses under our care has continued in

---

1   Although Mr Fletcher signed off the donation fund accounts on 12 January, Mr Jukes did not sign off the Red Cross accounts until 15 February, so the letter was probably not circulated until March.

its quiet even course during the year. I hope that the friendships between the tenants and those who are the landlords, or who represent them, deepen as the years roll on, and that there is a steady growth in that improvement in the appliances and in the buildings themselves which should keep pace with the rising modern standard that one is glad to see being gradually adopted.

One loss of work I have to regret during the past year. Ossington Buildings are no longer under our care, the directors having decided to adopt another system of management. I do not think my kind helpers there will feel that this change has been due to any failure on their part. The work was going on to my entire satisfaction, and I think the financial results cannot be called unsatisfactory, seeing that our collections steadily increased quarter by quarter as shown in the subjoined table,[2] and that on a collection of £1,175 we had only £1 15s 6d arrears when we closed our accounts at the end of the last quarter. The control of the repairs and the laundry had never been put into our hands, and this involved a dual management, which was found inconvenient, and a change of some kind became inevitable.[3]

On the other hand we had hardly given up the Ossington Buildings before we were requested by the owner to take charge for him of two groups of tenements in a far poorer neighbourhood, where it is possible we are more wanted. It is certainly much more uphill work than among the happy groups of respectable and well-conducted families who were fast becoming our real friends in Ossington Buildings. I trust that we

---

2   OSSINGTON BUILDINGS
Facts respecting Collection of Rents

QUARTER ENDING

Dec. 9th 1890	...	£360	12	3
March 10th 1891	...	£384	3	9
June 9th 1891	...	£430	6	9

[*Octavia Hill's note*]

Editor's note: The inclusion of this table of rents collected—unique in the letters, as Octavia habitually refused to divulge this information to anyone except the owners of the properties—shows how defensive Octavia felt about the removal of Ossington Buildings from her management.

---

3   This dual system of management was the downfall of the arrangement. Octavia needed to have absolute discretion in the management of her properties, or she felt her work would be compromised. See 1874, pp.32-3 and 38-9, for an exposition of the completeness of control which Octavia's managers exercised over arrangements.

shall rapidly get this newer area into order. Another owner shortly afterwards asked me to take charge of a very large number of tenements in Islington. It was quite too far from my other centres for me to undertake it myself, but I was able to introduce two of my best trained helpers, and they are now at work there under the direction of experienced friends of mine living in that part of London.

Red Cross Hall continues to be a centre of bright and, I hope, useful gatherings. The balance-sheet relating to it and to the garden are annexed. By the extreme kindness of friends we have been able to provide a series of entertainments of a very attractive character on Thursday evenings during the entire winter season. On Sunday afternoons also we have had beautiful music given by friends, as well as lovely flowers. The room, filled like a parish drawing-room with neighbours at tea, looking at illustrated books, or listening to music, is a very pleasant sight, with its bright fires and light, and with Mr Walter Crane's beautiful panel on the wall. The Hall is still further enriched this year by the present which the working men's carving class have made to it—a beautiful clock-case, carved by themselves, and designed by Mr Fletcher.[4] Miss Constance Fripp has also most kindly presented to the Hall a portfolio of water-colour landscapes, which have afforded great pleasure.[5] The cadet corps has continued to drill in the Hall, the gymnastic apparatus is available for men and boys one night weekly, a

---

4   In 1891 the Red Cross class of the Home Arts and Industries Association submitted to the association's annual exhibition an 'overmantel containing a clock', made for their hall. 'The class at the Red-cross Hall branch have executed an oak clock-case and overmantel for their hall in Southwark. It was designed by Mr Benton Fletcher, with German Renaissance-like foliations [sic] in the panel, which are rather thin and wanting in breadth. The cushioned frieze, on the other hand, is heavy looking.' (*The Building News*, 5 June, 1891, p.771.) Although this work may have been, to the artistic eye, in some ways deficient, its importance was as a gift from the 'working men who belonged to the carving class'. (*Red Cross Hall Annual Report*, 1907, p.5.) *The Studio* review of the 1895 exhibition singled out a medicine cupboard in the 'Olde English Renaissance' style designed by Benton Fletcher, but this time made by the Bankside Southwark boys' class, which he ran. In 1898 the class 'displayed some work really wonderful, considering the circumstances of its production. The hanging bookshelf will sufficiently indicate the refined lines and fitting carving of this centre.' (*The House*, vol.3, 1898, p.162.) Captain Fletcher, a military man, is mentioned in the 1890 letter in connection with the band of the cadet corps (1890, p.284).

---

5   Constance L. Fripp (1862–1892) was a landscape painter who exhibited from c.1883. She was an Associate of the Society of Women Artists, with whom she exhibited 26 works. She also exhibited one at the Royal Academy and five at the Royal Institute of Painters in Water Colours.

class of pupil teachers practice musical drill there on a Saturday afternoon, and the Hall has been again and again let and lent to the clergy, the Women's Settlement, and to others for various gatherings.

The garden forms a pleasant out-door sitting-room in hot weather, and a space of light and air always; but we have done little during the past summer in the way of special gatherings there. Such would require a good leader of workers and a large staff in addition. I do not know whether we may dare to hope for them in the coming summer.

My wishes in the future for both garden and Hall are that more local life should develop in and round them. I wish we could come more into touch with working men and women who would care to organise what should be a help to the neighborhood. The children's play, a great success, was the one example of what might be done by the people if well organised.

Before leaving the subject I would wish especially to record my warm thanks to Miss Plunkett, who came forward to fill a great want, and who has proved such an indefatigable and efficient centre of the gatherings there, both on Thursdays and Sundays.

May I also put here on record my sincere thanks for the happy days spent by our people in the country at Sir Frederick Pollock's, Mrs Cash's, Miss Johnston's, Mr Arthur Hill's and at Mr Edmund Maurice's—days not to be forgotten by many who will have no opportunity but through me to offer their hearty thanks.

I mentioned last year the hope I had of seeing a scheme of wise district visiting growing up from the Women's University Settlement in Southwark. That hope has been realised. But, as the Settlement will issue its own report, I will only add here now heartily I rejoice in what has already been done, how much I hope the work may gradually develop, and how thankful I am that it has secured such a leader as Miss Sewell,[6] than whom I know no one who could have given to the experiment so sure a security for being made wisely and well. I am more and more assured that it is only in continuous contact with people in their homes that our kind, but most sentimental, British public will learn the facts that will lead it to abandon specious theories of reform *en masse*, and plans for relieving misery by the million, to wait for the result of sound, steady work. How strange it seems that the Tower Hamlets Pension Society has had hard work to get money enough to

---

6 Margaret Sewell was the head worker of the Women's University Settlement, a position she held until 1901 when she was succeeded by Helen Gladstone, the daughter of the former prime minister.

pension in its quiet steady way the old who have saved money and lost it, and whose homes are worth keeping together, and yet now the nation is considering schemes which might involve a 1s. 6d. income tax, and which, I must say, appear to me only to provide the most gigantic scheme of inadequate relief ever dreamed of by men. What an odd form our pity takes, how sudden it is in its rushes. Believe me, if you will know and love and watch those with whom your lives have been thrown, learn how to come in contact with some few of the poor, you will find far better ways of helping than any *gigantic* scheme that deals with people *en masse*. Solid schemes of insurance, of saving, there are, and may be, but we can't do our *charity* thus; and I think at the heart of all these pension schemes there is a desire to equalise income, and to get rid of charity, and to substitute a rate distributed as a right. If you desire to equalise income I should advise you to do it by giving liberal wages, arranging for reasonable hours of work, and taking a large view of your duties to all men, and by making large well-considered gifts, not by giving from a compulsory tax upon your poorer neighbour as well as yourself. If you desire to take from charity its patronising tone, see that you yourselves from your heart believe that what is helpful to any man is verily due from you, so far as you can render it, at any sacrifice. See, too, that in administering a fund raised by law from a hard-working community you feel it no disgrace to the recipient, but a bounden duty on your part to see whether or not the subsidy will be helpful, and in what form it will be most wisely administered. I have been amazed to see what has been written about the indignity of poor-law enquiries. Would the writers really prefer an insufficient dole taken from the respectable and thrifty to pension in a life of license every drunkard of their parish? But I hope the common sense of England will recover itself as it has done, I believe, after the wave of excitement over General Booth's scheme,[7] and I hope it may be before it is too late, and that no party feeling, no uneasy consciences, may lead England into schemes which would, in my estimation, discourage thrift, dispirit

---

7   *In Darkest England and the Way Out* by William (General) Booth of the Salvation Army had been published in 1890. Thousands of copies were sold in the first year and it raised discussion of 'the social question' to a new level. Booth's Darkest England scheme was a blueprint for social regeneration, vast in its extent, and he costed it at £1 million. He claimed the Salvation Army could start work on it with capital of £100,000 and on 31 January 1891—before Octavia wrote this letter—he signed the Darkest England Trust Deed which established the social welfare work of the Salvation Army as a separate entity with its own distinct funds—an arrangement that continues to this day.

the industrious, and by no manner of means eradicate old age pauperism.

It is impossible writing now not to deal with the open space question as it stands in February. Several important matters are before us. There are two schemes which are needing money to carry them through, namely, those relating to West Wickham and Hilly Fields. The former is for securing 25½ acres of exquisitely wooded and sloping land which was threatened with enclosure. The spirited action of the Bromley District Commons and Footpaths Preservation Society led to its being discovered that there were still commoners living who had rights over it, and a suit was about to be commenced to assert these rights, when the Lord of the Manor came to terms, and offered to sell his entire interest in the land to the public for £2,000, a sum amounting to little more than he might possibly obtain for his manorial rights. Under these circumstances the local committee, after consultation with the Commons Preservation Society, decided that there was no question that they would do well to accept the offer. It now only remains for the money to be subscribed, which certainly ought not to be difficult in well-to-do districts like West Wickham and Beckenham, where residents will themselves greatly benefit by the additional open space in their neighbourhood, as well as by having the satisfaction of feeling that they are handing down in perpetuity a lovely space of wooded land for those who shall come after them—one that forms also an addition to Hayes Common, which is so greatly appreciated by thousands of Londoners in the summer. All honour and success to the gallant committee which has thus made the way easy for the preservation of such a site! I hope those who can, in the neighborhood, will now liberally subscribe what is needed.

Hilly Fields has occupied also much of our time. This is much nearer the metropolis, indeed it forms one of the very nearest hilly areas still unbuilt over—if not the nearest—to a poor part of London.[8] The extent will be 45 acres under the scheme as enlarged by the recent County Council decision. The entire cost will be some £42,000 of which the London County Council have voted £22,000, and the Greenwich

---

8   Octavia first heard of Hilly Fields when she was visiting one of the tenants in Deptford. Seeing a bunch of wild flowers in one of the houses, she asked where they had come from, and was told that Hilly Fields was the nearest country walk. 'I went to seek out the spot, and found it absolutely bounded on the London side by wastes of little houses, but commanding, on the south, a view far away to Knockholt Beeches.' ('An open space for Deptford', letter to the *Daily Graphic*, 1 February 1892.)

District Board, £7,000. The action of the Lewisham Board in refusing to vote anything, though the land is in their parish, appears to me disastrous, both as a precedent for other boards, and also as forming a very valid reason why many persons will not give. We have hoped to the last that the Board would reconsider its decision, have done our utmost in raising subscriptions, in which effort the public has been most generous, but if now, in spite of all this liberal aid, the Board still refuses, the failure of the scheme must rest on their shoulders.[9] I cannot see what we can or should do more. In one way or other the matter will probably be decided before these words are printed.[10]

By far the most important step forward which has been taken this year with regard to open spaces has, to my mind, been that of the formation of the Kent and Surrey Committee of the Commons Preservation Society. It is the first attempt to work in greater detail with regard to all the numberless small encroachments on public rights which are going on in country neighbourhoods. With this object the following arrangements have been made: a strong Executive meets frequently in London to receive, consider, and, so far as possible, deal with all cases brought to their notice in which rights are interfered with over commons, roadside strips, or foot-paths. Residents in Kent and Surrey are being enrolled on payment of a 1s enrolment fee, and correspondents in various parts of both counties are requested to communicate with an hon. secretary, who, if necessary, visits and reports

---

9   As the London County Council had declined to purchase Hilly Fields outright, a committee had been formed to raise the required funds—£42,000—involving the Kyrle Society, the Metropolitan Public Gardens Association, the Commons Preservation Society and the local Lewisham committee. It was anticipated that the LCC would pay half, the two local authorities of Greenwich and Lewisham one-sixth each, leaving one-sixth to be raised by public subscription. However, the Lewisham Board of Works, which had just paid for 47 acres of land beside the Ravensbourne river, was unwilling to spend any more money on open spaces, and passed the following resolution: 'That this Board considers the acquisition of the Hilly Fields a matter affecting the interests of London generally as a metropolitan environment, and declines to ask the ratepayers of the district of Lewisham to contribute so large a sum as £7,000, or any sum, and is of the opinion that the London County Council should be requested to acquire the Hilly Fields as an open space for the people, the cost of buying the land and laying it out as a public park to be obtained from the county rate.' (Kyrle Society report 1891, p.13.)

---

10 This was a very optimistic assumption: the negotiations dragged on for another two years. Although this is the first mention of Hilly Fields in the letters, the Kyrle Society had been co-ordinating the campaign since 1889. (Kyrle Society report, 1889, p.19.)

to the Executive on any case of encroachment brought to his notice. Donations and subscriptions for the ordinary work of the society, and for guarantee funds where action may have to be taken, are much needed. Even already some very valuable work has been done. Several months ago a small group of commoners and cottagers in the neighbourhood of an important and beautiful common in Surrey enrolled themselves as members of this Kent and Surrey Committee, and paid their shillings for enrolment. Some of them have practised rights as commoners, as did their fathers before them, for many years, and they are deeply convinced that they have rights, but recently they have been warned and fined for exercising them. Several were again summoned this winter, and wrote at once to the honorary secretary of the Kent and Surrey Committee, who was able to give them such advice and support as resulted in all the summonses against them being dismissed and costs being given.

I venture to think that the time has arrived when the effort to preserve such enjoyment of common land as has come down to us should be undertaken by the whole body of the residents in a county, poor and rich—at least so far as that they should share the onus which falls so heavily on those who are compelled to assert their rights against neighbours; and I hope that the support of the country by South London, of the rural cottager by the suburban districts, and of both by an experienced London executive, may result in arresting the progress by which path after path, common after common, and roadside strip after strip, are being lost. There is no part of my work which is just now more deeply engrossing me than this, and I shall be delighted to receive offers of help, or to give further information.

Some of my friends know how sadly much time and strength were taken up last year by the effort to save the approach to our earliest London playground, and to the six cottages which overlook it. They will want to know how it ended. It ended thus. The representations to the large landowner who proposed to so mar the approach as to render it one inconsistent with the requirements of the Metropolitan Building Acts, and in our opinion so objectionable as to be untenable by us, were wholly unavailing, until rights of light were discovered which, if enforced, would have considerably interfered with his building scheme. He then came to terms which, although they only secure our approach for 23 years, and have put my friends the owners to very heavy expenses for substantial alterations to alter the approach, do give access to our cottages, and enable the small playground to be used for that length of time.

What will happen then we little know; but that small playground bought by Mr Ruskin in 1864[11] has led up to more, larger, better, perhaps even more abiding ones being secured. What is done in generosity and with thought bears fruit in the long years. The playground where some of those who are now leaders in great work in important parts of London made their first acquaintance with the poor whom they have since helped so greatly, where year by year so many of us for 25 years have met at the May festival, the trees Mr Ruskin had planted, the cottages where tenants of 20 years' standing had lived, seemed last year as if they would be lost, by being cut off from access. I worked to save them, and of the extreme kindness of those who gave me help I cannot speak too gratefully, never shall I forget it, but— when it seemed as if all was going to be swept away, I felt most deeply how whatever was most valuable in the traditions *were* traditions, and would be handed down in the memories and lives of those who had met there, though every trace of the little place were to vanish.

But I must not end a letter about a year so full of blessing and growth with words about even the past shadow of a possible loss, but ask you all to unite with me in lifting up our hearts in thankfulness for the ever increasing blessings which come to us, and above all for the way in which our fragments of work, with all their short-sightedness and incompleteness, are accepted and taken up and moulded into parts of God's work, parts of those great schemes which He sees Who holds His world and all of us in the hollow of His hand, and Who can put into its place, and use, and bring good out of every effort, however small, however faulty, which is pure, and true, and unselfish.

OCTAVIA HILL

---

11 The purchase of the freeholds of five houses in Freshwater Place, together with a house in Old Marylebone Road that backed onto them, which provided Octavia with her first open space, had taken place in 1866, not 1864. Octavia describes the taking-over of Freshwater Place in 'Four Years' Management of a London Court', *Macmillan's Magazine*, July 1869, reprinted in Whelan, 1998, pp.51-64.

DONATION ACCOUNT, 1891

RECEIPTS

	£	s.	d.
Cash in hand	86	9	11
Rev. B.H. Alford	5	0	0
A.C. Allen, Esq	2	2	0
Anon.	10	0	0
Somerset Beaumont, Esq	55	0	0
Mrs Brander	1	0	0
Charles Bridgeman, Esq	5	0	0
Mrs Bridgeman	2	0	0
Mrs Darwin	5	0	0
Wm. Debenham, Esq	10	0	0
Mrs Scrase-Dickins	7	16	0
Lady Jane Dundas	10	0	0
Miss E. Erie	10	0	0
Miss Edith Fisher	1	0	0
Miss Forman	1	1	0
Miss Frankau	3	0	0
Mrs Gillson	5	4	0
Miss Head	5	0	0
Mrs Henry	0	10	0
Alfred Hill, Esq	10	0	0
For Entertainment	0	2	0
E.F.J.	30	0	0
Mrs Laycock	5	0	0
H. Luxmoore, Esq	2	2	0
Mrs J. Macdonell	1	6	0
Miss Meek	2	0	0
Frank Morris, Esq	1	1	0
Mrs Arthur Peile	1	0	0
Rev. C. Plummer	4	0	0
Per Mrs Powell	2	2	0
Mrs Ramsden Roe	1	0	0
Per Miss Alice Sargant	10	0	0
Mrs Siemens	5	0	0
Miss A.E. Shaen	2	0	0
Gordon Somervell, Esq	3	3	0
Mrs Leslie Stephen	10	10	0
Mrs Thompson	2	0	0
Mrs Tufnell	1	1	0
Miss Mary Wells	2	0	0
Miss Jane Wells	1	0	0
Mrs Whelpdale	2	0	0
Mrs S. Winkworth	80	0	0
Miss Yorke	10	0	0
	£413	9	11

DONATION ACCOUNT, 1891

EXPENDITURE

	£	s.	d.
Pensions and other Help to the Aged	64	11	0
Industrial Schools, Training of Children in	39	6	0
Boarding out (Partial Board and Clothing of Six Children)	35	18	2
Tower Hamlets Pension Fund	20	0	0
Help in Sickness	19	16	6
Education	29	7	8
Excursions to the Country and other entertainments	59	19	2
Red Cross Hall	10	0	0
Care of Playground	10	8	0
Improvement of Court	5	10	0
Kyrle Musical	5	0	0
Open Spaces	4	1	0
Employment	0	14	6
Toys, pictures, and flowers, carriage of	1	17	1 ½
Printing of Letter to Fellow-workers, Stationery and Postage	6	6	5 ½

Cash in hand:

Special Fund	80	0	0			
Available	20	14	4			
				100	14	4

£413	9	11

Examined and found correct, A.P. Fletcher, January 12th 1892.

RED CROSS HALL AND GARDEN ACCOUNT, 1891

RECEIPTS

	£	s.	d.
Balance at Bank	26	15	6
Cash in hand	4	13	3
G.B. Gregory	2	10	0
Miss Harris	1	0	0
Mrs Temple	1	1	0
A.M.P.	0	10	0
Per W.W. Cobbett	0	2	6
Women's University Settlement (subs.)	2	2	0
Per Miss Octavia Hill:			
For Garden	10	0	0
For Cleaning	6	4	6
For Odd jobs	0	9	0
Sale of Tickets for Operetta, Febuary 26th	3	4	3
Collected at Entertainments	3	7	3
Gymnasium Receipts	1	12	10
Letting of Hall and Committee Room	19	8	6
Rents: Working Men's Club and 10, White Cross Street	29	3	6
Interest, Red Cross Cottages	48	0	0
Interest, White Cross Cottages	13	6	8
	£173	10	9

RED CROSS HALL AND GARDEN ACCOUNT, 1891

EXPENDITURE.

	£	s.	d.
Caretaker	52	0	0
Caretaker extra fees	2	8	0
Cleaning	8	7	6
Water	10	15	6
Gas, Carbon and Footlights	13	10	0
Fuel	2	3	2
Tuning Piano	0	10	0
Entertainment Expenses	5	7	11
Printing	2	7	10
Postage	1	10	3
Music Stands	0	5	0
Frames for Water-colour Drawings	1	0	0
Fixing Clock-case	1	0	0
Sundry Repairs and small items	13	15	3
Distempering Walls of Club Room	2	2	6
Gymnasium, Superintendence	1	18	0
Fire Insurance	1	5	0
Insurance of Lamp	0	4	6
Rates and Taxes	2	1	1
Police Band	2	0	0
Garden:			
License of Balcony	0	10	0
Paint	3	1	0
Work, Plants and Materials	11	2	1
Pigeons' Food	1	4	5
Cheque Book	0	2	6
Balance at Bank	23	4	10
Cash in hand	9	14	5
	£173	10	9

Examined with books and vouchers and found correct, Ernest Jukes, February 15th 1892.

LETTER TO MY FELLOW-WORKERS

TO WHICH ARE ADDED

ACCOUNTS OF DONATIONS RECEIVED

FOR

WORK AMONG THE POOR

DURING 1892

BY

OCTAVIA HILL

LONDON:
PRINTED BY WATERLOW AND SONS LIMITED,
LONDON WALL, E.C.

SUMMARY

Housing work: Ecclesiastical Commissioners; Islington; Deptford... Red Cross Hall: Walter Crane's panel of the self-sacrifice of the navvies... a flower show planned for Red Cross garden... resignation of Sydney Cockerell junior... the Women's University Settlement and plans for training... open spaces: Hilly Fields; West Wickham; the need for more helpers.

EDITOR'S NOTE

Going, as usual, from the particular to the general, Octavia discusses Walter Crane's new panel in the series showing heroic deeds of the poor in terms of 'the help which beautiful and powerful art offers in districts like Southwark'; and an account of the struggle to preserve Hilly Fields and the forest at West Wickham leads into a moving appeal to 'secure for the agricultural labourer in his daily life, for the Londoner in his holiday... a sight of this fair land, which was meant to be a joy to its inhabitants'. Octavia writes with a sense of urgency about open spaces which are being lost 'yearly, yes, monthly' because she and her small group of helpers lack both time and resources to do the necessary work. 'How many commons will be enclosed illegally before 1894?' she asks. In fact, 1894 would see the founding of the National Trust to put the open spaces work on a firmer footing. However, the most significant announcement in this letter relates to the two-year training course that was being set up at the Women's University Settlement. Octavia, in common with others who were working in social reform movements at the end of the nineteenth century, realised that the problems they were dealing with were complex, and that the day of the well-meaning amateur was over. Training was essential for all, 'whether volunteers or those seeking paid posts'. It was the beginning of social work as a profession.

316

190, Marylebone Road, N.W.
Christmas, 1892

My friends,

I always like to begin my annual letter to you with a report on the houses which form so large a field of our work, and which constitute the sphere of steady, permanent intercourse with a settled body of friends among the poor. I say a report on the houses, not that I ever disturb the quiet regular course of silent work by referring to all the courts; but I try to record the important changes in them.

Running through my mind those groups which have had crises in their history during the past year, I come first to the fact that the Ecclesiastical Commissioners last winter handed over to our charge two additional courts in Southwark, and that last summer they again added to our area there by entrusting us with houses in three more.

The block in Islington, which I mentioned as entrusted by the owners to the charge of Mr and Mrs Blyth,[1] and where four of my fellow-workers are helping, has been very great success; order and cleanliness have been established; instead of sixteen tenements being unlet, there are now none; the central court, which was a black trampled waste, has been planted and made tidy, and the owners are in communication with Mrs Blyth, with the view of putting three more of their blocks under her charge. That would comprise a population of about 2,000 souls. It is doubtful whether she will be able to extend her operations so rapidly, but she hopes to arrange to take one more block at Christmas.

The other houses go on in their steady quiet course, the ladies in them becoming increasingly able to be, not only the friends of the tenants, but the wise managers of the houses; more and more able to decide independently and quickly, and with full knowledge of local circumstances, the various questions which a landlady alone can settle,

---

1 From now on, Patrick Blyth would be Octavia's most faithful auditor. He audited the Red Cross accounts in 1892/3/4, then both the Red Cross and donation fund accounts for most of the years until Octavia's death. In 1909 both sets of accounts were audited by William Blyth, who had been honorary auditor to the Kyrle Society for over 20 years.

and on which the order and comfort of a group of tenants so much depends. I should like in this relation to refer especially to the three small freehold houses bought and given by Mrs Scrase-Dickins, now some years ago, to be held in trust by Lord Wolmer, Miss Johnson, and myself.[2] They are situated in a street which has for years been proverbially one of the roughest in the neighbourhood; the houses themselves are very small, and have no special structural advantages at all, except, indeed, that they are small, and thus prevent families from being herded *en masse*; but they are houses of the very kind which might, under ordinary circumstances, be the scene of dirt and disorder: they were such for some time before and after they were handed to us. Now, how all is changed! The tiny little rooms look like real homes; instead of being let singly, the tenants have been encouraged to take two rooms; and a settled, firm, friendly rule has made them the happiest little places. The interest accruing from the gift is devoted yearly by trustees to some good object: this year it goes to the Tower Hamlets Pensions, and to the Boys' Home at East Barnet. This is one of many such groups. I single it out rather as it is a trust, than because there is anything different in the progress there and elsewhere. Wherever we have ladies willing and able to work on for a series of years in one place this sort of change is marked.

Poor Deptford! our black sheep continues black—at least I fear it does; I am, however, full of hope about it. We have had a necessary change in our staff there; and I have secured as my representative one who, if I mistake not, will make her mark there before the year is out. But we shall see. It is slow and up-hill work; but in St Christopher's Place, where we worked on for years, perhaps laying foundations, but with no very visible sign of progress, fresh helpers came in, and then the court took a turn, from which time its progress has been steady. I can't help thinking that there is a hope, that this change in Deptford, which clearly is a great added strength to us there, may be the beginning of a radical improvement. I hardly dare to trust myself to dwell on such a hope, but I think I see germs even there of a new growth.

---

2   The Horace Street Trust took its name from the street in which these three houses were situated in Marylebone. Anna Scrase-Dickins gave them to Octavia in 1886. The name of the street has now reverted to its original Cato Street to commemorate the Cato Street conspiracy of 1820, in which a group of men hired a stable in the street from which to carry out an assassination attempt on several government ministers who were supposedly dining with Lord Harrowby in nearby Grosvenor Square. The plot became known to the authorities who planted spies in the group. They were arrested, charged with high treason and executed or transported.

Red Cross Hall has gone on much as before during the past year. The cadet corps, the gymnasium, the Thursday entertainments and the Sunday afternoon sociable gatherings, have been steadily continued, all growing and doing better, but remaining essentially the same. The Committee, on which are representatives from the Working Men's Club, has just sent £5 as a voluntary offering towards the cost of materials, etc., for the panel, so generously painted by Mr Walter Crane for the Hall. A second most beautiful one has been received from him and fixed during this session; the subject is thus described:[3]

'In the summer of 1874 a number of navvies were at work upon the line of railway between Glasgow and Paisley. They stood back upon the approach of an express train, which, on passing them, would cross a lofty viaduct. The engine was in sight. One of the men, named Jamieson, saw that a sleeper had started, and that unless it were replaced the train would be wrecked—wrecked upon the viaduct. There was no time for words. The navvy made a sign to his nephew standing beside him, and the two rushed forward. They fixed the sleeper, saved the train, and were left dead upon the line.

'The funeral was largely attended, especially by fellow workmen, who had turned out to do honour to their comrades. "We laid them," writes the Rev. James Brown, St James' Manse, Paisley, "in an old churchyard on a hillside that slopes down to the very edge of the railway. As the two biers were carried down the hill, the bearers being the friends and comrades of the dead, the trains were coming and going. No fitter resting-place could have been found. I thought of Tennyson's lines on the Duke of Wellington's funeral in the crypt of St Paul's:

' "Let the sound of those he wrought for,
And the feet of those he fought for,
Echo round his bones for evermore.[4]

' "I hope some day to get a simple stone set up, that will be seen by passing travellers." ' '

---

3   By Miss Frances Martin, writing in *Macmillan's Magazine. See ill. 8.*

---

4   From the 'Ode on the Death of the Duke of Wellington', 1852—the year of Wellington's death. Tennyson himself had died during 1892.

The panel is most beautiful, the whole story being told wonderfully in the navvies' faces and action, and the steady advance of the fatal train along the curved line of rails giving a feeling of what is coming. We do very earnestly thank Mr Crane for the great gift he has made to us. There must be some who feel the teaching which lies in the memory of deeds like this, and the help which beautiful and powerful art offers in districts like Southwark. Let them secure this help by paying the mere nominal price which will enable the committee to take advantage of Mr Walter Crane's most generous gift, to use his unequalled power to complete the noble scheme of pictorial decoration of the hall. They can do so by sending the money to Mrs Russell Barrington for this object. She has been the originator of the whole scheme, and is kindly trying to get the money together for the next panel or panels to illustrate more heroic deeds of the poor. Mr Walter Crane has all the sketches ready.

We are much hoping that next summer we may be able to arrange for a flower show in Red Cross garden, in which the plants grown by our poorer neighbours in Southwark may be exhibited. The trustees have power to charge for entrance to the garden on four days of the year, if they think well. We might have the prizes given with some pretty ceremony; we might have a band and flags, and sell refreshments. In years now long past, when we organised such festivals in Marylebone, the flower show became an opportunity of gathering together the inhabitants of the parish who know, or would like to know, one another; such an opportunity as a London parish rarely gets. It not only promoted the culture of flowers, but was like a large garden party for rich and poor, old and young, present and former workers.

We shall accept exhibitors from any part of Southwark, and shall gladly seek co-operation from all clergy, ministers and workers there. We want the inhabitants of the locality to feel the garden theirs for all good uses possible.

The accounts are, as heretofore, printed at the end of this letter. It will be seen that the garden and Hall are mainly dependent on the most generous gifts of the late Mr Henry Cowper, and of Lady Jane Dundas, which bring in rents and interest nearly sufficient for the necessary expenses of maintenance and caretaking. The people's own contributions, and money from letting the Hall, bring in a further sum. Still, donations are gladly accepted, and enable us to do more with both garden and Hall, and to try such experiments as this of the flower show.

I note with profound regret the retirement from the honorary secretaryship of Mr Sydney Cockerell, who has acted for us from the day of the opening of the garden. He felt the duties incompatible with other work. I can only thank him for past help.[5] My friend Miss Plunkett, to whose zeal and genial sympathy the gatherings in the Hall owe so much in the past year, has kindly accepted the post.

My relations with the Women's University Settlement grow ever closer. I look upon it not only as a great added strength to my management of houses in Southwark, but still more as the most

---

5   Sydney Carlisle Cockerell (1867–1962) was the son of another Sydney Cockerell, the secretary of the club in Barrett's Court until his death in 1877 (1877, p.86). Young Sydney was only ten when his father died, leaving a widow and seven children in somewhat difficult financial circumstances. In 1884 Sydney joined the family firm of George Cockerell and Company, coal merchants. He disliked the work but applied himself conscientiously. In 1887, when still only 19, he became secretary to the Red Cross Hall committee. He admired Octavia enormously and ranked her, together with William Morris and John Ruskin, as one of the most outstanding people of the day. His diaries, now in the British Library, show how he became deeply involved with Red Cross, going far beyond his duties at committees and with the accounts, to attend the frequent plays, concerts and other events. He got drawn into Octavia's other projects, acting as a steward at the opening of Vauxhall Park by the Prince and Princess of Wales (1890, pp.286-87). He also became treasurer of the cadet corps. However, as the years went by his interest in the work waned, possibly owing to Octavia's obsessive attention to detail, which resulted in constant pestering over events that he regarded as not all that exciting (*see ill.9*). (Darley, 1990, p.242.) His diary entries for 1891 often note the poor quality of and low attendance at the events, and, in his review of the year, he notes that he is: 'still treasurer of the Red Cross Hall and cadet corps funds in Southwark, but the work does not wholly interest me'. His review of 1892 continues this theme: 'I have said nothing of my withdrawal from the Red Cross work on which I was so long engaged. I do not know how far this was due to selfishness and hatred of fatigue—still I felt that what little I did was done half-heartedly and that I was really helping no one'. On 17 May 1892 Octavia wrote to Sydney, regretfully accepting his resignation, which cannot have come as a complete surprise to her as she had been corresponding with him for several years about his dissatisfaction with his role in life. On 19 July 1892 she wrote to say: 'Far be it from me to say one word against any decision to stick to business. You know how much I honour it, and feel it worth sacrifices.' (Maurice, 1914, p.519.) However, Sydney was not resigning from Red Cross to concentrate on the family business. He resigned from that as well and went to work as William Morris's secretary. He was eventually to achieve prominence as director of the Fitzwilliam Museum, Cambridge, from 1908 to 1937. It was Sydney who healed the rift that had grown between Octavia and John Ruskin as a result of Ruskin's intemperate attack on her in *Fors Clavigera* in 1877. After a meeting with Sydney in 1888, Ruskin made a most abject apology. 'I've been obliged to make it up with Octavia Hill and am choked with humble pie' was Ruskin's account of it. (Hilton, 2000, p.550.) Sydney became a regular contributor to the donation fund, giving a pound a year from 1899 onwards.

promising centre for that training of workers, to which must be devoted so much of the energies of those who would see wiser methods of work among the poor prevail. As I am contributing an article on this subject to the January number of the *Nineteenth Century*,[6] I will only briefly mention here that Miss Sewell has drawn up, and the Committee are considering, a definite course of one or two years' training, which they will recommend as suitable for all workers, whether volunteers or those seeking paid posts; that they are prepared to receive suitable students ready to avail themselves of such a course either as residents or as students attending daily.[7] In order to set a standard of good trained work they are endeavouring to get two scholarships founded, each of the value of £50 a year, to be tenable at the settlement by some who may be unable to pay the fees for board and residence. Pending this desirable result, or in addition to it, they would ask any to whom the scheme commends itself either as a good way of improving work among the poor, or as a means of preparing women for really useful paid work, that they should offer a payment of £50 for some one suitable student for a year.

I attended the Church Congress this year at Folkestone, and spoke on the need of such training, though the definite scheme was not then so far matured as now. I may add that Miss Sewell, who spoke at the Bristol Conference on the same subject, and who has given much attention both to the principles and practice of such training, has drawn up a list of books for the reading of those who purpose to qualify themselves for wiser methods of work among the poor.

---

6   Octavia Hill, 'Trained Workers For The Poor', *The Nineteenth Century*, January 1893, 33, pp.36-43. Octavia announced in her article that the Settlement committee had applied to the trustees of the Pfeiffer bequest, 'left for the benefit of women and girls', for funding to endow two scholarships at £50 per annum at the Settlement. 'The Settlement is registered under the Limited Liability Act, as is Girton, and its constitution and by-laws have been settled by Lord Thring... It is governed by a committee elected by the various women's colleges, and therefore, though it is only five years old, we think it might be entrusted with such scholarships.' Meanwhile, she asked if individual benefactors would pay for one or two trainees 'without any paraphernalia of perpetual scholarships'. Both requests were successful. Two private sponsors came forward almost immediately (1893, p.342), and the Pfeiffer trustees made a grant of over £3,000 in 1894 (1894, pp.357-58).

---

7   Miss Sewell's course was a serious matter, involving four days work a week with other charity workers for practical experience, combined with theoretical studies and private reading of 'books helpful to those intending to take up work among the poor'. (Judge, 1994, p.13.)

With regard to open spaces there seem many things to report. The donations which have reached me for Hilly Fields have been large and generous; the inhabitants of the locality, too, at least those of Deptford, have given liberally.[8] The sum in the bank in October was sufficient to meet the requirements stated by the London County Council as necessary to enable them to go on with the immediate purchase of the controlling interests in the land, though a further amount of some £1,700 would have had to be ultimately raised to complete the entire scheme. But there would have been time for this, and the Committee had no fear of securing the remainder. Unfortunately, after the Council had passed a definite resolution for immediate purchase, their advisers raised a legal point with regard to their powers to purchase without the consent of Parliament. There is little doubt of sanction being granted by Parliament, and enabling clauses have been prepared for submission to it, but this must cause considerable delay, and the owners of the land, very naturally, feel that without some advance of price, or interest on the large sum involved, they hardly can consent to wait any longer. They have already given us much time; the Lewisham Board's refusal to help threw a great burden on private donors, and it takes long to collect so large a sum privately. These matters, even the powers of the London County Council, are still under consideration. I cannot myself believe that a scheme so largely beneficial to South East London, and for which a sum of £40,500 is provided, will be allowed to fall through.

The 25½ acres of lovely forest land at West Wickham, referred to in my last annual letter, have been secured in perpetuity.[9] The main honour is to those who struggled for it as a common, and so enabled the public to buy, not the land at freehold building value, but the rights of the

---

8   On 1 February 1892 the *Daily Graphic* had published a letter from Octavia under the heading: 'An open space for Deptford: Now if ever; now forever'. She reported that the purchase price for the land was £42,000, and that the larger part had already been raised thanks to the generosity of the Greenwich District Board, the London County Council and local donors. However, £5,980 needed to be promised immediately to secure the purchase, and she requested pledges to be sent either to herself or to Mr Walter Derham, hon. secretary to the joint committee representing the Commons Preservation Society, the Kyrle Society, the Metropolitan Public Gardens Association and residents in the neighbourhood.

---

9   'Most fortunately, the Corporation [of London] came forward with a grant of £500, and a promise to maintain the common forever. The legal difficulties having been settled, the Lord Mayor, in state, declared the common open on the 12th of last November.' (Kyrle Society report, 1892, p.16.)

Lord of the Manor over it. I wish that in every neighbourhood there were such a gallant committee with such a devoted and earnest honorary secretary as Mr Ritherdon. The thanks of the public are due also to Mr Shaw-Lefevre[10] and Mr Robert Hunter, who in this, as in every other

---

10   George Shaw-Lefevre (1831–1928) was the son of Sir John Shaw-Lefevre, who in turn was the younger brother of Charles Shaw-Lefevre, Viscount Eversley. The viscountcy became extinct on the death of Charles in 1888, but his nephew would be created Baron Eversley in 1906 in recognition of long service to the Liberal party. A barrister by profession, George Shaw-Lefevre entered parliament as MP for Reading in 1863. There was already concern about the rapid destruction of Epping Forest by enclosures, and in 1865 a select committee of the House of Commons was appointed 'to inquire into the best means of preserving for public use the forests, commons and open spaces in and around the metropolis'. Because Shaw-Lefevre had made the most effective speech in the debate, he was chosen to be a member of the committee, which was responsible, in the following year, for the passing of the Metropolitan Commons Act, which was designed to protect access to common land within a 15-mile radius of Charing Cross. As he became increasingly passionate about his cause, Shaw-Lefevre took the view that there was a need for a pressure group to insist upon common rights, and to precipitate court cases to test the law where necessary. On 19 July 1865 he convened a meeting at his chambers in the Inner Temple at which the Commons Preservation Society (CPS) was formed. Shaw-Lefevre attracted the support of, amongst others, Thomas Huxley, the eminent scientist and defender of Darwin, John Stuart Mill, then at the peak of his reputation as a writer on social and economic issues, and, from the world of letters, Thomas Hughes and Leslie Stephen. Within a few months £1,400 had been raised for the new society, and on 24 January 1866 the Lord Mayor of London chaired a meeting at the Mansion House for the public launch of the CPS, which by this time had attracted the support of the Bishop of London, the Deans of Westminster and St Paul's, members of parliament, fellows of learned societies and Henry Fawcett, whose garden in Lambeth would later become the basis of Vauxhall Park. Shaw-Lefevre made a speech complaining that the law had been too wary of insisting on rights of public access to open spaces. Whilst recognising the right of a village to its green, there was no 'analogy between the village and its green and the great city and its commons'. (Murphy, 1987, p.13.) The CPS was Britain's first national conservation body. It was enormously successful in its campaigns, particularly after the appointment of Robert Hunter as its solicitor in 1867. When Hunter became involved with Hardwicke Rawnsley and Octavia in forming what would become the National Trust, Shaw-Lefevre was initially opposed to the idea, suspecting (rightly, as it turned out) that such a body would draw support away from the CPS. He was eventually won round when he realised that insisting of rights of common access would not suffice to protect tracts of privately owned land that were coming on the market in the 1890s, and which had never been subject to such rights, such as those areas of the Lake District that would be acquired by the Trust. In 1899 the Commons Preservation Society merged with the National Footpaths Preservation Society to become the Commons and Footpaths Preservation Society. It still exists as the Open Spaces Society. Shaw-Lefevre married Lady Constance Emily Moreton, the only daughter of the Earl and Countess of Ducie, which would have created an even closer

effort to secure open space, have given unceasingly the benefit of their great influence and unique knowledge. I cannot think why, especially now that the improvement of rural districts is coming so much before the public, a larger number of young and ardent men, politicians and others, do not come forward to try and secure for the agricultural labourer in his daily life, for the Londoner in his holiday, the safe and undisturbed possession of the common, the green way-side strip, and the thousand footpaths which lead him into pleasant places, and to a sight of this fair land, which was meant to be a joy to its inhabitants. It remains the hardest of all things to get either workers or money for the preservation of paths and commons, which are among our people's best possessions, and are being yearly, yes, monthly, snatched from them. I had to write this year two such begging letters as I have seldom in my life had to write, to two old and tried friends of years' standing, who had already given to me largely and generously. Had they not again come forward the Kent and Surrey Committee would have been without the absolutely necessary funds for important action. They sent me the help I wanted instantly, and I don't write this, and I have never had to write one word, to complain of people's not giving. Far from it. I am always more and more impressed with how much they give; how gladly, too, they seem to give, whenever and wherever they believe that the sacrifice will do good. I, least of all, I, who have been so largely, so liberally, so affectionately, so unexpectedly and yet so surely helped, could never dare, could never feel tempted, to reproach people with parsimony. What I do sometimes wonder at is, how little the bulk of people see what they could do with money; how little they choose the far-reaching results, the undoubted blessings of certain forms of gift.

Think of Kent and Surrey, the play places of our wearied Londoners —not of the rough who robs the bank of its primrose roots, but of the doctor and his wife, of the young student, of the clergyman's convalescent child, of the busy merchant; of these and all who, whether from Saturday to Monday at a country inn, or on a day's holiday, or for a week in small country lodgings, or daily, after their city duties, revel in beauty and quiet. Kent and Surrey are the home of many a

---

bond with Octavia. His sister Madeleine Shaw-Lefevre was on the committee of the Metropolitan Association for Befriending Young Servants, founded by Octavia's friend Jane Nassau Senior, and in 1879 became the first principal of Somerville College, Oxford. During his term of office as first commissioner of works (1892–93), Shaw-Lefevre was able to use his position to open to the public Kew Gardens and the gardens of Hampton Court Palace.

simple English rustic, where he ekes out his low wages by having a donkey on the common, and cutting wood for his winter fire. How are we defending the inheritance of our land-less fellow countrymen? We are losing it, irrecoverably losing it, year by year. Only a handful of us are yet at work on the Kent and Surrey Committee of the Commons Preservation Society; not an honorary secretary is to be heard of by any enquiries I have made; at critical junctures its funds are dependent on my writing to two friends; the burden of its manifold decisions depending on the tried veterans in the cause! The agricultural labourers have found us out, and many a hard-earned shilling reaches us in postal orders from a village, many an illiterate but burning letter. But where are the educated workers? 'Oh', you will say, and say rightly, 'there is a great deal of sympathy and workers to be had, and you will get them gradually if you try'. Most true, my friends; no one knows this better than I. Many a fruitful letter I could write, much of the work I could do, and in time workers would be found; but the time to do all this is wanting to me. I am responsible for a large amount of regular work; duties have grown up that I dare not cast aside. 'Why', I ask myself, 'must the organising, or rather the vivifying, come all from me and my few tried fellow-workers, already overtaxed? Where are the young heroes who burn to help and to do? Why is all the energy to go into the slums of London, and none into the remote places from which our slums are fed; all to the free dinners and the pittance to the lazy unemployed; none to the honest rustic, who with difficulty supports himself with the addition of fuel and pasture dependent on his common rights? How is it that the rural labourers have heard of this work, and that it has attracted so little attention from the richer country residents, or from educated Londoners?'

Well, it will all come in time, I know; but meantime, how many commons will be enclosed illegally before 1894? How many footpaths will be lost for ever for want of local opposition? Now there is one thing the public can perhaps do during 1893. At present, if a public footpath is threatened which has been enjoyed by landless Englishmen from time immemorial, and a meeting of the inhabitants in vestry is called to decide on whether or no it is to be closed, the law allows the question to be decided by what is called the plural vote, unless anyone has spirit, knowledge and money enough to oppose at Quarter Sessions. This plural vote means that every man has votes according to the value of his property. The matter to be decided involves no expenditure of rates, where a man who pays most may have some right to more weight. It is a question where he who has least land is most concerned. Yet a

£50 assessment gives one vote, and every £25 additional assessment gives an additional vote, with a maximum of six. So that this year we have a footpath being closed—and legally closed—where 75 persons voted against the closing, and 46 for it; for the 46 cast 103 votes. I believe a clause will be inserted in a Government Bill altering the law; the public ought really to make sure that that alteration, at least, is made. I don't complain of the progress which our Kent and Surrey Committee has made: we have had some reverses which will do us good. I daresay we have learnt much and done some good. May we have strength in the opening year to do more; and may an ever-increasing body of fresh helpers come forward, for the work is at once manifold and urgent.

Lastly, my dear friends, let me thank you for the donations which you have trusted to me privately during the past year, an account of which is subjoined. They form but a small part of what you have sent me: the larger portion is accounted for in more formal public reports. This is what has been trusted to me personally, and forms the basis of much of that silent, personal help, which for years it has thus been granted me to do; that basis of support which makes me strong, in many a day when real need comes before me and before that ever nearer and ever dearer body of tried workers with whose almost daily presence and help it has pleased God to enrich and bless me. It seems impossible to thank the givers and the workers who stand nearest; I trust they know in their very hearts what they are to me.

OCTAVIA HILL

DONATION ACCOUNT, 1892

RECEIPTS

	£	s.	d.
Cash in hand	100	14	4
Anon.	0	2	0
A.C. Allen, Esq	2	2	0
Rev. B. Alford	5	0	0
Mrs Baynes	0	2	9
Mrs Bridgeman	2	0	0
Mrs Scrase-Dickins	3	18	0
Miss J. Forman	1	1	0
The late Charles E. Flower, Esq	3	3	0
Miss Frankau	2	2	0
Miss Fisher (for Summer Treat)	3	0	0
Miss O. Fowler (fares to Erleigh)	0	5	0
Miss Gossett	1	10	0
Mr and Mrs Gillson	2	12	0
Miss Howitt	0	10	1
Miss Johnston	20	0	0
Miss Johnston (for Vans to Hampstead)	3	0	0
H. Luxmoore, Esq	5	0	0
Mrs Langenbach (for Children's Holiday)	2	2	0
Francis Morris, Esq	1	1	0
Mrs Macaulay	0	10	0
Per Dr and Mrs George MacDonald (for Hilly Fields)	55	0	0
Per Mrs Macdonell (Convalescents)	1	10	0
F. Nettlefold, Esq	20	0	0
Sir Frederick Pollock, Bart. (fares to Haslemere)	3	11	8
Rev. Charles Plummer	5	5	0
Mrs Douglas Powell	4	4	0
Mrs Peile (Convalescents)	1	1	0
Miss Ravenscroft	0	5	0
Mrs Leslie Stephen	10	10	0
Gordon Somervell, Esq	3	3	0
Miss Jane Sharp	1	1	0
Mrs Siemens	5	0	0
Arthur L. Scott, Esq	3	3	0
Mrs Tufnell	1	1	0
Mrs Todhunter	1	0	0
Mrs Percy Thompson	2	0	0
Mrs Winkworth	35	0	0
Mrs Whelpdale	2	0	0
Miss Mary Wells	2	0	0
	£316	9	10

DONATION ACCOUNT, 1892

EXPENDITURE

	£	s.	d.
Boarding-out (Partial Board and Clothing of several Children)	38	5	4
Pensions and other Relief to Aged	41	12	0
Convalescents 4	6	10
Emigration 3	0	0
Excursions to Country and other Entertainments	37	16	11 ½
Hilly Fields (Special)	55	0	0
Red Cross Garden	10	12	6
Care of Playground	10	8	0
May Festival 6	15	4
Industrial School (Donation to Church Farm) 2	0	0
Employment 1	11	6
Plants, Flowers, Carriage, etc 1	7	7
Printing Letter to Fellow-workers, Stationery, Postage, etc 6	4	4

In hand:

	£	s.	d.			
Special Fund	50	0	0			
Available	47	9	5 ½			
				97	9	5 ½

$$£316 \quad 9 \quad 10$$

Examined and found correct, Herbert M. Broughton, December 22nd 1892.

RED CROSS HALL AND GARDEN ACCOUNT, 1892

RECEIPTS

	£	s.	d.
Balance at Bank	23	4	10
Cash in hand	9	14	5
Donation:			
W.W. Cobbett, Esq	1	10	0
Miss Black	1	1	0
Mrs Temple	1	1	0
F. Martelli, Esq	0	10	0
Per Miss O. Hill	10	0	0
Per Miss O. Hill for Cleaning	6	0	0
Hire of Hall and Committee Room	20	15	0
Programmes (sale of)	4	10	5 ½
Collected at Entertainments	3	15	10
Gymnasium Receipts	1	8	9
Sale of Bracket, Fuel, Breakage	0	8	0
Rents, Balance of, for Club and 10, White Cross Street	22	4	4
Interest: Red Cross Cottages	48	0	0
Interest: White Cross Cottages	6	12	0
	£160	15	7 ½

RED CROSS HALL AND GARDEN ACCOUNT, 1892

EXPENDITURE

	£	s.	d.
Caretaker	60	1	0
Caretaker, Extra Fees	3	2	0
Caretaker, Cap and Adrertisement	0	9	8
Cleaning	3	15	11
WaterRate	6	4	3
Gas, Carbon and Footlights	15	9	9
Fuel	2	7	10
Tuning Piano	0	18	6
Entertainments, Special	1	10	0
Entertainments, Expenses	2	6	3
Printing Programmes, etc	2	11	6
Postage, Stationery and Cheque Book	1	13	11 ½
Gasfitter	5	17	5
Repair of Hall Lamp	1	12	9
Stage Appliances	2	14	10 ½
Repairs in Hall and Distempering Committee Room	2	5	3
Wire for Second Panel	1	3	10
New Cupboard	0	12	0
Sundry Small Repairs	2	11	7
Gymnasium Instructor	0	4	0
Insurance, Two Panels	1	0	3
Land Tax	0	5	0
Sundry Small Expenses	0	5	10 ½

Garden:

					£	s.	d.
Grass Seed	3	3	0				
Gravel	2	7	0				
Repair of Seats	0	11	0				
Tools and Plants	0	18	2				
Pigeons' Food	1	2	11				
					8	2	1
Contribution to Second Panel					5	0	0
Memorial, Balance for					3	10	3
Balance at Bank					20	7	2
Cash in Hand					4	12	8
					£160	15	7 ½

Examined and found correct, Patrick Blyth.

331

LETTER TO MY FELLOW-WORKERS

TO WHICH ARE ADDED

ACCOUNTS OF DONATIONS RECEIVED

FOR

WORK AMONG THE POOR

DURING 1893

BY

OCTAVIA HILL

LONDON:
PRINTED BY WATERLOW AND SONS LIMITED,
LONDON WALL, E.C.

SUMMARY

A spiritual reflection... housing work: Southwark; Lisson Grove; Mrs Russell Gurney's block in Paddington handed over to the Horace Street Trust; Deptford; training of workers from Dundee and Amsterdam; 999-year lease offered on Red Cross cottages and Hall by the Ecclesiastical Commissioners... open spaces: Kent and Surrey Committee of the Commons Preservation Society; Hilly Fields is saved... Women's University Settlement: first scholarships for training courses funded... donation fund... outings and entertainments for tenants, first Red Cross flower show... deaths of two fellow-workers.

EDITOR'S NOTE

The opening paragraphs of this letter form an almost transcendental meditation on the need to achieve 'an atmosphere of prayer and stillness' in 'an age of hurry'. This passage shows how important Octavia felt the spiritual dimension of the work to be, with her fellow-workers 'shining, like the souls Dante saw, each growing rosier and brighter with fulness of light'. We can see why Ruskin described her as 'the best lady abbess you can have for London work' (Rawnsley, 1923, p.29). The other-worldly tone returns towards the end of the letter in the passage on defeat: 'Defeats have a singular blessing about them... May I be with the defeated in the early struggles of a great cause!'. Octavia took a long-term view of everything, always trusting to divine providence to bring her work to fruition. The final passage describes the body of fellow-workers, dead and alive, as a sort of communion of the saints.

Dear friends,

Once more I am sitting down to write to you a record of some of the incidents of a year's work, and to render an account of my stewardship. Each year that I do so there is an ever larger group of fellow-workers to whom I feel it is due that so much has been accomplished. As I pause their faces arise before me, and the memory of what they *are* seems to me more than what *they do*. The words, 'a crowd of witnesses',[1] occur to me. Witnesses of what? witnesses of Whom? Where faithful work, struggling to be perfect, is done; wherever loving lives are led longing to bring blessing, there is a witness of a God of love, of order, of peace, sometimes unseen by those who witness for Him, but shining through them, and in time, we trust, revealing Himself to them—sometimes about their path and about their bed, present in very deed, and known to them.

With a continually larger amount of business detail to see to, let us each strive in our very hearts that, while working steadily to get these in good order, as faithful stewards bound to have all we are put in trust of well done, we yet keep around ourselves such an atmosphere of prayer and of stillness that the spirits of those we serve, and our own no less, may be filled with peace. It is an age of hurry, an age too of strenuous endeavour, let us see that in our own lives we secure such pause and such peace that we can hear the still small voice, or the angels proclaiming glad tidings. We are allowed to offer our service, but it is a part of a great whole over which our Father watches, and we, and all his other children, are to *be* what He would have us, no less than to *do* it. Of all, therefore, of the many causes of thankfulness with which this letter must be full, its deepest and most heartfelt is for what you all are. As I think of you, each in your place, I feel as if you might, in all the dark places where you are shining, be like the souls Dante saw, each growing rosier and brighter with fulness of light. Better this than the

---

1 Presumably this Octavia's version of the 'cloud of witnesses' of Hebrews 12:1.

tangible work, though that, transfigured by the spirit in which it is done, is preparing the way of the Lord too.

Quite immeasurable is the spiritual influence: I can but report concerning the actual work. First, of the places put under our care, or rather of those specially to be mentioned this year.

Encouraged by the satisfactory result of Red and White Cross cottages and Gable cottages, I suggested to the Ecclesiastical Commissioners that they should themselves build similar cottages on their own ground in Southwark. They met my suggestion most cordially, and, after careful thought, decided to build nine new cottages. These are just completed, they have been put under our care, and the first tenants are moving in.[2] They are very near Red Cross Hall and garden, close to the new public library, and opposite to a new church.[3] The sun comes brightly in at their back windows. We begged the Commissioners to leave small borders against the walls of the tiny yards, so that tenants may plant creepers, and, at least, a few crocuses and ferns.

The daughter of a former fellow-worker and friend this year offered to help with money for building for the people. She at the same time came to work in one of our courts, so that she will know better how wisely to manage houses in the time to come. Encouraged by her offer, I approached the ground landlord of an estate near Lisson Grove, for whom we were managing a block of dwellings,[4] with the result, finally,

---

2   *See ill. 15.* These are the cottages known as 1-9 Winchester Cottages on Orange Street (now Copperfield St). The EC authorised expenditure of £2,500 on the erection of cottages in Orange and Pepper Street (now Risborough Street) (Letter from EC to Cluttons, 24 June, year illegible, possibly 1892). They still exist and now change hands for sums in the region of £350,000.

---

3   This was All Hallows in Pepper Street (now Risborough Street), founded as a memorial to a beloved child and opened in 1892. The living was in the gift of Keble College, Oxford, and the church was controversial as a centre of Anglo-Catholic worship. Rev. R.H. Duthy, vicar from 1892 to 1912, was the subject of numerous complaints to the bishop from a Mr Side and other residents of Union Street, who protested against his ritual practices. However the bishop, who was himself a staunch evangelical, refused to take action against Fr Duthy when he found it was men of his persuasion who were of most use to him in his work amongst the poor of Southwark. Dr Duthy ran a large Sunday school and a mission hall in Red Cross Street, where he would no doubt have met Octavia. The church was bombed and burnt out in the Second World War. It was rebuilt, but little of the original fabric remains. (Higham, 1955, pp.270 and 289.)

---

4   This was Christchurch Buildings in Lisson Street, built in 1856 by the Marylebone

that my young friend took from him the lease of a plot of ground immediately behind his own block of dwellings. Here she is erecting six cottages; the foundations are now being dug, and we are with keen interest watching the work. Not only will the cottages be delightful in themselves, but, being low, they will let light and air into the block behind them in a far larger degree than such buildings as would probably have been erected. We are hoping to plant a hawthorn and almond tree or two in the small yards, and a poplar in the yard of the block which is at a lower level. I hope it will grow tall, and that its top will catch the

---

Association for Improving the Dwellings of the Industrious Classes. In this letter Octavia begins to describe how her supporters bought one site after another in a street in Lisson Grove and built charming, tile-hung cottages designed by Elijah Hoole, which are still there today (see 1894, 1895, 1896, 1897, 1906). However, Octavia never mentions the name of the street, and with good reason, as it had been the scene of a recent sex scandal. In the early part of the 1880s a vigorous campaign was being waged by the moral purity movement to raise the legal age of consent to sexual intercourse from 13 to 16. A bill had been introduced into parliament, but Gladstone's government, by now in its last days after the death of General Gordon at Khartoum, was inclined to drop it. In June 1885 W.T. Stead, the editor of the *Pall Mall Gazette*, injected new life into the campaign by publishing a series of scandalous articles called 'The Maiden Tribute of Modern Babylon' in which he described how he had been able to purchase a 13-year-old girl, Eliza Armstrong, for £5 from her mother, after making it plain that she was required for prostitution. As a result of the sensation caused by the articles, parliament passed the bill in August 1885, raising the age of consent to 16, but Stead was sent to prison for three months for 'kidnapping' the girl, as her father claimed he had never consented to her being removed from the house. The Armstrong family lived in Charles Street, Lisson Grove, which, according to E. Moberly Bell, 'had at no time enjoyed an enviable reputation, [and] now became so notorious that no respectable family would willingly live in it'. (Moberly Bell, 1942, p.201.) It was at this point that Octavia was asked to undertake the management of Christchurch Buildings in Lisson Street, which she accepted, clearing out the 'evil-living' tenants and keeping their rooms empty until she could find respectable ones. The land at the back of Christchurch Buildings sloped down steeply to Charles Street, much of which had already been demolished and which Octavia realised would remain virtually unlettable unless it underwent a radical transformation, so she persuaded her supporters to buy up sites and rebuild, until she controlled almost the whole street. She also persuaded the LCC to change the name of the street to Ranston Street in 1896. (Moberly Bell calls it, incorrectly, James Street, but she may have been confused by the fact that Charles Street was a turning off Great James Street, now the eastern part of Bell Street.) The first new group of cottages, which Octavia refers to here, was built for Stella Duckworth and called Almond Cottages, presumably because of the almond tree in the yard. They are now 32-37 Ranston Street. *See ills. 17 and 18.* Christchurch Buildings, together with all the other buildings on the east side of Lisson Street, have now been demolished and the land laid out as a garden.

sunlight often in an evening when the tenants watch it from their windows. But this planting is for next year.

I came down to breakfast one morning lately, and found on my table a letter from Mrs Russell Gurney, whom I had not seen for many years, saying she had left to me in her will a block of model dwellings which she and her husband had built years before, but that she would like me to take it now.[5] The gift went right to my heart, and I was delighted. But I asked her to make it a trust, and she kindly consented to let it be added to the trust I mentioned to you in my last letter.[6] The deeds are now being drawn. The houses are quite in the West End, and must be, I should think, a very great comfort to the many poorer people who want to be near their work, yet for whom rents are prohibitory, except where a little oasis has thus been preserved for them among the acres covered with huge houses. I think that some of my fellow-workers who cannot go into the out-of-the-way places will find it a very delightful thing to have thus a small group of tenants under their charge, and I believe that real friendships and much personal intercourse will be possible between them.

---

5   This block of model dwellings was Westbourne Buildings in Elms Lane, now Elms Mews, off the Bayswater Road. It no longer exists. Mrs Gurney died three years after making this gift to Octavia, who always remembered her as a key benefactor, and mentioned her in the list of departed fellow-workers when she was accepting her portrait by John Singer Sargent in 1898 (1898, pp.420–21). Emilia Gurney, *née* Batten (1823–1896), married Russell Gurney in 1852. Gurney, Conservative MP and Recorder of London, was a statesman of some note, being an ardent supporter of women's rights, especially with regard to education and the vote. He steered the Married Women's Property Act through parliament, and followed this up in 1876 with the Enabling Act, which empowered medical examining bodies to educate and graduate women on the same terms as men. Emilia shared her husband's interests, especially in women's education, and was on the original committee of Girton College, Cambridge. Emilia was deeply religious, and became interested in spiritualism and mysticism. Following her husband's death she instigated a spiritual meeting at their house every year on Ascension Day (her husband had died on the morning after Ascension Day). She acquired a disused cemetery chapel on the Bayswater Road, attached to St George's, Hanover Square, and turned it into a magnificent frescoed Chapel of the Ascension. She was extremely well-connected, numbering amongst her close friends Lady Mount-Temple, Julia Wedgwood, General Gordon, Louise Galton, wife of Francis, the pioneer of eugenics, and Lady Elizabeth Eastlake, wife of the director of the National Gallery. She produced a version of Dante's *Divine Comedy* called *Dante's Pilgrim's Progress*. She shared with George MacDonald, another friend, an immense admiration for Bunyan's *Pilgrim's Progress*.

---

6   The Horace Street Trust, formed to receive the three houses given by Anna Scrase-Dickins in 1886 (1892, p.318).

Mr and Mrs Blyth have taken over the additional blocks in Islington which I mentioned in my last letter.

So much as to new areas. Of the courts and buildings formerly under our charge all have gone on well, and are happy in having no very remarkable changes to record.

Only Deptford I must mention, because it has been for such years our great difficulty. Here we have to record the loss of our friend and fellow-worker Miss Chase, who has returned to America, and whose zeal and sympathy can never be forgotten by those who knew her.[7] In spite of this loss, assuredly the street has made very distinct advance this year. The change of staff to which I referred last year has produced

---

7   This is the only reference in the letters to Ellen Chase (unless she is the 'young Bostonian' of 1887, p.229), who had arrived from America in the summer of 1886 and been thrown in at the deep end, replacing Miss Ironside in Deptford (1886, p.207). Ever since taking over the street in 1884, Octavia's accounts of the goings-on there had introduced a note of gloom into the letters: 'My poor Deptford... continues the great difficulty to us... a source... not only of anxiety but of pain... our black sheep continues black' and so on. In the 1894 letter Octavia announces that she has cut her losses and withdrawn from the street's management. However, we have the fullest account we possess of any of Octavia's projects in Ellen Chase's book *Tenant Friends in Old Deptford*. Ellen Chase, who was a gifted writer, paints a vivid picture of life with the tenants in Queen Street (which she calls Green Street) which is completely at odds with Octavia's dismal observations. She describes the usual problems with tenants who gave false references and refused to pay the rent, but her account is more positive and light-hearted than Octavia's articles describing her early struggles in Marylebone. How can we account for the discrepancy between the two women's narratives of Deptford? And how can we account for the fact that Octavia makes no mention of Ellen Chase in the letters until she has returned to America, in spite of the fact that she was clearly a talented housing manager and deeply imbued with Octavia's values? The answer is probably that they were just too similar and, like many leaders of movements, Octavia was more comfortable with her foot soldiers than her fellow officers. Ellen Chase's account of life in Deptford makes almost no mention of Octavia. There is an opening chapter called 'Management of Houses on the Octavia Hill Plan' which makes a couple of brief references to Octavia, but Octavia does not appear in the main body of the text at all. The reader is left with the impression that Ellen Chase was managing everything on her own, when we know from Octavia's correspondence that she was constantly at Deptford. The peculiar publishing history of *Tenant Friends in Old Deptford* also suggests a problem between the two women. It was not published until 1929, and although the title page advertises 'a preface by Octavia Hill', there is no reference to the fact that Octavia had been dead for 17 years by then. The fact that Ellen Chase appears to have been a woman of independent means probably made relations between her and Octavia even more difficult. Ellen gave £14 to the donation fund in 1887 and appears regularly in the lists of donors from then on, giving what would have been substantial amounts. She gave £7 for Deptford Park in 1894 (after she had returned to America) and £5 for Mariner's Hill in 1908.

better effect than I had dared to hope.[8] Under a continuous, a firm, a vigilant and a wise rule, even these poor people are beginning to feel the blessings of government. Much loving and heroic service is also being done for them, but this is easier to secure than the patient and wise firmness of quietly thoughtful government, indifferent to popularity because based on conscience, which it has been our great satisfaction at last to secure there. The charity we had, the continuous rule, we never achieved before. Under it the people and the place show marked improvement, though it is still the court which is distinctly behind all the others in its condition.

In connection with the houses I may mention that during the past year two ladies, one from Dundee, and one from Amsterdam,[9] have come to stay some months with us, to study further the management of houses as we do it in London. Both were ladies of considerable power, and during the time they were with us they managed to make themselves of very real service to us, so that we have to thank them, while I hope that what they saw will be of use to their respective towns. I am sure they will be wise enough not to adopt anything we do here as if it were necessarily suitable for other places. It is only our best effort to meet the local and present needs. They will, I hope, only use their experience here as suggestive, and to be adapted to the wants of their own cities.

Before I leave the question of the houses, I ought to record that the Ecclesiastical Commissioners have decided to endeavour to give to those who hold leases under them the advantages of fixity of tenure, by offering to them leases for 999 years on a very slightly advanced ground rent. The trustees of Red Cross Hall and cottages have decided to avail themselves of this offer of the Ecclesiastical Commissioners, and the deeds are to be ready for signature before March. The garden was already held on a 999 years' lease, and as the amenities of this greatly depend on the Hall and cottages, and all the life of the one is bound up with the others, I am very glad to think the long tenure will be thus rendered possible.

---

8   On 22 November 1893 Octavia had written to Ellen Chase: 'Queen Street goes wonderfully. Miss Gee does wonders there.' (Maurice, 1914, p.527.) She clearly did not want Ellen to labour under the impression that she was indispensable.

---

9   'I have with me... a charming young lady, Mis Ter Meulen from Amsterdam, who is spending a few months in England, to prepare for taking up houses in her own country. She is full of power, brightness and sweet human sympathy.' (Letter from Octavia to Ellen Chase, 22 November 1893, Maurice, 1914, p.527.)

I wrote to you last year about the Kent and Surrey Committee, and the great need there was of fresh workers for it, and specially of an honorary secretary. The report of this Committee will be issued soon, so I will only say here that, in consequence of my appeal in the last year's letter, the matter was brought to the notice of Mr Thomas Farrer, who undertook the hon. secretaryship, and this has been an immense help to the committee. I have chronicled successes, and here I must record a defeat, one which has greatly disappointed us. We have not succeeded in preserving the footpath to which I referred last year. This has not arisen from any want, however, of our being heartily supported, and being able to fight for it to the last. We had money enough given us to carry the case up twice to Quarter Sessions. Once we were successful, owing to the irregularity of proceeding on the part of the enclosers. The second time the matter went to a jury, who took into consideration the relative value of the widening of a road to the station, which the landowner who wished to close the path offered to do at his own cost. The two questions were quite distinct: in our estimation either the Highway Board, or the landowner whose building on adjacent land renders the widening advisable, should have paid for it. If such equivalents are to be taken into consideration, the public may lose any field path in England in order to save the ratepayers from paying a highway rate when building operation necessitates fresh roads in other parts of the parish. I hope those who trusted us with their money will not feel too disheartened. I think myself that it was by no means thrown away. I believe that the fact of a fight is a help in preventing closure. I also think a point was secured by the first trial, when the landowner had to pay costs and to begin again in proper legal form. Besides this, I feel we cannot always foretell the result, and must advance in hope of a victory, when sure that, whether it come or not, we ought to struggle for it. I have never been unmindful of, or inconsiderate to, donors; it would be dreadful if I were so, when they are so very responsive and good to me; but I do believe that many would desire to stand by us in our struggles when they are right, and would be as proud to take defeat with us as victory—prouder, perhaps. Defeats have a singular blessing about them. Every one is ready to help the winning cause. It is on the defeats that the victories are built, as a bridge upon piles out of sight. May I be with the defeated in the early struggles of a great cause! never shall I be more useful. After the defeat one can slip out of the way.

Not but that we glory in victories very thankfully when they come, though, perhaps, our hallelujah has a deeper sound for the memory of defeats of long ago, and of those who stood beside us in them. Here at least is a very bright one. Hilly Fields is won! Mr Hunter[10] and Mr Derham have struggled on during the whole past year, as during the previous ones, through obstacles that would have daunted less persistent leaders. They had the great satisfaction this month of seeing the last obstacle overcome, and in the most satisfactory way. The Lewisham Board of Works, which ought to have led the van, had the grace at last to vote the balance of money needed, and the Hilly Fields are saved.[11]

I have several times mentioned in these letters the Women's University Settlement, with which I have been so much bound up during the last few years. That connection continues and strengthens. I find there the training for many of my new volunteers, while, as they grow in knowledge, they return to form some of my best workers. I think the Settlement finds my work, too, one of its best training fields, and a sphere that would afford scope for some of its well-trained workers.

I spoke of the scholarships we hoped to found there, and asked if anyone would provide, for a year, the £50 necessary for a year's training and residence for a scholar. Two friends most kindly responded. By this means within the year two ladies have been started in remunerative posts, and two are still under training.

---

10 Robert Hunter was knighted in the New Year's honours list a few days after Octavia had written this letter. It is sometimes said that he received his knighthood for services to the Post Office, and sometimes for his work for open spaces. As honours were not attributed to categories of achievement in those days, we will never know.

---

11 The list of subscribers to the appeal ran to 31 pages and included William Morris and F.D. Mocatta, the well-known Jewish philanthropist. The Kyrle Society contributed £1,000, and other generous benefactors included the Duke of Westminster and many of the city livery companies such as the Goldsmiths', Fishmongers' and Leathersellers'. Sir Arthur Arnold, chairman of the LCC, which had spent £4,685 on laying out the grounds, opened the park to the public on 16 May 1896. Sir Robert Hunter, in his capacity as chairman of the committee set up to save Hilly Fields, attended the opening ceremony and paid tribute to the hard work of Octavia Hill, 'so well-known to many of them by reason of her public-spirited labours, in the course of her work in Deptford'. (*Lewisham Gazette*, 22 May 1896.) In fact, the success of the campaign probably owed more to Robert Hunter's unstinting dedication and perseverance in reconciling the conflicting interests of the various parties. Octavia's brief references to the campaign give no idea of its complexity, which was described in the Kyrle Society's report for 1892 (pp.12-14). There were legal and financial ramifications involving the Ecclesiastical Commissioners, the Bishop of Lichfield, the New Land Development Company, the Trustees of the Bridge House Estates and the executors of a Mr Lee. The amount of detailed and highly skilled work involved must have been enormous, and it is easy to understand why Henry Fawcett said of Robert Hunter that he had never known a professional man do so much professional work for nothing.

Now we come to donations. Our labour would be comparatively fruitless, and oh! how much harder, if it were not for the ever ready, ever generous help that reaches us from farther off. In large measure have I been thus trusted this year. I have received quite lately three large donations, which greatly swell my balance-sheet, and which it will be my business at once to distribute, with the careful co-operation of my fellow-workers. The money for our group of orphans, pensions, and others for whom we have undertaken definite responsibilities so long as we are able to fulfil them, is independent of these special funds. I wish the donors of both could know all the blessings they bring, but that is impossible without seeing the brightened faces and the cheered homes where the help comes.

We have had delightful summer parties again for our people. Miss Johnston and Mr and Mrs Arthur Hill again entertained a large group of tenants, and Sir Spencer Wilson most cordially and kindly received another group at Charlton Park on the August Bank Holiday.

Besides this, Dr and Mrs Longstaff arranged to entertain on Saturday or Sunday afternoons every week for a very long summer season, groups of about 20 at their lovely place at Putney. These formed the most enjoyable opportunities for many London workers to gather together a group of those to whom such an afternoon's rest and pleasure was specially helpful. They were received by Dr and Mrs Longstaff themselves in the most sympathetic and hospitable way, and the real personal interest shewn, and the quiet summer beauty have made a deep impression on many.

The work at Red Cross Hall and garden has gone on most successfully on the old lines. Our thanks are very heartily given to the many kind friends who have come down on Thursdays and Sundays to sing, to act, to show microscopes, and to help; also to those who, for our Sundays as on other occasions, have been so good as to send us flowers. The drill and gymnastics have gone on as usual.

The new feature at Red Cross this year has been the flower show, which was held on July 15th. A separate report has been printed, so I will only here add how very pleased I was to see how much the people responded, how large the number of the exhibitors was, how cordially Southwark furnished the local committee, and what a very happy day we had on our one out-door summer fête in Southwark. I hope this year may see such another day, and that as the years go on, more garden fêtes may be possible there.

We have no fresh panel commemorating heroic deeds to record this year. We have, however, succeeded in getting the money for the last one, and are hoping soon to see another. Mrs Barrington is getting out, at my request, a balance-sheet of the donations received, and the expenses. The plaster of the panels is paid for, for the entire set. The other Sunday a gentleman recited a beautiful ballad about a heroic rescue from fire, ending with an adjuration to us all to forget ourselves in thought for others, and so to be found ready should the call come for great and sudden sacrifice. The hall was hushed in breathless attention while the words re-echoed through it. As I passed down among the audience just afterwards I was twice stopped. One man said, 'Did you see how every eye was turned to her', pointing to the Alice Ayres. A woman said, 'I couldn't but think of Alice Ayres'. 'Did you know her?' I asked. 'Yes I always dealt there', she said, 'and I was glad when they put up that panel there.'

My friends, two have passed away from us since I wrote to you, who have left a memory behind them which, in its way, is to us, too, a trumpet call: Miss Brooke, whose faithful, humble, loving work and generous gifts will long be a witness of the noble out-of-sight lives which exist in England, to which Mr Hughes refers so beautifully in his preface to his *Memoir of a Brother*,[12] and which he says so truly form the strength of England, which would come out in a crisis, and which is always telling in out-of-the-way places. Miss King, too, in the full energy of high-hearted and high-souled youth, snatched from among us while we were all rejoicing in her help, and prophesying of her future. It opened to her in ways we did not dream of. May we live here in memory of such gone before, and be as ready to step into His nearer presence when we are called!

OCTAVIA HILL

---

12 In the preface to his book *Memoir of a Brother* (Macmillan, 1873) Thomas Hughes, the author of *Tom Brown's Schooldays* and a prominent member of the Christian Socialist movement, had written: 'In a noisy and confused time like ours, it does seem to me that most of us have need to be reminded of, and will be the better for bearing in mind, the reserve of strength and power which lies quietly at the nation's call, outside the whirl and din of public and fashionable life, and entirely ignored in the columns of the daily press. The subject of this memoir was only a good specimen of thousands of Englishmen of high culture, high courage, high principle, who are living their own quiet lives in every corner of the kingdom, from John O'Groats to the Land's End, bringing up their families in the love of God and their neighbour, and keeping the atmosphere around them clean, and pure and strong, by their example—men who would come to the front, and might be relied on, in any serious national crisis.' It is easy to understand why Octavia should have cited this book with approval.

DONATION ACCOUNT, 1893

RECEIPTS

	£	s	d
In hand	97	9	5 ½
Rev. B.H. Alford	5	0	0
A.C. Allen Esq	2	2	0
Miss Austin	1	0	0
Charles Bridgeman, Esq	5	0	0
Mrs Bridgeman	2	0	0
Duchess of Cleveland	25	0	0
Miss Chase	1	6	0
Miss Chase for training boy to December 1894	18	0	0
The Countess of Ducie	20	0	0
Lady Jane Dundas	20	0	0
Lady Jane Dundas (for the blind)	40	0	0
Miss E. Erle	10	0	0
Hon. T.C. Farrer	5	0	0
Miss Forman	1	1	0
Miss Fowler	2	10	6
Miss Frankau (Convalescents)	2	2	0
Mrs Gillson (pension)	2	12	0
Miss Gossett	1	1	0
Lady Hobhouse (country pleasures)	3	3	0
M.E.J.	20	0	0
M.E.J. (Vans to Hampstead)	3	0	0
Miss Kirby	0	2	6
Mrs Langenbach	2	2	0
Miss Lewis	1	0	0
Mrs Lynch (balance from Donation for Deptford party)	0	11	10
Mrs Macaulay	4	5	0
Per Mrs Macdonnell	2	13	4
Frank Morris, Esq	1	1	0
Lady Nicholson	1	1	0
Mrs Oldham (for the aged)	3	3	0
Rev. Charles Plummer	5	0	0
Rev. Charles Plummer (for 1894)	5	0	0
Mrs Peile (Convalescents)	1	0	0
Sir Frederick Pollock (excursions)	10	0	0
Miss Richardson	2	10	0
Mrs Scrase-Dickins	1	9	3
Mrs Leslie Stephen	10	10	0
Miss Jane Sharp	1	1	0
Miss Stephens	0	5	0
Miss Singleton	10	0	0
Lindsay Scott, Esq	3	3	0
Mrs Charles Thompson	2	0	0
Mrs Tufnell	1	1	0
A. Vaughan, Esq	10	0	0
Mrs Winkworth	20	0	0
Mrs Winkworth (pension, special)	30	0	0
Mrs Winkworth (pension, special)	10	0	0
Miss Mary Wells	2	0	0
Mrs Whelpdale	2	0	0
Interest on Investment	8	15	3
	£439	1	1 ½

DONATION ACCOUNT, 1893

EXPENDITURE

	£	s	d
Training and Boarding out in Homes …………………………………………………	76	13	4
Pensions and other Relief to Aged ………………………………………………	54	8	6
Cottages (preserving) ……………………………………………………………	49	16	0
Help in Sickness and Convalescence, &c. ………………………………………	23	12	1 ½
Country Excursions and other Entertainments …………………………………	13	11	10
Blind, donation to Home, and pension …………………………………………	13	0	0
Playground, care of ………………………………………………………………	10	8	0
Printing Letter to Fellow-Workers, Stationery, Postage, &c. …………………… 8	2	4 ½
May Festival ……………………………………………………………………… 6	6	4 ½
Kyrle Society …………………………………………………………………… 5	17	0
Industrial School (donation to Church Farm) ………………………………… 5	0	0
Boys' Club (donation) …………………………………………………………… 2	0	0
Employment …………………………………………………………………… 0	15	0
Guard for Trees and Fee at Flower Show ………………………………………… 0	7	3
In hand: Special Fund …………………………………………………………	60	0	0
In hand: Appropriate …………………………………………………………	65	0	0
In hand: Available ……………………………………………………………	44	3	4

£439   1   1 ½

Examined and found correct, A.P. Fletcher, January 12th 1894

RED CROSS HALL AND GARDEN ACCOUNT, 1893

RECEIPTS

	£	s	d
Balance at Bank, January 1893	20	7	2
Cash in hand	4	12	8
Interest, Red and White Cross Cottages	92	8	3
Rents, Balance of Club and 10 White Cross Street	22	19	11
Hire of Hall	17	3	0
Programmes, sale of	12	2	8
Donations:			
Miss Peto	5	0	0
Women's University Settlement, per Mrs Braby	2	2	0
Mrs Temple	1	1	0
Mrs Mansfield	1	0	0
Miss Harris	1	0	0
F. Martelli, Esq	0	10	0
Gymnasium Pupils' Fees	5	18	10
Collected at Entertainments	2	1	5
Insurance Co: broken lamp	0	10	6
Returned Paint Cans	0	3	0
Sale of Pigeons	0	2	3
	£189	2	8

RED CROSS HALL AND GARDEN ACCOUNT, 1893

EXPENDITURE

	£	s	d
Caretaker	58	18	3
Garden:			
Gravel, Mould, &c. ... 19 12 6			
Hose and reel ... 3 16 6			
Paint and Soda ... 2 1 9			
Plants ... 2 0 3			
Tools ... 0 9 2			
Pigeons' Food ... 1 5 6			
	29	5	8
Curtain, Gymnastic Appliances, Furniture, &c.	13	3	2
Repairs	12	8	0
Gas	8	2	1
Water Rate	6	4	8
Printing, Stationery, Advertisement	7	15	4
Sundries	5	1	8
Cleaning	4	0	0
Entertainment Expenses	3	15	3
Fuel	2	12	6
Insurance: two Panels	1	7	0
Insurance: Fire	1	2	6
Insurance: Plate Glass	0	9	0
Land Tax	0	5	0
Cash at Bank, January 1984	31	11	5
Cash in hand	3	1	2
	£189	2	8

Audited and found correct, P.L. Blyth, January 13th 1894.

LETTER TO MY FELLOW-WORKERS

TO WHICH ARE ADDED

ACCOUNTS OF DONATIONS RECEIVED

FOR

WORK AMONG THE POOR

DURING 1894

BY

OCTAVIA HILL

(FOR PRIVATE CIRCULATION ONLY)

LONDON:
PRINTED BY WATERLOW AND SONS LIMITED,
LONDON WALL, E.C.

SUMMARY

Housing work: Lisson Grove; Ecclesiastical Commissioners... tenants should pay their own rates... work at Deptford handed over... White and Red Cross cottages, Hall and garden: Walter Crane's panel of the child in the well... outings for tenants... donation fund and list of grants made by the Horace Street Trust... Women's University Settlement: Pfeiffer trustees provide £3,000 to endow scholarships; two adjacent properties purchased... Kyrle Society in need of funds... open spaces: Deptford Park... foundation of the National Trust; Dinas Oleu.

EDITOR'S NOTE

At the opening of this letter Octavia expresses her concern with the expansion of the role of local government and the consequent increase in its expenditure. She is especially worried by the fact that local authorities can borrow money to fund current projects in ways that will impose burdens of debt on the community for decades to come. The rest of the letter is fairly routine— Deptford, Red Cross, Women's University Settlement—until we come to to the last paragraph. Its opening words—'I am, naturally, deeply interested in the foundation of the National Trust'—give little idea of the key role that Octavia had played in bringing into existence this institution, which was to assume such impressive dimensions and significance in the life of the nation.

190 Marylebone Road, N.W.

My dear friends,

Another year has come and gone, and I have prepared the account of the money entrusted to me for donations.[1] With this I must send you all, not only some little record of other work, but my heartiest thanks for the co-operation on which it has all depended.

Our work in the houses has in some directions expanded. The cottages near Lisson Grove, to which I referred in my last letter, were completed last June, and immediately occupied.[2] A friend and fellow-worker of many years' standing is in treaty for ground in the same street, whereon to erect seven more, and the plans for these are ready.

The Ecclesiastical Commissioners, pleased with the success of the nine cottages built by them in Southwark, have built five more adjoining them, which are completed and occupied.[3]

They have also erected, on a site belonging to them in Westminster,[4] 19 cottages,[5] which they have put under our care, and they are rapidly

---

1   Although it is not possible to date this letter, Patrick Blyth signed off the Red Cross accounts on 3 January 1895, which is quite early. Unfortunately Mr Broughton did not date his approval of the donation fund accounts.

---

2   Almond cottages, designed by Elijah Hoole for Stella Duckworth, can be seen in ills.17 and 18.

---

3   These were additions to Winchester cottages on Orange Street (now Copperfield Street) built at a cost of £1,450. (Letter from Cluttons to the EC, 9th May 1894.)

---

4   The EC purchased the land, on which these properties were built, from a Mrs Brown in July 1894, at an undisclosed cost. (Letters from Cluttons to the EC, 3 April 1894 & 10 July 1894.)

---

5   *See ill. 19.* Fifteen of these cottages were located on the north-east side of Garden Street and three were in Dorset Street. They consisted of nine four-room cottages, seven six-room cottages, and two eight-room cottages. The total cost of this development was £6,150. (Letter from Cluttons to the EC, 4 November 1894.) Garden Street and Dorset Street no longer exist.

proceeding with others in the same street.[6]

In all these new cottages I am introducing the plan of arranging that the tenants should pay their own rates, the rent being fixed much lower to enable them to do this. Now that the rates are steadily rising in all parts of London, and threatening not only to be a heavy incubus for the current year, but to lay a burden of municipal indebtedness for 60 or 80 years, which may seriously cripple the future; now that the expenditure is decided on by multitudes of voters little trained to look forward, keen for immediate result; now that those who own the land or buildings have next to no voice in local government; in pity for those thousands of poor who depend so much for their prosperity on sound and far-seeing finance, I feel such an arrangement of very deep moment to our city. I have, therefore, devoted much thought to it, and my fellow-workers have very cordially helped, struggling through what has been most up-hill work. It has not, even on the present small scale, been without result, as our tenants are now keenly alive to many of the facts about the rates which they, and they only, can alter: first, they realise that a defaulting ratepayer throws additional burdens on his neighbours; second, they are angry, and rightly, at the ambiguity which exists in the notices issued in many parishes. These do not state clearly up to what date rates are paid. Rates are now very generally asked for in advance, and a tenant has a right to claim them back if he leaves; but as this does not appear clearly on the claims or receipts, numbers lose what they have a right to. The plan of making weekly tenants responsible

---

6   This rebuilding came at a turbulent time for the Ecclesiastical Commissioners. As with the other estates managed by the EC, there was a lot of controversy over the condition of their properties. In the case of Westminster, this controversy centred around Garden Street. Mr J. Hunter Watts of the Social Democratic Front condemned the properties on Garden Street as being 'unfit for human habitation' in the 19 February 1894 edition of *The Daily Chronicle*. He severely lambasted the EC: 'No improvements seem to have been made on your initiative except when you benefit yourselves pecuniarily...' The authorities concurred with Mr Watts. The EC were summoned to a Westminster police court hearing on 10 November 1894, where 26-36 (even) Garden Street were declared unfit for human habitation. (Letter from Cluttons to the EC, 11 November 1894.) A series of notices were served on the EC, and on residents of Garden Street by the LCC. They were informed that the LCC wished to demolish the above houses, which had been condemned by a surveyor working on behalf of the LCC. These notices were legislated by the Metropolitan Building Acts, 1855 and 1869, and the Local Government Act, 1888. Other parts of the EC estate in Westminster were condemned to a lesser extent. For example, the St Margaret's and St John's parish medical officer deemed Regency Street as unhygienic in the same year. (Official Petition, 23 February 1894.)

for rates is very difficult to work; not being general, the machinery and arrangements do not help us. But I have felt it to be so important as to be well worth a great effort. It may be that some of those in authority will realise its value, and that we may get some help in time. What could conduce most to make the plan succeed would be if *some* allowance could be made for tenants paying their rates in advance, analogous to, though naturally not so great as, that made to landlords who compound. Also some plan by which the various payments might be spread over the year, falling due at different quarters. This would go far to mitigate the difficulty for working people of paying a lump sum down twice a year, as is demanded in some London parishes. Weekly or fortnightly collection, which I hear is arranged for in Edinburgh, would manifestly be more costly, but our tenants would manage a quarterly payment pretty easily. However, at present there is no hope of any modification of existing arrangements, we must do our best to learn to fit in with the present regulations in the several parishes. I hope that, if we lead the van, others may follow, and co-operation may come in time from officials. All newly elected vestrymen might, meantime, do well to try to secure that fuller facts should be inserted on claims and receipts. The words 'made' 'due' and 'payable' are used in a way not always clear to the ratepayer, while the option of paying in separate instalments is often not shewn clearly on the claims.

This subject, however, is somewhat technical, and I only refer to it here because it is interesting me deeply. I think it would tend towards municipal economy, likely to tell to the advantage of the time to come. I dread these large loans lightly voted by thousands who little know what they mean in the future, and I think the greatest blessing, as well as the greatest justice, would be for those who vote the expenditure to feel that it mattered, and that economy benefited them.

The hope of gaining time which I might devote to carrying through this experiment greatly weighed with me in my decision to resign my work at Deptford. I resolved to do this at Christmas. It is naturally very sad for me to part from friends among whom I have worked for so many years, and to give up control of the places I have cared for. But it was a choice between refusing to manage the new cottages in Westminster and giving up Deptford. I, therefore, introduced my principal worker at Deptford to the owner of the houses there, and she will carry the management on for him; so Queen Street is no more under my care. It is a great satisfaction to me that I left the street in far better condition than at any other time during our stay there. When I did the accounts for the last time, and reviewed the state of people and place, I really did feel that all was in a far sounder position than of old.

Westminster will be a far better centre for training workers than Deptford could be for me, and I feel such training very important.

I hear from my friend at Amsterdam that she has met with strong support, and has had houses put under her care. Also that a gentleman is about to build houses of which she will have charge. From Dundee also I hear that the work progresses.

The trustees of White and Red Cross cottages and Red Cross Hall have accepted the lease for 999 years, making their tenure the same as that of the garden.

Another of Mr Walter Crane's panels has, owing to his kindness and that of Mrs Russell Barrington and her friends, been placed in the Hall this year. It commemorates the saving of a child who had fallen into a well, by the brave action of a man who descended at the risk of his life.

The work at the Hall and garden has gone on better and better each year. The Flower Show was a great success. There was also a May Festival there for the first time. The regular work has gone on as of old. Words will not say how grateful we are to the faithful groups of friends who come down on Sundays and Thursdays to sing and play, and act, and lecture. Some of the songs and recitations on Sundays have seemed to me like angel voices, coming among us to lift the veil and show us the great and noble and eternal spiritual beauty that lies around us when we forget it most. We have received lovely presents of flowers, too, telling much in the same way.

Dr and Mrs Longstaff, Mr and Mrs Arthur Hill, Sir Frederick and Lady Pollock, Mr and Mrs Edmund Maurice, and Miss Johnston have given our people delightful summer parties.

We have received, as in former years, munificent donations of pictures and magazines from Messrs Cassell,[7] and kind and welcome presents of clothes from others.

With regard to money given, the balance sheet shows how steadily kind our friends have been, and how their help has been applied. It will be seen how very large a proportion of the money goes to training and boarding-out and to pensions. These headings cover grants to orphans or the children of widows, and to blind or aged forlorn people; and as

---

7   Cassells were leading publishers of arts books and journals. They published the *Magazine of Art* from 1878, and, in the same year, their catalogue included Gustav Doré's *Paradise Lost* and *Don Quixote*. Cassell's *Family Magazine* was a high-class, illustrated publication. Their books and journals were far from cheap. They would later publish Miranda Hill's plays (1903, p.505).

any failure in such help would be very serious, I have thought it right to keep a fair sum in hand for the coming year. All I have in hand is thus appropriated. Any fresh sums which reach me, and some have done so even since this balance sheet was audited, will enable me to help fresh people. The £49 16s. spent in 1893 in 'preserving cottages' has been returned to me, the owners feeling that the result of the expenditure had been recouped by the receipts. This grant came from a special fund, and I shall hope to use it again in some such way; practically, it was a guarantee.

The Women's University Settlement in Southwark has occupied a good deal of my time this year. The 'scholars' trained there by the grants of £50 a year made by two of my friends have been well floated in independent work in consequence of this training. The idea of the importance of such training has taken root, and more than £3,000 has been granted by the Pfeiffer trustees, the interest of which will be an endowment for scholarships tenable at the Women's University Settlement. Dr J.G. Fitch[8] has kindly interested himself in the scheme, and has been mainly influential in securing this munificent grant. I

---

8   Sir Joshua Girling Fitch (1824–1903)was an educationalist associated with the New Education or the idea of 'Learning by Doing', the introduction of workshops into schools: 'The advocates of this view cite Rousseau, and Frobel, and Pestalozzi, and urge with truth that the brain is not the only organ which should be developed in a school; that to do justice to the whole sum of human powers and activities, there should be due exercise for the senses, and definite practice in the use of the fingers and the bodily powers.' (J.G. Fitch, *Educational Aims and Methods*, 1900, p.158). According to Fitch, the supreme end of education 'is the harmonious development of all the powers of a human being'. The second son of Thomas Fitch, Joshua Fitch was born in Southwark. His parents were poor but intellectually inclined, and at an early age Fitch started work as an assistant master in the British and Foreign School Society's elementary school in the Borough Road, founded by Thomas Lancaster. He continued to educate himself, taking his BA degree at London University in 1850 and his MA two years later. He rose quickly through the system, becoming a government inspector and commissioner. He was transferred to East Lambeth in 1877. In 1883 he was made a chief inspector and in 1885 chief inspector of training colleges, a post he held until he retired in 1894. He was knighted in 1896. Fitch was a recognised authority on all branches of education, his official reports and books being highly influential: *Lectures on Teaching* (1881), *Thomas and Matthew Arnold and their influence on English Education* (1901)and *Notes on American Schools and Training Colleges* (1887). *Educational Aims and Methods* (1900), originally delivered as lectures and addresses, encapsulated his philosophy. He was an advocate of the movement for higher education for women and was constantly looked to for counsel and direction on every sort of educational subject; his wide knowledge, safe judgement and amiable character made his co-operation highly valuable.

believe that the scholars thus trained, going out as they do, whether as volunteers or as professional workers, will be of immense value in these critical times of social change; their intimate knowledge of the poor, and the affection which grows up in the intercourse with them, joined to the careful study of past history, and of present law, will render them very valuable.[9]

One other great change in the life of the Settlement has occupied me. It became evident that better accommodation for the residents, as well as for the numerous out-workers, was urgently needed. Nelson Square is the only place in the district in which conditions of quiet and air seemed to make living in the district bearable for ladies. It was very difficult to obtain a freehold there, and as a good deal of alteration in the houses was necessary, it appeared essential to obtain a freehold. After much negotiation the freehold of the house the Settlement occupied and that of the two adjoining houses were obtained. Since then we have been busy with the necessary alterations, which have been both costly and troublesome. Our requirements were very humble and simple, but in old houses repairs are expensive, and I am sorry to say that, in spite of the liberality of many kind donors, we still want £600 at least to provide the bare cost of what is necessary. When all is done we shall have three houses united by openings on each floor, thus securing all the bedrooms under one roof, a good-sized dining room, drawing room and library for the residents, an office for out-workers, a private room for the Warden, and a bathroom. The little garden at the back, with a large plane tree, and the square in front, make the houses airy and quiet.[10] Seeing what an amount of good is done for all the neighbourhood by the Settlement, and that it is a place of training for women, I hope funds may be forthcoming to strengthen the hands of those who are at work, and set the minds of the Committee at rest.

I have had from a former pupil and fellow-worker, who is an artist,

---

9   The first person to hold a Pfeiffer scholarship was Miss Sharpley, who went on to become head worker of the Settlement.

---

10   Numbers 44, 45 and 46 Nelson Square, Southwark are still standing, as is the plane tree in the garden. In 1961 the Women's University Settlement changed its name to the Blackfriars Settlement, partly in order to reflect the involvement of men (there had been a male warden since 1959) and partly to involve the local community more with the work. In 1999 the Blackfriars Settlement sold the Nelson Square property and moved out in 2001. It continues to provide services from a number of sites in the Waterloo area.

the offer of a cast of a series of bas-reliefs from subjects taken from Chaucer.[11] The words are:

> For thilke ground that bears the weedes wick,
> Bears eke the wholesome herbe and full oft,
> Next to the foule nettle, rough and thick,
> The lily waxeth pure and white and soft.
> And next the valley is the hill aloft;
> And next the darke night is the glad morrow;
> And also joy is near the fine of sorrow.[12]

The words seem to me singularly appropriate to the hope which should inspire dwellers in a poor part of London, and I thought the ladies would appreciate the delicate beauty of the design. I have therefore offered the bas-reliefs to the Settlement, and am hoping to have them fixed in the drawing room. Mr Hoole, with that generous helpfulness to which for now some 20 years we have owed so much, is planning the setting of them.

I am sorry to say that the Kyrle Society is in sore need of funds. The

---

11 *See ill. 13.* The 'former pupil' was Ellen Mary Rope (1855–1934) who, at the age of 15 in 1870, had been sent to the girls' school run by Miranda and Octavia Hill in their home in Nottingham Place. In an interview published in 1900 Ellen Rope described how 'she received lessons in drawing from Miss Octavia Hill, who was the sister of the schoolmistress and—no small advantage—a pupil of Ruskin. Her attention was now directed towards the study of great works of art, and a collection of Old Masters at one of the RA winter exhibitions was a revelation to the young girl, who had never before had the opportunity of seeing pictures of this kind.' From 1877 until 1884 Rope studied at the Slade, as a pupil of Professor Alphonse Legros. During this period Mrs Mary Watts, Lady Mary Lovelace and Evelyn De Morgan were also at the Slade, which had established itself as one of the most progressive London art schools, initially under the direction of Sir Edward Poynter. In 1880 she became interested in sculpture and modeling in clay, the same direction taken by Mary Watts, and was clearly influenced by the Italian Renaissance. From 1889 Rope exhibited at the Arts and Crafts Exhibition Society. One of her most important commissions was for four six-feet spandrels in relief for the vestibule of the Women's Building at the World's Columbian Exposition, Chicago, in 1893. 'Faith', 'Hope', 'Charity' and 'Heavenly Wisdom' were to find a permanent home in the Ladies' Dwelling, Chenies Street. ('Hope' and the greater part of 'Charity' have survived.) From 1896 to 1906 Rope produced work for the Della Robbia Pottery, Birkenhead, a prominent HAIA class founded by Harold Rathbone. (Crawford, 2002, pp.288-92.)

---

12 From Geoffrey Chaucer's *Troilus and Criseyde*, book 1, lines 946-52. Modern scholarly editions of the text have 'rose' instead of 'lily'.

decorative and musical branches have steadily been pursuing their quiet and most useful course for years without puffing, and with the greatest devotion on the part of the artists, carrying beauty and noble thoughts into many an out-of-the-way place. I am sorry that the small regular support which would enable the Society to carry on this work should be wanting. Sometimes I see my way to hand over some of the kind help which reaches me to societies, if I know a time of difficulty has come; but as a rule, unless I know the sympathies of donors to lie that way, I take it that money sent to me, rather than to well-known societies issuing their own reports, is meant for such individual cases of sorrow and need as can only be reached through those who know the sufferers.

I hope my friends will think the Hall balance sheet encouraging. What with the income from the cottages, and what with the most satisfactory receipts from the people themselves, who have contributed £12 6s 8d in pennies for programmes, and £3 1s 1d freely given on Sundays, and with £21 for hire of Hall, all of which represents good work, it depends little on donations, and it is wonderful to think how much has been done there during the year.

I always seem to have to end my letter with some words about open spaces. Another has been secured at Deptford, about which we have helped. It is somewhat grandly called in the locality Deptford Park.[13] It

---

13 There is a certain irony in Octavia's news of the opening of Deptford Park in the same letter as her announcement of the formation of the National Trust, as the two things were intimately linked. In 1884 Mr W.J. Evelyn, a descendant of the famous seventeenth-century diarist, had approached Octavia offering part of his ancestor's celebrated garden at Sayes Court in Deptford as a public park. He wished to include in his gift a garden building to be used as a museum. Octavia consulted Robert Hunter, who warned her that there was no public body capable of receiving and managing such a gift. The fact that a building was included ruled it out for the local authority, as it was not purely an open space, and none of the campaigning bodies such as the Commons Preservation Society or the Kyrle Society were in a position to hold and administer property. Octavia wrote back to Hunter on 8 August saying that Evelyn had decided to hand over the property to trustees, with the power to pass it to a public body later. Hunter pondered on the problem, and in September 1884 he gave a paper to a social science conference in Birmingham calling for the establishment of a new type of body, capable of acquiring land and buildings and managing them in the public interest. To illustrate the need for such a body, he gave the example of 'a gentleman in the neighbourhood of London' who had 'offered to dedicate to the public a couple of acres of open land with a building capable of being used as a museum or lecture theatre'. Hunter's speech was printed and circulated, and on 10 February 1885 Octavia wrote to him to suggest that the new body should be set up as a trust rather than a company, and called the Commons and Gardens Trust. Across the top of her letter Hunter wrote, in pencil, '?National Trust'. (Waterson, 1994, pp.25-

consists of 17 acres of flat land, admirably adapted for playground, and forming a great contrast to Hilly Fields, which is valuable for its slope and its view. The new land is much nearer London and the centres of population, and many a game at cricket will be possible there when there is not time for the players to get as far as Hilly Fields; many a child will enjoy a swing, or a game at ball there, between morning and afternoon school.

The Kent and Surrey Committee have completed no definite bit of successful work this year, but I must say I am well satisfied with the progress they have made: for they have steadily worked on at the maps, and other things that opened out, have secured a good secretary to assist Mr Farrer, and have increased capacities for dealing with the many cases that come before them. It is, however, very uphill work, and one cannot help hoping they may be able to advise and reinforce the parish councils, finding in them the local knowledge and power of which the Committee's special knowledge is the complement.

I am, naturally, deeply interested in the foundation of the National Trust for the Preservation of Places of Historic Interest and Natural Beauty.[14] It gives for the first time a body able to hold such places for

---

32.) However, it took another decade for the new body to come into existence, and Mr Evelyn tired of waiting. In July 1886, 'the garden and playground at Sayes Court, Deptford, were formally opened... by the Baroness Burdett-Courts. Resolutions thanking Mr W.J. Evelyn... for giving the ground, and the Kyrle Society for laying it out, were passed on the motion of the Rt Hon. G.J. Shaw-Lefevre, MP, and the Rev. Brooke Lambert, vicar of Greenwich, respectively.' (*Charity Organisation Review*, August 1886, p.312.) With the creation of the London County Council in 1888, the political climate became more receptive to the idea of using public funds to acquire open spaces, and Mr Evelyn sold a further seventeen acres of land to the local authority for £36,000, which, according to the borough surveyor, was below its market value as building land. The LCC, which normally limited its contribution to half of the value of open spaces, made an exception and contributed two-thirds in this case, as the local authority had been called upon to provide about £10,000 for Hilly Fields and Telegraph Hill within only a few years. Mr Evelyn donated two further strips of land to widen the access to the park from its main entrance on the Deptford Lower Road, now Evelyn Street. The Park was declared open, and dedicated to the public forever, on 7 June 1897 by Dr W.J. Collins, the chairman of the LCC. Dr Collins was welcomed by Sidney Webb, who represented Deptford on the LCC, and who rather tactlessly congratulated the local people on acquiring their third open space within a few years 'practically without cost to the people of Deptford', by passing the cost on to other ratepayers in London. 'Deptford was reaping the benefit of its partnership with the greatest city in the world.' (*Kent Mercury*, 11 June 1897.)

---

14 Although 1895 is generally given as the date of the National Trust's foundation, the first meeting took place at Grosvenor House, the London home of the Duke of

the nation, and, I hope, likely to treat them with taste and thought. It is delightful to think that one beautiful sea-cliff has already been given to them—a bit of British coast held in trust for the nation.[15] Will there be more such gifts to record this time next year? Let us hope so; and let us resolve that we for our own part will not be wanting. It may not be given to us to make our offering by contributing to the purchase of land or building, but in some form, tangible or invisible, let us resolve that some sacrifice shall be made, some lasting gift devoted, by us, for our own dear England.

OCTAVIA HILL

Westminster, on 16 July 1894. The Duke was a long-standing supporter of Octavia's projects, including open spaces, and had been chairman of the Hampstead Heath Extension Committee, formed by Octavia, Shaw-Lefevre and Baroness Burdett-Coutts in 1884 (1884/5, pp.189–90). Although Parliament Hill Fields had been purchased, largely with funds raised from public bodies, and vested in the London County Council, it was becoming increasingly obvious that there were many open spaces threatened by development, in the private as well as the public sector, that could not be preserved in this way. There had been proposals as early as 1884 for a land-holding company that could receive and manage property in the public interest, but nothing came of the idea for several years, partly owing to the opposition of Shaw-Lefevre, founder of the Commons Preservation Society, who feared (correctly, as it turned out) that the new organisation would attract support to the detriment of the CPS. By the early 1890s several private properties, especially in the Lake District, were under threat as there was no hope of their purchase by the local authorities. This was the impetus for the formation of the National Trust. In 1893 Hardwick Rawnsley travelled to London to impress upon Octavia the urgent need for the sort of land-holding association they had been talking about for nearly a decade, if sites such as the Lodore Falls were to be saved. 'Not ten minutes elapsed before she said: "If Sir Robert Hunter will help us and the Duke of Westminster will allow us to meet in Grosvenor House, the scheme will go forward."' (Rawnsley, 1914, p.237.) The scheme did go forward; the Duke chaired the meeting at Grosvenor House and became the first president of the National Trust, a position he retained until his death in 1899. Octavia foresaw that the Duke's position as a major landowner would inspire confidence in those who might endow the fledgling Trust with land and legacies. The memorandum and the articles of the Trust, dated 12 December 1894, were registered on 12 January 1895.

---

15 This was Dinas Oleu, the 'Fortress of Light'. The gift of Dinas Oleu was accepted at the first meeting of the executive committee of the National Trust in February 1895. The four-and-a-half acres of land in the parish of Llanaber were given to the National Trust on 29 March 1895 by Mrs Fanny Talbot, a wealthy philanthropist and friend of Ruskin, Octavia and Hardwicke Rawnsley. Dinas Oleu forms a natural balcony

over Barmouth harbour. Mrs Talbot had a hatred of 'the abomination of asphalt paths and cast iron seats of serpent design' and donated the first National Trust property believing such tasteless additions would be avoided. Hardwicke Rawnsley's 1891 'Mawddach Poem' was engraved in the rock below Dinas Oleu:

> Who planned upon this mountain rock to build
> High o'er the shifting sands of Mawddach's flood,
> They knew the soul of man had need of food
> From Heaven and that the world's Creator willed
> That from far hidden deeps should hearts be thrilled
> With touch of ocean's wild infinitude.
> They drank the dews of morning as they stood,
> And with the sunset's latest awe were filled.

See 1911, pp.659-60 for Octavia's account of her visit to Dinas Oleu, which by this time had a seat, albeit cut into the rock.

DONATION ACCOUNT, 1894

RECEIPTS

	£	s	d
In hand January:			
Special Fund 60 0 0			
Appropriated 65 0 0			
Available 44 3 4			
	169	3	4
Allen, A.C., Esq	2	2	0
Booth, Charles, Esq	5	0	0
Bridgeman, Charles, Esq (Cadet Corps)	5	0	0
Bridgeman, Mrs	2	0	0
Barnes, Miss A.	0	10	0
Bartlett, Miss	2	0	0
Cleveland, Duchess of (General Fund)	25	0	0
Cleveland, Duchess of (Cadet Corps)	25	0	0
Chase, Miss (for Deptford Park)	7	0	0
Dundas, Lady Jane	20	0	0
Ducie, Countess of	25	0	0
Erle, Miss E.M.	5	0	0
Ewart, Miss	25	0	0
Forman, Miss	1	1	0
Frankau, Miss	3	0	0
Gillson, Mrs		10	0
Hill, Alfred, Esq	5	0	0
Harris, Miss (for panels, Red Cross Hall)	2	2	0
Harris, Miss E.M.	1	1	0
Howitt, Miss	0	10	4
Johnston, Miss (for vans to Hampstead)	3	0	0
Langenbach, Mrs	2	0	0
Morris, F., Esq	1	1	0
Macaulay, Mrs	4	5	0
Macaulay, Mrs (for Cadet Corps)	0	5	0
Powell, Dr and Mrs Douglas	2	0	0
Pollock, Sir Frederick (fares to Haslemere)	5	2	1
Stephen, Mrs Leslie	10	10	0
Stone, Rev. E.	2	0	0
Somervell, Gordon, Esq (Kent & Surrey Committee)	3	3	0
Stephens, Miss L.	0	5	0
Todhunter, Mrs	1	0	0
Tufnell, Mrs	2	2	0
Thompson, Mrs	2	0	0
Temple, Mrs	2	2	0
Vaughan, Miss F.O.	5	0	0
Webb, Mrs Randall	2	0	0
Winkworth, Mrs	20	0	0
Whelpdale, Mrs	1	0	0
Wells, Miss Mary	2	0	0
Interest on Investment	5	16	3
Returned on sum advanced for preservation of cottages	49	16	0
	£457	7	0

364

DONATION ACCOUNT, 1894

EXPENDITURE

	£	s	d
Training and Boarding out in Homes	81	11	11 ½
Pensions and other Relief to Aged	52	3	9
Cadet Corps	31	5	0
Country Excursions and Entertainments 14 9 4			
Fares, Haslemere 5 1 2			
Vans, Hampstead 3 0 0			
	22	10	6
Emigration	22	10	0
Aid in Sickness and Convalescence	17	1	3
Deptford Park	15	2	0
Playground, care of	10	8	0
Blind, pensions to	10	4	0
Industrial School (donation to Church Farm)	10	0	0
Printing Letter to Fellow-Workers, Stationery, &c.	7	4	6
Employment	6	1	5
Kent and Surrey Committee of Commons Preservation Society	6	1	0
Cripples, Moore Street Home for	5	0	0
May Festival, Freshwater Place	5	0	0
Apprenticing lad	5	0	0
Contesting license of public-house	2	10	0
Panels, Red Cross Hall	2	2	0
Trees, plants, &c.	1	5	0
Cash in hand: Special Fund	50	0	0
Cash in hand: Appropriated (pensions and schools)	96	6	7 ½

| | £457 | 7 | 0* |

* *Editor's note:* The total should be £459 7*s.* Error in original.

Audited and found correct, H.M. Broughton

RED CROSS HALL AND GARDEN ACCOUNT, 1894

RECEIPTS

	£	s	d
Balance at Bank, January 1894	31	11	5
Cash in hand	3	1	2
Interest, Red and White Cross Cottages	50	14	6
Rents, Balance of Club and 10 White Cross Street	12	4	7
Hire of Hall	21	1	9
Programmes, sale of	12	6	8
Donations:			
Anon. for Singing Class	5	5	0
Miss M.M. Eve	5	0	0
Women's University Settlement	2	2	0
Mrs Phillips	2	0	0
Mr Cobbett, for May Pole	1	10	0
Mrs Orr	1	6	0
Mrs Temple	1	1	0
Colonel Westmorland	0	10	0
Miss Leith	0	6	0
Miss Heppel	0	3	0
Gymnasium Pupils' Fees	5	2	10
Collected at Entertainments	3	1	1
Library	0	7	6
Singing Class	0	4	6

	£158	19	0

RED CROSS HALL AND GARDEN ACCOUNT, 1894

EXPENDITURE

	£	s	d
Caretaker	59	0	0
Garden:			
Balcony, Pond, Tiles … 15 15 3			
Plants, &c. … 1 6 11			
Paint … 1 6 0			
Pigeons' Food … 1 4 1			
Tools and Stakes … 1 0 7	20	12	10
Cupboard, Fanlight, Gymnastic Appliances, &c.	15	19	0
Printing, Stationery, Advertisements	8	10	6
Entertainment Expenses	7	15	4
Gas	7	12	2
Cleaning	6	1	6
Secretary's Expenses	6	16	0
May Pole	5	12	6
Water Rate	4	15	0
Sundries	4	7	1
Repairs	2	11	6
Fuel	2	4	7
Insurance: three Panels	1	1	6
Insurance: Lamp	0	4	6
Bank charges	0	10	6
Balcony License	0	5	0
Cash at Bank	4	3	2
Cash in hand	0	16	4
	£158	19	0

Audited and found correct, P.L. Blyth, January 3rd 1895.

LETTER TO MY FELLOW-WORKERS

TO WHICH ARE ADDED

ACCOUNTS OF DONATIONS RECEIVED

FOR

WORK AMONG THE POOR

DURING 1895

BY

OCTAVIA HILL

(FOR PRIVATE CIRCULATION ONLY)

LONDON:
PRINTED BY WATERLOW AND SONS LIMITED,
LONDON WALL, E.C.

SUMMARY

Housing work: St Christopher's Place; Westminster; St Botolph's cottages in Charles Street (Ranston Street), Lisson Grove; Southwark... tenants pay their own rates... outings for the tenants... the programme at Red Cross Hall: departure of Miss Plunkett... the donation fund... Women's University Settlement... open spaces: Kent and Surrey Committee of the Commons Preservation Society; National Trust... Sarsden Buildings in St Christopher's Place (Barrett's Court) passes into Octavia's possession on the death of Lady Ducie.

EDITOR'S NOTE

In an effort to raise awareness of 'the gigantic accumulation of municipal indebtedness' Octavia has arranged for tenants in the new cottages to pay their own rates, although she has not been able to extend the system to tenants in blocks. The intention was to bring home to people the consequences of voting for candidates who promised benefits based on high levels of public expenditure. The brief mention of the National Trust pinpoints one of the reasons for its success: 'Whatever is given to it is a gain. It has not the fighting.' The Trust was not a controversial campaigning body. In its early years its main role was to accept gifts of land from other organisations that had done the 'fighting', rather than running campaigns of its own.

190 Marylebone Road, N.W.

My dear friends,

I am about to prepare the annual balance sheet, giving the account of donations committed to my care during the past year.[1] And I set myself once more to render what further account of my stewardship I can: to weigh, so far as may be, those other intangible gifts which have reached me, gifts of time, and strength and health; suggestive thoughts from books, or living men; memories and experiences gathered in past years; and helpful offerings of time and power from many faithful and devoted fellow-workers. How have all these been accepted and used? How has the song of praise for them risen in my heart day by day? What are the definite gains they have procured? Who is better for them? Who is happier for them? What places are fairer and brighter for them? What failures have been given us to humble us, and to purify us, and show us that we must plant and sow and water, but that it is God Who gives the increase, and to carry our thoughts forward in hope to the fruits which so often spring from those efforts which have seemed to fail most? Very solemn questions for us all, questions which, with the closing and opening year, all human souls are apt to ask themselves with special solemnity and heart searching, whether they fill a large or a small sphere. Like Pippa, we have been given a day.[2] What have we done with it? Like Rabbi Ben Ezra, we are bound to 'take it and prove its worth' now it is ended. And let us see to it that we weigh:

> ...All the world's rude thumb
> And finger failed to plumb,

---

1   Although it is not possible to date this letter, Patrick Blyth signed off the donation fund accounts on 8 January 1896, so it was probably mailed out in late January.

---

2   Robert Browning's 'Pippa Passes' is a long dramatic poem published in 1841. The heroine is a young Italian girl who works in a silk factory in Asolo in northern Italy, which Browning knew, although it is said he drew the character of Pippa from a girl he saw in the Dulwich Woods. It is she who utters the famous line: 'God's in his heaven, all's right with the world.'

So passed in making up the main account;

. . . .

Thoughts hardly to be packed
Into a narrow act;
Fancies that broke thro' language and escaped.[3]

And yet when we have done all that, we come back to ask what definitely we have achieved; what has been given to us; how stands our account of gain or loss in all we have hoped and striven for in 1895.

So far as I can measure, then, with regard to my public work, it stands thus:

All the houses in our care have done well under their various managers, St Christopher's Place very naturally leading the way. It combines a very high standard of business management, cleanliness and order, with much social intercourse, great development of the tenants' own powers and energies, and much affection and friendship gained by the long years of work there. All the courts and blocks have their special advantages and characteristics, many, perhaps most, of them have greater physical advantages, which makes it more impressive to me that nearly all the suggestions of new and helpful measures are apt to come from St Christopher's Place.

I have to record the completion of 19 fresh cottages, built by the Ecclesiastical Commissioners, in Garden Street, Westminster. They form the opposite side of the street so built in 1894.[4] They have been placed under our care, are all well let, and are most satisfactory.

One of my fellow workers has erected seven new cottages in the street, near Lisson Grove, where, in 1894, six were built. These are called St Botolph's cottages.[5] Three other schemes for building in the same street are progressing, two of them being nearly settled.

One other house which had been a great annoyance to the

---

3   Part of stanzas xxiv and xxv of Robert Browning's 'Rabbi Ben Ezra', from *Dramatis Personae*, 1864. The first stanza actually begins: 'But all, the world's rude thumb...' Browning had been a friend of Octavia's grandfather Thomas Southwood Smith, and had consequently known Octavia as a girl. He was one of her favorite poets, and she was in the habit of reading from 'Rabbi Ben Ezra' to her guests. (Darley, 1990, p.323.)

---

4   *See ill. 19.* In an undated (c.1917) list of workmen's tenements, the following were recorded as having been built in 1895: 13 six-room cottages, two five-room cottages, 20 two-room cottages and the 19 four-room cottages mentioned by Octavia. In total this development came to 54 separate holdings consisting of 204 rooms.

---

5   Still standing as 5-11 Ranston Street.

neighbourhood, owing to its bad management, has been handed over to our care, and is at present thoroughly orderly, quiet and clean. It belongs to a small tradesman in a neighbouring street. The experiment is the first we have made of representing an owner who had had every facility for detailed management, and had not secured order. It remains to be seen whether we can continue to satisfy him. So far we have done so. It is a question of finance. We should not have undertaken this house but for the sake of those in the neighbourhood.

I have also undertaken one house very trying to deal with, as standing by itself in a very difficult street, but this is the property of one of the best workers in the parish, and I am sure of his hearty co-operation, besides setting him free for more important work.

One of the courts we have long managed in Southwark has to be demolished.[6] The Ecclesiastical Commissioners have met us most kindly in retaining it as long as possible; but it occupied ground which interfered with building on the frontage to a new street, and we have always foreseen that is must be destroyed when that land was let. The external walls proved this autumn to require such very extensive repair that it would have been quite unreasonable to ask for it to be undertaken. To our great regret we are, therefore, scattering our old friends, and must see many of the smaller cottages in Southwark thus disappear. The change is inevitable, but sad. The court had one, to me, unique feature—that of a tiny bed of flowers and creepers in the open court, kept by the tenants, and in perfect order.

The Commissioners are hoping to erect some new buildings for working people in the neighbourhood, and to place them under our charge.

I receive very encouraging accounts of the progress of similar work in Amsterdam, under the lady who came to be trained with us. Another lady of very great power and promise has been with us for the last four months, and is returning to Amsterdam to carry on similar work under a committee. I feel sure of her success. I have no late news from friends at Dundee, but have been asked recently to talk over some schemes for Edinburgh.

---

6   It is not clear which property this refers to, but there is discussion in the archives around mid-1892 concerning six small cottages in Union Court, Gravel Lane that are to be pulled down following the sale of land to the South Eastern Railway Company. However, later correspondence, closer to the time of this letter, also discusses the possibility of selling houses to the north of Union Street and west of Gravel Lane to the LCC for model dwellings, although the final existing letter discussing this sale states that the EC had dismissed the LCC's offer as inadequate. (Note of EC, May 1894.)

The Mansion House Council on the Dwellings of the Poor asked leave to photograph some of our cottages, and published a short account of them in their annual report. They thought the experiment of building a limited number of cottages in towns a valuable one.[7]

The tenants in all our new cottages pay their own rates. The plan is one of which I continue to feel the great advantage. It gives them and us trouble, but some of our difficulties are over, and I think the plan well worth the effort. I have made no attempt to apply it to the blocks, partly for want of time to arrange for joint action with other bodies. Joint action would be essential where we had not a unique article like the cottages to offer. Partly I have delayed taking action because I am not sure that some movement may not be set on foot for the local authorities themselves to arrange for direct payment, with discount for payment in advance. This would be manifestly far better than our doing it, but, if it is not organised by others, we must try this experiment also. The rise of rates, and, what is to my mind far worse, the gigantic accumulation of municipal indebtedness, have become so serious, direct payment would so obviously counteract the tendency simply and naturally, that one thinks it must be arranged for soon. It was interesting to me to notice that I had a larger number of responsive letters with regard to this subject than I had ever had before to any paragraph I had written, they came from all over England, and many were very thoughtful and wisely far-seeing.

We have had the same kind hospitality offered to our poorer friends during the summer as in past years. Mr and Mrs Arthur Hill invited a large group of tenants this year, not to Erleigh, but to Shere, to the house of the rector, their son, where the beautiful rural village and welcoming kindness gave a most perfectly enjoyable day.[8] Sir Frederick

---

7   *The Dwellings of the Poor: Report of the Mansion House Council for the year ending December 31st, 1894*, London: Cassell. This edition of the council's annual report included a two-page section headed 'Cottage homes in London under the management of Miss Octavia Hill'. It contained brief descriptions of Gable Cottages, Southwark, Almond cottages in Charles Street (now Ranston Street), Marylebone, Red Cross and White Cross cottages, Southwark, and cottages in Garden Street and Dorset Street (both now demolished) Westminster. The report was illustrated with photographs (*see ills. 2, 14, 17, 19*). The closest the report comes to endorsing Octavia's pro-cottage views is the sentence: 'The tenants greatly prefer these cottages to the sets of rooms in the blocks adjoining', which was probably written by Octavia.

---

8   Rev. Frederick Hill was rector of Shere from 1893 to 1919. He would assist at his aunt Octavia's funeral in 1912. His hospitality is mentioned again in the letters for 1897, 1899 and 1900. The September 1895 edition of the *Shere Parish Magazine*

and Lady Pollock again invited us to Hindhead; the driving in the lovely country, the dinner in the tent, and, above all, the sympathy and kindness, gave great joy. Mr and Mrs Edmund Maurice and Miss Johnston again welcomed us to their homes, and sent many back with a memory of peace and kindness. Several of my fellow-workers organised a day in the country for their own tenants. Dr and Mrs Longstaff entertained repeated parties during the summer. They also offered during the whole summer the cottage in their garden, to be occupied for a fortnight at a time by two guests. We had the extreme pleasure of thus inviting many an old couple, many hard-worked sisters, many delicate people to have a summer fortnight of quiet country life.

Red Cross Hall has this year sustained the very greatest loss in the departure for a long voyage of our able and valued honorary secretary, Miss Plunkett. She had for some five years borne the real weight of all the work there; indeed, it had grown from small beginnings to be what it is under her fostering care. The business was done so excellently that I never had an anxiety about it. She had made her place. The people's hearts had grown round her. I do not think her place can ever be filled. It remains for us to see whether we can carry on the same work or not. So far we have managed the autumn session with great success, but it will not be possible to me in the further future to devote so much strength to this one work, what can be done there in the future will depend on what capable help gradually comes round me. It is the central place which is so difficult to fill, and into which no one can step, they must grow into it. Of the loyal, the hearty, the kind co-operation of the many friends who have helped there I cannot speak too gratefully. We have had again a successful May Festival, a flower show, a regular course of winter entertainments and Sunday gatherings with much beautiful music.

I have also to thank many friends for presents of bulbs, plants and flowers. May I here add grateful thanks to a former pupil, now a missionary in India, who has yearly sent to us and to the Kyrle Society beautiful Indian draperies.

I do not this year attach the Red Cross account to this letter; it is printed with a separate report.

---

contained an account of the outing: '…on the first of August… we were enabled to entertain the large party of London poor brought down by Miss Octavia Hill, under the best possible conditions. The Londoners enjoyed "a real good day in the country", and went away thoroughly impressed with the wonderful beauty of Shere and its surroundings.'

The donation balance is attached to this letter, as heretofore. It records as of old, in its own dry way, much living help. There will be absent from it in the years to come the name of one whose faithful help is stayed by death. Mrs Leslie Stephen has passed from among us, and leaves blanks not to be filled here below. That she has left behind her living help—one of my noblest young workers, and the owner of a small group of cottages—is a point I note and think of often.[9]

I should like here to acknowledge gratefully £100 from the Parochial Charities Fund, sent to the Kyrle Society in consequence of an application from me. It has been the very greatest help to the Society, especially to the musical and decorative branches.

I have mentioned in previous years the gifts of houses, which have been placed under the care of myself and two trustees,[10] who have the glad privilege of giving away in whatever way seems to us helpful the money which would else go to pay interest to the owners.

I subjoin a list which, I think, will be pleasant reading for you all of the gifts made from these funds during the past years:

		£	s	d
December 1886	Church Farm Industrial School	21	16	8
March 1887	Special cases of poverty in Southwark	23	9	4
October 1888	St Andrew's Home for Boys	22	11	2
October 1889	Girls' Home, Charlotte Street, W.	10	0	0
October 1889	Mrs Watts Hughes' Boys' Home	5	0	0
October 1889	Tower Hamlets Pension Fund	5	0	0
October 1889	Charity Organisation Society	2	0	0

9 Before becoming the second Mrs Leslie Stephen, Julia Stephen (1858–1895) had been Mrs Julia Duckworth, and before that Julia Jackson. She was a member of the famous Pattle clan, as her mother, Maria Jackson, was the sister of Julia Margaret Cameron, the photographer, Lady Virginia Somers and Mrs Thoby Prinsep, with whom the painter G.F. Watts had lived for 30 years. Julia was a renowned beauty, and often sat for the artists of the Little Holland House circle. She may have been the model for the Virgin in Burne-Jones's Annunciation (1876–79, Lady Lever Art Gallery). Penelope Fitzgerald, Burne-Jones's biographer, suggests that she may have been pregnant with Vanessa Bell at the time. Julia's daughter by her first marriage, Stella Duckworth, became one of Octavia's fellow-workers, but died herself only two years after her mother, just after having six cottages built in Charles Street (now Ranston Street), Lisson Grove (1897, p.401).

10 Octavia, Lord Wolmer and Janet Johnson were the trustees of the Horace Street Trust, which at this time still consisted of the three houses in Horace Street given by Anna Scrase-Dickins and Westbourne Buildings in Paddington given by Emilia Gurney.

October 1890	Oxford Home for Friendless Girls	16	12	7
October 1891	Kyrle Society open spaces	8	13	9
December 1892	Church Farm Industrial School	5	11	1
December 1892	Tower Hamlets Pension Fund	5	11	1
October 1893	Nursing Fund, Westminster	10	8	6
October 1894	Rural Nurses, Hampshire	9	14	7
October 1894	Parochial Mission Fund	20	0	0
October 1894	Boarding Out and Training	20	0	0
October 1894	Women's University Settlement	10	0	0
October 1894	Kent and Surrey Commons Preservation Society	10	0	0
April 1895	Training of Rural Nurses	9	0	0
April 1895	Kent and Surrey Commons Preservation Society	10	0	0
April 1895	Cadet corps, Southwark	5	0	0
April 1895	Hampshire Rural Nurses	5	0	0
April 1895	Red Cross Hall	9	0	0
October 1895	Pensions, &c.	3	19	0
October 1895	Training Rural Nurses	19	0	0
October 1895	National Society of Epileptics	10	0	0
October 1895	Special Cases COS	2	19	0
October 1895	Church Farm Boys' Home	5	0	0
October 1895	Red Cross Hall	2	7	10
October 1895	Charity Organisation Society	5	0	0
October 1895	Kent and Surrey Commons Preservation Society	2	0	0
October 1895	Training and Boarding Out	6	10	0
		301	4	7

The settlement workers are satisfactorily established in the new houses, their garden laid out by the kindness of a friend; the whole of their great work going forward. The value of the training seems to be widely recognised, almost more than I could have believed; the numbers wishing to come, either as paying students or as free Pfeiffer scholars, exceeding those who come trained and ready for settled work. This may be helpful in the years to come and in distant places, but it makes the present work heavy for the leaders, and I often wish more trained volunteers, capable of being leaders, were to be had there. However, it will perhaps right itself in time. Meantime the training is most useful, and the other work does get done, and well done; only it tells heavily on those who do it. The deficit for the alterations to the houses is still £192. It is most important this should be cleared off.

The freehold of the house adjoining the Settlement was for sale this year. The Committee did not all wish to enlarge the Settlement, nor could they rightly have incurred any further expenditure even with the hope of recouping. Yet it was of the utmost moment to them to secure unobjectionable neighbours, especially as the back garden or yard might have been built over; this would have shut out the sunlight from the Settlement. Moreover, this same yard contained two large plane trees, visible from all the Settlement windows. It was, therefore, a great relief when Miss Harriot Yorke volunteered to buy the house. This has been done, and it is now put in order and let to those who are a great help to the local work.

The Kent and Surrey Committee of the Commons Preservation Society has several very important cases in hand; a very warm response reached us to an appeal for money help for them. I can honestly say that a great deal of good work has been done—work that I am sure must be done before good can result. I do not think we, who are the leaders, could have done more. I have myself withdrawn all my strength from London open space work, which is progressing, to devote it to the country, which is losing day by day; many are doing the same, though it is most disappointing to meet with so little immediate result. Still, I look to the time when these efforts will tell—they do tell already by encouraging many people—may tell indirectly in discouraging some enclosures. We are gaining friends, perfecting our machinery, the response to our appeal for money greatly cheered us, but for tangible result, for visible victory, we must wait.

The National Trust bids fair to have a brighter record. Whatever is given to it is a gain. It has not the fighting, and will appeal to the generous hearts of many.

One change the past year has brought, which touches too nearly my own life for it to be possible to do more than refer to its outward result. Sarsden Buildings, that part of St Christopher's Place which was first rebuilt—rebuilt when it was still 'Barrett's Court'—that part which contains the old clubroom where the Princess Alice went with me,[11]

---

11 This is the only reference in the letters to the visits that Octavia received in November 1876 from Princess Alice of Hesse-Darmstadt (1843–1878), Queen Victoria's second daughter, who was keenly interested in Octavia's work, and wished to replicate it in Darmstadt. Octavia took her on a tour of properties in Marylebone and Whitechapel, and to the Monday night gathering in the club in Barrett's Court.

the clubroom which contains Mr Cockerell's memorial and his last letter to the men of his club, has become my own. It has become so in fulfilment of the wish of the late Lady Ducie, one of my oldest friends, and one of those who helped when my work was small and out of sight. She laid out Red Cross garden, and we have just a small stone in the wall there saying that she did.[12]

Not long before she left us, she arranged to throw into one the two back courtyards at Sarsden Buildings; they were of different levels, and we arranged to leave a slope, thinking the children would like it. When this was done a little girl ran to her home, exclaiming with joy, 'Mother, there is a hill in my playground.' For the small child whom from far off she helped, and for the friends whose privilege it was to walk beside her through life, and to share something of her thoughts, blessing followed her wherever she went, and, as the vision of her rises before me, the words that come oftenest to my mind are: 'When the eye saw her then it blessed her'.[13]

OCTAVIA HILL

This was a concert at which Octavia warned the Princess: 'They have a standard, they do care to keep to it, it is improving but I could not promise that you would not hear strange, rather low-toned songs, remarks on the rich and great, discontent with things as they are.' The Princess, however, was game for all this and came incognito, '*quite alone, in a big hat and old black gown, ran about like a young girl, and would not have the least notice taken of her*', according to Emily Shaen. Octavia remained in touch with the Princess until the latter's death from diphtheria in December 1878, at the age of 36. The story of the royal supporter is told in chapter ten of Gillian Darley's *Octavia Hill: A Life* (1990).

---

12 Julia Reynolds-Moreton, Lady Ducie, died on 3 February 1895 aged 68. On 9 February Octavia wrote to Sydney Cockerell: 'I can hardly yet realise what the void in my life will be from the loss of the friend of some 30 years, and of such a friend. She was quite unique, the majesty of intellect being only equalled by the depths of her affection, and the greatness of her spirit.' (Maurice, 1914, p.533.) Lady Ducie had been one of Octavia's most enthusiastic supporters since the earliest days. Born Julia Langston, the daughter of a MP, she had married her cousin, Henry Reynolds-Moreton, the MP for Stroud, in 1849. Sarsden Buildings was named after Lady Ducie's birthplace in Oxfordshire. The stone inscription is still in the garden, set below the mosaic of the Sower (*ill. 5*).

---

13 'When the ear heard me, then it blessed me;
    And when the eye saw me, then it gave witness to me.'
                              Job 29:11.

DONATION ACCOUNT, 1895

RECEIPTS

	£	s	d
In hand January:			
Special Fund	50	0	0
Appropriated	96	6	7½
	146	6	7½
Per Miss Yorke	20	0	0
Austin, Miss	1	0	0
Allen, A.C., Esq	2	2	0
Alford, Rev. B.H.	5	0	0
Brooks, Miss	1	0	0
Baumgartner, Miss (for Women's University Settlement)	25	0	0
Booth, Charles, Esq	5	0	0
Bridgeman, Charles, Esq	5	0	0
Bridgeman, Mrs	2	2	0
Blyth, Patrick, Esq	1	1	0
Barnes, Miss A.M.	0	10	0
Cleveland, Duchess of	50	0	0
Cockerell, Sydney C., Esq	2	0	0
Dundas, Lady Jane	20	0	0
Davenport-Hill, The Misses (Excursion)	7	0	0
Erle, Miss E. (Women's University Settlement)	10	0	0
Erle, Miss E. (Relief)	10	0	0
Forman, Miss	1	1	0
Frankau, Miss	4	4	0
Gossett, Miss	1	1	0
Gillson, Mrs	5	0	0
Gardiner, General	1	1	0
Hatfeild, Miss (for improvement of houses)	5	0	0
Harris, Miss E.	1	0	0
Harrison, J. Mason, Esq	1	1	0
Hill, Alfred, Esq	10	0	0
Howitt, Miss	0	10	2
Johnston, Miss	20	0	0
Johnston, Miss for 1896	20	0	0
Lee-Warner, Miss	0	10	6
Litchfield, R.B., Esq	3	0	0
Langenbach, Mrs	2	2	6
Manning, Miss	2	0	0
Mallett, Rev. H.	2	10	0
Morris, Frank, Esq	1	1	0
Macaulay, Mrs	4	5	0
Macdonell, Mrs James	5	0	0
Oldfield, E., Esq	5	0	0
Plummer, Rev. Charles	5	0	0
Plummer, Rev. Charles (for 1896)	5	0	0
Phillips, Mrs	1	0	0
Pollock, Sir Frederick (for tenants' fares to Haslemere)	5	3	11
Stephen, Mrs Leslie (the late)	10	10	0
Schuster, Mrs	3	0	0
Singleton, Miss	2	10	0
Stone, Rev. Edward	2	2	0
Slack, Mrs	1	1	0
Stephen, Miss	0	5	0
Todhunter, Mrs	1	0	0
Todhunter, Mrs (for 1896)	1	0	0
Thomasson, J.P., Esq (for Women's University Settlement)	20	0	0
Tufnell, Mrs	1	1	0
Thompson, Mrs Charles	2	0	0
Wells, Miss Mary	2	0	0
Webb, Mrs	50	0	0
Yorke, Miss Harriot (special for invalid)	10	10	0
Interest	2	18	1
Anon. (for invalid)	0	7	6
	£534	17	3½

380

DONATION ACCOUNT, 1895

EXPENDITURE

	£	s	d
Women's University Settlement*	161	13	6
Training and Boarding Out	97	4	2
Pensions and other relief	37	5	4
Excursions and Country Holidays	15	19	11
Red Cross Hall	14	1	0
Kent and Surrey Committee of Commons Preservation Society	13	10	6
Cadet Corps (Southwark)	11	1	0
Invalid (special case)	10	10	0
Playground, Freshwater Place (Caretaking)	10	8	0
Help in Sickness and Convalescence	7	15	1
May Festival, Freshwater Place	6	9	5
Blind (Pensions to)	5	2	6
Stationery, Postage, Carriage, &c.	5	2	11 ½
Houses (Improvement of), Special Donation	5	0	0
Printing Letter to Fellow-Workers	4	3	0
Education	3	12	0
Plants	0	19	0 ½
Cash in hand: Special Fund	20	0	0
Cash in hand: Available†	104	19	10 ½

* Much of this was sent for the permanent improvement of the settlement houses in response to my letter of 1894.

† The amount I have in hand seems to me so satisfactory that in spite of the amount I feel it necessary to keep in hand for those old pensioners and boarded-out children, for whom I am already responsible, I hope to be able in the opening year to take charge of one or two more.

Audited and found correct, P.L. Blyth, January 8th 1896.

£534	17	3 ½

LETTER TO MY FELLOW-WORKERS

TO WHICH ARE ADDED

ACCOUNTS OF DONATIONS RECEIVED

FOR

WORK AMONG THE POOR

DURING 1896

BY

OCTAVIA HILL

LONDON:
PRINTED BY WATERLOW AND SONS LIMITED,
LONDON WALL, E.C.

SUMMARY

Housing: its importance in underpinning all other work; new houses in Lisson Grove; Ecclesiastical Commissioners and other properties in Southwark; more volunteers needed for housing work; extract from the 1879 letter on housing work as a bond and a duty... the desirability of tenants paying their own rates... St Christopher's Hall and Red Cross Hall... outings for the tenants... donation fund... National Trust: Barras Head.

EDITOR'S NOTE

If the letters had titles, this would be the Housing Letter. In recent letters Octavia had tended to take the housing work somewhat for granted, with assurances that all was progressing satisfactorily, as she concentrated on newer enthusiasms such as open spaces, of which she had said in the 1891 letter that 'there is no part of my work which is more deeply engrossing me than this'. However, in this letter she traces all of the various branches of her activities back to their roots in the London houses and tenements with which she had by now been familiar for upwards of 30 years. Open spaces, cultural philanthropy, social activities, all owe their existence to her knowledge of what life was like in 'the narrow space in rooms and crowded alley' for working-class tenants. Octavia even reproduces a section of the letter of 1879—the only such self-quotation in the letters—in which she expatiates on the advantages of housing work over district visiting. In the concluding paragraph Octavia reports on the acquisition by the National Trust of Barras Head (now Barras Nose) in Cornwall, the first property acquired by a public subscription 'as the common playground, study, resting place, vantage ground for seeing the lovely things of nature'. Octavia hopes that it will not be the last of such places 'which shall thus become in a new and very real sense the common land of England'. It certainly wasn't.

190 Marylebone Road, N.W.

(January, 1897)[1]

My friends,

After wishing you all a very happy New Year, I will begin my letter to you, as usual, by an account of the houses under our care. They seem to be the most tangible trust committed to us, and the knowledge of people and needs acquired in them seems the foundation of the greater part of our work. It is from the narrow space in rooms and crowded alley that I first learned how the small garden near the narrow court or huge block was the necessary complement of the home—hence Mr Ruskin's first playground—and all that followed; it was in their colourlessness and unloveliness that I learnt how the colour and music brought by the Kyrle Society were needed; it was in seeing the want of larger out-door space for holidays for bigger children that I learnt to perceive the use of park and hilly ground, and to notice that where the population was poorest and thickest there was least of such breathing space; hence came my desire to join in efforts for Parliament Hill and all subsequent schemes; it was in watching the lives of the poor in long-ago days that I learnt the need of amusements for them, now so largely met on all sides, and the importance of companionship in these; it was watching in near relation to our people how much what they did themselves interested and developed them, that led to the training of the tenants' children to act little plays, and of the tenants themselves to sing, to act, to cultivate flowers. Even the country work, the preservation of meadow path or upland common, has grown out of the sense of what these are to us all after long work in court and alley and London street, how Kent and Surrey are the natural playground and resting place for those, rich or poor, whose home is in our smoky, noisy London. In fact, whatever we have found to do has been suggested by the need as we saw it affecting the homes, and members of the homes, with which charge of the houses brought us in contact. The houses, therefore, stand first in this my annual record.

---

1   Octavia begins by wishing the fellow-workers a happy New Year. Patrick Blyth signed off the donation fund accounts on 18 January 1897.

Of new houses I have to record the completion by my friends, Mrs Schuster and Mrs Rix, of five more cottages in the same street near here where we have built before.[2] It is now pretty well settled that the remainder of the street will be completed by our friends and fellow-workers, the deeds and plans are in course of preparation. This will give us 10 more cottages, making 28 in all in that street.

The Ecclesiastical Commissioners have just completed 45 more tenements in Southwark.[3] These are handed over to our management, and we are now proceeding with the letting.

They have also handed over to us for management six more old cottages, the leases of which have fallen in to them. On the other hand, I regret to say that when four old cottages under our charge required substantial repair, it was thought better to remove them and throw the space occupied by them into extra yard space for others that we have care of, which are at their rear. I am glad of the extra yard space, but old cottages are of immense value to the poor, and the longer they can be preserved the better. They are quite irreplaceable. No one now can, under present conditions and cost of building, give to the poor anything like the amount of home-peace, comfort, and accommodation at so small a cost. The old cottages look shabby, and those who do not know the life of the people, object to owning them, and they are looked upon without favour; but well managed, and essentials secured, they are an inestimable boon to those who live there, and every one that can be preserved with security for health should be jealously guarded. The separate yard for chair for invalid, swing for child, place for creepers, and bulbs, space for man to make little workshop, the separation from other families, the amount of accommodation in proportion to cost, often the playground for children of neighbours near their mother's door and safe from wheeled vehicles afforded by the paved court make them, supposing they be well drained, well roofed and dry, incomparably better for a family than anything, however spick and span, we can build now. And so you will find the respectable working man knows well. He

---

2   These cottages, now 27-31 Ranston Street, stand beside the first group of cottages built by Stella Duckworth (1893, pp.336-38). The Schusters paid for four and the Rixes for one. Following the deaths of Mr and Mrs Rix, the Schusters acquired their cottage (1906, pp.558-59) to prevent 'alien management' from coming to the street.

---

3   It is likely that this refers to tenements in Union Street. While no details of this can be found in the files, lists compiled at later dates note 44 tenements (seven double-fronted tenement blocks) built in 1896 in Union Street, Southwark.

will prefer them for his family, so long as they are left him, to anything we can now provide, unless he can afford a *new* cottage. So, at least, I have found. Though, doubtless, as manners and morals improve, and as we managers learn better how to secure perfect order in blocks, the difficulties of the aggregation of many families will diminish; meantime let us keep all small cottages we can which can be rendered healthy.

A friend has just taken a long lease of nine cottages in a court running at the back of the Women's University Settlement in Southwark. Two of these will be immediately rebuilt, and the rest will be rebuilt during the next ten years. There also will be placed under our management.

This completes the number of fresh houses under our own immediate care. The old ones are all going on remarkably well. I do not know that there are any fresh developments to record, but the steady work goes on. Our trained leaders are increasing in power and knowledge, and it is owing to this that we are able steadily to increase our area of work.

This increase of area makes me very anxious to secure, if possible, four more volunteers fitted for work in the houses; two of them might be placed in houses which are under constant care of experienced leaders, so that younger workers might begin thus. In two other blocks, though we would gladly teach those who had not done similar work before, we should want ladies who would be likely after a time to be able to take some responsibility, as the blocks stand alone, and would not be under the continuous and watchful eye of experienced workers.

It is so long since I made any statement of what such work should become, that I think it may be helpful to insert here an extract, addressed to my fellow-workers in houses, from my letter of 1879, which is out of print.

'I should like to note down what it appears to me you are all feeling as to the differences between the charge of a court where people are your tenants and much other visiting among the poor. I do not deny that all work should possess some of these characteristics; but I do not think that other kinds gain them so easily. The care of tenants calls out a sense of duty founded on relationship; the work is permanent; and the definite character of much of it makes its progress marked. Have you ever asked yourselves why you have chosen the charge of courts, with all its difficulties and ties, rather than other benevolent undertakings which are more easily taken up and thrown down? The burthen of the problems before you has been heavy, and the regularity of the occupation has often demanded of you great sacrifices. Why have you not chosen transitory connection with hundreds of receivers of soup, or pleasant intercourse with little Sunday Scholars, or visiting among the aged and bed-ridden, who were sure to greet you with a smile when you went to them, and had no right to say a word of reproach to you about your long absences in the country? Why did you not take up district visiting, where, if any family did not welcome you, you could just stay away? Because you preferred a work where duty was continuous and distinct, and where it was mutual. And then all the petty annoyances brought before you at such awkward moments, with so little discretion or good temper—all the smoky chimneys, broken water-pipes, tiresome neighbours, drunken husbands, death, disease, poverty, sin—call not only for your sympathy, but for your action. From the greatest to the least the problems have implied some duty on your part. "What ought I, in my relation to the tenants, to do for them in this difficulty?" you have each had to ask yourself. From the merest trifle of a cupboard key broken in a lock, to the future of some family desolated by death, or sunk into misery from drink, all has asked for your sympathy, much has demanded your action. Nor have you chosen for whom these duties shall be undertaken: the family are tenants, that fact implies your relation to them. Thus you have not felt the duty a self-chosen one; the tie has been closer, more like that in your own homes—deep, real, lasting, not always easy, often involving management of trifles, giving no sense of self-congratulating pride as in a work of supererogation. It has implied a share in the people's pain—as we bear one another's burthens at home; but bringing, I know you have all felt by this time, something of the same quiet sense of indestructible connection, a solemn blessing in fulfilment of simple duty. It has brought to you also, I feel sure, a real attachment to your people. You know they are yours; they know it; and as the years go on this sense of attachment will deepen and grow. Sometimes, when the difficulty of dealing with the manifold technical matters is very heavy upon you, you will all remember that these grow much lighter the more experience you gain—that the power among your little flocks increases tenfold after a time—above all, that the burthen of absolutely right action in this, as in all positions of life, is not with you, only the duty of trying to see and do right. If you keep this steadily before you, your Father will be continually bringing out of all your feeble efforts and clumsy mistakes all manner of great joy, and help, and wonderful results you never thought of; and a great sense of supporting help will be with you, a sort of cloud to shelter you by day, and fire to light you by night; you will feel that it is He who gave you the relation to your tenants, is helping you in it, as He helps us each in whatever duty He calls us to, never giving the command without the power.

'The charge of tenants has been valued by you too, because the duty is mutual; it implies your determination, not simply to do kindness with liberal hand, popular as that would be, but to meet the poor on grounds where they too have duties to you. The fulfilment of these takes away the glamour of almsgiving; it substitutes the power of meeting the people as they are, on simple human ground, as fellow-citizens, not mere receivers of your alms. You have all felt the effort of trying to keep them up to the mark; the effort, I know, will be less and less to you each as time goes on; the love that springs from the duty will be more and more. The day will come to each of you who are happy enough to go on working long, when the business will seem easy routine, and the tenants will be to you like a large family of friends or of children, with many memories in common; when even the places—those ugly London courts—will be to you so dear; for you will remember how and where you made them lighter, cleaner, better: the rooms, the yards, the streets will be associated with faces that brighten when they see you, and with victories over evil which you helped to achieve by your presence, or which you had the great privilege of seeing achieved—you hardly know which it was—you felt so one with the spirit that conquered the wrong.'

I have most cheering and delightful reports of the progress of the work in Amsterdam. It appears as if the two leaders there who came to us for training had taken up the work *con amore* and saw on all its sides what it should be—personal, sanitary, financial. We very heartily wish them God speed.[4]

Mr Loch[5] and I lately met some of the representatives of the societies

---

4   By the time she was writing this Octavia had another Dutch trainee: 'I am most anxious to do all I can to help Miss Maas in learning what she can of our work. She has made great sacrifices in coming to England to learn, and I fear it is not easy for her to do so.' (Letter from Octavia to a friend, 2 November 1896, Maurice, 1914, p.539.)

---

5   Charles Stewart Loch (1849–1923) was the secretary of the Charity Organisation Society (COS) from 1875–1914, and became so closely identified with it that, according

for improved building for working people, who have been the leaders of most of the wise public action with regard to such building, that we might see whether concerted action could be arranged so as to make weekly tenants, who are now the majority of voters in all municipal matters, feel, before it be too late, the weight of municipal indebtedness they are piling up against themselves and their successors for 60 years to come. There was no divergence of opinion as to the importance of the matter, none as to the right way of meeting it being to make the tenants pay the rates, or in some way to make the weekly sum, which includes rates, rise and fall in some proportion to the rise and fall of rates. But those who represented the larger bodies did not see their way to adopt the plan as pursued in Edinburgh, nor any other of a similar kind, unless either the law, or the authorities, supported them and made the plan general.

As to myself, I continue to arrange for the direct payment of rates by the tenants in the new cottages under my care. I am aware that it is a drawback in letting, especially as the rates never fall. But we let very well; I think even this small nucleus valuable, and the experiment may be useful. I am sure it makes more intelligent voters, and more careful ones. What would seem to me better, would be for landlord and tenants to pay each half rates, but that would be still more complicated, and the authorities do not help. Practically, too, the landlord does pay his share, as he is unable to let without lowering rent when rates go up.

I purpose, if all be well, trying in the current year a second experiment, which would turn the attention of weekly tenants, not occupying

---

to his *Times* obituary: 'He made the COS; he was the COS.' He studied at Balliol under Jowett and T.H. Green. He decided, after a struggle, not to enter the church, and became a clerk at the Royal College of Surgeons. In his spare time he became involved with the COS, appearing as a member of the Islington district committee in 1874. In 1875, at the age of 26, he was appointed to the paid position of secretary to the Society. He wanted the COS to bring together all people of good will to solve social problems, helping to realise 'the religion of charity without the sectarianism of religion'. He believed that the aim of charity should be to restore people to a condition of independence, wherever possible. He opposed socialism, because he believed that it ignored the ethical dimension of life and treated people like animals, consuming goods and services provided by the state. He believed that it was the responsibility of the state to provide sanitation and education, but not school dinners or old-age pensions. He was an admirer and close friend of Octavia's, and married Sophia Peters, her secretary. He became a trustee of both the Red Cross Hall and the Horace Street Trust in 1900, and entertained parties of Octavia's tenants at his home in Oxshott in 1904 and 1907. He wrote a glowing, two-part tribute to Octavia after her death in the *Charity Organisation Review*. (Rooff, 1972, pp.35-52.)

separate cottages, to the increase of taxation, and which would not be nearly so great a drawback in letting. I propose to diminish the rent in some selected blocks by the amount of the present rate, then to collect, each week, the amount of rent *plus a varying rate to be calculated half-yearly*. I shall compound, but the tenant will see how large, and how steadily rising, is the sum he pays for rates. But this is in the future.

At St Christopher's Hall and Red Cross Hall the work has proceeded on the same lines as in previous years. The opera, with choruses performed by tenants, the play acted by the tenants' children, the library, the planting of bulbs, the sociable evenings, and the drill, proceed at St Christopher's as of old. Red Cross Hall now issues its own Report; but I may mention here two important matters outside the usual yearly record. One is the gift by Miss Minet of a mosaic for the garden. The subject is 'The Sower'. The panel, a circular one, has been executed at Messrs Powell's by the same workmen who did the mosaic at St Paul's. It is not complete, and we are daily expecting that it will be fixed.[6] The second matter also concerns the garden. We have it in contemplation, if funds allow, this year to substitute an arcade of brick for the wooden structure which now forms our children's covered playground, and the raised balcony. We all regret the thought of losing our beautiful wooden one, but in any case it would require substantial repair this year, and as the London County Council only licenses wooden outside structures for two years as temporary erections, it seems, although they do renew the license, as if it might be well, if we could manage it, to get this most valuable adjunct of our garden into a firm and permanent form. Mr Hoole has drawn a very tempting sketch of what might be done, but it is a long stretch of space to cover, and the building must be strong, as we use the roof for our summer parties. It will cost £200, of which the trustees have £50 available. We thought of making an appeal in Southwark, as well as to our kind friends elsewhere. It is not a necessity; we can repair the wooden structure, and get it relicensed. But it would be pleasant to get the playground more permanent. Anyone who saw in rainy weather the children from the courts round playing at battledore and shuttlecock, with the fresh air blowing in, anyone

---

6   *See ill. 5.* This mosaic roundel, by James Powell after a sketch by Lady Waterford, has been re-sited, and is the only one of the garden features and ornaments described by Octavia to survive. Miss Minet also donated a sundial inscribed with the legend: 'As hour follows hour, God's mercies on us shower'. She must have been a woman of some means as she gave £50 to the donation fund in 1909, which was divided between the National Trust, the Commons Preservation Society, the Kyrle Society and Red Cross Hall (1909, pp.627 and 629).

who saw the balcony illuminated on a summer night for the garden party arranged by a neighbouring clergyman for his congregation, and realised what the added space on the balcony was for Southwark people on such occasions, would feel that to provide it for them was a good thing.

This is the best place to record my own personal grateful thanks to all who have helped me, whether at St Christopher's, or at Red Cross Hall, at the many gatherings and entertainments in an unusually bright and full year.

For summer parties we have had once more a most enjoyable one at Erleigh Court. Mr and Mrs Arthur Hill received us, as always, in a most hospitable way, and the memories of former happy days there added to the delight of this. Miss Johnston, too, again invited a party, who were greatly delighted with their reception. And Mr and Mrs Edmund Maurice entertained a group of our people, and this was a great success. We were to have gone to Sir Frederick Pollock's, an excursion much prized by our people, but such incessant and tremendous rain came on that, after various days had been planned, the excursion had to be abandoned, to our great regret.

Dr and Mrs Longstaff through the whole summer again lent the cottage in their garden to old or delicate couples, for a fortnight's stay. They also invited a group to see the chrysanthemums in bloom one Sunday, and have helped besides in many ways.

And now I come to the record, written in my heart, as well as in these pages, of those who have once more so bountifully helped with money. The list of those who gave to my own donation fund is attached, with the bare record of how it was spent. But what all this has meant to the recipients will never be known except to those who have had the glad privilege of distributing it. I wish we *could* convey to the donors any idea of the little homes kept together by pension, or timely aid; of the children of widows trained for service, or fortified in health by country sojourns. Nor must the great causes which, in their early or critical times, have been tided over difficulties, be forgotten in setting down what these moneys, thus entrusted to my care, have been. Moreover, the donation balance sheet contains not one-half of what reaches me, because where money is sent me for any organised Society, it is by that Society that it is set down and accounted for, and not here, and yet it has come to me often from faithful friends and fellow-workers of many years' standing. And many a great gift reaches me, like the offer to educate and support an orphan child, to pay a worker for some pioneer work, which finds no record here, but for which a sort of song of thankfulness is always rising in me. For the unrecorded, out-of-sight gifts, grateful thanks should be herein expressed.

One great success we have to set down as accomplished in 1896. The promontory of Barras Head has been purchased by the National Trust, and will be henceforward the possession of the people for ever. It is not quite the first, nor will it, I hope, be the last, of such places which shall thus become in a new and very real sense the common land of England. But it is the first which has been, not given by one far-sighted and generous donor, but purchased by the combined help of many—rich and poor, near and far, American and English—giving each in their measure to buy a bit of England as the common playground, study, resting place, vantage ground for seeing the lovely things of nature, open to all, and for long years. Surrounded on three sides by the great sea dashing among its black rocks; hollowed into great caves like that of Merlin just opposite into which the Atlantic waves roll; sailed over by sea birds; set with great clumps of heather, gorse, and sea thrift; looking across the narrow space of King Arthur's Cove to the Island Rock, with ruins of Tintagel Castle so dear to us all from legend and poem, bound up with noble thoughts of British history, of British legend—it seems a fitting first-fruit of the combined gifts of members and friends of that National Trust, which has been founded to keep for her people for ever, in their beauty and accessible to all, some of England's fairest and most memorable places.[7]

OCTAVIA HILL

---

7 Barras Head, now called Barras Nose, was purchased by public subscription for £505. This eighteen-acre site is near Tintagel in North Cornwall. Celtic myth has it that the baby King Arthur was washed into this cave by the same Atlantic waves Octavia describes. It is in this area, possibly in a cave similar to this one, that the King is said to sleep awaiting his return to lead the people. Tintagel was the site of King Arthur's legendary cliff-top castle. Octavia was interested in the Arthurian legend, as were many artists of the time including Rossetti, William Morris and Tennyson. 1896 was also the year that the National Trust acquired the fourteenth century Clergy House in Alfriston, its first building, purchased for £10 as a ruin from the Ecclesiastical Commissioners and costing £350 to restore. It is surprising that Octavia does not mention this, since, as the accounts with this letter show, she had been actively involved in the campaign to save it. This brought her into contact with William Morris's Society for Protection of Ancient Buildings (SPAB), founded with much enthusiastic support from Ruskin in 1877. The SPAB awarded Octavia honorary membership in 1897 and introduced her to architects such as Thackeray Turner and C.R. Ashbee, who spent his honeymoon in the Clergy House in 1898. (Ashbee, 2002, p.34.)

DONATION ACCOUNT, 1896

RECEIPTS

				£	s	d
In hand January:						
Special Fund	20	0	0			
Available	104	19	10 ½			
				124	19	10 ½
Allen, A.C., Esq				2	2	0
Austin, Miss				1	0	0
Bannerman, Miss Lilias				1	0	0
Bannerman, Miss Lilias for 1897				1	0	0
Blyth, Patrick, Esq				1	1	0
Bartlett, Miss				3	3	0
Bridgeman, Charles, Esq				5	0	0
Bridgeman, Mrs				2	0	0
Cleveland, Duchess of				50	0	0
Duckworth, Miss				10	10	0
Duckworth, Miss (for fares Tenants' Excursion)				3	0	0
Erle, Miss E.				10	0	0
Evans, Richardson, Esq				1	1	0
Forman, Miss				1	1	0
Fowler, Miss (for fares Tenants' Excursion)				0	5	0
Frankau, Miss				4	4	0
Harrison, Mason, Esq				1	1	0
Highfield Benevolent Society				5	5	0
Howittt, Miss				0	10	5
Johnston, Miss				20	0	0
Johnston, Miss (Vans for Tenants' Party)				3	0	0
Langenbach, Mrs				2	2	0
Macaulay, Mrs, General Fund	2	5	0			
Macaulay, Mrs, Special, Alfriston Clergy House	2	0	0			
				4	5	0
Macaulay, Mrs, for 1897				4	5	0
Mallett, Rev. H.F.				2	10	0
Morris, F., Esq				1	1	0
Nicholson, Lady				1	1	0
Plummer, Rev. Charles				5	0	0
Roe, Mrs Ramsden				1	0	0
Rolfe, Mrs (for Trees)				1	15	0
Singleton, Miss				2	10	0
S.C.				1	0	0
Stephens, Miss (for Flowers)				0	5	0
Thompson, Mrs C.				2	0	0
Todhunter, Mrs (for Flowers)				1	0	0
Tufnell, Mrs				1	0	0
Vaughan, E.L., Esq				1	1	0
Wells, Miss Mary				2	0	0
Winkworth, Mrs				20	0	0
Winkworth, Mrs for 1897				20	0	0
Interest on deposit				7	0	4
				£331	18	7 ½

DONATION ACCOUNT, 1896

EXPENDITURE

	£	s	d
Training and Boarding Out	63	17	6
Pensions and other relief	42	11	6
Alfriston Clergy House Preservation (from special funds)	22	0	0
Southwark Cadet Corps	15	0	0
Help in Sickness and Convalescence	13	12	10
Red Cross Hall	11	14	0
Playground, Freshwater Place, care of	10	8	0
Kyrle Society	10	0	0
Excursions	9	5	4
Blind	5	10	6
Education	5	8	0
Employment	5	0	0
Working Women's Club	5	0	0
Maurice Girls' Home	5	0	0
Plants and Trees	3	19	6
Printing Letter to Fellow-Workers	3	18	6
Stationery and Carriage	3	8	8 ½
May Festival	2	17	3
Seats for Laundry Women	1	0	0
In Hand	92	7	0

£331	18	7 ½

Examined and found correct, P.L. Blyth, January 18th 1897.

LETTER TO MY FELLOW-WORKERS

TO WHICH ARE ADDED

ACCOUNTS OF DONATIONS RECEIVED

FOR

WORK AMONG THE POOR

DURING 1897

BY

OCTAVIA HILL

(FOR PRIVATE CIRCULATION ONLY)

LONDON:
PRINTED BY WATERLOW AND SONS LIMITED,
LONDON WALL, E.C.

SUMMARY

Housing work: the Strand; Southwark; Lisson Grove and the development of maisonettes… no further housing work can be undertaken unless more volunteers are forthcoming… Red Cross Hall… St Christopher's Hall… outings for tenants… open spaces: Churchyard Bottom Wood and the need for wilderness to be left untouched… donation fund: death of Lady Jane Dundas and her bequest of £1,000 to be distributed at Octavia's discretion among the poor.

EDITOR'S NOTE

Octavia begins by apologising for the monotony which must creep into such a series of letters reporting on steady and continuous work. Whilst it is true that her account takes us into familiar territory—housing work, outings for tenants—she then surprises us with one of those striking passages that make these letters so arresting. The plea for the preservation of wilderness, rather than turning every open space into 'a conventional park', puts Octavia way ahead of her time, and shows how far she anticipated the concerns of the modern environmental movement. 'Why spend large sums draining with pipes… why should there not be some damp hollows for the marsh-marigolds… left?' Octavia's antinomian instincts are reflected in her objection to iron railings around open spaces.

190 Marylebone Road, N.W.
(January 1898)[1]

My friends,

Continuous work, which is in many ways the most valuable form of help, necessitates a certain monotony in an annual letter, which, I hope, does not feel painful to you. It is not lifeless, believe me; but, because it is continuous, there is not much new to record. Yet it is a good thing for us to review what has been accomplished during the year, to note how far the great stream of the world has borne us, what forces it is bringing to help, or what dangers threaten which we must oppose. Also, I long to write a few words, once a year, at least, to the many friends and fellow-workers now settled in foreign lands, in the colonies, and in other parts of England, with whom now, or in the past, my relation has been so near, or to whom I owe so much. Also, I must print and circulate an audited account of money sent to my donation fund; and I could not send it without a word. So, all things considered, it seems best to write a letter this year to you all; and if, to some of you, there seem in it little beyond the old story, you will forgive it, I think, partly for the sake of the deepening interest and affection the old story gathers in the added years, and partly for the record of steady progress and of what new facts there are to be set down for 1897.

The directors of a company have, during the past year, given into my charge a block of buildings in a court off the Strand.[2] It was a place where the detailed supervision of ladies seemed as if it would be specially helpful, and it has been pleasant to install a superintendent, and to begin securing order and cleanliness. It is a new district for us, but the

1 Octavia wishes the fellow-workers 'a happy and blessed New Year' in the last paragraph of this letter. Patrick Blyth signed off the donation fund accounts on 18 January 1898.

2 See 1899, p.431 for Octavia's description of the demolition of this block, belonging to the Strand Buildings Company, as part of the LCC's Strand Improvement Scheme, which resulted in the construction of Kingsway and the Aldwych.

certainty that the directors would support us in our work, and the fact that the able help of my friend, Miss H. Sim, was available, encouraged me to undertake the charge.

The copyhold of one more cottage in the court at the back of the Women's University Settlement has been purchased by the same lady who last year took the lease of nine others. Two out of the nine have been rebuilt, and are well occupied.

The lease of a plot of land in Southwark has been taken from the Ecclesiastical Commissioners by a lady who has been working in the houses, and five cottages are about to be built on it.[3]

The freehold of a cottage adjoining some already managed by us in Marylebone has been purchased with money recouped from the other three cottages. These form a part of the Horace Street Trust previously mentioned in these letters. After due expenditure in improvements and repairs, which should be abundant for a few years, the proceeds of this Trust are available for gifts.[4]

The two more groups of tenements spoken of in my last letter, which will complete the street near Lisson Grove under our charge, are very nearly ready for occupation.

One of these is very interesting. It consists of compound houses, each of which comes to be practically two distinct cottages one on the top of another. One front door and passage leads to a five-roomed cottage, containing three ground-floor rooms and two rooms below with coal-cellar, wash-house and small back yard. Another front door leads by a separate staircase to a seven-roomed cottage, containing three rooms on first floor and four above. This tenement, too, has separate wash-house, coal cellar, and an iron outside staircase which leads down to a small yard. The same principle may be applied to smaller cottages. It has the great advantage of enabling us to build what are practically separate cottages, with little yards, and yet get a somewhat greater height of building than two storeys; so diminishing ground rent, without resorting to high blocks, or to so much life in public as many buildings necessitate.[5]

---

3 33-39 Orange Street (now Copperfield Street) and 2 Lemon Street (now Sawyer Street). Octavia Townsend, the developer, was introduced to the EC by Octavia Hill, and took the land on an 80 year lease at a rent of £35 per annum. (Letter from Cluttons to EC, 14 March 1897.) These five two-storey cottages became known as Walpole cottages. They were sold to the EC in 1921, but have now been replaced by an office block.

---

4 See 1895, pp.376-77 for a list of grants made by the trustees.

The other buildings being finished are six more cottages. They were undertaken by Miss Duckworth, who had worked with us so devotedly, who was so beloved by all among whom she worked, who had taken up as an inheritance her mother's help to our donation fund, whose marriage and tragic death during the year filled us first with warm sympathy and then with deep sense of loss.[6] These cottages, her last work for us, will come with all solemn sense of trust from her and as dear for her sake.

The number of volunteers in our houses has increased during the past year; several very valuable ones having joined our ranks. But I would earnestly press upon any who may know suitable ladies, likely thus to give help, kindly to remember my urgent need of more, for our tenements have increased in a larger proportion than our workers. I am glad to say I look upon myself as strong in good leaders; indeed, it is because of this that I have dared steadily to increase the area under my charge during the last few years. Leaders are by far the most difficult to secure; also they make the houses far more independent of my life and strength. But the strain will be considerable unless we largely add to our staff of volunteers, and that before the houses in progress come into letting. Also, I must undertake no new work till this staff is larger. I explained last year what kind of duties there were to perform.

---

5 *See ill. 24.* These cottages, called Herondale Cottages, are still standing as 14-19 Ranston Street. Maisonettes (as we now call them) were to figure in the laying out of the Walworth Estate for the Ecclesiastical Commissioners, which was carried out under Octavia's supervision (1904, p.520).

---

6 Stella Duckworth (1869–1897) was the daughter of Julia Duckworth, who became the second wife of Leslie Stephen, man of letters and first editor of the *Dictionary of National Biography* (1895, p.376). Julia was a staunch supporter of Octavia's work, appearing as a donor in every set of accounts from 1872 until her death in 1895. From 1872–1878 she is listed as Mrs Duckworth, then from 1879 to 1895 as Mrs Stephen. She gave substantial amounts—almost always £10 or ten guineas. As in several other families, support for Octavia was passed down the generations 'as an inheritance', and Stella became one of Octavia's fellow-workers. In the year after her mother's death she appears herself for the first time in the donation fund accounts, giving ten guineas—her mother's amount. In the following year, soon after her marriage, Stella died of peritonitis. She was the sister of Gerald Duckworth, the publisher, and of George Duckworth who, as director of housing at the Ministry of Munitions during the First World War, made sure that women were appointed to manage the housing along Octavia Hill lines. Stella was the half-sister of Virginia Woolf and Vanessa Bell. These cottages, now 21-26 Ranston Street, were her second 'batch' in Charles Street: she had been responsible for Almond cottages—Octavia's first new-build in the street— in 1893. (1893, pp.336-37.)

Red Cross Hall issues its own report, which will reach all who have helped there. But I may here thank all my own friends who have so generously aided my efforts there during the past year. Entirely through their gifts will the covered playground and balcony be reconstructed. The scheme of reconstruction has had to be modified; but I hope it may do well as it is now planned. Two new successes are so great a delight and help to me, that they should be specially mentioned here. One is the most generous help given by Mrs Julian Marshall and her daughters. They have entirely undertaken more than half the Sundays in the Hall; they have organised and directed a small violin class, which seems likely in time to fulfil our long-cherished hope of training the working people to join in the performances as well as listen to them. Moreover, to have Mrs J. Marshall in constant communication with the Hall has enabled us to avail ourselves of her advice on the arrangements for the music, which has considerably raised its whole character.[7]

The second great gain there has been that Miss Sewell has joined the committee of management, so giving much more possibility of local work by bringing the Hall into near touch with the Women's University Settlement. This desirable object has been further aided by the kindness of Miss Eardley Wilmot, who has taken the full responsibility of all the Thursday entertainments during the past session, and who has just accepted the post of honorary secretary.

The Hall and garden are the natural complement of the Women's University Settlement, as they afford scope for larger social gatherings in and out of doors than are possible in Nelson Square.

At St Christopher's the work has gone on as of old; former volunteers are entering into new duties, but the relation between them and their friends in the court remains firmly knit, and younger helpers are beginning to come in and learn to know and care for the tenants.

---

7   This is the first reference in the letters to Florence Ashton Marshall (1843–1911) who will re-appear frequently in accounts of the musical activities at Red Cross Hall, especially the annual performance of the *Messiah*. Gillian Darley quotes from a memoir, written in 1935 by one who had known Mrs Marshall, describing 'the slim, springy, fighting figure of Mrs Julian Marshall conducting her orchestra for the entertainment of Miss Octavia's Southwark tenants. And there is Miss Octavia herself, benignly surveying the scene from the utmost back of the Hall, not that she may hear the better, but because, as she says, she likes to watch their faces—the faces of her poor whom she is slowly but surely civilising.' (Darley, 1990, p.244.) As well as being a composer herself, Mrs Marshall wrote a highly acclaimed biography of Mary Shelley, the creator of *Frankenstein*, which was published in 1889 as *Life and Letters of Mary Wollstonecraft Shelley*.

I mention with special pleasure the play performed by tenants' children, undertaken by Miss MacDonell; and the excellent dramatic entertainment given by Mr Arthur Heathcote and Mr Bernard MacDonald.[8]

The summer parties were many and very successful. Mr and Mrs Arthur Hill and the Rev. Frederick Hill entertained two hundred of the Southwark tenants in the vicarage grounds at Shere.[9] The directors of the Dwellings Company gave the fares as a Jubilee offering.[10] Never did I see people enjoy a day more, and the extreme kindness and sympathetic thought for them went to the hearts of the guests. Then a Jubilee excursion to Southend for two hundred tenants was given mainly by the owner of one of the courts, and a most successful day it was; much was due to the kindness of Mr Frederick Crump, who managed all the business both beforehand and on the day.

Our faithful friends, the Misses Johnston, Miss Davenport Hill, Sir Frederick Pollock, the Countess of Selborne, Miss Maud, Miss Russell and Miss Townsend, again entertained groups of our people.

Dr and Mrs Longstaff lent their cottage during the whole summer to a succession of guests, from whom we are continually hearing of the great delight and benefit the visits gave.

With regard to open spaces, the main definite success achieved this year by the societies with which I am connected has been, I think, the

---

8 Bernard MacDonald was a son of Octavia's great friend George MacDonald (1905, pp.537-38) and younger brother of Greville (1902, pp.486-87). Born in 1865, he wanted to become an actor, but, instead, was persuaded to set up as a teacher of elocution and voice production. Greville, who was an ear, nose and throat specialist, promised him a line of patients from his surgery, but these failed to materialise.

---

9 The September 1897 edition of the *Shere Parish Magazine* notes: 'On August 18th, Miss Octavia Hill brought a party of her "London poor", about 200 in number, to spend a happy day in the country, which they were most successful in doing. Mr Cooper very kindly lent us two wagons, and Mr Weller his brake, to convey the old and infirm from and to the station, and Mr Killick most kindly lent the old recreation ground for the treat, and many kind friends lent us a hand in entertaining the people, several of whom had never been to the country before... Altogether a happy day was spent. Miss Octavia Hill writes later: "Will you thank all our kind friends at Shere: those who sent the lovely flowers; our kind and willing guides and helpers; the leaders of the wagons and brake, and all who helped to the great enjoyment of the people."' The recreation ground no longer exists.

---

10 1897 was the year of Queen Victoria's Diamond Jubilee. The accounts for this year show that several donors paid for Jubilee excursions.

purchase, now almost completed, of the 53 acres of Churchyard Bottom Wood, in the north of London. It is an area which for many years has been before us as one which it was of the utmost importance to secure for London. The Ecclesiastical Commissioners had offered it on most favourable terms. It lies on a slope, the lower part of which is close to a district now rapidly being covered with multitudes of small houses, and where omnibus and tram routes from crowded parts of London converge. From the higher parts of the land there is a view. A view is a great refreshment to those of us who live habitually enclosed by near and high walls.[11] Beside this, Churchyard Bottom Wood is a real wood; and if the local authorities will only be sensible enough to leave it unspoiled in its natural beauty, instead of turning it into a conventional park, it will be a source of special delight to Londoners.[12] I never can see why open spaces dedicated to the public should be elaborately fenced from them with iron railings. Hampstead Heath is not enclosed, nor Blackheath, nor Wimbledon Common. Why should the public be forced to go far round to enter through rare gates, instead of reaching their open space at the nearest point to their own homes? Again, why spend large sums draining with pipes, and so destroying some plants and some beauties? Surely, if paths are well and solidly made up with stones, and a good crown to them, that would do well for a path through

11 The Ecclesiastical Commissioners offered the 52-acre site, north of Highgate, for £25,000. A committee was formed of local residents and representatives of the Kyrle Society, the National Trust, the Commons Preservation Society and the Metropolitan Public Gardens Association. Robert Hunter was elected chairman. Hornsey District Council immediately voted £10,000 and undertook to maintain the site as an open space forever, as long as it was handed over to them in such a state as to involve no further expenditure. In order to allow public bodies to contribute, it was felt prudent to enact a bill in parliament, which became law on 6 August 1897. The costs of the bill, plus the requirement of the District Council, pushed the total required up to £30,000. This was raised as follows: Hornsey District Council £10,000; London County Council £5,000; Middlesex County Council £5,000; Islington Vestry £2,000; St Pancras Vestry £2,000; City of London Parochial Charities £1,000; private subscription £6,000. As the sum raised was slightly in excess of requirements, some small plots of land were added to the boundaries of the wood, bringing it up to 53 acres. The wood was declared open to the public on Saturday 23 July 1898 by HRH the Duchess of Albany, who declared that it would be known henceforth as Queen's Wood in honour of Queen Victoria's Diamond Jubilee. (Kyrle Society reports, 1897, pp.11-12; 1898, pp.21-23.)

12 In 1990 Queen's Wood was designated a statutory local nature reserve by Haringey Council. It is also listed as a site of metropolitan importance by the London Ecology Unit.

a wood! Why should there not be some damp hollows for the marsh-marigolds and some look of nature left? Well! this is a diversion; let us be thankful that the wood bids fair to be soon in the hands of the public.

The Commons Preservation Society, the Kent and Surrey Committee, and the National Trust, all issue their own reports; but I may remark generally, that they appear to me to be distinctly growing in power and influence; that their organisation seems to me far better and on a sounder footing. The critical question respecting the preservation of footpaths and roadside wastes now is, how the parish, district and county councils are going to fulfil the duties committed to their care as guardians of public rights. At present many members of them are eagerly communicating with our societies with regard to possible action. But a few members of these public bodies, some of them nearly concerned with the subjects under dispute, seem able to bar action. However, public opinion is growing, and it now has a legal organisation through which to act, and I am hopeful. There is no doubt that the London societies are fully and most usefully employed; they are doing excellent work, and are appealed to as specialists with regard to law and procedure.

The donation accounts are attached. I have to thank all friends heartily who have by these gifts strengthened our hands for good. They will see that, in the main, except such sums as are given for special objects, the money has been spent in regular relief to the old, the children, and for sick cases where clubs could not help, or not sufficiently. It is strange to me that in a year when so much has been given to transitory, and sudden, and therefore not duly thought-out relief, there should be real difficulty in meeting the wants of quiet old people in the far East of London; those, too, who in their youth, have given evidence of thrift. Yet I hear on all sides of such organisations as the Tower Hamlets Pension Fund being obliged to draw on the Treasurer, or else actually stop the little pensions they give to such old people as I describe, and of there being serious difficulty in obtaining help for such cases as those advertised in the COS *Review*.[13] Surely this sort of steady, well thought-out gift is far better than huge sudden funds given impetuously, distributed at high pressure, and, when gone, leaving behind nothing but false hopes and disappointment.[14]

---

13 *Charity Organisation Review*, the monthly journal of the Charity Organisation Society, was published from 1885 to 1921, when it was replaced by the *Charity Organisation Quarterly*.

The desire to give in a steady, sober, gradual way, the desire to let money go, so far as I can control it, to the poor and incurable and aged, the endowments for whose benefit are every year being diverted to the strong, the clever, and the capable, has influenced my decision as to the distribution of a fund which came to me at the end of 1897, and respecting which I propose to render an audited account next year. The late Lady Jane Dundas, who had again and again both helped me in my work and asked my advice as to other gifts, has passed away.[15] We owe to her the building of Red Cross cottages, and our grateful thought must always follow her. She left £1,000 to be given according to my direction among the poor. My idea is to spread it over a few years, so as to give more continuity to its usefulness, and to devote it, in the main, to the old, the infirm, and the incurable. I have already found, through experienced friends, many such, and shall, please God, in quiet deliberate course, select others, or continue to those whom I have selected such small grants as may seem well. I shall report yearly till the fund be exhausted.[16]

I am thankful to say that these new pensioners have been all in addition to my own old ones, my friends having kindly, as heretofore, given me money for my regular work independent of this legacy. I am sure they will be glad to know that, thanks to their goodness, it is available for new help in other parts of London.

And now, my friends, let me heartily wish you, one and all, a happy

---

14 This is another thinly veiled reference to the notorious Mansion House Fund of 1886, organised by the Lord Mayor to benefit the unemployed (1884/5, p.186; 1908, p.598). Samuel Barnett had written an essay on the Fund for the November 1886 *Nineteenth Century*, describing how damaging the 'brutal generosity' of large sums of money hurriedly given away had been to long-established, patiently administered philanthropic schemes: 'The fund... like a torrent, swept away the tender plants which the stream of charity had nourished.' (Whelan, 2001, p.87.)

---

15 Lady Jane Dundas, one of Octavia's most devoted supporters who had paid for the Red Cross cottages, died on 26 August 1897. She was the daughter of the seventh Earl of Wemyss. Born in 1811, she had married Colonel Philip Dundas in 1858. According to her obituary in *The Times* (28 August 1897): 'Despite her advanced age she retained to the last the full use of all her faculties, and had a large circle of friends. She had been a liberal contributor to many philanthropic institutions in Edinburgh.' And, it could have been added, in London.

---

16 In fact, Octavia would give only an incomplete account of the distribution of the bequest. See accounts for 1898, 1899, 1900, 1901 and 1902, by which time she reports that 'the bequest... is drawing towards its close' (1902, p.487)—even though only £641 8s 1d had been accounted for.

and blessed New Year. Each year as it passes over us leaves us richer in memory, stronger therefore in love, and let it be also firmer in hope. For we wrestle, not in our own strength, but in that of Him who cares for and loves all His children and His earth with a love besides which ours is but a faint reflex. Surely His hope must be as much above ours as His strength and love. So let us go on bravely, whether we see clearly or not, sure that He is teaching and guiding us, and that, if we follow Him, He will unfold more of His Eternal purpose.

OCTAVIA HILL

DONATION ACCOUNT, 1897

RECEIPTS

	£	s	d
Cash in hand January	92	7	0
Allen, A.C., Esq	2	2	0
Austin, Miss	1	0	0
Ashmead, F.A., Esq (Jubilee Excursion)	1	0	0
Bannerman, Miss Lilias	1	0	0
Bartlett, Miss Hannah	3	0	0
Beckwith, E.L., Esq	5	0	0
Bleckley, Mrs	1	0	0
Beaumont, Somerset, Esq	50	0	0
Bridgeman, Mrs Charles	2	2	0
Bridgeman, Colonel (Jubilee Excursion)	2	0	0
Brooks, Miss	1	0	0
Cockerell, S.C., Esq	2	1	0
Cleveland, Duchess of	50	0	0
Erle, Miss E.	20	0	0
Evans, Richardson, Esq	1	1	0
Forman, Miss	1	1	0
Field, Rogers, Esq (for training cripples)	5	0	0
Farrer, H.R., Esq (Jubilee Excursion)	2	2	0
Frankau, Miss (Country Holidays)	3	3	0
Gillson, Mrs	5	0	0
Hills, Mrs (The late)	10	10	0
Howitt, Miss	0	10	0
Hunt, H.A., Esq (Jublilee Excursion)	2	0	0
Hanbury, George, Esq	2	0	0
Hooper, G.N., Esq	2	0	0
Hope-Edwards Miss E. (Emigration)	25	0	0
Johns, Miss	1	1	0
Johnston, Miss	20	0	0
Johnston, Miss, for vans taking party to her house	3	0	0
Lee-Warner, Miss (Excursion)	0	10	0
Lloyd, E.H., Esq (Jubilee Excursion)	0	10	0
Lucas, Sir Thomas, Bart	3	0	0
Mallet, Rev. H.F.	2	10	0
Murray, J., Esq (Jubilee Excursion)	1	1	0
Morris, Frank, Esq	1	1	0
Macaulay, Mrs	3	0	0
Parkes, F., Esq	1	0	0
Plummer, Rev. Charles	5	0	0
Praed, Herbert, Esq (Jubilee Excursion)	3	0	0
Pearson, Miss (Excursion)	1	0	0
Penn, John, Esq (Jubilee Excursion)	1	0	0
Pollock, Sir Frederick, Bart (fares of party entertained at Haslemere)	5	14	8
Selborne, Countess of (special case)	0	10	0
Simpson, Joseph, Esq	3	0	0
Somervell, Gordon, Esq	3	3	0
Singleton, Miss	2	10	0
Stephens, Miss Louisa	0	10	0
Scully, Mrs	5	0	0
Tufnell, Mrs	1	1	0
Thompson, Mrs C.	2	0	0
Todhunter, Mrs	1	0	0
Tyrrell, Miss Amy	0	5	0
Thomasson, John, Esq (for Balcony Red Cross Hall)	20	0	0
Tait, Mrs (Excursion)	2	2	0
Wells, Miss Mary	2	0	0
Yorke, Miss Harriot (for Deaf and Dumb)	1	0	0
Interest, &c.	11	4	7
	£400	12	3

DONATION ACCOUNT, 1897

EXPENDITURE

	£	s	d
Pensions and similar Relief … … … … … … … … … … … … … … … …	68	0	1
Training and Boarding-out … … … … … … … … … … … … … … … …	55	19	5 ½
Excursions, mainly from special gifts for the purpose … … … … … … …	36	15	0
Balcony, Red Cross Hall (special gift) … … … … … … … … … … … …	20	0	0
Emigration …	15	1	9
Southwark Cadet Corps (special) … … … … … … … … … … … … …	15	0	0
National Trust for places of Historic Interest or Natural Beauty … … … …	10	0	0
Playground, Freshwater Place (care of) … … … … … … … … … … …	10	8	0
Churchyard Bottom Wood (special) … … … … … … … … … … … … … 8	7	0
Red Cross Hall … … … … … … … … … … … … … … … … … … … 7	5	0
Help in Sickness and Convalescence … … … … … … … … … … … … 5	17	6
Cripples, training of (special) … … … … … … … … … … … … … … 5	0	0
Relief, per Charity Organisation Society … … … … … … … … … … … 5	0	0
M.A.B.Y.S., Southwark … … … … … … … … … … … … … … … … 5	0	0
Church Farm Home … … … … … … … … … … … … … … … … … 5	0	0
Deaf and Dumb … … … … … … … … … … … … … … … … … … 2	0	0
May Festival … 2	0	0
Armenian Home … … … … … … … … … … … … … … … … … … 1	10	0
Employment … … … … … … … … … … … … … … … … … … … 1	2	9
London Fever Hospital … … … … … … … … … … … … … … … … 1	1	0
Plants … 0	7	3
Printing Letter to Fellow-Workers … … … … … … … … … … … … … 4	13	0
Stationery and Carriage of Parcels … … … … … … … … … … … … … 2	11	8
In Hand, allotted to special cases … … … … … … … … … … … … … 107	2	0
Available Balance … … … … … … … … … … … … … … … … … … 5	10	9 ½

£400 12 3

Examined and found correct, P.L. Blyth, January 18th 1898.

LETTER TO MY FELLOW-WORKERS

TO WHICH ARE ADDED

ACCOUNTS OF DONATIONS RECEIVED

FOR

WORK AMONG THE POOR

DURING 1898

BY

OCTAVIA HILL
(FOR PRIVATE CIRCULATION ONLY)

LONDON:
PRINTED BY WATERLOW AND SONS LIMITED,
LONDON WALL, E.C.

SUMMARY

Housing: Southwark; Marylebone; Westminster... the successes of three fellow-workers... Red Cross Hall... outings for the tenants... open spaces: Postman's Park, Toy's Hill, Ide Hill... donation fund, Lady Jane Dundas's bequest... portrait of Octavia by John Singer Sargent.

EDITOR'S NOTE

This letter was sent out with a separate pamphlet, in an identical format, entitled 'Presentation of Miss Octavia Hill's Portrait, Grosvenor House, December 1st 1898'. It runs to 18 pages, including a two-page list of subscribers (including John Ruskin) which informs us that 'Mr Sargent R.A. gave the frame for the picture'. The gift commemorated Octavia's 60th birthday (on 3 December), and the pamphlet contained the text of her acceptance speech. This is the source of the much-quoted passage in which Octavia asks her followers not to form an association to perpetuate any special system after her death. Octavia was much given to contemplating her own demise—see 1874 (p.31), 1876 (p.66), 1880 (p.135), 1906 (p.563) and 1908 (p.601)—but she still had 14 years to live and a great deal of work ahead of her.

190 Marylebone Road, N.W.
(February, 1899)

My friends,

I am very late in writing to you; here we are in February, and I am only now sitting down to report for last year. You must kindly excuse the delay. I have had to prepare three papers lately—one on the 'Management of Houses', addressed to a gathering of the workers from all the London women's settlements; this had to be rather technical. It is reprinted in the January number of the *Charity Organisation Review*,[1] and may interest some of you who are engaged in the management of courts or blocks. Then I gave two lectures at the request of my friend, Mr Loch; one on the same subject as for the settlement workers, but less technical, and dealing with the recent action of the London County Council with regard to the housing question, specially as bearing on our own future work. The second lecture was on 'open spaces', and the new duties which are opening before us with regard to them.

Not only have I set down in these three lectures much of what I specially had to say just now, and should naturally have embodied in this, my annual letter, but preparing them has absorbed what little time I can spare, consistently with carrying on the large amount of practical business for which I am responsible, so that it has been impossible until now to write to you.

Let me, as usual, begin with the houses. Those in our hands have been all, I think, carried on satisfactorily. We have lost one of the Southwark groups of cottages belonging to the Ecclesiastical Commissioners, owing to the land on which they stood being required for a parish mortuary. The people, old tenants, felt leaving very much, and owing to the great and increasing need of rooms in Southwark, they found it difficult to get in elsewhere. I deeply regret that the action of the London County Council with regard to housing the poor is stopping independent building on sound financial lines by the good

---

1 Octavia Hill, 'Management of Houses For The Poor', *Charity Organisation Review*, No. 25, New Series, January 1899.

companies; thus it is unconsciously creating the very evil it wishes to mitigate.[2]

During the past year the following additions have been made to the properties under our care. The five cottages I mentioned as about to be built in Southwark by Miss Townsend are now complete and well let.

The Horace Street trustees have bought still another house, adjoining those in Marylebone previously owned by them. A large part of the purchase money was met by the fund accumulated to recoup capital.

The compound houses I referred to last spring are let and greatly appreciated.[3]

I then said that these would 'complete the street under our charge', but I spoke inaccurately. It is true they were the last houses which required rebuilding, but there were two comparatively new houses in amongst ours which were not under our care. These, owing to unsatisfactory management, were a very great drawback to our tenants, and we felt them a difficulty in every way. My friend, Miss Sim, who has worked with us so long, and than whom there is no one who has more thoroughly mastered the work in all its branches, has herself purchased the lease of these two houses.[4] They are thoroughly cleansed and reduced to order, and will be not only satisfactory in themselves, but a help to neighbours. There remain still two other houses under indifferent management, but, being at one end of the street, they interfere with us less.

Lady Selborne has taken from the Ecclesiastical Commissioners the lease of a piece of ground in Southwark, whereon she is building 24

---

2 The London County Council, created in 1888, had been quick to avail itself of the powers conferred on local authorities by the 1890 Housing of the Working Classes Act to build and manage housing. In 1893 the LCC began work on the Boundary Road Estate, a 15-acre site in Shoreditch, which was given a completely new road layout and a series of blocks to accommodate 5,100 people. This was the first council estate, soon to be followed in 1897 by the Millbank Estate, behind the Tate Gallery.

---

3 Herondale cottages are now 14-19 Ranston Street.

---

4 Miss Sim was one of Octavia's closest associates. She had been living with Octavia, Miranda and Harriot Yorke in 1891 at the time of the move to 190 Marylebone Road. Having started as Octavia's secretary and housekeeper, she progressed to housing management (1897, p.400). The fact that she was able to purchase these two houses— now 12 and 13 Ranston Street, between St Botolph's cottages and Herondale cottages—suggests that she was a single lady of some means, like a number of those who surrounded Octavia.

three-roomed tenements. There have been almost insuperable difficulties in getting a satisfactory scheme for these, owing to the very high price for building and exceptional requirements for working-class dwellings. But the building is begun at last. She proposes to spend little in extra appliances, but to make a point of securing the maximum of light, air and space in sound, well-drained buildings, so meeting the needs of the larger families who wish to obtain adequate space in healthy surroundings, and who prefer cheapness to additional appliances. The need of rooms is so great now that we long to see the building progress quickly.[5]

The Ecclesiastical Commissioners have placed six more houses under our care. They also tell me that they are about to erect a large number of dwellings for artisans on a site in Westminster. I have been consulting with them as to the plans for these. The tenements will be placed under our care when complete. They are very near the cottages we now manage for the Commissioners.[6]

---

5   These tenements, at 17-19 Lemon Street (now Sawyer Street), became known as 1-3 Whitehill Houses. (Letter from Cluttons to EC, 29 June 1898.) Between 1951 and 1958 Whitehill Houses (later known as 5-9 Sawyer Street), were transferred to the Horace Street Trust, initially by transfer of the lease and then through the purchase of the freehold. Whitehill Houses still exist, and are managed by Octavia Housing and Care. The Countess of Selborne, née Lady Maud Cecil, was the wife of the second Earl, who had been one of Octavia's original trustees of the Red Cross Hall (see 1887, pp.217-18), a role he fulfilled until his appointment as First Lord of the Admiralty in 1900 made it impossible for him to continue (1900, p.451). The Countess had become involved with Octavia's work through her entertainment of the tenants (see 1897, 1900, 1901, 1904), but the construction of Whitehill Houses took her involvement to another level. The fact that the Countess of Selborne was concerning herself with which appliances should and should not be supplied to working-class tenants shows how successfully Octavia had made the detailed arrangements for working-class housing the objects of consideration for those of the highest social position.

---

6   Although uncertain, it appears these tenements were on Regency Street, Vincent Street, and Hide Place. In May 1897, a letter from the clerk for the parish of St Margaret and St John's highlighted the continued demolition of undisclosed property over the previous seven years, which covered five-and-three-quarters acres of land. For the parish this came to £4,000 in lost revenues (in terms of lost rates). The clerk requested they start building new housing and that this should be for the working classes. In response, Alfred de Bock Porter instructed Cluttons to inform the clerk of their intention to erect cottages on this land (letter, 17 May). A letter from Cluttons to the Commissioners, dated 23 May 1899, discusses 12 tenement houses, four with shops, that were to be built upon vacant land in Regency Street, Vincent Street and

It may be interesting to some of you to know how large some off-shoots of our work have now become, undertakings for which I have no responsibility, but which have grown up independently, under the charge of friends and fellow-workers. I would refer specially to three which are conducted by those who have taken up the work professionally. One friend who worked for me a very short time, but of whose power I thought highly, was introduced by me in 1886 to the chairman of a large company. He took the responsibility of putting her, though untrained, at the head of about 350 houses in the suburbs. He felt they were so badly managed they must be put in other hands at once. She succeeded so well, that in the second year she collected £1,000 more in the year for the company than had ever been received before. She is still representing the same association, and has since undertaken management for other owners also.

Another fellow-worker who had helped me in my courts I introduced to the late Lord Northampton's notice 14 years ago, when Lord W. Compton consulted me about their Clerkenwell property. I recommended him to engage a lady manager. I advised him also not to pull down, but to improve, existing buildings, where leases fell in, of such houses as were capable of improvement, and which had good space front and back. This lady found able and ready support given by Lord Northampton's agents. The combination of skilled professional advice, and sympathetic and conscientious detailed work, proved successful. She represents the present Lord Northampton, and now collects £8,000 yearly in rents on the Northampton estates.[7]

A third lady, who helped me in Deptford, and who took over the

---

Hide Place at a cost of £19,341. Although there is no explicit connection made here, Octavia's commentary in her 1900 letter about this development mentions three streets, which appear to be Regency Street, Vincent Street and Hide Place.

---

7   Following the dissolution of the monasteries, the land belonging to St Mary's convent and St John's priory in Clerkenwell was given to the new Tudor nobility, and the Earl of Northampton built himself a mansion half way up St John Street. However: 'In London's expansion after the Napoleonic wars, as Clerkenwell's population rocketed, its fine streets became slums—especially the new Northampton Estate, laid out round Northampton Square with streets named after family titles and estates (Spencer, Ashby, Crompton) but without control over sub-division of plots. The manor house, long abandoned to become a private asylum and then a school, was demolished... Houses were turned into workshops and tenements; squalid courts and alleys were notorious; the Fleet river had long been a rank sewer.' (Weinreb and Hibbert, 1983, pp.186-87.)

12. The Prince and Princess of Wales opening Vauxhall Park, 1890.

'Those only who were working with us at the time know… how the responsibility of a large public ceremony at which the Prince and Princess of Wales were to preside, had to be undertaken pretty suddenly by the Kyrle Society. Never shall I forget the devotion, or the power, of some of the men and women who came in then to help; never shall I forget the extreme and most willing and gracious kindness shewn by the Prince and Princess of Wales. It was to me a very solemn scene, because all classes were so entirely gathered in, each to do what in them lay to accomplish the good work.'

LETTER TO MY FELLOW-WORKERS, 1890

Engraving from the 'Illustrated London News', 12 July 1890.

13. Plaster panel by Ellen Rope for the Women's University Settlement, Southwark.

'Miss Rope is a very hard worker and a very rapid one; she is an enthusiast, and puts all her heart into her work. The set of panels in coloured plaster, illustrating verses of Chaucer, and placed in the Women's University Settlement in Nelson's Square, is a very beautiful embodiment of the poet's idea.'

Text and photograph reproduced from 'The Artist: An illustrated monthly record of arts, crafts and industries', vol. XXVI, September to December 1899, p.209.

14. Gable cottages, Little Suffolk Street (now Sudry Street), Southwark, 1894.

'Eight dilapidated two-storeyed cottages stood formerly on this site, having yards of some depth behind them, which were choked up with lumber and trade refuse. The local authorities condemned the old cottages, and the problem arose how to lay out the site to the best advantage. As the street was narrow a space in front of the new cottages seemed desirable, where trees might be planted and seats placed. Space in front seemed more useful than at the back, as it gave frontage for more cottages, while a yard in the rear of each gave all the accommodation of this kind that was really required, and afforded no waste space for rubbish and lumber. Twenty cottages were accordingly planned and built at a cost of £175 each. Every cottage is complete in itself, containing two cheerful rooms on the ground floor, which can be used as parlour and kitchen, or as living room and bedroom in case three bedrooms are required, the remaining two bedrooms being on the first floor. A separate yard with the necessary conveniences is provided for each cottage, which has, in addition, the use of a wash-house, one being provided to every two cottages. The exterior is of red brick with red tiled roofs, contrasting with the cream-coloured rough-cast plastering of the first floor, while the diamond lattice windows are an agreeable variation from the ordinary glazing. These cottages were at once let on completion, and have been continuously occupied ever since.'

Text and photograph from: 'The Dwellings of the Poor: Report of the Mansion House Council for the year ending December 31st, 1894', London: Cassell. Reproduced by permission of the British Library.

15. Winchester Cottages, Orange Street (now Copperfield Street), Southwark, 2003.

'The third main departure for the Commissioners from their original course was to begin building their own housing. They had explicitly ruled this out in 1884, but in June 1893 the Ecclesiastical Commissioners authorised the expenditure of £2,500 for the erection of cottages in Orange Street (now Copperfield Street) and Pepper Street (now Risborough Street). These became 1-9 Winchester Cottages. Five more cottages were added in May 1894. These tiny 'two-up, two-down' cottages can still be seen on what is now Copperfield Street in Southwark. They are no longer in possession of the Commissioners, however, and one property was valued at £360,000 in 2003 on the open market— suggesting that they are no longer occupied by the working poor either.'

Ian Ginsberg, Appendix 3. 'Octavia Hill and the Ecclesiastical Commissioners'.

'Encouraged by the satisfactory result of Red and White Cross Cottages and Gable Cottages, I suggested to the Ecclesiastical Commissioners that they should themselves build similar cottages on their own ground in Southwark. They met my suggestion most cordially, and, after careful thought, decided to build nine new cottages.'

LETTER TO MY FELLOW-WORKERS, 1893

16. St John's Church, Waterloo, with the inscription by George Herbert.

'I believed the words might go home to many a man as he hurries along the crowded thoroughfare near, if he caught sight of them between the trees, their colour attracting his notice, perhaps, first, in its contrast with the dreary dinginess all round. I liked to think some busy man might renounce a profitable bargain, or might even dream, for a minute or two, of renouncing it, for the sake of some good deed. Or I have sometimes liked to fancy a working man, from among the men who sit in that public garden, might be reminded, as he read the words, that though his life was out of men's sight and seemed occupied with little things, seemed perhaps somewhat broken and wasted, there was the possibility of nobleness in it, if bravely and unselfishly carried on. But to whatever heart it might or might not go, the words seemed fit to be spoken to each one of the multitude, hurrying in and out, or pausing there, and worthy to be set , with some care, in lovely colour, to last for years.'

LETTER TO MY FELLOW-WORKERS, 1883

Photo: Gavin Young

17. Almond cottages in Charles Street (now Ranston Street), Lisson Grove, 1894.

'Six cottages have been built at Charles Street, Marylebone, on a site from which the old buildings had been removed. In front is a small forecourt paved with red tiles, enclosed with a light wrought iron railing and gates. Behind each is a yard which, as it abuts on the yard of a block of dwellings in the next street, leaves the back quite open and airy. These cottages are gabled in front and have the upper storey rough-cast with cream-coloured spar; below this is a band of tile-hanging which, as well as the rough-cast, not only varies the front, but increases the warmth of the rooms within, and the lower storey is faced with red bricks. Ample window space has been provided and is filled with lattice glazing, while the roofs are covered with red tiles. Each cottage has four rooms, two on the ground floor and two above, and is well provided with cupboards and fittings. As the ground floors are first concreted, then asphalted, and then boarded, the rooms are warm and free from dust. In the yard of each is a detached scullery, furnished with sink and copper, and separate detached conveniences are provided for each cottage. A quantity of foul rubbish which had been thrown upon the site had to be removed, and owing to the unsoundness of the subsoil the foundations had to be carried to a considerable depth. These cottages cost £218 each.'

Text and photograph from: 'The Dwellings of the Poor: Report of the Mansion House Council for the year ending December 31st, 1894', London: Cassell. Reproduced by permission of the British Library.

19. Garden Street cottages, Westminster, 1894 *(opposite)*.

'The cottages at Garden Street and Dorset Street were erected upon the sites of a number of old cottages which it was necessary to remove on account of their insanitary condition, caused partly by age and partly by structural defects. The new cottages, all of which contain two storeys, are designed to accommodate several classes of tenants, and consist shortly of 19 four-room cottages, 13 six-room cottages and 5 double-fronted cottages—37 in all. The double-fronted cottages contain eight rooms each, and are severally designed to accommodate four tenants requiring two rooms each. There are ample paved yards at the rear of the cottages, and washhouses, and WCs at the end of the yards. The cottages are erected in grey stock bricks, relieved by red brick double ring arches to the windows, and string courses, red tiled roofs, and tiled pent-house porches over the entrance doors. The cost of the 37 cottages amounted to about £12,000.'

Text and photograph from: 'The Dwellings of the Poor: Report of the Mansion House Council for the year ending December 31st, 1894', London: Cassell. Reproduced by permission of the British Library. Garden Street no longer exists.

18. Almond cottages, 2003.

20. Figure of St Christopher on St Christopher's Buildings, Barrett's Court (now St Christopher's Place), Marylebone.

'The figure is one which I began enlarging long ago, from Albert Dürer; friends have most kindly finished it, and are getting it carved. The confidence, to which service brings St Christopher, that God is the strongest of all powers, had always made him a saint I liked to remember in Barrett's Court.'

LETTER TO MY FELLOW-WORKERS, 1879

21. Barrett's Court (now St Christopher's Place), Marylebone, 2004

The block in the foreground in now called St Christopher's House. It was rebuilt by Octavia in 1882 and replaced some of the first houses that Lady Ducie bought in Barrett's Court. The blue building beyond it is St Christopher's Buildings, now called Greengarden House, opened in 1877 to replace Mrs Stopford Brooke's houses that had been condemned by the Medical Officer of Health. Whilst both blocks retain their original format of flats over shops, the flats are now let as serviced apartments, and the decrepid slum that Octavia knew is a smart shopping precinct. However, Lady Ducie's Sarsden Buildings, on the opposite side of the court, is still used for social housing.

management of the houses there from the owner when I left, sends me, at my request, the following list of properties under her charge:

	Locality	No. of Tenements	Yearly Rental		
			£	s	d
1	Islington	236	3,045	18	0
2	Hoxton	72	1,235	0	0
3	Shoreditch	24	418	12	0
4	Bow	20	289	18	0
5	Wapping	(122 and 8 shops)	1,950	0	0
6	Fulham	28	742	6	0
7	Deptford	41 (five small properties)	464	15	0
8	Southwark	234	3,276	0	0
9	Notting Hill	12	176	16	0
			£11,599	5	0

Of course, all this is very different from the near personal interest, and the close link between owner and tenants, which is rendered possible in my own work, with all its wealth of volunteers helping, and where the separate court or street is put into the hands of one lady, who becomes as nearly as she can be the living head of a small group of tenants. But these three workers have achieved, on an independent footing, that a lady's influence should be brought to bear on a large number of tenants, and of their zeal, devotion and energy I feel sure.

The Red Cross Hall report will reach all of you who care to have it, or who are in any way connected with the Hall and garden. We have had most successful sessions there. Friends continue to help with ever faithful and generous kindness. The violin class now numbers 20 members, steadily learning, and who, we hope, will perform in the Hall itself in time to come. The balcony has been restored to efficient usefulness.

We again had delightful summer parties at Erleigh, at Haslemere, at Hampstead and at Chenies—thanks to the kindness of Mr and Mrs Arthur Hill, Sir Frederick Pollock, the Misses Johnston and the Duchess of Bedford. And again Dr and Mrs Longstaff lent their cottage to a succession of guests for the whole summer—guests who are never weary of recounting their happiness there.

With regard to the open spaces movement, I have to record the steady continuous development of all the bodies charged with their preservation.

We have two marked successes to record. One was that of the Kyrle Society in so supplementing those endeavouring to secure the Postman's Park, by strenuously coming to the rescue when all seemed lost, and carrying the matter through in a wonderful way, so that the first part of the garden was absolutely saved and conveyed to trustees for the public, and that option of purchase was granted for the rest of the ground for two years from June 1898. A large amount of the purchase money for this latter portion is secured, but unless the main movers in the scheme exert themselves resolutely and at once to collect the balance, it seems as if they might again risk defeat at the last moment. The Kyrle Society handed over £1,600 towards the purchase money. It has a further sum in hand towards the amount needed for the last portion of the ground, and will thankfully receive additional donations.[8]

The second triumph was the vindication of public right over an important field-path in Kent, commanding a beautiful view. This success was greatly due to the action of the Kent and Surrey Committee, the members of which have for eight years been struggling to preserve this path. The owners are to pay the costs, and to put up a swing-gate.

My friends, Mr and Mrs Richardson Evans, presented last year to the National Trust some land on the spur of Toy's Hill, commanding a beautiful and distant view. It was given as a memorial to their brother, Mr Feeney, and was, so far as I know, the first beautiful site in England dedicated as a memorial. The area is small, but it was all that was to be sold at the time, and it secures for ever a sight of the distance.

We have now, thanks to Mr Derham's help, settled all the preliminary

---

8   Postman's Park, so called because it provided a place of relaxation for postal workers from the main post office in St Martin Le Grand, was created as an open space by combining the churchyards of St Leonard's, Foster Lane and St Botolph's, Aldersgate. The total required was £12,000, and it was agreed that the sale could be effected in two 'halves', with two years to find the second £6,000. The first £6,000 was raised as follows: City Sewers and Treasury £1,250; London County Council £250; Corporation of London £500; Kyrle Society £1,600; Metropolitan Public Gardens Association £950; subscriptions via the vicar and churchwardens £1,325; balance temporarily advanced by B. Norman, churchwarden, £125. The Kyrle Society contribution was the largest, and had saved the scheme from collapse. On 24 June 1898 the vicar and churchwardens signed a contract with the City of London Parochial Charities, who were the vendors, and took possession of the first half of the site. The Kyrle Society open spaces sub-committee estimated that, of the remaining £6,000 needed, they had £3,750 in hand and in pledges. The remaining £2,250 proved so difficult to raise that 18 months later Octavia offered to put in £1,000 from the In Memoriam fund, if the remaining £1,250 were found immediately (1899, p.435). (Kyrle Society report, 1898, pp.23-24.)

business securing for the National Trust the option of purchase of a larger area on another of the Kentish Hills.[9] We have been fortunate enough to be early in the field, and have not had to deal with building land values, nor to buy at high prices the fragments of land which happen to be left unbuilt on. The land is quite rural still in its character, commanding one of the loveliest views in Kent; it comprises 15 acres, and consists of a slope of fields, of a woodland hollow on the hill-side, and a spring and a field at the foot of it. Whether all of it, or what part, will really be secured to the Trust, will depend on the amount of money given within the time that the offer of purchase remains open. £1,600 would secure the whole. You will know how earnestly I shall desire that this should be forthcoming.

I subjoin the balance-sheet of my donation fund. It seems like a widow's curse. Whenever we think we are about to be crippled for means to relieve a needy person, some fresh gift is sure to arrive and make us feel the thoughtful generosity of friends at a distance. Seeing so large an amount in hand, it may be a little difficult for you to realise how often we have to say, 'Can we make a grant?' for orphan, or widow, or sick friend. But so large a proportion of what we give is for some want which will go on for a considerable time—training or pension— that I feel it necessary to keep in hand a fixed proportion for every such dependent, so that at any rate we may not *suddenly* fail those whom we have taken under our care. Whenever that proportion is secured, new gifts enable us to help additional people.

I add a second balance-sheet this year. It contains the record of what I have thought it best to do with a portion of the great bequest of Lady Jane Dundas. I hope to print such an account yearly for the next few years. You will see that I have appropriated two large sums for purposes of lasting good for a number, and that the remainder has been given to the sick, the old, and the broken down. To deal with the two large grants first, I knew that Lady Jane Dundas cared for London open spaces, and in devoting £50 to the Postman's Park, and so helping

---

9 Octavia is referring to Ide Hill, west of Sevenoaks and close to Toy's Hill. She gives more details of the appeal in the letter for 1899. Both Toy's Hill and Ide Hill are east of Crockham Hill where Octavia and Harriot Yorke had been living for part of the year since 1884 in a house called Larksfield, designed by Elijah Hoole and paid for by Harriot Yorke—the sole owner. Octavia's residency in Kent is the obvious reason for the early accumulation of National Trust properties in the area, as well as the vigorous campaigns waged by the Kent and Surrey committee of the Commons Preservation Society.

at a great crisis to save a City garden for the people, I knew I was doing what she would have wished. Between the high walls, under the shade of trees, near to the splashing fountain, what blessing that garden will bring.

Then, secondly, I knew a village where there is no resident squire or clergyman, a little group of cottages on a sandy hill. The cottagers were obliged, when their little stores of rain-water were exhausted from their butts, to toil up a long hill with heavy buckets. A bit of land on the spur of the hill close to the cottages was given to the National Trust for the sake of securing a view. I found there was water to be had on the land close to the road, and on the top of the hill. The National Trust had no duties of giving water, but I obtained their leave to sink a well on their ground. I could not easily manage the whole cost, but thinking that Lady Jane Dundas, Mrs Russell Gurney, and Mrs Scrase-Dickins, would all approve the object, I devoted £20 of Lady Jane's bequest, and £20 from the Horace Street Trust, to this permanent gift to the villagers.

A part of Lady Jane Dundas's money has been devoted to poor ladies. Some of these I learned to know of through the Ladies' Guild. I remember how much Lady Ducie had felt was wanted for the incurable, or old and utterly forlorn. In order to secure much personal thought and care for the recipient, and to share among many who are working face-to-face with the poor the joy of being able to help, I sent £5 each to several friends in various parts of London, asking them to keep the money till the real case of need presented itself, to give it when and how they thought best to people they knew. I chose, naturally, experienced people, most of them COS workers in poor districts, and I believed that with a free hand, and a small sum given to such, more good would be done in a human friendly way than anyhow else. I have not been disappointed. I have received most careful and very encouraging letters. I have given a few dry facts gathered from these in the account, but I cannot convey therein the impression I receive of the good done.

A certain part of this relief was given direct to people I myself knew much of. Altogether, I feel well satisfied with the result of the disposal of the money, and I wonder sometimes whether, far-away from us though she be, any knowledge of the blessing of her gift can reach and rejoice the giver. How little one knows!

I cannot close a letter giving any report of 1898 without adding a few words of heartiest thanks to the givers of the portrait of myself by Mr Sargent.[10] I said what little I could to those who were present at

Grosvenor House on December 1st, but I wish my thanks could reach, with something of living speech, my dear friends who were not there.[11] Let them be sure that this proof of their remembering kindness must ever be deeply valued by me; that it will speak to me of them; that it will be a proof of their sympathy in all that I have tried through life to do; that it shall make me try more earnestly to be more worthy of their goodness; and that I look upon it as a memorial not of my own work, but of that joint work to which they have all, each in their various ways, contributed, and that in so large a measure that we can none of us say 'this is mine', and 'that is yours', but all of us may say it is 'ours'. In fact, that old phrase that touched me so when the tenants began to use it long years ago when we all had drawn together with memories, hopes,

---

10 When John Singer Sargent (1856–1925) was asked by a group of her admirers to paint Octavia Hill's portrait, to mark the philanthropist's 60th birthday, he was at the height of his powers. Born in Florence to American parents, he had settled in England in 1885, being elected to the Royal Academy in 1897. Why Lady Pollock and Mary Booth selected him is something of a mystery, as he was famous for painting glamourous society women. Indeed every woman wanted to be portrayed by Sargent, as his flamboyant, virtuoso, some might say 'slick', style made any woman look good. He was the inheritor of the Grand Manner, producing life-size canvases, but he was criticised for a lack of psychological insight. He carried out the commission in August and September of 1898. By this time Sargent was himself quite choosey about whom he portrayed, and it was not just a question of money. He had so many calls for his services that he was denied the time for anything else and, like many painters, he saw 'face' painting as a means to an end, providing the resources for 'subject' pictures. Octavia no doubt would have appealed to him as something of a challenge. According to Darley, a lavish oil by the greatest portraitist of the age was not to Octavia's taste. She had certainly resisted such extravagance before, refusing to have a portrait of herself donated to Red Cross Hall. Evidently she would have been happy with a chalk sketch. But in the event the sitter and the artist grew to admire each other, and, according to Mary Booth, 'our modern Velasquez seized his chance and he succeeded in transferring to his canvas... something of the inward spirit which we have reverenced'. Harriot Yorke commented that Octavia never looked sideways and most of the accounts 'refer to her enormous dark eyes and penetratingly direct gaze' (Darley, 1990, p.267). But Sargent was probably simply following artistic convention, as the direct gaze of a woman from a picture was still seen by many as immodest and 'unladylike'. He does convey a sense of determination, but at the same time the warmth of her personality. Some 200 subscribers contributed, with Sargent giving the frame. The portrait now hangs in the National Portrait Gallery.

---

11 In the absence of the Duke, the Duchess of Westminster presided at the ceremony. C.S. Loch and Revd Fremantle spoke, as did Octavia. She thanked her friends, including the dead ones, especially Mrs Nassau Senior, William Shaen, F.D. Maurice, Mrs Russell Gurney and Sydney Cockerell senior.

and life which were common to us, 'He' or 'She' is 'one of us', sprang again into my mind as I looked down the goodly list of donors, and thought of the many others also who were with us in heart and aim. For surely we may believe that in our desire to help the poor, to better the earth our Father made, we are bound into one great fellowship, not only with friends here, not only with those scattered in various places, not only with the living, but with the great company that has gone before, whom we are passing on to meet when we are needed here no more.

OCTAVIA HILL

DONATION ACCOUNT, 1898

RECEIPTS

	£	s	d
Cash in hand January	112	12	9 ½
Andrewes, Mrs H.	1	1	0
Allen, A.C., Esq	2	2	0
Austin, Miss	1	0	0
Anon. (for apprenticing crippled boy)	5	0	0
Anon., K.L.	1	0	0
Bartlett, Miss Hannah	3	0	0
Booth, Charles, Esq	5	0	0
Bridgeman, Charles, Esq	5	0	0
Bannerman, Miss Lilias	1	0	0
Brooks, Miss	1	0	0
Cleveland, Duchess of	50	0	0
Cornish, Rev. T.F.	1	0	0
Evans, Richardson, Esq	1	1	0
Erle, Miss Eleanor	20	0	0
Forman, Miss	1	1	0
Field, Rogers, Esq	6	0	0
Frankau, Miss (for Country Holidays)	3	3	0
Gillson, Mrs	5	0	0
Hills, John, Esq	10	10	0
Harrison, Mason, Esq, The late	1	1	0
Hill, Alfred, Esq	10	0	0
Howitt, Miss	0	10	1
Johnston, The Misses	20	0	0
Johnston, The Misses (for vans taking party to their house)	3	0	0
Langenbach, Mrs	2	2	0
Mallet, Rev. H.F.	2	10	0
Macaulay, Mrs	5	0	0
MacDonnell, Mrs (per Country Holidays)	1	10	0
Morris, F., Esq	1	1	0
Parkes, F., Esq	1	0	0
Pearson, Miss (tenants' fares)	1	0	0
Powell, Sir Richard Douglas	2	2	0
Pollock, Sir Frederick (fares to Haslemere)	4	18	6
Plummer, Rev. Charles	5	0	0
Schuster, Mrs	3	0	0
Stone, Rev. E.	1	1	0
Somervell, Gordon, Esq	3	3	0
Stephens, Miss	0	10	0
Singleton, Miss	2	10	0
Tufnell, Mrs	1	1	0
Thompson, Mrs Charles	2	0	0
Tyrell, Miss Amy	0	10	0
Thornton, T., Esq	1	1	0
Todhunter, Mrs	1	0	0
Webb, Mrs Randall	5	0	0
Wells, Miss Mary	2	0	0
Winkworth, Mrs Stephen	40	0	0
Winterton, Percy C., Esq	1	0	0
Interest on Deposit	3	15	6
	£363	16	10 ½

DONATION ACCOUNT, 1898

EXPENDITURE

	£	s	d
Postman's Park, towards purchase (special)	95	6	0
Pensions and similar Relief	47	10	2
Training and Boarding-out in Homes	38	1	3 ½
Apprenticing Cripple	25	0	0
Excursions and Country Holidays	20	3	4
Southwark Cadet Corps	15	0	0
Playground, Freshwater Place, care of	10	8	0
Balcony, Red Cross Hall	10	0	0
Gardens and Plants	9	2	10
Printing and Postage of Letter to Fellow-Workers	4	18	1 ½
Aid in Sickness and Convalescence	4	6	0
Violin Class at Red Cross Hall (special)	3	10	0
District Nursing	2	2	0
Employment	1	7	5
London Fever Hospital	1	1	0
Stationery and Carriage Parcels	0	17	9
In Hand, mainly allotted to special cases	75	2	11 ½

£363　16　10 ½

Examined and found correct, P.L. Blyth, January 3rd 1899.

LADY JANE DUNDAS'S BEQUEST, 1898

EXPENDITURE

	£	s	d
Postman's Park	50	0	0
Well on National Trust land	20	0	0
Ladies (various help for)	31	1	0
Pensions, etc, from *Charity Organisation Review*	20	10	6
Aged couple ruined by Liberator failure	13	0	0
Blind people	7	8	10
Epileptics, National Home for	5	0	0
Tower Hamlets Pension Fund	5	0	0
Crippled Boy (training for trade)	5	0	0
Per Mr Toynbee	5	0	0
Widow, aged 70 (relief during illness)	5	0	0
Per Miss Sewell	5	0	0
Orphan Child (boarding in country)	3	18	0
Widow, aged 70, with a blind daughter	3	0	0
Incurable Invalid, kept a long time on Mother's savings	2	12	0
Thrifty Widow (C.) aged 74	2	12	0
Thrifty Widow (K.) aged 82	2	8	0
Aged Sailor (W.) and Wife	2	8	0
Invalid Pensioner (bedding for)	2	9	0
Compositor suffering from blood-poisoning	1	19	0
Aged Couple (man past work)	1	18	6
Perfumer, consumptive	1	14	6
Cabinet-maker (savings in two Clubs exhausted)	1	6	6
Bedridden woman (for attendance to clean room)	1	6	0
Old man suffering from accident	1	1	6
Various gifts	7	4	0
	£207	17	4

LETTER TO MY FELLOW-WORKERS

TO WHICH ARE ADDED

ACCOUNTS OF DONATIONS RECEIVED

FOR

WORK AMONG THE POOR

DURING 1899

BY

OCTAVIA HILL

LONDON:
PRINTED BY WATERLOW AND SONS LIMITED,
LONDON WALL, E.C.

SUMMARY

Housing work: Lady Selborne's new houses in Southwark; the beginning of the work in Notting Hill; Westminster; Strand Improvement Scheme; private-sector rented property threatened by municipal building, the drawbacks of lodging houses for men and the advantages of suburban developments… outings for the tenants… St Christopher's Hall and Red Cross Hall… open spaces: Brockwell Park and Postman's Park… Ide Hill goes to the National Trust… the donation fund, Lady Jane Dundas's bequest and the anonymous In Memoriam fund… death of John Ruskin.

EDITOR'S NOTE

Beginning with a paragraph about the Boer War, this is the only letter to refer at any length to external political circumstances that lie outside Octavia's field of operation. However, Octavia's conclusion is that the 'crisis in our country's history' means that everyone should do whatever it is they are called upon to do to the best of their ability, which 'makes a nation strong'. The message for the fellow-workers was obvious. Octavia's public-spiritedness did not extend to public authorities, and this letter contains a heart-felt objection to local authority housing—or 'windy talk about municipal building'—which she believed was paralysing more worthwhile attempts to provide working-class housing. She also takes the opportunity, when reporting on the progress of Lady Selborne's block in Southwark, to point out that it has been held up by the 'needless, and even objectionable, requirements to which those who build in these days are liable'. Octavia could see that both issues—over-regulation which was driving up costs and the access to public money to avoid the discipline of the market in municipal housing—would conspire to undermine the principle upon which she had based her housing work: 'the houses of working men are to be on a sound financial basis, and not charities'. In this letter Octavia reports on the beginning of her work in Notting Hill, which would become so important that it is mentioned in every subsequent letter.

190 Marylebone Road, N.W.
(January, 1900)[1]

My friends,

In sending you New Year's greeting, and thanks for all your help during
the past year, I always give some short statement of achievements, of
continuous endeavour, and of hope. Writing this December, how all
seems dwarfed and abased by the overwhelming sense of the crisis in
our country's history through which we are passing! National
responsibilities, national duty, national endeavour, national sorrow,
absorb us. Our desire that England should do what England ought,
that she should be given strength to secure free speech, uncorrupted
justice, equal rights in South Africa, that she should be brought through
all her sorrow and effort triumphant and ennobled, seems so to fill our
hearts, that all our own work looks worth nothing. Yet this is not so; to
some of us there is no way in which directly we can help. We cannot
fight, we cannot nurse, money is being given abundantly. Where then,
except in prayer, is our help to England in this great struggle? Is it not
in steady performance to the best of our power of whatever daily duty
lies before us, in intelligent and diligent study of events, in cultivation
of such calm and sympathy as will be helpful because it forms a part of
public opinion, in tenacious adherence to a noble and practical ideal?
And is not this, in fact, what makes a nation strong, that her members,
however insignificant, should be doing honest, thorough work, that
they should each in their place do well and be their best? One cannot
see how it tells, but it does tell. Where men and women are honest,
great and true-hearted, there is strength. Corruption is for ever weak,
however strong it looks. And we who cannot offer to England our lives
on the battlefield, the statesman's directing intellect, or the doctor's
and nurse's skill, must look to it that our own path is strenuously trodden,
our own hearts are doubly purified, and that we fill, worthy of our high
calling and nationality, whatever humble place we have to fill. Let us,
looking across the seas to those who are representing us in this crisis,
whisper to ourselves:

---

1 Ruskin's death, referred to in the PS, occurred on 20 January 1900.

> Here and here did England help me,
> how shall I help England?

So we come back to London and the houses, and our records for 1899.

There are only two additional groups of houses which have been put under our care this year.

One is Lady Selborne's, in Southwark, spoken of in my letter of 1898 as then building. Its completion has been long delayed owing in great measure to the—to my mind—needless and vexatious, and even objectionable, requirements to which those who build in these days are liable. These, and the greatly increased cost of all building, have disappointed us in our hope of letting out these tenements at a low rent if we are to adhere to the principle we think so all-important, that the houses of working men are to be on a financial basis, and not charities. But now, at last, our building troubles are over, and the rooms are being let. They certainly are excellent tenements. Each consists of three rooms, divisible, if it seems good, into lettings of two and one room. This, for families varying in size, seems to us a great point. A man can take one, two, three, four, or more rooms, according to the number of his family. The rooms are light, airy, dry and cheerful; the small forecourts to each house will form a delightful playground for little children, and the backyard will be available for drying clothes. So many two-roomed tenements have been built, that these three-roomed ones will fill a distinct want, especially considering the higher standard of accommodation now required by working-class families.

Our second expansion in 1899 is in quite a new neighbourhood. The clergyman of a parish in Notting Hill[2] has asked us to take charge

---

2   This was Rev. Charles Robers, vicar of St Clement's, Notting Dale. Although Octavia referred to her properties as being in Notting Hill in every letter except the last one (1911), they were in fact in Notting Dale, which was a very different area. The houses in Notting Hill accommodated prosperous families, who had no need of the services of Octavia and her ladies. Notting Dale, at the foot of the hill, was a community scarred by its history of brick-making and pottery kilns, based on the clay soil, made worse by the influx of pig-keepers. By 1840 there were 3,000 pigs sharing 260 hovels with 1,000 human beings. The pig-slurry filled up the excavated brick fields, resulting in a one-acre lake of slurry known as the Ocean. In 1893 the *Daily News* published an article on Notting Dale called 'The West-End Avernus' in which the author claimed that he had 'never seen anything in London more hopelessly degraded and abandoned than life in those wretched places'. Partly as a result of this article, a programme of public and private works sought to deal with the situation

of five houses adjoining his parish room. He had not been satisfied with the management of them, and, indeed, it sorely needed reform. He and his colleagues have given us every support, and we have reason to believe he is pleased with the progress made during the short time the houses have been under our care.

But we soon saw that, if much good were to be done there, more houses must be acquired. The neighbourhood seems corrupt, not poor; only too much money seems to reach the inhabitants from the rich people of Kensington. This district is filled with beggars and others who feed on the lavish alms of the ignorant or careless donors. Vice seems rampant, and whole streets are let in furnished lodgings, an extravagant form of tenure, not likely to attract the steady workman, and lending itself readily to the loafer and shiftless or vicious. I drew the attention of a gentleman who consulted me about ways of helping, to the possibility of purchasing 20 more houses almost contiguous to those of which we have charge. He has, I understand, secured them, and as soon as the legal business is complete, he has arranged to put them under our care. We should like to hear of more still in that district.

The large group of dwellings in Westminster now being erected by the Ecclesiastical Commissioners, of which I spoke last year, is not yet complete; but it will be entrusted to us for letting when ready.

On the other hand, a block belonging to the Strand Buildings Company is situated in the area comprised in the London County Council's scheme for the great new street from Holborn to the Strand.[3] It will therefore be purchased by the London County Council, and our connection with it will cease.

All the courts, blocks, and houses which we have been in charge of from earlier dates have gone on well. The tie between our workers and

---

that was seen as a reproach to the greatest metropolis in the world. The Rev. Robers's invitation to Octavia was a part of this initiative. (Whetlor, 1998, pp.19-32.)

---

3   The Strand Buildings Company had been formed in 1857. The 'great new street' was Kingsway, which opened in 1905. The Strand Improvement Scheme, referred to again in the 1900 letter, involved the destruction of 28 acres of narrow streets, with their tenements and workshops, to make way for the Aldwych and Kingsway, named in honour of Edward VII. It was the last major thoroughfare to be built in the West End of London. To accommodate the large numbers of poor people who were displaced, the London County Council acquired two-and-three-quarters acres between Clerkenwell Road and Portpool Lane and developed what became known as the Bourne Estate. It accommodated 2,642 people in blocks five stories high, and still exists. (Tarn, 1973, p.136; Barker and Jackson, 1990, pp.146-47.)

tenants becomes always stronger as the years go on; in some cases we have had two or three generations of one family in a court, and our workers have grown up in friendly intercourse with present tenants. We have been able hitherto, in spite of steadily rising rates, to keep our rents at the old figures, but if the expenditure of the municipal authorities continues to rise, this will manifestly soon become impossible; meantime, by most careful economies it has been achieved.

The housing question is occupying the attention of many, of some who know little about it. It is a very grave one for all who do. I regret that the extension of their building by the good companies and good builders is paralysed by the windy talk about municipal building, which so cuts off the healthy forms of supply. I see no hope of large, well-considered schemes for metropolitan building on a financial basis, which alone can supply the need, till municipal building is abandoned. The municipality cannot, in my opinion, be good landlords to its own constituents; it cannot supply the huge requirements of London. It is entirely checking the healthy natural development of independent schemes. I also much regret that some large landowners are arranging for the erection of huge lodging houses for men. I cannot believe these luxurious abodes, providing for large numbers in a very unnatural way of living, will be helpful. Nor do I think the conscience of those who own areas where leases are falling in, and who think they ought to accommodate some proportion of the poor displaced for the erection of higher-rented flats, can be rightly satisfied by this provision for the strongest and best able to shift for themselves, leaving the families unprovided for. I believe myself that the next great scandal about houses will arise in connection with this luxurious accommodation for men. But this is in the region of prophecy.

To my mind, the most helpful schemes for now meeting the difficulties of housing will be the increase of suburban building—with good means of access. They will by no means do away with the immense value of such provision as is possible in central areas, but will lighten the pressure on these, and will afford nicer homes for those who can go further afield. I have been very glad to be consulted about two such schemes, and I am glad to see public attention directed to similar undertakings.

Our tenants have again had the privilege of being invited to the country to see kind friends of now many years' standing. A large party went to Shere, by the invitation of Mr and Mrs Arthur Hill, and were most kindly entertained by members of their family. Mr and Mrs Hill were not able to be present, but their spirit pervaded all the arrangements; the day was exquisite, and one of unbroken happiness.[4] Another group went to Haslemere, by the invitation of Sir Frederick and Lady Pollock, and one party to the Misses Johnstons', at Hampstead. On each occasion we had fine weather and much enjoyment.

Dr and Mrs Longstaff again lent, towards the end of the summer, their charming cottage for longer visits for two people at a time.

The social side of the work has been steadily carried on at St Christopher's Hall and Red Cross Hall. In the former, the fortnightly social gatherings contribute to the happy life of the tenants, and enable workers to meet other members of the families, and in other ways than in their day-time calls; while the occasional dramatic performances bring in also, by Miss Yorke's kindness, various tenants living further away. At Red Cross the gatherings both on Thursdays and Sundays are planned for the neighborhood; not exclusively for the tenants. Nothing can exceed the kindness of our friends in giving these entertainments; the trouble they take, the excellent music and acting they provide, their goodness in putting up with make-shift arrangements, make us feel under a great debt of gratitude. The Sunday music at Red Cross and the violin class, thanks greatly to Mrs Julian Marshall, continue, and are greatly valued. We have deeply to regret the resignation of Miss Eardley Wilmot as hon. secretary to the Hall. She has ably and zealously carried on the work, but finds it now incompatible with other duties. It is a great blow to us—the greater that she was a living link between the Settlement, its workers, its poor and the Red Cross Hall. I am earnestly hoping that the Settlement may be able to send us someone in her stead. The work for the moment devolves on me. The Hall has been distempered this year for the first time for twelve years. It looks very bright and nice, but the outlay has been a great tax on the funds, especially as it follows so closely upon the renewal of the balcony, and as it is found essential to do something to improve the soil of the flower beds. The audience both on Thursdays and Sundays has improved. They are mainly the same people, but they have learned to care more for the real beauties of music and refined acting; many are still very rough and unpolished, but distinctly improved

---

4   The August edition of the *Shere Parish Magazine* records the day: 'On July 4th, 200 of the London poor were brought down by Miss Octavia Hill, and some of her fellow workers, for a day in the country; they were entertained on the recreation ground, and altogether spent a most delightful day. Our best thanks are due to the many kind friends who helped us with gifts of flowers, the loan of carriages, & c.'

since the old days.

Now in due course comes the report on open spaces. As I shall have to tell you presently, I have been, during this year, the recipient of a very large gift, and, in consequence of it, I have been able very materially to assist towards securing two London open spaces.

The first I will name is one I have not mentioned for many years—Brockwell Park. It is situated in the South Eastern quadrant of London, which, as you know, has by far the smallest amount of open space. The parish of St George the Martyr, Southwark, has only one acre of garden or recreation ground for 48,222 inhabitants.

Brockwell Park is one of the few natural outlets for our crowded Southwark population. It is reached from the Elephant and Castle for a fare of $1\frac{1}{2}d$. Years ago we recommended that the park should be bought; this was done, and it is vested in the London County Council. It was reopened by Lord Rosebery, who pointed out in his speech that, if ever the adjacent land were to be had, it ought to be added to the park. The present park is 86 acres in extent, it is prettily wooded, and part of it hilly, but it greatly needs enlarging. The demand for space for cricket and games is in very great excess of what can be supplied; the frontage is so small that the access to the park is most limited. My own tenants have told me they have sometimes not got down from the tram that took them there on a bank holiday, the crowd near the gates being so great. This year an opportunity arose for securing neighbouring land which was most suitable and beautiful; its acquisition would not only add to the area of the park 42 acres, but would open out access to it from a large new neighbourhood, and give ample frontage and means of entrance all along a broad road. But land is of great value there, and the cost was great.[5] If half the purchase money could be raised the committee could approach the London County Council. How was it to be raised, however? The local committee were hopeless. At an opportune moment I was able through the Kent and Surrey Committee[6] to offer £1,000 if the remainder was obtained. It struck the chord of hope; a gentleman present at once offered £500; the scheme was started. The amount now promised is £23,000, and I believe the land will be purchased.

The completion of the Postman's Park purchase scheme has been in abeyance, owing to the starting, before the last portion of land had

---

5   The amount needed was £66,800.

---

6   Of the Commons Preservation Society.

been secured, of Mr G.F. Watts's scheme for commemorating heroic deeds there.[7] This necessitated a faculty being obtained, and all the delays of legal action.[8] The faculty is obtained, but a year and a half of the two years granted for option of purchase is over. I was therefore very fearful that this last bit of land might be lost, as £2,250 of the £6,000 required were still needed. I therefore offered £1,000 on the single condition that the remaining £1,250 be at once raised. On the strength of this large grant the promoters of the scheme applied once more to the London County Council and the Corporation; and we now await their reply. If they refuse to make up the balance, my £1,000 goes elsewhere, and, so far as I see, this last piece of a treasured city

7 On 5 September 1887 G.F. Watts had written to *The Times* suggesting that Queen Victoria's golden jubilee should be commemorated by a monument celebrating 'stories of heroism in everyday life'. He argued that 'the character of a nation as a people of great deeds is one... that should never be lost sight of... The material prosperity of a nation is not an abiding possession; the deeds of its people are.' He used as an example Alice Ayres, 'the maid of all work' who lost her life whilst rescuing three children from her employer's burning house. Watts' plan for a series of illustrations of heroic deeds of the working classes was taken up for Red Cross Hall, but Walter Crane was the artist who carried out the commission, including the Alice Ayres picture (1890, p.281). Watts would have to wait for more than a decade to get his chance in Postman's Park, but he did at least have the satisfaction of knowing that his tiled memorials would survive, while Crane's panels were flaking off the walls of Red Cross Hall during his lifetime. Nothing of them now remains. George Frederick Watts (1817–1904), 'England's Michelangelo', was the most 'high-thinking' of the Victorian 'Olympians', those artists, including Lord Leighton, who were committed to classicism. During his very long career he steadfastly refused the bestowing of any titles, until he finally accepted the Order of Merit in 1902. Watts, known in his circle as 'Signor', was indeed noble. His personal motto was 'The Utmost for the Highest'—very close to the Kyrle's 'To the Utmost of our Power'. Like Ruskin, Watts believed in the social mission of art and, under the influence of Renaissance Italy, was committed to public art, especially in the form of fresco or mural painting. Any project that Watts undertook was 'serious', his outlook 'earnest'. Many of his paintings would, at the behest of Canon Barnett, be sent to educate the East Enders. Watts was a shrewd business man, exacting the maximum from his clients, but generous to his charities. Watts's mission was to paint walls. Given his interests, Watts was bound to respond to the pleas of the Kyrle to paint public spaces with uplifting tales. Watts was a founding member of the Kyrle in June 1877, serving on the general committee. Watts did not supply the Kyrle with designs—he would not trust his grand schemes to another's hands—but he did offer gifts: 'Mr G.F. Watts, RA, has very kindly executed for the Decorative Branch... a drawing in red chalk from his beautiful picture of "Hope". This picture will shortly be placed in the Seaman's Institute, Ratcliffe, the institution selected by Mr Watts for this valuable gift.' (*Charity Organisation Review*, March 1895, p.129.)

8 Alterations to church property required a faculty from the Dean of Arches.

garden is lost. You will remember we saved one half in June of 1898.

Now let us come to the country open spaces. For these I feel, as I have often told you, bound to give, not only money, but whatever time is possible to me. For it is now or never that they will be saved for the people and times to come, and we who are working for them, and realising their importance, are few. How many subscribers and donors do you think there were this year to the gallant little Kent and Surrey Committee of the Commons Preservation Society? Think, first, how Kent and Surrey are the natural playground, and refreshment area, for London; think, too, of their beauty, estimate the number of cyclists and excursionists and walkers, the villas of the suburbs, the country houses over the whole area—how many do you think sent money to the Committee which is saving for them, by strenuous up-hill work, rural pathways, commons and road-side waste? Only 64 sent help. Well may those who realise what depends on swift, wise, defensive action have to work to their utmost till the reinforcements come in!

Think, then, my joy in recording that the past year has seen the acquisition of a hillside slope at Ide Hill, the one of which I wrote to you last year. It is really bought and conveyed to the National Trust for the people of England for ever. My own faithful friends helped, the press helped cordially, we appealed widely; the Kyrle Society, ever ready in the quiet help of pioneer work, unobtrusive, and thorough, gave great support, handing in £769 of the £1,640 collected. We still want just over £100, but we could not lose the ground, and we hope this sum may come in later. So it is saved: breezy hill, wide view, woodland glades, tiny spring, all yours and mine and every citizen's for all time to come, given to you for ever for your joy and teaching.

Now let me draw your attention to the accounts, showing how I have used your gifts to my donation fund, and the portion of Lady Jane Dundas's bequest which I resolved to spend this year. The first fund supplies the needs of our near poor, the radical help of those whom I and my fellow-workers know—widow, orphan, old pensioner, convalescent—as well as supplying special gifts for special objects. Lady Jane's has this year been expended in large measure for the help of poor ladies. For next year I have already allotted it in my own mind for helping to provide the water supply for a poor outlying country parish, where the promise of it has encouraged the adoption of a scheme to which, now it is started, others are largely contributing; to the education and support of an orphan boy; and to the boarding out of a delicate motherless child, whose father is dying of consumption.

Now let me record that this year I have received by far the largest gift that I had ever received, or could have dreamed of having to administer. It is to be called In Memoriam, and is to be otherwise quite anonymous. It comes to me from the living, in memory indeed of one who helped in life, and is gone before.[9] It was so large that I thought it well to give it in large sums, as you will see from the list. I consulted my wisest and nearest fellow-workers about some of the gifts. A good many of the separate hundreds and fifties were given to people I had known for years working for causes I had watched. To many, such sums represented quite unforeseen opportunities of blessing, quite infinite relief from anxieties as to ways and means for important work. Besides the gifts here recorded, I have made some conditional promises, which will, I hope, be carried through next year.

To my fellow-workers, to my friends, to the many donors, all thanks are due, all thanks are felt. We are, I know, so bound together that few words are needed, but at the solemn Christmas time, bright with promise for mankind, at the fresh New Year, bringing us we know not what, we only know from Whom, I would like to quote some lines of my sister's written long ago, and to ask each of you to take them to yourselves, as what I would say to you each, and for our country:

Since whatever is, is best,

---

9 Octavia gives very few clues to the identity of the helper who had 'gone before', but the most likely candidate is the Countess of Ducie. Lady Ducie, who had died in 1895, had been one of Octavia's earliest and most enthusiastic supporters. She and her husband were also extremely rich, which the donor of the In Memoriam fund would have needed to be. It is difficult to get a complete picture of the fund, as Octavia only published accounts for it with the letters for 1899, 1901 and 1902. These showed gifts amounting to £6,792, which would be worth well over half a million pounds today. However, there were other gifts that were not recorded in the published accounts, and some grants referred to in the letters are difficult to identify with certainty in the accounts. The largest sums given were £1,000 for Brockwell Park and £1,000 for Postman's Park, which are presumably included in the £2,050 shown for 'open spaces' in the 1900 accounts. In 1901 Octavia placed a further £1,000 to the credit of the Kent and Surrey Committee of the Commons Preservation Society which was intended as bait for a local authority in South East London, tempting them to buy a hilltop, but Octavia does not say which one, so we do not know if the purchase took place (1901, p.472). Octavia gave £500 for TB sufferers in 1902, then in 1903 she reports using the last of the In Memoriam fund to buy Mariner's Hill for the National Trust (1903, p.510). Unfortunately she prints no accounts for the fund after 1902, so we do not know how much was spent on Mariner's Hill. Presumably it would have been a significant sum, as £1,500 was required for the extension to the site in 1908 (p.579). Octavia gave £100 for emigration in 1905 (p.547), which

> Loving hearts content may rest;
> And the prayer I breathe for thee
> Is the prayer for what shall be.[10]

OCTAVIA HILL

Since my letter to fellow-workers went to press, I have seen that Mr Ruskin is gone before. The earth seems indeed sadder and poorer that such a man lives on it no more.

To me the news brings up such a crowd of holy and lovely memories of all that he was and did in the far-away years, that I am lost in the sense of tender reverence.

That penetrating sympathy, that marvellous imagination, that noble generosity, that grasp of all that is beautiful, that wonderful power of expression, that high ideal of life, have not only blessed his friends, but have left their mark on England. His thoughts have so pervaded thousands of homes that England is better, greater, and more attuned to noble ideals than she could have been but for his life and writings.

To me personally the loss is irreparable. I have cared to think of the master and friend of my youth in his lovely home, and to feel that he was among us still.

I know that for him, the gain is great: he has passed to the great beyond, all his noblest aspirations are opening before him, the incompletenesses passed away, the companionship of the mighty dead around him, the work accomplished, the love fulfilled, the peace complete, the blessing of thousands upon him.[11]

21 JANUARY 1900

---

must have really represented the end of the fund because there are no further references to it in the letters.

---

10 These lines must be from one of Miranda's unpublished works, probably one of the children's plays, because they do not occur in any of the three plays published by Cassells in 1903 (1903, p.505), nor in *The Fairy Spinner and Out of Date or Not?* (1875), Miranda's volume of fairy tales illustrated by Kate Greenaway, which was her only other published work.

---

11 This is a remarkably generous posthumous tribute to Ruskin, who had died on 20 January, considering that Ruskin's attack on Octavia in *Fors Clavigera* had been one of the factors that precipitated her breakdown in 1877. He had then made life difficult for her by insisting on disposing of Paradise Place and Freshwater Place in 1881, just

as she was getting back to work. Although the rift had been officially healed in 1888 thanks to the intervention of the 20-year-old Sydney Cockerell (1892, p.321, n.5), Ruskin's biographer Tim Hilton has portrayed that as a cruel triumph over a bewildered old man on the brink of insanity (Hilton, 2000, p.111). There was very little contact between Ruskin and Octavia thereafter, although he contributed towards the cost of the John Singer Sargent portrait in 1898. As Octavia grew older she became less sympathetic to Ruskin's views on economics, as they strayed over the border from socialism into communism. She commented in 1912 on a biography of Ruskin that: 'the writer esteems his political economy higher than I should do, in comparison with his art work'. (Maurice, 1914, p.579.)

DONATION ACCOUNT, 1899

RECEIPTS

	£	s	d
Cash In hand January 1899	75	2	11 ½
Allen, A.C., Esq	3	2	0
Austin, Miss	1	0	0
Bannerman, Miss	1	0	0
Bartlett, Miss H.	3	0	0
Bridgeman, Charles, Esq	5	0	0
Baumgartner, Miss	20	0	0
Cleveland, Duchess of	50	0	0
Cockerell, Sydney C. Esq	1	0	0
Dawson, Mrs	1	0	0
Erle, Miss Eleanor	20	0	0
Evans, Richardson, Esq	1	1	0
Forman, Miss	1	1	0
Frankau, Miss	4	0	0
Hills, John Waller, Esq (two years)	20	10	0
Howitt, Miss	0	10	1
Johnston, The Misses	3	0	0
E.F.J.	20	0	0
Langenbach, Mrs	2	2	0
Lowndes, Miss	1	0	0
Luxmoore, Henry, Esq	2	0	0
Macdonell, Mrs, per (convalescent cases)	2	10	0
Macaulay, Mrs	5	0	0
Mallett, Rev. H.F.	2	10	0
Parkes, F., Esq	1	1	0
Pollock, Sir Frederick (fares of party entertained at Haslemere)	5	7	6
Plummer, Rev. C.	5	0	0
Schuster, Mrs	3	0	0
Singleton, Miss	2	10	0
Somervell, Gordon, Esq	3	3	0
Stephens, Miss	0	10	0
Thompson, Mrs C.	2	2	0
Todhunter, Mrs	1	0	0
Tufnell, Mrs	1	1	0
Wells, Miss Mary	2	0	0
Given for Employment	21	5	6 ½
Interest on Deposit of In Memoriam Fund	22	7	11
	£314	17	0*

* *Editor's note:* The total should be £315 17s. The error, which occurs in original, results from the fact that A.C. Allen's annual donation of £2 2s has been set as £3 2s. The accounts for this year were not audited.

DONATION ACCOUNT, 1899

EXPENDITURE

	£	s	d
Pensions …	41	10	6
Training and Boarding Out in Homes … … … … … … … … … … … … … …	22	12	5 $\frac{1}{2}$
Sickness and Convalescence, aid in … … … … … … … … … … … … … …	16	15	3 $\frac{1}{2}$
Cadet Corps …	15	0	0
Red Cross Hall …	12	10	0
Excursions and Entertainments … … … … … … … … … … … … … … … …	10	6	2
Playground Freshwater Place (care of) … … … … … … … … … … … … …	10	8	0
Printing Letter to Fellow-Workers … … … … … … … … … … … … … … … …	3	16	0
Maypole Festival …	3	0	6
Stationery and Carriage of Parcels … … … … … … … … … … … … … … …	2	2	3 $\frac{1}{2}$
Employment of Aged Pensioner … … … … … … … … … … … … … … … …	1	14	0
Gardens and Plants …	1	4	9
Fever Hospital …	1	1	0
Wells, Toy's Hill (padlock and keys) … … … … … … … … … … … … … …	0	18	0
Pensioners in advance … … … … … … … … … … … … … … … … … … …	9	7	0
In hand, mainly allotted to special cases … … … … … … … … … … … …	162	11	0 $\frac{1}{2}$

£314 17 0

IN MEMORIAM, 1899

EXPENDITURE

	£	s	d
Open Spaces	2,050	0	0
Country Home for Epileptics	1,000	0	0
Cripples and Invalid Children	400	0	0
Training Homes, M.A.B.Y.S. and Church Farm	250	0	0
Society for Relief of Distress	250	0	0
Cadet Corps	250	0	0
Orphanages	200	0	0
Pensions and similar relief	192	1	1
Provident Dispensary, Southwark	100	0	0
Training Rural Nurses	100	0	0
Home for Training Feeble-minded Children	100	0	0
Red Cross Hall	100	0	0
	£4,992	1	1

LADY JANE DUNDAS'S BEQUEST, 1899

EXPENDITURE

	£	s	d
Ladies, help in Sickness, etc … … … … … … … … … … … … … … … … …	35	0	0
Orphan, Boarding out … … … … … … … … … … … … … … … … … … …	15	19	0
Education and Training for Work … … … … … … … … … … … … … … …	12	0	0
Charity Organisation Society Pensioners … … … … … … … … … … … …	10	0	0
Aged couple ruined by Liberator failure … … … … … … … … … … … … … 9		15	0
Allowances during illness … … … … … … … … … … … … … … … … … … 2		3	0
	£84	17	0

443

LETTER TO MY FELLOW-WORKERS

TO WHICH ARE ADDED

ACCOUNTS OF DONATIONS RECEIVED

FOR

WORK AMONG THE POOR

DURING 1900

BY

OCTAVIA HILL

(FOR PRIVATE CIRCULATION ONLY)

LONDON:
PRINTED BY WATERLOW AND SONS LIMITED,
LONDON WALL, E.C.

SUMMARY

Housing: Ecclesiastical Commissioners in Westminster; getting rid of middlemen in Notting Hill; purchase of the Strand Buildings by the London County Council; the need for trained professional workers in housing... St Christopher's Hall and Red Cross Hall... Horace Street Trust... outings for the tenants... In Memoriam fund: Red Cross garden and Hall; boys' club in Southwark; Brockwell Park; Postman's Park... Lady Jane Dundas's bequest... donation fund... National Trust: Courthouse in Long Crendon; Toy's Hill.

EDITOR'S NOTE

In 1892 Octavia had emphasised the importance of training for all those working on her housing projects, whether volunteers or paid staff. In that case, the training was to be handled by the Women's University Settlement and Octavia was appealing for scholarships. In this letter she returns to the theme, arguing that property owners should have a housing manager in the same way that they have a lawyer, an architect or an auditor. Octavia is thus insisting on the professional status of her fellow-workers by suggesting that they should be afforded the same respect as that given to other more established professions. She argues that training has raised standards in nursing and teaching, and could be expected to have the same effect in 'the management of dwellings let to the poor'. She was looking way beyond her own concerns, as she now realised that she and her band of fellow-workers would never be able to keep up with the demand for managers, even using her devolved system. She therefore wanted to establish a training course for all involved with working-class housing, whether under her or not. Those women who had worked with Octavia, and who formed the Society of Women Housing Estate Managers (SWHEM) after her death, continued the tradition of training. As late as the 1930s they were still the only body offering training in housing management, and in 1943 it was decided to admit men from the Institute of Housing to the courses, as the Institute provided no training courses of its own (Whelan, 1998, pp.27-28).

190 Marylebone Road, N.W.
December, 1900

My friends,

I am writing to you at the close of one year to tell of thankfulness for the past, at the opening of another year to suggest hope for the future.

My record will deal first with the houses under my care. The most important addition during the year has been that of the large group of dwellings in Westminster, which I mentioned in my last letter as being in process of erection by the Ecclesiastical Commissioners. More than half of these are now finished and let. They consist of houses facing three streets, substantial, light and airy, divided into four-roomed and three-roomed tenements, with pleasant outlook, and abundant space at the back; they have been eagerly sought, and very satisfactory tenants have been secured.[1]

The 20 houses in Notting Hill to which I referred in my last letter have also been purchased and placed under our care. They have been a source of much anxiety, as the cost of obtaining direct control has been great. To do this it was necessary to get rid of middlemen, who too often permit a very low standard as to morality, order and

---

1 Despite this glowing report, all was not well between Octavia and her charges. In May 1901, residents of 1-6 Hide Place filed a petition with the commissioners. In the petition, the residents demanded a reduction in rent because the middle room in each tenement was too dark and the scullery was too small. Neither Octavia nor the Commissioners had any sympathy for these complaints. In a letter to Cluttons, dated 30 May, Octavia remarked: 'I think that any yielding to the request would only lead to fresh requests and would not lead to harmony or good government of the tenements...' There had been a similar protest in Regency Street in October 1900. Twenty-four tenants had signed a petition over the state of the new tenements, in particular the washrooms, which they did not like being indoors. Octavia dismissed their complaint in a letter to Sir Alfred de Bock Porter, dated 24 October: 'Considering that each tenant has four rooms it seems to me that, by a little arrangement, they could easily plan to use another room as a living room on wash day. I therefore cannot see that the present arrangement is unhealthy.'

cleanliness. The rooms were let by the night, they were furnished, and so, when the middlemen went, the tenants had necessarily to go, and we had no opportunity of trying whether any of them were, or could be raised into being, fairly satisfactory tenants. Judging by what we saw there was little hope of this, and certainly the breaking up of such a group, the cessation of an extravagant and homeless way of living, the removal from power of an unsatisfactory class of middlemen, is an unmitigated good. The process of cleansing the houses was long and costly, is not even yet nearly done; but the result of converting the houses to the use of hard-working decent families, having their own furniture, and ensuring that cleanliness and order should succeed to dirt and anarchy, is most cheering. The employment given is good, wholesome cleansing processes are carried out, and I hope the owners feel with me that the money spent has done far more good than twice the amount spent in gifts. At present, however, it is all up-hill work, and needs energy and courage and patience.

A small company has been formed by a group of ladies and gentlemen to improve working-class houses in Notting Hill. They have purchased four quite close to those we manage, and have placed theirs under our care.[2]

We are also in treaty for one more house in the same street as those already under our control; we have come to terms with the owner, and have a lady ready to buy, and before this is in print I hope the matter may be concluded. The conduct of one house in a street tells so much

---

2   The Improved Tenements Association (ITA) was formed in August 1900 by Reginald Rowe (1868–1945), under-treasurer of Lincoln's Inn and a member of the stock exchange, and his cousins Amy and Arthur Hayne. Amy Hayne, who worked with the Harrow School Mission in Latimer Road, had been shocked by the housing conditions she came across. She met Octavia, who had just become involved with housing in the area, and was impressed by her system of management. The report of the first general meeting described the ITA as being 'formed… for the purpose of buying houses in the Harrow Mission district and neighbourhood, putting them in proper sanitary condition and repair, and placing them under the control of Miss Octavia Hill, who would be responsible for the letting, choice and number of tenants, collection of rents and general management of the houses'. These four houses, their first purchases, were numbers 2-8 in Walmer Road (demolished in the 1960s to make way for the Westway) which were let as 13 two-room tenements. ITA was a commercial company, not a charity, and paid four per cent dividends to shareholders in every year but one up to 1909. When dividends became more problematic the directors wrote to Octavia, who replied in 1911 that: 'The demand for rooms in London is nowhere what it once was, and the rowdy character of this neighbourhood is a drawback'. (Malpass, 1998, pp.25-29.)

on the rest that, when we have begun at all in a street, we greatly rejoice to secure any additional property there.

The Strand Buildings, which are situated within the area comprised in the Strand Improvement Scheme, have been acquired by the London County Council, and have therefore ceased to be managed by us.[3]

In the immediate proximity to the cottages built a few years ago by the Ecclesiastical Commissioners, there are 35 of which the leases fell in at Michaelmas, and the Commissioners asked whether we would take the temporary management of them; some of them will necessarily come down and be rebuilt, some will be held for a few years, some retained for a considerable time, and some will, I hope, be replaced by new cottages. It is a curious thing to realise, as one does in a case of this kind, how wholly owners delegate their responsibility in a long lease, how income is drawn by them, and little or no control is exercised. I felt in looking over these houses how glad I was that the Commissioners were now keeping this class of property, which is so liable to abuse, in their own hands.

This thought had long ago been realised by me. Being so prominently again before me, I have been thinking a great deal lately about how responsible bodies can, in the future, secure such management by trained ladies as has been found helpful in the past. This has turned my attention much more than heretofore to the thought of how to provide more responsible professional workers, for I felt that, however much volunteers might help, it was only to professional workers that responsible and continuous duties could, as a rule, be entrusted, especially by large owners or corporations.

Up to now my professional workers have been among my most zealous and self-sacrificing colleagues, always ready to take onerous duties, to fill vacant places, to slip out of the way and go to new fields when volunteers came forward, to change their work when it seemed best, however fond they were of tenants, however interested in courts, always willing to help to train others for management in houses whether in London, the provincial towns, Scotland, Ireland, America, Holland, or any other place from which workers came, taking their holidays when best they could be spared, and in every way proving themselves my colleagues by their hearty recognition that what we had to do was to teach, initiate, and supplement as many earnest workers as we could. What I owe to them in the past for the devoted help they have thus rendered for now many years, no one will ever know.

---

3   See 1899, p.431.

But up to this year I, or my sisters, or my friend Miss Yorke, or some tried and experienced volunteer, have been the responsible persons to whom private owners, or men of business, or corporations, have entrusted their houses, and it is we who have reported on all business. As a matter of fact, as you all know, we have wished to put all the management on a business footing, and, with few exceptions, have charged the owners the ordinary five per cent on rental usually paid to collectors.

Thinking over all this with regard to the further future, and to larger areas than we can cover, it seemed to me that the present plan had its limitations. Even if many more such leaders were found, how would they be known? Could responsible bodies make plans dependent on them? Then I realised that my best plan for the future would be, not only to train such volunteers as offered, and the professional workers whom we required, but to train more professional workers than we ourselves can use, and, as occasion offers, to introduce them to owners wishing to retain small tenements in their own hands and to be represented in them by a kind of manager not hitherto existing. The ordinary collector is not a man of education having time to spare, not estimating his duties as comprising much beyond a call at the doors for rent brought down to him, and a certain supervision of repairs asked for. If there existed a body of ladies trained to more thorough work, qualified to supervise more minutely, likely to enter into such details as bear on the comfort of homelife, they might be entrusted by owners with their houses. We all can remember how the training of nurses and of teachers has raised the standard of work required in both professions. The same change might be hoped for in the character of the management of dwellings let to the poor. Whether or no volunteers co-operated with them, would settle itself. At any rate, owners could have, as I have often told them they should have, besides their lawyer to advise them as to law, their architect as to large questions of building, their auditor to supervise their accounts, also a representative to see to their people, and to those details of repair and management on which the conduct of courts or blocks inhabited by working people depends. Where people live close together, share yards, wash-houses and staircases, too often there is no one whose business it is to supervise and govern the use of what is used in common, or to see how one tenant's conduct affects others.

Having decided that it was desirable to provide workers qualified to take such responsible posts beyond the areas which I and my friends had under our charge, I at once invited two ladies to come and be trained, whom I might introduce to owners as soon as they were needed. I see two areas likely to open out almost before they are ready. When they are started, I shall put on two more if all be well.

So much for the extension of our work. The old courts and blocks and streets have gone on successfully, much as in former years, our relation to tenants, and interest in the places, deepening with time. The standard of life in London is continually rising, and an ever-increasing number of tidy respectable people are wanting and obtaining more comfortable homes. Our rents have hitherto not risen, careful management having enabled us to keep them at the same amount, but increased assessments and increased rates will probably compel us to raise them soon; meantime, wages have risen and work is most abundant.

Our two Halls—St Christopher's and Red Cross—continue full of life. Sociable evenings, dramatic performances, music, flower-show, May festival, cadet drill, all continue, and are highly appreciated. I have to regret, at Red Cross, the first change in our trustees, but the cause of it is not a sad one. Lord Selborne, now that he is First Lord of the Admiralty,[4] feels that he must resign the trusteeship. He has long been a faithful and kind friend, and I much regret his leaving. Mr Herbert Praed is also retiring from the trusteeship; his other duties have precluded him from giving us active help, and the group of tenants in Stanhope Buildings, opposite to the garden, which is managed by a company of which Mr Praed is chairman,[5] is well linked to the work in

---

4   Lord Selborne was First Lord of the Admiralty from 1900 to 1905. Working with Admiral Fisher, he presided over far-reaching reforms, uniting economy with efficiency. These reforms included the introduction of the Royal Fleet Reserve, known as Selborne's Light Horse, the setting up of the naval colleges at Osborne and Dartmouth, the setting up of the design committee which produced the Dreadnought, and the introduction of submarines into the service. The first submarine was launched in 1901, and orders were placed for another 40 during Lord Selborne's term of office. According to Lord Jellicoe: 'our superiority in capital ships at the outbreak of the last war was due to the efforts of the Boards presided over by Lord Selborne and his successors'. (*The Times*, 27 February 1942.)

---

5   Stanhope Buildings belonged to the Victoria Dwellings Association, a commercial property company that opened its first block in Battersea in 1877, and its second in Islington in 1879, both designed by Charles Barry. Stanhope Buildings in Southwark was its third development. (Tarn, 1973, p.94.) This is the last mention of Herbert Praed in the letters, although he crops up in the accounts between 1908 and 1911, giving a guinea to the Red Cross flower show. He was created a baronet in 1905, but the title died with him as he produced no heir.

the Hall by Miss Ironside. My friend Mr C.S. Loch has kindly consented to become a trustee. We shall find in him a helpful counsellor should changes occur requiring new departures, and it is a great pleasure to me, personally, that my work should be thus associated with a tried friend of many years' standing, and one in whose wise and sympathetic decisions as to both cottages and Hall, and knowledge of local workers who might help on the committee of management for the Hall, I should have great confidence. Lord Stamford[6] has kindly consented to be the other trustee. He and Lady Stamford have helped us in many ways for some years. His having been chairman of the Selborne Society[7] and of the Charity Organisation Society, show his interest both in the provision of a garden and Hall for the people, and in the wise management of houses.

With respect to the Horace Street Trust, from which, to my great regret, Lord Selborne feels he must also retire, I came to the conclusion that it would be well to make another change. Here the number of

---

6   The ninth Earl of Stamford (1850–1910) had been born William Grey, the son of a missionary in Newfoundland. He had come to the title indirectly, the eighth earl having died without producing a male heir, despite being married three times. The ninth earl was an indefatigable supporter of good causes, especially those relating to the Church of England. As well as having been chairman of both the Selborne Society and the Charity Organisation Society, he was connected with the Bible Society, the Additional Curates Society, the Church Building Society, the Metropolitan Hospitals Sunday Fund, the Queen Victoria Clergy Fund and the Colonial Bishoprics Fund. He was a free-trader and a Liberal Unionist in his politics.

---

7   Lord Selborne's title derived from the parish of Selborne in Hampshire, where his father, Sir Roundell Palmer MP (later created the first Earl of Selborne) had bought land at Blackmoor in 1865. He then commissioned Alfred Waterhouse to build a model Victorian estate village. Waterhouse (architect of the Natural History Museum in South Kensington) designed the church of St Matthew, a village school (now the village hall), a number of smaller houses and then Blackmoor House. The house displayed the motto *Ego autem et domus mea serviemus Domino* ('But as for me and my house, we will serve the Lord', Joshua, 24:15). According to Lord Selborne's obituary in *The Times* (27 February 1942) the family lived up to this: 'His home reflected the finest virtues of the Victorian age.' The Selborne Society was founded in 1885 to commemorate the eighteenth-century naturalist Gilbert White of Selborne in Hampshire. It was originally a national organisation, founded to continue the traditions of this pioneer of environmental study by correspondence between members about their observations of natural history. Today's Selborne Society was originally the Brent Valley branch of the national Society, and continues the work of its founders, observing and recording wildlife in part of west London and managing and conserving Perivale Wood Local Nature Reserve as the Gilbert White Memorial.

trustees has been three only.[8] I thought it had better be raised to five. Mr Loch most kindly takes Lord Selborne's place, and I am delighted to have made sure of his help on the Trust. The houses which form the Trust are, however, in this neighbourhood, and, looking to the future, I thought we ought to secure wise local help. To my great satisfaction my friend Mr Francis Morris has consented to act. He is, as many of you know, hon. secretary of the Marylebone Charity Organisation Society. He is also a poor law guardian here, and has devoted many years to helping the poor with all wise and deep individual sympathy. He has himself purchased houses for letting to working people, and, busy as he is, I know that, if it were needed, no one more ably and readily would see that the management of the houses was well organised. He will also know, as well as any one in London, how to give away the money arising from the Trust so as to be really helpful. In addition to these two, I have suggested and obtained for my colleagues the approval of the nomination of my niece, Elinor Lewes. She formerly collected in one house belonging to the Trust, and now collects with me in the cottages in Westminster. She is one of my ablest and most zealous accountants, and has helped me of late much with organisation of records and papers. She is thus much with me in the centre of things, and no one better than she would know in the years to come how things had been managed, where records were, and, best of all, which workers knew how to carry on what had to be done. I hope her young, bright, intelligent sympathy would know how never to follow past methods mechanically, but to keep heart and mind ever readily open, and listening for the signs of the changes which the years ought to bring, the 'new occasions' which 'teach new duties'[9] only recognised by the 'attentive ear'[10] of the 'good and obedient servant'.[11]

All this deals with the future. It is a great satisfaction to me to be getting it thus carefully planned legally. The spiritual heirship settles itself in gradual ways which we hardly note; it is well from time to time to bring documents and legal conditions into keeping with them. May

---

8   The trustees since the formation of the trust in 1886 had been Octavia, Janet Johnson and Lord Wolmer, now the Earl of Selborne.

---

9   From 'The Present Crisis' by James Russell Lowell (see 1902, p.483).

---

10 Proverbs 25:12 and Ecclesiasticus 3:29.

---

11 Presumably Octavia's version of 'good and faithful servant', Matthew 25:21.

I here record that, in consulting over the Horace Street deeds, I could not but be struck by the ready way in which they lent themselves to the modifications needed by time. It recalled vividly my friend Mr Shaen, and the way he had thought them out. Like all good work they seemed so thoroughly right, and like work conceived by a noble intellect they permit the growth which time demands. It seemed almost like a message from him saying: 'See, I planned what you wanted then, so that it should help what you want now'.

But now to return to the records of the past year. Again the tenants have been to Shere, and again to Sir Frederick Pollock's and to Miss Johnston's; all the days were most successful, and the tenants very heartily enjoyed themselves.[12] As the years pass on, too, there is a sense of personal affection and gratitude on the part of the invited guests which adds much to the value of the day. Lady Selborne asked 50 of the Southwark tenants to Hatfield on the August Bank Holiday.[13] It was a day of steady rain, which was disappointing, but the great interest of the place, and the extreme kindness of all who entertained us, will never be forgotten. Miss Boord invited a group of tenants to Leatherhead, and Miss Townsend one to Weybridge. Both parties were much appreciated.

Dr and Mrs Longstaff again lent their cottage for visits of a fortnight's duration for old couples. It has been a great privilege to invite such from crowded parts of London for a time of peace and restful refreshment.

I have no report on the In Memoriam fund, except to record the expenditure of £150 of the balance. £100 of this was given to Red Cross garden and Hall. I knew it was an object with which the donors would deeply sympathise. There has been a good deal of important work to be done in the garden in radical improvement of soil and other matters. We receive no local help in money, and my ordinary funds would be quite insufficient to make the Hall full of bright life for the neighbourhood, and the garden a place of healthy enjoyment. I have been, therefore, most thankful thus to secure strong support for the

---

12 The *Shere Parish Magazine* again records the day in its August edition of that year: 'On Thursday, July 19th, we had the pleasure of entertaining a large party of Londoners, the tenants of Miss Octavia Hill, in the vicinity of the Marylebone Road. They came down 200 strong, and we spent a very hot but very happy day on the recreation ground... The Londoners declared that they had never had a happier day.'

---

13 The Countess of Selborne was born Lady Maud Cecil. Hatfield is the ancestral home of the Cecil family.

work there. The balance of this £100 is in the Post Office Savings Bank, in the name of the Red Cross trustees, and we are drawing on it weekly for all manner of good things.

Fifty pounds from the In Memoriam fund was given to a boys' club in Southwark,[14] in connection with the cadets. It is being kept together, as well as the cadet corps, under great difficulties, while so many of the officers are away in South Africa, and I was specially glad thus to lighten financial anxieties for those gentlemen who are left.

Brockwell Park, the scheme which was really started by the In Memoriam fund last year, is now an accomplished fact, and 45 more acres are thus added to London's pleasure and playgrounds in the quarter which is most densely populated in proportion to open space.[15] It is true that quite all the money has not been provided, owing partly to the London County Council refusing to pay the legal expenses of the scheme, and partly to the fact that the ground was found on measurement to be rather larger than had been thought. But the land is actually secured, and the liberal guarantors of the balance of purchase money will, one hopes, not be allowed to lose by their public-spirited action. The £1,000 promised and contributed by the In Memoriam fund is held till the purchase is completed by the Kent and Surrey Committee of the Commons Preservation Society. It is on deposit, and has been a most valuable source of revenue to that Committee, pending the final completion of the purchase of Brockwell Park.

The long struggled-for Postman's Park has at last been secured, and was opened last summer.[16] You will remember how at a very critical juncture in the negotiations last year I was able to offer £1,000 from the In Memoriam fund, and how, when I wrote last year to you, I was

14 Although there are no accounts for the In Memoriam fund with the 1900 letter, these two sums for Southwark are shown in the 1901 accounts.

15 The deal took rather longer to complete than Octavia anticipated. £66,800 was needed for the project, and it took most of the following year to get the last £3,500. The purchase was completed on 28 September 1901, when the London County Council became the owners of the property. (Kyrle Society report 1901, p.21.)

16 The combined churchyards of St Leonard's, Foster Lane and St Botolph's, Aldersgate were laid out as a public garden in stages. The way in which Octavia involved herself in this campaign shows how useful it was to for her to have access to different sources of funding. First, in 1898, she reports that the Kyrle Society has given £1,600 towards the purchase (1898, p.418), and that it has 'a further sum in hand towards the amount needed for the last portion of the ground'. Then she mentions that she has added £50 from Lady Jane Dundas's bequest (1898, p.419). In 1899, when the

not sure that this would save it. However, by the combined effort of many friends to 'open spaces' the matter was finally achieved, and the whole garden is now dedicated to the public. A very interesting ceremony its opening was. There was a service in the church, at which the Bishop of London gave an address, with special reference to the records of heroic deeds of the poor, which Mr G.F.Watts has had placed in the garden. They are recorded on simple tiles let into the wall. The tiles are executed by Mr De Morgan,[17] a sort of cloister is formed of

---

campaign was at a crisis point, she promised £1,000 from the In Memoriam fund, over which she had complete discretion, if the other £1,250 needed were raised quickly (1899, p.435). This technique, which has become a standard method of charity fundraising, was successful. The land was known as Postman's Park because postal workers from the main post office in St Martin Le Grand, which bordered the site, used it for relaxation.

---

17 William Frend De Morgan (1839–1917) was in effect William Morris's potter and one of the founding-fathers of British Art Pottery. From 1859 De Morgan studied painting at the Royal Academy Schools, where he met Henry Holiday, a fellow Kyrle supporter. By 1861 De Morgan was involved in stained glass design and it was through his experiments with glass that he noted the effects of iridescence. Later he would apply his discoveries to pottery, emulating the appearance of historic Hispano-Moresque wares, running a successful pottery manufacture from c.1872 to 1907. De Morgan began designing tiles and glass for Morris's firm in 1863. Pottery was one of the few crafts that Morris was not really interested in, although during these early years of the firm, Morris, Marshall, Faulker and Co. founded in 1861, Morris did try his hand at decorating tiles. Once De Morgan showed an interest in ceramics, Morris was happy to let him take over that side of the business. After 1875, when Morris bought out his partners, De Morgan supplied all the firm's ceramics, both tiles and vessels. Being handcrafted and made on a limited scale, first in Chelsea (1872–82), then at Merton Abbey (1882–88) and finally in a purpose-built factory at Sands End, Fulham (1889–1907) De Morgan's wares were not cheap. His patrons were rich, like Lord Leighton, who commissioned him to tile the Arab Hall of his famous house in Holland Park with original antique 'Persian' tiles, filling in any gaps with his own (1879). Under the aegis of the Kyrle Society, 'Whitechapelians' would be brought from the 'East' to see the beauty of the Arab Hall in the West End. Although he was a close friend of Morris, even moving to Merton Abbey where Morris had established his workshops, De Morgan was not interested in his politics. He was first and foremost a designer, chemist and potter, inspired by the past, especially the Italian majolica of the Renaissance.

---

18 Following Renaissance precedent, Watts was committed to didactic and morally edifying public art. He had supported the project to decorate Red Cross Hall with panels commemorating working-class acts of heroism, although the commission went to Walter Crane. However, he fulfilled his dream, at his own expense, in Postman's Park. Watts's homage to the people took the form of a number of tablets by William

wooden pillars and tiled roof, and a long bench for wayfarers runs along it. It is all very simple, very beautiful; and strangely peaceful it looked in the heart of the great city, and with the blue sky showing above the little garden ground, with its fountain and its flowers.[18]

This is what the In Memoriam fund has achieved. The balance I still hold has been used during 1900 mainly as a lever to try to get some more good schemes into working order; but not one of the new large schemes is so far settled and advanced as to enabled me to feel it well actually to pay over the money. I shall hope to succeed in doing so a little later.

The proportion of Lady Jane Dundas's bequest, which I settled to use this year, has been, as you will see, some of it spent in providing water to a country village where no one seemed to have hope enough to start a fund. This gift led the way, and neighbouring owners and others helped largely when the scheme was started. The water is now available for the village, and a thanksgiving service was held this autumn. Another part of the money from this bequest has been lent for an emigration case, and is being conscientiously returned. It has enabled a disabled man to join relatives in the colonies who could support him, and has relieved those who could not do so in this country.

My own donation fund, of which the accounts are appended, has, as you will see, been in the main spent for the old and the sick, and for preparing young people for life. It is a never-ending source of blessing and strength to me to have this fund to turn to. One case among so many which specially interested me was that of a poor woman dying of

---

De Morgan, protected from the weather by a kind of cloister (dated 1898) described by Watts's biographer Wilfrid Blunt as resembling a bicycle shed and, like the heroes it commemorates, rather humble. Thirteen tablets were placed there during the artist's lifetime, 34 by his widow and a further five by public subscription, the last being unveiled by the postmaster general in 1930. The later tablets were made by Doulton, who presumably stepped in when De Morgan's pottery closed in 1907. Space for 90 more remains, but according to *The Times* (5 December 1962): 'no suitable names have been put forward to fill the gap'—a surprising observation, given the occurrence of the Second World War. Several children are commemorated who gave their lives for others even younger than themselves: Solomon, aged 11, 'died of injuries, 6 September 1901. After saving his little brother from being run over in Commercial Street, he said, "Mother I saved him, but I could not save myself"'. Younger still was Harry Bristow, aged eight, who at Walthamstow on 8 November 1890 'saved his little sister's life by tearing off her flaming clothes, but caught fire himself, and died of burns and shock'. Blunt notes that these plaques go unnoticed by users of the garden today, who have little time to spare to remember Ernest Benning, a young composer who 'upset from a boat one dark night off Pimlico Pier, grasped an oar with one hand, supported a woman with the other, but sank as she was rescued'. (Blunt, 1975, pp.218-19.)

cancer, whom it enabled to remain with her husband to the last. One is that of a fine old woman, a tenant of many years' standing, who manfully worked to the last possible day, but who became blind; she is now, thanks to this fund and to a son's help, in a home for the blind, where she is well cared for. There is a large balance in hand. I have subdivided it, as two large items are allotted to special objects not ripe for transfer of the amounts. Even the remaining balance is large, but I can assure my friends who kindly trust me with these moneys, that it is a little difficult to steer clear between opposite evils: on the one hand, I hate hoarding money meant to be generously spent, and which sympathy and time should bring to do living good at once; and, on the other hand, I do feel it incumbent on me to secure a reasonable amount in hand to provide against sudden failure for pensioners and young people's training. I have decided, as a rule, to reserve half-a-year's money for each case. I do not think anyone would feel that too much. I think it enough, for should donations not continue it gives me time to consider cases, and I think I ought rather to trust those who may come after me loyally to carry through responsibilities such as these, should I leave them incomplete, than lock up money intended to be given, not hoarded. I have rather more than this half-year's pledged income in hand at present, but not much more.

We have no new ground secured in the country this year by the National Trust, but we hope for a good scheme for next year in which you may all help. This year the National Trust has been occupied with two schemes for saving some of those charming small buildings which enrich English villages, handed down to us from past ages to tell us what men built and were in the far past, and what loveliness, now increased by the hand of time, buildings once had. One is a Courthouse in Buckinghamshire, a long, low building of the 14th century, timber and tile and plaster, eaves and lattice windows, low doors, and long room with timbered roof, formerly used as a parish room, but, when the Trust took it, condemned as a dangerous structure, and about to be swept away, with its quaint beauty and speaking history. It has been secured, and is being strengthened and made livable in and useful to the parish at a cost of £350: of this about £125 is still needed.[19] The

---

19 The Courthouse, Long Crendon was bought in 1900 from Lady Kinloss, All Souls College and the Ecclesiastical Commissioners for £400. This half-timbered and two-storey building is attributed to the fourteenth century. Court was held there from the reign of Henry V until Victorian times. It was brought to the Trust's attention by the Society for the Protection of Ancient Buildings of which the architect, C.R. Ashbee, was a leading light, as well as being a Council member of the Trust. In 1901

other old building before the Trust is one at Tintagel, for which it also needs funds.[20]

Under the ægis of the Trust, too, the small bit of terrace-like hillside at Toy's Hill, given in memory of Mr Feeney by his relatives, is being made ready for use and enjoyment. Seats have been placed where villagers and visitors can sit and watch the lights and shadows over the whole magnificent sweep of country of which the terrace commands a view. A small tiled roof is being put over the village well, dug by permission of the Trust on its ground; heather, broom and other wild flowers are being brought in and planted, so that the little place will soon look dedicated to all, in memory of one who would have rejoiced that a memorial should take a form so helpful, so unobtrusive, and so lovely.

This letter has, I fear, something monotonous in its character. But, I ask myself, is it not a source of thankfulness that, instead of brand new schemes every year, I have to tell of steady perseverance in those which have been found good; that those who help from year to year are so many of them the same; that the record tells of their faithful and continuous help? Not only thus do the various works prosper and gradually develop, but the places, the people, the outward things, gain a wonderful value to us; the passing years reveal their capacities, their beauties; the steady passing of time among them endears them with a wonderful sense of preciousness. It is a life rather of growth than of change, of development rather than crisis, and this year has been built up on foundations laid and tested in the now far away past.

I am, my friends,
Always yours faithfully,
OCTAVIA HILL

Ashbee became involved with the restoration of the property, which he intended to use as a holiday home for London boys taking art classes—the boys to come via his Guild of Handicraft in Whitechapel. Octavia initially supported the proposal, then suddenly raised such strong objections that Ashbee's plans were overturned, and he resigned from the Trust in protest.

20 This is the Tintagel Old Post Office, a fourteenth-century manor house furnished with local oak furniture. One room used to be used as a letter-receiving room for the district. The building was purchased from Miss Catherine Jones in July 1903 with £200 raised by public appeal. Miss Jones had herself saved it from destruction by raising £300 in funds by selling work by herself and other local artists and by hiring the architect Detmar Blow to renovate the building. She was granted a lifetime interest in the property.

DONATION ACCOUNT, 1900

RECEIPTS

	£	s	d
Cash In hand January 1900	162	11	0½
Allen, A.C., Esq	2	2	0
Anon.	1	1	0
Austin, Miss	1	0	0
Bannerman, Miss Lilias	1	0	0
Bartlett, Miss H.	2	0	0
Beaumont, Somerset, Esq	40	0	0
Blyth, Patrick, Esq	1	1	0
Bridgeman, Charles, Esq	5	0	0
Bridgeman, Mrs	2	0	0
Brooks, Miss	1	0	0
Burgess, Miss S.	0	10	0
Cleveland, Duchess of	50	0	0
Cockerell, Sydney C., Esq	1	0	0
Erle, Miss Eleanor	20	0	0
Forman, Miss	1	1	0
Frankau, Miss (Convalescents)	4	4	0
Gillson, Mrs	10	0	0
Hill, Alfred, Esq	5	0	0
Holy, Mrs	20	0	0
Howitt, Miss	0	10	0
Johnston, The Misses	20	0	0
Johnston, The Misses (vans to Hampstead)	3	0	0
Lee-Warner, Miss	0	7	6
Lowndes, Miss	1	0	0
Lynch, Mrs	100	0	0
Macaulay, Mrs	5	0	0
Mallet, Rev. F.H.	2	10	0
Morris, Francis, Esq	1	1	0
Parkes, F., Esq	1	0	0
Plummer, Rev. Charles	5	0	0
Pollock, Sir Frederick (tenants' fares to Haslemere)	6	10	6
Richardson-Evans, Mrs	1	1	0
Richardson-Evans, Mrs (plants and seats, Toy's Hill)	2	16	3
Roberts, Mrs	2	2	0
Schuster, Mrs	3	0	0
Stone, Rev. E.	2	0	0
Somervell, Gordon, Esq	3	3	0
Singleton, Miss	2	10	0
Todhunter, Miss Annie	1	0	0
Tufnell, Mrs	1	1	0
Wells, Miss	2	0	0
Interest on In Memoriam balance	13	18	10
Loan returned, emigration	14	0	0
	£525	1	1½

DONATION ACCOUNT, 1900

EXPENDITURE

	£	s	d
Pensions	43	2	7
Training and Boarding Out	47	12	1 ½
Relief in Sickness and Infirmity	44	9	1 ½
Excursions and Holidays	22	0	6
Open Spaces	21	16	11
Special Cases	18	16	3
Cadet Corps	15	0	0
Playground, care of	10	8	0
Emigration	9	18	3
Plants, &c.	5	0	5
Craft School	5	0	0
Printing Letter to Fellow-Workers	3	16	0
Stationery and Carriage of Parcels	2	11	3 ½
Labour	2	2	0
London Fever Hospital	1	1	0
In Miss O. Hill's hands (for special object)	100	0	0
In Miss O. Hill's hands (for special object)	55	0	0
Balance (of which a large part is allotted for Pensions, Training, &c.)	117	6	8
	£525	1	1 ½

Examined and found correct, P.L. Blyth.

LADY JANE DUNDAS'S BEQUEST, 1900

EXPENDITURE

	£	s	d
Training of Orphans	29	2	0
Well	25	0	0
Pensions	16	5	0
Emigration	14	1	9
Education	6	4	0
Cadet Corps	5	0	0
Relief	0	10	0
	£96	2	9

Examined and found correct, P.L. Blyth.

LETTER TO MY FELLOW-WORKERS

TO WHICH ARE ADDED

ACCOUNTS OF DONATIONS RECEIVED

FOR

WORK AMONG THE POOR

DURING 1901

BY

OCTAVIA HILL

(FOR PRIVATE CIRCULATION ONLY)

WATERLOW & SONS LIMITED, PRINTERS, LONDON WALL, E.C.

SUMMARY

Housing: Notting Hill, Westminster, Southwark; Ecclesiastical Commissioners' properties in Southwark and Lambeth... tenants in Southwark to pay rates... activities at St Christopher's Hall flourishing, Red Cross Hall less successful... outings for the tenants... donation fund, Lady Jane Dundas's bequest, In Memoriam fund... National Trust: Brandelhow... the inadequacy of the letters to fellow-workers.

EDITOR'S NOTE

In this letter we see Octavia's work expanding on several fronts in a way that takes it up to another level. This year represents the tipping-point in her relationship with the Ecclesiastical Commissioners. In the 1880s they had given her only small groups of properties to manage, often those that were most run-down and due for demolition, whilst keeping an eye on her activities at Red Cross in Southwark on land that they had leased to her. Then, in the 1890s, the Commissioners began building new properties, including many in Westminster, for Octavia to manage. In 1901, however, they involved her in what was to be a major re-development of the Lambeth Estate, involving the complete demolition of several acres of properties and a new road layout. She takes us through this in the next three letters. This would be followed in 1903 by the even more important re-development in Walworth, the largest estate Octavia would manage. Although she never held any official position with the Ecclesiastical Commissioners, Octavia was by this time effectively their residential property consultant. The acquisition of the Brandelhow Park estate on Derwentwater by the National Trust was also significant. It represented by far their largest landholding to date, and the beginning of the enormous influence that the Trust would exert over the management and preservation of the Lake District. Typically, however, Octavia starts the letter with a microcosmic example of why she succeeded in everything she attempted: her 'ever-increasing band of fellow-workers' had complete trust in her judgement. When she needed to buy seven more houses to raise the tone of a street in Notting Hill, Lady Pollock, who had been entertaining her tenants for years, bought one, Miss Christian bought one and got her uncle to buy another, while Mrs Hall, 'who has long been working with me in other parts of London', bought the remaining four. Octavia ends this letter with the longest of her several apologies (see 1873, 1888) for sending out a circular letter at all, rather than writing to her supporters separately.

My friends,

Another year has come and gone, and I write again to tell you of extended and sustained work carried on by an ever-increasing band of fellow-workers, and of the many blessings which have come to us during 1901.

The courts long under our care have continued centres of happy and easy work, where tenants and workers draw closer in bonds of sympathy as time rolls on.

The 20 houses in Notting Hill, to which I referred in last year's letter, have continued a source of grave anxiety financially, and involve most difficult problems with regard to means of raising the standard of life there. But my spirited and faithful workers there do not lose heart, and are supported by the patience and sympathy of the owner. He and we must, I think, feel, in spite of many discouragements, that very sensible progress has been made during the past year. All the houses sublet by non-resident middlemen have now been recovered, and are under our direct control. They have been thoroughly cleansed, and instead of being let furnished by the night, are occupied by families. Tenants of a high class do not readily come into a street long known as disreputable, but we hope our poor friends there—though many of them broken by difficulty, temptation and physical infirmity—may be braced to better things by wise rule in the houses, and by the constant presence among them of those who are set on helping them to do better. We also believe that the light, large, cheerful, cheap, healthy houses, will attract gradually respectable working-class families, as confidence in our steady and firm management increases: these will benefit themselves, and help to influence our poor broken-down tenants. I mentioned last year that we had hope that one more house in the same street would be purchased by a lady, and placed under our management. This was done. Last spring another friend also bought a house and placed it under our care. Late in the year, through the spirited action of our principal worker in the street, we secured the option of purchase of seven more houses, if they were taken all at once. Miss Hewson, who had already bought one house, arranged to take one of

465

these seven. Miss Christian, who had already one, interested her uncle, Colonel Bainbrigge, who bought one. Lady Frederick Pollock bought a third, and Mrs Hall, who has long been working with me in other parts of London, bought the remaining four. The newly acquired houses are immediately opposite some of those previously bought, and the possession of them will greatly strengthen our hands in the effort to redeem the street from disorder. These seven houses were purchased in November, and we are now getting the middlemen to surrender them to us one after another. Each house is thoroughly cleansed and done up, the existing tenancies are considered, some tenants are retained in hope that they may improve, and vacant rooms are offered at reasonable rents to working-class families.

The old houses in Westminster, which we undertook to manage for the Ecclesiastical Commissioners at Michaelmas, 1900, form now part of our regular group,[1] and are in good order, though reduced in number, as some of them have been pulled down and replaced by another kind of building. The Commissioners felt justified in pulling down, partly because the cottages were worn out, partly because they had provided numerous and excellent dwellings for working people in the immediate neighbourhood. Twenty-three of the houses remain and are under our care. I am glad of this, as, greatly owing to the price of buildings, and, in my estimation, to the somewhat Quixotic and unnecessary standard for new houses, it has become most difficult to accommodate the very poor in new buildings. Happily, wages improve, and 'the very poor' are fewer each year.

My friend, Miss Curteis, has decided to build in Southwark a quite small nice block, three storeys high, and containing 29 rooms. Mr Hoole has devised an excellent plan for rendering available an irregular and difficult site. A variety of tenements of three, two, and one rooms are provided with a common yard and common wash-house. They are very simply planned, and, I believe, will be as cheap as rooms can be now, and, I hope, may meet a need. The ground-floor rooms have

---

1   The names of a few streets in Westminster where old properties were turned over to Octavia are known, but their chronology is not. Octavia mentions leases falling in on two occasions: 1900 and 1905. By 1904 Octavia was collecting in Dorset Place and Vauxhall Bridge Road (Minute of the EC Estates Committee, 4 February 1904), and a later list of workmen's tenements notes 127 holdings in old properties in Upper Garden Street and Regency Street. It is possible that the cottages here, and those mentioned subsequently in the 1902 and 1903 letters, are those in Dorset Place and on Vauxhall Bridge Road.

separate front doors, so that they feel like cottages. This block is now in course of erection.[2]

But by far the largest increase of our work has been in consequence of the Ecclesiastical Commissioners asking us to take charge of some of their property, of which the leases fell in, in Southwark and Lambeth.

In Southwark the area had been leased long ago on the old-fashioned tenure of 'lives'. That is, it was held, not for a specified term of years, but subject to the life of certain persons. The lease fell in therefore quite suddenly, and 50 of the houses, which were occupied by working people, were placed under my care.[3] I had only four days' notice before I had to begin collecting. It was well for us that my fellow-workers rose to the occasion, and at once undertook the added duties; well too, that we were just then pretty strong in workers. It was a curious Monday's work. The houses having been let and sublet, I could be furnished with few particulars. I had a map, and the numbers of the houses, which were scattered in various streets over the five acres which had reverted to the Commissioners, but I had no tenant's name, nor the rental of any tenement, nor did the tenants know or recognise the written authority, having long paid to other landlords. I subdivided the area geographically between my two principal South London workers, and I went to every house accompanied by one or other of them. I learnt the name of the tenant, explained the circumstances, saw their books and learnt their rental, and finally succeeded in obtaining every rent. Many of the houses required much attention, and since then we have been busily employed in supervising necessary repairs. The late lessees were liable for dilapidations, and I felt once more how valuable to us it was to represent owners like the Commissioners, for all this legal and surveying work was done ably by responsible and qualified men of business, while we were free to go in and out among the tenants, watch details, report grievous defects, decide what repairs essential to health

---

2   Nelson Buildings. Octavia applied on behalf of Miss E.L. Curteis for a lease on land occupied by 32-40 Holland Street. She had built three three-roomed suites, seven two-roomed suites and six one-roomed suites. These were later sold to the Commissioners in the 1920s, as the owners feared the neighbouring bidders on the property would not prove good landlords.

---

3   A note of 1904, officially sanctioning Octavia's management, lists properties on the following streets as coming into her care in 1901: Argent Street, Loman Street, Golden Place, Great Suffolk Street, Pepper Street, Suffolk Grove, Victoria Place and Whitecross Street.

should be done instantly. We have not half done all this, but we are steadily progressing.

The very same day the Commissioners sent to me about this sudden accession of work in Southwark, they asked me whether I could also take over 160 houses in Lambeth. I had known that this lease was falling in to them, and I knew that they proposed rebuilding for working people on some seven acres there, and would consult me about this.[4] But I had no idea that they meant to ask me to take charge of the old cottages pending the rebuilding. However, we were able to undertake this, and it will be a very great advantage to us to get to know the tenants, the locality, the workers in the neighbourhood, before the great decisions about rebuilding are made. In this case I had the advantage of going round with the late lessee, who gave me names, rentals and particulars, and whose relations with his late tenants struck me as very satisfactory and human. On this area our main duties have been to induce tenants to pay who knew that their houses were coming down (in this we have succeeded), to decide those difficult questions of what to repair in houses soon to be destroyed, to empty one portion of the area where cottages are first to be built, providing accommodation elsewhere for tenants so far as is possible, and to arrange the somewhat complicated minute details as to rates and taxes payable for cottages partly empty, temporarily empty, on assessments which had all to be ascertained, where certain rates in certain houses for certain times only were payable by the owners whom we represent.

All this is occupying our attention at present; the interesting, important, but more straightforward matters relating to the rebuilding

---

4   The poor condition of the Lambeth Estate had been a problem for the Ecclesiastical Commissioners, particularly since the publication of *The Bitter Cry of Outcast London* in 1883, owing to its proximity to Lambeth Palace, the official residence of the Archbishop of Canterbury. On 5 October 1895 the *Clarion* had published an article claiming that: 'Within a stone's throw of the Bishop's palace are some of the ugliest slums and housing in London... To what a pass have our modern ideas of Christianity come, when we have bishops and clergy living in affluence upon the proceeds of the sale, body and soul, of our poor sisters?' The writer was referring to the belief, so common that it passed into folklore, that Church of England property was being used for prostitution. Whatever the truth of this (and it was probably greatly exaggerated), it may have contributed to the willingness of the Commissioners to put their property under the management of Octavia and her ladies, who would not have tolerated such behaviour for a minute. The *Clarion* was a socialist paper founded and edited by Robert Blatchford, a follower of William Morris and author of *Merrie England*. Walter Crane was an illustrator for the paper in 1900s, and Bernard Shaw was a contributor in the years before the Great War, when its circulation peaked at about 74,000.

are for the coming year; about these the Commissioners ask me for suggestions.

Owing to the extension of the work, I am anxious to secure more volunteer workers both in the houses and for accounts.

It may interest some of my readers to know that a movement has taken place in Southwark among almost all the owners of cottage property, to refuse any longer to compound for payment of rates. By this refusal the duty devolves on the occupying tenants. It has long been my belief that the duty ought to rest with the tenants, as they alone elect the local authorities who levy and expend rates, and you will remember that this arrangement has for years been made in many of the cottages under my care. I also attended a conference, many years ago, called by the Charity Organisation Society, in which owners of working-class dwellings were urged to discontinue compounding.[5] At that time no general movement took place. But last year the Southwark Borough Council decided to reduce the allowance for compounding so much that the owners *en masse* allowed their compounding agreements to determine, reduced the tenants' rents in proportion, and now the Council is collecting from the tenants. How the plan will work, whether the owners will remain firm should the Borough Council offer them better terms, or what will happen, I cannot tell. All I am sure of is, that if the owners persevere, and if other parishes follow suit, we shall secure keener criticism of expenditure, which may restrain extravagant measures in London municipal government. At present in Southwark all is chaos. The tenants hate the plan, and profess their utter inability to put by the amount allowed out of their rent weekly. They also feel bitterly that the rates are asked for half-a-quarter in advance. So far as this is done to secure payment it seems right, but surely some allowance ought to be payable to the tenant who pays beforehand analogous to, though not as large as that, to the large owner who compounds; and surely some such arrangement would be to the advantage of the Council, if it be, or could become, legal. So far as the collecting before the date may be due to forestalling income it seems unadvisable, and might be abolished when the bulk of the electors cared to urge it. The landlords, at present, are so united, that the tenants who wish to stay in Southwark have to arrange to pay their rates, though they dislike it; and if they learn to put by their money it may be the

---

5 Compounding was an arrangement for paying the rates on rented property whereby the landlord undertook responsibility for payment, but could claim a 50 per cent reduction if the annual rent was below £7 4s. (Tarn, 1973, pp.34-5.)

beginning of more thrift. One family in our buildings is putting by 1*s* 6*d* a week, which is the amount of the present borough rate, and 2*d* a day in a box to provide once over for the money which will have to be paid in advance on February 14th. Whether the borough council is losing or not we do not yet know. They have the compounding allowance to meet some deficiencies, and at present the tenants are much scared by the summons, 3,000 of which were issued in one day, when the greatest confusion and injustice arose. People were summoned who had paid their rates, and many were summoned for their predecessor's rates. But all this confusion will abate soon, and the tenants will learn how to defend themselves. Let us hope they will be, on the whole, honourable and thrifty. We are not the leaders in this sudden and extended movement. Personally, I should have preferred for the poorer tenants some intermediate step, with a fixed rent and movable rate collected weekly—at any rate, for a time. But if the far more educational plan can be carried through—and it is marvellous how soon our people now learn things—it will be incomparably better, and may save London from much debt and from much waste. In our own houses we issued a form of agreement to each tenant not previously paying rates, stating the present rate, the amount at which his tenement was assessed, the amount we were prepared to reduce his rent now that he would be responsible for the rates. These were almost all returned duly signed, except in one block, where a few tenants led a sort of revolt against the proposed arrangement, and where consequently we were obliged to make many changes of tenants. The new ones are coming in with full recognition of the fresh conditions, and it is in this very block that the satisfactory instance of saving for rates, to which I referred, has occurred.

I can only repeat that the plan has by no means settled into working order, and with the uncertainty of what the Borough Council and what the landlords will do, one can prophesy nothing for the future.

Now to happier and more peaceful thoughts. Our Halls, both St Christopher's and Red Cross Hall, have continued in much use during the past year. At St Christopher's the tenants, old and young, have become, under Mr Hamer's inspiration and guidance, more and more themselves the performers. *Ruddigore* is to be acted in the spring, and last year they came to Red Cross Hall to perform *Pinafore*, which was a great success. The children have been acting a play about King Alfred, written especially for them. We have no such work going on at Red Cross, but friends from a distance are most kind in giving us excellent music and performances. In the pressure of work in the new houses, and in default of an honorary secretary, we had, for the first time in fourteen years, to intermit for a session the entertainments at Red Cross during this autumn, but we managed the Sundays, and now again the Thursdays will be begun, one of my nieces[6] having undertaken to arrange them.

Dr Longstaff's cottage has again been placed at our disposal, and several old couples rejoiced in a fortnight there. The tenants were again invited to Sir Frederick Pollock's and to Miss Johnston's, and greatly enjoyed it, and Lady Selborne took her tenants for a day to Winchester, a great event in the life of several. Miss Townsend also took her tenants into the country.

The donation fund has, as in the days of old, helped many feeble, old and forlorn people, and started some young ones better equipped for the battle of life, and fitter to be useful to men and women in their day. One case only let me mention, that of a lad in a workhouse school known to my sister. He was so incapacitated by asthma as to be unable even to attend the school, and was growing up without any trade or prospect of earning. He was boarded in the country, where he at once got better, attended school and drill, walked, and learnt and enjoyed life, and is now in the Scilly Isles learning bulb gardening, which is lighter work than ordinary gardening, and farm work, and under the watchful care of a clergyman who has started many lads well there.[7]

---

6   This was Elinor Lewes, who in the 1902 letter is described as entertainment secretary (1902, p.486). Elinor was the daughter of Octavia's sister Gertrude. (Gertrude was by this time a widow, her husband Charles Lewes having died at Luxor in 1891.) Elinor had gone to work for Octavia as her secretary in 1899, to the latter's great relief: 'I do really feel as if at last there was someone who could help me with the papers... Please thank your mother for lending you to me thus!' In the 1900 letter Octavia had given a glowing account of her work in connection with her appointment as a trustee of the Horace Street Trust (1900, p.453). Elinor married Carrington Ouvry, Octavia's solicitor, and temporarily gave up working for her aunt, although she then went back to it until her children began to arrive in 1904. Even then, Elinor continued as a Horace Street trustee. Octavia wrote what was probably her last letter to Elinor, explaining that she had left property to her. This was Sarsden Buildings in St Christopher's Place, left jointly to Elinor and her sister Maud. The property was still showing a four per cent return. (Darley, 1990, pp.319, 326, 333.)

---

7   Miranda Hill came into contact with this boy in her capacity as poor law guardian, a position she took up after the closure of the girls' school in Nottingham Place. In 1908 Octavia wrote to her friend Mary Booth to tell her that: 'This room is gay with daffodils sent as a present to [Miranda], with such a nice letter—from a pauper boy she started in the Scilly Isles who is learning to cultivate bulbs.' His health must have improved, because he later emigrated to Australia and went into the hotel trade (1911,

We have several gaps in the ranks of our donors, which in all gratitude should be specially mentioned; one, that of a dear former pupil of ours, who has lovingly followed our work and helped it continuously through her sweet short life, and who desired that a gift should be sent to me after her death for our people;[8] the other, that of the Duchess of Cleveland, who, unknown except by her welcome gift, and unasked, has, for the last few years, munificently helped us. Her large gift will be greatly missed, and I have thought it well, in view of many pensioners, to keep a slightly larger balance in hand this year. My sister-in-law, Mrs Arthur Hill, has also passed away. For many years she has been the kind hostess at Erleigh Court to a large group of tenants, who will long remember her gracious and sympathetic reception of them.

The part of Lady Jane Dundas's bequest, which I decided to expend this year, has been mainly used for training a young lady, an orphan, for useful and independent work, for the support of an orphan child, and for a well in a country village.

Brockwell Park, to which, as I reported, £1,000 of the In Memoriam fund was devoted, has been finally secured and opened to the public. Forty-five more acres of open space have thus been permanently dedicated to the needs of South-East London, which was the worst provided quadrant.

A second £1,000 from the In Memoriam fund has been placed to the credit of the Kent and Surrey Committee of the Commons Preservation Society in order that it might form the inducement to a South-East London parish to organise a scheme for securing as an open space a very important hill-top, commanding a fine view, and close to numberless small houses. Subject to the scheme going through, and that without delay, and to the arrangements being approved by the Kent and Surrey Committee, that £1,000 will be devoted to the acquisition of the hill. Meantime, the interest on the deposit will be available for the general funds of the committee, which is doing most valuable work further afield, that taxes to the utmost its small funds.

And now I come to record the great new achievement of the year,

---

p.659). After Miranda's death his mother wrote to Octavia to tell her that her son owed his life to Miranda. (Darley, 1990, pp.320-21.)

---

8   The 'dear former pupil' was Lilias Bannerman, who had been giving one pound a year since 1896. The gift in her memory was £25. In a reversal of the usual process, her mother inherited the role of Octavia's supporter from her daughter and gave a guinea every year until 1911. In addition, there were donations of one pound (Lilias's amount) made 'In memoriam' of L.B. between 1904 and 1911.

the marvellous success of the appeal for the land on Derwentwater.[9] Little did I think when I referred last year to the large scheme which I hoped would get into practical shape so that you might help to carry it through, that long before the end of the year it would be triumphantly concluded. Many a great anxiety I had before the money really was obtained; the £7,000 we wanted seemed so large a sum; the gifts, welcome as they were, seemed to make so little impression on it; the time for collecting passed so rapidly, the year was said to be so bad a one for collecting money. On the other hand, I had such hope; so many things in my life which had seemed impossible to do had got done in time, the scheme itself was so good a one, the English public had always seemed so appreciative and responsive, and then, too, the letters were so encouraging. Day after day Canon Rawnsley[10] (to whose

---

9   This was the Brandelhow Park estate of 108 acres, with nearly a mile of shoreline, which was offered to the Trust by its owner Colonel Hills for £6,500, providing the purchase price could be raised in six months (*see ill. 32*). The beginning of the Trust's now enormous landholding in the Lakes (it currently controls a quarter of the Lake District National Park) was a tiny plot on Friar's Crag, opposite Brandelhow Park, on which, in October 1900, Hardwicke Rawnsley erected a simple memorial to John Ruskin on which were inscribed the great man's reminiscence: THE FIRST THING/WHICH I REMEMBER/AS AN EVENT IN LIFE/WAS BEING TAKEN BY/MY NURSE TO THE BROW/OF FRIARS CRAG ON/DERWENTWATER. The few square yards round the memorial were the first bit of the Lake District to become the property of the National Trust although, peculiarly, the land is not held, like almost all NT property, in perpetuity, but on a 'tenancy at will' basis. The Lake District was of immense importance to John Ruskin and thus to Octavia. The appeal for Brandelhow, of which the opening by Princess Louise is described in the next letter, was addressed to 'lovers of Ruskin, who once said: "If there is one thing I can boast of, it is that I can be a guide to all the beauty of Derwentwater"'. The Kyrle Society, which had contributed £500, reported that: 'All must feel much gratified at the prospect of securing for the public so beautiful a tract of land in one of the great playgrounds of England, in the country of Wordsworth, Southey and Ruskin.' (Kyrle Society report 1901, p.19.)

---

10   Hardwicke Rawnsley (1851–1920) was educated at Uppingham, under the famous headmaster Edward Thring. He then went to Balliol College, Oxford, where he fell under the spell of Jowett, Thomas Hill Green (the mentor of Arnold Toynbee) and Ruskin, who inspired Rawnsley to join the 'diggers' on the Hinksey Road. He read for holy orders, and his life was destined to be 'one of service', his first contact with the poor coming in 1875 when he volunteered to work in Seven Dials and Soho. Ruskin directed him to Octavia, 'the best lady abbess you can have for London work' (Rawnsley, 1923, p.29). However, the strenuous work in Seven Dials soon broke his health and he went to the Lake District to recover, staying with Mr and Mrs John Fletcher of Ambleside, whose daughter Edith was to become his wife in 1878. In December 1875 Rawnsley was ordained a deacon and soon took charge of the Clifton College

indefatigable energy and unwearied perseverance the scheme owes its success) and I kept receiving letters, one more delightful than the other; some from the young in their exuberance of life; some from the old, rich in memory; some from the rich, with solemn sense of duty; some from the poor, eager to contribute their mite; some from the north, from sense of neighbourhood; some from the south, in gratitude for holiday; some from America, from friends and in thought of kinship and common inheritance of literature; some from our colonies and abroad in thought of English loveliness and dearness.[11] And at last, by the multitude of gifts, the large sum was amassed, and now stands

---

Mission in Bristol. Again he was working with the 'roughest class' but in the company of Frank Barnett, brother of Canon Barnett, Rawnsley made every effort to improve the social life of the poor, with debating clubs and musical evenings. 'Crippled by want of noble surroundings', Rawnsley worked for two years in Bristol, beginning his career as a conservationist. He won the hearts of the locals around to saving the condemned Tower of St Werburgh, which was removed stone by stone to Mina Road, Montpelier. Rawnsley's two passions were the countryside and architectural beauty, a heritage only held in trust which 'we to our children must transmit or die'. (Rawnsley, 1923, p.36.) At the end of 1877 Rawnsley accepted the offer of the living of Wray on Windermere, where his career as champion of the Lake District began. Rawnsley involved himself in local campaigns to protect the countryside from 'rash assault' and 'trains and trippers', and formed the Lake District Defence Society in 1883 (later the Friends of the Lake District) with Tennyson, Browning, Ruskin and the Duke of Westminster amongst its members. In 1883, after five years at Wray, he moved to St Kentigern's Church, Crosthwaite, just outside Keswick. Rawnsley's next project was the founding of the Keswick School of Industrial Art in 1884 (KSIA), with his wife teaching metalwork in the evenings to the local labourers. The idea was to offer a leisure activity for the long winter evenings and training for seasonal employment. This was education for the 'whole working man—to his eye, to his hand, to his heart as well as his head'. (Rawnsley, 1923, p.67.) The battle cry of the Arts and Crafts movement would be head, hand and heart or the 'Three H's'. The KSIA was part of the Home Arts and Industries Association, founded by Mrs Eglantyne Jebb of Ellesmere, and designed to foster rational recreation and seasonal employment. The KSIA developed into a thriving 'peasant industry', and Rawnsley was an integral part of the movement from the first, appearing on the platform at the Art Congress held in Liverpool in 1888, 'where he stood surrounded with shining pots and pans, which he waved before a delighted audience as he expatiated on their merits, their cheapness and their moral influence in raising the tone of the life of their makers'. (Rawnsley, 1923, p.67.) The KSIA lasted until 1986. The National Trust would not have come into being without the shared sympathies, talents and dedication of Rawnsley, Octavia and Robert Hunter.

---

11 'One contributor, referring to himself as "a working man", apologised for being able to send only two shillings: "I once saw Derwent Water and can never forget it. I will do what I can to get my mates to help." Octavia Hill recalled a contribution of 2s

ready in the hands of the National Trust, waiting for the deeds to be completed, and for this lake-side, green with wood and meadow, gray with rock, and commanding view of purple mountain and blue lake, to pass into the possession of the people, for their joy, for their teaching, for their rest and refreshment, the gift of the many, each in due measure, to the many, to be loved and used in honour and gratitude to those who gave, in hope and trust that the gift would be for the joy of all through long years to come.

Now, how shall I thank you all who have helped during the past year, not only with Derwentwater, but in all our work, in houses, for open spaces, with our poor; with all our writing and accounts, our entertainments? How can I thank you all who make our work what it is, so full of helpfulness, so thorough, so full of love and life? This poor little letter, sent once a year, and necessarily so brief and general, seems utterly unsatisfactory, and I would so gladly write to each, individually, some little word of thanks about what I, as we all, owe to him or her. But it cannot be; and I hope each will read between the lines something of the thought that goes with the letter—so various, so living, so individual—as I write my name on the cover, and think just how this or that friend has helped, and what I should like to say in sympathy with the life of each one of my friends and fellow-workers.

Believe me, I am,
Yours gratefully always,
OCTAVIA HILL

6d from a factory worker in Sheffield who said that: "All my life I have longed to see the Lakes" and then added, "I shall never see them now, but I should like to help keep them for others".' (Waterson, 1994, p.45.)

DONATION ACCOUNT, 1901

RECEIPTS

	£	s	d
In hand, January 1901	272	6	8
Allen, A.C., Esq	2	2	0
Austin, Miss	1	0	0
Barlett, Miss H.	2	0	0
B.S. (special pension)	26	8	0
Blyth, Patrick, Esq	1	1	0
Bailey, John, Esq	5	0	0
Bridgeman, Charles, Esq	5	0	0
Bridgeman, Mrs	2	0	0
Booth, Mrs Charles	5	0	0
Beckwith, E.L., Esq	5	0	0
Bannerman, the late Miss Lilias	25	0	0
Brooks, Miss	1	0	0
Cleveland, Duchess of (the late)	50	0	0
Cockerell, Sydney, Esq	1	0	0
Ducie, Earl of	5	0	0
Dawson, Miss	2	0	0
Erle, Miss Eleanor	20	0	0
Evans, Mrs Richardson	1	1	0
Forman, Miss	1	1	0
Frankau, Miss	5	0	0
Fisher, Miss	1	0	0
Fleming, Owen, Esq	1	1	0
Hatfeild, Miss	20	0	0
Haynes, Edmund C., Esq	10	0	0
Howitt, Miss	0	10	1
Hills, J.W., Esq	10	0	0
Johnston, The Misses	23	3	0
Lee-Warner, Miss'	0	10	0
Luxmoore, H., Esq	2	0	0
Leon, Dr John	1	1	0
Lowndes, Miss K.	1	0	0
Langenbach, Mrs	2	2	0
Morris, F., Esq	1	1	0
Martineau, John, Esq	50	0	0
Macaulay, Mrs	5	0	0
Mallet, Rev. H.F.	2	10	0
Parkes, F., Esq	1	0	0
Paddock, Francis, Esq	5	0	0
Pollock, Sir Frederick, tenants' fares	6	15	0
Plummer, Rev. Charles	5	0	0
Roberts, Mrs	2	2	0
Schuster, Mrs	3	0	0
Simpson, Joseph, Esq (the late)	1	1	0
Somervell, Gordon, Esq	2	2	0
Singleton, Miss	2	10	0
Tufnell, Mrs	1	1	0
Thompson, Mrs C.	2	2	0
Tyrrel, Miss Amy	0	10	0
Todhunter, Miss	1	0	0
Wells, Miss	2	0	0
Whelpdale, Mrs	1	10	0
Interest on deposit	2	19	2
	£608	9	11

DONATION ACCOUNT, 1901

EXPENDITURE

	£	s	d
Derwentwater (special gifts)	201	11	5
Pensioners	72	18	5
Training and boarding out	33	11	9 ½
Well, &c.	23	17	8
Relief in sickness or misfortune	18	0	0
Excursions, Holidays and Entertainments	16	6	0
Playground, care of	10	8	0
Long Crendon Court House (special donations)	9	4	0
Convalescent cases	4	2	0
Printing Letter to Fellow-Workers	3	16	0
Stationery and Postage	3	2	2
Labour	2	3	0
London Fever Hospital	1	1	0
Balance, December 1901*	208	8	5 ½

£608	9	11

* The whole of this balance, with the exception of £17, is allocated to special purposes

477

RED CROSS HALL AND GARDEN ACCOUNT, 1901

RECEIPTS

	£	s	d
Balance at Bank, January 1900	4	16	10
Cash in hand	3	7	0 ½
Hire of Hall	12	10	0
Hire of Office	10	8	0
Donations:			
Allen, A.C., Esq	1	1	0
Anon.	0	2	6
Gardiner, Miss	1	1	0
Girton College	1	16	0
In Memoriam, per Miss O. Hill	35	0	0
Lukor, Mrs	0	2	6
Martelli, Francis, Esq	0	10	0
Sheard, Miss	0	10	0
Stevens, Mrs Bingham	0	1	0
Temple, Mrs	1	1	0
Webb, Mrs Randall (for Maypole)	0	10	0
Webb, Mrs Randall	2	0	0
Interest, Red and White Cross Cottages	84	14	4
Programmes, Sale of	4	7	9
Violin Fees	4	3	6
Collections	2	15	9 ½
Gas	0	17	10 ½
Miscellaneous	0	1	0
	£171	17	1 ½

RED CROSS HALL AND GARDEN ACCOUNT, 1901

EXPENDITURE

	£	s	d
Caretakers	58	19	0
Violin Lessons	18	0	0
Entertainment Expenses	16	2	5
Repairs	12	2	11

Garden:			
Repairs	6	9	3
Pigeon Food	1	3	0
Rent	1	0	0
Shears	0	6	0
Grass Seed	0	2	6
Sundries	0	3	0

	£	s	d
	9	3	9
Borough Rates	8	1	6
Printing, Postage and Stationery	7	11	11
Gas	7	9	7
Cleaning	6	7	8
Water Rate	6	2	0
Fuel	3	8	6 ½
Maypole Festival	4	14	0
Fire Insurance	2	9	9
Income Tax	1	17	10
Bank Charges	0	13	0
Cash in hand, December 31st 1901	3	3	2
Balance at Bank	5	10	1
	£171	17	1 ½

479

IN MEMORIAM FUND ACCOUNT, 1901

EXPENDITURE

	£	s	d
South London Open Space (Kent and Surrey Committee)	1,000	0	0
Derwentwater	100	0	0
Red Cross Hall and Garden	100	0	0
Southwark Cadet Corps (Boys' Club)	50	0	0
Tower Hamlets Pension Fund	25	0	0
Kyrle Society	25	0	0
	£1,300	0	0

Examined and found correct, W.O. Ussher

LADY JANE DUNDAS'S BEQUEST, 1901

EXPENDITURE

	£	s	d
Training for work	47	10	0
Well	25	0	0
Orphan Child (boarding in Country)	12	6	6
Pension Case	1	12	6
	£86	9	0

Examined and found correct, W.O. Ussher

LETTER TO MY FELLOW-WORKERS

TO WHICH ARE ADDED

ACCOUNTS OF DONATIONS RECEIVED

FOR

WORK AMONG THE POOR

DURING 1902

BY

OCTAVIA HILL
(FOR PRIVATE CIRCULATION ONLY)

WATERLOW & SONS LIMITED, PRINTERS, LONDON WALL, LONDON, E.C.

SUMMARY

The need to be open to new ideas whilst holding on to old values... housing: Lambeth; Southwark; Westminster; Notting Hill... an office for Octavia... outings and entertainments for the tenants... donation fund, In Memoriam fund and Lady Jane Dundas's bequest... open spaces: Hainault Forest; opening of Brandelhow by Princess Louise... a visit to Edinburgh... the fellowship of fellow-workers... Kymin Hill... death of Caroline Hill.

EDITOR'S NOTE

The 'sameness' and 'monotony' of the letters becomes one of Octavia's regular themes as the years go by—'rather a steady development... than any new departure'—even though the scale of the work was changing. In this letter Octavia reports on the continuing transformation of the seven-acre site in Lambeth for the Ecclesiastical Commissioners, and on the opening of Brandelhow, a major Lake District acquisition for the National Trust. However, she insists that, apart from the scale, nothing else is changing. 'If we keep firm hold of the dream of our youth... and if we tune our spirits to the heavenly harmonies, then... our life's work develops in slow progressions, like a tree growing.' Octavia's fellow-workers always knew that they could rely on her to hold onto the dream of her youth. No matter how big the budget, she would never waste money; no matter how complex the arrangements, she would never allow a bureaucratised 'system' to replace the individual attention she gave to every problem and every person she came into contact with.

(190 Marylebone Road, N.W.)

(December, 1902)[1]

My friends and fellow-workers,

Another year has rolled over, leaving us, I trust, better, stronger in hope, more united to one another, and richer in gathered memories. It does not seem to me, looking back over this past year, that I have anything very striking to record. The work which I have to chronicle is rather a steady development on the old lines than any new departure; it is growth rather than change. And this is best so, provided we are all sure that we have kept ourselves attentive to the low whispers which should teach us where and how we were wrong, or how the new times call us to different methods. We who grow old specially should strive to keep an open heart, a quick eye and a ready ear for the facts which should teach us how:

> New occasions teach new duties; Time makes ancient good uncouth;
> He must onward still and upward, Who would keep abreast of Truth.[2]

But there are the things that do change, the methods, the special needs, the readiness of men to do or to see, and there are things which do not change, the aims, the motives, the right spirit; and if we keep

---

1   Octavia's mother Caroline Southwood Hill died on 31 December 1902, when Octavia was sending this letter to the printer. It had been written earlier in the month when Octavia was staying with her mother at Tunbridge Wells. From 1902 onwards, Octavia occasionally omitted her address from letters. Where the address is supplied by the editor, it is given in brackets.

---

2   From 'The Present Crisis' by American poet James Russell Lowell (1819–1891). The line is actually: 'They must upward still, and onward...'. Born in Cambridge, Massachusetts, in 1877 Lowell was appointed minister to London, where he remained until 1885. Lowell did much to increase the respect for American letters in Europe, and was a favourite of Octavia, who used to read aloud from his works to her guests. Octavia had met him in 1882 at Tortworth Court, the country house of the Earl and Countess of Ducie. She was invited to the unveiling of the memorial to him in Westminster Abbey in November 1893. (Maurice, 1914, pp.446 and 528.)

firm hold of the dream of our youth, if that dream was a right one, and if we tune our spirits to the heavenly harmonies, then sometimes we need have no sudden revulsions and changes, but our life's work develops in slow progression, like a tree growing, and the changes are almost unnoticed except when one looks back over many years. So I do not regret to have no special new departures to record, only let us be sure that there is growth, and that the absence of change is not because of dulness in apprehension of the new needs which life must bring.

To turn first to our work in the houses. It has continued much as before. The seven acres in Lambeth which the Ecclesiastical Commissioners are rearranging and rebuilding are getting into shape.[3] Twenty-six new cottages,[4] light, dry, convenient and clean, now stand where the old ones did, and all were let before they were finished. Eighteen tenements of three rooms each will, before this is in your hands, probably be completed and occupied;[5] the same number are now being built, and the larger part of the scheme, comprising many other dwellings, the new streets and public recreation ground, will be at once proceeded with. They have been postponed hitherto in order not to displace too many families at once. The high cost of building, the rise of rates, the—sometimes absurd—requirements of local bodies make it impossible to reaccommodate families at the same rents as in the old houses. This makes it, to my mind, a very great duty on the part of owners and local authorities to preserve so far as possible all old

---

3   This refers almost certainly the land now bounded by Webber Street to the west, the Cut to the north, Short Street to the east and Ufford Street to the south. The leases were to fall in at Michaelmas 1901, and plans were being made for rebuilding at least as early as February. The initial proposals from Cluttons to the EC were fairly ambitious. They made provision for 36 tenements and 24 new cottages at a cost of £71,000. The plans also included building a new road in lieu of Caffyn and Mitre Street, and making space for a public library, two mission houses and a recreation ground. (Letter from Cluttons to the EC, 13 February 1901). An article in the *Daily Express* at the time calculated that 212 houses were to be demolished, displacing 277 families, including 630 adults. (*Daily Express*, 13 April 1901.)

---

4   The first wave consisted of 26 cottages, built for £10,000 on the south side of Ufford Street, and comprising 20 four-room cottages and six five-room cottages, each with a washhouse and yard. (Letter from Cluttons to the EC, 20 February 1902.) Another three were added in May 1902. (Letter from Cluttons to the EC, 9 May 1903.) *See ills. 22 and 23.*

---

5   This refers to three tenement buildings, each with six three-room suites, built on Short Street in July 1902. (Letter from Cluttons to the EC, 9 July 1902.)

houses occupied by the poor, always supposing the drains and roofs are sound, and the rooms dry and light. The fashion of clearing away, which makes a grand show, has, in my estimation, gone quite far enough. Of course, where, as in Lambeth, an area has to be rearranged, the duty is wholly different. But then it becomes no longer a question of housing the poorest, one must build as cheaply as possible and as simply, but the standard will be more in keeping with modern requirements, and one must look to the steady workman who spends all he can on his home, who lays by against the time of slack work, whose wages correspond to his value, to occupy rooms in the new surroundings, in an area which then fulfils a different public requirement, that of providing happy, healthy, cheerful and really comfortable houses for the workmen who are better off, leaving to the old houses, thoroughly supervised, the provision of the cheapest homes for the poorest, till the happy day when rates fall, or building costs less, or migration to the suburbs diminishes pressure. So pause before you destroy an old house which is, or can be made, healthy. But I have wandered from our own new area in Lambeth. I think if you saw it you would be happy in it, and would feel that it was meeting a really great need, for it is not easy now in London at any reasonable price to secure anything like such pretty comfortable home-like places for the tidy families who care for their homes. It has been a great labour during the past year to deal with this area. The management of the old houses on healthy conditions, yet without large expenditure on cottages which were to be pulled down in a few months, has needed much judgment; the regularity with which tenants have paid their rents under such circumstances has won my respect, it has only been when under notice that arrears have accumulated, and this is far more in consequence of the absurd and unjust state of the law than owing to the tenants' own action. The payment and recovery of rates and taxes for all sorts of various intervals for individual small cottages has been most complicated, and the new cottages have required much care and labour in the selection from a large number of applicants of the most suitable residents. I owe very much to the zealous and able help of my friend Miss Lumsden, who has done the bulk of this work for some little time, and who will, I hope, enter now into permanent charge of the steadily increasing new colony.[6] I should like here to record how much I owe to the unwearied, kind and efficient co-operation of the officers of the Ecclesiastical

---

6 But not for long. In the following year Octavia would move Miss Lumsden to Walworth, to oversee what would be a much bigger and more coherent development.

Commissioners, who have advised and supported us ably and promptly about all technical matters.

So much for Lambeth. Far different are the circumstances at Nelson Buildings, the new block of 29 rooms built by Miss Curteis, in Southwark, which came into letting last July. There we have an instance of what can now be done with economy and care in new buildings of the simplest construction, in one-, two- or three-roomed tenements; we are able there to let at 3s a room, and each family can take more rooms directly they need them. These rooms appear to have met a want, and are well let.

We have taken over the management during the past year of a number of old houses in Westminster, and the Ecclesiastical Commissioners are building two more new cottages there.[7]

In Notting Hill the seven houses which I mentioned in my last letter as purchased by a group of my friends, have been taken over, a good deal done to them to make them fitter homes for working people, and though the reputation of the streets and its surroundings are still a great difficulty, we feel that real progress has been made there. One friend has bought three more houses there, and another friend has leased a fourth, so that we now have in that district 45 houses.

I have this year taken an office adjoining our house and communicating with it. This gives me room for papers and place for a secretary to work, and allows me, for the first time, to have responsible permanent help at the centre of my work without interfering with home quiet. The mere business connected with so large a number of houses and owners involves much detailed clerical work, and the possibility of delegating some of it ought to leave me freer for the larger duties which open out before me.

The halls and the summer parties have gone on much as in previous years. One of my nieces has kindly undertaken a great deal of the work at Red Cross Hall, she is now entertainment secretary.[8] The same kind groups of friends continue to help us on Thursdays and Sundays. Miss Johnston and Lady Pollock again invited the tenants to summer parties, which were greatly enjoyed, and we were again able to go to my brother's at Erleigh, recalling many a happy day of long ago. Dr Greville MacDonald, too, invited us to Haslemere, a fact which vividly recalled

---

7   Erected in Dorset Street at a cost of £790. (Letter from Cluttons to the EC, 23 October 1902.)

---

8   See 1900, p.471, n.6.

the days we spent in his father's garden, when all the conditions of work and life were so much harder, when the work was small and unknown, and the sympathetic hospitality such a cheer in difficulties.[9] Dr Longstaff's cottage has received its fortnightly guests from among the old, the desolate and the weakly.

The donation fund, concerning which the accounts are attached, has kept up its perennial spring, and the names of many faithful helpers will be again found among the donors. The In Memoriam fund has helped with a large sum towards remedial treatment of consumption, a greatly needed and costly form of help.[10] The bequest from Lady Jane Dundas, of which I decided to spend a certain amount annually, is drawing towards its close.[11] There would be much to tell of what it has done if we were to review its use since the bequest reached me. This year I devote it to the Hainault Forest scheme for getting a tract of land for the benefit of East London and its Essex off-shoots. The land is

---

9   Greville MacDonald (1856–1944) was the fourth child and eldest son of Octavia's great friend George MacDonald (1905, p.537, n.5). As a boy he always felt that his father had a 'down' on him and favoured his elder sisters. He was backward in his lessons. Staying with the MacDonalds in Bude in 1867, Octavia befriended Greville and gave him coaching in Latin. After that he never looked back. He qualified as a doctor and became a distinguished Harley Street ear, nose and throat specialist. He was chairman of the Peasant Arts Fellowship, which became the Peasant Arts Guild in 1917. It had begun as the Haslemere Peasant Industries, a class affiliated to the Home Arts and Industries Association. He wrote an authoritative biography of his father, *George MacDonald and His Wife*, which was published (with an introduction by G.K. Chesterton) in 1924.

---

10   The accounts at the end of this letter shows £500 given for the 'open air treatment of consumption'. Tuberculosis was, in those days, incurable and almost invariably quickly fatal.

---

11   Octavia included lists of grants made from Lady Jane Dundas's bequest of £1,000 with the letters for 1898, 1899, 1900, 1901 and 1902, by which time the grants totalled £641 8s 1d. The reason for the slowness in distributing the legacy is the approach Octavia adopted: most of the beneficiaries were individuals who had fallen on hard times, for whom £5 would have been a lot of money. Thus, we come across a 'thrifty widow, aged 74' (£2 12s), 'perfumer, consumptive' (£1 14s 6d) and an 'aged couple ruined by Liberator failure' (£9 15s). The only substantial grants were £50 for Postman's Park (1898) and £100 for Hainault Forest (1902). This leaves about £400 unaccounted for, given that the sum would have been earning interest, but of course Octavia was under no obligation to give a full account to the fellow-workers. Presumably Lady Jane Dundas's executors would have received the complete list of grants. In 1904 Octavia reported that interest was still accruing on the balance (1904, p.524), and in 1905 she lent £50 'for the professional education of a lady' (1905, p.547).

within 12 miles of St Paul's, nearer of course to the East End, within easy access on foot, by bicycle, tram, and train, to the teeming population of our poorest part of London. Ours was one of the first gifts in the early beginning of the scheme, and we are proud to think that we met the initiators of it in their difficult beginnings.[12]

Beginnings how difficult, accomplishment how triumphant! Let us turn from Hainault to Brandelhow.[13] In October we had the great joy of seeing the land, longed for so much, bought with such effort, opened for the nation. It was a wild windy day,[14] but the lights could not have been lovelier, gleams of glorious sunshine sweeping over russet fern, golden beech, greenest grass, chasing cloud shadows on Skiddaw and Blencathara,[15] shining on the lake far below studded with its islands. The Princess Louise was there to open it in the name of the National

---

The accounts for 1908 show £13 4s 6d given to the Red Cross Hall, and those for 1909 show the 'balance' of £50 going to the donation fund. Presumably this represented the end of the bequest fund, more than a decade after Octavia had received it.

---

12 See 1903, p.509 for further developments on Hainault.

---

13 The Brandelhow estate of pasture and woodland lies on the west shore of Derwentwater, at the foot of Catbells. At the time when Octavia and Hardwicke Rawnsley were struggling to raise the funds to buy it, Beatrix Potter used the lake in some of the illustrations to her third tale—*The Tale of Squirrel Nutkin*. St Herbert's Island is recognisable as Owl Island in the story. Beatrix Potter's father Rupert was a friend of Hardwicke Rawnsley and the first life member of the National Trust. It was he who introduced his daughter to the Lake District, with which she fell in love. She used the royalties from her tales to buy Hill Top farm in Sawrey, and sold her drawings in the USA to raise funds to buy properties for the Trust on the shores of Lake Windermere. When she died in December 1943 she bequeathed to the Trust 14 farms and 4,000 acres, together with her extensive flocks of Herdwick sheep, so-called after Hardwicke Rawnsley who founded the Herdwick Sheep-Breeders Association in 1899 to save a threatened species.

---

14 *See ill. 31.* 'The scene was really most beautiful and very funnily primitive. The great tent was blown to atoms; and the little red daïs was out under the free sky... and the nice north country people quite near, and so happy and orderly.' (Letter from Octavia to her sister Emily, 16 October 1902, Maurice, 1914, p.553.)

---

15 These are two of the finest sites in the Lake District. It was the issue of protecting the Latrigg footpath skirting Skiddaw that first brought Hardwicke Rawnsley into contact with the Commons Preservations Society. The issue almost went to court but a settlement secured public access to the path. Both Skiddaw, the 'top with rosy light' and Blencathara's 'rugged feet' where 'Sir Lancelot gave safe retreat' are mentioned in William Wordsworth's 'Benjamin the Waggoner' Canto IV.

Trust, of which she is now president;[16] her presence recalled a day now many years ago when she came, an early friend to the open space movement, to open a little walled-in garden in London, one of the first churchyards turned into a people's garden, a little oasis still among the bricks and mortar, a space where children can play and the feeble may rest in the open air, but all surrounded by smoky London, and where even the spring leaves soon are blackened.[17] 'That day to this', I seemed to hear whispered in my ear, 'such progress one lives to see', for I thought of the growth of interest in open spaces, of the few helpers in the old time, of the thirteen hundred donors to Brandelhow, sending donations from crowded Lancashire towns, from quiet English country homes, from distant India and South Africa, some rich, some poor, some old, some young, all caring and giving, to preserve for the nation one of its fairest spots. And a triumphal song of thanks and joy seemed to be ringing around us as if the spirits gone before, and the English scattered over the far-away parts of the earth, and the dwellers in crowded courts, and the men and women that shall inherit the earth after we have gone, were rejoicing with us.

I have had another happy visit North this autumn. I went to Edinburgh to see a group of managers of houses who asked me to come and see their work.[18] I found a much larger piece of work going

16 This was the first National Trust property to be opened by a member of the royal family. Princess Louise, Queen Victoria's fourth daughter, became the second president of the National Trust following the Duke of Westminster, who had died in 1899. Octavia told her mother that the Princess had requested the presidency for herself at this ceremony. 'I hoped you would ask me, I should really like to do more for the work, and I should like Lord Carlisle as vice president.' (Moberly Bell, 1942, p.239.) Lord Carlisle represented the trustees of the National Gallery on the Council of the Trust. The Princess, the Duke of Argyll, Octavia Hill, Hardwicke Rawnsley and Robert Hunter each planted an oak tree.

17 Octavia is referring to the opening of the burial ground of St George's, Hanover Square as a public garden on 1 July 1884 (1883, p.169, n.1). On 25 April 1884 Octavia had written to her sister Emily saying that the opening of the churchyard would have to take place in late June, depending on the state of the grass. 'I think the absence of any square space a difficulty. There is no space for speaking or gathering people together. If we could have had anything like our May festival, and had the poor in, I should have liked it; but I see no space for anything but a procession, which would hardly do. Perhaps some brilliant idea will be suggested...' (Maurice, 1914, p.450.)

18 The Edinburgh Social Union had been set up by Patrick Geddes (1854–1932), pioneer of town planning, and Elisabeth Haldane (1862–1937) in 1885. Elisabeth

on than I had realised, much of it was of the very kind which seems to me most useful, and to depend most on such a set of workers. They have tried what could be made of the old Edinburgh houses, just securing cleanliness, light, ventilation, good water, and preventing overcrowding. Doing this, they are able to accommodate the same tenants at the same rents, and to make order and friendliness succeed to disorder and misrule. They are also managing new tenements. They are collecting some £6,500 per annum in rents, are about 30 in number, and the movement has been going on steadily for many years. One day the delegates from Glasgow, Perth and Dundee were good enough to come over; in all these cities similar organisations are at work. It was very pleasant to realise how many ladies were thus managing houses, and to talk over our common difficulties and successes.

And now may I end my letter with again thanking my own great and good group of ever ready and helpful workers, some new, some old, some helping this way, some that, some still in our immediate circle, some colonising, as it were; we have no formal bond of membership, we need none; our common work, our common hope, our common fellowship, makes us somehow into one body, not the less nearly bound because the bond is wholly spiritual and no way rigid. I remember long ago the workers and tenants used to amuse me by talking about 'one of us' when there was no definite describable link, but I think the

---

Haldane had gone to work for Octavia at the age of 20, and had acquired sufficient sympathy with, and technical knowledge of, the work to carry it north of the border. She was the sister of Richard, later 1st Viscount Haldane, who, when he was secretary of state for war, would preside at a display put on by the cadets at Caxton Hall (1908, p.596). The ESU became the first such body to take on the management of local authority housing and by 1900 it was managing Edinburgh City Council's entire housing stock. Unfortunately, the ESU experienced the sort of political interference which Octavia always warned would bedevil municipal housing, and they eventually withdrew from the arrangement. However, according to C.S. Loch: 'the outcome was a triumph for [Octavia's] method. So great was the confusion and the maltreatment of property by the tenants that the lady collectors were invited to return to their work, the efficiency of which is now fully acknowledged.' (Loch, 1912, p.162.) The ESU is listed as a 'provincial' Kyrle Society in the Kyrle's annual reports, although its members may not have seen themselves in quite that light. The scope of its activities varied over the years, sometimes covering industrial art, industrial law and health, but its core areas of concern were housing, decoration and 'window gardening'. The text of Octavia's address to the AGM of the ESU on 21 November 1902 can be found in Whelan (1998) pp.114-21. The chairman of the meeting spoke of Maurice, Kingsley and Ruskin as 'the giants from whom we have learnt and drawn inspiration', and referred to the privilege of hearing about them from Octavia, who had known all three. (Maurice, 1914, p.554.)

years have justified the phrase and that there is among those I am proud to call 'my fellow-workers' a certain real link, though sometimes now their duties lie in far other fields, and their work is larger than mine, and quite independent of mine, something that would make it true still to feel, even if one would hesitate to say, that he or she is 'one of us'. It would mean fellowship in a large and noble company.

As I have spoken of open spaces, I may commend to your notice the one for which we are now working, the nine acres forming the top of Kymin Hill, near Monmouth. It seems to combine the advantages of the town and the country ones, as it is accessible, like the town ones, to many thousands in the year, and has the wide view over hill and dale which, in general, belong more to the country ones. It has also its associations with Nelson and Britain's admirals, and our nation's sea life, to which we owe so much. Only £100 remains to be raised. I know many of you do give, and have given, largely to open spaces and other objects, and the last thing I should wish would be to spoil the joy of gift by undue asking or pressure. But I mention it as a good thing that needs doing by any who have the power and a spontaneous wish to give towards a permanent possession for England's good.[19]

OCTAVIA HILL

This letter was written while I was staying with my mother at Tunbridge Wells. Now that I am sending it to the press, I have to record that she has left us, that no more on this earth we can carry to her our completed work for her approval, nor turn to her for sympathy in its progress.[20] But that inspiration which has been for now our long lives drawn from her love, from her lofty nature and utter devotion to duty, will not cease because she has passed before us into light, and we have to trust our hearts to hear what she would teach us.

---

19 The top of Kymin Hill overlooks Monmouth and the Wye Valley. The people of Monmouth donated the Kymin in 1902 after having used this beauty spot for many years as the site for Tuesday open-air lunches for the gentlemen of the town. The Kymin came with a monument—the Naval Temple, opened in 1802 as a tribute to great British admirals including Lord Nelson. The nine acres around it were purchased for £300. Hardwicke Rawnsley was outraged by early graffiti: 'The abominable habit of scribblers who visit Kymin Hill has rendered the inscription almost illegible'. (Rawnsley, 1920, p.41.)

---

20 Caroline Southwood Hill had died on 31 December 1902 at the age of 93. She was staying with her daughter Gertrude Lewes at 6 Cambridge Terrace, St Pancras.

DONATION ACCOUNT, 1902

RECEIPTS

	£	s	d
In hand, December 1901	208	8	5 ½
Allen, A.C., Esq	2	2	0
Andrewes, Mrs F.W.	1	1	0
Andrewes, Mrs Herbert ...	1	1	0
Anon.	0	10	6
Ashe, Mrs	3	0	0
Austin, Miss	1	0	0
Bailey, J., Esq	10	0	0
Bainbridge, E.P., Esq	2	2	0
Bainbrigge, Colonel	4	10	0
Bannerman, Mrs	1	1	0
Bartlett, Miss H.	2	0	0
B.S.	15	0	0
Blyth, Patrick, Esq	1	1	0
Bosanquet, Charles B.P., Esq	1	0	0
Bridgeman, Charles, Esq ...	5	0	0
Brooks, Miss	1	0	0
Chase, Miss	1	0	0
Cockerell, Sydney, Esq	1	0	0
Covington, Mrs Stenton ...	0	5	0
Cudworth, Mrs	2	2	0
Dawson, Mrs	2	0	0
Ducie, The Earl of	5	0	0
Evans, Mrs Richardson ...	1	1	0
Fisher, Miss	2	0	0
Forman, Miss	1	1	0
Frankau, Miss	5	0	0
Friend, A, per Mrs Greene	10	0	0
Gillson, Mrs	3	0	0
Greene, Mrs	20	0	0
Hills, J.W., Esq	10	0	0
Hoole, Elijah, Esq	2	2	0
Howitt, Miss M.	0	10	1
Hutton, Mrs John	3	3	0
In Memoriam, L.B.	1	0	0
Johnston, The Misses ...	20	0	0
Johnston, The Misses (Vans for Party entertained at Hampstead)	3	0	0
Langenbach, Mrs	2	2	0
Leon, Dr	1	1	0
Luxmoore, H., Esq	2	0	0
Macdonell, Mrs James	1	15	0
Macaulay, Mrs	4	0	0
Mallet, Rev. H.F.	2	10	0
Martelli, Miss A	0	10	0
Morris, F., Esq	1	1	0
Paddock, Francis, Esq	5	0	0
Plummer, Rev. Charles	5	0	0
Poynter, Ambrose, Esq	2	0	0
Roberts, Mrs	2	2	0
S.B. for Coronation Treat	70	0	0
Schuster, Mrs	5	0	0
Schuster, Miss	5	5	0
Simpson, Miss	1	0	0
Singleton, Miss	2	10	0
Somervell, Gordon, Esq ...	3	3	0
Sprague, Dr	10	0	0
Stanhope Buildings (Directors for Coronation Treat)	33	0	0
Stone, Rev. E.D.	5	0	0
Todhunter, Miss	1	0	0
Tufnell, Mrs	1	1	0
Tyrrel, Miss	0	10	0
Wells, Miss	2	0	0
Yorke, Miss H.	1	0	0
Interest on Deposit	41	0	8
	£563	11	8 ½

DONATION ACCOUNT, 1902

EXPENDITURE

	£	s	d
Excursions, for Tenants, from two Special Gifts from Owners of Houses for this purpose	112	3	9
Pensions	67	8	8
Training and Boarding Out	59	7	3
Relief in Sickness and Infirmity	33	7	10
Planting and Laying Out Gardens in Westminster	10	10	11
Playground, Care of	10	8	0
Employment	9	3	6
Excursions and Holidays (ordinary)	11	7	6
Houses, Gift to	2	10	0
Stationery and Carriage of Parcels	2	8	8
London Fever Hospital	1	1	0
Printing Letter to Fellow-Workers	3	16	0
In Hand★	239	18	7 ½

£563	11	8 ½

★ This sum includes interest on the In Memoriam deposit just received, otherwise it is all appropriated for pensions, training and other special objects.

RED CROSS HALL AND GARDEN ACCOUNT, 1902

RECEIPTS

	£	s	d
Balance at Bank, January 1902	5	10	1
Cash in hand, January 1902	3	3	2
Interest, Red and White Cross Cottages	65	7	4
Hire of Hall	17	15	0
Hire of Club Room	9	1	0
Hire of Office	7	16	0
Sale of Programmes	6	3	2
Violin Class Fees	4	8	0
Collections on Sundays	3	1	0
Donations:			
Allen, A.C., Esq	1	1	0
Anon.	6	5	0
Blyth, Patrick, Esq	1	1	0
Bridgeman, Mrs	2	0	0
Elliman, Mrs	1	1	7 ½
In Memoriam	10	0	0
Macaulay, Mrs	1	0	0
Martelli, F., Esq	0	10	0
Nicholson, Lady	0	10	0
Schmitz, Miss	0	10	6
Schuster, Mrs	5	0	0
Stevens, Mrs Bingham	0	1	0
Temple, Mrs	1	1	0
Townshend, Miss	1	0	0
Webb, Mrs Randall	2	0	0
Williams, Mrs	0	5	0
Yorke, Miss	5	15	0
Gas	0	7	0
	£161	12	10 ½

RED CROSS HALL AND GARDEN ACCOUNT, 1902

EXPENDITURE

	£	s	d
Caretaker	59	2	0
Violin Lessons	18	10	0
Borough Rates	12	7	11
Entertainment expenses	10	11	0
Garden:			

	£	s	d			
Repairs	3	3	0			
Paint	1	17	6			
Pigeon Food	1	3	10			
Rent	1	0	0			
Sundries	0	5	0			
				7	9	4

	£	s	d
Printing, Postage and Stationery	6	19	4 ½
Cleaning	6	16	7 ½
Gas 6	2	9	0
Water Rate	6	2	0
Repairs	4	15	5
Maypole Festival	4	2	5
Fuel	3	10	0
Income Tax	2	6	8
Fire Insurance	2	5	3
Bank Charges	1	3	6
Land Tax	0	4	7
Plate Glass Insurance	0	4	6
Cash in hand, December 31st 1902	1	15	11 ½
Balance at Bank	7	3	7
	£161	12	10 ½

Verified and found correct, P.L. Blyth, January 12th 1903

LADY JANE DUNDAS'S BEQUEST, 1902

EXPENDITURE

	£	s	d
Open Space (Hainault)	100	0	0
Training for Profession	66	2	0
	£166	2	0

IN MEMORIAM FUND ACCOUNT, 1902

EXPENDITURE

	£	s	d
Open Air Treatment of Consumption	500	0	0
	£500	0	0

LETTER TO MY FELLOW-WORKERS

TO WHICH ARE ADDED

ACCOUNTS OF DONATIONS RECEIVED

FOR

WORK AMONG THE POOR

DURING 1903

BY

OCTAVIA HILL

SUMMARY

Ecclesiastical Commissioners: 22 acres in South London taken on for the creation of the Walworth Estate; management by the Ecclesiastical Commissioners preferable to the sale of long leases... other housing work: Notting Hill... Ecclesiastical Commissioners: seven acres in Lambeth coming to completion and additional cottages in Westminster... difficulties in Notting Hill... the need for additional workers: six months' training offered... Red Cross Hall and St Christopher's Hall... a new building for the cadet corps... fundraising for the Kyrle Society... fewer outings for the tenants... open spaces and the National Trust: Hainault, Kymin Hill, Mariner's Hill... the donation fund.

EDITOR'S NOTE

1903 is the Walworth Letter. In this letter and the following two, Octavia relates, in unusual detail, the process by which she became involved with the demolition and rebuilding of 22 acres in Walworth under the Ecclesiastical Commissioners. Cluttons were, as usual, the Commissioners' managing agents, so Octavia could not appoint her favourite architect Elijah Hoole, but it is clear that her input was considerable. The estate, which is still intact, is a splendid example of urban planning which reflects all of Octavia's most deeply held views. The roads are spacious and tree-lined, there is a large open space, and the properties are all built on a human scale in a picturesque style. It was the largest estate which Octavia managed and it became her showpiece. She was so keen to make it work that she moved Miss Lumsden from Lambeth, to which she had only recently been appointed, to take charge. It seems peculiar that the Ecclesiastical Commissioners were once again toying with the idea of disposing of 80-year leases on the estate, 20 years after Octavia had persuaded them to drop the practice. She was worried enough about it to give the difference of opinion an airing in this letter. Predictably, she was able to report in 1904 that the Commissioners had backed down.

190 Marylebone Road, N.W.
(January, 1904)[1]

My friends,

I am writing to you in the opening year, and my thoughts are dwelling on the past and on the future; on the past with thankfulness, on the future with hope. How deep the causes for thankfulness are! Even those great losses which have marked our lives with an impression which no time can efface are but fresh proofs that, in the deepest sense, there can be no loss, that:

There shall never be *one* lost good.[2]

We know that all we have loved is ours now, and shall be for all eternity. So we clasp closer the memory of our past, and walk on fearless towards the future.

The past year has brought one very large expansion of our work, larger than that in any previous year; and it is started on independent lines, in a way which gives hope for future growth. The Ecclesiastical Commissioners wrote to tell me in the autumn that an area in South London containing 22 acres, and with between 500 and 600 houses on it, was falling in to them at the expiration of a long lease, and they asked me to undertake the management of the property. Bearing in mind what they themselves had said as to providing for the continuity of such work, and with a deep desire not to lose near touch with my own old tenants, workers and places, if I spread my time over still larger areas, I set myself to think whether this new work might not be started from a new centre. Never during the 40 years I have been at work could I have done this under such favourable circumstances. My friend, Miss Lumsden, whom I mentioned in last year's letter as helping in Lambeth, was settled in London, and though she would be a great loss in Lambeth, I felt that the new work was far more difficult to get done,

---

1   Octavia was writing 'in the opening year'.

---

2   From 'AbtVogler', ix, by Robert Browning. See also 1876, p.68.

and that she had rare capacity to do it. She consented to undertake the work, and I introduced her to the Commissioners, and advised that they should appoint her for this new centre. I could have supervised the new area with a larger staff, but it would have separated me more from my own old haunts; it would have wasted force, for, had I been responsible, I must have followed all decisions, whereas Miss Lumsden was quite capable of making them, and would do so more quickly, and with more living knowledge of the people and places if she were really in authority.

But it was a huge undertaking and needed much care and labour to start it well, and naturally we were all keen to help. It was a great day when we took over the place. Our seconds in command took charge manfully for a fortnight of all our old courts, and fourteen of us, including all my own most responsible workers, one lady who had gained experience in Edinburgh, and one or two married ladies who used to help long ago, met on Monday, October 5th, to take over the estate, and collect from 500 or 600 tenants wholly unknown to us. We organised it all thoughtfully, we had fifteen collecting books and all the tenants' books prepared, had opened a bank account, had found a room as office, and divided the area among our workers. Our first duty was to get the tenants to recognise our authority and pay us. I think we were very successful, we got every tenant on the estate to pay us without any legal process, except one who was a regular scamp. We collected some £250, most of it in silver, and got it safely to the bank. Then came the question of repairs; there were written in the first few weeks 1,000 orders for these, although, as the whole area is to be rebuilt, we were only doing really urgent repairs and no substantial ones. All these had to be overlooked and reported on and paid for. Next came pouring in the claims for borough and water rates. We had to ascertain the assessments of every house, the facts as to whether landlord or tenant was responsible, whether the rates were compounded for or not, what allowance was to be claimed for empties. There were two water companies supplying the area, and we had to learn which supplied each house.

The whole place was to be rebuilt, and even the streets re-arranged and widened, and I had promised the Commissioners I would advise them as to the future plans. These had to be prepared at the earliest date possible, the more so as the sanitary authorities were pressing, and sent in 100 orders in the first few days we were there. It is needless to say with what speed, capacity, and zeal the representatives of the Commissioners carried on their part of these preparations, and they rapidly decided on which streets should be first rebuilt and what should be erected there. But this only implied more to be done, for we had to empty the streets swiftly, and that meant doing up all possible empty houses in other streets and getting the tenants into them. Fortunately there were several houses empty, the falling-in of the lease having scared away some tenants. The Commissioners had decided to close all the public houses on the estate, and we let one to a girls' club[3] and had to put repairs in hand to fit it for its changed destination.

Meantime my skilled workers had to be withdrawn, though Miss Lumsden's staff was new to the work, and I do not know how the business could have been done but for her immense power, devotion and zeal, and the extreme kindness of friends in offering special help.

The matter now stands thus: We have got through the first quarter; have collected £2,672—mostly in silver; the quarter's accounts are nearly ready to send in; we have completed the most pressing repairs; have emptied two streets, and plans for rebuilding them are decided on; tenders have been accepted for those, and they are begun. Plans have been prepared for rebuilding and rearrangement of the whole estate, and these are now before the Commissioners for their consideration. They provide a site for rebuilding the parish school—an area of about an acre—as a public recreation ground, the substitution of four wide for three narrow streets, and afford accommodation for 790 families in four-roomed and six-roomed cottages, cottage flats, and flats of three and two-roomed tenements in houses in no case higher than three storeys.[4]

But there remains one most important point still under the consideration of the Commissioners. It is whether this domain is to be leased to builders and managed by them and their successors for some 80 years, or whether it is to remain under the direct control of the Commissioners. All of you who know anything of how much depends on management, will realise how earnestly I trust that they may decide to retain the area, and may feel confidence in finding in the future worthy representatives to manage it for them on sound financial principles, and in the best interests of tenants and landlords. Those

---

3   Run by the Hon. Maude Stanley. See 1906 p.558.

---

4   The details of this development were as follows: 100 cottages of between four and six rooms, 108 three-roomed cottages, 581 flats and one shop. They were built in approximately a dozen waves between 1903 and 1908. Initial rents were between 4s 6d for the smallest flats to 11s for the largest cottages.

who know what a country landlord can do in a village will realise the influence of wise government in such an area. This land is church land, it adjoins the parish church, it is quite near the Talbot Settlement, established by, and named after, the bishop of the diocese;[5] surely it should not pass from the control of the owners. If clauses in leases were as wisely planned, and as strongly enforced as possible, they could not be like the living government of wise owners, were it only that the needs and standards are for ever changing, and during the next 80 years many decisions involving change may be desirable.

---

5   Edward Stuart Talbot (1844–1934) was the one hundredth Bishop of Rochester from 1895 until 1905, when the diocese split in two and he elected to become the first Bishop of Southwark. The Diocese of Southwark was created to include the whole of the county of London south of the Thames and the Parliamentary divisions of east and mid Surrey. The Bishop of Southwark was confronted by the challenge of building up the church through parishes that ranged from prosperous villages such as Reigate and Kew and highly respectable Edwardian suburbs to appallingly over-crowded and insanitary tenements. Charles Booth's survey of the life and labour of the people of London described much of the new diocese as 'the largest area of unbroken poverty in any city in the world'. Talbot, the nephew of Lord Shrewsbury, was the son of a highly successful barrister and an adherent of the Oxford Movement. He studied at Charterhouse and Oxford. Thanks to his parents, he grew up with a keen sense of social responsibility. His mother was devout and clever, with a grasp of politics, as well as a gifted artist in watercolour. In 1860 she had been a prime mover in founding the Parochial Mission Women's Association, an Anglican initiative aimed at reaching the poor in London by means of their own 'class'—its guiding rule was that the mission women should be '*bona fide* of the lower class'. Edward fell in love with Lavinia, the third daughter of Lord Lyttelton, when she was only 15, and subsequently married her. After a brilliant career at Oxford, Edward was ordained at 26. He resigned as the first warden of Keble College, Oxford, to become Vicar of Leeds. Lavinia Talbot (1847–1939) was such a strange mixture of spirituality and somewhat glittering wordliness that she was said to have the best of both worlds. When her husband left his position in Leeds the ladies of the parish asked her what sort of gift she would like, and somewhat to their surprise she said diamonds. When presented with the jewels she held them up to the light and said: 'O diamonds, diamonds, I think I could sell my soul for diamonds'. (Lockhart, 1949, p.89.) Nevertheless, she shared her husband's social concerns and together they helped to found Lady Margaret Hall in Oxford. They also set up Talbot House in Walworth in 1900, a settlement house that worked in close co-operation with nearby Cambridge House. Cambridge House had been established in 1889 as a lay settlement to support and develop the activities of the Trinity College Mission in its work to combat the effects of poverty and deprivation in the poorest parts of South London. By 1897 Cambridge University as a whole was involved in the work, with graduates and undergraduates living in Cambridge House and undertaking voluntary work in the local community. Talbot House focused on the specific needs of women and children, but the two settlements worked in close collaboration until 1972, when they amalgamated to form Cambridge House and Talbot, which still exists.

I can only trust that these considerations may come home to those who control the church lands, and that they may find a sufficient group of trained workers to faithfully and well represent them. I believe Miss Lumsden's acceptance of this particular post may have an important bearing on their decision. I am satisfied she has the power to do the work well, and I look forward with hope to the establishment on sound lines of work beneficent in itself, and possibly bearing fruit in far-reaching ways.

There are other additions to the houses under our care to record this year. In the spring twelve freehold cottages in the street where we are managing at Notting Hill came into the market and friends came forward to purchase the whole group. Every house purchased there is a help and limits the area controlled by those who let furnished lodgings without enquiry.

The Improved Tenements Association has purchased and put under our care two more houses in Notting Hill.[6]

The seven acres in Lambeth belonging to the Ecclesiastical Commissioners are getting rapidly covered with the excellent new buildings planned by them; every week now ten or twelve new tenements are completed and handed over to us for letting. This keeps us very busy. The streets there are being completed, but the laying-out of the garden is not yet begun.[7]

The two new cottages in Westminster are completed and let, and some more old ones there have been put under our care; on the other hand, a few of the old ones are likely to be sold and pass from us, being rebuilt for other purposes than letting to the poor.[8]

---

6   The two houses mentioned here were in Mersey Street, described by Reginald Rowe as 'slummy little houses in a slummy little street'. They proved a bad investment. (Malpass, 1998, p.27.)

---

7   Building certainly continued apace between 1902 and 1903. Following the letting of one block of the tenements built earlier that year, four more blocks were built on the north side of Ufford Street, containing 24 three-room suites. (Letter from Cluttons to the EC, 15 July 1902.) Another 13 blocks were built on the north side of the new street (known as Mitre Street—now Mitre Road), containing 75 three-room suites and six two-room suites. (Letter from Cluttons to the EC, 25 March 1903.) Finally 15 tenements were built, 12 on the south side of the new street and three on the north-east side of Webber Street. They had three storeys and contained 59 three-room suites and 43 two-room suits, with common washhouses and WCs.

---

8   This policy towards older architecture would stir great public controversy for years to come, when the Ecclesiastical Commissioners resorted to demolishing large

The work in our dear old courts continues steadily as of old, and each year adds to the interest of it. By far the most difficult is that in Notting Hill; but, even there, we certainly see much good resulting from it, and we hope and believe that, as time goes on, the financial success will follow, as it so generally does, on thoughtful and careful management. Some very satisfactory sanitary improvements have been effected there by the provision of damp courses, rendering the parlours drier. To this expense the Horace Street trustees have contributed from the profits on their houses.

All this extension of work makes me most eager to secure additional workers, and I would earnestly ask all my friends to consider whether they know anyone who would be willing to give help in what I cannot but think would be a very interesting sphere. We sadly want help in Westminster, Southwark, Lambeth, and Walworth.

Surely we may hope for more volunteers ready to work, heart and soul, side by side with us, and form part of the general company who are sharing our labour, our joy, and who are feeling the steady progress which their generosity is securing in one court or other. I here refer to volunteer work. We have enlarged our staff as much as we intend to do, so that applications for paid work are useless. But Miss Lumsden and I are each able, and would be willing to give six months' training to any really promising candidate who would like to train for a chance of professional work opening out. I have had three applications for paid managers in London during the past year, which I have been unable to fill, owing to all our trained, and even partially trained, helpers being absorbed by our own extended area, and there are openings in provincial towns from time to time; but it should be borne in mind that such would only be open to those capable of taking the whole responsibility of management. They are far more difficult posts than those side by side with us as leaders.

Red Cross Hall has gone on as heretofore on much the same plan.

---

tracts of their land in old Westminster for commercial redevelopment. Opposition to this policy came from many quarters: the residents, press, Parliament, the Royal Society of Antiquaries and the National Trust. The redevelopment scheme covered Great College Street, Cowley Street, Barton Street and North Street. None of these came under the jurisdiction of Octavia or any of her successors. (Sources: *St. James's Gazette*, 1 August 1903; *The Times*, 4 August 1903; *The Globe*, 4 August 1903; National Trust Petition, 22 June 1904; *The Westminster Gazette*, 5 December 1904; *Pall Mall Gazette*, 10 December 1904; letter from Westminster Housing Association to the EC, 23 April 1930.) (See Appendix 3, pp.745-46.)

Its bright entertainments are a joy to many. We had a specially interesting May Festival, as, in addition to the ordinary school performance and merry child gathering, we took the opportunity of inviting friends to come and see the rebuilding in Lambeth, and the needs of the cadet club and corps. The Sunday gatherings are far larger than of old, and the thanks of all concerned are due to the many friends who have provided the music then, and the entertainments on the Thursday evenings. Much is due, too, to Mrs Elliman's kind and faithful help as honorary secretary; in fact, I do not know how the work there could have gone on next session but for her help, now that my niece is unable to continue her valuable help as entertainment secretary. It is interesting to notice how much more, now, the Hall is in request as a place for entertainments to be given by the various organisations at work in the neighbourhood.

St Christopher's Hall is still used as of old, and is a pleasant meeting place for the tenants. They are gathered in as performers there in a way we cannot manage at Red Cross. This is a great advantage, where possible. In this connection I should like to mention that some of my sister Miranda's children's plays,[9] written for the children's performances there, are now published separately. I think many interested in children's entertainments may care to know this.

This year it was thought desirable to place the headquarters of the cadet corps, and the club in Southwark which grew out of it, on a more satisfactory footing as to house-room, and to do it in memory of the zealous and able colonel to whom it owed so much, and to the cadets who fell in South Africa. The cadets drill weekly at Red Cross Hall, but the club met at an old house in Union Street, which it had quite outgrown. The house was dilapidated, dirty, incommodious, and

9 Cassells published Miranda Hill's plays as two editions of a children's monthly magazine called *Little Folks*, priced at 6d each. *Rumpelstiltskin and Dummling* formed one edition, and *Cinderella* the other. A third edition, written by Maggie Brown and called 'How to get up a children's play', gave detailed directions for performing the plays. *Rumpelstiltskin* had already been printed and offered for sale at 3d by means of a slip enclosed with the letter for 1891 which described it as: 'One of a series of plays written for, and acted by, the tenants' children at St Christopher's Place during the last nine years.' C.S. Loch, the secretary of the Charity Organisation Society, wrote one of the songs for *Rumpelstiltskin* and had the play performed in his home. Miranda's plays were like pantomimes with every suggestion of coarseness removed and replaced with uplifting moral instruction. Cassells were longstanding supporters of the Red Cross library, making donations of books, magazines and pictures (1888, p.245, 1889, p.263, 1894, p.356).

wretchedly ventilated, and the boys and the officers who devote themselves to the movement did so under conditions most trying. There was also a very deep desire on the part of many to raise a memorial to Colonel Salmond and the boys who fell, and the Bishop of Rochester preached a memorial sermon in St Saviour's, Southwark. A committee was formed to raise a fund, and it was decided to devote it to the reconstruction of the house in Union Street, and to a tablet in St Saviour's.[10] Among other plans to arouse interest and secure support, the Countess of Selborne was so very kind as to allow us to hold a drawing-room meeting at the Admiralty,[11] at which Lord Methuen took

---

10 St Saviour's is now Southwark Cathedral and the memorial is situated on the wall of the north aisle, opposite the main south-west door. It carries the words:

> To the glory of God and in memory of Lieut Colonel Albert Louis Salmond (3rd Derbyshire Regt Sherwood Foresters) who for the benefit of London working boys raised the 1st Cadet Battalion 'the Queen's' (Royal West Surrey Regiment) with headquarters in this parish and was its commanding officer for thirteen years (1889–1902). He died 4 August 1902 at Deelfontein South Africa of wounds received whilst commandant of Stormberg. Also to the memory of the former members of the cadet battalion who died during the Boer War in the service of their country: Corpl G.W. Pritchard (Southwark) 1st Border Regt; Lce Corpl A.J. Rhodes(Southwark) 2nd Queen's; Pte A.V. Underwood (Southwark) 1st Welsh Regt; Drmr G.E. Yeeles (Southwark) 2nd Queen's; Pte Harry J. Daw (N Kensington) 1st Royal Dragoons; Pte H.H. Chilvers (Paddington) 1st Border Regt; Pte Percy Chatterton (Westminster) Paget's Horse; Sergt W. Griffen (Pimlico) Comr in Chf's Body Guard; Pte G.H. Weber (Bethnal Green) RAMC; Pte Harry Parker (Stepney) 1st Border Regt. 'Quit you like men.' Set up by their cadet comrades and friends.

Henry Nevinson, the commander of the Whitechapel corps which pre-dated the Southwark corps by four years, described Albert Salmond as an unlikely choice to be a leader of men - or boys: 'He had the look of a melancholic pessimist, incapable of enthusiasm or decision... but within a few weeks I perceived that he was one of the few inspired and unselfish enthusiasts I have ever known... Though he had business of his own, as solicitor and coal-owner, his whole heart was fixed upon the battalion, and, being untrammelled by humour, he took it with a seriousness that no general in command of an army upon the front in the Great War could have surpassed... Often... I have stood at his side in front of the little line of shabby, ill-fed, anaemic cockney boys, and heard him say with the assurance of perfect sincerity... "Remember this: the eyes of the Horse Guards are upon this battalion."' (Nevinson, 1923, pp.93-94.)

---

11 Where her husband, the Earl of Selborne, was First Lord from 1900 to 1905. The term 'drawing-room' is misleading, as this had been a packed public meeting, held on 30 April, and addressed by Lord Methuen, the Bishop of Stepney, Sir Alfred Turner, Sir Frederick Maurice, Sir Arthur Conan Doyle and Octavia herself.

the chair. The Bishop of Stepney[12] and others spoke, the meeting was a great success, and I would gladly record my hearty thanks to all who so zealously helped.[13] The money has come in well, the building has been ordered and is nearly completed. It will make the club and corps

---

12 The Bishop of Stepney from 1901 to 1908 was Cosmo Lang, whose rise through the church hierarchy had been nothing short of spectacular. A bishop at 37, he was made Archbishop of York at the age of 44, and was the only obvious candidate for Archbishop of Canterbury. Unfortunately for him, his predecessor, Davidson, lived to a ripe old age, and Lang did not take his place on St Augustine's throne until 1928, by which time he was 64. Lang inherited the bitter controversy surrounding the refusal of parliament to authorise the new Prayer Book. He was Archbishop at the time of Edward VIII's abdication, for which many people blamed him (although he had almost no involvement at all), and then he had to cope with the challenges posed to the church by the Second World War. He was convinced that the radical changes in society that would inevitably accompany the end of the war would require a younger man to steer the church through them, and he resigned in 1942. Lang was a curious mixture of deep spirituality with outrageous snobbishness and pomposity. Nevertheless, he had a genuine concern for the welfare of the poor, and in 1883, as an undergraduate at Balliol, he had attended the meeting at which Samuel Barnett read his paper on university settlement houses. Barnett inspired his young audience to set up a settlement house in memory of Arnold Toynbee, a lecturer at Balliol whose life of service to the poor had been cut short by an early death. Lang became one of the two undergraduate secretaries of what would become Toynbee Hall in Whitechapel, and the first meeting of undergraduates connected with the project was held in his rooms. His dedication to the cause was such that he was warned by the Master—the forbidding figure of Benjamin Jowett—that his business at Oxford was not to reform the East End of London but to get a first class degree. (Lockhart, 1949, p.40.) His relationship with Toynbee Hall appears to have been more distant after his undergraduate phase, but he was chairman of the council from 1933 to 1945. At Stepney he was Samuel Barnett's bishop, and, in the year of this letter, Lang would become involved with Barnett in organising the very last of the Lord Mayor of London's traditional Mansion House Funds for the relief of distress. The 1886 Fund had turned into such a notorious shambles (1884/5, p.186 and 1908, p.598) that the few funds attempted after that were organised on completely different lines. The Bishop's scheme was little more than a small-scale labour colony in Essex, where work was provided for 467 heads of families from Stepney, Poplar, Bethnal Green and Shoreditch. According to William Beveridge, it represented the beginning of the end for private attempts to relieve large-scale cyclical unemployment. (Whelan, 2001, p.89.)

---

13 Octavia followed up the meeting at the Admiralty with a sort of 'open day', connected to the annual Maypole festivities in Red Cross garden. On 23 May 1903 her sister Gertrude was persuaded to join Octavia and Harriot Yorke in Southwark, where Octavia had asked 'a good many people (some influential) to come down and see the Maypole and the cadet headquarters and the new houses. They are to have tea and be personally conducted by herself and others.' (Darley, 1990, p.326.) Miss

far better. About £200 is still needed, but I hope that will be forthcoming.[14]

There was another meeting held this year to help forward work with which I am closely connected. The Kyrle Society was much needing funds, and, by the kindness of the Countess of Ellesmere, a meeting was held at Bridgewater House.[15] Lord Stamford took the chair, and there was a full attendance. Such gatherings are a great lift to a cause, and this one was a great service to the Society, which has since also been helped by grants from various city companies. I hope it may receive an increased number of annual subscriptions. The large amount of really good volunteer work it secures commends it to all who care to brighten the lives of the poor.

Owing to my absence for annual holiday we were not able to accept my brother's invitation to our tenants this year, to our great regret, and Sir Frederick and Lady Pollock were in America, so the summer parties were fewer than in previous years, but we had some small ones, and Miss Johnston again entertained a large group at Hampstead.

Ironside was responsible for the children, the flowers and the band, while Octavia looked after 'the dignified people'. Presumably the intention was to demonstrate the inadequacy of the old building, as work on the new structure did not begin until August (see below).

---

14 Writing in April 1904—three months after the composition of Octavia's letter—Lieut Colonel Cyril Bennett, commanding officer of the 1st Cadet Battalion, recorded in the Battalion's annual report: 'The plans involved an outlay of over £1,000, but, thanks to the energetic assistance of Miss Octavia Hill and other constant friends, enough money was obtained to permit of the work being commenced in August, and I am pleased to report that it is now completed, to the great advantage of the Battalion, but more especially of course to the local companies in Southwark, since the useful little drill hall provided is available every evening. The deficit on the building fund is now £160, which I trust will soon be cleared off.' A letter published in The Times on 18 April 1903, signed by Octavia and others, had put the cost of the project at £2,000, and appealed to the public for support on the grounds that: 'Cadet battalions receive no government grant and are entirely dependent on private subscriptions'. The money seems to have come in more slowly than was usual with Octavia's appeals, because in the 1904 letter she is still concerned that '£36 is still needed to complete the cost. I am afraid this fact is causing grave anxiety to the leaders of the movement'. (1904, p.524.)

---

15 Bridgewater House had been designed by Sir Charles Barry and built for the Earl of Ellesmere between 1847 and 1850. It faces Green Park, and the whole of the first floor was designed as a picture gallery to display what was regarded as the finest private collection of paintings in London, including Raphael's *Madonna and Child* and Titian's *Holy Family*. It still exists, as 14 Cleveland Row.

With regard to open spaces, I have not very much to record. The Hainault scheme is, I believe, practically secured. It owes its success mainly to Mr Edward North Buxton.[16] The scheme I referred to in last year's letter for securing Kymin Hill for the public has been carried through, and it is now in the possession of the National Trust, that means that it is preserved for the enjoyment of the nation.

One other addition to the National Trust land has been made this year. Three-and-a-half acres on the very top of a Kentish headland, commanding a wide view, have been bought and are being conveyed to the Trust.[17] Rights of way have been secured on three sides of it, so that, in a sense, it fulfils the idea I have so often suggested of a strip of land forming a pleasant walk from one place to another, being itself beautiful and commanding a view. One pathway leads to a country lane, one to a field walk, one on to a common, and when the winding paths up a bank, covered by copse wood, and set with primrose and wild hyacinth roots, shall have been cut, and the openings in the hedges made, and the rustic seats set on the grassy sloping table land, which

---

16 This is now the Hainault Forest County Park, near Romford on the London/ Essex border. The site was handed over to the London County Council and officially opened on Saturday 21 July 1906. Earl Carrington, president of the Board of Agriculture, was the guest of honour, and in his speech he paid tribute to Edward North Buxton, to whose efforts the saving of the forest as an open space was mainly due. Edward North Buxton was one of the original members of the Commons Preservation Society and its long-time vice-president. He had been actively involved in the campaign to save Epping Forest. When, together with his eldest son Gerald Buxton, he led the campaign to acquire 900 acres of Hatfield Forest, which was vested in the National Trust, this was described as 'the third Essex forest to be saved largely through the efforts of the Buxton family'. (Legg, 1994, p.21.)

---

17 This was Mariner's Hill. 'We had a most interesting afternoon yesterday... going both to Mariner's and Ide Hill. We all agreed in favour of the former; partly because of the magnificent view, partly because it is now or never for it.' (Letter from Octavia to Miranda Hill, 17 May 1903, Maurice, 1914, p.556.) Octavia had originally thought that it might prove necessary to build some properties on the land to help finance the purchase. Although this did not happen, she wrote to her solicitor Carrington Ouvry, telling him that restrictive clauses limiting the use of the land to 'institutions, holiday homes etc.' were acceptable, as the Trust 'by no means plan to give access to the tramp, the London rough, the noisy beanfeaster, or the shouting crowds of children, they offer no attractions for them, but plan to preserve the land in its natural beauty for the artist, the professional man, and such of the public as appreciate and respect natural beauty'. (Letter from Octavia to Carrington Ouvry, 8 September 1903, quoted in Darley, 1990, p.312.) Part of Ide Hill had already been purchased and conveyed to the National Trust in 1899 (1899, p.436).

forms the summit of the hill, I can imagine many happy groups walking there or pausing to gaze at the wide extent of blue hill and plain. East, south and west, all is open to view, and as the fresh wind blows, or the sun sets behind the distant promontory, or the moon rises over the plain, many may enjoy that sight of nature's beauty which seems meant for man's joy and refreshment.

The land has been mainly bought with the last of the In Memoriam fund.[18] It seemed well to me, having devoted the bulk of it to the relief of suffering, to the blind, the hungry, the feeble, or the aged, that a portion should be given as a provision for, and recognition of, the need of that joy and peace which beauty gives. It will be, too, I hope, a suggestion to some who are providing a memorial to those whom they love who have gone before them; how suitable is the dedication in the memory of them, of a space of God's earth to be kept beautiful and quiet, one set apart for the inspiration of many, and from which all the marvellous beauty and manifold changes of God's heaven may be seen by the human watchers. At any rate this is an offering and a dedication In Memoriam.

Now lastly, as to the donation fund. Again let me offer sincere thanks to the many generous and faithful donors, and try to tell them how many and how much their gifts have helped. I wish they could know something of the histories which lie hidden behind the figures in the account I print. But this cannot be, and we must be content to remember that blessings unknown to them have followed their gifts. One large donation which will materially help that portion of our work which is most difficult—the houses in Notting Hill—has also something of the In Memoriam feeling about it. It comes from one who represents the founder[19] of the Horace Street Trust. She to whom we owe so much of

---

18 In fact, this was not quite the end of the fund. In 1904 Octavia reported adding the interest from In Memoriam to her donation fund, and in 1905 she gave £100 from it towards the cost of emigration (1904, p.524 and 1905, p.547).

---

19 The 'founder' of the Horace Street Trust was Anna Scrase-Dickins (1831–1901), whose gift of 'three small freehold houses' in 1886 led to the setting up of the Trust. Mrs Scrase-Dickins had died on 23 June 1901 in Hawkhurst, Kent, at the age of 69, but presumably it had taken some time to settle her estate. The only large donation shown in the accounts for 1903 is £100 from a Miss Burrage. Miss Burrage had first appeared in the donation fund accounts in 1888. In the same year Anna Scrase-Dickins made her first contribution to the accounts, with a gift of £110 to the Red Cross fund (p.270). Miss Burrage appears again in 1904 (£17 3s 6d), 1905 (£25 13s), 1907 (£16 3s), 1908 (£15 4s), 1909 (£14 3s 10d) and 1910 (£14 2s 6d). In the 1910 accounts she is described as 'the late Miss Burrage'. These sums are so odd—

the power to help, and who has left that power as a Trust to us in the years to come, has passed away, but this fresh gift for one of our most forlorn places recalls her. Another large gift comes from one whose property we have managed for many years, and who sends it with words of encouragement and blessing. So the present grows out of the past and makes one with it, each year gathering up the memories and the blessings of those that came before.

I am, always, my dear friends
Yours faithfully,
OCTAVIA HILL

---

most people gave round sums in pounds or guineas—that it looks as if Miss Burrage was giving away the interest on a capital sum—perhaps an inheritance. Mrs Scrase-Dickins herself had first appeared in the donation fund accounts for 1890 giving £1 16s 7d, the 'interest on Mrs Scrase-Dickins's gift', then £7 16s in 1891, £3 18s in 1892 and £1 9s 3d in 1893. It looks as if Miss Burrage had inherited from Mrs Scrase-Dickins the investment on which the dividends were being paid to Octavia. Anna's widower, Major-General (later Sir) William Scrase-Dickins, gave £5 14s in 1907. He was the third son of Charles and Lady Elizabeth Scrase-Dickins of Coolhurst in Horsham, and both he and his wife were buried in the chapel there.

DONATION ACCOUNT, 1903

RECEIPTS

	£	s	d		£	s	d
In hand, December 1902	239	18	7 ½	In Memoriam, 'L.B.'	1	0	0
Andrewes, Mr and Mrs H.	1	1	0	Johnston, The Misses ...	20	0	0
Allen, A.C.	2	2	0	Johnston, The Misses			
Austin, Miss	1	0	0	(for vans to party at			
Andrewes, Mrs	1	1	0	their house)	3	0	0
Bartlett, Miss H.	2	0	0	'L.'	0	10	6
Booth, Mrs	5	0	0	Lowndes, Miss	1	0	0
Blyth, Patrick	1	1	0	Langenbach, Mrs	2	2	0
Bridgeman, Charles	5	0	0	Matheson, P.E.	1	1	0
Bannerman, Mrs	1	1	0	Morris, F.	1	1	0
Burrage, Miss	100	0	0	Macaulay, Mrs	5	0	0
Barlett, Miss C. (for				Mallet, H.F.	2	10	0
Kentish Headland) ...	10	0	0	Pollock, Lady (for Kymin)	5	0	0
Brooks, Miss	1	0	0	Poynter, Ambrose	2	0	0
Bridgeman, Mrs	2	0	0	Paddock, F.W.	5	0	0
Cockerell, Sydney	1	0	0	Pollock, Sir Frederick			
Covington, Stenton	2	4	3	and Lady	10	0	0
Cudworth, Mrs	2	2	0	Roberts, Mrs	5	5	0
Ducie, The Earl of	5	0	0	Rolfe, Mrs (for Kymin) ...	5	0	0
Dawson, Mrs	2	0	0	Somervell, Gordon			
Erle, Miss	20	0	0	(for Kymin)	3	3	0
Evans, Mrs Richardson ...	1	1	0	Sprague, Dr	10	0	0
Fellow-workers in houses (for				Schuster, Mrs	10	0	0
Kentish Headland) ...	50	0	0	Singleton, Miss	2	10	0
Fleming, Owen	1	1	0	Tufnell, Mrs	1	1	0
Forman, Miss	1	1	0	Thompson, Mrs	2	2	0
Fiertz, Miss	3	3	0	Thompson, Mrs (for Kymin)	4	4	0
Frankau, Miss	5	0	0	Todhunter, Miss	1	0	0
Hills, J.W., for 1903, 1904	20	10	0	Wells, Miss	2	0	0
Hoole, Elijah for 1903, 1904	4	4	0	Wright, Mrs Caleb	1	0	0
Hill, Alfred	10	0	0	Returned for children			
Hutton, Mrs	3	3	0	boarded out	5	10	5
Harris, Miss E.M.	3	3	0	Interest on Deposit of			
Howitt, Miss	0	10	1	In Memoriam fund ...	64	11	4
Hewson, Miss	1	0	0		£684	18	2 ½

DONATION ACCOUNT, 1903

EXPENDITURE

	£	s	d
Open Spaces:			
Kentish Headland 248 0 0			
Kymin Hill 17 7 0			
Hainault 0 10 6			
	265	17	6
Pensions	65	1	9
Training and Boarding Out	40	10	5 ½
Relief in Sickness and Infirmity	14	19	0
Red Cross Hall	11	0	0
Playground, Care of	10	8	0
Boots for Orphanage	10	0	0
Cadet Corps	8	15	6
Houses, improvement of	7	13	6
Entertainments	7	6	6
Employment	5	15	3
Poor Parish in Southwark	5	0	0
Kyrle Society (meeting)	3	10	0
Stationery and Carriage of Parcels	2	0	0 ½
London Fever Hospital	1	1	0
Printing Letter to Fellow-Workers	3	12	6
In Hand	222	7	2 ½
	£684	18	2 ½

Examined and found correct, P.L. Blyth, January 14th 1904

RED CROSS HALL AND GARDEN ACCOUNT, 1903*

RECEIPTS

	£	s	d
Balance at Bank, January 1903	7	3	7
Cash in hand, January 1903	1	15	11 ½
Hire of Hall	30	12	6
Hire of Club Room	13	0	0
Hire of Office	10	8	0
Donations:			
Allen, A.C., Esq	1	1	0
Blyth, Patrick, Esq	1	1	0
Gladstone, Miss	4	0	0
Harris, Miss	2	2	0
Lewes, Miss M.	0	3	6
Lee-Warner, Miss	0	10	0
Martelli, F., Esq	0	10	0
Orr, Mrs	1	0	0
F.P., per Miss O. Hill	1	0	0
Pollock, Sir Frederick	10	0	0
Stevens, Mrs Bingham	0	1	0
Temple, Mrs	1	1	0
Webb, Mrs Randall	2	0	0
Interest, Red and White Cross Cottages	77	7	4
Programmes, sale of	7	2	5
Violin Fees	4	2	0
Collections	3	17	3
Gas	3	15	6
	£183	14	0 ½

* *Editor's note:* in the original this date is incorrectly given as 1904.

RED CROSS HALL AND GARDEN ACCOUNT, 1903*

EXPENDITURE

			£	s	d
Caretaker			58	13	0
Furniture and Repairs			27	3	0 ¼
Violin Lessons			17	15	0
Borough Rates			12	13	7
Entertainment Expenses			10	7	6 ¾
Gas 8			7	2	0
Garden:					
Repairs	4	6	5		
Rent	1	5	0		
Pigeon Food	1	1	4		
Notice Board	0	16	0		
License for Balcony	0	5	0		
Grass Seed	0	2	6		
			7	16	3
Cleaning			6	4	7
Water Rate			6	2	0
Printing			6	17	2 ½
Maypole Festival			4	13	9
Fuel			3	10	2
Insurance			2	9	9
Income Tax			2	6	2
Bank Charges			0	2	6
Cash in hand			1	15	11
Balance at Bank			6	16	5
			£183	14	0 ½

Audited and found correct, P.L. Blyth, January 18th 1904

515

LETTER TO MY FELLOW-WORKERS

TO WHICH ARE ADDED

ACCOUNTS OF DONATIONS RECEIVED

FOR

WORK AMONG THE POOR

DURING 1904

BY

OCTAVIA HILL

SUMMARY

*Ecclesiastical Commissioners: Walworth and the Lambeth Estate, Waterloo...
other housing work: Notting Hill and the need to preserve cottages;
Westminster; Freshwater Place... outings for tenants... club and
headquarters for the cadets... donation fund... open spaces: Purley Beeches;
Brockwell Park; Ullswater.*

EDITOR'S NOTE

*Octavia begins with the triumphant admission that the Ecclesiastical
Commissioners have backed down over the question of assigning 80-year
leases on the Walworth Estate. She attributes this to the fact that 'there is
growing up a certain number of ladies capable of representing them'. She
then repeats the claim, first made in the letter for 1900, that her housing
managers should enjoy the same professional status as architects, lawyers
and surveyors. As these managers were 'ladies', it was a bold claim for a
new profession at a time when women were still struggling to be taken
seriously in any professional capacity. Octavia announces the completion of
the work on the Ecclesiastical Commissioners' Lambeth Estate, which had
seemed vast at the start, but was now somewhat dwarfed by Walworth. On
the open spaces front, she appeals for 700 acres of Ullswater, which would
become another enormous landholding in the Lake District for the National
Trust. In a moving passage, Octavia links the beauty of nature with the
cultural associations of Turner and Wordsworth to make a plea for open
access for the whole of the people, rather than 'one or two families'. She
reminds us that man does not live by bread alone, and that England should
be rich enough to provide some areas where every person can 'commune
with his God in the mighty presence of mountain, sky and water'. All for
£18 an acre!*

190 Marylebone Road, N.W.

My friends,

I am again writing to tell you of a year's work, helped and cheered by your ever generous and ready co-operation. It is on the old lines, and I do not think that I have any new kind of work to record, only a widening and deepening of interest in the old spheres, and fresh development of new schemes growing out of those realised in former years.

The Walworth area, the largest I have anywhere, is progressing admirably under my friend Miss Lumsden, who is realising all my hope as to proving able to fulfil, strongly and wisely, the duties of a manager. When I wrote to you last it was still doubtful whether the Ecclesiastical Commissioners would decide to undertake the responsibility of rebuilding, and retaining in their own hands, the whole of the area which was to be devoted to dwellings for the working classes. It was still undecided whether they would not lease a part to builders or companies. They have resolved to retain the whole in their own hands, and to manage it by their own agents, of whom Miss Lumsden is the first. The advantages of this plan are obvious. The Commissioners will be directly responsible for good arrangements and government, instead of being powerless to interfere for 80 or 90 years; they will be freer than any lessees can be to modify, should change be needed owing to development of science, or alteration of requirements as time goes on; they can determine conditions of life in a large area occupied by working people, which may have as deep an influence as the churches and schools, which, up to now, they have felt it their duty to supply. All this they have felt it possible to do, because they realise that there is growing up a certain number of ladies capable of representing them, and possessing special knowledge. So that in the years to come, as they will have lawyers to do legal business, surveyors and architects to see to the fabric of their houses, so they will have managers to supervise in detail the comfort and health of their tenants, so far as these depend on proper conditions in the houses in which they live; managers who will be interested in the people, and will have time to see thoroughly to the numerous details involved in management of such areas.

There have been completed up to now in Walworth the following: 39 four-roomed cottages, 12 six-roomed, and 18 three-roomed tenements. Besides these there have been built 28 cottage flats, as we call them.[1] These are like two cottages, quite distinct from one another; each with three rooms and a scullery, one being on the ground floor, with the yard nearest to the house, the other being on the first floor, approached by a separate front door and staircase, and having a separate yard, beyond the other, approached by a distinct staircase at the back, so that each tenement forms a separate cottage. The yards are a good size, and small beds of earth have been left, so that those tenants who choose may make for themselves gardens. A considerable number of other tenements are nearly ready. A good deal of the remainder of the area to be devoted to such building has been cleared, and the formation of the new and wider streets is authorised, and will shortly be begun, as will also the laying out of the space given by the Ecclesiastical Commissioners as a recreation ground for the public. When all is finished, there will be accommodation for 800 families on the estate.

The Lambeth Estate, near the Waterloo Station, is finished. The last houses there were handed over to us for management in July. The public garden, given by the Commissioners, is nearly ready for opening.[2] The estate provides accommodation for 256 families, and forms a wonderful contrast to the forlorn neighbourhood of the New Cut; the pretty, comfortable, well appointed cottages, the light and commodious flats, the liberal allowance of yard space, and the fact that none of the buildings is more than three storeys high, the large group of respectable tenants resident there, make it quite an ideal place for the home life of quiet working-class families.[3]

We had a very pleasant gathering there in the spring, when I asked

---

1   Now known as maisonettes, which Octavia had been referring to as 'compound houses' in 1897 (1897, p.400).

---

2   *See ills.22 and 23.* The garden opened out onto Ufford Street. It appears to have been delayed by disagreement between the EC and Lambeth Borough Council over who would maintain it. It was finally conveyed to Lambeth in July 1904. (Letter from the EC to White, Bossett & Co., 15 July 1904.)

---

3   The New Cut scheme, as this development became known, ultimately extended over approximately 2.5 acres. Rebuilding would cost £60,000. Twenty-nine cottages and 51 tenements were built, covering an area of 90,000 sq. ft, and averaging a gross rent of £4,000 per annum. The scheme encompassed New Cut (1-27 odd), Webber Street (1-33 odd), Caffyn Street (1-51) (demolished to make way for Mitre Road) Mitre Street (1-42) (also demolished to make way for Mitre Road) and Ufford Street

the owners and their representatives, who had co-operated so heartily, to come and see all that they had done, and to meet many of my fellow-workers and friends, and others likely to care to see the place. The weather was propitious, and as many of the houses were just being finished, but not quite ready for occupation, we were able to wander about at will, and see all that was to be seen without disturbing the occupants.

Our property in Notting Hill is going on slowly, but steadily, towards distinct improvement. There are gradually gathering under our care a group of those of the very poor who desire to live decently and to pay their way; they greatly appreciate the remarkable cheapness of the light, comfortable rooms, and the order and quiet for which we are struggling, and which, in a measure, we are able to secure, and they will form, as time goes on, a most satisfactory group of tenants. We are able to secure this cheapness, and to come in contact with this very poor class of tenant, because we have not had either to clear the area, or to rebuild, but, having been fortunate enough to buy small houses, with good light and air back and front, we have taken them over, often full, have given every tenant a trial, have steadily improved the houses, and are providing for a poorer group than could ever be introduced into rebuilt houses. One advantage in these houses is their great adaptability to the varying requirements of families. They contain seven rooms, one of which is quite small, and we can let one, two, three or more rooms together according to circumstances. Our cheapest floor is 5s for two rooms; the small room is 1s 6d.

I wrote an article in the *Daily Chronicle*,[4] pointing out the extreme value, in the best interests of the very poor, of preserving such houses where they could be made healthily habitable. Their being small,

---

(1-53). The *Daily Telegraph* termed the whole development a 'garden city' (31 March 1902). The New Cut was renamed the Cut in 1938.

---

4 'Housing Difficulties: Management versus Re-construction' appeared in the *Daily Chronicle* during 1904 (date unknown) and was then published in pamphlet form. This pamphlet is bound into the volume of letters in the collection of the Goldsmith's Library of Economic Literature, University of London Library, and was probably distributed with the 1904 letter. It is reproduced in Whelan (1998) pp. 122-25. Octavia, who was always keenly aware of the extent to which negative pre-conceptions got in the way of her work, complained that: 'It is inadvisable to stigmatise a neighbourhood with such names as "Modern Avernus"'. She was referring to a notorious article about Notting Dale which had appeared in the *Daily News* in 1893, entitled 'A West-End Avernus'. In classical mythology, Avernus was the lake at the entrance to hell of which the waters were so poisonous that birds flying over it dropped dead. It was a

adaptable and cheap, seems to me most important. Block building, elaborate appliances, unalterable suites of rooms are quite unfit for the people whom there is a difficulty in housing, however valuable they may be for the well-to-do mechanic. I reprinted the article as being suggestive for those contemplating schemes for the provision of accommodation for working people, and I wish it might reach many before small houses are destroyed.

In one way, this Notting Hill area is the most satisfactory to me of any we have. It is so steadily improving, and the people with it. It is meeting so much the needs of those who find it hardest to get on. The group of ladies who manage it are eminently fitted to help on any who can be helped there, whether it be by introducing the young people to better work, by recommending widows for charing, by giving the labourer an odd job of rough work, by immediately calling attention to cases of illness or extreme want, by bringing a little healthy amusement into somewhat monotonous hard-working lives, and in many other ways. The work is much more like that which I was able to do in earlier years than any which is possible in most new buildings.

We have had a great alarm about the work there, owing to a proposal by the Kensington Borough Council to take possession of these cottages in connection with a scheme for municipal housing. I very earnestly hope that the danger is averted, but I cannot feel sure.

Six more houses have been bought in Notting Hill and placed under our care during 1904, by a friend who had previously purchased nine. The Horace Street Trustees have also purchased the leases of two more.

At the Westminster estate all goes well. We have resident there a total of 238 families.

That estate, as well as all our other groups, has prospered well, the tenants becoming dearer to us as the years roll on, and the children and grandchildren of tenants of former years are themselves becoming tenants.

In Freshwater Place a memorial stone is being placed to the late Mr William Shaen,[5] who bought the court to prevent it going into strange

---

peculiarly apt image for Notting Dale, where the excavation of clay-pits for brickmaking, coupled with the influx of a large colony of pig-farmers, had resulted in the creation of a lake of pig-slurry covering one acre. By the time of Octavia's article, the lake, known locally as the Ocean, had been drained and reclaimed as Avondale Park.

---

5   The memorial has disappeared and so has Freshwater Place, although the site, on Homer Row, Marylebone, is still occupied by social housing, and still has a small garden.

hands, when Mr Ruskin sold it, and whose wise and ever ready counsel and help guided me in the very earliest beginning of all my work.

Before leaving the subject of houses I may mention that in 1903, and also in 1904, I acceded to a request from the School of Sociology that I would allow some of their students to work side by side with my workers in order to see some of our methods. They were painstaking and reliable workers, helpful to us so long as they stayed, and I hope they learned something; but they were not, as a rule, thinking of continuous management of houses.[6]

I have been glad that of late some of those whom we have been introducing as our students have come with a more direct object of continuing such work. Birmingham, Liverpool, Oxford and Manchester have all been contemplating introducing trained ladies to the management of houses. A lady from Birmingham came up to work with us for some time; she showed considerable power. There is a hope that she will begin work in Birmingham early in the year. A lady from Oxford is now with us, and will return to reinforce the group now managing such property in Oxford. Manchester, I hope, is securing a trained worker from Edinburgh.

St Christopher's Hall and Red Cross Hall have been going on much as of old. The former owes much, as in previous years, to Mr S. Hamer, and the latter to Mrs Elliman's valuable help as hon. secretary.

Our summer parties were a great success. We were again able to meet at my brother's, at Erleigh Court. The weather was most lovely, the tenants extremely happy, and all went very well. Sir Frederick and Lady Pollock again entertained us, and I think the guests were almost happier than ever, and more touched by the kindness shown to them.

---

6   The School of Sociology had been set up in 1903 by the Charity Organisation Society at Denison House, their headquarters on the Vauxhall Bridge Road, partly as a result of their involvement with the formal training programme for social work established by Octavia and Margaret Sewell at the Women's University Settlement. The COS was always keen on training, and saw the School as a means of achieving academic recognition for social work. Its first director was E.J. Urwick, and its programme of lectures, which were extremely popular, drew on the leading speakers of the day, such as Patrick Geddes, Bernard Bosanquet, William Beveridge and Karl Pearson. It was established as a separate legal entity, with minimal control from the COS Council, but the COS was ultimately responsible for the bills, and in 1912 was forced by shortage of funds into a merger with the newly created social science department of the London School of Economics. 'That confounded School of Economics has mopped up our little School of Sociology in London', Bernard Bosanquet wrote to his nephew. 'We have made the best terms we could and are putting up the shutters with heavy hearts.' (Harris, 1989, pp.35-41.)

We had with us a few tenants from Notting Hill for the first time. Miss Johnston's party, too, was most successful; we prize it specially because, as we drive all the way, we can take the mothers with tiny children, who get so little break in their hard-working lives. Lady Selborne took a party up the river, Mr and Mrs Clutton Brock entertained a group at Weybridge, Miss MacInnes at Hampstead, and Mr and Mrs C.S. Loch at Oxshott.

The rebuilding of the club and headquarters for the cadets is completed. It has been most satisfactory, as it gives much more and better scope for all the useful work there, and must be much more healthy for boys and officers. I regret to say that £36 is still needed to complete the cost. I am afraid this fact is causing grave anxiety to the leaders of the movement. It really ought to be forthcoming, as the corps is doing a great deal for lads on whom so much of the future depends.

Once more let me thank all kind donors to my donation fund. It has been the means of much most valuable help to many an out-of-sight poverty-stricken person in the past year—man, woman and child. What it is to us, who are face to face with them, to be able to help, even to help largely, when the time of need comes, no words will say. I have carried to this account a large amount received for interest mainly accruing from the In Memoriam fund and Lady Jane Dundas's bequest, both of which I decided to spend gradually.[7] This interest I am holding for a special object. Almost all the balance in hand is appropriated for the various pensioners, children in schools or boarded out. We have a large number of these at present, and failure to continue help to any of them would be so serious, that I always keep two quarterly payments in hand for each. Hence my apparently large balance.

The open spaces work goes on well. The Kent and Surrey Committee is doing more and more each year. It has done much in defending paths and commons, and regulating commons. It has before it just now no less than three most important schemes for acquisition of land: first, Purley Beeches, a lovely country spot within reach of Londoners, and still nearer to the increasingly populated area of Croydon;[8] second,

---

7   The interest during the year amounted to £24 5s 11d.

---

8   This 18-acre site in Sanderstead was not secured until 1907 when, on 23 January, the parish council met in the school in Sanderstead village to discuss the purchase of Purley Beeches by the ratepayers. For a number of years previously some of the residents of Sanderstead had subscribed for the rent and maintenance of the Beeches, but the option to purchase the site expired in February 1907. They had succeeded in raising

another addition of six acres to Brockwell Park, which would add more frontage to a recreation area of quite inestimable value to South-East London;[9] and, third, another larger and most important scheme of which the particulars will be made known later.

Of our great scheme for open spaces most of you will have heard, and I have to return heartfelt thanks to so many of you who have sent me generous help for it. I hardly realised how many friends I had till the donations for Ullswater came pouring in from so many of you, and I feel that I have made many new friends in 1904 from the letters I have received from far and near—letters showing such deep interest in schemes for others, for the years to come, and such readiness to make sacrifices for them.

I have been able from the funds received for collection in the houses to devote £100 to Ullswater. The possibility of sparing the money is due to the large amount of voluntary help given by so many devoted and steady fellow-workers. I have always charged the owners the ordinary commission on rents collected, because I hold that such property should be managed on a sound financial basis. The fact that we have volunteers secures to the tenants a far larger amount of personal care than would be possible without them, but it also diminishes the cost, and I should like here heartily to thank all who have helped, both in the courts and with the accounts, and to ask them to realise that it is practically they who have made this large gift to the Ullswater fund. I

---

the sum of £1,474 towards the price of £5,400 asked by the owner, Mr E. Arkwright, for the freehold, this price being about half the value of the land for building purposes. It was proposed that a rate of 2d in the pound should be levied in order to raise the necessary money. The resolution was put to the meeting of the Warlingham parish council and carried by 50 votes to 30, but a poll was demanded and the chairman agreed. As a result, a poll of the whole parish took place on 2 February 1907. 178 ratepayers voted for the purchase and 114 against. The land was purchased and opened to the public on 30 November 1907, but the strength of the opposition and the uncertainty of the councillors shows how controversial the use of public money for open spaces still was. In 1953 the Coulsdon and Purley Urban District Council was granted a coat of arms which included two trees, one for the Purley Oaks and the other a beech for Purley Beeches.

---

9   This was one of the very few open spaces appeals with which Octavia associated herself that failed. It proved impossible to raise the purchase price and the land was sold for £2,000 more than it had been offered at as an open space. However, the open spaces sub-committee of the Kyrle Society was able to persuade the owner to preserve a fine avenue of trees, and to grant access to the Park from Trinity Road. (Kyrle Society report 1905, p.20.)

have also given £100 from Lady Jane Dundas's bequest. These two sums will appear in the National Trust accounts.

And yet with all this help, and with all that has reached Canon Rawnsley and my other colleagues, we have not yet quite half of what we need, £5,500 out of £12,000. We have some little time before us still, and I do not abate one jot of heart or hope, but I admit that I have not a notion where this large balance will come from. Whether from the great manufacturing towns, six of which are now, I believe, forming committees to help, whether any larger donors will come forward, or whether the multitude of generous givers who are continually sending smaller gifts will have time to accumulate the great balance I do not know. I believe the money will come; it is coming daily. My colleagues are doing their utmost; but I fear that I personally can do little more. You, my friends, have responded to my published appeal in far larger measures than I had ever hoped. I have spoken at Oxford. I have made known through the press the facts about this 700 acres of land on the slopes of Ullswater, commanding views of its head, surrounded by the great company of mountains, as Turner painted them for us;[10] its mile of lake shore with the waves breaking on the shingle; its association with Wordsworth in his noblest utterances;[11] its boulders and heather, its wooded ravine, its mountain meadows, its bird and plant life, and its herds of deer; its great slopes, from which such views are visible, and how it lies open to sun, and shower, and storm. I have told how it may either be free to foot of man, woman and child for all ages, or appropriated to one or two families, and fenced off with barbed wire; shut off from artist, naturalist, hard-worked professional man, smoke-grimed city dweller, workman and child; of how £18 buys one acre of it for all time. All this have I said; I am going in the spring to say it all once more at Cambridge. After that, what more can I do? It rests with

---

10 The fact that Turner had painted the scene would have made its preservation especially important to the three founders of the National Trust, all of them disciples of Ruskin, whose multi-volume *Modern Painters* (1843–1860) had been intended to persuade the public that Turner was the greatest British painter. (Ruskin's original title had been *Turner and the Ancients*.) According to Octavia's sister Emily, Octavia knew volume I of *Modern Painters* well by the age of 12. She contributed some copies of paintings for inclusion in volume V, and in 1875 she wrote to Ruskin telling him how much *Modern Painters* had influenced her life and work. (Darley, 1990, pp.66 and 146.)

---

11 Ullswater is famous for being the place from which sprang the daffodils of Wordsworth's most famous poem 'Daffodils' (1804).

others now. I cannot believe that the land will be lost. There are too many who know that man does not live by bread alone;[12] that when all material wants have been duly recognised and attended to, there does remain in England enough wealth for her to set aside a few areas where man may contemplate the beauty of nature, may rest, may find quiet, may commune with his God in the mighty presence of mountain, sky and water, and may find that peace, so difficult to realise in the throng of populous cities.[13]

Yes, it will be given, I know it will, and I think all of you who have given will rejoice that you have shared in the gift. It may seem arrogant to assume that one knows what good our Father holds in His hand to give us in the coming year, and one may be wrong, the year may bring disappointment which may be better for us than success. And till one knows one must walk humbly, and wait, and watch, and say, 'Will it be thus, or thus, that Thou dost purpose for us?' But sometimes one seems to see, and I believe that the land on Ullswater will be preserved, that the gifts reaching us from so many will lead up to the realisation of their object, and that among all the blessings which, judging from past years, I am sure are laid up for us in the opening year, there is this one more, that Gowbarrow, in all its beauty, shall be consecrated to the nation.

I am always, my dear friends,
Yours faithfully,
OCTAVIA HILL

---

12 Matthew 4:4.

---

13 *See ill. 33.*

DONATIONS DURING 1904

	£	s	d
Allen, A.C., Esq			
Andrewes, Dr and Mrs F.	2	2	0
Austin, Miss A.	1	1	0
Anon.	1	0	0
Bailey, John, Esq	0	10	6
Beckwith, E.L., Esq	5	0	0
Blyth, P.L., Esq	5	0	0
Boulter, A.E., Esq	1	1	0
Bridgeman, Charles, Esq	1	1	0
Bridgeman, Mrs	5	0	0
Bartlett, Miss H.	2	0	0
Beaumont, Somerset, Esq	2	0	0
Bannerman, Mrs	10	0	0
Brooks, Miss	1	1	0
Burrage, Miss	1	0	0
Cockerill, Miss	17	3	6
Covington, Mrs Stenton	0	10	0
Cockerell, Sydney C., Esq	0	10	0
Cudworth, Mrs	1	0	0
Chase, Miss	2	2	0
Ducie, Earl of	2	2	0
Dawson, Miss (Notting Dale)	5	0	0
Erle, Miss	3	0	0
Evans, Mrs Richardson	20	0	0
Forman, Miss	1	1	0
Fortescue, Earl	1	1	0
Frankau, Miss (Convalescence)	2	0	0
Hutton, Mrs	5	0	0
Howitt, Miss	3	3	0
Harris, Miss E.M.	0	10	6
Hope-Edwards, Miss Ellen	13	3	0
Hill, Miss Octavia's Fellow-Workers	10	0	0
Johnston, The Misses	50	0	0
Johnston, The Misses (for brakes taking party to their house)	20	0	0
Luxmoore, H., Esq	3	0	0
Lowndes, Miss	11	0	0
In Memoriam, L.B.	1	0	0
Morris, F. Esq	1	0	0
Macaulay, Mrs	1	1	0
Mallet, Rev. H.	5	0	0
Macfie, Mrs (per)	2	10	0
Parker, Mr. and Mrs Perey	15	0	0
Poynter, Ambrose	2	2	0
Plummer, Rev. Charles	2	0	0
Pollock, Sir Frederick (fares to party at his house)	5	0	0
Somervell, Gordon	6	3	9
Schuster, Mrs	3	3	0
Schuster, Miss	10	0	0
Singleton, Miss	10	10	0
Temple, Mrs	2	10	0
Tufnell, Mrs	1	1	0
Thompson, Mrs C.	1	1	0
Todhunter, Miss	2	2	0
Wells, Miss Mary	1	0	0
Walker, Miss	2	0	0
Welbury-Milton, Mrs	0	10	0
Wright, Mrs Caleb	2	0	0
Winkworth, Mrs	1	0	0
	20	0	0
	£306	16	3

DONATION ACCOUNT, 1904

RECEIPTS

	£	s	d
In hand, January 1904 (including Interest on Deposit)	222	7	2 ½
Donations	306	16	3
Interest on Deposit	24	5	11
	£553	9	4 ½

DONATION ACCOUNT, 1904

EXPENDITURE

	£	s	d
Training and Boarding out	64	17	9
Pensioners (allowance and special gifts)	62	0	2
Summer Excursions and Entertainments	35	1	5
Open Spaces (special gifts)	34	17	0
Employment	30	0	6
Playground, care of	10	8	0
Sickness and Convalescence	10	0	4
Invalid Children	10	0	0
Apprenticing	10	0	0
Migration	9	6	7
Houses (improvement)	5	10	9
Workhouse Girls' Aid Society	5	0	0
Trees and Planting	4	10	5
Printing Letter to Fellow-Workers	4	9	6
Shoreditch Charity Organisation Society (special cases)	3	10	0
Reformatory Case	3	2	6
Carriage, Stationery, Postage	2	12	8 ½
Epileptics	2	10	0
Fever Hospital	1	1	0
In hand:			
Interest	85	15	4
Donations	158	15	5
	£553	9	4 ½

Examined and found correct, P.L. Blyth

RED CROSS HALL AND GARDEN ACCOUNT, 1904

RECEIPTS

	£	s	d
Balance at Bank, January 1904	6	16	5
Balance at Bank, January 1904	1	15	11
Hire of Hall	28	16	6
Hire of Office	10	8	0
Hire of Club Room	16	3	0
Donations:			
Allen, A.C., Esq	1	1	0
Blyth, Patrick, Esq	1	1	0
Gladstone, Miss	2	0	0
Harris, Miss S.J.	5	0	0
Stevens, Mrs Bingham	0	1	0
Webb, Mrs Randall	2	0	0
Interest, Red and White Cross Cottages	77	7	4
Programmes, sale of	8	4	7
Gas 4	18	0	0
Collections on Sundays	4	8	2
Violin Fees	3	18	0
Miscellaneous	0	1	0
	£173	19	11

RED CROSS HALL AND GARDEN ACCOUNT, 1904

EXPENDITURE

	£	s	d
Caretaker	59	9	0
Violin Class	17	10	0
Borough Rates	11	18	0

Garden:

	£	s	d		£	s	d
Repairs	4	12	3				
Hurdles and Wire for Creepers	2	0	3				
Pigeon House	1	19	6				
Pigeon Food	1	1	4				
Rent	1	0	0				
Creeper, training of	0	15	0				
Grass Seed	0	2	6		11	10	10
Entertainment Expenses					8	15	11 ½
Furniture and Repairs					9	3	7 ½
Gas 8					13	3	0
Cleaning					7	2	3
Water Rate					6	2	0
Printing, Postage and Stationery					5	14	2
Maypole Festival					4	8	4
Fuel					3	18	4 ½
Insurance					1	16	3
Income Tax					1	10	6
Land Tax					0	4	7
Cash in hand, December 31st 1904					4	1	3 ½
Balance at Bank, December 31st 1904					12	1	6
					£173	19	11

Audited and found correct, P.L. Blyth.

LETTER TO MY FELLOW-WORKERS

TO WHICH ARE ADDED

ACCOUNTS OF DONATIONS RECEIVED

FOR

WORK AMONG THE POOR

DURING 1905

BY

OCTAVIA HILL

SUMMARY

Ecclesiastical Commissioners: opening ceremony of the garden in Walworth; Red Cross flower show and good fellowship in Southwark; Lambeth garden open; Westminster… other housing: Marylebone; Notting Hill; unnecessary municipal building in Lambeth; Manchester… the reckless expenditure of local authorities and the advantages of the payment of rates by tenants… Octavia is asked to join the Royal Commission on the Poor Law… National Trust: Ullswater; Hindhead; Anglesey; Gowbarrow… outings for tenants… cadet corps… Cheap Cottages Exhibition… In Memoriam fund; Lady Jane Dundas's bequest; donation fund.

EDITOR'S NOTE

This letter contains Octavia's most extended discussion of the damage that was being done to economic development in general, and to the housing sector in particular, by 'the reckless and useless expenditure which we see everywhere incurred by local authorities'. Her most serious objection to the system of rates was that 'we seem… to have lost sight of the old connection between taxation and representation'. Weekly tenants could burden a community with debt for the next 60 years by voting for politicians who made extravagant promises, whilst being able to remove themselves from the indebted area at a week's notice. The property owner, on the other hand, who 'spends thousands on a building, to which he is committed as long as it stands, has no vote'. The only answer, as Octavia saw it, was to make tenants realise what proportion of their rent went in rates, or, even better, to get them to pay the rates themselves. She had begun several schemes along these lines in the previous decade (see 1894, 1895, 1896) but she clearly felt the problem was getting worse. However, just when she was gearing herself up to mount a campaign over it, she was asked to join the Royal Commission on the Poor Law, and she felt that her membership of the Commission made campaigning inappropriate. In fact, Octavia would never run this campaign, and she mentions that matter only once more, in 1906.

My friends,

You who year by year increase in number, and in readiness, and in power of help, some known to me personally, some only by letters of help and cheer, it is to you I dedicate this short record of some of the main features of our common work during 1905.

I will begin as usual about the houses, and first about the largest scheme, that on the Ecclesiastical Commissioners' estate at Walworth. It is rather a question whether I ought to report upon it here, as it is so distinctly under my friend Miss Lumsden. But she and I are in such close touch and perfect agreement, it has grown so directly out of my own work for the Commissioners, and it is still in its infancy, so that important questions affecting its permanent form are needing our joint settlement, that it feels more or less under my wing. Besides I am sure that you will all be glad to hear about it.

The rebuilding is now completed for nearly 300 of the families who are to be rehoused there in cottages, cottage flats, or sets of rooms in three-storied houses. The remainder of the building is progressing fast; the resident superintendent has been appointed. The public garden is laid out and opened. The letting is a considerable and very responsible task, and has made great calls on the time and the wisdom of Miss Lumsden and her group of able fellow-workers. The whole character of the area depends and will depend for many a year on the selection of tenants, their character and way of life will decide that of the neighbourhood. They appear an interesting and thoroughly respectable body of residents, and should help and cheer one another. Their little gardens are, many of them, already well cared for and crowded with flowers, and some of the families had their meals out of doors last summer, and had put up little tents for shade. The Commissioners have carefully preserved every tree which could be left in the former back yards, and have varied the position of the spaces left for flowerbeds so as to include any tree or lilac bush which was there. This encourages

---

1   The letter ends 'with best Christmas wishes'.

the tenants about their gardens.

The public garden given by the Commissioners has been handed over to the London County Council. I was present at the opening ceremony.[2] A platform was erected at one end, a railing in front of it separated us from the rest of the ground which was absolutely filled from end to end by a solid mass of people. The yards belonging to neighbouring owners, which bound the garden on one side, were also full of spectators; wretched untidy yards; but one felt what the outlook over the garden would be to the dwellers in those houses. The sun was shining brightly, and I could see the beautifully clean fresh buildings on every side which the Commissioners had built, or were building. I saw the pleasant bow-windows; I knew what capital space there was at the back of each house. I looked straight up one wide street, newly formed and replacing the narrow one which had been; I knew something of what the life now was within the houses, and my mind could not but revert to the day in October of 1903, when the estate reverted to the owners; of the rotten and leaking roofs; of the falling plaster; of the dangerous staircases; of the forlorn dirt and over-crowding. I thought of the far-sighted wisdom which had led the Ecclesiastical Commissioners to resolve to rebuild the area, of all the silent, patient, swift and experienced labour which had effected the transformation I was looking at; and I was thankful to know that they had decided to retain the estate in their own hands so that, in the years to come, the future condition and the management should be determined by them. I was thankful, too, to know that there were many ladies qualified, or qualifying, to be the representatives in the future of landlords minded thus to retain the government of their own estates. Miss Lumsden was abroad, and I happened to be alone, and I sat and thought while the speeches went on, thought how few of the speakers knew what quiet work had gone to the making of what they saw, and as I felt the silence of one who had been the moving spirit of it all, and who had brought us all in to do our several parts, Browning's words recurred to me:

The town's true master did the town but know.[3]

---

2   On 15 July 1905. 'The Ecclesiastical Commissioners were represented by Sir Lewis Dibdin and Sir A. de Bock Porter. The former made a most satisfactory speech, showing that he grasped the main points of the work.' (Letter from Octavia to her sister Emily, 16 July 1905, Maurice, 1914, p.562.) *See ills. 29 and 30.*

---

3   From Robert Browning's 'How It Strikes a Contemporary' in *Men and Women*,

It is in such work that England's real strength lies, and happy are they who can assist it in their own sphere.

Curiously enough, I went back straight the same afternoon to our Red Cross flower show. The warehouses were high, the streets were littered with refuse, the sun had little power of reaching the houses, our little garden, surrounded by high buildings, was but a tiny space compared with the Walworth one. Still it was an oasis, and it was one with a history. One felt what Walworth, with its better outside conditions, lacked, and what the years must bring it. There the personal relations, the friendships of years, had had no time to grow; it was clean, airy, hopeful, a space for life to come into—but the life was in Southwark. Such memories crowded round it, such visions of friends who had been there, and given and done things since the day of the opening in 1887, when the motto on the wall showed the words:

The wilderness shall rejoice and blossom as the rose.[4]

London air has forbidden the actual flowers, but, spiritually, how true has been the promise. How our Good Shepherd has looked down on us; how the records of Lady Ducie, Mr Cowper, Lady Jane Dundas speak to some of us; how we remember Mr George MacDonald and his family giving us, as the first performance at the Hall, the representation of *The Pilgrim's Progress*;[5] and on and on through the

---

1855. The line is actually: 'The town's true master, if the town but knew!'

---

4   Isaiah 35:1.

---

5   On 22 September 1888 (1888, p.245, n.6). George MacDonald (1824 –1905) was a writer of many talents. Famous in his own day as a novelist, he was also a poet, essayist, lecturer, critic and preacher, but above all a writer of fantasy for both adults and children. His best-known children's stories are *At the Back of the North Wind*, *The Princess and the Goblin* and *The Princess and Curdie*. His adult fantasies, *Phantaste* and *Lilith*, have been influential on later writers. C.S. Lewis, in particular, regarded him as his 'master'. MacDonald was educated at Aberdeen University and later came to London to train as a minister in the Congregational Church. He married Louisa Powell (by whom he had 11 children) and took up his first pastorate at Arundel in Sussex in 1851. He left this post because the elders of the church did not like the 'advanced' German theology he preached and, after a short period in Manchester as an independent preacher, he settled in London and thereafter earned his living as a writer and lecturer. He got to know Frederick Denison Maurice and under his influence became a member of the Church of England. It was through Maurice that he got to know Octavia Hill. They met when MacDonald came to lecture on poetry at the

years, the place has gathered sacredness, not only from those who are gone before, but from the many who remain to help, and next Sunday, when we gather to hear the *Messiah*, we shall remember them all, and feel them near in our Christmas gathering. At Walworth the crowd was all unknown, but as I entered Red Cross garden there were friendly greetings of poor and rich, and these most hearty among themselves, for those who frequent the Hall know one another, and to them, too, the place is crowded with their memories of those who have been with them there in past years. Again, another contrast struck me. At Walworth the platform was decorated with a few grand plants, hired or lent; at Red Cross it was the neighbourhood itself which furnished the decorations, not so grand by any means, but very important in our eyes. For it was the people's flower show, and here were their little plants, tenderly watched and watered, and brought to the show; and those who gave the prizes, or led them to the steps of the platform, lived among them and knew them.[6] To such end Walworth has yet to

---

Working Men's College in Red Lion Square, Holborn (which had been established by Maurice) in 1859. As the family grew up, they began to give dramatic performances of John Bunyan's *The Pilgrim's Progress*. These were first put on as private entertainments at the family home in Hammersmith known as The Retreat, later occupied by William Morris and re-named Kelmscott House. In later years the MacDonalds travelled the country giving performances of the play. MacDonald himself often took the part of Mr Greatheart. During a tour of the north of England in 1880 his daughter Grace, who was playing the part of Piety, was taken seriously ill with a lung haemorrhage. At Harrogate a hall had been booked for the performance and Octavia Hill was drafted in at the last minute to play the part. As a result of the closeness between the Hills and the MacDonalds, *Pilgrim's Progress* was frequently performed for Octavia's various groups of tenants, and Ellen Chase records the impact it made on those in Deptford: 'The tale was very likely received with better understanding in some of the more favoured properties, but never with more appreciation than in our own in the far-away South-East. We heard later that it was well into the early morning before the players reached home, but they must have felt their trouble of small account compared with the delight of the audience, the smaller children even leaving their seats to press against the platform and feast their eyes on the glow of colour and candlelight, flowers and fruits, when the curtain rose on the House Beautiful. It was a new and unimaginable world brought before them, one we might hope they would never quite forget.' (Chase, 1929, p.13.) MacDonald's 1868 novel *Robert Falconer* contains an idealised portrait of Octavia as 'Mary St John', a beautiful and angelic young woman whose work among the poor includes the provision of housing.

---

6   A copy of the programme for this flower show, called the West Southwark Flower Show and covering the parishes of St Saviour, Christ Church and St George the Martyr, survives in the Church of England Record Centre. The show took place

grow; with its better conditions it should do better, but there is something sacred in the small beginnings and early unnoticed effort which it is hard for the later schemes to come up to.

And yet my heart sang for joy when I went over the Walworth Estate the other day.

The Lambeth Estate, too, is all now in letting, the public garden is open, and it all seems very satisfactory. It forms a large respectable area, which must be a great comfort to those tidy families whose work takes them to that neighbourhood; and one would think such a group of residents would do something to reform the locality of the New Cut.

In Westminster we have under our charge a large and various community in the new and old houses belonging to the Ecclesiastical Commissioners. They have put under our care a good many more old houses, the leases of which have fallen in during the year, and are giving us 11 more at Christmas.[7] But the largest extension there will be in March, when the leases fall in of two streets which are back to back with the great number of three-roomed houses rebuilt for workmen's dwellings a few years ago, and which are under our charge. The Commissioners purpose completing the area in much the same way, and we are already busy preparing suggested plans by their request.

All the Marylebone houses have gone on in much the same quiet and satisfactory way, St Christopher's Place, with its facilities for social meetings, its library, and bulb show, its steady and regular improvement, and its large group of tenants, taking the lead.

Notting Hill has distinctly made progress. There has been a very

---

between 3.00 and 6.30 pm on Saturday 15 July. Admission was two pence—and 'no children will be admitted after five o'clock'—with prizes presented at 4.30 pm by the Hon. Mrs Talbot. The prize-giving must have taken quite a while, as there were no fewer than 29 categories, with a total of 114 prizes, varying in worth from four shillings to one shilling. Cut flowers and window boxes could be entered, as well as potted plants. Eight of the prize categories were for geraniums, the flower of working-class respectability, modest but dependable. In the well-known Victorian language of flowers, the geranium stood for 'comfort': in the working-class cottage it signalled a comfortable cosiness. Caroline Stephen had stipulated geraniums by the door in Hereford Buildings (1882, pp.156-57), and the Countess of Lovelace had her estate workers' cottages designed to ensure that the windows would not disturb 'the geranium and the family Bible'. (Lovelace, 1928, p.717.) In 1905 and 1906 the Princess of Wales sent gifts of geraniums to the Kyrle Society for its work in 'window gardening'. (Kyrle Society reports 1905, p.21; 1906, p.21.)

---

7   This possibly refers to Upper Garden Street and Regency Street.

wise mayor of Kensington during the past year,[8] and we have heard nothing of extension of municipal schemes. Whether municipal buildings be advisable or not, it certainly in no way takes the place of our work, which we consider very important, and we hope their area will be settled independently of ours. Four additional houses in the street where we are mainly at work have been bought by friends and placed under our care during this year. This is a cause of great satisfaction to us, as every house in the hands of uncertain landlords is a possible difficulty and drawback. Wherever there are quarrels, bad conduct or neglect, it is not only bad in itself, but prevents tidy, striving, poor families from availing themselves of the light, healthy, cheap rooms in a pleasant locality, and tends to bring into temptation the tenants we are hoping to keep in better ways.

One interesting feature of the Notting Hill scheme has been the opportunity it has given us of employing and gradually developing the power of several of the lower grade of workmen who are the first to suffer when trade is slack. The small jobs needed in old houses enable us to try them, to teach them, and to advance them as they show industry, capacity and will to work. The ladies there have shown both patience and skill about such supervision as enables us to employ such men. There is less disturbance of tenants in inhabited houses by getting repairs done thus, bit by bit, as opportunity allows; and it is delightful to watch men improve and to know that several are thus pretty constantly at work, and the condition of the houses also gradually bettered.

The Improved Tenements Association has placed two more houses in Notting Hill under our care.

I do not know that there is anything specially to record about Southwark. The exodus towards the suburbs tells on the letting, and the matter will have to be carefully watched.

---

8   The mayor of Kensington from 1905–07 was Alderman Henry Robson JP. In the previous year Octavia had turned down a request from Kensington borough council to manage some of their housing stock, owing to her opposition to municipal housing in principle: 'they are disappointed, and rather angry, at my refusal to manage for them what they have got. They have no right to be so, I have always opposed municipal building and it would ill become me to accept office!' (Darley, 1990, p.282.) In fact, the councillors were not much more enthusiastic themselves, as Octavia's warm tribute to Alderman Robson makes clear. 'Generally speaking, Kensington Council, which has been Conservative since its formation, has been an unenthusiastic supporter of municipal housing... by the 1930s the Kensington Housing Trust, the Sutton Dwellings Trust and the Peabody Trust between them had built almost twice as many new homes as had the borough council.' (Denny, 1993, p.86.)

By the way, I wonder why the London County Council is about to build again in Lambeth. Sir Richard Farrant and the Peabody trustees have drawn attention to the way in which South London, near the centre, is overbuilt. Everyone who knows anything about it confirms this, the local papers advertise for weekly tenants to whom a month's or a fortnight's rent free is offered. Mr Nettlefold, who has been doing such wise work on the Birmingham Corporation with regard to their policy as to housing, tells us in his admirable and helpful pamphlet that Birmingham counted the empty tenements before deciding about building.[9] This natural course does not appear to suggest itself to the London County Council.

---

9   John Sutton Nettlefold (1866–1930) was a member of one of Birmingham's most successful industrial dynasties. The Nettlefolds were Unitarians and members of an exceptional group of Birmingham non-conformist families, including the Kenricks and the Bunces, who read Ruskin with enthusiasm and acted on his precepts. John Sutton Nettlefold's grandfather (also John Sutton: 1792–1866) had founded Nettlefold and Chamberlain, an engineering company producing screws, with his brother-in-law Joseph Chamberlain in 1854. Chamberlain sent his son—young Joseph, aged 18—to work at the factory and keep an eye on his father's investment. Young Joseph —later known as Radical Joe, mayor of Birmingham and member of parliament— made such a success of the business that he was able to sell his share of it in 1874 for £120,000. In 1902 Nettlefold Ltd merged with Guest, Keen and Co., which still exists as GKN, a major supplier of parts to aerospace and automobile manufactures. Octavia's Mr Nettlefold—young John Sutton—was active in Birmingham politics and chairman of the Birmingham housing committee. Interest in social housing, and in Octavia's methods in particular, seemed to run in the family. John's uncle Frederick (1833–1913) sent £20 to the donation fund in 1882, 1883, 1886, 1888 and 1889, and John's brother Oswald (1864–1924) sent £5 in 1886. John Nettlefold wrote a series of books and articles addressing housing and open spaces issues, in which he advocated town planning as a means of accommodating large numbers of people in good housing, with land left for open spaces. He was generous in his praise of Octavia: 'Miss Octavia Hill's work is... so well known that I need not describe it here. Suffice it to say that owners of property under her management have always received four or five per cent on their investments, and tenants are so well treated that there are always plenty looking for houses "under the ladies". Her success is largely due to the individual attention given to the tenants. The housing problem is largely a question of individual character. Landlords who complain of the dirty and destructive habits of their tenants are very often themselves directly responsible for what they complain of in that they treat their tenants as mere rent-producing animals, and ignore the human element.' (Nettlefold, 1909, pp.195-96.) Nettlefold was not reticent about using his published work to promote his own committee, and it is easy to see why Octavia followed his progress with interest. He favoured slum clearance by using the Housing of the Working Classes Act 1890 to force slum landlords to bring their properties up to an acceptable standard at their own expense, and claimed that, between January 1902 and June 1905, 560 houses in Birmingham were rendered habitable, 225 were repaired without

I am glad to hear that Manchester has secured the services of a lady trained in Edinburgh for the management of a block of buildings for a company formed for providing dwellings. The problem appears to be a difficult one, partly because of the time it takes to redeem a place from the bad name resulting from unsuccessful management. Those who have had it to do know how difficult the task is; but they know too, that it can be done with time, patience, knowledge, and, above all, the right person. I heartily wish Manchester success. It is a most important beginning, and, well carried through, may have large and beneficent results in that city, and other cities.

Before quite leaving the subject of housing, I should like to refer to the important question of the compounding for rates. The practice is, I feel sure, at the root of the reckless and useless expenditure which we see everywhere incurred by local authorities. The very moment that the large body of electors felt that they paid the rates, that moment we should have deliberate expenditure. If it were large it would at least be incurred because it was believed to be really good. At present the large body of electors do not realise that it affects them; weekly tenants have the votes; weekly tenants don't realise that their rent includes rates; weekly tenants vote expenditure involving loans for 60 years, but can themselves remove from the burdened area at a week's notice. It is neither fair nor wise.

For some years we have ourselves arranged for a considerable number of tenants to pay their rates direct. We have also arranged for a great many to pay a fixed rent and a weekly instalment for rate, which varies with the rise and fall. This latter plan is not quite so educational, but it is certainly effectual for its object, and it has the great advantage of being far more adapted to the habits of the tenants; they prefer paying weekly. It also prevents their accepting lower rent till rates fall due, and then absconding, which is bad for them, their landlords, and local authority. It also saves the local authority the expense and trouble of

---

notices, 283 were undergoing repairs and 258 were demolished. (Nettlefold, 1905, p.45.) He boasted that, as a result of his policies, there was no town in England where the average rise in house rent owing to slum reform had been so small as in Birmingham, *viz.* 10$\frac{1}{2}$d per week. He also claimed that town planning had created 12 acres of open space in congested inner city areas. (Nettlefold, 1910, p.4.) In his 1905 book *A Housing Policy*, to which Octavia seems to be referring in this letter, he makes frequent reference to her *Homes of the London Poor* as a guide to best practice, and he claims that, in Birmingham, the housing committee would not even consider building municipal housing unless their programmes of slum clearance had 'created a scarcity of good cheap houses' in an area. (Nettlefold, 1905, p.21.)

collection, and enables the landlord to avail himself of the discount for compounding, out of which he can pay himself for the trouble of collecting, checking claims, and for having to advance money; the rates now in London being always demanded in advance.

I am glad to know that the Peabody trustees have adopted some such arrangement with their tenants on several of their estates; also that the Artisans', Labourers' and General Dwellings Company have arranged in 2,100 of their tenements that their tenants should pay the rates direct.

But the advantages of the direct payment need to be pressed very emphatically on all London owners. Also there are one or two more difficulties put in the way of the plan by the local authorities which, to my mind, ought to be removed.

I should like strongly to urge the repeal of Clause 4 in the Act for Amending the Law with respect to the Rating of Occupiers for short terms, 32 & 33 Vict., Ch. 41, which empowers local authorities to compel owners to pay rates direct for tenements under £20 annual value.

This seems to me distinctly undesirable on grounds of public policy. Westminster adopted this course and, with a few strokes of the pen, took away from a large number of intelligent and careful tenants on the Peabody Estates, and from some under my care, the main effective incentive to watchful criticism of local expenditure.

Again an anomaly takes place with regard to rating in some parishes which appears to me distinctly unfair on tenants paying their own rates. The LCC table, published with a view to get London boroughs to adopt a uniform plan as to assessing weekly tenements, recommends a certain deduction, which it calls for 'contingencies', meant, of course, to meet the uncertainties of weekly tenancies and enhanced cost of repairs for such properties.

Such reduction in assessment is, so far as my experience goes, made in London boroughs, except in cases where tenants pay rates direct. There a higher scale of assessment is adopted so that you may have houses in a row precisely similar in every respect assessed at different amounts. The annual value must be identical, but the allowance for contingencies not being set down by law it cannot be demanded, and the loss falls on the tenant paying rates direct, and on his landlord. This appears unfair.

Were I dealing with the matter I should recommend that some much smaller discount should be allowed to small tenants paying rates punctually before a prescribed date. It should be less than that made to landlords for compounding for a large group of tenements, but I think there should be such an allowance, it would encourage thrifty tenants and save collectors trouble.

We seem quite in this matter to have lost sight of the old connection between taxation and representation. The owner who spends thousands on a building, to which he is committed as long as it stands, has no vote; his passing weekly tenants help to burden it with debt for 60 years.

I was about to try to bring these facts out at some conference, composed of those conversant with and interested about such matters, and to get them considered in the true interests of the whole community, when I was asked to become a member of the Royal Commission on the Poor Law.[10]

The questions to be dealt with are so important, the experience I have had, actually in the homes of the poor for years, is so great, and has been exceptional in as far as we have met one another with mutual duties, that I did not feel I could refuse, glad as I should have been could I rightly have gone on quietly in the old paths.

But the call seems clear and it implies many things. First, I must not, for the moment, take up any conference or public action with regard to the direct payment of rates. I can only, as of old, hope that the practical plan we are carrying out may gradually spread, in spite of the artificial hindrances which it meets with. I am glad to find that Mr Nettlefold is bringing forward the subject in Birmingham.[11]

Then, secondly, I have so to rearrange the work for which I am personally responsible that it shall not suffer from the claims on my time which this Commission will make. I do not yet know what these will be, they must be considerable, but I have quite a splendid band of

---

10 Octavia received a letter from the Prime Minister, Arthur Balfour, asking her to join the Commission in November 1905. 'The new Commission was a legacy of the outgoing Conservative administration. Balfour confided to Beatrice Webb, in the carriage on the way to the first performance of Shaw's *Major Barbara*, that he had had great problems keeping politicians out of the Commission and in finding a chairman. He had chosen Lord George Hamilton, who, he explained to her, "is not such a fool as he looks".' (Darley, 1990, p.287.)

11 John Nettlefold shared Octavia's concerns about the damage inflicted by high rates, and the unfairness of the system which made some people pay for other people's choices. In 1908 Nettlefold had a series of his newspaper articles published in a penny pamphlet as a 'Message to the Citizens' of Birmingham. Amongst other things, he deplored the fact that 'at present nearly half the population of actual Birmingham enjoys benefits for which they pay nothing'. He favoured spreading the burden and thus lightening it. (Nettlefold, 1908, p.16.)

fellow-workers, who I know will do their utmost that I should not be missed, and they are so experienced, so zealous, so united, that I feel no alarm at all at the prospect of partial withdrawal. I think a small amount of time will go far in keeping things together. I sometimes think they may even go better. At any rate it need not be for always, but all my appointments, all my plans, all my organisation must be reviewed, and this will be my first duty so soon as I see what time, even at the beginning, the Commission will require. That will demand my full, best and very deliberate strength.

It is well that the call comes just as one great open space scheme is nearing completion. The land on Ullswater is practically secured, although we are still collecting, both for the expenses, and for some adjoining fields, mentioned in our appeal. For these latter we have, however, five years' option of purchase. This undertaking has required a good deal of time in many ways, a good deal of writing has had to be done, and more speaking than I ever had to do in any one year before. I have attended meetings in Cambridge, Manchester, and Liverpool, besides two in London. But now it is done, and all who have so generously and affectionately helped may feel sure that the lovely stretch of country is indeed henceforward open to everyone who loves and can visit it. My very deep thanks are due to all who have co-operated. I wish my thanks could reach you all in far away places from which gifts have come. It is a very large sum of money to have raised and to have raised in time, and we must all be thankful to have been permitted to help.

The National Trust has this year also been endowed with the 700 acres of Hindhead,[12] and with six acres of grand headland in Anglesey, as well as with Gowbarrow, its largest possession. So it has been a record year for open spaces.

We had not many summer parties this year; we could not go to my brother's, nor to Sir Frederick Pollock's; but our kind hostesses the Miss Johnstons (one of whom has since passed away) again welcomed us at Manor Lodge. Mrs Sharp gave a delightful small garden party at

12 Sir Robert Hunter, co-founder with Octavia and Hardwicke Rawnsley of the National Trust, lived in nearby Haslemere, so once again we can see the pattern of early National Trust acquisitions reflecting the concerns of the founders for their own immediate areas. Hunter had moved to Haslemere with his family in 1883, as the railway enabled him to commute to his job as legal adviser to the Post Office in London. However, he worried about the effect of the railways in opening up Surrey to commuters like himself, and wanted to preserve the tranquillity that had drawn him there.

Wimbledon, Mr and Mrs Clutton Brock again entertained a group of tenants at Weybridge, and the Hon. Mrs John Talbot invited a party to Edenbridge.[13]

The Southwark cadet corps and its club are happily established in the rebuilt premises, and the full money has been obtained for the building. They are greatly in need of more annual subscriptions to meet current expenses, being almost reduced to refusing cadets.

It was thought desirable to have ladies among the judges to decide on the best cottages built at Letchworth for the Cheap Cottages Exhibition,[14] and Miss Yorke and I were asked to act. This we were able to do, and we spent several days in visiting the various cottages. It was very interesting work and I think the scheme will prove very useful, specially do I think that the detailed catalogue will be of more than temporary service. It is full of helpful and definite suggestions to those about to build, and they can modify their buildings according to local conditions and needs. These are manifestly so various, that no one type of cottage can be of universal fitness, but the respective merits of

---

13 Hon. Mrs John Talbot (1840–1925) presented the prizes at the flower show, mentioned earlier in this letter. Née Meriel Lyttelton, eldest daughter of George, fourth Lord Lyttelton, Mrs Talbot was the sister of Lavinia Lyttelton who married Edward Talbot, with whom she set up the Talbot Settlement in Walworth (1903, p.502.) Two Lyttelton sisters thus married two Talbot brothers. After her mother's premature death, Meriel had to look after the family home, Hagley, and raise the family. In 1860 she married Johnny Talbot, who was Conservative MP for West Kent. She was very close to her mother-in-law, the philanthropic Mrs Caroline Talbot.

---

14 On 16 July 1905 Octavia wrote asking her sister Emily to join Harriot Yorke and herself on a trip to Letchworth: 'Miss Yorke says we are to have a carriage reserved for us, and to be driven to the cottages, of which there are 120!' (Maurice, 1914, p.562.) Letchworth was the creation of the First Garden City Co. Ltd., formed in 1903 to turn the theories of Ebenezer Howard into reality. Howard's book *Tomorrow* (1898), republished in 1902 as *Garden Cities of Tomorrow*, advocated a new way of building that would bring together the best aspects of town and country life. Industrial development in Letchworth brought with it the need for workmen's cottages, but those built by the Garden City Company proved too expensive. The Cheap Cottages Exhibition was intended to show how attractive and suitable working-class housing could be built more economically. The winning cottage was of brick and tile. 'In the intervening years before the First World War a variety of societies were set up to build cheap cottages and the district council was also persuaded to build, since it could obtain loans on less onerous conditions than private organisations... The early cottage building societies became expert at the problem of designing an economic yet attractive small house, and in this sense, Letchworth was developing the work started at Bourneville and, of course, still going forward at this time.' (Tarn, 1973, pp.164-68.)

those built for competition could be thoroughly studied at Letchworth and in the catalogue.

I have during the past year given £100 from the In Memoriam fund for emigration, carefully carried out for selected families by experienced workers with knowledge of the candidates.[15]

From Lady Jane Dundas's bequest I have lent £50 for the professional education of a lady, who, I believe, will thus become a valuable worker.[16]

Both these funds are drawing to an end. I cannot be grateful enough to the donors who have thus for now some years strengthened my hands for important action. I am glad I resolved to spend the amounts during a term of years; they have thus been better spent. The interest on deposit, as will be seen from the accounts, has always been added to my donation fund.

And now last I come to the donation fund, strong in all your gifts, and filling so large a part in the well-being and training of many. It has no surprises, no great sensations, no sudden bursts of action; quietly, steadily, efficiently and accompanied with much loving care, it provides what is really needed for those who are really known. Thank you all, my friends, for helping me to achieve this by your gifts, and with earnest thanks to all my beloved fellow-workers, and with best Christmas wishes,

Believe me to be,

Affectionately yours,

OCTAVIA HILL

---

15 This is the last reference to the In Memoriam fund, which was presumably thus exhausted. For an assessment of the fund, see 1899, p.437, n.9.

---

16 This is the last reference to Lady Jane Dundas's bequest in the text of the letters, but the accounts for 1908 show £13 4s 6d given to the Red Cross Hall from the fund, and those for 1909 show £50 given to the donation fund. As this is described as the balance, this presumably represented the end of the fund (1909, p.626).

DONATIONS DURING 1905

	£	s	d
Andrewes, Mr and Mrs	1	1	0
Allen, A.C., Esq	2	2	0
Austin, Miss	1	0	0
Blyth, P.L., Esq	1	1	0
Bailey, John, Esq	5	0	0
Bannerman, Mrs	1	1	0
Bartlett, Miss H.	2	0	0
Bridgeman, C., Esq	3	0	0
Bridgeman, Mrs	2	0	0
Burrage, Miss	25	13	0
Cockerell, Sydney C., Esq	1	0	0
Cudworth, Mrs	2	2	0
Ducie, The Earl of	5	0	0
Dawson, Miss	3	0	0
Evans, Mrs Richardson	1	1	0
Erle, Miss	20	0	0
Forman, Miss	1	1	0
Frankau, Miss	6	0	0
Hutton, Mrs	3	3	0
Hoole, Elijah, Esq	1	1	0
Heberden, Mrs	5	0	0
Howitt, Miss	0	10	0
Hewson, The Misses	1	0	0
In Memoriam, L.B.	1	0	0
Johnston, Miss	20	0	0
Johnston, Miss (for vans for party to her house)	3	0	0
Lewes, Mrs	0	10	0
Lowndes, Miss	1	0	0
Macaulay, Mrs	6	0	0
Montefiore, Claude J., Esq	10	10	0
Morris, F., Esq	1	1	0
Nicholson, The Dowager Lady	5	0	0
Plummer, Rev. C.	5	0	0
Roberts, Mrs	2	2	0
Somervell, Gordon, Esq	3	3	0
Simpson, Mrs	1	1	0
Tufnell, Mrs	1	1	0
Thompson, Mrs C.	2	2	0
Todhunter, Miss	1	0	0
Wells, Miss Mary	3	0	0
Walker, Miss M.A.	1	0	0
Welbury-Mitton, Mrs	3	0	0
Winkworth, Mrs	20	0	0
	£184	6	0

DONATION ACCOUNT, 1905

RECEIPTS

	£	s	d
In hand, January 1905 (including Interest)	224	9	9
Donations	184	6	0
Interest on Deposit	19	2	5
	£447	18	2

DONATION ACCOUNT, 1905

EXPENDITURE

	£	s	d
Pensioners	112	2	8
Gowbarrow (transferred from General Fund)	51	0	0
Training and Boarding-out in Homes	43	14	6
Relief in Sickness or Distress	36	6	8
Excursions and Parties	11	2	0 ½
Playground, care of	10	8	0
Parish Room (poor district)	10	0	0
Cadet Corps	5	0	0
Crippled Boys' Workshop	5	0	0
Emigration	5	0	0
Club Room (poor district)	5	0	0
Soil for Gardens	1	13	6
Employment	1	5	0
London Fever Hospital	1	1	0
Printing Letter to Fellow-Workers	3	12	6
Stationery, Postage, &c.	1	14	7
In hand:			
Interest	54	17	9
Balance	88	19	11 ½
	£447	18	2

Examined and found correct, P.L. Blyth

RED CROSS HALL AND GARDEN ACCOUNT, 1905

RECEIPTS

		£	s	d
Balance at Bank, January 1905		12	1	6
Cash in hand, January 1905		4	1	3 ½
Interest, Red and White Cross Cottages		77	7	4
Hire of Hall		27	17	6
Hire of Office		13	0	0

Donations:

	£	s	d	£	s	d
Allen, A.C., Esq	1	1	0			
Barnett, W.H., Esq	1	0	0			
Blyth, P., Esq	1	1	0			
Bridgeman, C., Esq	2	0	0			
Causton, R.K., Esq	1	0	0			
Gladstone, Miss	2	0	0			
Harris, Miss	1	1	0			
Hill, Miss	0	10	0			
Martelli, F., Esq	1	0	0			
Morshead, Mrs	1	0	0			
Temple, Mrs	1	1	0			
Webb, Mrs	2	0	0			
Wigan, Sir F.	1	1	0			
Willcox, W.H.	1	1	0			
				16	16	0
Clubroom Rent				9	15	0
Programmes, sale of				9	7	5 ½
Violin Fees				4	17	0
Collections on Sundays				4	14	9
Gas 3				10	0	0
				£183	7	10

RED CROSS HALL AND GARDEN ACCOUNT, 1905

EXPENDITURE

				£	s	d
Caretaker				57	7	0
Garden:						
Labour	6	12	6			
Architect's Fee	6	6	0			
Lawn Mower	2	16	6			
Concreting Walk	2	3	6			
Plants	1	12	6			
Pigeon Food	1	4	4			
Repairs	1	2	6			
Rent	1	0	0			
Notice Board	0	7	6			
				23	5	4
Violin Class				17	10	0
Entertainment Expenses				11	5	6 ½
Repairs				11	2	9
Gas 11				1	8	
Borough Rates				11	10	11
Water Rate				10	7	6
Cleaning				7	0	3 ½
Stationery				5	3	7 ½
Fuel				3	19	11
Maypole Festival				3	16	9
Insurance				2	9	9
Income Tax				1	13	3
Land Tax				0	4	7
Cash in hand				5	8	11 ½
				£183	7	10

Examined and found correct, P.L. Blyth.

LETTER TO MY FELLOW-WORKERS

TO WHICH ARE ADDED

ACCOUNTS OF DONATIONS RECEIVED

FOR

WORK AMONG THE POOR

DURING 1906

BY

OCTAVIA HILL

SUMMARY

Housing: Notting Hill... Ecclesiastical Commissioners: Westminster; Lambeth; Walworth... Marylebone; Southwark; Chelsea; Lisson Grove... a new scheme for making tenants pay their own rates... Poor Law Commission and its impact on other work... National Trust: Gowbarrow... Red Cross Hall... entertainments for tenants... donation fund... Octavia contemplates her own demise.

EDITOR'S NOTE

After several years during which the housing sections of the letters have been dominated by accounts of the grand re-building schemes of the Ecclesiastical Commissioners, Octavia gives pride of place in this letter to Notting Hill. Her supporters were buying up more and more houses in Katherine Street (now Wilsham Street), so that Octavia now controlled 51 out of 113 in her campaign to ensure that 'cleanliness, order and sobriety succeed disorder, dirt and drunkenness'. She takes the opportunity to restate one of the key principles on which her housing work had been founded over 40 years before: old and run-down properties are better than smart new re-builds because they afford the opportunity to reach the 'lowest class of tenants' and raise them, together with the structures. New 'model tenements', on the other hand, require model tenants to go in them, so the opportunity to reach the lowest class is lost. Perhaps Octavia felt the need for this re-statement because she had been moving away from this approach in the demolition and re-building of considerable acreages of South London for the Ecclesiastical Commissioners.

My dear friends,

There seems much to be thankful for in looking back over the past year.

I will begin by chronicling the new work in the houses.

In Notting Hill much depends on our obtaining more and more control in the street, as we are mainly struggling there with bad conditions in houses not under our care. We have happily been able to purchase five more leasehold houses here, making 51, in all, out of 113. One has been bought by Miss Wedgwood, two by Miss Eva Boord, one by Lady Farrer, and one by Colonel Bainbrigge. The two latter had previously bought one house each. These houses had been in the possession of a man who let them furnished. This system does not encourage thrift, nor does it attract those tenants who care for their homes. Besides this, the management usually leaves much to be desired, and streets so let get a bad name, and usually are inhabited by a very low class of tenants. This fact makes a great difficulty in taking them over. One cannot retain tenants living in vice, irregular in their payments, or violent in their habits. The more decent and self-controlled are shy of such localities, and the problems of letting become very difficult. We have felt these to the utmost. But my experience teaches me that the question is one of time, and that with patience on the part of owners, and earnest and prolonged perseverance on the part of those who manage, the neighbourhood gradually improves, and cleanliness, order and sobriety succeed disorder, dirt and drunkenness. Moreover, this purchase of old and badly used property has the great advantage that, by means of it, one really reaches the lowest class of tenants, accommodates them at a much more moderate rent than is possible in the new buildings, and raises a certain proportion of them with each house, or group of houses, thus obtained. Also one protects from annoyance and degradation the respectable tenant who, through poverty, has sunk into such a district.

The work at Notting Hill, therefore, is one after my own heart, and I feel that there we are meeting, so far as in us lies, with the most difficult of all the housing problems, and doing good in ways which no new building schemes can achieve. I am earnestly anxious that full strength should be given to this kind of undertaking, and feel deeply grateful to those who are devoting their time and thought to this branch of work, which needs so much hope, resolution, and patience.

One interesting feature there has been the opportunity offered by these old buildings to employ several of the tenants in various simple repairs and improvements. The inhabitants are a poor lot, physically weak, old, and without character or skill—just the class that are first to feel depression of trade. And they are, many of them, untrained men attached to the building trade, who have felt severely the recent depression, which has specially affected this trade. It has been most satisfactory to be able to set them to small jobs of white-washing or painting. It has done good all round, improved the houses, taught the men a little, tided them over a crisis, and kept up their heart and hope.

We are also much rejoiced to welcome to the parish a new vicar, the Rev. R.M. Carrick,[1] who has experience of the harm to the recipients done by ill-considered doles, and who has set himself to abolish them in his parish. A parish like this, in the near neighbourhood of richer ones, suffers most of all from these doles, which are deadly in their influence. The task of abolishing them will be hard and unpopular, and I am glad that our group of workers is rendering help willingly and efficiently.

The Improved Tenements Association, who put their houses under our management, has purchased 15 more cottages during 1906.[2] They are of the kind eagerly sought after by tenants, and we are glad to add them to our area.

The next most important addition to our work has been the completion of the tenements in Westminster, built by the Ecclesiastical Commissioners, and referred to in my last letter. They are 42 in number and are contiguous to some of those which we have managed for the last seven years. They are excellent in every way; they have been eagerly sought, and were let and occupied in an incredibly short time.[3]

---

1   Robert Carrick was vicar of St James Norlands in Notting Dale from 1906 to 1916.

---

2   Thirteen of them were in Prince's Place. (Malpass, 1998, p.27.)

---

3   The files mention 20 tenements built in this year: eight in Chapter Street, six in

It is satisfactory that the Commissioners still have in Westminster large numbers of old houses, under our care, which meet the needs of poorer people.

In Lambeth the group of tenants is, I think, very satisfactory,[4] and the estate with its public garden forms a pleasant area in a central situation, in marked contrast to the New Cut, and is a nice residential small district for those who wish to live near their work. The inhabitants are near enough to share somewhat in the social life so strongly developed round Red Cross Hall and the Southwark houses, and at the Sunday music, flower and bulb show, and other gatherings, we gladly welcome such as care to come.

The letting on this estate has suffered lately from the opening of a large block of London County Council dwellings, erected although the over-building in South London was well known. I believe myself that, as in other districts, families will be found in the long run to prefer dwellings managed by private owners; but, for the moment, we have lost some tenants, and, where there is other provision, it seems to me a pity that those who represent the ratepayers should erect additional houses.

We had, in May, a very pleasant gathering of friends and fellow-workers at Walworth, in order that they might all see the excellent cottages and flats provided in such numbers on this, the largest estate committed to our care. The weather was bright, and many of our friends were present. The public garden, thanks to the skill and care of the London County Council, looked most cheerful, and it was satisfactory to see the numerous happy homes. We prepared for this gathering a short pamphlet, giving an account of all which has been done by the Ecclesiastical Commissioners in providing and managing houses for

---

Fredrick Street and six in Hide Place. One cottage in Fredrick Street was also converted into tenements. (Letter from Cluttons to the Ecclesiastical Commissioners, May 1906.)

---

4   The New Cut development remains in the Church Commissioners' hands today. We know less about the rest of the seven acres, to which Octavia constantly refers, but concerning which there is a lack of detailed information, and the Commissioners' Lambeth Estate is now only a small remnant of what it once was. London County Council bought parts of Westminster Bridge Road, Lambeth Palace Road, Stangate Street, York Road and Addington Crescent in 1949 as part of its preparations for the 1951 Festival of Britain. St Thomas's Hospital purchased property on Boniface Street, Carlisle Lane, Royal Street, Stangate Street, Finck Street, Upper Marsh, Waxwell Terrace and Westminster Bridge Road as part of its extension a short time later. This area is now covered by a local authority tower block estate. Precisely how much of this property was in the hands of Octavia's fellow-workers one can only speculate.

working people. I am not sending it to you all, because I do not know which of you would care for it, but I have plenty of copies, and will gladly send one to any and all who will let me have a card asking for one.[5]

The buildings on this estate are not yet finished, but the last will soon be in hand. It is proposed that the only shop which is being built here shall be taken by a Co-operative Society, if such can be formed among the tenants, and a meeting will shortly be held to consider this point. There will be room for coal to be stored, and there is no article on which co-operative arrangements would tell more than in the purchase of coal. Miss Stanley has built on the estate a club for working girls, and a hundred were present at her last gathering. Her large room is sometimes available for gatherings for other estate purposes.

I do not know that I have anything fresh to tell you about the dear old places—St Christopher's Place, all the Southwark groups, and those in Marylebone and Chelsea. They go on much as of old, only the passing years give us an added depth of affection for them; we become more conscious of how we are bound to the people, and they to us, and how sure and real has been the progress made.

One loss we have sustained—Mr and Mrs Herbert Rix have passed

---

5   The pamphlet was called *The Ecclesiastical Commissioners' Housing of the Working Classes: London Estates*. The first nine pages were taken from the 1904 Report of the Estates Committee on Metropolitan Housing (21 January 1904) which was presented to parliament. This was followed by a lengthy extract from Octavia's letter for 1903, and a report from Miss Lumsden. It explains how the Commissioners have met their 'moral obligation to see... that the claims of the working classes to be provided with healthy homes... at reasonable rents should not be neglected'. There were three main tactics. First, land was made available at nominal rates to philanthropic individuals and bodies like Lady Selborne, Miss Curteis and, of course, Octavia's Red Cross trustees. Second, land was made available at below market value (usually two-thirds) to reputable commercial companies providing working-class housing, like the Metropolitan Industrial Dwellings Company and the Victoria Dwellings Association, as well as to local authorities like Hammersmith and Westminster. Finally, the Commissioners undertook to erect and manage certain properties themselves, using Cluttons as their agents, 'but an arrangement has been made by which the actual supervision and collection of the rents has been delegated... to Miss Octavia Hill and other ladies trained by her to deal with this particular class of property'. These properties were managed to show a four per cent per annum return on the investment. The Mitre Street scheme (the two-and-a-half acres in Lambeth) is described as costing £61,000, and the Walworth redevelopment £200,000—still showing a four per cent return. Miss Lumsden describes how tenants are made to pay their own rates, as 'they take a much keener interest in municipal affairs, and watch very carefully the expenditure of the council'.

away. They had built one of the cottages near Lisson Grove, and, though their removal to the country prevented their seeing much of people or place, they were always interested in the scheme, and most cordially sympathetic and helpful when anything had to be settled. A day or two before his death, Mr Rix wrote that he desired that their cottage should be offered to one of those interested in the district, so that no alien management should come into the street. This wish his executors have arranged should be carried out, and Mr and Mrs Schuster, who own four adjoining cottages, are buying the fifth, so the management goes on as before. This was of the greatest importance, and I am grateful to all who have rendered it possible.

Before I leave the question of the houses, I should like to mention one small but practical point. I have mentioned in previous letters how important I consider it that tenants who vote for bodies levying rates should realise their amount and incidence, and that we had ourselves devised various plans for securing this end. One of these was the weekly collection of a fixed rent and variable rate. Our plan required good accountants, as the exact amount of rate was collected, and required quarterly adjustment, because it did not necessarily divide easily into weekly payments. The Popular Municipal Alliance has, however, devised a plan far more available for common use. They have prepared a scale, which shows the amount payable per week on each assessment, and for every amount of rate. They are prepared to sell rent cards showing this scale, which can be had by writing to 52 Bow Road, London, E. The method is so simple that anyone can use it; and I venture to say that, if extensively adopted, it would do more to moderate the present reckless extravagance on the part of those who represent the ratepayers than almost anything. Compounding would become comparatively harmless; and, as it suits the tenant, the landlord and the local authority, this is a great point.

My time has been much occupied during the past year with the duties of the Poor Law Commisson. Till it reports, its members are not ready to speak of the results of its enquiries, nor would it be advisable that they should do so; so I will only write of it in its relation to my other duties. As it is now proceeding to visit various parts of Great Britain, the claims on my time may be in the future even greater than during the past year; and it will require great care to decide how the claims of the new work can be fulfilled without injuring my permanent work. To this my best thought must be devoted. So far, I am delighted to feel that the new duties have not interfered with the old. Thanks to the most zealous and able help of my trusted representatives in their several districts, I believe the work to have been absolutely as well done as before. I have only to regret the impossibility of seeing my workers, and seeing or hearing about our tenants weekly on Mondays and Tuesdays, as for 40 years I had been in the habit of doing. But we have found other possible days and ways of meeting more or less, and a good deal of detail has been, by better organisation, delegated; so that, perhaps, when the glad day comes that the Commission is over, we may find the times of meeting better used; and I sometimes think the work may have gained by the interruption. The very morning I received the request to join the Commission I saw that this might be so.

To turn now to the question of open spaces. I have to record the entire completion of the Gowbarrow purchase, additional fields and all; it is now absolutely and entirely bought and dedicated to the public.[6] There was a ceremony in August to open it; the weather was beautiful, many were present, and it was a great success.[7] I was sorry that I could not be there, but I thought much about the gathering, and was glad to see from Canon Rawnsley's speech how he had dwelt on the memory of all the various donors and what the nation owed to them all. It certainly was a marvellous gift, and a wonderful group of givers.

For myself, I was very anxious to see the place again. I had not visited it since the scheme was proposed, and I much wanted to look at it in the new light of its having been secured for the people. Miss Yorke, Miss Lumsden, my sister and I, therefore went up there quite quietly for a few days at Whitsuntide; and we saw it all, and thought much over it. It is a magnificent piece of ground, and I was more than ever impressed with it. It is so beautiful, so large, so various. I have written of it so often that I fear to weary you, and its salient features have been

---

6　*See ill. 33.* In *The National Trust: A Record of Fifty Years' Achievement* (1945), D.M. Matheson, the secretary of the Trust, cited the success of the Gowbarrow appeal as one of the most significant events in the history of the Trust (p.123). £12,800 was raised (more than was originally appealed for) to purchase 750 acres—the largest landholding to date.

7　The ceremony took place on 9 August 1906 and was performed by James Lowther, speaker of the House of Commons and the largest landowner in the Lake District. He congratulated: 'the sixteen hundred persons who had fallen victim to the solicitations of Canon Rawnsley and Miss Octavia Hill, and who had so generously and so unselfishly planked down the money, not for their own enjoyment altogether, but for that of their fellow citizens. We have all heard of the mountain in labour that brought forth a mouse. This time the mice have been in labour and have brought forth a mountain.' (Rawnsley, 1923, pp.112-13.)

described so well, that it seems needless to repeat any description. I will only say, therefore, that, from the low margin of the lake to the high and lonely upland fell, every yard of it is rich in beauty; and that as we walked by the rising Aira, or up the Hunter's path, I blessed God that He had made the earth so lovely, and that He had enabled those who had united to save it for His children to fulfil their purpose and realise their dream.[8]

I have nothing much besides to say about open spaces. The National Trust, the Kent and Surrey Committee[9] and the Kyrle Society go steadily on with one scheme after another, and quietly add space after space, or path after path, to be a permanent possession for our city dwellers to inherit. The two latter societies are sorely in need of pecuniary support.[10] It has been a very serious question with both how they could possibly continue their operations, yet both are doing excellent work and that most economically.

Red Cross Hall prints its own report this year, which contains also that of the flower show. The two committees have decided to amalgamate, which will save much labour.[11] I will only record that we had a most successful flower show, May Festival and bulb show.[12] We

---

8   The Aira Force waterfalls were the inspiration for at least three poems by Words-worth, most famously 'The Somnambulist'. The association of history, art and natural beauty was a potent one for Octavia, and she never missed the opportunity to make the link in her pleas to preserve sites. These scenes were more than beauty spots: they represented for Octavia important sources of strength in the formation of the national character. This is the reason for the frequent use of spiritual imagery when she is talking about the work of the National Trust. Thus, in 1904 Octavia had asked for Gowbarrow to be 'consecrated to the nation' (1904, p.527).

---

9   Of the Commons Preservation Society.

---

10   On 29 November 1906 *The Times* had published an appeal for funds for the Kyrle Society from Lord Monkswell (chairman) and Octavia (treasurer): 'For nearly 30 years the society has pursued its objects... There is scarcely any important open space which has been secured for the public during that time with the acquisition of which it has not been connected... Work for all branches of the society is waiting to be done; but our resources are quite inadequate for our work, and the society greatly needs additional help if its efforts are not to be seriously crippled.'

---

11   Although the committees had merged, the accounts for 1907 onwards show that Octavia continued to keep a separate account for the flower show.

---

12   The bulb show took place on 3 March, the Maypole festival on 25 May and the

---

also had a most beautiful performance of the *Messiah*, which Mrs Julian Marshall gave with her unfailing kindness.[13] I should also like here to express thanks to Mrs Elliman for taking, and fulfilling so excellently, the duties of honorary secretary to the Hall, which never was fuller of life.[14] Miss Connell and her friends arranged there a party for all the children of the Southwark tenants. While speaking of entertainments, I may mention that three of my sister's plays for children are republished by Messrs Cassell, in one volume, price 1*s* 2*d*.

We have had four capital parties this year, given by Lady Pollock, Mrs Thackeray Turner, Mrs Sharp and Mrs Troup.

As to the donations which have reached me, I should like to express heartiest thanks to all the faithful and kind friends who have given. We are face to face, in Notting Hill, with a large group of impotent folk, and I have been rejoiced to feel that I have been able, through the help which reaches me, to set on foot the useful work to which I referred earlier, and to render assistance to the widow, the sick or the child, who, there and elsewhere, have needed support.

My old friend, Miss Manning, left me in her will £100, which I am spending thus for my people, with many a thought of her and of her noble life. My brother also sent me a very large gift. On the strength of these I have somewhat increased the number of those I can permanently benefit by way of pension or education.

Perhaps I might note here, too, the permanent income we receive from two large gifts in the past—that from the late Mrs Scrase-Dickins, and from the late Mrs Russell Gurney. Each of them gave a freehold

---

flower show on 21 July. '[The flower show] was a most successful one. Seven hundred and twenty-one plants were registered. Lady Pollock was good enough to distribute the prizes.' (*Red Cross Hall and Garden Report*, 1906, p.6.) Lady Pollock had also been good enough to give £5 towards the cost of the show, making her the biggest donor. The flower show and the bulb show cost £41 13*s* 11½*d*, of which £10 9*s* was given out in prizes.

---

13 On 16 December 1906. Mrs Marshall had already arranged the Sunday afternoon musical entertainments on 7 and 21 January, 4 and 18 February, 4 and 18 March, 4 and 18 November and 2 December.

---

14 Entertainments during the year had included *Popping the Question*, performed by the boys of Dulwich College, *The Girton Girl and the Milkmaid*, performed by students from Kings College, *Scenes from King John*, *Scenes from Nicholas Nickleby*, *Dick Whittington and His Cat* and, on 21 March, 'the New Zealand Twins danced a native dance'.

on which working people lived,[15] and not only have these been carefully managed, but the trustees to whom they are conveyed annually devote, as by the trust deed they are bound to do, the money which would have gone to the owner as interest, to open spaces, or other beneficent objects.

So we go on from year to year, blessed and helped by many, by some who have passed away, as well as by those who are with us still, and an ever deeper sense of gratitude ought to be, and I think is, ours, and the hope, too, that, as in the past efforts begun in difficulty have borne fruit, and small beginnings have grown to larger and larger schemes—so the same Hand will support and direct us to the end.

Some of you will know how nearly that end of labour for me, here on earth, came this autumn, and as the years go on, one knows that that end draws nearer. When it comes, I feel no fear in leaving all for which I have striven, and all that I have loved, in the sure keeping of Him who has been with me through a long life, and of you all, my friends, who have alone made possible much of what it has been given to me to accomplish.

I am,
Yours affectionately,
OCTAVIA HILL

I should like here to record, what some of you will be interested to know, that my mother's book, *Notes on Education*, has been this year published by Seeley.[16]

---

15 Anna Scrase-Dickins (1831–1901) gave three houses in Horace Street in 1886. Emilia Gurney (1823–1896) gave Westbourne Buildings in Paddington in 1893.

---

16 *Notes on Education for Mothers and Teachers* by Caroline Southwood Hill, London: Seeley, 1906. This was a posthumous publication: Caroline Southwood Smith had died on 31 December 1902.

DONATIONS DURING 1906

	£	s	d
Allen, A.C., Esq	2	2	0
Andrewes, Mr and Mrs H.	1	1	0
Austin, Miss	1	0	0
Bailey, J.	5	0	0
Bannerman, Mrs	1	1	0
Bartlett, Miss H.	2	0	0
Beckwith, Edward	10	0	0
Blyth, Patrick	1	1	0
Bridgeman, Charles	5	0	0
Christian, Miss G.E.	5	0	0
Cockerell, Sydney	1	0	0
Covington, Mrs	0	10	0
Cudworth, Mrs	5	0	0
Dowson, Felix N.	1	1	0
Ducie, Earl of	5	0	0
Evans, Mrs Richardson	2	2	0
Forman, Miss	1	1	0
Frankau, Miss	5	0	0
Harris, Miss E.M.	3	3	0
Heberden, Mrs	5	0	0
Hewson, Miss	1	0	0
Hill, Arthur	50	0	0
Howitt, Miss	0	10	0
Hutton, Mrs	1	1	0
In Memoriam John Hamer	1	1	0
In Memoriam	1	0	0
Kirby and Lowndes, The Misses	1	1	0
Macaulay, Mrs	6	10	0
Manning, Miss, the late, £100, less legacy duty	90	0	0
Marshall, Miss Louisa	10	0	0
Morris, Frank	1	1	0
Paddock, Francis	3	0	0
Plummer, Rev. C.	5	0	0
Schuster, Mrs	10	0	0
Somervell, Gordon	3	3	0
Thompson, Mrs C.	2	2	0
Todhunter, Miss	2	0	0
Tufnell, Mrs	1	1	0
Wagner, H.	5	0	0
Walker, Miss M.	1	0	0
Welbury-Mitton, Mrs	3	0	0
Wells, Miss	2	0	0
Willink, H.G.	15	0	0
Winkworth, Mrs	20	0	0
	£297	12	0

DONATION ACCOUNT, 1906

RECEIPTS

	£	s	d
In hand, January 1st 1906	143	17	8 1/2
Donations	297	12	0
Interest	42	5	2
	£483	14	10 1/2

DONATION ACCOUNT, 1906

EXPENDITURE

	£	s	d
Pensioners	110	6	3
Training and Boarding-out	36	4	5
Emigration	25	0	0
Employment	14	3	6
Sickness and Convalescence, help in	13	16	0
Excursions and Entertainments	13	4	3
Cadet Corps	13	0	0
Relief, various grants for	11	9	0
Playground, care of	10	8	0
Red Cross Hall	6	0	0
Southwark Diocesan Association (Friendless Girls)	5	0	0
Kyrle Society	5	0	0
Kent and Surrey Preservation Society	5	0	0
Rating Reform	5	0	0
Blind Institution	3	3	0
Marylebone Nursing Association	2	0	0
Stationery	1	13	11
Plants	1	10	6
Printing Letter to Fellow-Workers	4	14	6
In hand:			
Interest	54	17	7
For Pensions and other liabilities	142	3	11 $\frac{1}{2}$
	£483	14	10 $\frac{1}{2}$

Examined and found correct, P.L. Blyth.

LETTER TO MY FELLOW-WORKERS

TO WHICH ARE ADDED

ACCOUNTS OF DONATIONS RECEIVED

FOR

WORK AMONG THE POOR

DURING 1907

BY

OCTAVIA HILL

SUMMARY

Housing: Notting Hill; changes in the housing market mean that there is no need to build more working-class housing in London... Ecclesiastical Commissioners: Southwark; Westminster... training of new workers... Poor Law Commission... donation fund... community activities in Southwark, Marylebone and Notting Hill... St Christopher's Hall, Barrett's Court... entertainments for the tenants... cadet corps... open spaces: a forthcoming campaign to add to Mariner's Hill; a seat in memory of Caroline Hill.

EDITOR'S NOTE

In this letter Octavia confronts a big question that must have been on her mind for some years: 'Is the need for my special work [in housing] over?' The obstacles that were being placed in the way of her system were getting larger. Octavia mentions, among these obstacles, a depression in trade and the 'exodus of working people to the suburbs' that cheap railway fares had made possible. However, the real villain in Octavia's scenario is, as always, 'the alarming extravagance on the part of local authorities'. In this letter she draws the vicious circle. Local authorities—particularly the London County Council— were using their new powers to enter the housing market in a big way. They were funding their activities by raising the rates, which enabled them to let at below-market rents. Private landlords, therefore, had to lower their rents to compete with local authority housing, and they had to pay higher rates to meet the expenditure incurred by their public-sector rivals. The consequence was that, for the first time in 44 years, Octavia had to tell some of her owners that no dividend was payable. This was a set-back of the most momentous nature for Octavia, who had always operated according to the golden rule that: 'the houses of working men are to be on a sound financial basis, and not charities' (1899 p.430). In spite of all this, Octavia decides that her work is more necessary than ever, because it has always been about management more than building and, whether or not new housing is built in central London, someone is going to have to manage what is there already. Octavia foresees more property owners seeking the services of her lady managers to secure a return on their investment in an increasingly hostile market. What she did not foresee was that the local authorities themselves would eventually call upon the services of ladies trained in Octavia Hill methods of housing management. After Octavia's death her managers formed themselves into an association to keep alive her principles. In 1932 this became the Society of Women Housing Estate Managers (SWHEM). By 1936 the Society had 143 qualified members, 62 of whom were working for local authorities. (Whelan, 1998, pp.26-29.)

190 Marylebone Road, N.W.
December, 1907

My dear friends,

How quickly the years now seem to go by, and how much there is to record in them; each is full of life and of value as built up on those that are past. Once more am I preparing to chronicle progress; as usual I begin with the houses.

Those acquired during the year in Notting Hill district are sixteen small old-fashioned cottages which have been bought by our ever faithful friends, Mr and Mrs Schuster. They are all inhabited by tenants who have been there many years at low rents. In this case we rather hope to be able to preserve a small oasis, than to rescue a bad property from unsatisfactory management.

It is different with four others bought this year in our old street, where, if not obtained by us, the baleful rule of the landlord who lets in furnished rooms is at once set up. The first two thus rescued were purchased by Mrs Banks, one a cottage, and one a larger house which we sublet in floors or single rooms at low rents. The rooms are large, light, dry and cheerful, there is a good wash-house and yard. Two similar ones were bought at an auction in December by Miss Schuster,[1] they adjoin some we already manage, and it will be a great help to obtain control over them. Three others sold at the same time, which we should like to have secured, were purchased by a man who will turn out all the tenants and let in furnished rooms. The price at which they were sold was so high that we did not feel justified in purchasing, though we had kind friends who would have risked the purchase even at the advanced price.

The cost seemed to us prohibitory, the more so that a great change has come over the demand in London for rooms for working people, and the difficulty of letting tells most in the worst streets. But all over

---

1 Octavia had written to Paula Schuster about these cottages on 14 August 1907: 'They are right in the middle of those we have struggled so hard to improve and we know that two of the worst landlords will try to get them to let in furnished lodgings. You can imagine how eager I am to secure control of them if it be possible, were it only to preserve our people from harm.' (Darley, 1990, p.279.)

571

London the same change has taken place, and the local papers are ringing with accounts of the thousands of tenements unlet. It is sad for the owners, and it has been a great grief to me, that, at last, the unlet tenements have reached such a point that, for the first time for 44 years, I have had in one or two small properties to report to the owners that actually no dividend had been earned, and in one or two others it had diminished. One hopes that the disaster may not in the future be as serious as this; things do usually adjust themselves more or less, and there has been a depression in trade, and an alarming extravagance on the part of local authorities which has increased the difficulty of the financial problem, which one hopes will come to an end.

Two things, however, must be borne in mind. Time was when I could say with confidence that, if owners saw their way to steady, wise management, working-class houses would secure a regular interest on their cost, full provision being made for the due expenditure of money in the gradual improvement of the houses; and it has been this fact which has enabled our work to go on regularly extending itself year by year. But, from the moment when rate-supported bodies began to compete with private enterprise, so that houses in private ownership were liable to higher rates in consequence of extravagance of local bodies, or suffered from the competition of rate-supported building schemes, I knew that this steady natural growth in the work of the large good companies, and of conscientious owners, to which there was up to then practically no limit, might be seriously impeded. I am very thankful that from that time, now very many years ago, I have consistently warned all would-be buyers, and have accepted capital only from those who could judge of the probable financial problem, and advised them only to invest capital which they felt justified in thus risking.

One cause in the difficulty in letting is the exodus of working people to the suburbs. This is in many ways to be rejoiced at. I could wish it had been in every case wholly due to schemes based on a sound financial basis; because so the expansion would have been unlimited, and would not have pressed hardly on industry and on ratepayers. The facilities of means of travelling have carried thousands of families to the outskirts of London, where they get more and much cheaper accommodation. High rates have made many manufacturers migrate, and their workmen and their families will find more spacious living room in less crowded districts. This migration is satisfactory and it will leave more and cheaper rooms available for those whose work is in London, and who feel the daily going and returning very fatiguing, and that it separates them much from their homes. But there is really no necessity for building now for working people in London.

Time was when the expenditure was providing a sorely needed article, and when the pressure for rooms was great, and those who then met it may be glad they did so. This has ceased, and naturally I ask myself: 'Is then the need for my special work over, and do I look henceforth to other duties?'

Far from it, the need is greater than ever. I have built, I am glad to say, much in the old days, as many a court and street bears witness, and I have lived near enough to the people to have realised early what kind of home they wanted, and what a variety; and our houses now let incomparably better than others in their respective districts. But building never was what I felt our main duty. It was always the right government of the houses which I felt the greatest need. Almost the worst house, if the household be wisely managed, is better than ever so costly a one ill-managed. And it is this wise, firm and sympathetic management which it is so difficult to obtain and for which trained ladies are so fitted. The need for such government is in no way abated; indeed, sometimes I think it increases, and it is far better exercised by her who represents the owners than by any sanitary inspector, or health visitor, partly because she controls the house, and can voluntarily improve it as the years go on, partly because her area is more limited and her knowledge of, and intimacy with, the tenants is greater, partly because she has to call on them for fulfilment of duty, which tests them, and makes the relationship more natural.

If it be true that the need of our work is greater than ever, how is it likely to be extended should the present difficulties of letting continue, and so limit the purchasing of additional houses by our generous group of willing owners? It will grow, as far as I see, by those who already own houses turning increasingly to us to manage for them. It always has grown thus, but the more the pressure comes on them the more the owners will need the intelligent and resourceful assistance of those who know the people, and can adapt the house to modern requirements and bring the attractions of order and wise rule to their estates. If there are fewer residents in the central districts there are more in these flimsy and insubstantial pretentious little villas, with far more appliances than tenants know how to use, and so costly to keep in order, and which are built over acres of ground without any richer neighbourhood near. These will rapidly become as forlorn and rowdy as their old haunts, unless something of thoughtful rule be established in them. And the huge blocks of flats will equally need the presence of trustworthy leaders and human government. So the call is still for us, and we must train and send out all the wise managers we can.

We have moreover, independent of extension, a very large area that demands our constant care. Walworth and Notting Hill moreover are in the radius to which the tide is setting;[2] in Westminster the demand for rooms is as great as ever; and in some of our neighbourhoods we have so good an article, or the years have linked us so firmly with an established group of tenants, that the upheaval does not touch us in the least.

The Ecclesiastical Commissioners have during 1907 handed over to us 41 cottages in Southwark and one larger house, the leases of which fell in to them. They are also building 54 new tenements in Westminster.[3] These are not nearly finished, but we could have let them three times over, and to desirable tenants.

Before I leave the question of the housing, I ought to record that a group of earnest workers in Manchester seem really desirous of securing houses which may be put under the charge of a qualified lady. It will be a very important step and a very critical one. We have been fortunate in finding a very promising worker, not without links in Manchester, who has come to us for a year's training, and now is looking to return there for definite work when her year here is over. Two ladies are also planning to come from Leicester for some training.

A lady also has, by will, founded a scholarship for such training in the future. The scholarship will be tenable at the Women's University Settlement, which is associated with those likely to have special experience in management, and which is itself so constituted as to be

---

2   The Walworth scheme was completed in 1908, although some smaller additions were made later. The main changes to the estate came after the Second World War, when the Commissioners made a virtue of necessity and turned the tenements into self-contained flats while rebuilding following bomb damage. Every fifth flat was absorbed by its neighbours to make space for bathrooms and kitchens. The estate remains largely in the hands of the Church Commissioners.

---

3   These were in six more tenement houses on Chapter Street, Fredrick Street and Hide Place (distribution unknown), all three storeys high. There were 18 four-room tenements, nine three-room tenements, and 20 two-room tenements built at a cost of £11,136. (Letter from Cluttons to the EC, 17 July 1907.) These were the final properties to be built by the Commissioners in Westminster. Unlike other estates, it was ultimately given over to commercial use. A limited number of streets remained reserved for social housing, to be run by lady collectors. These were in Chapter Street, Fredrick Street, Hide Place, Dorset Street, Garden Street, Vincent Street and Regency Street.

an authority with regard to the future conditions on which the selection of scholars should be made.[4]

The Poor Law Commission has necessarily occupied much of my time, and bids fair to continue to do so. It is naturally very interesting. We have visited Lancashire, Yorkshire, the Midlands, South Wales, the Eastern counties, the Western counties, and Scotland. My colleagues went also to the neighbourhood of Shrewsbury and to Northumberland, but I could not go. Next year we purpose visiting Ireland. The time has not arrived for making any remarks on the vast field which has opened before us; it is deeply interesting, partly by the great and important questions it suggests, partly by the large number of individuals of whose life-work we get some idea.

These latter have often and often recalled to me Miss Alexander's beautiful legend of the Hidden Servants,[5] and as I have got a glimpse of the righteous manufacturer, the devoted leader of the friendly society, the generous founder of some out-of-sight charity, the faithful nurse, the energetic matron or teacher, the self-sacrificing wise guardian, the humble and gentle pauper, I have heard echo in my ear the thankful words: 'How many Thy Hidden servants are!'

Or course there is the other side; and the problem appears to me the more puzzling the more the solution of it depends—not on machinery which Commissions may recommend and Parliaments set up—but on the number of faithful men and women which England can secure and inspire as faithful servants in their manifold duties.

---

4   Miss Hankinson, in Manchester, endowed a scholarship for training women in housing management. Unfortunately, by the time of her death in 1930 the expected £2,000 had become just over £200. This is the last reference in the letters to the Women's University Settlement, with which Octavia had been loosening her ties since the beginning of the century. Her last recorded attendance at an AGM had been in 1903. (Judge, 1994, p.15.)

---

5   Francesca Alexander's long, pious and moralistic poem *The Hidden Servants* was published in 1900. It concerns Hermit, who wants to know what God thinks of him, and is sent to see a clown and two village women, whose souls reflect his own. At first he is disappointed, but then recognises that they have all served God in their own ways. Hence the realisation: 'As he saw the star-like glow/ of light, in the cottage windows far,/ How many God's hidden servants are!' Francesca Alexander was a protégé of John Ruskin, who had met her in Florence in 1882. For the rest of his working life, Ruskin devoted time to developing, editing and publishing her work, the majority of which was based on illustrated translations of Italian (particularly Florentine) folk tales. Ruskin was attracted to the beauty and simplicity of her work, which he dwelt on is his Oxford lecture 'Francesca's Book'.

Among the many blessings which I have to dwell on during the past year is the fact that I have received three large gifts which are accessions of strength. One is the bequest of £250 under the will of my dear friend and ever faithful helper Mr Henry Mallet. It has greatly assisted good works which needed it much. A second gift, that of £200, comes from Miss Mayo. It is specially devoted to houses, and it will, I believe, enable me, unrestrained by any question of whether it will produce interest, to rescue from the hands of the low-class landlords one of the houses that may henceforward become the house of hard-working families, but that else would be given up to demoralising influences, and be the haunt of the thriftless, the immoral and the drunkard, and which would corrupt and disturb the neighbours. The third gift is that of £100 for a London open space to be selected by the Kent and Surrey Commons Preservation Society.

I was able, too, after consultation with my large group of volunteers working in and for houses, to distribute quite a large sum for the following objects:

	£
The National Trust for Places of Historic Interest and Natural Beauty	50
Kent and Surrey Committee of Commons Preservation Society	50
Southwark Girls' Refuge	20
Purley Beeches Preservation	15
Tower Hamlets Pension Fund	15
East End Emigration Fund	10
Epileptic Colony at Chalfont	10
North London Nurses	10
Invalid Children's Aid Society	10
St Crispin's Workshop	10
Southwark Boys' Aid	10
M.A.B.Y.S.	10
Red Cross Hall	10
Southwark Cadets	10
Southwark Cadet Club	5
Registration and Apprenticeship	5

These latter gifts are independent of my usual donation fund which by the contributions annually sent to me by generous friends supports many a friendless orphan, forlorn widow, or sick family, besides starting in independent life young people, and supporting at critical moments important work.

It has been even more needed this year because Westbourne Buildings and Horace Street, which usually afford large grants to us for various good work, have during this year required all their surplus, the one for an entire new system of drainage, the other for large substantial repairs which afforded opportunities for improvements also. I expect in 1908 again to want all their contributions for a great open space scheme.

I am printing with my letter the accounts for Red Cross Hall and garden, and the flower and bulb shows. Their illustrated report last year was so full and so good that it seems unnecessary to say much this year. I have to thank most heartily all who have at the Hall provided entertainments and music for our people, they have been greatly appreciated and have been a great pleasure to us. To Mr Wood, our kind treasurer, and to Mrs Elliman's ever helpful service our great thanks are due.

My appeal for money to reinstate the balcony met with a very generous response, £93 coming in specially for it. It has been completed, and is sound, strong and looks very pretty.

St Christopher's Hall continues as in past years the centre of its large and established group of families, its library is much appreciated, and all goes on well there. It is a cheer to us in contemplating Notting Hill, and realising what uphill work it is there, to reflect how insuperable the same problem once seemed in St Christopher's, now so orderly and happy.

Notting Hill is this year beginning to follow humbly St Christopher's lead, in that one of our fellow-workers is getting up there a children's cantata. She has 30 boys and girls in training, and it is pleasant to think of their learning all together and thinking of butterflies, witches and fairies instead of lingering in the degrading streets.

From various causes we had fewer summer parties last year, but Mr and Mrs Stenton Covington gave a large party in their beautiful garden at Streatham; Mr and Mrs Loch entertained a group at Oxshott; Mrs Clutton Brock, at Weybridge; and Miss Stacey took a party to Greenwich.

To our very great pleasure Dr Longstaff's cottage was again this year put at the disposal of a succession of old couples. The ever generous individual consideration and kindness which meets the guests, the quiet, the beauty, the ease which it affords, make a visit there quite an epoch in the lives of many a worthy couple who in their old age have few enjoyments.

The cadets have done well during the past year. A battalion committee has been formed which will, we trust, bring the various companies in the different districts of London more together, promote still more corporate feeling among them, and enable us all to know better when and where difficulties arise, and how we can help one another. It is pleasant to me to know more of the officers and their work among the boys. A display and assault-at-arms was held on December 14th at Caxton Hall, when members of all the companies performed. General Hon. Sir Neville Lyttelton was so good as to preside, which was a great encouragement to us all. It was delightful to see the exercises and gymnastics, and to realise what the training must do, were it only for the boys' physique. But the obedience, discipline, corporate life, and above all the companionship of the officers, must make all the difference to the whole future life of many a lad.[6]

Of the open space work I have not much this year to record, its steady progress is set forth so fully in the reports, by the National Trust, Kent and Surrey Committee, and Commons Preservation Society. Among other things they tell of the scheme now in hand for preserving 540 acres of Ludshott Common, near Haslemere, of many a footpath which has been saved and many a triumph won, and friend secured for the movement. But this year I have not myself had in hand any great scheme such as Brandelhow or Gowbarrow.

Next year I believe it will be different. I have in view a lovely bit of land, part heath-like, part woodland, part meadow, which I hope to secure. It adjoins a common, and is bounded on one side by a country lane.[7] It is in a growing neighbourhood and is threatened by building.

---

6   Sir Neville Lyttelton (1845–1931) was Chief of the General Staffs. He remarked in his speech that: 'he had been both pleased and astonished at the excellence of the performances he had just witnessed, [and] said he had been much struck by the evidence which their annual reports afforded of the success of those cadets of the corps who had joined the ranks of the army. That success seemed to have been invariable: they got their promotion very rapidly and went on advancing. That proved that in that corps they had learned the qualities of cleanliness, prompt obedience, good manners, and strong sense of duty—qualities which would carry them far.' (*The Times*, 16 December 1907.) Sir Neville Lyttelton was the brother of Lavinia and Meriel, who married the brothers Edward and John Talbot respectively. (1905, p.546, n.13)

---

7   This was an extension to Mariner's Hill in Kent, near to Octavia's home with Harriot Yorke at Crockham Hill. Part of the Hill had already been acquired for the National Trust in 1903, using the In Memoriam Fund (1903, p.510). This extension was added to the site in 1908 (1908, p.600). It would be extended yet again in 1912

But it is quite rural in character still, though near enough to London to be reached in a Saturday afternoon ramble. But its special value is that the lowest slope, which is a mass of primroses and wild hyacinths in spring, and foxgloves in summer, leads up to, and forms part of, one of those wonderful inland promontories which for the special blessing of Londoners seems to have been ordained to overlook what Rudyard Kipling calls 'the dim blue goodness of the Weald';[8] but beyond the weald it commands a marvellous view of hill and wood and far away even to the South Downs. There is always a breeze there, and from the meadow which crowns the height, the sun as it rises and sets, and all the majesty of changing cloud, of shower, or storm, or gleam of light is spread before the beholder. Such vantage grounds of view all along the chain of hills in Kent and Surrey are being sought, occupied, and enclosed by the richer purchaser, and many a happy home is growing up on them. But it would seem well that some portion of them should be kept for the enjoyment, refreshment, and rest of those who have no country house, but who need, from time to time, this outlook over the fair land which is their inheritance as Englishmen, whose view is too often bounded by houses the other side of their street, and from whom more and more, woods, fields and hills are closed, as residences spring up in the country. This land will cost about £1,500. I see my way to £1,000. I earnestly trust my friends will now be able once more to help me, even with the small sums, so that when the balance is forthcoming we may ensure a great gift for the years to come for the young, for the old, for the artist, for the poet, a possession held in common by many. Let us secure it before it passes into the hands of the builder and before

---

as a result of Octavia's last open spaces appeal—in fact, the last words she would write to her fellow-workers (1911, pp.663-64).

---

8   No tender-hearted garden crowns,
    No bosomed woods adorn
    Our blunt, bow-headed, whale-backed Downs,
    But gnarled and writhen thorn—
    Bare slopes where chasing shadows skim,
    And, through the gaps revealed,
    Belt upon belt, the wooded, dim,
    Blue goodness of the Weald.

From 'Sussex' by Rudyard Kipling, 1902. Kipling lived near the village of Burwash in Sussex for 30 years until his death. Here he wrote *Puck of Pook's Hill* amongst other works in the house called Bateman's, now, together with the writer's Rolls Royce, owned by the National Trust.

that hill crest is devoted to one family only, which might be the common joy of a great succession of happy, though landless, workers.

We have placed on one such bit of land, given to the National Trust in memory of my mother, a stone seat designed by Mr Hoole.[9] Near it her eldest great grandchild[10] has planted an oak; we hope he will remember it in years to come and connect the future with the past where it had its root. The seat bears words from Lowell's Commemoration Ode, from the passage:

> Blow, trumpets, all your exultations blow!
>   For never shall their aureoled presence lack:
>   I see them muster in a gleaming row,
>   With ever-youthful brows that nobler show;
>   We find in our dull road their shining track;
>   In every nobler mood
>   We feel the orient of their spirit glow,
>   Part of our life's unalterable good,
>   Of all our saintlier aspiration;
>   They come transfigured back,
>   Secure from change in their high-hearted ways,
>   Beautiful evermore, and with the rays
>   Of morn on their white Shields of Expectation![11]

In memory has it been given, but in glad memory, and with such thoughts as should be present to him who shall there watch the spring growth, and look out on the beauty of the England he loves and which is the inheritance of her sons.

OCTAVIA HILL

---

9   This was also on Mariner's Hill. It is noticeable that Octavia does not mention the name of the site she is talking about, either in this letter or in the 1903 letter in which she reported the acquisition of the first part of the hill for the National Trust.

---

10 Arthur Ouvry, then aged three, was the eldest son of Octavia's niece Elinor and her husband Carrington Ouvry. Arthur wore a red cap and cape, 'that made him look like a little gnome'. (Letter from Octavia to Elinor, 16 June 1907, quoted in Darley, 1990, p.317.)

---

11 From stanza VIII of James Russell Lowell's 'Ode Recited at the Harvard Commemoration, 21 July 1865'. The line beginning: 'For never shall...' was inscribed on the seat. See 1902, p.483.

DONATIONS DURING 1907

	Red Cross Hall and Garden			Balcony			Flower Show			Donation Fund		
	£	s	d	£	s	d	£	s	d	£	s	d
Allen, A.C.	1	1	0	—			—			2	2	0
Andrewes, Mr and Mrs H.		—			—			—		1	1	0
Austin, Miss		—			—			—		1	0	0
Bannerman, Mrs ...		—			—			—		1	1	0
Bailey, J.		—			—			—		5	0	0
Bayley, G.F.		—			—		1	1	0		—	
Baumont, Somerset		—		50	0	0		—			—	
Beckwith, E.		—			—			—		10	0	0
Bennett, Major ...		—			—		0	10	0		—	
Blyth, Patrick L. ...	1	1	0		—			—		1	1	0
Bonsor, Cosmo ...		—			—		1	1	0		—	
Boxes on Balcony		—		1	5	2		—			—	
Bridgeman, Charles		—			—			—		5	0	0
Bridgeman, Mrs ...		—			—			—		2	0	0
Bridgett, Miss		—			—		0	5	0		—	
Brooke, Rev. W. Ingham		—		1	0	0		—			—	
Burrage, Miss		—			—			—		16	3	0
Clutton, Ralph ...		—		5	0	0		—			—	
Chase, Miss		—			—			—		2	2	0
Cockerell, S.C. ...		—			—			—		1	0	0
Cockerill, Miss ...		—			—			—			2	6
Covington, Mrs ...		—			—			—		0	10	6
Cudworth, Mrs ...		—		5	0	0		—		5	0	0
Dakin, Miss E. ...		—		2	0	0	1	0	0		—	
Dawson, Miss		—			—			—		4	0	0
Dowson, F.N.		—			—			—		1	1	0
Ducie, The Earl of		—			—			—		5	0	0
Erle, Miss Eleanor		—			—			—		20	0	0
Evans, Mrs Richardson		—			—			—		2	2	0
Fellow-Workers, Miss O. Hill's	10	0	0		—			—			—	
Fierz, Miss	2	2	0		—			—			—	
Forman, Miss		—			—			—		1	1	0
Frankau, Miss		—			—			—		5	0	0
Gillson, Mrs		—		5	0	0		—			—	
Gladstone, Miss ...	2	0	0		—			—			—	
Hamilton, Miss ...		—			—		1	1	0		—	
Harris, Miss E.M.		—		5	0	0		—		3	3	0
Harris, Miss S.J. ...	1	1	0	5	0	0		—		1	1	0
Herberden, Mrs ...		—			—			—		5	0	0
Hills, John W.		—			—			—		10	0	0
Hon. Treasurer ...		—			—		0	12	6		—	
Howitt, Miss		—			—			—		0	10	0
Hurry, Dr and Mrs		—			—			—		1	1	0
Hutton, Mrs		—			—			—		2	2	0
Inglefield, Miss ...		—		0	5	0		—			—	
In Memoriam, J.H.		—			—			—		2	2	0
In Memoriam, L.B.		—			—			—		1	0	0
Johnson, Miss ...		—		5	0	0		—			—	
Kirby, Miss		—		0	10	6		—			—	
Lees, H.		—			—			—		0	10	0
Llangattock, Lady		—			—		1	0	0		—	
Luker, Miss	0	2	6		—		0	5	0		—	
Macaulay, Mrs ...		—			—			—		6	6	0
Mallet, The late Rev. H. (bequest of) ...		—			—			—		250	0	0
Martelli, Francis ...	0	10	0		—			—			—	
Mayo, Miss		—			—			—		2	17	0
Morris, F.		—			—			—		1	1	0

DONATIONS DURING 1907 (continued)

	Red Cross Hall and Garden			Balcony			Flower Show			Donation Fund		
	£	s	d	£	s	d	£	s	d	£	s	d
Morshead, Mrs ...	1	0	0	—			—					
Nicholson, Lady	—			—			—			5	0	0
Orr, Mrs	1	11	6	—			—			—		
Paddock, F.W. ...	—			—			—			2	0	0
Pascall, —	—			—			0	10	0	—		
Penrhyn, Lady	—			2	0	0	—			—		
Perkins, Mrs ...	—			—			2	2	0	—		
Plummer, The Rev. C.	—			—			—			5	0	0
Pollock, Sir Frederick and Lady	10	0	0	—			—			10	0	0
Post Office	—			0	2	0	—			—		
Praed, C.	—			—			1	0	0	—		
Schuster, Mrs ...	—			—				5	0	10	0	0
Sale of Bulbs ...	—			—			1	3	5½	—		
Scrase-Dickins, General	—			—			—			5	14	0
Sewell, Miss ...	—			0	10	0	—			—		
Somervell, Gordon	—			2	2	0	—			3	3	0
Sprague, Dr ...	—			—			—			10	0	0
Thompson, Mrs ...	—			—			—			2	2	0
Todhunter, Miss ...	—			—			—			2	0	0
Tufnell, Mrs	—			—			—			1	1	0
Tupper, Miss	—			—			—			20	0	0
Wagner, H.	—			—			—			5	0	0
Walker, Miss M.A.	—			—			—			1	0	0
Ward	—			—			1	1	0	—		
Warner, Miss Lee	—			—			0	10	0	—		
Webb, Mrs Randall	2	10	0	—			—			—		
Wedgwood, Miss ...	—			—			—			5	14	0
Welbury Mitton, Mrs	—			—			—			3	0	0
Wells, Miss ...	—			—			—			2	0	0
Whelpdale, Mrs	—			1	0	0	—			—		
Wilcox, Miss ...	—			—			2	2	0	—		
Winkworth, Mrs ...	—			2	0	0	—			—		
Wood, W.	—			—			1	1	0	—		
Yorke, Miss	5	15	6	—			0	10	0	—		
	£38	14	6	£92	14	8	£16	19	11½	£470	14	0

DONATION ACCOUNT, 1907

RECEIPTS

	£	s	d
In hand, January 1907	197	1	6½
Donations	470	14	0
	£667	15	6½

DONATION ACCOUNT, 1907

EXPENDITURE

	£	s	d
Emigration …	135	11	7
Pensions …	78	14	0
Training and Boarding-out … … … … … … … … … … … … … … …	66	11	3
Open Spaces … … … … … … … … … … … … … … … … … …	34	14	7
Cadet Corps … … … … … … … … … … … … … … … … …	32	0	0
Sickness and Convalescence … … … … … … … … … … … … … …	27	16	2
Employment … … … … … … … … … … … … … … … … … …	23	10	5
Playground, care of … … … … … … … … … … … … … … …	10	8	0
Kyrle Society … … … … … … … … … … … … … … … … …	10	0	0
Entertainments … … … … … … … … … … … … … … … … … …	5	7	6
Printing Letter to Fellow-Workers, Stationery … … … … … … … …	5	7	0 ½
London Fever Hospital … … … … … … … … … … … … … … …	1	1	0
Bulbs and Mould … … … … … … … … … … … … … … … … …	0	10	3
Allotted for Pensions, Training and Open Spaces, about … … … … …	200	0	0
Available balance, about … … … … … … … … … … … … … … …	36	3	9
	£667	15	6 ½

Examined and found correct, P.L. Blyth.

RED CROSS HALL AND GARDEN ACCOUNT, 1907

RECEIPTS

	£	s	d
Bank, January 1907 ...	13	10	3
Cash, January 1907 ...	0	0	10 ¾
Interest, Red and White Cross Cottages ...	91	6	7
Hire of Hall ...	53	12	3
Donations:			
Balcony ...	92	14	8
Hall and Garden ...	38	14	6
Flower and Bulb Show ...	16	19	11 ½
Rent of Clubroom ...	16	5	0
Rent of Office ...	13	0	0
Sale of Programmes Thursday Entertainments ...	5	19	11
Collections on Sundays ...	2	19	1 ¾
Violin Fees ...	2	3	0
Gas 1 ...	10	6	0
Miscellaneous ...	1	5	0
Post Office Savings Bank withdrawn ...	26	7	0
Sale of Tickets, Bulb Show ...	0	10	0
	£376	18	8

RED CROSS HALL AND GARDEN ACCOUNT, 1907

EXPENDITURE

	£	s	d
Balcony, Renewal of … … … … … … … … … … … … … … … … … …	172	0	3
Caretaker … … … … … … … … … … … … … … … … … … …	60	12	0
Printing, Illustrated Report, etc … … … … … … … … … … … …	23	0	9
Flower Show … … … … … … … … … … … … … … … … … …	20	10	11
Entertainments, Expenses for … … … … … … … … … … … … …	18	15	0 ½
Borough Rates … … … … … … … … … … … … … … … … …	12	0	10
Violin Class … … … … … … … … … … … … … … … … … …	12	0	0
Gas 9 …	3	4	0

Garden:						
Plants … … … … … … … … … … …	3	9	6			
Sundial Repairs … … … … … … … … … …	2	17	6			
Pigeons' Food … … … … … … … … … …	1	5	0			
Rent … … … … … … … … … … … …	0	19	0			
Tools and Netting … … … … … … … … …	0	10	7			
				9	1	7

	£	s	d
Repairs and Furniture … … … … … … … … … … … … … … … …	8	9	2
Water Rate … … … … … … … … … … … … … … … … … … …	6	2	0
Cleaning … … … … … … … … … … … … … … … … … … …	6	14	3
Fuel …	4	14	3
Maypole Festival … … … … … … … … … … … … … … … … …	4	7	11 ½
Insurance, Fire, etc … … … … … … … … … … … … … … … …	1	19	3
Income Tax … … … … … … … … … … … … … … … … … …	1	13	6
Land Tax … … … … … … … … … … … … … … … … … … …	0	4	7
In hand, Bank, December 1907 … … … … … … … … … … … … …	1	8	1
In hand, Cash, December 1907 … … … … … … … … … … … … …	4	0	11
	£376	18	8

Examined and found correct, P.L. Blyth.

LETTER TO MY FELLOW-WORKERS

TO WHICH ARE ADDED

ACCOUNTS OF DONATIONS RECEIVED

FOR

WORK AMONG THE POOR

DURING 1908

BY

OCTAVIA HILL

SUMMARY

Housing work: Ecclesiastical Commissioners in Westminster; finding work for tenants in Notting Hill; more courts for the Ecclesiastical Commissioners in Southwark; falling demand for rented property owing to unfair competition of public bodies; cottages in Manchester... Red Cross Hall: flower shows, the Messiah *and other events... outings for tenants... the cadets... the Poor Law Commission... the National Trust: Brandelhow; Ludshott Common and Waggoners' Wells; Hindhead; Morte Point; Mariner's Hill... Octavia contemplates her own demise and changes in her team.*

EDITOR'S NOTE

For the past three years Octavia had been heavily involved with the Royal Commission on the Poor Law, but she had been able to say very little about its work, for reasons of confidentiality. However, she timed the 1908 letter to go out after the publication of the Commission's report on 17 February 1909, so that she could express her views for the first time in print. The Commission had conducted the most thorough review of the poor laws since 1832, in a climate of opinion that meant that the hated workhouses had to go. Octavia herself recognised that this was inevitable, and she had therefore put her name to the majority report, which called for radical change. This was in spite of the fact that her natural inclination was for slow and steady reform of existing institutions, rather than the sweeping away of 'a system which has the advantages of centuries of experience'. Even Octavia had to acknowledge, however, that the time for gradual reform had passed. She blamed the loss of confidence in the system, shared by both the working classes and the middle classes, on its failure to separate the idlers and wastrels from those in genuine distress. She then characteristically blamed the growing number of idlers and wastrels on the demoralisation caused by 'unwise charity'. Her plea to the fellow-workers to read her agreement to the conclusions of the majority report with the qualifying words 'so far as I can see' in mind, shows how great her reservations about its recommendations really were. On two points, however, she put her foot down. Octavia had entered a memorandum dissociating herself from certain aspects of the majority report: she objected to extending free health care, and she opposed the creation of 'artificial work' by the state in periods of depression. (Octavia mentions the second objection but not the first in the 1908 letter.) She felt that both would undermine the independence of working people by discouraging them from saving for a rainy day. It was for a long time a commonplace of social historians that the majority report, put together by stalwarts of the Charity Organisation Society, represented the last gasp of Victorian individualism, while the minority report, signed by Beatrice Webb and George Lansbury, was supposed to be the forward-looking prefiguration of the twentieth-century welfare state. More recent scholarship has tended to emphasise the similarities between the two reports, rather than their differences, which have been described as 'mere differences of emphasis' rather than radically opposed world-views (Vincent, 1999, p.85). Both sets of recommendations would have resulted in the destruction of the old poor law, and both wanted to send able-bodied idlers to penal detention colonies. Although there was no direct new legislation resulting from the Commission's report, a system of state old-age pensions, of which Octavia strongly disapproved, had been introduced just a few weeks previously on 1 January 1909. Octavia would also live to see the introduction, in 1911, of national insurance. The Charity Organisation Society had been strongly represented on the Poor Law Commission by Octavia, C.S. Loch and Helen Bosanquet, but the tide was going out for their views on the relief of poverty.

(190 Marylebone Road, N.W.)
(February 1909[1])

My dear friends,

I will follow precedent and first record the progress of the various courts and houses under our charge.

The new flats in Westminster have been completed and are all successfully let. They are most satisfactory, and meet the wants of a superior class of tenants. We have an active and zealous superintendent there who has encouraged the tenants to lay out their gardens, and prizes were given for those which were best kept. This is hopeful, as it has been a great success.

Mr and Mrs Schuster have just bought two more houses in Notting Hill. They had been twice cleared by the local authorities, as they were being badly used. I fear they may not be a financial success. But it is a great blessing to know they are safe from bad use; and we look forward with great satisfaction to getting them put in order structurally and thoroughly cleansed. The purchase of them will also help the other houses we have charge of in the street, one of which they actually adjoin.

The great feature in our operations in Notting Hill this year has been the extension of the plan of giving odd jobs to tenants of a low and shiftless class, who have been unusually out of work this winter. It is, of course, very difficult to manage this well. The men need almost constant looking after, the price must be enough to encourage them to persevere, and to enable them to get material and, by degrees, tools, yet not too high to prevent their trying for regular work under proper foremen and for full hours. It is essential that it should appear to them like a proper commercial transaction; yet it is manifest to them that they are not skilled. On the whole, I hope that, by the earnest care and patience of my representatives there, we have steered clear of the dangers of such schemes; certainly the money has been of quite immense importance to the families. Several of the men have become more handy

---

1 Octavia says (p.596) that her letter will not be circulated until after the publication of the Poor Law Commission's report, which occurred on 17 February 1909. The auditor did not date the signing off of the accounts, except for the Red Cross accounts, dated 9 February 1909.

and capable than they were, some we begin to feel of real use in more skilled work, employment has kept them out of mischief, and the houses have been improved by many jobs which we should not otherwise have put in hand. I have thought it well, during this slack season, to use some donations for thus improving houses, training some of the poorest, and I hope we may continue to steer clear of the evils of 'relief' works. I have received from Miss Louisa Marshall a munificent gift, which will be available for similar employment and improvement in the future.

There have been many structural repairs to do in the courts in Southwark last handed over to us by the Ecclesiastical Commissioners, in order to bring them up to anything approaching the standard of those which have been under us for some years. But this is gradually being achieved.

Horace Street and Westbourne Buildings have completely paid for the substantial repairs referred to in my last letter, and stand again on a sound financial footing.

Miss Wedgwood has been so good as to hand over to the Horace Street trustees the lease of the house she held in Notting Hill. So this will now be managed as part of that trust.

I said so much in my last letter about the changes which had come over London letting that it is unnecessary to repeat it. The difficulty still remains; and I find that the best authorities find it impossible to predict how far it is likely to be permanent, and how far it is connected with the present depression. Certainly some of the causes will continue. On the other hand, there is a wonderful power of adjustment which seems to take place in such matters with a little time. The difficulty has not told on us very seriously as yet, except in our most difficult area, that of Notting Hill, where other causes operate, some of which, we hope, are removable with patient work and with time. To me the most anxious features in the matter are the rise of rates, the unsound competition of rate-supported bodies, and the ignorance of trustees of large new charities. The LCC is feeding nearly 100,000 children,[2] the Chelsea Borough Council is arranging for rebuilding on a large scale,

---

2   In 1906 an act of parliament had enabled local authorities to provide school dinners for poor children. Although this seems a relatively unimportant event in the history of state welfare, it polarised the debate around the proper role of the state with regard to welfare services. For those who opposed it, like Octavia, it was an example of the way in which the state was undermining the family by taking over its roles: 'do you think the old dole demon is dead? Not so... he comes to us now in the shape of free dinners... he will weaken the parents' sense of responsibility... he will teach the father to spend in drink the money which he would have expended on the children's dinners,

and the Sutton Charity, which surely should have been devoted to pioneer work in rural building, is arranging schemes for overbuilt London.[3]

Whatever be the demand for London tenements, our management continues to be wanted as much as ever; whatever happens about building, the people will be somewhere, and the poorer and less disciplined, above all, need trained ladies as managers in their dwellings.

May I mention here, though it is in no sense any part of my work, my great satisfaction in watching the growth of the co-partnership housing work.[4] It is, I think, the most hopeful development with regard to housing, and on a thoroughly sound footing. Naturally, however, it does not as yet help those who have sunk lowest.

---

the mother to pass the time in which she might have cooked the dinners in gossip.' (Hill, 1889, p.455.) Those who supported it saw it as a vital measure in making society face up to its obligations. According to B. Kirkman Gray, in his book *Philanthropy and the State* (published in the year of this letter), the school dinner was: 'an education in citizenship. Without a word being said, the child gradually absorbs a knowledge of its own dependence on and place in the social life. He finds himself a guest at the common table of the nation.' (Kirkman Gray, 1908, pp.294-95.)

---

3   The Sutton Trust had been established in 1900 under the will of W.R.Sutton, founder of a firm of London carriers. For legal reasons it was unable to start building before 1909, just as Octavia was writing this letter. It first housing development was in Sceptre Road, Bethnal Green. The Trust catered for a higher class of tenant than many of Octavia's schemes. Most of its flats had two or three rooms, and all had their own lavatories and sculleries. (Tarn, 1973, p.106.)

---

4   'Co-partnership tenants organisations... were intended to enable a group of working-class families to build and own a group of houses. The co-operative movement grew out of the mid-nineteenth-century desire amongst working men to protect their own welfare as well as their own jobs... Tenant Co-operators Ltd built several housing estates but it was not until 1901 when Henry Vivian, at that time secretary of the Labour Association, founded Ealing Tenants Ltd that a true co-partnership organisation came into existence.' (Tarn, 1973, p.178.) In 1908 John Nettlefold, whose admiration for Octavia's methods was fully returned (see 1905, p.541), wrote: 'I cannot do better than conclude this article with a short account of the methods and results of the co-partnership tenants' housing societies that are federated together under Co-Partnership Tenants, Ltd., 6 Bloomsbury Square, London, W.C. There are now nine of these societies, at Hampstead, Harborne [Letchworth] Garden City, etc., owning land and buildings that have cost nearly £400,000 and are worth considerably more. The idea is that eventually the tenant members shall have shares in their society, equal to the value of their houses, but it takes most of them many years to get together the necessary money, and therefore it is necessary to find capitalists to take up four per cent loan stock, so that the houses may be built at once. As the years go by, the shareholdings of the tenant members will increase, and loan stock be paid off, unless the investor

I mentioned last year that there was a hope that a scheme for managing poor property in Manchester, under a trained lady, might be set on foot. This has been done. A gentleman has purchased a group of cottages in a central district, is thoroughly reconstructing them so far as is necessary to meet sanitary requirements, and the lady who was trained here is established in charge there. Necessarily, it is up-hill work at first, but I confidently hope it may be a thorough success. I think it bids fair to be so. I wish that we could hear of more houses in Manchester to be put under the same worker, who seems to me most capable and likely to make a real success of whatever is entrusted to her.

Before leaving the question of the houses, I should like to mention how very glad I should be of additional volunteer help in them. At Westminster and at Southwark we are wanting ladies to undertake, as regularly as possible, the collecting among a group of tenants. This must necessarily be done on Monday or Tuesday, and would occupy a long morning. I think it would be found very interesting, as it would be side by side with experienced workers, and the relations with the tenants are very pleasant.

---

wishes it diverted to another society, of which there will undoubtedly be a very large number all over the country in the near future. This co-partnership tenants' loan stock is, in my opinion (based upon intimate knowledge and practical experience), a safe four per cent investment. Any surplus there may be after paying four per cent on loan stock and five per cent on shares will be divided among the tenant members as dividend on rent. There is no more certain way of ensuring interest on capital than by dividing profits with your customers. Human nature being what it is, the tenant members will do everything in their power to take care of their houses and the property generally, thereby ensuring the four per cent on loan stock, because until that is paid there will be nothing for them. The co-partnership tenants' housing system has this great advantage over the ordinary building society, in that if a thrifty working man has to leave the district in search of employment, he does not have the house left on his hands. The house never belongs to him individually, so that on leaving he merely has to give the ordinary week's notice. But his holding is in shares in the society, and he can either leave it in or sell at par. This arrangement greatly facilitates the mobility of labour, which is most important to the working classes. The co-partnership housing movement, not yet ten years old, has already made wonderful progress. It is founded on two great principles, association and self-help, and will, if combined with common-sense state development on town-planning lines, not only provide better housing conditions and reasonable rents; it will also make for better men and women and healthier children, building up character and improving the national physique. The children of today are the citizens of tomorrow, and nothing is of greater national importance than that our future citizens should grow up in healthy environments with every opportunity for sensible recreation.' (Nettlefold, 1909, pp.200-02.)

Red Cross Hall has during the past year lost the inestimable services of Mrs Elliman, who has for so long helped there. Illness in her family prevents her further co-operation, but Mrs Orr is most kindly taking the full burden of the largest bit of responsible work—that of the flower show—and also comes on the Thursday nights which are so difficult to fill.

The year's work has been most successful, except as to finance. The flower show was a great success, so was the maypole. Mr Maller, who for 20 years has given us his valuable aid in organising the show and judging the plants, felt that he could no longer thus help. We are grateful to him for his unwearied support and interest. Miss Agar was so very good as to devote two whole days to visiting the various courts and judging the gardens and plants. Many kind friends enabled us to fill in the whole course of concerts and entertainments for Sundays and Thursdays with a set of really beautiful performances. These culminated on December 20th with the *Messiah*, arranged for us by Mrs Julian Marshall. This was almost more beautiful than ever, and we all feel it like a united Christmas service. The Hall was crowded to overflowing, and it was wonderful to watch the faces of rough men and toil-worn women listening with rapt attention to the music and carefully following the words. Another notable feature this year is the way in which the Hall has helped the development in church work which has taken place in the parish. St Saviour's now has a service there each Sunday, and gatherings twice weekly connected with the church. The last Thursday evening entertainment this year was by St Saviour's Guild. It was given by those of various ages, first by the infants, last by young men. The Hall was crowded by neighbours and friends, 15*s* being taken in pence.

The balcony was reconstructed last year, and that is all paid for, but I feel anxious about finance there this year. It is long since the Hall was distempered. It looks now very dirty, and I do not feel that it is helpful to the people for it to look as it does, nor worthy of its traditions. We ought to have it distempered as soon as it can be spared in the spring. It is very high, which is a good thing for beauty and ventilation, but it therefore needs scaffolding when cleaned, and I fear it may cost some £30 or so. Red and White Cross cottages have had heavy expenses and have been unable to make their full contribution to the Hall during 1908, so, as the balance sheet shows, our funds are low.

Many of the tenants were again entertained at summer parties. Again they were invited to Erleigh by my brother. It was a perfect day and all enjoyed it thoroughly, not only the rose garden, the rowing on the lake, the hayfields, the music; but the memory of the past occasions, when they had been there, and of the kindness received, deepened the pleasure. Groups of tenants were also most kindly entertained by Sir Frederick and Lady Pollock. Also a new opening was given us by the kind invitation of Mr Bell, of Pendale Court, Bletchingley, where some of our Southwark tenants spent a most happy day. Dr and Mrs Longstaff were kind enough to entertain two large parties at Putney; and they also invited aged poor couples in turns to spend a fortnight at the cottage in their lovely garden. I think this has been almost more appreciated than ever. My sister arranged for the various couples to follow one another in unbroken succession from May to September, and many were the longing and grateful letters we received.

The cadets have had a satisfactory year. At the display which was again held at Caxton Hall on December 5th, Mr Haldane[5] was so good as to preside. We felt it a great honour to be thus recognised by a cabinet minister, and are grateful to him for the help he thus gave. It is very delightful to see the relation between the officers and the boys, and to realise what the training is, and how radically the exercise and camp life tell on the physique of the lads.

A very large part of my time this year has been occupied by the Poor Law Commission. I shall not issue this letter before its report is made public,[6] so I am free to write of its conclusions.

The reference to the Commission was so wide that there was hardly any subject outside its scope, and one felt that it was impossible to do full justice to all the problems which had to be dealt with. It seems to me that an immensely painstaking and most careful study has been devoted to these, a huge amount of evidence has been taken, facts innumerable have been recorded, and very thoughtful consideration has been devoted to the conclusions arrived at. I was very glad to decide that I could sign the report with my colleagues, diverging from them on only one or two points. I sign it, however, assuming that any friends who care for my opinion will take a common-sense view of the signature, and will realise that many of the conclusions must be understood to be approved as with the addition of the words 'to the best of my belief' or 'so far as I can see'. I was fortunate in being able to attend every meeting

---

5   Richard Haldane (1856–1928), later 1st Viscount Haldane, was a Liberal statesman and, from 1905–12, secretary of state for war. He remodelled the army and founded the Territorials. He was the brother of Elizabeth Haldane who had become one of Octavia's housing managers at the age of 20, and who would later, with Patrick Geddes, set up the Edinburgh Social Union. (1902, pp.489–90.)

---

6   The report was published on 17 February 1909.

in London, but one, during the three years the Commission sat, and most of those in Scotland and the provinces; and I gave the best of my thought to the evidence and to every proposal, but I often and often thought that many of the decisions might have well been prepared for by years of practical work, or experimented on with advantage on some small scale. So the word 'recommend' I had to interpret as meaning 'I recommend to the best of my knowledge'. The problem was before us, and recommendations were submitted to which one was bound to say Yes or No.

I found the problem, moreover, incomparably more difficult because, by the nature of it, I was precluded from advising what my instinct would have led me to consider the only prudent course, namely, a gradual reform and development in the poor law itself. Such reform has taken place in regard to the treatment of children and of the indoor sick, and might have been urged and carried forward for other classes also with good hope and with certainty of gradually inspiring confidence in the public, as these two branches of the poor law administration have done. Many of the clearly wise recommendations of our report might have been carried out without a great upheaval of arrangement, tradition and nomenclature in a system which has the advantage of centuries of experience, but for one insuperable difficulty. The larger area, the detention of certain classes, the further classification, the rendering our workhouses real houses of work by development of agricultural and industrial employment, the personal visitation of out-relief cases by volunteers or women officers—all these, and many other wholesome and necessary reforms, might have been adopted; in fact, I could have signed Dr Downes's[7] paper confidently; it was in accord with all my instincts of gradual improvement; but there was one obstacle which seemed to me invincible. There has grown up outside the poor law a great body of people untouched by it, and this of two kinds. There is the idler and the wastrel, fostered by an unwise charity: for him, indeed, we might have recommended detention on a colony, under the Home Office, when he was proved a beggar and a ne'er-do-well, and so have cleared poor law institutions of their worst element and left them freer from corrupting influence on those who enter them. But how to distinguish these men from the genuine unemployed through misfortune? Some offer there must be which would eliminate these latter, and that one which they could honourably accept. In justice

---

7   Arthur Downes, one of the commissioners, was senior medical inspector for poor law purposes to the local government board for England.

we were bound to devise such; in wisdom we must do it; or free dinners for children, Mansion House Funds[8] and artificial work—ruinous financially and injurious educationally—were inevitable.

Had our workhouses happily been reformed in time, as the schools and infirmaries have been, so that our legislators, charitable people, and working classes could trust them, had they so classified the inmates that the loafer and drunkard were not made to associate with the industrious and unfortunate, had they developed schemes of work or training in surroundings fit for worthy men and women, we might have re-affirmed the advisability of a resident test and training—at any rate as under the modified workhouse test for the man—still keeping the old names of poor law, guardian, relieving officer, and we might have proceeded more gradually.

But the names, the system, associated with the general workhouse, are not accepted either by working or benevolent people as rightly to be associated with such help as should be available. There is no time to reform and redeem them. All round there have been growing up schemes of relief, overlapping one another, without proper enquiry, without any test. School feeding must be subsidising drunken and idle parents and duplicating poor law aid; charitable alms are scattered wide, causing demoralisation; old-age pensions are administered and decided on by a separate body from the main state relief agency, and divorced from it; and instead of work in an institution, recognised as relief, we have perilous schemes of artificial work, costly, deceptive to workers, lowering their standard—and sure to collapse.

You will see, therefore, why I have given my adhesion to a scheme of change more radical than I should else have done. You will notice, however, that I break away from my colleagues in so far as I would have no unreal outside made-work at all. The work should be recognised as relief or training, wherever it was not needed and carried on in the real market of the open world. So only does it seem to me we can really test poverty or re-establish independence among our people. We seem to be confusing ourselves and deluding them by made-work under artificial conditions.

I am not hopeful that my three years' work has been very helpful. I

---

8 More than 20 years after the Lord Mayor's 1886 Mansion House Fund for the relief of the unemployed, it was still a byword for waste and demoralisation (see p.186, n.1). In his book *Unemployment*, first published in 1909, William Beveridge recorded that: 'There are men experienced in observing and dealing with distress who say the East End and South London have scarcely yet recovered from the demoralisation of that orgie [*sic*] of relief'. (Whelan, 2001, p.90.)

have tried to do my best, and I am glad that I did not refuse the call. I do not consider my training particularly fitted me for the post; certainly, in many ways, several of my colleagues were much better qualified for the duties; still, I had a certain amount of special experience, I have tried to render it useful as it was asked for, and now I may return to my own sphere of duty.

I now turn to a brighter subject, that of open spaces. I must not pause to dwell on the great progress in the provision of these which has taken place. You will see, in the National Trust and Kent and Surrey[9] reports, accounts of the securing of all the land at the head of Derwent Water, and of many acres of lake shore connecting this with Brandelhow; of the 500 acres of Ludshott Common and Waggoners' Wells;[10] of the two large areas of land near Hindhead[11] given by Miss James; of Morte Point, in Devonshire, about to be given to the Trust;[12] and of many another acquisition or victory. I will here only enumerate two most nearly connected with my private work. First the magnificent gift to

---

9   i.e. the Kent and Surrey committee of the Commons Preservation Society.

---

10 This area—actually 540 acres—near Grayshott in Hampshire was home to the rambler and novelist Flora Thompson, who wrote much about the countryside. The Waggoners' Wells were old ironworkers' hammer ponds. A tract of woodland adjoining the Wells was purchased by public subscription and donated to the National Trust in 1919 in memory of Sir Robert Hunter, six years after his death.

---

11 This land is near Beacon Hill in Surrey. The National Trust now owns land to the west, east and south of Beacon Hill, including the famous Devil's Punchbowl and the Hindhead Common, which includes a 'Sir Robert Hunter Trail'. The Devil's Punchbowl was, prior to its becoming National Trust property in 1906 after Robert Hunter's campaigning, the property of the tycoon Whitaker Wright, who notoriously committed suicide by taking a capsule of cyanide in the ante-room of a London court prior to being sentenced for fraud. Before this the American/British millionaire businessman had become an unpopular lord of the manor after he had dug up Hindhead Common in order to landscape his garden. This collection of holdings which Robert Hunter was putting together in the Hindhead area, like Octavia's clutch of properties in Kent, illustrates the tendency of early National Trust acquisitions to reflect the founders' own locations. In an obituary of Robert Hunter, published in the *Cornhill Magazine* in 1914, Canon Rawnsley noted that National Trust holdings already included: 'In his own countryside in Surrey, Hindhead Common and the Devil's Punchbowl—750 acres in extent—Ludshott Common, Bramshott Chase, Nutcombe Down, Grayswood Common, Waggoners' Wells and Marley Common'. (Rawnsley, 1914, p.237.)

---

12 This is near the town of Woolacombe in North Devon. The land was given to the Trust by Miss Chicester in memory of her parents, the late Sir Alexander and Lady Chicester, and was called the Morte Point Memorial Park.

me by an anonymous donor of £1,000 for open spaces. Part of this I have already thankfully spent, of part I shall render an account in the future. I must not speak of the plans for it yet.

Secondly, let me mention with great thankfulness the completion of the purchase, and dedication to the public through the National Trust, of the area added to Mariner's Hill at Crockham, of which I wrote last year.[13] It is a wonderful piece of land, beautiful itself, and more beautiful in its command of view of blue distance and of sky. Let me here set down my heartiest thanks to all who helped. I have transferred for this object some of the gifts, the disposal of which was left to my discretion. I print the full list of donors; so that friends who have kindly sent donations, will find my acknowledgment in one list or the other.

To all who have contributed to my ordinary fund for the poor and struggling let me express my earnest gratitude. The fund has met and is meeting the needs of many.[14]

I have again recorded for you some of the chief events of our year's work—work which many of you have shared and many have followed with interest, and many are glad to hear of, though they may be far off. It is helpful, too, to me to be called on to survey the year with its many

13 On 25 June 1908 Octavia had organised an open day on Mariner's Hill to celebrate the purchase. 'Miss Yorke was in charge of catering—beef and lamb (ham was rejected) and no sweets. A brake would meet guests at Oxted station... Carrington Ouvry threw a damper on the plans by pointing out that it was hayfever season but Sir Robert Hunter was already invited and it was decided to go ahead.' (Darley, 1990, p.313.)

14 The only way in which Octavia had been able to meet the needs of the poor and struggling from the fund in 1908 had been by raiding the reserves. The accounts for this letter reveal just how determined she was to secure the additional part of Mariner's Hill for the National Trust. For the first and only time, she created a separate account for one specific open space, which shows where the £1,500, which she had correctly anticipated in 1907 would be the cost, came from. She had transferred £188 from the donation fund to the Mariner's Hill appeal, which came to £40 more than the fund had received in the year. In addition, the Mariner's Hill donors' list includes £75 from Miss Miranda and Miss Octavia Hill. This represents the only occasion on which Octavia appears as a donor in her own accounts, apart from small donations to the work-room account in 1875 and to the flower show in 1909. Octavia put in £250 from the fellow-workers, representing money that would have been used to pay the housing managers, had not some of them been working voluntarily, £120 from the Horace Street Trust and £25 from the Kent and Surrey Committee of the CPS. There follows a list of donations received per the National Trust, including £150 from the Trust's own assets, of which Octavia's faithful companion Harriot Yorke was the treasurer.

hopes and labours, to stand, as it were, like Rabbi Ben Ezra, and to feel with him when he hears a voice saying:

> Note, when evening shuts,
> A certain moment cuts
> The deed off, calls the glory from the gray:
> A whisper from the west
> Shoots—'Add this to the rest,
> Take it and prove its worth: here ends another day'.[15]

This thought comes home to me, perhaps, more than usual, and with deeper solemnity this year, because, I have myself been called to go through a rather serious illness, when I had to decide how my various work would stand if I suddenly had to leave it, and the answer was full of satisfaction and of hope. There was then still at the head of the Ecclesiastical Commissioners' business a man who had learnt what was the importance of their keeping their poorer tenants under their immediate control, and how they could recognise as their representatives ladies animated by devotion, skilled in practical work, and ready to watch over tenants and houses. I looked round and I saw in each of my groups of houses one or more trained fellow-workers, bound to a company of tenants by years of service, and inspired by traditions of fellow work one with another. I had nothing to do but to write a few words to Sir Alfred de Bock Porter, to tell him what lady was at the head of each district and to recommend her appointment. I could feel sure he would listen, and the decision was in safe hands. Since then he has been called to leave us, a brave and great spirit has been summoned from his place of influence on earth, and we can only hope that he has left his traditions and worthy colleagues behind to carry on what he has so nobly and so silently begun. Never again, let us hope, will owners of the church estates give up control for a term of years of the guardianship of their poorer tenants, or of the conditions governing the estates of which they are in charge. But Sir Alfred himself is gone, and as if to call me still more to be thrown back on God Himself and His care for whatever is good in our work, a singular concurrence of events has broken into my band of workers. It is such an upheaval as bids fair to break up traditions and make me feel that I have to begin

---

15 Stanza xvi of Robert Browning's 'Rabbi Ben Ezra' from *Dramatis Personae*, 1864. The first line actually runs: 'For note, when evening shuts,..' and the last line should be: 'Take it and try its worth: here dies another day.'

rebuilding. First, one young worker left to begin fresh, and, we hope, happy, life in New Zealand; next, circumstances obliged a second helper to retire this Christmas; then one of my best leaders, in charge of, and devoted to, a large group of tenants, had to leave London on account of health; and lastly, another such leader, who had been the head of many courts for ten years, who was much beloved by the inhabitants, felt that she must give up her charge during 1909.

I stand almost awed by the upheaval, and pause to ask, as the *Guardian* newspaper tells us Sir Alfred used to do, 'Well, what is the way through?'[16] And the answer comes clear and sure. First, I cannot be thankful enough that the blows fall just as I have finished with the Poor Law Commission. When I undertook this, I was able to do so because I knew I had in every district a faithful and wise representative, able to carry everything on, possibly really better for my partial withdrawal, and I had been pondering what new development my own work would take so soon as the Poor Law Commission was over, as I could not dream of intervening where all was going so well. I had visions of new developments into which I would throw my strength; but now it is clear that the well-known places want me once more, and that I must be there side by side with younger and new workers to carry on the government on the old lines.

My first duty is to re-organise, promoting my junior fellow-workers to the more responsible posts, and trying to select fresh ones to worthily take up the duties, and to link themselves with us in the years to come. This I will try to do wisely, and already I begin to see how, rightly

---

16 The obituary that Octavia refers to appeared not in the *Manchester Guardian*, but in the London-based church paper *The Guardian* on 2 December 1908. Sir Alfred de Bock Porter KCB (1840–1908) had died of typhoid fever on 25 November 1908 at his home in East Barnet. He had entered the service of the Ecclesiastical Commissioners at the age of 20 and worked for them for the rest of his life. He was appointed financial secretary in 1880, and secretary in 1888, a post he still held at the time of his death— 'in harness', as the obituarist put it. The obituary makes clear why Octavia would have felt his loss keenly: 'Too much praise could hardly be given to Sir Alfred Porter in connection with the large schemes undertaken by the Commissioners for the provision of houses for the working classes upon their property in Westminster, Walworth and elsewhere. It is not in the least detracting from the credit due to the Commissioners for these undertakings to say that without the whole-hearted support of Sir Alfred Porter... the way could hardly have been found of carrying them into execution... The laying out of building estates in such a manner as to secure the healthiest conditions was a matter to which he gave attention... Judicious schemes for the preservation of open spaces and the provision of recreation grounds were sure of his sympathetic support.'

met, these changes may be ordered to be the beginning of added strength and new growth; those who pass from among us may carry on traditions in fresh places; and the new band of recruits may bring an accession of hope and vigour to us.

Alas! I cannot without pain, however, see those leave us who shared the old memories, and who had been linked with the past histories of families of tenants, who remembered those noble friends who have been with us in times of crisis, and on memorable days, and who may have since gone to their rest. The younger helpers may be strong, but they cannot have the same nearness as those with whom the past is a common inheritance.

Wherefore let my thanks be the deeper and more fervent to those, both of my staff, and among my volunteers, who still see their way to stand beside me in the dear old places, and to help, strengthened by the memory of the progress, and the realising of the ideals of our work, to carry it on still, and to welcome the newcomers in hope. In this connection I will as among those of oldest standing link the names of Miss Ironside, and Miss Covington, and close this letter with heartfelt thanks to all my fellow-workers in the past.

OCTAVIA HILL

DONATIONS DURING 1908

	Donations			Red Cross Hall			Flower Show		
	£	s	d	£	s	d	£	s	d
Allen, A.C.	2	2	0	1	1	0	—		
Andrewes, Mr and Mrs H.	1	1	0	—			—		
Anon.	—			1	1	0	—		
Austin, Miss	1	0	0	—			—		
Bailey, John	5	0	0	—			—		
Bainbrigge, Col	2	0	0	—			—		
Bannerman, Mrs	1	1	0	—			—		
Bayley, E.	—			—			1	1	0
Blyth, Patrick, Esq	1	1	0	1	1	0	—		
Bonsor, Cosmo	—			—			0	1	0
Braginton, Miss	—			1	1	0	—		
Brander, Mrs	1	0	0	—			—		
Bridgett, Miss	—			—			0	5	0
Burrage, Miss	15	4	0	—			—		
Causton, Rt Hon. R.K.M.	—			—			5	0	0
Cockerell, S.C.	1	0	0	—			—		
Christian, Miss G. Eleanor	5	0	0	—			—		
Covington, Mrs	0	10	0	—			—		
Curteis, Miss	—			0	5	0	—		
Dakin, Miss	—			—			1	0	0
Dawson, Miss	2	0	0	—			—		
Dowson, Felix	1	1	0	—			—		
Ducie, Earl of	5	0	0	—			—		
Dundas, Lady Jane's Bequest	—			13	4	6	—		
Erle, Miss	20	0	0	—			—		
Evans, Mrs Richardson	4	14	6	—			—		
Fordyce, Miss	—			2	2	0	—		
Forman, Miss	1	1	0	—			—		
Frankau, Miss	3	3	0	—			—		
Fry, John	—			0	10	6	—		
Gladstone, Miss	—			2	0	0	—		
Hamer, Mrs	2	2	0	—			—		
Hamilton, Captain	—			—			0	10	0
Harris, Miss A.B.	2	0	0	—			—		
Harris, Miss S.J.	—			1	1	0	—		
Hewson, The Misses	1	1	0	—			—		
Hill, Miss M.	—			0	10	0	0	5	0
Horace Street Trustees	—			5	0	0	—		
Howitt, Miss	0	10	0	—			—		
Hutton, Mrs	1	1	0	—			—		
In Memoriam, L.B.	1	0	0	—			—		
Llangattock. Lord	—			—			1	0	0
Lowater, Mrs	—			3	0	0	—		
Macaulay, Mrs	2	2	0	—			—		
Macfie, Mrs	1	0	0	—			—		
Martelli, F.	1	0	0	0	10	0	—		
Martinengo Cesaresco, Countess	1	0	0	—			—		
Montefiore, Mr and Mrs	10	0	0	—			—		
Morris, F.	1	1	0	—			—		
Morshead, Mrs	—			1	0	0	—		
Nicholson, Lady	5	0	0	—			1	0	0
Orr, Mrs	—			1	1	0	0	10	6
Paddock, F.W.	2	0	0	—			—		
Pascall, J.	—			—			0	10	0
Plummer, Rev. C.	5	0	0	—			—		
Pollock, Sir F.	6	1	6	—			—		
Praed, Sir H.	—			—			1	1	0
Randall Webb, Mrs	—			2	10	0	—		
Schuster, Mr and Mrs	10	0	0	—			0	5	0
Scott, Mrs	2	0	0	—			—		
Sewell, Miss	—			0	10	0	—		

DONATIONS DURING 1908 (continued)

	Donations			Red Cross Hall			Flower Show		
	£	s	d	£	s	d	£	s	d
Temple, Mrs	—			1	1	0	—		
Thompson, Mr C.	2	2	0	—			—		
Todhunter, Miss	2	0	0	—			—		
Tufnell, Mrs	1	1	0	—			—		
Tupper, Miss	8	0	0	—			—		
Tweeddale, Lady	—			1	0	0	—		
Wagner, Henry	5	0	0	—			—		
Walker, Miss	1	0	0	—			—		
Warner, Miss Lee				—			0	10	0
Wells, Miss	2	0	0	—			—		
Willcox, W.H.	—			—			2	2	0
Wood, Miss	—			—			1	1	0
Wood, W.R.	—			—			1	1	0
Yorke, Miss H.	—			0	4	0	0	10	0
	£148	0	0	£39	13	0	£18	12	6

DONATION ACCOUNT, 1908

RECEIPTS

	£	s	d
In hand, December 31st, 1907	236	3	9
Donations	148	0	0
Interest on Deposit	34	3	8
	£418	7	5

DONATION ACCOUNT, 1908

EXPENDITURE

	£	s	d
Paid to Mariners	188	3	3
Pensions	46	6	0
Employment	45	9	7
Sickness and Convalescence, help in	30	4	3
Training and Boarding-out	25	4	2
Excursions and Entertainments	15	0	3
Relief, various grants for	10	10	0
Playground, care of	10	8	0
Girls' Club	5	3	6
Blind Institution	3	3	0
Gardens, Mould for, etc	1	10	5
Printing Letter to Fellow-Workers and Stationery	5	19	11
In hand, December 1908	31	5	1
	£418	7	5

Examined and found correct, P.L. Blyth.

MARINER'S HILL, 1908

LIST OF DONATIONS PER MISS OCTAVIA HILL

	£	s	d
Allen, A.C.	2	2	0
A London Clerk	5	0	0
Anon.	75	0	0
Ashe, Miss	1	0	0
Baring, Hon. F.H.	25	0	0
Beckwith, E.L.	10	0	0
Berridge, Miss	5	0	0
Bland, Miss	0	5	0
Blandy, Mrs	10	0	0
Bowan, Mrs	1	0	0
Brown, A.	50	0	0
Browne, Mrs	2	0	0
Chase, Miss	5	0	0
Cocks, Miss	1	0	0
Donation Fund, smaller sums transferred from Miss Octavia Hill's*	141	3	3
Duff, Miss	5	0	0
Duff, Miss Gordon	0	5	0
Evans, Mrs Richardson	1	1	0
Ewart, Miss	30	0	0
Fellow-Workers, Miss Octavia Hill's	250	0	0
Fleming, Mr and Mrs	10	10	0
Fortescue, Hon. Dudley	3	0	0
Gimson, Miss	3	3	0
Gladstone, Rev. H.	5	0	0
Gosling, L.D.	1	1	0
Hartley, Mrs	2	0	0
Head, Miss	1	0	0
Heberden, Mrs	5	0	0
Hesketh, E.	3	3	0
Hill, Miss Miranda and Miss Octavia	75	0	0
Hill, Walter, the late	1	1	0
Hills, J.	10	0	0
Horace Street Trustees	120	0	0
Hurry, Dr and Mrs	1	1	0
Hutton, Miss	0	10	6
Interest on deposit	36	11	9
Jackson, Miss	2	2	0
Jardine, Miss	2	0	0
Kaufmann, L.H.	0	1	0
Kent and Surrey Committee	25	0	0
Lazenby, Mrs	5	0	0
Loch, Mr and Mrs C.S.	1	1	0
Longstaff, Dr	25	0	0
L.W.B.	1	1	0
Lowndes, Miss	1	0	0
Macaulay, Mrs	3	3	0
Macdonell, Mrs George	1	1	0
Mallet, Rev. H. (The late, part of bequest)*	25	0	0
Marshall, Miss	10	0	0
Martelli, The Misses	1	4	0
Maurice, Mr and Mrs Edmund	1	1	0
Mitton, Mrs Melbury*	2	0	0
Parker, Mr and Mrs Percy	2	2	0
Powell, Miss	50	0	0
Roberts, Mrs	2	2	0
Robinson, Miss J.	0	10	0
Schuster, Mr and Mrs	20	0	0
Schuster, Miss	52	10	0
Scott, Mrs	0	10	0

MARINER'S HILL, 1908 (continued)

LIST OF DONATIONS PER MISS OCTAVIA HILL

	£	s	d
Sewell, Miss	3	0	0
Sim, Miss	10	0	0
Somervell, Gordon	3	3	0
Sprague, Dr	5	0	0
Stacy, Miss	2	2	0
Stone, Rev. E.D.	1	1	0
Strachey, J.S. Loe	5	5	0
Tait, Mrs	1	1	0
Thank-offering from a Manchester Worker	2	0	0
Tupper, Miss*	20	0	0
Wagner, Henry	5	0	0
Whelpdale, Mrs	5	0	0
Wood, Miss Daisy	0	5	0
Yorke, Miss	50	0	0
	£1,244	2	6

LIST OF DONATIONS PER THE NATIONAL TRUST

Astley, Miss	5	0	0
Boyle, Rev. R.	0	10	0
Chamberlain, W.	1	0	0
Cockerill, Miss	0	2	6
Colquhoun, Rev. J.C. Campbell	3	3	0
Chute, J.L.	0	10	0
Dodgson, Campbell	5	0	0
Earl, E.A.	1	1	0
Eastbourne, per Miss Macdonald	1	0	0
Ewing, Dr	5	0	0
Fry, Lewis	2	2	0
Horace Street Trustees	4	17	5
Janson, Percy	2	2	0
National Trust	150	0	0
Ouvry, E.C.	12	0	0
Rougement, C.J. de	2	2	0
Scorer, F.K.	2	0	0
Stubbs, Rev. C.A.	1	0	0
Snelling, W.	0	10	6
Warburg, Miss Agnes	2	2	0
Weardale, Lord	10	0	0
Yarborough Anderson	3	3	0
Sale of wire	1	0	0
	£1,459	7	11

The land has now been purchased at a cost of £1,400; legal expenses and Copse Wood cost £58; printing 30s. The fencing is not yet paid for.

* Transferred from Donation Fund.

RED CROSS HALL AND GARDEN ACCOUNT, 1908

RECEIPTS

	£	s	d
To Bank, January 1908	1	8	1
Cash, January 1908	4	0	11
Hire of Hall	57	15	6
Interest on gifts for Red and White Cross Cottages	38	13	8
Donations:			
Garden and Hall	39	13	0
Flower Show	18	12	6
Rent of Clubroom	13	15	0
Rent of Office	10	8	0
Sale of Programmes, Thursday Entertainments	6	6	5
Collections on Sundays	4	7	8
Gas, received from tenants	2	6	0
Violin Fees	2	5	0
Sale of Tickets, Flower Show	0	15	0
Miscellaneous	0	6	0
	£200	12	9

RED CROSS HALL AND GARDEN ACCOUNT, 1908

EXPENDITURE

	£	s	d
Caretaker	61	10	0
Flower Show	30	1	9
Violin Class	23	10	0
Rates and Taxes	16	18	6
Repairs	11	15	3
Gas	14	3	0
Entertainments, Expenses of	8	9	3
Cleaning	7	17	6
Water Rate	6	8	10
Stationery and Printing	6	5	9
Fuel	4	13	4
Maypole Festival	3	18	11
Garden, Expenses for	3	15	10
In hand, Bank, December 1908	3	10	6
In hand, Cash, December 1908	0	3	1
	£200	12	9

Examined and found correct, P.L. Blyth, February 9th 1909.

LETTER TO MY FELLOW-WORKERS

TO WHICH ARE ADDED

ACCOUNTS OF DONATIONS RECEIVED

FOR

WORK AMONG THE POOR

DURING 1909

BY

OCTAVIA HILL

SUMMARY

The need to trust in God... housing: Southwark; Hoxton; Horace Street; Amsterdam... more volunteers needed... training of tenants in Notting Hill has been a success... Red Cross Hall and garden: performances by the people, as at St Christopher's Place... Ecclesiastical Commissioners: vacant plot in Southwark benefits cricket team... cadet corps: Octavia objects to War Office's proposed rules... conference of workers in voluntary and statutory bodies in Notting Hill... donation fund... open spaces: Morte Point; Cheddar Cliffs; Windsor Fields.

EDITOR'S NOTE

In striking contrast to the last letter, in which Octavia spoke of her work on the Poor Law Commission with its momentous recommendations for the relief of poverty, in this letter she is going right back to basics, stripping off 13 layers of wallpaper from houses in Hoxton, putting on the annual performance of the Messiah *at Red Cross Hall, and turning her 'forlorn tenants' in Notting Hill into odd-job men. One of the key aspects of Octavia's approach to her work was her insistence that success depended on carrying out these fiddly little jobs with the same care and perseverance as were applied to grand national schemes, and she lived up to her own ideal. The grand schemes certainly get short shrift in this letter. The only reference to the Ecclesiastical Commissioners is her description of the way in which she got them to lend a piece of land in Southwark for cricket practice, and the whole open spaces movement, which had dominated some of the recent letters, is covered in one final sentence which mentions, almost as an aside, the acquisition of the Cheddar Gorge by the National Trust. The only part of the letter that gives an idea of her ability to see the big picture as well as the details, is her expression of concern for the cadet corps, now that the War Office was moving in to take it over. The corps had never been totally independent of the state. It had been necessary to seek authority from the War Office back in 1889 to form the first corps, and Octavia had to get permission when she changed their uniforms from dark green to 'British scarlet', but the relationship had been a loose one. The direction of the corps had been largely in the hands of Octavia and her helpers. By the early 1900s, with the Boer War making enormous demands on the capacity of the armed forces, the government had begun to view the by now extremely successful cadet movement as a way of increasing the nation's military might.*

614

Consequently, as Octavia reports in this letter, 'the War Office are about to link on the cadets to the general organisation for military service', and with government control came regulations. The specific regulation to which Octavia objects here was the termination of the lads' association with the cadets at the age of 17, when they could not join the armed forces, or any working-men's club, until they were 18. They would thus be abandoned, at a vulnerable age, to 'the temptations of the streets'. Behind this objection there may have been a growing uneasiness on Octavia's part about the way in which the cadet movement was going. She had originally intended it to be a means of character building, based on the healthy comradeship of gentlemen and working-class boys. She had assured her mother (who was a pacifist, like Octavia's Quaker friends), that it was not primarily intended to funnel boys into the army. Now things seemed to be changing, and Octavia was obliged to use the argument that the boys would be 'far more likely to enlist' if the arbitrary cut-off age of 17 was abandoned. With unprecedented informality, Octavia signs this letter as 'your affectionate old friend', a form she uses once more in 1910.

My dear friends,

I am again writing to you to record what has been done during the past year, and to tell of hopes for the new one; and as I do so, a song of thankfulness seems to be singing in my heart as I think of the many and great mercies which have been with us, of the joy which has been sent to us, and of how day by day strength has been given to follow the way, and light to see it, not far ahead, but sufficient for daily guidance. The world seems in a turmoil; grave political changes, bearing for good or evil on the life of our people, are impending; passions run high; but one seems the more thrown back on the certainty that the Lord is King, that He leads the nations by ever new and wonderful ways, that He accepts the least and humblest service, guides it and guards it, and that, however small, however out of sight, in so far as it is done earnestly and thoughtfully, it has strength, and forms part of His plan for His children here below.

With regard to our own work, let me record for you what I can, in a short letter, of its progress.

I have undertaken, since I last wrote, two fresh courts. One is situated close to those I have long managed in Southwark and to the Hall and garden, so forming naturally a part of our work there and under my own immediate supervision. It belongs to a lady, a near relative of an old friend of mine, who has asked me to take charge of it. It is a difficult court, forming a narrow passage between two streets, a large public house has a back entrance into it, the houses are in some cases without through ventilation and hardly any of them have yards. But a great deal has been spent on thorough sanitary reconstruction; moreover, Red Cross garden is very near; only the children have not learned to come there. The owner sincerely cares to do what is right about the place; and if anyone can make it satisfactory and a success in the present conditions of letting in Southwark, we ought to be able to do so. One of my fellow-workers has gallantly thrown herself into the undertaking, and is, among great initial difficulties, making way, I believe.

The other group is a much more hopeful one. It consists of about

617

40 small cottages, each with good yard or garden space, forming a street which feels wide because of the low houses; it has a good school and playground in it, and no public house at the corner. It belongs to owners who approached me about it, and who will certainly be conscientious with regard to it.[1] Unknown to them, the condition of the houses was far from satisfactory. Structurally they were going to rack and ruin, the roofs were not weather-tight, and the interiors of the houses were very dirty. We were only just in time to prevent the collapse of part of the fabric, and it will need careful watching, and considerable expenditure on repairs before the little street reaches a satisfactory condition. Needless to say, there had been no one in charge in and out of the houses whose duty it was to think about the people, to care for and keep order among them. This court is in Hoxton, quite away from my own neighbourhoods. I was fortunate, therefore, to be able to enlist the help of a lady whom I had known for years as a wise and capable manager of houses, who was ready to undertake all the personal work, and all the ordinary supervision, even at so difficult a time as the initiation of the scheme. Naturally, however, I have been obliged to visit the street very frequently; especially as the decisions about repairs have been urgent and important, and at the beginning there is much to be decided as to repairs and finance. We only took over the street at Michaelmas. It has been most happy and interesting work there. The lady in charge knew a small builder whom she had employed for years, just the sort of man we wanted, and he has been constantly there with a man or two to help, putting in new drains and gutters, supporting roofs, pointing defective brickwork, painting most shabby outside woodwork, to cheer the place up and preserve the fabric. Then a respectable man out of work has been constantly engaged on the inside repairs—stripping the walls, on which sometimes 12 or 13 dirty papers had been left, whitening ceilings, patching defective plaster, mending stairs and floors, and generally cleaning and refreshing all. We began with the empty cottages, of which there were nine, these were let as they were ready, care being taken about the references. The damp was seen to as quickly as possible everywhere, and now we shall, I hope, be

---

1   These houses were in Redvers Street and belonged to the Montefiore family. The wealthy philanthropist Sir Moses Montefiore had been admired by Octavia's mother Caroline Hill. She told Sydney Cockerell, after reading Tolstoy's polemical pamphlet *What shall we do then?*, that Tolstoy and his followers should imitate men like Sir Moses and '*use* their advantages for the good of mankind instead of *renouncing* them'. (Darley, 1990, p.316.) Redvers Street, a small cul-de-sac off Kingsland Road, still exists, but there are no houses there now.

making way with internal cleansing of inhabited houses. When spring comes, we may be able to encourage the tenants to get the gardens into order.

So far about the new courts, now about the old ones. I think all the houses under my care have been going on much as in the past; most of them are very satisfactory, though the difficulty of letting shews itself more or less in many of them. Horace Street has needed further structural repairs, these gave an opportunity for fresh improvements. The financial difficulty of executing these would have been great, but as these houses form part of the same trust as Westbourne Buildings,[2] the funds from the latter, which would otherwise have been available for gifts, have been devoted to paying for repairs and improvements in Horace Street. This clearly is the first duty of the trust, and the best way of spending the money.

I mentioned last year the development of a scheme in Manchester for the management of houses by ladies. This assumed rather larger proportions during 1909, as fresh houses have been bought and a company has been formed. There has had, however, to be a change of worker. The newly appointed one has spent a few weeks with us in London, that we might shew her what little we could in so very short a time. We hope now she will gain her own experience in her own city, under the able and earnest supervision of Miss Hankinson who is the life and soul of the movement there.

It is pleasant to be able to point out how well housing schemes have developed in Amsterdam; there seem to be quite a number of improved or rebuilt houses under the care of ladies, and a wonderful school of sociology with far more practical experience in managing houses than ours gives. Two very promising young students thereof recently visited England, I believe with a sort of travelling scholarship, returning to work in Amsterdam. Since then a young Dutch lady has come over for six months to thoroughly learn our ways here. She is residing at the Talbot Settlement,[3] sees much of general social undertakings in South London on her off days, and is most kindly helping me at Red Cross Hall. I receive very cheering letters from my friend who first undertook the charge of houses in Amsterdam and has continued it steadily for some years.

---

2   Westbourne Buildings were in Elms Lane, now Elms Mews off the Bayswater Road, and the trust was the Horace Street Trust.

---

3   See 1903, p.502.

I have been in correspondence during the past year with those interested in houses in Birmingham, Tunbridge Wells, Oxford, Nottingham, Torquay and many other places; but it is little one can do to help unless some resident can come and be regularly trained; one hopes, however, that some ladies may be feeling their way through small beginnings to do practical good in managing houses.

I should be very glad if more volunteers would come forward. I need them much in Westminster, Lambeth and Southwark. The work would occupy some hours in the middle of the day on Monday or Tuesday, and we want those who in the main can come pretty regularly; but we are able to take up the duties during necessary absences, and I think those would find the occupation most interesting who care to make real friends among a small group of poor families, whom they would meet on an independent footing, and that as time went on satisfactory ways of knowing and of helping such families would open out. They would also be interested to advise about the gradual improvement of the houses, and to note their progress.

Before leaving the question of fellow-workers, as I wrote last year of the considerable changes in my staff, may I add how more than satisfied I am with the zeal and power of my new helpers? They have done real good service, have been loyal and, I think, interested, and are daily gaining experience.

I mentioned in my last letter the extent to which we were using and training the more forlorn of our tenants at Notting Hill, by employing them to do useful repairs and improvements in the houses. They needed much teaching and endless supervision, but they grew in skill and habits of industry, and my fellow-workers devoted much time to making the scheme possible. These repairs were partly necessary ones, paid for out of the rents received, but were partly improvements or jobs given principally for the sake of the men; and I have received large and most welcome gifts to enable me to extend such beneficent action as far as possible. One result has been that two of the Notting Hill men employed there in past times, have this year been really valuable in Southwark, doing needed repairs on an entirely independent footing, earning more, and employed more steadily; they are off our hands, which leaves us able to train fresh men at Notting Hill.

I do not know that there is anything further that I should record about the dear old courts except how thankful I have been that, the Poor Law Commission being over, I have been able to be more down in them again.

Red Cross Hall and garden have, as I anticipated, required a large expenditure on substantial repairs. I have received, as you will see, very generous gifts towards the cost for these; I am very grateful, and am glad to see the results.

The *Messiah* was again given by Mrs Julian Marshall, who has also continued her most beautiful concerts on alternate Sundays for the winter sessions. The other Sundays also have been kindly undertaken by various friends. They have been very successful and the attendance is markedly increased and improved.

The Thursdays, too, are going on very well, we are greatly obliged to the kind friends who have come from far off to give entertainments. I am also glad to record that, under our spirited young secretary, a great impetus has been given to performances by the people themselves; local club, and class, and guild have been approached, and have given concerts and dramatic entertainments full of spirit. This development is one I have long desired; it has been possible for many years past at St Christopher's Place, but never till now, to any extent, in Southwark, and I look upon this change as most satisfactory.

The Ecclesiastical Commissioners have acceded to my request that they would allow us to use a piece of vacant ground in Southwark[4] until it is required for building. It was placed under the charge of the Red Cross committee, and has been continuously used by the clubs in the neighbourhood for cricket and other games. Such vacant ground near their homes is of great value.

Perhaps this extract from a letter from the secretary of one of the clubs will be of interest:

'We have now finished our programme, and I thought you would be interested to hear how we have fared. We have played 17 matches, won 12, lost 2, and drawn 3. We have also won the championship of the Clapham and District Cricket Association, Division A. One of our members, Mr G. Ford, leads the batting averages of the division, and another, Mr G. Asplin, is second in both batting and bowling. My members have requested me to tell you that we attribute our success in no small measure to the practice we have been able to have on the ground so kindly lent to us by you, how much we appreciate your kindness, and how thankful we are to you, words of mine cannot express. I can only

---

4   This was between Orange Street (now Copperfield Street) and Loman Street. (Letter from OH to the EC, 29 March 1909.)

say that we believe, in fact we are positive, that you have had a big share in our winning the cup this season. On behalf of all my members I again thank you for your great help and kindness to us.'

There were several summer parties, as of old, to Dr Longstaff's, to Mr Bell's, and to Miss Peake's. One, the last there can ever be, to Erleigh Court,[5] was to many of us sacred to memories of goodness and generosity in the years that are past.

We are many of us much exercised now as to the future of the cadet corps. The First London Battalion, founded in 1887,[6] has always been linked closely with our work in Southwark, two companies drilling in the Hall, and the headquarters of the Battalion being quite near. The health, the physique, and the moral training of our lads has owed much to it. More than eight thousand boys have passed through its ranks, and many have done honourable service for their country both by sea and land. They day has now come when the War Office are about to link on the cadets to the general organisation for military service. They have issued suggested regulations which appear to me, and to all the devoted group of gentlemen who have acted as officers to these lads for now so many years, to be full of peril to the whole movement. It is proposed to make the severance of the cadet from his officers, comrades, and club, compulsory at the age of 17. This regulation is not proposed for the higher-class boys, and it would seem hard indeed to make it for such lads as ours. We have always felt the club life, the camping out together and with their officers, part of the most valuable influences possible. If it is to cease at 17, when the cadet is not a man, when he is open to all the temptations of the streets, and to the undisciplined life there, most of the good gained from 14 to 17 will be lost. Moreover, no workman's club is open to him till he is 18. Setting aside the moral and physical training, it appears to us a great mistake from the point of view of those who desire to link such lads on to the organisation for the defence of our country. It is true that if they desire to do so they can join the territorials. But these boys are not in a strong position to arrange

5   Octavia's half-brother Arthur died in 1909. He had entertained groups of tenants for many years at his home, Erleigh Court in Berkshire, and at Shere, where his son was rector (1895, p.374). In 1906 he had made 'a very large gift' of £50 to the donation fund (1906, p.562). His wife had died in 1901 (1901, p.472).

6   The Southwark cadet corps had been formed in 1889 (1889, p.263), but the battalion was not formed until 1890 (1890, p.285).

with their employers to be given time, nor can they afford to sacrifice time or wages. Some do and would join the territorials at 17, and we should not propose their being barred from doing so; but we think their severance from the cadet corps at 17 should be optional. If they are inclined for a military career they are far more likely to enlist in the regular army where they would be provided for. This they cannot do till they are 18. For the sake of that unique and wonderful reforming power which we have found the cadet corps to be for our London lads, we very earnestly deprecate the adoption by the War Office of the suggested rule of breaking its influence off at the early age of 17.

A report generally deals only with what is done; but I have never cut myself off from asking you to share with me my hopes for the future, and to see something of my dreams. So I will add that I am seriously thinking of trying to carry the Notting Hill work a little further by endeavouring to get together a conference of good local workers, official and voluntary, to try to put in force there some of the many good laws which exist, but which do not somehow get applied. We ought to see whether this need continue to be so. If it were possible also to get more co-operation between the various agencies, so as to prevent any disorganised work there, it might mitigate the evil. But many wise people have tried for this, and the unwise stand aloof. However, we shall, if all be well, try this year what we can do in this way.

And now let me add a few heartiest words of thanks to you all far and near, for all your manifold help and sympathy during the past year. I think a great blessing has been upon our donation fund; I love to remember the individual people helped, and to feel how you are all linked with me in doing this good work.

And if I am recording reasons for a song of thankfulness, let me include the continually increasing success of the open-space movement, Morte Point, Cheddar Cliffs,[7] Windsor Fields,[8] and many another being

---

7   More commonly known as the Cheddar Gorge. The National Trust only owns the north side of the gorge, the south side being part of the Longleat estate. The cliffs that run either side of the gorge are Britain's highest inland limestone cliffs. It was purchased with £1,100 raised by public subscription. An agreement between the Trust and Lord Bath, who owned the opposite white cliffs of the gorge, meant that the quarrying that would have destroyed this beauty spot ceased.

---

8   From the 1909 annual report of the Kyrle Society: 'The National Trust… has been successful in its appeal for the £3,000 required to secure the land adjoining the recreation ground at Windsor, and necessary to preserve one of the finest views of the castle.' (p.23.)

added to our long list of places secured to the people to form not only playgrounds and breathing spaces, but areas of beauty for joy and meditation.

Once more adding hearty thanks,

I am,
Your affectionate old friend,
OCTAVIA HILL

DONATIONS DURING 1909

	Donations			Red Cross Hall			Flower Show		
	£	s	d	£	s	d	£	s	d
Allen, A.C., Esq	2	2	0	1	1	0	0	10	6
Andrewes, Mr and Mrs	1	1	0	—			—		
Austin, Miss	1	0	0	—					
Bailey, J., Esq	5	0	0	—			—		
Bannerman, Mrs	1	1	0	—			—		
Barclay, Mrs	1	0	0	—			—		
Bayley, E.	—			—			1	1	0
Beckwith, Edward L. (The late)	10	0	0	—			—		
Blyth, Patrick, Esq	1	1	0	1	1	0	—		
Bonsor, H. Cosmo, Esq	—			—			1	1	0
Brander, Mrs	2	2	0	—			—		
Bridgeman, Chas, Esq	5	0	0	—			—		
Bridgeman, Mrs	2	0	0	—			—		
Bridgett, Miss	—			—			0	5	0
Brinton, Miss	—			0	10	6	—		
Burrage, Miss	14	3	10	—			—		
B.S. (Fares to Erleigh)	6	18	0	—			—		
Causton, The Rt Hon. R.K.	—			—			5	0	0
Cockerell, S.C. Esq	1	0	0	—			—		
Cockerell, Miss Olive	—			0	10	0	—		
Cocks, Miss	—			1	0	0	—		
Collecting boxes, etc	—			—			0	10	6
Covington, Mrs	0	10	0	—			—		
Curry, The Misses M. and E.	—			—			0	5	0
Curteis, Miss	—			0	5	0	—		
Dakin, Miss E.	—			—			1	0	0
Dawson, Miss	5	10	0	—			—		
Dowson, Felix, Esq	1	1	0	—			—		
Ducie, The Earl of	5	0	0	5	0	0	—		
Dundas, Lady Jane (Balance of bequest of the late)	50	0	0	—					
E.R.B.	—			1	0	0	—		
Erle, Miss	20	0	0	—			—		
Evans, Mrs Richardson	2	2	0	—			—		
Fellow-Workers, Miss Octavia Hill's	—			50	0	0	—		
Fisher, Mrs	—			1	1	0	—		
Fordyce, Miss	—			2	2	0	—		
Forman, Miss	1	1	0	—			—		
Frankau, Miss	2	2	0	—			—		
Friend, A.	—			1	1	0	—		
Fry, John, Esq	—			—			0	5	0
Gillson, Mrs	10	10	0	—			—		
Gimson, Miss	1	1	0	—			—		
Gladstone, Miss	—			2	0	0	—		
Hamer, Mrs	2	2	0	—			—		
Hamilton, Captain de Courcy	—			—			0	10	0
Harris, Miss	2	0	0	1	1	0	—		
Harris, Miss S.J.	—			2	2	0	—		
Heberden, Mrs	3	0	0	—			—		
Hewson, The Misses	2	0	0	—			—		
Hill, Miss Miranda	—			10	0	0	0	10	0
Hill, Miss Octavia	—			—			1	0	0
Hill, Miss Octavia, per	—			41	19	6	—		
Hills, John, Esq	10	0	0	—			—		
Howitt, Miss		10	0	—			—		
Hutton, Mrs	1	1	0	—			—		
In Memoriam	30	0	0	—			—		
Kirby, Miss	0	10	0	—			—		
L.B. In Memoriam	1	0	0	—			—		
Llangattock, Lord	—			—			1	0	0
Lowndes, Miss	0	10	0	—			—		

DONATIONS DURING 1909 (continued)

	Donations			Red Cross Hall			Flower Show		
	£	s	d	£	s	d	£	s	d
Lumsden, Miss … … … … … … … … …	—			23	12	11	—		
Luxmoore, H.E., Esq … … … … … …	2	0	0	—			—		
Macaulay, Mrs … … … … … … … …	2	2	0	—			—		
Macdonnell, Mrs G.P. … … … … … …	2	0	0	—			—		
Marshall, Mrs C.J. … … … … … … …	—			—			0	2	6
Marshall, Miss L. … … … … … …	20	0	0	—			—		
Martelli, F. … … … … … … … … … …	—			3	10	0	—		
Minet, Miss … … … … … … … … …	50	0	0	10	0	0	—		
Mitton, Mrs Melbury … … … … …	5	0	0	—			—		
Moggridge, Miss Dorothy … … … …	1	0	0	—			—		
Morris, Francis, Esq … … … … …	1	1	0	—			—		
Morshead, Mrs … … … … … … … …	—			1	0	0	—		
Nicholson, Lady … … … … … … …	5	0	0	—			—		
Orr, Mrs … … … … … … … … …	—			1	1	0	0	10	6
Paddock, F.W., Esq … … … … … …	2	0	0	1	0	0	—		
Pascall, James, Esq … … … … … …	—			—			0	10	0
Plummer, Rev. C. … … … … … …	5	0	0	—			—		
Praed, Sir Herbert … … … … … …	—			—			1	1	0
Roberts, Mrs … … … … … … … …	—			2	2	0	—		
Rotch, Miss … … … … … … … …	1	0	0	—			—		
Schuster, Mrs … … … … … … … …	10	0	0	—			0	5	0
Scott, Mrs … … … … … … … … …	2	0	0	—			—		
Sewell, Miss … … … … … … … …	—			0	10	0	—		
Somervell, Gordon … … … … … …	3	3	0	—			—		
Stone, The Rev. E.D. … … … … …	1	1	0	—			—		
Thompson, Mrs Percy … … … … …	2	0	0	—			—		
Todhunter, Miss … … … … … … …	2	0	0	—			—		
Townsend, Miss … … … … … … …	—			1	0	0	—		
Tufnell, Mrs … … … … … … … …	1	1	0	—			—		
Tupper, Miss … … … … … … … …	50	0	0	—			—		
Wagner, Henry, Esq … … … … … …	5	0	0	—			—		
Walker, Miss M.A. … … … … … …	1	0	0	—			—		
Warner, Miss Lee … … … … … …	0	10	0	—			0	10	0
Webb, Mrs Randall … … … … … …	—			2	0	0	0	10	0
Wells, Miss … … … … … … … … …	2	0	0	—			—		
Willcox, W.H., Esq … … … … … …	—			—			2	2	0
Wood, Miss … … … … … … … … …	—			—			1	1	0
Wood, W.R., Esq … … … … … …	—			—			—		
Yorke, Miss Harriot … … … … …	—			—			0	10	0
	£380	16	10	£167	9	11	£20	0	0

DONATION ACCOUNT, 1909

RECEIPTS

	£	s	d
Cash in hand, January 1909 …	31	5	1
Donations …	380	16	10

	£412	1	11

DONATION ACCOUNT, 1909

EXPENDITURE

	£	s	d
Pensioners	60	0	3
Relief (chiefly in Sickness and Convalescence)	39	12	6
Gardens and Plants	32	2	9
Excursions and Country holidays	24	15	2
Training and Boarding-out	23	16	4
Houses (improvement of)	20	14	5
National Trust (Miss Minet's Gift)	20	0	0
Red Cross Hall (Miss Minet's Gift)	10	0	0
Kyrle Society (Miss Minet's Gift)	10	0	0
Kent and Surrey preservation (Miss Minet's Gift)	10	0	0
Emigration	13	8	0
Mosaic (repairs and architects' fee)	11	19	6
Walworth Cadet Corps (special donation)	10	0	0
Playground, care of	10	8	0
M.A.B.Y.S.	10	0	0
Marylebone Workhouse Girls' Aid	6	6	0
Red Cross Hall	5	0	0
Apprenticeship	3	10	0
Aged Blind	3	3	0
London Fever Hospital	1	1	0
Flower Show	0	10	0
Printing Letter to Fellow-Workers, Stationery, Carriage, &c.	9	8	7 ½
In hand for Pensions, Training, &c.	76	6	4 ½
	£412	1	11

Examined and found correct, W.M. Blyth, January 14th 1910.

RED CROSS HALL AND GARDEN ACCOUNT, 1909

RECEIPTS

	£	s	d
Bank, January 1909	3	10	6
Cash, January 1909	0	3	1
Hire of Hall	36	8	0
Interest on gifts for Red and White Cross Cottages	33	19	0
Donations:			
Garden and Hall	167	9	11
Flower Show	20	0	0
Rent of Clubroom	28	17	0
Rent of Office	10	16	0
Sale of Programmes, Thursday Entertainments	4	8	6
Collections on Sundays	4	19	1 ½
Gas, received from tenants	0	9	0
Violin Fees	1	17	0
Sale of Tickets, Flower Show	0	10	6
	£313	7	7 ½

RED CROSS HALL AND GARDEN ACCOUNT, 1909

EXPENDITURE

	£	s	d
Caretaker	59	18	0
Flower Show	18	15	1
Violin Class	16	10	0
Rates and Taxes	18	7	5
Repairs	70	19	3
Gas 14	5	6	0
Entertainments	9	8	11 ½
Post Office	25	0	0
Cleaning	7	2	5
Compensation	14	14	10
Water Rate	6	15	8
Stationery	5	4	1
Cricket Net	0	11	6
Fuel	4	10	4
Maypole Festival	4	4	9
Garden, Expenses for	34	18	1
In hand, Bank, December 1909	2	1	9
	£313	7	7 ½

Examined and found correct, W.M. Blyth, January 13th 1910.

LETTER TO MY FELLOW-WORKERS

TO WHICH IS ADDED

ACCOUNT OF DONATIONS RECEIVED

FOR

WORK AMONG THE POOR

DURING 1910

BY

OCTAVIA HILL

SUMMARY

Housing: Southwark; Hoxton... training of the unemployed: a large donation received to extend this work... visitors from Holland... Red Cross Hall and garden... entertainments for the tenants... cadet corps... National Trust: properties in the West of England; four acres of Grange Fell given in memory of Miranda Hill... Notting Hill and the Horace Street Trust... a cadet corps for Notting Hill... donation fund... death of Miranda Hill

EDITOR'S NOTE

The 'unsound competition' of local authority housing is one of the recurrent themes of the later letters, and in this letter Octavia repeats all of the points she had already made in 1907: local authorities can build extravagantly and manage carelessly because all of their risks and all of their losses can be passed on to ratepayers. Some of these ratepayers are themselves landlords, struggling to keep down rents as they are in competition with local authority rents, which are not market-based, whilst at the same time facing rising demands for rates. Octavia even repeats the 'for-the-first-time-in-40-years' claim from the 1907 letter. But on this occasion she reaches a different conclusion. Whereas in 1907 she had decided that the time for new purchases and new building had passed, and that management of existing properties was the thing to concentrate on, she now faced a situation in which the owner of some of the first properties that had been placed under her management in Notting Hill wanted to bail out. Octavia could not bear to think of her years of careful work being undone by unscrupulous landlords, but nor could she honestly recommend anyone to buy the properties as an investment. The solution she came up with was to use some of the various charitable funds with which she had been entrusted to purchase the properties and vest them in the Horace Street Trust. The Trust was committed to spending the profits from its properties on open spaces. If these Notting Hill properties incurred losses, it would mean less money for the Trust to give away, but it would not mean that any individual's assets were being reduced in value. Although Octavia would have regarded this arrangement as far from ideal, it was better than the alternative.

190 Marylebone Road, N.W.
December, 1910

Dear Friends,

I begin my annual letter to you as usual with a short reference to the houses under our charge.

Those taken over last year have progressed. The court in Southwark, however, is a very difficult one. It has manifest drawbacks, several houses are unlet and all that we as managers can do is to deal with those conditions which are dependent on us; this we are trying to do, and certainly the place is improved, but some evils, such as the fact that the back entrance of a public house opens into the court, ought to be dealt with by other agencies. The street in Hoxton has made very great progress. We have taken over six more cottages there and now have control of the whole street. There is only one cottage unlet there now; there were nine when I last wrote. A great deal has been spent in drainage, thorough repair of roofs, rebuilding of chimney stacks, replacing of unsound beams, supply of gutters, as well as painting and papering. In short, the renovation of the houses, structural as well as decorative, is steadily progressing. Much remains to be done, however; I do not consider that the standard of regular payment in either of these courts is what it should be. I hope to be able to record progress next year: at Hoxton this ought to be easy.

The older courts have gone on much as before; there are good, experienced, and devoted workers in each. I have been fortunate in securing some fresh helpful volunteers, but we much need some more. In Southwark the collapse of some old workshops at the rear of one of the courts, belonging to the Ecclesiastical Commissioners, gave an opportunity of giving yard space, and additional through ventilation to several cottages. The Commissioners gave us leave to thus use the ground. It was most interesting, and not an easy problem to rearrange so as to use the ground to the best advantage, and give access thereto in the best way. But this is now completed. It was done gradually, bit by bit, and gave good employment to some of those out-of-work men

635

whom we had trained. It was also a great satisfaction to see doors broken out which gave the children access to even the smallest yard, and allowed space for the drying of clothes; or to see the bedroom windows enlarged; or the little gardens formed.

The vacant ground at Southwark, lent by the Commissioners, has been increasingly used. The cricket clubs have practised there, football has been organised, and now the teachers of the neighbouring board school, who asked to use it in school hours, write gratefully of the opportunities of open-air exercise classes.

The plan of training and using certain men out-of-work, who are not in the running for steady independent employment, has continued with success. We have almost forgotten that some of those whom we first thus employed were ever so stranded, so helpful are they; four of them are now regularly employed at Southwark and really wanted there. A generous and large donation makes me strong to develop the scheme further so far as seems advisable, and so far as supervising help is available. I do not print the account of this fund. It is audited, but I think it well to keep it as far as possible from appearing prominent as a donation fund. Often it is used as a guarantee only, and the owners of the houses in which it is used repay the amount; but sometimes the work is distinctly made-work, though it is far better if it does not appear to be so. Donations for this object are needed and would be most helpful.

We have this year again welcomed among us two Dutch ladies who have come to study our methods with the view to hereafter managing houses in Holland. They have been most satisfactory students, came well prepared, arranged to stay a reasonable time, and appear to return to hopeful and well organised schemes in their own land.

Red Cross Hall has gone remarkably well during the past year. Miss Casson[1] has still further developed her plan of bringing in the local clubs and other institutions to undertake the entertainments; this develops power in local workers and creates local interest. The

---

1   Elizabeth Casson (1881–1954) was the sister of Lewis Casson and consequently the sister-in-law of Sybil Thorndike. Octavia may have hoped that she would use her glamorous showbusiness connections to spice up the programme at Red Cross Hall, but Miss Casson's talents took her in a different direction. According to her obituary in *The Times* (20 December 1954): 'She became interested in the experiment that Miss Octavia Hill was carrying out in Southwark to improve housing conditions among the poor and worked as secretary at the Red Cross Hall until 1913. During the war she studied medicine, and... was awarded her diploma in psychological medicine... She set up a residential clinic at Bristol in 1929 and in the following year founded the school of occupational therapy.' From 1930 until her death she was the medical director of the Dorset House School of Occupational Therapy at Churchill Hospital, Oxford.

audiences, too, increase, as friends of the performers naturally come to see and hear those they know, and many a society is glad of a bright, large hall for an annual performance. Last winter *Eager Heart* [2] was acted by the members of a working girls' club. I heard that it was most impressive, being almost like a religious service. It has been repeated this year, the girls being keen to act it again, and I was glad to see it. I was much impressed with the grave earnestness of the young actors, and glad to know that such thoughts should be in their minds, and that their hearts should be tuned by such impressions. It was sweet to hear the young voices, to see a few of our own violin class in the small orchestra, and to be again indebted to Miss Hope Jackson for her kindness in singing the solos.

Mrs Orr again undertook the very considerable duties of honorary secretary of the flower show, which was a great success. Miss Agar most kindly judged all the plants and gardens for us, and Lady Dibdin[3] distributed the prizes. It was pleasant to welcome her and Sir Lewis Dibdin[4] as representing the Ecclesiastical Commissioners, to whom our whole work in Southwark owes its initiation and continuance.

---

2   *Eager Heart* was written by A.M. (Alice) Buckton and published in 1904. Subtitled 'A Christmas Mystery-Play', it is a religious drama featuring a character named Eager Heart and her sisters, Eager Fame and Eager Sense. *Eager Heart* seems to have been a very popular piece with amateur companies, especially with companies connected with the church. It probably owes something to the success of William Poel's production of *Everyman*, which was staged in 1901 and frequently revived and toured during the following 12 years. *The Times* of 19 December 1912, reviewing a production of *Eager Heart* at Church House, Westminster on the previous day, noted that this was the 60th time *Eager Heart* had been given in London. We only have one reference to a production by professional actors, at Sadler's Wells on 10 January 1933 (two performances only— matinee and evening), and these were charity performances in aid of the restoration funds of two London churches. The director, who also acted in the play, was Philip Ben Greet (who had taken Poel's production of *Everyman* on tour to America). The programme asks the audience not to applaud and only lists the names of the actors, not their roles.

---

3   Lady Dibdin gave two guineas to the donation fund in 1911 (1911, p.666).

---

4   Sir Lewis Dibdin (1852–1938) was an ecclesiastical lawyer, judge and administrator. His talents, combined with his scholarship and breadth of experience, gave him a unique degree of influence for a layman on the affairs of the Church of England. From 1903 to 1934 he was Dean of the Arches, the highest ecclesiastical appellate court of the Church of England. It is said that he was the last ecclesiastical lawyer to serve in this position, and that his term of office covered the last period in which ecclesiastical law and the judicial system of the Church of England were matters of pressing concern to its members. From 1905 to 1930 he was first church estates

We had last winter a most beautiful lecture from Dr Greville MacDonald, illustrated with graceful and lovely slides of birds and flowers. We are again having a performance of the *Messiah*; Mrs Julian Marshall continues as heretofore her wonderful and never wearying goodness to us. A good deal has been done to the garden by the great kindness of donors, and under Miss Lumsden's supervision I hope we shall succeed in getting more flowers to bloom in it.

I have to record the loss by death of one of our trustees. Lord Stamford had been a kind and sympathetic friend. Miss Lumsden has been good enough to allow herself to be made a trustee to fill the vacancy.

We did not have many summer parties this year, but a pleasant one for the Notting Hill tenants was given by Mr and Mrs Charlesworth, and we arranged an expedition to Kew Gardens for a small party of 35 tenants in August.

I stated last year some of our anxieties as to the future of the cadet battalion. These anxieties have continued during the year, but a greater desire to make the permanent arrangements such that London boys may continue successfully to be trained, disciplined, and rendered available to help their country, has recently been shown by the authorities, and the commanding officer of the battalion has decided to apply for it to be affiliated to the county association on January 1st. We shall see, as time goes on, how the scheme works, and whether our boys can helpfully continue in the new organisation.[5]

---

commissioner, responsible, with two other estates commissioners and two ecclesiastical commissioners, for the management of the property of the Church of England entrusted to them. He represented the Ecclesiastical Commissioners at Octavia's funeral in 1912. In 1938, the year of his death, the Ecclesiastical Commissioners named Dibdin House in Maida Vale, a four-storey block of accommodation for 237 families, after him. (Sunderland, 1995.)

---

5   According to C.S. Loch, in his obituary essay on Octavia: 'Miss Hill cared very much for the cadet corps at Southwark. She was heartily patriotic... A cadet corps led to healthy enthusiasm, to new and widening relations, the relations especially of the cadets to their officers, to cleanliness and unselfishness, and an expansion of interests. She regretted greatly the official checks that threw back the growth of the movement, now, it is hoped, altogether removed.' (Loch, 1912, p.219.) Octavia's concerns for the future of the cadets went deeper than she let on in her letters to fellow-workers. In the summer of 1910 she wrote to Major Cyril Bennett, commanding officer of the Southwark battalion: 'I am fairly and entirely puzzled by the government's action about the cadets. Do they really want to kill the movement?' (William Hill, 1956,

With regard to open spaces I ought to record that I visited this autumn three of the National Trust possessions in the West of England: the Cheddar Cliffs, Coleridge's cottage at Nether Stowey,[6] and Morte Point. I was much pleased and encouraged. Cheddar is certainly very impressive. Morte Point is a wonderful possession for the public. Its wild beauty; the rocky cliffs against which the sea always breaks; the fact that, as a promontory, it stands alone and complete in itself; the sense that there is nothing but the ocean between it and America; the birds that frequent it; and the turf and thrift which soften the rocky surface, make it a splendid headland to be owned by the people.

I should like to record here my grateful thanks to all those who have contributed to give four acres of Grange Fell in memory of my sister

---

p.143.) It was not only about whether the boys should leave the cadets at 17 or 18; Octavia had been concerned about the way in which the cadets were seen as a means of funnelling boys into the army. When her mother, who was a pacifist, had objected to the militaristic nature of Octavia's scheme, before the formation of the Southwark corps in 1889, Octavia had denied that the cadets would 'strengthen a love of war'. She saw the cadet corps mainly as a means of providing working-class boys with 'exercise, discipline, obedience, *esprit-de-corps* [and]... manly companionship with the gentlemen who will be their officers'. (Maurice, 1914, pp.491-92.) However, the demands made on the armed services by the Boer War caused the War Office to become much more interested in the cadet movement as a source of recruits. As early as 1899, at the public meeting held to commemorate the tenth anniversary of the Southwark corps, Lord Wantage announced that 'the object of those who were at the head of the movement was, first, to add to the strength and power of the nation, especially for defence, and, secondly, to improve the moral character of young soldiers'. (*The Times*, 31 May 1899.) However, according to Moberly Bell, whose biography of Octavia was written with the co-operation of the family: 'Octavia... regarded the corps simply as an instrument of education, in her mind its value lay in what it could do for the lads who composed it, not in what they corporately could do in the army'. (Moberly Bell, 1942, p.198.)

---

6   Samuel Taylor Coleridge and his family moved to Nether Stowey in Somerset on 31 December 1796. Whilst there he wrote *The Ancient Mariner*, and it was there that he was disturbed in his composition of *Kubla Khan* by the 'person from Porlock'. Coleridge had been an admirer of F.D. Maurice, one of the formative influences on Octavia's youth (the other being Ruskin), and 'to Octavia... the purchase of the cottage by public subscription in 1909 was significant because of Coleridge's association with F.D. Maurice'. (Waterson, 1994, p. 44.)

---

7   Octavia gives thanks to those who have helped purchase four acres of Grange Fell in Borrowdale in memory of her sister Miranda, but in the next letter she gives thanks for seven acres. She may have been confusing two memorial appeals. When Grange Fell came on the market in 1910 it was Hardwicke Rawnsley who secured a five-year

Miranda.[7] She loved beautiful places and cared that they should be devoted to the nation.

To return to the houses, I have had a very anxious time lately about Notting Hill, owing to the fact that the gentleman who first bought houses there to put them under our charge, felt that he must part with some of them. This was a great blow. Not only is our presence more important here than in any other neighbourhood where we are supervising, but no purchaser would be found for any houses in this district except such as would increase the evil so rampant in the neighbourhood. All the houses that change hands are purchased by those who let furnished lodgings, and that means, almost necessarily, evil. We manage about 100 houses in the neighbourhood, 63 of which are in one street, but they are not all contiguous, and wherever others intervene there is difficulty and deterioration. My great hope is always to increase, not to diminish, the number I can control. For 40 years there has never, till now, been a time when I could not say confidently to anyone that (always supposing they saw their way to wise management) they might, when investing money in houses, be sure of a moderate interest. The need of money has, therefore, till now never limited my work. But things have changed, and I can no longer conscientiously tell my friends that a moderate interest is sure. The unsound competition of municipal and county building schemes (which do not secure good management), the rise of rates, the exodus towards the suburbs and, above all, the recent legislation, makes all house property, certainly a very troublesome, and possibly a losing speculation. Yet wise management is more than ever needed, in Notting Hill above all places. I dare not ask prudent people to purchase; things may right themselves, but one cannot see any distinct hope of reaction. I could not possibly see our ten years' work checked, gentle and helpful influence and rule withdrawn, and houses which had been steadily improved fall back into the hands of unscrupulous owners, and especially where such houses adjoin those still under our care. What

---

option to buy, and then launched an appeal for the sum. In the same year King Edward VII died and his sister the Princess Louise, who was president of the National Trust, decided to commemorate him by her purchase and then giftmaking of Grange Fell to the National Trust. In September 1913 a stone tablet was set into the rock, inscribed with the following words, cut in letters designed by Canon Rawnsley's wife Edith: 'In loving memory of King Edward VII, Grange Fell is dedicated by his sister Louise as a sanctuary of rest and peace. Here may all beings gather strength, and find in scenes of beautiful nature a cause for gratitude and love to God, giving them courage and vigour to carry on His work'.

22. Cottages in Ufford Street, Lambeth, 1906.

This photograph is taken from a postcard sent to Octavia Hill in 1906. It shows some of the new cottages on the Ecclesiastical Commissioners' Lambeth Estate, seen from the recreation ground on the other side of Ufford Street.

Reproduced by permission of the Church Commissioners.

23. Cottages in Ufford Street, Lambeth, 2004.

24. 'Compound houses' in Charles Street (now Ranston Street), Lisson Grove, 2004.

Herondale cottages in Charles Street (now 14-19 Ranston Street) were early experiments in what we now call maisonettes, and what Octavia called:

> 'compound houses, each of which comes to be practically two distinct cottages one on the top of another. One front door and passage leads to a five-roomed cottage, containing three ground-floor rooms and two rooms below with coal-cellar, wash-house and small back yard. Another front door leads by a separate staircase to a seven roomed cottage, containing three rooms on first floor and four above. This tenement, too, has separate wash-house, coal cellar, and an iron outside staircase which leads down to a small yard… It has the great advantage of enabling us to build what are practically separate cottages, with little yards, and yet get a somewhat greater height of building than two storeys; so diminishing ground rent, without resorting to high blocks, or to so much life in public as many buildings necessitate.'

LETTER TO MY FELLOW-WORKERS, 1897

26. Merrow Street, Walworth, 1906, after redevelopment (*top*).

From 'The Ecclesiastical Commissioners' Housing of the Working Classes, London Estates, 1906'. Reproduced by permission of the Church Commissioners

27. Merrow Street, Walworth, 2003 (*below*).

25. Brettell Street, Walworth, 1903, before redevelopment (*opposite*).

From 'The Ecclesiastical Commissioners' Housing of the Working Classes, London Estates, 1906'. Reproduced by permission of the Church Commissioners.

28. Interior of cottage kitchen, Walworth, 1906.

This is one of the few surviving photographs of the interior of a property managed by Octavia Hill.

From 'The Ecclesiastical Commissioners' Housing of the Working Classes, London Estates, 1906'. Reproduced by permission of the Church Commissioners.

29. Recreation ground, Walworth, 1906.
From 'The Ecclesiastical Commissioners' Housing of the Working Classes, London Estates, 1906'. Reproduced by permission of the Church Commissioners.

30. Recreation ground, Walworth, 2003.

31. The opening of Brandelhow Park by Princess Louise, 1902.

'In October we had the great joy of seeing the land, longed for so much, bought with such effort, opened for the nation. It was a wild windy day, but the lights could not have been lovelier, gleams of glorious sunshine sweeping over russet fern, golden beech, greenest grass, chasing cloud shadows on Skiddaw and Blencathara, shining on the lake far below studded with its islands. The Princess Louise was there to open it... her presence recalled a day now many years ago when she came, an early friend to the open space movement, to open a little walled-in garden in London, one of the first churchyards turned into a people's garden... "That day to this", I seemed to hear whispered in my ear, "such progress one lives to see", for I thought of the growth of interest in open spaces, of the few helpers in the old time, of the thirteen hundred donors to Brandelhow, sending donations from crowded Lancashire towns, from quiet English country homes, from distant India and South Africa, some rich, some poor, some old, some young, all caring and giving, to preserve for the nation one of its fairest spots. And a triumphal song of thanks and joy seemed to be ringing around us as if the spirits gone before, and the English scattered over the far-away parts of the earth, and the dwellers in crowded courts, and the men and women that shall inherit the earth after we have gone, were rejoicing with us.'

LETTER TO MY FELLOW-WORKERS, 1902

Photo: National Trust Photographic Library, c. Rosalind Rawnsley

32. Derwentwater, looking towards Brandelhow Park and Catbells.

'Day after day Canon Rawnsley ... and I kept receiving letters, one more delightful than the other; some from the young in their exuberance of life; some from the old, rich in memory; some from the rich, with solemn sense of duty; some from the poor, eager to contribute their mite; some from the north, from sense of neighourhood; some from the south, in gratitude for holiday; some from America, from friends and in thought of kinship and common inheritance of literature; some from our colonies and abroad in thought of English loveliness and dearness. And at last, by the multitude of gifts, the large sum was amassed, and now stands ready in the hands of the National Trust, waiting for the deeds to be completed, and for this lake-side, green with wood and meadow, gray with rock, and commanding view of purple mountain and blue lake, to pass into the possession of the people, for their joy, for their teaching, for their rest and refreshment, the gift of the many, each in due measure, to the many, to be loved and used in honour and gratitude to those who gave, in hope and trust that the gift would be for the joy of all through long years to come.'

LETTER TO MY FELLOW-WORKERS, 1901

Photo: National Trust Photographic Library, Joe Cornish

33. Ullswater, from Gowbarrow Fell.

'I have made known through the press the facts about this 700 acres of land on the slopes of Ullswater, commanding views of its head, surrounded by the great company of mountains, as Turner painted them for us; its mile of lake shore with the waves breaking on the shingle; its association with Wordsworth in his noblest utterances; its boulders and heather, its wooded ravine, its mountain meadows, its bird and plant life, and its herds of deer; its great slopes, from which such views are visible, and how it lies open to sun, and shower, and storm. I have told how it may either be free to foot of man, woman and child for all ages, or appropriated to one or two families, and fenced off with barbed wire; shut off from artist, naturalist, hard-worked professional man, smoke-grimed city dweller, workman and child; of how £18 buys one acre of it for all time… I cannot believe that the land will be lost. There are too many who know that man does not live by bread alone; that when all material wants have been duly recognised and attended to, there does remain in England enough wealth for her to set aside a few areas where man may contemplate the beauty of nature, may rest, may find quiet, may commune with his God in the mighty presence of mountain, sky and water, and may find that peace, so difficult to realise in the throng of populous cities.'

LETTER TO MY FELLOW-WORKERS, 1904

was I to do? At last a plan occurred to me. There is, as you know, a small group of four trustees,[8] all great friends of my own, in whom, with myself, are vested the freehold houses given to me years ago by Mrs Scrase-Dickins and Mrs Russell Gurney.[9] More recently these trustees have acquired three small leaseholds at Notting Hill. If they would purchase the leases of five of the houses there, that would meet the need of our friend who has felt he must sell some. As the Horace Street trustees now own houses, they must always have a machinery for management which can deal with the business arising out of the new complicated arrangements relating to house property. As they own two freeholds, they have some security as against loss on leaseholds. By their trust they are bound to give away for open spaces, or other objects which are helpful to the people, any profits arising from the houses after expenses are paid. The result of their purchasing these Notting Hill leaseholds, even should no interest accrue from them, would be loss of money to give, not personal loss. They were clearly the people who could and should hold the leases. But they had very little money and a great deal was wanted. However it was a great point to see anyone who could hold the houses without fear of loss.

The trustees, one and all, consented to do so if I could find the money. I really believe that I have done this, always supposing that some friends, who I quite believe will agree, authorise my thus applying some funds which are now in my hands. Strangely enough, a gift of £400 made to me 30 years or more ago, suddenly becomes again available, and forms more than a third of the purchase money. The transfer will therefore take place, no one will risk what they are not prepared to risk, and if, happily, interest accrues it will be available for direct gift in the years to come.

I mentioned last year that I hoped to carry forward the work in Notting Hill so that it might generally influence the district, and I wished this the more because I then felt the difficulty of further purchase of houses which might come into the market. I have made enquiries as to the possibility of repressive measures being taken with regard to the public houses and furnished rooms. These enquiries may bear fruit later, but, for the moment, there seems more hope of advance in the

---

8   They were Janet Johnson, C.S. Loch, Elinor Lewes and Francis Morris (1900, p.453). Octavia was the fifth trustee.

---

9   Anna Scrase-Dickins (1831–1901) gave three houses in Horace Street in 1886. Emilia Gurney (1823–1896) gave Westbourne Buildings in Paddington in 1893.

more congenial and more thorough way of developing and organising the agencies—many and good they seem to be—in the district itself; this is going forward, and I shall hope to report on these larger reforms next year.

For the present I will only write of one hope I have of a fresh organisation for good in the district in that there seems a possibility that we may arrange for a company of cadets to be enrolled there, and so benefit the boys' when they begin work. There is no organisation which I have found influences so powerfully for good the boys in such a neighbourhood, or gathers them in so eagerly as that of our cadets, and I should be most hopeful that, if we succeed in arranging for a company there, it would be a powerful influence among them. I should like to see it in touch with the Rugby mission where Mr Donald is at work.[10] The cadets learn the duty and dignity of obedience; they get a sense of corporate life and of civic duty; they learn to honour the power of endurance and effort; they get exercise which develops their bodies and improves their health, and they come in contact with manly and devoted officers. The summer camp too is a great gain. These ideals are in marked contrast with the listless self-indulgence, the pert self-assertion, the selfishness and want of reverence, which are so characteristic of the life in a low district, and if such ideals can be brought before the young lad before he gets in with a gang of loafers, it may make all the difference to his life.

My donation fund has been generously supported all the year, and I know it has done good work. You will notice that we have a larger balance than usual. As in previous years a great part of this is pledged. As my receipts are from voluntary sources only, and I am supporting orphans,

---

10 The Rugby Mission had started as a boys club, founded by Arthur Walrond in 1885. An old Rugbeian, he had persuaded the school to support the venture, and in 1899 an old bus yard in Walmer Road was purchased, and club premises built on the site. The Rugby Home Mission contained a meeting room and a gymnasium, beneath which there was a swimming bath. The Mission ran a programme of educational and cultural activities, social events and sports, especially boxing in which several of the mission boys were to make their names, including Digger Stanley, the Lonsdale Belt holder. C.S. Donald was a Church of England clergyman who was appointed missioner in 1905 and remained there for 20 years. 'We who lived in the Dale found the drama of life', he wrote many years later in his memoirs. 'I am a nonentity whose story is of no moment to any other. But there is a debt to pay—owed to my chums, the plucky, generous, vivacious boys and girls of the old London streets... Few of them got much out of the kitty of life. In the strata of life they belonged to the lias, the monotonous blue-grey clay. But, as geologists know, and I discovered over 60 years ago, grey mud is the locus for diamonds.' (Whitlor, 1998, pp. 12 and 35-38.)

pensioners, &c., I feel bound to have a certain reserve, not a large one, but one which would give time to reconsider responsibilities if funds should fail. But beyond my ordinary balance I have received this year one great gift on the strength of which I am, in great joy, extending my gifts. I am encouraged to hope that its usefulness may be increased, and that I may be brought into nearer touch with recipients in the more forlorn districts of London, owing to the fact that a very experienced friend has come to me who will specially take up this duty. I cannot tell the donors what great and radical good their gifts have done during the past year, nor what it is to us all to feel ourselves thus fortified to help at once and thoroughly when need arises.

I have been writing, and I know you have been reading, all this with an undercurrent of thought as if, important as it all may be, and necessary as it may be not to forget the larger issues in private ones, all the same the thought of one loss overshadows all my year's record. The friend, the counsellor, the companion of all my life has passed from me beyond the veil.[11] Life is necessarily changed for me, and it is only with bowed head, and with continual prayer for courage that I can take it up. But it is not here or now that I can speak of this, nor even of the marvellous blessing which seems to have been over all that she had done here below, it has been one chorus of love and gratitude from all whom she had known in every relation of life—poor law children, pupils, friends, servants, colleagues—all have felt something of the gracious holiness with which she walked through life. Of this I will not write, for I cannot, but I must add a word or two of loving thanks to all the many friends who have stood near me, and have rendered such loving service through all my great need.

I am, in ever greater gratitude,
Your affectionate old friend,
OCTAVIA HILL

---

11 Octavia's sister Miranda had died in May 1910 and Octavia was devastated by the loss. She had been closer to Miranda than to her three other full sisters. Although Octavia was the dominant sibling, she had always recognised the extent to which she depended on Miranda's faithful support in all of her projects. 'When Octavia herself was dying, she told her companions that the prospect of joining Miranda was cheering her on.' (Darley, 1990, p.329.)

DONATIONS DURING 1910

	Donations			Red Cross Hall			Flower Show		
	£	s	d	£	s	d	£	s	d
Allen, A.C.	2	2	0	1	1	0	0	10	6
Andrewes, Mr and Mrs H.	1	1	0	—			—		
Austin, Miss	1	0	0	—			—		
Bailey, J.	5	0	0	—			—		
Bannerman, Mrs (In Memoriam)	1	1	0	—			—		
Barclay, Mrs	1	0	0	—			—		
Bayley, E.	—			—			1	1	0
Blyth, P.L.	1	1	0	1	1	0	—		
Bonsor, H. Cosmo	—			—			1	1	0
Brander, Mrs	1	1	0	—			—		
Bridgett, Miss	—			—			0	5	0
Brinton, Miss	—			0	10	0	—		
Brogentin, Miss	—			0	10	6	—		
Burrage, Miss (The late)	14	2	6	—			—		
Cockerell, S.C.	1	0	0	—			—		
Covington, Mrs	0	10	0	—			—		
Curry, The Misses M. and E.	—			—			0	10	0
Curteis, Miss	—			0	5	0	0	2	6
Dakin, Miss E.	—			—			1	0	0
Dawson, Miss	2	0	0	—			—		
Dowson, Felix N.	1	1	0	—			—		
Ducie, The Earl of	5	0	0	—			—		
Dunn, Sir William	—			—			1	1	0
Edwards, Colonel H.									
(Part of Donation from)	130	0	0	—			—		
Erle, Miss	20	0	0	—			—		
Evans, Mrs Richardson	2	2	0	—			—		
Fellow-Workers, Miss Octavia Hill's	—			10	0	0	—		
Frankau, Miss	5	0	0	—			—		
Forman, Miss	1	1	0	—			—		
Fry, J.	—			—			2	2	0
Fordyce, Miss	—			2	2	0	—		
Gladstone, Miss	—			2	0	0	—		
Griffiths, Miss	—			2	2	0	—		
Hamer, Mrs	2	2	0	—			—		
Harris, Miss S.J.	1	1	0	1	1	0	—		
Herberden, Mrs	3	0	0	—			—		
Hill, Miss	5	0	0	—			—		
Hill, Miss Octavia, per	0	5	8 ½	0	3	6	—		
Howitt, Miss	0	10	0	—			—		
Lowndes, Miss	1	1	0	—			—		
Llangattock, Lord	—			—			1	0	0
Macaulay, Mrs	3	8	6	—			—		
Macfie, Miss	1	0	0	—			—		
Marshall, Miss L.	10	0	0	—			—		
Marshall, Miss L. 'In Memory of									
Miss Hill'	10	0	0	—			—		
Marshall, R.C.	—			—			1	1	0
Martelli, F.	—			0	10	0	—		
Mills, F.C.	5	0	0	—			—		
Morris, F.	1	1	0	—			—		
Morshead, Mrs	—			1	0	0	—		
Nicholson, Lady	5	0	0	—			—		
Orr, Mrs	—			1	1	0	0	10	6
Paddock, F.W.	2	0	0	1	0	0	—		
Pascall, J.	—			—			0	10	0
Plummer, Rev. C.	5	0	0	—			—		
Pollock, Lady	—			2	5	2	—		
Praed, Sir H.	—			—			1	1	0
Price, Miss C.R.	0	10	0	—			—		
Schuster, Mrs	10	0	0	—			0	5	0

DONATIONS DURING 1910 (continued)

	Donations			Red Cross Hall			Flower Show		
	£	s	d	£	s	d	£	s	d
Sewell, Miss	—			0	10	0	—		
Somervell, Gordon	3	3	0	—			—		
Somervell, Mr and Mrs	1	0	0	—			—		
Stone, Rev. E.D.	2	2	0	—			—		
Strachey, J. St. Loe	5	5	0	—			—		
Strauss, E.A.	—			—			1	1	0
Thompson, Mrs C.	2	0	0	—			—		
Todhunter, Miss	2	0	0	—			—		
Tuffnell, Mrs	1	1	0	—			—		
Tupper, Miss	15	10	0	—			—		
Wagner, H.	5	0	0	—			—		
Walker, Miss	1	0	0	—			—		
Warner, Miss Lee	—			—			0	10	0
Webb, Mrs Randall	—			2	0	0	0	10	0
Welbury-Mitton, Mrs	5	0	0	—			—		
Wells, Miss	2	0	0	—			—		
Willcox, W.H.	—			—			2	2	0
Wood, Miss	—			—			1	1	0
	£306	2	8 ½	£29	2	2	£17	4	6

DONATION ACCOUNT, 1910

RECEIPTS

	£	s	d
In hand, January 1910 …	76	6	4 ½
Subscriptions and Donations … … … … … … … … … … … … … … …	306	2	8 ½
Returned by Emigrant … … … … … … … … … … … … … … … … … … …	1	0	0
	£383	9	1

DONATION ACCOUNT, 1910

EXPENDITURE

	£	s	d
Pensions	68	13	0
Relief (mainly in Illness)	55	9	1
Training and Boarding-out	52	7	7
Playground	10	8	0
London Playing Fields	10	0	0
M.A.B.Y.S. (Special Gift)	5	0	0
Workhouse Girls' Aid (Special Gift)	5	0	0
Entertainments	3	11	8
Blind	3	3	0
London Fever Hospital	1	1	0
Stationery	0	1	7
Printing Letter to Fellow-Workers	6	10	0
In hand*	162	4	2
	£383	9	1

Examined and found correct, P.L. Blyth, January 12th 1911.

* A large part of this balance is allocated to chronic cases, but it is more than usual owing to one great gift which will enable me to help a larger number. — O.H.

RED CROSS HALL AND GARDEN ACCOUNT, 1910

RECEIPTS

	£	s	d
Cash, January 1910	2	1	9
Interest from Red and White Cross Cottages	73	17	0
Hire of Hall	30	14	0
Donations:			
Garden and Hall	29	2	2
Flower Show	17	4	6
Flower Show Sale of Tickets	0	7	2
Rent of Clubroom	16	12	0
Rent of Office	12	0	0
Sale of Programmes, Thursday Entertainments	6	6	4
Sale of Programmes, *Eager Heart*	5	1	6
Collections on Sundays	4	11	6
Violin Fees	4	1	0
Gas, received from tenants	0	12	0
	£202	10	11

RED CROSS HALL AND GARDEN ACCOUNT, 1910

EXPENDITURE

	£	s	d
Caretaker	61	18	6
Flower Show	20	4	2
Violin Class	17	10	0
Borough Rate	13	3	6
Taxes	3	5	4
Water Rate	6	15	8
Repairs	6	14	7
Gas and Fuel	19	1	10
Entertainments	13	1	2 ½
Cleaning	6	11	9
Expenses for Garden	4	14	11
Stationery	2	19	7
Fire Insurance	2	9	9
Cash in hand, December 1910	24	0	1 ½
	£202	10	11

Examined and found correct, P.L. Blyth, January 12th 1911.

LETTER TO MY FELLOW-WORKERS

TO WHICH IS ADDED

ACCOUNT OF DONATIONS RECEIVED

FOR

WORK AMONG THE POOR

DURING 1911

❧

BY

OCTAVIA HILL
(FOR PRIVATE CIRCULATION ONLY)

SUMMARY

Housing: Legislation makes private provision of working-class housing very difficult; 15 cottages added to the stock in Notting Dale and another 12 purchased from the owner who was withdrawing; housing projects in Manchester, Cambridge, Holland, Sweden… more volunteers needed… Red Cross Hall: music, flower show, electric light installed to protect Walter Crane's panels… employment for tenants… more order required in Notting Dale… cadets in Paddington and Notting Dale… donation fund: previous successes… National Trust: Barmouth; One Tree Hill in Sevenoaks; Wandle; Grange Fell; Mariner's Hill.

EDITOR'S NOTE

In 1933 Octavia's niece Elinor edited a selection of the Letters to Fellow-Workers in which extracts from the printed letters were mixed together with some of Octavia's earlier personal correspondence to give a brief, first-hand account of Octavia's career in housing management. The concluding words of the book are attributed to the 1911 letter: 'As I write to record what has been done… I think of the many and great mercies which have been with us, of the joy which has been sent to us…' In fact, in order to elicit the appropriate 'dying fall' for Octavia's last letter, Elinor had transposed this passage from the beginning of the 1909 letter. Octavia was fond of contemplating her own demise, and had first speculated on what would happen to her work after her death in the letter for 1874 (p.31), when she was only 36! There were similar gloomy speculations in the letters for 1876, 1880, 1906 and 1908— but not 1911. When Octavia sat down to write this letter in December 1911 she did not realise that it would be her last. On the contrary, it was business as usual on all fronts, still trying to enforce 'law and order' and raise 'the moral standard' in Notting Dale, still extending the work in Cambridge, Manchester, Holland and Sweden, still putting on the Messiah at Red Cross Hall, and, above all, still appealing for open spaces. However, by the spring of 1912 Octavia realised that she was seriously ill and began divesting herself of responsibilities. On 9 March she wrote to the Commissioners, handing over responsibility for the Westminster Estate to Ada Covington; on 22 April she wrote to transfer her work in Southwark to Miss Mitchell, and on 17 July she proposed to hand over the final part of her work, in Mitre Street (Lambeth), to Joan Sunderland. (The Walworth Estate was so much Miss Lumsden's responsibility that no formal transfer was required.)

The benefit of Octavia's devolved system of management, under which she had always encouraged her fellow-workers to think and act on their own account, without referring everything to her, became apparent now, just as it had done at the time of her breakdown in 1877. 'I might have given it a few more touches, but I think it is nearly all planned now, very well', was her verdict on the future of her work. She made a brief trip to Larksfield, the house that Harriot Yorke had built for them in Crockham Hill, then returned to the house in Marylebone Road in June. She died on 13 August, the day after receiving the cheque that secured the addition to Mariner's Hill, the very last open space for which she had appealed. (Maurice, 1914, pp.580-83.) On 20 August the Morning Post *carried a report of Octavia's funeral, at which Sir Robert Hunter had represented the Princess Louise. The Princess's wreath was accompanied by the message: 'In deepest admiration and esteem for one who devoted her whole life and energy to the advancement and welfare of her fellow countrymen.'*

190 Marylebone Road, N.W.
December, 1911

Dear Friends,

The question of the housing of the working classes satisfactorily, so far as it depends on private owners, has, in my opinion, become more than ever difficult of late years. The trend of recent legislation renders it almost impossible to find those who can undertake the responsibilities of house-ownership. The extension of our work in the future is, for this reason, to be looked for in the direction of managing houses for present owners, rather than in that of finding new purchasers. Yet wise management is more needed than ever.

I am therefore especially glad that, in spite of the new legal and financial difficulties, we have been able during the last year to extend our area of work. One friend—a barrister, and consequently capable of realising to the full the risk and trouble involved—has ventured to buy fifteen cottages situated in the heart of Notting Dale, the district in which, of all others, we are the most eager to extend our control and influence. These cottages were in great need of substantial improvement, and the carrying out of these improvements, such as the excavations under floors; the putting in of damp courses; the opening out of windows; the laying down of new paving, in addition to the pointing, painting and other general repair, has provided beneficent work, for now many weeks, to our men, thus giving them steady employment. There remains still more of this useful work to be done in order to complete the improvement of the cottages.

The threatened danger of losing houses already under our care has this year been further averted. I mentioned in my last letter the pleasure we had felt in retaining five houses in Notting Dale which we had managed for ten years but which the owner then felt himself obliged to sell. These, if sold in the open market, would almost inevitably have fallen into bad hands, and the work of our ten years would have been broken off; but, happily, the houses were bought during 1910 and were placed under the Horace Street Trust—a Trust of which most of you know.

But that did not meet the whole difficulty as there remained, in the

655

same street and belonging to the same owner, twelve more houses which he very reluctantly felt he should be obliged to sell during 1911. I set myself therefore to see what could be done and, by the generosity of friends, we have succeeded in arranging for all to be bought and to continue under our charge.

Two ladies each gave the price of one house, a gentleman for whom we have for 40 years managed property in another part of London gave a third (the cheque being accompanied by a most appreciative letter), and a fourth was bought by those of my fellow-workers who, having themselves helped in the management of houses, realise the good that may be accomplished by it. These four houses have also been given over to the Horace Street trustees, the donors preferring to make their money a gift rather than to undertake the responsibilities of leaseholders. It may be repeated here, that, according to the terms of the trust, all monies not needed for the upkeep or other expenses of the houses must be given to open spaces or some other beneficent object, so that if any financial success is attained these gifts will serve a double end. The remaining eight of the twelve houses were bought by friends interested in the welfare of this difficult and forlorn locality and willing to hold the leases themselves.

If anyone had told me some time ago that, in spite of difficulties, we could have purchased all these seventeen houses I could scarcely have believed them!

With regard to our work in other parts of London, all the districts hitherto under our care remain as successful as ever and grow in interest. I feel deeply thankful for the sagacity, devotion, and judgement shewn by my representatives in each place. As the years pass, more of the living intercourse with tenants, more of the responsibility of decisions devolves on my fellow-workers, and I know that their work is excellent.

We have lost from amongst us, by her early death whilst on a visit to South Africa, Miss Florence Joseph, one of my noblest, most capable and dearly loved workers. Tenants, colleagues and I myself, feel the loss deeply. But we must be thankful for the memory of such a character, and must strive to fill the gap as best we can.

The scheme for the purchase and management of poor courts in Manchester, in the early stages of which we were able to give help, is progressing most satisfactorily. The initial difficulties, which were very great, seem to have been overcome by the spirited and patient efforts of those in charge. The undertaking is financially successful, and a good many additional houses have just been taken over.

A lady from Cambridge came to us last summer to study our ways of work, and I hear that the cottages under her charge there, a gift from Mrs Henry Sedgwick to the COS, promise to be very satisfactory.

We continue to be able to help kindred work in foreign countries. Two more capable Dutch ladies have been over to learn house management. One of them obtained a good post on her return to Holland. She takes over the charge of 80 families and of a garden for their common use and enjoyment. A Swedish lady is just beginning a course of training with us. I hope that on her return to Stockholm she may find help by associating herself with Mlle. Lagerstadt who came to us for training some 20 or 30 years ago and has been carrying on work there ever since.

May I remind my friends how gladly I would welcome more volunteer workers in our own courts? There must inevitably be breaks in our band of workers, sometimes in a happy way by their marriage, sometimes from other causes, and fresh recruits are needed to fill the ranks. I believe that often those who take up this form of helpfulness find that their intercourse with the tenants is on a delightful footing, that they learn much, and are supported by being side by side with my experienced representatives. No municipal or state ownership can supply the place filled by the representative of conscientious owners. Such a one can secure more elasticity in the rule; has greater power of swift decision; finds a place for generous action; has the possibility of making various arrangements for various families; and may, above all, realise the human relationship which, where it exists, makes life full and happy.

At Red Cross Hall all has gone well.[1] Mrs Julian Marshall continues her regular help on Sundays, and before Christmas again gave us a performance of the *Messiah*. It seemed to me almost more beautiful

---

1   Apart from the occasional change of trustee, the status of the Hall, garden and cottages appears to have remained the same for Octavia's lifetime. On 21 May 1921 Miss Lumsden wrote to the secretary of the Ecclesiastical Commissioners asking him to consider a change to the lease structure of the Hall and garden. This was, according to Miss Lumsden's letter, part of an attempt to put the housing operation on a more permanent and professional footing. It was requested that the lease of the Hall and garden be transferred to the permanent trusteeship of the diocesan trustees, and the cottages be given over to the Horace Street Trust. This was agreed to and the rents were reapportioned accordingly. In February 1922 the Rochester Diocesan Trust requested that the garden be passed to Southwark Borough Council. In 1934 the Rochester Diocesan Trust were asked by the War Office to change the name of the Hall, and agreed to re-name it Bishop's Hall. The freehold of the Hall was eventually sold to the Rochester Diocesan Trust for £25 in 1961, and the Hall was subsequently sold into private commercial ownership.

than ever, and more like a Christmas service for us all together there.

The teacher of the violin class at the Hall has decided that the time has arrived when he can form an orchestral class from the more advanced students. He told me that he had classes of the same kind in various parts of London, but that he found the Southwark pupils more in earnest than the others. Has this anything to do with the 24 years of Sunday music in the hall, so much of it inspired by Mrs Julian Marshall?

The entertainments on Thursdays go on as in former years under Miss Casson's guidance. She is bringing in more and more of the local clubs and associations.

The flower show was a great success, Mrs Orr and Miss Agar again giving their invaluable help; Miss Lumsden watches over the garden; many kind friends come and help on Sundays and the place is full of happy life. I am glad to say we have had electric light installed, partly for the sake of better preserving the Walter Crane panels.[2]

Mr and Mrs Carter and Miss Sayle gave a delightful party at their country house to some of the Notting Dale tenants.

I do not know that I need repeat what I have said in previous letters about the usefulness of the employment given to poor and not over-skilful tenants. The value of the plan impresses me more every year as I watch the feeble and helpless man growing—simply by the practice he gains, and the careful and patient supervision of ladies—into one whose work we prize, and whom we desire to retain as a permanent workman. The money given in previous years for employment has indeed borne rich fruit.

I promised in my last letter to report further on whether it had been possible to get anything radical done in the Notting Dale district by way of enforcing law and order in the houses *not* under our charge. Some radical reforms seem not only called for but most urgently needed; such are the further diminution of public houses; the closing of their back doors when they open upon poor courts; the control of furnished lodgings; better police protection, and, above all, a raising of the moral standard by the banding together of the better intentioned of the residents themselves. Alas, I have nothing, even now, to record except hope. But the hope is there, and let us trust that it may, in some measure, be realised in the course of the present year.

One step forward which seems full of promise has, however, been

---

2   The Red Cross Hall accounts show that £20 17s was spent on the electric lighting (1911, p.671). Unfortunately, it was too late to save the panels, which had already been severely damaged by the gas lamps.

made. A meeting was held last March at the house of my sister, Mrs Lewes, to consider the formation, in the worst parts of Paddington and Notting Dale, of two companies of the 1st Cadet Battalion, which has done so much good amongst working lads since it was started in Southwark 20 years ago. These companies, each with its club, have been successfully started and we are very hopeful as to the result, the commanding officer of the Battalion, Colonel Beresford, having been able to give these newly formed companies much of his personal supervision.

Let me here say how grateful I am to all who have so generously supported my donation fund. Instances are constantly coming before me which shew the present results of past help. Two of these I should like specially to mention as examples, because the two people to whom they relate were among the many cared for of old by my sister, Miranda, in her capacity as guardian, and their history shows how fruitful through the years the result of wise and loving help may be. One is that of a young man who sailed this year to Australia and from whom we have good news. He was so delicate a boy of eight that he could not even get from the infirmary ward across the yard to the school. He was growing up without teaching and without health. Helped by the donation fund my sister boarded him out in the country; he began to get strong; when he was old enough she placed him in Scilly to learn bulb growing. Later he returned to his mother in London, but memories of the country haunted him and he saw more openings for advancement in the colonies. He was not vigorous-looking and could not get an assisted passage, but out of his small earnings he saved £16 of passage money. He is now employed in an hotel in Melbourne earning £1 a week, and with no expenses. All through the years he has felt the care and thought bestowed on him, and it has blessed his life.[3] The other instance I should like to mention as interesting to many who loved my sister, is that of a girl from Southall, who once seemed as low and hopeless a person as could be. We had felt almost in despair about her, but she was watched over and helped for a long time, and lately she has written from a good situation in the country where she is earning £18 a year, and seems in every way established in right paths and well doing. Such results light us on our way.

And now about open spaces. I visited in the spring the cliff at Barmouth, which was the first possession of the National Trust. It was given by Mrs Talbot, a great friend of Mr Ruskin's. It is steep and wild,

---

3   See 1901, pp.471-72, for the beginning of this story.

the path along its face is cut in the rock high above town and sea; at one place the path is widened, a semi-circular seat is hewn in the face of the cliff, and above the seat is cut an inscription telling of its dedication to the people for ever. As we stood there the rain clouds suddenly parted and cleared off, the sun broke out and lighted up the whole magnificent view of sea, and bay, and headland, and one felt what an abiding possession such a view was for the townspeople, and the many visitors from all parts of England.

One interesting event of my year was being present at the dedication to the public of One Tree Hill, near Sevenoaks, which has been given to the National Trust by Dr and Mrs Jamieson Hurry in memory of my brother.[4] The day was lovely, the view most beautiful, and the gift one which rejoiced my heart.

There is another open space with which I have been very closely connected this year, and which therefore, I must mention. It is on the banks of the Wandle. I have long been anxious to impress upon people the importance of connecting larger existing open spaces by pleasant walking ways, away from dust and noise; these connecting walks need not necessarily be very broad, but should be set with trees, have near them grass and flowers, if only at the edges, and should be provided with plenty of seats. To women and young children who cannot get to far-off parks these pathways would be of inestimable value, and they would save stronger walkers, too, from having to tramp through ugly streets, or go by train or tram before reaching the open common or park. Doubly useful would these walking ways be if they could be along the banks of a river. The Wandle, which flows from Carshalton to Wandsworth, seemed to offer an opportunity of carrying out such a plan, if, one after another, we could get hold of portions of land on its banks, purchasing them from the various owners as opportunity offered, and so making a river path as continuous as it is still possible to make it. Before this year several such spaces had been secured and we set ourselves to get more. After colouring our map to see what land was still unbuilt upon, we selected two areas to begin with. We have so far

---

4   This is south-east of Sevenoaks, on the other side of the town from Ide Hill and Toy's Hill. Octavia's half-brother Arthur had entertained her tenants at his home Erleigh Court in Berkshire on many occasions. He had died in 1909 (1909, p.622). Mrs Jamieson Hurry was his daughter. 'How glad Arthur would be that his children showed a large generosity for a public object.' (Letter from Octavia to her sister Emily, 28 February 1911.) Arthur Hill's children and grandchildren also paid for a public swimming bath in Reading in his memory. (Maurice, 1914, p.576.) It still exists as the Arthur Hill Pool and Fitness Studio, the oldest sports facility in Reading.

succeeded that one of these will form a walk some 40 feet broad on the left bank of the river. It will be vested in the local authority and will go a long way to connect two wider areas on the shores.

Of the second Wandle space I must tell you even more, because it is a very special one, and we are thinking much about it. It is about 10½ acres in size, and is close to Mitcham station. The river here takes a wide curve and its banks are set with loose-strife and meadow-sweet. It also forms a largish pond, or tiny lake, surrounded by trees, and there is an island, a lovely meadow, and a public path which skirts the land; we shall be able to open up our land to this path. The whole money for the purchase has been obtained, though to do all we want with the land, more gifts will be needed. For it is intended to vest this land in the National Trust in order that it may be available for various purposes. First, we want its wild flowers carefully preserved, kingcups and forget-me-nots should do well; and as in private grounds a few yards off the lovely single anemone flowers luxuriantly, we may hope to introduce it into our own wood. Kingfishers are numerous. Can we preserve them? Then we hope to have a boat there, a great pleasure to Londoners out for a holiday, and we want a caretaker in charge of boating, bathing, skating, who will supply tea. We may too, with care, get some fish in the pond. At present teachers and pupils of the neighbouring LCC school enjoy the bathing—teachers in the river, scholars in the safe little backwater. Had the land been sold for commercial purposes this privilege would have been lost, we hope to preserve it for them and many others.[5]

---

5   This property is known as the Watermeads, and is one of the most important nature reserves in the London area. The wildflowers have been preserved, but access has to be limited, and admission is by key, which can be purchased annually from the property manager. Although this is the first reference to it in the letters, the scheme to clean up the river Wandle had been going on for some years, and Octavia had formed the River Wandle Open Spaces Committee with Robert Hunter and a Miss Mary Parton to cleanse and open up what had become a very polluted stretch of suburban landscape. The Committee, composed of delegates from the Kyrle and other open spaces amenity groups, went about the creation of the riverside walk with customary thoroughness, assembling parcels of land from private owners, builders, Magdalen College, Oxford and Wimbledon corporation. Octavia's determination to clean up the Wandle may have owed something to the debt she still felt she owed John Ruskin. Ruskin had visited the Wandle as a little boy and records in *Praeterita* his delight in its rivulets and minnows. As the nineteenth century progressed, the river became polluted by industrial waste. Mitcham was the centre of the paint and varnish industry for London, while William Morris and Arthur Lazenby Liberty set up their factories within a few hundred yards of each other on the banks of the Wandle, discharging

I thanked, last year, those of my sister's friends and pupils who had given, in memory of her, seven acres of Grange Fell[6] in the Cumberland she loved so well. This year I record with deepest thanks that a part of this Wandle land has been given by a large group of her former pupils in memory of her. They have sent their offerings from far and near.[7]

---

dyes and gums into the stream. (There is a certain irony in the fact that two of the greatest exponents of the 'house beautiful' should have contributed to the pollution that caused so much distress to the Master, especially as Morris was a devoted Ruskinian, and actually called one of his fabric designs 'Wandle'.) In 1866, in the introduction to *The Crown of Wild Olives*, Ruskin had written of the pollution of the Wandle: 'just in the very rush and murmur of the first spreading currents, the human wretches of the place cast their street and house foulness; heaps of dust and slime, and broken shreds of old metal, and rags of putrid clothes; which… they thus shed into the stream, to diffuse what venom of it will float and melt… in all places where God meant those waters to bring joy and health'. Ruskin had made an attempt to purify the stream by clearing a spring at Carshalton and erecting a tablet in memory of his mother. Like most of Ruskin's schemes, this one was failure, and by 1880 even the tablet had been lost. (Hilton, 2000, p.221.) In 1900 Octavia had refused to contribute towards the cost of a memorial to Ruskin in Westminster Abbey, on the grounds that Ruskin would not have wanted to desecrate a medieval building with a modern memorial. On the other hand, she said she would gladly support any scheme to preserve 'a mountain top, or lake, or river side' as a memorial. (Maurice, 1914, p.543.)

---

6   In the 1910 letter Octavia had referred to this as four acres. (1910, pp.639-40.)

---

7   The Kyrle Society accounts for 1911 show donations amounting to £67 15s from Miranda's former pupils, and a further £9 14s given in her memory from seven other donors, including £5 from her sister Emily. 'The Committee greatly appreciates this tribute to one who was the founder of the Society and a greatly loved colleague.' (Kyrle Society report 1911, p.7.) These donations formed part of the grant of £426 9s 8d made by the open spaces branch of the Kyrle to the River Wandle Open Spaces Committee during the year for the purchase of 'a particularly charming tract of land, amounting to just over ten acres in extent, situated a little below Mitcham Bridge'. (Kyrle Society report, 1911, p.7.) Within a few months of Octavia's own death, Mr Richardson Evans had purchased another 'delightful and picturesque' parcel of land on the riverbank in memory of Octavia. He was continuing what had become a family tradition: in December 1907 he had purchased a strip of land on the Merton side of the river that had already been laid out in building plots and given it to the National Trust, while earlier in the year his wife had given the Trust another stretch of land bordering the river in memory of her brother, John Feeney. (Kyrle Society reports, 1907, p.19; 1908, p.18; 1912, p.14.) The process of adding plot to plot continued, and in 1934 Morden Hall and its 125-acre estate, through which the Wandle flows, passed to the National Trust. Octavia's vision of putting together a 'river path' has now been so successfully realised that the Wandle trail runs for 11½ miles, with two-thirds of the riverside accessible to the public. In his memorial tribute to Octavia,

They wish to place somewhere on the ground a small tablet with her name. I hope that the National Trust will accede to this request.

So far I have written of what has been accomplished or of permanent undertakings going on their steady way. And now, do you know, I am really going to ask you, in spite of all you have done and are doing, whether you will help me, in any way not difficult to you or your friends, in my next great scheme which I have deeply at heart? You will remember helping me, now some years back, to secure a most beautiful bit of ground at Mariner's Hill, near Crockham Hill, Kent. Some of you have seen it, and know what wonderful air there is, what an expanse of sky, what a space of lovely country can be seen from it far away into the blue distance! It has been a great joy. But now a fear seizes us that, unless we can procure some more land, our eastern view may be ruined by building, for building is going on fast thereabouts and we are not safe unless we get more of the slope. By the great generosity of the owner we can now purchase for not quite half of its real value, if used for this purpose, all the land which would permanently secure our view. She will let the Trust have it for £1,500. Of this I have already got £600 and I greatly want the rest. You know how much open space we have preserved by small gifts, and I feel there is a great blessing in them, and a rightness in that which is enjoyed by the many being purchased by the many, so do not scruple to send small gifts if these are possible. But you know, too, how anxious I am that giving should remain a joy, which it cannot be if it is pressed for, so don't give or ask any one to give who does not really wish to help. But if you know any one who would care to hear of the opportunity tell them about it and remind them how delightful these southern slopes of the Kentish hills are; tell them this land would more than double our area and carry us up to the common. There is no view from the common itself, but it would form a delightful hinterland with heather, gorse and fir trees leading up to our open fields which have the view; tell them that the right of way which we now have to the common can never, if this land be purchased, be enclosed by a high black-tarred fence; tell them that,

---

C.S. Loch had written that: 'there could be no better memorial of Octavia Hill than the restitution of the Wandle... One day we remember last summer when with the map of the river before her she explained to us as we sat under the trees what pieces of land were purchased or given, what was purchasable, what was first of all desired, and so on, with a childlike pleasure in every circumstance, as if, from having seen how people were enjoying the banks and fields already open to them, she saw what a multitude would enjoy them in the future, sitting and wandering and playing there.' (Loch, 1912, p.161.)

if we do get this additional slope, all our view to the east will be unimpeded, land and sky giving delicious sense of space; ask them to imagine the joy of that hill-top with all its view and air; and ask them to help to leave it free for those who love it and will find joy and peace there in the years to come.[8]

OCTAVIA HILL

---

8   Three-and-a-half acres of Mariner's Hill had been acquired for the National Trust in 1903 (1903, pp.509-10) and a further eight acres were added to the site in 1908 (1908, p.600). However, according to the 1911 annual report of the Kyrle Society: 'the builder is ever invading the country anywhere within easy distance of town, and the view from these eleven-and-a-half acres is seriously threatened. Through the generosity of a landowner in the neighbourhood there is the opportunity of securing just over 14 more acres at the most moderate price of £1,500. If it be possible for the National Trust to avail itself of this offer a most delightful hill slope will be obtained, and the view will be safely preserved forever.' It is gratifying to be able to report that Octavia's last, heartfelt plea for an open space was successful. According to her brother-in-law Edmund Maurice: 'Up to within three days of her death [which occurred on 13 August] she continued to see her friends and fellow-workers, using to the utmost her failing strength, and endeavouring to arrange for the efficient carrying on of the many works in which she took such a keen interest. She was much cheered by the money sent to secure the purchase of Mariner's Hill, and she watched eagerly for letters or news of donations. Miss Rosamond Davenport Hill had bequeathed £500 to her sister, Miss Florence Davenport Hill, on the understanding that the latter should leave it to Octavia. When, however, Miss F.D. Hill heard how very ill Octavia was, she generously sent a cheque, which came the very day before Octavia died. This £500 was more than enough to secure the purchase of Mariner's Hill, and Octavia's delight and thankfulness were great.' (Maurice, 1914, p.581.) Florence Davenport Hill (no relation) was the daughter of Matthew Davenport Hill, the Birmingham prison reformer, and one of Octavia's oldest friends and supporters. She had been a guest at Octavia's 32nd birthday party in 1870 when Samuel Barnett first met, and fell in love with, his future wife Henrietta. Three years after Octavia's death, Hydon Heath, 126 acres near Godalming in Surrey, was purchased in her memory and given to the National Trust.

DONATIONS DURING 1911

	Donations			Red Cross Hall			Flower Show		
	£	s	d	£	s	d	£	s	d
Allen, A.C.	2	2	0	1	1	0	0	10	6
Andrewes, Mr and Mrs H.	1	1	0	—			—		
Atkinson, C.T.	5	0	0	—			—		
Austin, Miss	1	0	0	—			—		
Anon.				0	1	0	0	1	0
Anon. (per Mrs Tait)	1	0	0	—			—		
Bailey, Mrs J.	5	0	0	—			—		
Bannerman, Mrs (In Memoriam)	1	1	0	—			—		
Bayley, E.	—			—			1	1	0
Blyth, P.L.	1	1	0	1	1	0	—		
Bonsor, Cosmo	—			—			1	1	0
Bridgeman, Mrs	6	0	0	—			—		
Bridgeman, C.	5	0	0	—			—		
Bridgett, Miss				0	5	0	—		
Brinton, Miss M.	—			0	10	0	—		
Cockerell, Sydney	1	0	0	—			—		
Covington, Mrs	0	10	0	—			—		
Curry, The Misses	—			—			0	10	0
Curteis, Miss	—			0	5	0		2	6
Dakin, Miss	—			—			1	0	0
Dibdin, Lady	2	2	0	—			—		
Dowson, F.	1	1	0	—			—		
Ducie, The Earl of	5	0	0	—			—		
Dunn, Sir W.	—			—			1	1	0
Erle, Miss	20	0	0	—			—		
Evans, Mrs Richardson	2	2	0	—			—		
F.D.D.	1	1	0	—			—		
Fordyce, Miss	—			2	2	0	—		
Forman, Miss	1	1	0	—			—		
Frankan, Miss	5	0	0	—			—		
Fry, J.	—			—			1	0	0
Gladstone, Miss	—			2	0	0	—		
Griffiths, Miss A.	2	2	0	—			—		
Hamer, Mrs	2	2	0	—			—		
Harris, Miss	—			2	2	0	—		
Harris, Miss A.B.	2	0	0	—			—		
Hill, Mr and Mrs Alfred	3	3	0	—			—		
Hills, J.W.	10	0	0	—			—		
Howitt, Miss	0	10	0	—			—		
L.B., In Memoriam	1	0	0	—			—		
Llangattock, Lord	—			—			1	0	0
Lowndes, Miss	1	1	0	—			—		
Luxmoore, H.E., 1910 and 1911	4	2	0	—			—		
Macaulay, Mrs	2	0	0	—			—		
Marken, Miss V.	—			1	0	0	—		
Marshall, Miss Louisa	10	0	0	—			—		
Martelli, F.	—				10	0	—		
Moggridge, Miss	1	0	0	—			—		
Morshead, Mrs	—			2	0	0	—		
Morris, Frank	1	1	0	—			—		
Nicholson, Lady	5	0	0	—			—		
Orr, Mrs	—			1	1	0	0	10	6
Paddock, F.W.	1	0	0	1	0	0	—		
Parton, Miss	0	10	0	—			—		
Pascall, J.	—			—			0	10	0
Plummer, Rev. C.	5	0	0	—			—		
Praed, Sir Herbert	—			—			1	1	0
Schuster, Mrs	10	0	0	—			0	5	0
Sewell, Miss	—			0	10	0	—		
Somervell, Mr and Mrs Robt	1	0	0	—			—		
Somervell, Gordon	3	3	0	—			—		

DONATIONS DURING 1911 (continued)

	Donations			Red Cross Hall			Flower Show		
	£	s	d	£	s	d	£	s	d
Strauss, E.A., M.P.	—				—		4	4	0
Tanner, Mrs Slingsby T.	—				—		1	1	0
Thompson, Mrs	2	0	0		—			—	
Todhunter, Miss	2	0	0		—			—	
Tuffnell, Mrs	1	1	0		—			—	
Wagner, H.	5	0	0		—			—	
Walker, Miss	1	0	0		—			—	
Warner, Miss Lee	—				—		0	10	0
Webb, Mrs Randall	—			2	0	0	0	10	0
Welbury-Mitton, Mrs	3	0	0		—			—	
Wells, Miss	2	0	0		—			—	
Willcox, W.H.	—				—		2	2	0
Wood, Miss	—				—		1	1	0
	£148	17	0	£17	8	0	£19	1	6

DONATION ACCOUNT, 1911

RECEIPTS

		£	s	d
In hand, January 1911	...	162	4	2
Donations	...	148	17	0
Interest on various Deposits	...	17	12	6
Returned by Emigrant	...	4	0	0
Returned, not required for case	...	0	7	0
		£333	0	8

DONATION ACCOUNT, 1911

EXPENDITURE

	£	s	d
Pensions	68	4	7
Training and Boarding-out	39	15	8
Relief (mainly in Sickness)	32	12	11
Open Spaces (Wandle)	25	0	0
Boys' Club	24	8	6
Emigration	15	10	0
Playground	10	8	0
Employment	10	7	0
Excursions, &c.	4	15	11 $\frac{1}{2}$
Blind Pensioner	3	3	0
Printing Letter to Fellow-Workers and Stationery	6	18	1 $\frac{1}{2}$
In hand (for Pensions, &c.)	91	16	11
	£333	0	8

Examined and found correct, P.L. Blyth, January 16th 1912.

669

RED CROSS HALL AND GARDEN ACCOUNT, 1911

RECEIPTS

	£	s	d
Cash, January 1911	24	0	1 ½
Interest from Red and White Cross Cottages	72	11	0
Hire of Hall	42	1	2
Donations:			
Garden and Hall	17	8	0
Flower Show	19	1	6
Flower Show Sale of Tickets	0	7	10
Rent of Clubroom	13	0	0
Rent of Office	12	0	0
Sale of Programmes	4	13	1
Violin Fees	4	1	0
Collections	3	19	10
Gas, received from Tenants	0	10	0
	£213	13	6 ½

670

RED CROSS HALL AND GARDEN ACCOUNT, 1911

EXPENDITURE

	£	s	d
Caretaker	58	19	3
Electric Light, Instalment of	20	17	0
Repairs	19	15	10
Flower Show	19	9	10
Violin Class	18	0	0
Gas and Fuel	17	6	0
Entertainments	16	11	5
Borough Rate	13	12	0
Taxes	2	3	5
Water Rate	6	15	8
Cleaning	6	13	2
Fire Insurance	2	9	9
Stationery	1	14	7
Expenses for Garden	1	9	1
Ground Rent	0	18	10
Cash in hand, December 1911	6	17	8 ½
	£213	13	6 ½

Examined and found correct, P.L. Blyth, January 16th 1912.

The Walmer Street
Industrial Experiment

EDITOR'S NOTE

These two short accounts of the scheme adopted by Octavia and the Rev. Fremantle to offer work instead of handouts to the poor in the parish of St Mary's, Bryanston Square, both of which were written for the parish annual report and then published as pamphlets, are really the first in the series of letters to fellow-workers. They establish the basic format of a short essay in which Octavia explains what she has done, gives the reasons for her actions, places the work in a spiritual context, and concludes with a list of donations and expenditure.

The 'industrial experiment' was part of Rev. Fremantle's complete overhaul of the charitable work in his parish, which included the setting up of the Marylebone district committee of the Charity Organisation Society in 1869. However, it seems unlikely that he would have attempted such a bold and innovative scheme as that described here without the input of an exceptional young woman who had been making something of a reputation for herself in the parish with her method of housing management. By the time the industrial experiment got underway, Octavia was already managing houses in Paradise Place, Freshwater Place and Barrett's Court. She had always made it part of her role to find work for the unemployed tenants, so she had the relevant experience to help the rector, but the Walmer Street experiment put it on a more formal basis. Able-bodied people would be offered the option of work—or nothing. Only those who were not receiving assistance from other sources would be helped. Those genuinely unable to work would be given adequate pensions. The reasons that Octavia gives for her approach show how, in spite of a complete lack of any formal education, she had acquired a firm grasp of the principles of economic theory—what the Victorians called political economy. She objects to handouts not just because they are demoralising to the recipient—the most obvious objection—but because they depress wages. Employers find that they can get people to work for them by paying less than a living wage, knowing that they rely on free coals, free medical assistance, free school meals etc. to top up the wages. Octavia also points out that schemes such as she describes should be regarded as temporary or emergency measures for connecting the unemployed with the world of work. If allowed to turn into long-term sources of employment, they will have the negative effect of sheltering those assisted from the imperatives of the market: people must learn to supply the goods and services for which there is a demand. There is no point in paying women to do needlework that no one wants to buy if it would be more sensible for them to train for domestic service. Octavia also objects to handouts on the grounds that they sour the relationship between rich and poor by reducing the parties to the roles of giver and receiver. There were, in Octavia's view, many things that people of education and influence could, and should, do for the poor, apart from giving them money, but 'a working man, with delicacy of feeling, will not come to the more educated among the rich for advice which might be of value to him in difficulty, lest he should seem to be indirectly begging'. The need for genuine good fellowship between rich and poor would become a major driving force behind Octavia's life's work. The second, shorter account adds nothing significant beyond the fact that the personal loathing felt by the beneficiaries of the experiment for Octavia seems to be subsiding, and it has been judged such a success that the method has now been extended to cover the whole parish.

Finally, Octavia reports that various individuals have been giving her money for her work among the poor, 'and, as it is difficult for me always to find time to render an account of these sums to the separate donors, I must ask their permission to insert one here'. This need to render an account of the various monies entrusted to her for her own work, quite apart from the Walmer Street experiment, must have suggested to Octavia the idea of a printed circular that would contain a balance sheet, accompanied by a brief account of what she had been doing during the year. The first of the letters to fellow-workers appeared a year later.

EMPLOYMENT OR ALMS-GIVING?

BEING AN ACCOUNT

OF THE

PLAN OF RELIEF NOW ADOPTED

IN A

DISTRICT OF MARYLEBONE

BY

OCTAVIA HILL

LONDON: JAMES MARTIN, PRINTER
9, LISSON GROVE, N.W.
1871

PRICE, TWOPENCE

MISS HILL'S ACCOUNT OF
THE WALMER STREET DISTRICT

Having been asked by Mr Fremantle to give a short account of the system of relief adopted in one part of his parish, I beg to furnish the following particulars.[1]

I may say first that the object of the whole system is to substitute, in cases where the poor require help, the giving of employment for the giving of doles.

I had already tried this experiment on a somewhat different footing for six years previously in this parish,[2] and with marked success, when, in January 1870, Mr Fremantle arranged to adopt it in a small district which he committed to my charge. He has now no other organisation there for relief, and though the details of the management have been necessarily in my hands, and the funds have hitherto been collected by me, both he and I regard it as part of his organisation, and even the details have been submitted to those working with him.

The district is that comprising Walmer Street, Walmer Place, and Virgil Place, and was chosen as being the poorest under Mr Fremantle's direct control. There are in this district 200 resident families. They are all of a low class, most of them being labourers, or unskilled workmen. Any resident in the district who falls into distress, can apply at the room in Walmer Street, where I, or one of those working with me, attend for half-an-hour daily to receive applications. We learn full particulars as to the wants of the family and learn the qualifications for work of every member of it. Unless the father is in full employment, or

---

1 'This account was originally written at the request of the Rev. W.H. Fremantle, rector of St Mary's Bryanston Square, for his annual report, of which it forms an appendix.' (*Octavia Hill's note.*)

---

2 Octavia had always made it part of her work in housing management, which had begun in Paradise Place in Marylebone in 1865, to assist unemployed tenants to find work.

I know the applicant to be receiving gifts from private people in the neighbourhood, I am prepared to give work *in every case.* I do not profess to give full work, but I do give much more in wages than is ordinarily given in doles. In cases where illness leaves no one capable of doing work, I give help in money, but as a rule I find that even in cases of illness there is some one member of the family who is able to work. As to the sort of work, it varies in almost every instance. I have a large connection of friends who are good enough to tell me of work of any kind they may want done, and it almost always happens that some one of the applicants is able to do this. I may give, as examples of this work, carpentering, whitewashing, window-cleaning, or porter's work, for men; charing, washing, upholstery or needlework for women; and situations as under-servants, or errand boys for younger people. And when I do not know of any available employment through this channel I provide it from the funds placed in my hands for the purpose. I have always found that I could pick out some useful work—something which will make someone better or happier, or the world a little richer, towards which to direct labour, and I have that done and spend upon it some part of the donations entrusted to me.[3]

Every week I send in to the clergy a list of applicants, together with a statement of the amount they have received, the kind of work upon which they have been employed, and of the manner they have been introduced to employers or have been otherwise dealt with. I am also in constant correspondence with the organisation committee.

The number of applicants for relief during the year ending 31st December, 1870, was 133. Of 90 who were offered work only 51 accepted it, though in every case the work was specially chosen from its fitness to the applicant. This refusal proves that in these cases free gifts, and not honestly earned wages, were desired. The remainder of the applicants—43 in number—were not offered work, as they were those to whom loans were made, or those who applied for hospital letters, or the wives of men in full work, or those, very few, who were ill and had no member of the family who could work for them, or lastly, those to whom it seemed well to give pensions.

The amount of wages paid for each kind of work is given on p.13.[4]

---

3 'As an instance of this sort of employment, I may say, that if a carpenter had applied to me this winter for whom I could not obtain independent work, I should have set him to make a wooden fence to protect the ivy in our poor children's playground.' (*Octavia Hill's note.*)

---

4 Page 687 in this edition.

The amount received by me for the work done has been £108 9s 7½d, and £5 13s 7d of the money lent has been repaid by the borrowers, which leaves the actual cost of the undertaking £84 6s, making an average of 8s 5⁴⁄23d, for the relief of each resident family per annum.

It had been feared that the experiment would be found very expensive, and it is true that we have spent more than would have been the case under the ordinary system.[5] But it must be borne in mind that we have voluntarily chosen a liberal scale of relief, and that the poor have benefited accordingly. It would have been perfectly possible to give less, and it is no necessary part of the system to give as much, although I do not myself consider that the scale adopted was in the least higher than in these courts under the circumstances is really desirable. It may be a satisfaction to those who have placed the donations in my hands that I should here express my belief that all the applicants have had as much relief as, taking all the circumstances of their character and position into consideration, was desirable.

Though I have never departed from my principle of refusing all aid except by means of work to the strong and able-bodied, in the case of old and respectable people past work I have been most anxious to make some permanent and adequate provision. I have tried to give them small weekly pensions, believing that it is seldom working people can save for their old age, and though the workhouse may supply the necessaries of life, there is a charm about a little home of one's own, which the rich may fairly provide for those who have worked hard as long as they were able. A small fund has been entrusted to me for this purpose by a friend.

I may take this opportunity of saying that if one desiring to give help to any of the poor in this particular district will communicate with me, I shall be happy to render them all assistance in my power to put their aid in the form of work.

It may be well that I should give a few of the reasons which led me to adopt the plan above described.

The first was that it was *non-pauperising*, having no tendency to lower the rate of wages. The more I have watched during many years, the more it has seemed to me that the present habit of providing necessaries by means of alms had a tendency to make both working men and their employers calculate on its being possible to live on a low rate of wages, trusting to charity to back them up. It is true that some

---

5 'Mr. Fremantle tells me that he would have spent about £40 under the old system in these courts in the year.' (*Octavia Hill's note.*)

classes of workmen can now earn sufficient to keep a family well, but continual gifts make it possible to support one on less wages, and should the system of giving alms continue, there is a danger that, in the future, there may be no class of workmen receiving sufficiently high wages to be independent. I am certain that gifts of coals, clothes, grocery, and meat, will have nearly as distinct an influence on wages as the old poor law system had. A working man in London now need pay for no medical attendance; he seldom buys all his coals; he pays only a part of the value of the clothes of the family, if his wife buys them at a work-society; she need purchase no baby-linen; at many schools his children are provided with a dinner once or more in the week; and his blankets are perhaps lent him during the cold weather. So that we act as if a man's wages were so low that he could not be expected to meet the most ordinary and necessary expenses of life, and our doing this will still further lower them; whereas, by the plan I have adopted—by refusing to give help when he is in full employment—we distinctly throw him for the support of his family on the resources which his own work affords. We help him to other work during a slack season, but we do not encourage his living habitually on means which are partly wages and partly doles.

The second advantage of this system is that is *raises the self-respect* of those helped. We must not suppose that our gifts will do instead of adequate wages. We cannot dispense them fairly; we can never give back the sense of dignity and responsibility to the head of the family; and we cannot restore to him the natural joy he feels in winning by work the comforts of life for those who trust in him, if we have once destroyed those feelings by our alms. Then too, all happy, natural, human relation between rich and poor is rendered impossible by their meeting so continually on the footing of givers and receivers of alms. A working man with delicacy of feeling will not come to the more educated among the rich for advice which might be of value to him in difficulty, lest he should seem to be indirectly begging.

A third advantage, and perhaps the greatest, is that this system is distinctly *educational*. Not only is it a test of the industry and energy of the applicant; not only does it enable us to know him, and often to recommend him to better and more permanent kinds of employment, but every farthing thus spent, on relief given in the form of work, represents a distinct bit of education, and wherever the plan is adopted, every reckless and extravagant idler, every incapable workman, every self-indulgent, unpunctual, listless man, every stupid, heavy boor, gets, whenever want overtakes him, a little bit of discipline and the encouragement of effort crowned by its natural reward.

Thus while, on the one hand, I am able at once to help the more worthy of these poor people to higher and more responsible positions than they would have attained without my enquiries, test work, and introductions, on the other hand, there is no one among them so low or fallen that I am not at all times able to meet him if he is willing to make some effort himself. I have never been able in my own mind to divide those whom I have tried to help into the two classes of the 'deserving' and 'undeserving'. I have always found that there was bad in the best, and good in the worst; and it has been a constant pleasure to me to see that this plan enables one to recognise and aid every effort towards better things made by the so-called 'undeserving'.

As I am receiving from many quarters questions respecting the advisability of extending the plan, I may add a few words of advice. Let those who propose adopting it remember that it may be open to very serious objections if it is allowed to slip into a system of permanent employment. It should be a *substitute for occasional gifts*, a *means of training*, and best of all, where that is possible, a *means of introduction to independent employment*.

There are two reasons why a gigantic system of work supported by charity would become harmful—though it would appear to me that it would always be safer than a gigantic system of gifts. One reason is, that workers ought to adapt themselves to the wants of their times, that is to say, to learn to make, and to do, what employers of labour want to have done; and what that is, is proved by the natural demand. Thus, for example, it is not well to encourage women who might be useful in domestic service, to drag on a miserable existence at home by means of an artificial supply of needlework. Some women are too ready to wish for such aid rather than make the effort and submit to the restraint which entering service implies.

The second reason why independent work is better than that supported by charitable aid is, that it is very difficult to keep up the standard of work of the latter kind. Things which people want sufficiently to pay for they usually want done well, and it is this effort to do the work well which is the best industrial training for the shiftless and skill-less, who form the principal body of applicants for relief.

But there seems to me no possible reason why there should not be a small portion of work set apart for the training and support of the less worthy, which should enrich them in proportion to their effort; why there should not be a little work reserved to be offered instead of alms to those whose work is irregular, whenever it fails. If they cannot save for such times, it is the best form of assistance; if they can, they are much more likely to do so when they are met with work and not with alms at times of slackness.

Let me also earnestly advise anyone about to adopt this scheme of help to try and make terms with those distributing doles in their neighbourhood. If wages are given plus doles, it will prolong the dole system indefinitely. Endeavour to substitute work for doles, but steadfastly refuse to give work to those who are in receipt of them.

Another important thing is that work for men should always be offered in preference to that for women. For it is not good that artificial work given to the wife should back up a man's small wages or enable him to spend his time at the public house.

A great deal has been written on the importance of giving adequate help, if any be given at all. It is true that the wages given by me to people in need have rarely been sufficient to maintain them, but all such people have other resources of some kind. The small shop gives them credit, so does the landlord; the clothes and furniture can be pawned; the relations and friends, of whom the visitor rarely knows, give help; and though this is terribly indefinite, and it is impossible to estimate such resources accurately, it would be very fatal to ignore them. Were they ignored, and much more assistance given, the applicant would be placed in a position above that of the thrifty labourer. He would still avail himself of his other resources, and have *more* than adequate help. It is the fact of these other resources which explains the otherwise inexplicable mystery how applicants for relief contrive to tide over times of distress by means of some small help, which were there no other resources in the background, would be hopelessly insufficient.

In conclusion, I can only add that I believe the undertaking has achieved much and real good, and that I feel confident we are on the right tack. But I cannot honestly write at this time of the work, without confessing that it has wholly failed hitherto to do what I had cared most that it should do. It has not appeared to the people merciful, helpful, or loving. They have not yet seen that the thing which is stern may be the fullest of real love. They have never imagined what measure of love it needs to do what will hereafter help them most, instead of what would call down their blessings at the moment, and brighten their faces with delight, but would leave them later on, weaker, meaner, more helpless, and poorer men and women. All this is hidden from them, and God knows I do not blame them or much wonder. Charity has shown herself to them hitherto in more gracious, if in less wise and far-sighted forms; they do not recognise her when she comes so strangely.

And so the best object of all work among them is, for the moment, lost. For the best thing one dare hope for in one's work among rich or poor is that somehow the love that is in one may be a witness for the greater Love that watches and guards and blesses. Then it is a failure indeed if one's life looks like cruelty. But we must leave appearances to Him who is certainly able to reveal Himself without our little light, and who though He sometimes deigns to use us as His messengers will not let His children want for witnesses of Him when He does not use us. We may go steadily with what seems right, and leave it to Him to reveal our motives, or to hide them forever as He sees best.

OCTAVIA HILL

DONATIONS DURING 1870

	£	s	d
J. Ruskin, Esq	20	0	0
Mrs Macaulay	5	15	0
S. Brown, Esq	3	0	0
Mrs Edwin Hill	2	0	0
Miss Trevelyan	6	0	0
Mrs Scaramanga	2	2	0
Dowager Lady Stanley of Alderley	1	0	0
Robert Moon, Esq	5	0	0
Mrs Bonham Carter	5	0	0
Mrs Sheffield Neave	6	10	0
Lady Constance Moreton	1	0	0
Hon. Julia Dutton	1	0	0
Somerset Beaumont, Esq, M.P.	43	9	10
Miss Florence Hill	2	0	0
Mrs Gillson	5	0	0
Mr and Mrs Lewis	5	0	0
J. Wickens, Esq	10	0	0
Mr and Mrs P. Bayne	2	2	0
Hornsby Wright, Esq (for Reports)	0	5	0
Mrs Shaw	1	1	0
Mrs Lindesay (for Pensions)	5	0	0
For Special Cases	0	18	0
Mrs Gerald Goodlake (subscription)	0	10	6
	£133	13	4

THE INDUSTRIAL EXPERIMENT FOR 1870

RECEIPTS

	£	s	d
Donations	133	13	4
Men's work (from various employers)	28	19	9
Women's work (from various employers)	3	5	7
Sale of Needlework*	76	4	3 ½
Loans Repaid	5	13	7
	£247	16	6 ½

THE INDUSTRIAL EXPERIMENT FOR 1870

EXPENDITURE

	£	s	d	£	s	d
Men's Work:						
Distempering, Varnishing, and Plastering	10	19	0			
Carpentering	8	0	3			
Bricklaying	4	16	0			
Porterage, Window-cleaning, and Messages	4	14	9			
Smiths' Work	3	5	6			
Painting	2	6	9			
Glazing	0	11	0			
Mending Boots	0	1	10			
				34	15	1
Women's Work:						
Needlework	47	17	2 ½			
Cleaning	3	7	10			
Nursing	1	18	6			
Knitting	1	15	2			
Washing	0	13	6			
Messages	0	1	6			
				55	13	8 ½
Boys' Work:						
Messages	1	3	6			
Loans	8	15	5			
Pensions	0	10	0			
Gifts:						
Clothes	1	1	6			
Food	0	18	6			
Premium	0	10	0			
Money	0	7	0			
Wedding Ring	0	7	6			
Spectacles	0	1	6			
Cab to Hospital	0	1	0			
				3	7	0
Materials				61	10	10
Superintendence of Workroom				20	16	8
Coals, Wood, Soda, etc				4	16	5
Printing				3	10	6
Furniture				1	16	0
Account Books				1	6	2
Carriage of Parcels				0	7	11
Cash in Hand				49	7	4
				£247	16	6 ½

* Clothes to the value of upwards of £25 are now in stock.

FURTHER ACCOUNT

OF THE

WALMER STREET

INDUSTRIAL EXPERIMENT

❦

BY

OCTAVIA HILL

LONDON:
PRINTED BY GEORGE PULMAN, 24 THAYER STREET, W.
1872

Nearly a year ago I issued, at Mr Fremantle's request, to accompany his pastoral address for 1870, a report of an experiment I had tried in a certain district of his parish, the object of which was to make charitable relief elevating and educational, instead of degrading. I had attempted to do this by substituting work for the able-bodied and pensions for the old, in place of small and irregular doles.[1]

Having already fully explained the details of the plan and my reasons for considering the principles on which it is founded of extreme importance, I need not here go into these questions again. But it will be a satisfaction to those whose aid has enabled me to carry on the experiment for a second year, and to others interested in it, to hear that it has succeeded beyond my best hopes.

The past year's work has been to my mind a great success, and what I have to record with the deepest thankfulness is, that I believe the spirit in which the work has been undertaken and carried on is far better understood. I had to speak last year of general misconception, and a bitter sense of resentment amongst the people. I do not wish to underrate whatever may remain of this spirit, and perhaps others, who see the district from a different point of view, may see more of it remaining than I do; but certainly there is this year a strong force telling on the other side, and when I look back on the state of feeling that existed towards me at the time I closed my last report, I cannot but see the change in a very striking light.

No doubt individuals still feel annoyed, especially at times; but I believe that many in the district are growing to feel that all the personal effort used to train and help them to better things must spring from some true care of them—is a help to them—nay, may even be better than the coal tickets of which they are deprived. That this last stage is reached yet, I will not be too sure, but certainly between them and ourselves there has been some very happy intercourse during the last

---

1   'This report was also printed separately in the form of a pamphlet, entitled *Employment or Alms-giving?*'. (*Octavia Hill's note.*)

year; we have come to know each other better, and sometimes the bitterness of feeling has seemed to me wholly gone.

As I spoke in my last report of evil feeling and misunderstanding, I am bound to record my strong sense that a really blessed success, which has gathered strength with time, has now been achieved. I am not sorry, however, that I so spoke while the full sorrow of disappointment was weighing upon me, in order that no one may undertake such work unprepared. The work of reformation can never be unopposed, and those who enter upon it must gather up their courage to meet the necessary pain.

The arrangements of the plan have been precisely like those of the previous year. The details of expenditure are given at page eight.[2]

And now the friends who have helped me will be still further glad to hear that our work in Walmer Street district will henceforward be merged in one spread over a wider field, but carried on according to the same principles. The charities of St Mary's are now so managed that my work in the Walmer Street district (which is one small portion of it) will form a consistent part of the general scheme. This report of my work there will be the last; but the last, not because of the failure and death of the plan, but because of its success and life. The work is now part of a larger one, and will in future be silently comprehended in all reports of that.

The workroom for women, established as part of the industrial experiment, will now be available for the whole of St Mary's, and whatever work I have for men will be at the disposal of the St Mary's committee of poor relief.

I trust I shall remain district visitor for Walmer Street under Mr Fremantle and that with the machinery now organised I shall be able to carry on any good I have been able to do there better than ever. My position now differs from that of all Mr Fremantle's district visitors in no way, except that I am in more constant communication with the committee than most of them have hitherto cared to be.

One other bright spot in the future of this little Walmer Street district I must here mention. The whole of it (with the exception of five houses in Walmer Street) has been purchased by my friends, the Misses Sterling. The letting and control of the houses will henceforth be in their hands, and I have undertaken to assist them in the management. The people living there will therefore, in future, be additionally helped in all those

---

2 Pages 696-7 in this edition.

numerous ways by which a landlord who has the interests of his people really at heart is able to influence their lives for good.

In addition to the sums entrusted to me for the industrial experiment in Walmer Street, various others have from time to time been given me for helping the poor known to me elsewhere in different ways. And, as it is difficult to me always to find time to render an account of these sums to the separate donors, I must ask their permission to insert one here, and to offer to them, as well as to those who have supplied the funds for Walmer Street and for the children's playground, my heartiest thanks for the help so liberally and kindly given.

The sympathy and encouragement of these friends has come sometimes with a wonderful power of consolation to myself when all was very difficult, or when I have been weighed down with the amount of wrong and suffering I have seen around me. The actual possession of the money entrusted to me has enabled me to confer much and lasting good on many who very sorely needed help; it has given me the power to cheer and brighten, by some pleasant excursion or evening's entertainment, a few hours of many lives which are habitually ground down by care and monotony.

These gatherings, besides giving pleasure to those invited, give real opportunities of meeting the people face to face, and of talking with them from time to time in a way we cannot do when we encounter each other only in the hurry of work, or amidst the cares of business. I and my friends have been enabled to know our people better, and so to judge better in the future how to help and serve them.

I wish I could communicate to those whose money has enabled the good to be done, some knowledge of the histories that come crowding up in my mind, as I glance at the different items that make up the expenditure side of the balance sheet. They recall to me children rescued from disease, and worse than disease, women restored to health, and people started in work which has lasted in some instances until now. They recall all the trembling hopes and fears about each individual, the long waiting till they would avail themselves of the path opened which would lead them away from their wretched state, the triumph of joy when at last the choice was made—the right course taken. All these rise before me as I write, bringing a deep sense of thankfulness for the year's work.

And even the two names in the list which record our failures, do not lessen the thankfulness. It is something to have been able to aid people in their moment of trial, to have endeavoured to strengthen their sense of right, to have fought on their side with them against evil. Though they wandered away then, the time may come when the memory of those who loved, and would have saved them, may come back to them with a wonderful force, and may bring to their hearts, in tones which cannot be withstood, the thought of ONE who loves them more, and WHO is mightier to save.

Could those who have contributed to this fund know all the escape from misery, all the good, and all the happiness which this little balance-sheet represents, I am sure they would feel it a joy to have shared in the work.

THE INDUSTRIAL EXPERIMENT FOR 1871

RECEIPTS

			£	s	d
Cash in hand			49	7	4
Sales			87	16	7 ½
Loans repaid			2	2	4
Various employers for Men's work			28	18	9 ½
Donations:					
F.D. Mocatta, Esq	1	0	0		
Miss Trevelyan	3	0	0		
Mrs Lawford	5	0	0		
Mrs Macaulay	0	6	1		
Hornsby Wright, Esq	1	0	0		
Rev. W. Berry	1	1	0		
Miss Shiels	3	0	0		
A. Whately, Esq	1	1	0		
Mrs A. Whately	0	10	6		
Mrs Nassau Senior	1	0	0		
Miss Bell	0	5	0		
Sir Charles Trevelyan	1	0	0		
Mrs Lindesay	5	0	0		
Miss Rowland	0	12	0		
A. G. Crowder, Esq	10	0	0		
Miss Waggett	0	5	0		
M.E.R.	1	0	0		
			35	0	7
			£203	5	8

THE INDUSTRIAL EXPERIMENT FOR 1871

EXPENDITURE

	£	s	d	£	s	d
Men's Work:						
Distempering, Varnishing, and Plastering	12	11	10			
Carpentering	0	2	0			
Bricklaying	3	11	3 ½			
Porterage Window Cleaning, and Messages	6	6	4			
Smiths' Work	5	7	5			
Painting	0	12	0			
Glazing	0	3	0			
Mending	0	12	11			
Sweep	0	19	8			
Tailoring	0	2	6			
Playing Violin	0	2	6			
Making Brooms	0	5	4 ½			
Paving	0	8	6			
				31	5	4
Women's Work:						
Knitting	0	9	0			
Needlework	55	11	9			
Cleaning	2	8	3			
Message	0	1	0			
Model	0	2	0			
				58	12	0
Boys' Work:						
Messages				0	7	0
Gifts:						
Clothes	1	13	5 ½			
Food	1	4	4			
Advertisement	0	6	0			
Printing Cards for Candidate for Marylebone						
Church School	0	6	0			
Travelling for E.K., J.H., and K.O.	1	3	10 ¾			
				4	13	8 ¼
Loans				2	12	9
Pensions				6	6	0
Stationery				0	12	5
Packing, Carriage, &c.				1	7	9 ½
Coals, Gas, Soap, Soda, &c.				2	1	5
Furniture				0	19	2
Superintendence of Work				26	0	0
Materials				50	14	4
Printing Report				2	0	6
Cash in hand				15	13	3 ¼
				£203	5	8

N.B. — There are clothes in stock suitable for sale to working people, for which we should be very glad of orders. Also we desire to receive orders for private work. The women are much improved and can do it nicely.

Clothes to the value of £30 have been sent to New Zealand, where we hope to sell them.

PLAYGROUND ACCOUNT

RECEIPTS

	£	s	d
Miss Hughes (first donation)	0	2	6
Sir Baldwyn Leighton, Bart.	5	0	0
Mrs Stephen	2	10	0
Mrs Snelling	1	0	0
Miss Ridley	5	0	0
Mrs Bell	0	2	6
Sir Charles Trevelyan	2	0	0
Miss Hughes (second don.)	0	1	0
W.M.	20	0	0
Miss Mirelees	2	10	0
The late Mrs Whittaker	1	0	0
	£39	6	0

PLAYGROUND ACCOUNT

EXPENDITURE

	£	s	d
Balance due from 1870	5	14	6 ½
Salary of Superintendent	10	8	0
Fence to protect Creepers	3	5	0
Fence to protect Creepers	0	11	0
Swing	0	15	6
Balance in hand	18	11	11 ½

£39	6	0

DONATION ACCOUNT, 1871

RECEIPTS

	£	s	d
In hand from 1870	14	13	10 ½
Mrs Herbert Duckworth	5	0	0
Mrs Macaulay (for Boys' Home)	0	5	0
For Mrs M.'s Mangle	2	10	0
Lady Stanley of Alderley	1	0	0
Mrs Stopford Brooke	3	0	0
Miss Sterling	5	0	0
Mrs Sheffield Neave	2	13	0
Miss Rowland	0	2	6
Miss Pipe	4	10	0
Mrs Arthur Mills	3	5	0
Edward Spender Esq (for Excursion)	5	0	0
Mrs Arthur Whately	0	5	0
Somerset Beaumont, Esq, MP	2	0	0
Lady Caroline Charteris	1	0	0
Miss Lovegrove (for Excursion)	0	7	6
Miss Rowland (for Mrs N.)	0	4	0
Mrs Lindesay (for Excursion)	1	5	0
Miss Russell (for Excursion)	1	0	0
Prize for Flower Show	0	1	6
Miss Barker (for Excursion)	1	0	0
Miss Mirrlees	2	10	0
Miss Barker (for Mrs H.)	0	10	0
Miss Dawbarn (for Mrs M.)	0	2	0
Mrs Stephen Ralli	0	4	0
Lady Caroline Charteris	0	10	0
Mrs Atkinson	2	0	0
Mrs Stephen Ralli (for Lambeth)	5	5	0
Lady Abercromby	5	0	0
Mr and Mrs Arthur Whately	5	0	0
Miss Sterling	5	0	0
Lady Eastlake (for M.T.)	1	4	0
Mrs Stephen Ralli	0	3	4
Miss Barrington	1	0	0
Mrs Scaramanga (for St Barnabas)	5	0	0
Miss Scott (for Girls' Party)	0	2	0
Miss Miller (for Girls' Party)	0	2	0
Sale of Clothes at work-class	4	13	11
Sale of Tea given by S. Cockerell, Esq	0	10	9
	£92	19	4 ½

DONATION ACCOUNT, 1871

EXPENDITURE

		£	s	d
Jan 7	Tea for Tenants	0	5	4
14	Interest on Tenants' Savings	0	6	8
28	Party for Walmer Street	3	8	9
Feb 4	E. A. at Eastbourne	0	6	8
11	H, Upper Park Place	0	5	7
18	Boots for F. to go to situation	0	5	0
25	Cards for Savlngs	0	2	3
Mar 12	Adams per Miss Holland	2	0	0
	Portrait for old Mrs C	0	2	6
	Concert for the Blind	2	1	6
	Fever Hospital (Admission for patient)	2	2	0
	Clothes (E.K.)	0	7	2
	E. A. at Eastbourne	0	10	0
	Clothes, Girl going to servlce (E. K.)	0	1	5
May 20	Boys' Home (Mrs Macaulay's donation)	0	5	0
	Vaccination Fees, Walmer Street	1	10	0
27	Playground Festival	0	17	8
	Mangle	2	10	0
June 2	Whit Monday excursion for Barrett's Court	7	19	11
July 8	Rowing Expedition for Singing Class	0	1	6
	Tenants' Excursion (Freshwater Place)	3	1	4
	Vaccination Fees, Walmer Street	1	3	0
	E. W.'s Fees at Industrial School	4	10	0
	Mrs H.'s journey	1	10	0
Aug 12	E. T. at Industrial School	6	16	6
Sept 9	R. R. at Brighton Home	2	10	0
Oct 7	Fees for Evening Classes for Student	0	3	6
14	Clothes M. going to Canada	0	2	10 ½
	Lambeth	5	5	0

Walmer Street Excursion up the River*

		£	s	d
	Musicians	1	11	6
	Boat	6	0	0
	Food	8	9	0

		£	s	d
		16	0	6
21	Flower Stand for Show	0	2	6
28	A. W. going to Canada	2	0	0
Nov 4	Fees in Hospital for J.	2	7	6
11	Play for all Tenants and Walmer Street	5	9	10 ½
18	Employment at various times	0	8	0
	Pension M.T.	0	8	0
	Party Freshwater, and Paradise Place	1	4	0 ½
	Party (Singing Class)	0	13	9
	Mrs M. (Miss Dawbarn's gift)	0	2	0
	Mrs N. Pension (Miss Rowland's gift)	0	4	0
	Flower Show Prize	0	1	6
	St Barnabas, (Mrs Scaramanga's donation)	5	0	0
	Cash in hand December 31st 1871	8	6	7
		£92	19	4 ½

* We have to thank W. M. Matheson, Esq, A. Smither, Esq, and Messrs Hanbury, for considerable contributions for this expedition which are not included in these accounts.

Bringing Beauty Home to the People: The Kyrle Society 1877–1917

ANNE HOOLE ANDERSON[1]

The Kyrle Society… was one of the very earliest to bring before the public the great need that exists for brighter surroundings for the poor. In London especially, where there is so much that is squalid and ugly, it is important that the necessity of changed surroundings should be recognised. Men, women and children want more than food, shelter and warmth. They want, if their lives are to be full and good, space near their homes for exercise, quiet, good air, and sight of grass, trees and flowers; they want colour, which shall cheer them in the midst of smoke and fog; they want music, which shall contrast with the rattle of the motors and lift their hearts to praise and joy; they want suggestion of nobler and better things than those that surround them day by day.

OCTAVIA HILL, 1905.[2]

A suggestion to those who love beautiful things

The Kyrle Society is usually seen as growing out of Octavia Hill's desire to provide space and fresh air for the poor of London through 'beautiful outdoor sitting-rooms', but with its decorative branch, music branch and literature branch, its mission was much more ambitious: what we would now call civic reform. At its heart lay 'rational recreation', the

703

House Beautiful and a wholesome life-style; in effect the working classes behaving more like the middle classes.

In December 1875, Miranda Hill read a paper, 'A suggestion to those who love beautiful things', before the National Health Society, which focused on the conversion of disused burial grounds into gardens as a 'cheap and convenient beginning'.[3] The first efforts of a small committee, formed in October 1875, had been to plant flowers on barren land, the draping of ugly buildings with creepers, the painting of walls in St Jude's church in the slums of Whitechapel with panels of wild flowers,[4] and the provision of window boxes and flowers. The Kyrle Society was established in 1876, becoming operative one year later,[5] as a means of 'introducing colour and beauty in all respects to grim lives'.[6] The rather obscure name of the Society was taken from the philanthropist John Kyrle (1637–1724) of Ross-on-Wye, Herefordshire, celebrated in Pope's *Epistle to Bathurst,* as one who served the poor on limited means without blowing his own trumpet.[7] The Kyrle was to share the benefits of wealth with the working classes, diffusing 'a love of beautiful things among our poor brethren'.[8] As McBrinn notes, the concept of beauty was the lynchpin of the Kyrle, as derived from Ruskin's 'Lamp of Beauty' in his *Seven Lamps of Architecture*.[9] Ruskin discerned the civilising effect of a 'noble rendering of images of Beauty' and promoted the use of mosaic and fresco in architecture to that end.[10]

The Kyrle Society was formally constituted a national organisation in June 1877, with William Morris, the poet, designer and socialist, George Frederick Watts ('England's Michelangelo'), George Augustus Sala, journalist and illustrator, and Mrs Alfred Hunt on the committee. The society took its motto from Morris who said, at the first public meeting in 1881, that everybody should try to change society 'To the Utmost of Our Power'.

Although Miranda Hill has traditionally been given the credit for founding the Kyrle Society, it was her sister, Octavia, who was its driving force. Octavia was treasurer for over thirty years and the prime mover in the open spaces branch.[11] The Kyrle grew out of a concern for 'space', with Octavia determined to safeguard both urban and rural land for the 'recreation' of city dwellers, but the Society was also determined 'to bring beauty home to the poor' by decorating public spaces, such as hospital wards, parish rooms, school rooms, working-men's clubs and mission halls, with murals, mosaics and paintings, by distributing books and magazines and organising 'musical performances for poor people'. The Kyrle strove to implement environmental improvements through its branches: decorative, open spaces, music, literature distribution and pamphlets.[12]

Despite its importance at the time, marking the emergence of an 'environmental lobby', the Kyrle has been largely overlooked in recent accounts of Victorian philanthropy and social history. This neglect can be partly accounted for, as the Kyrle was superseded by organisations such as the Metropolitan Public Gardens Association (MPGA) and the National Trust, the latter literally spawned by the Kyrle. The Kyrle can also been seen as the progenitor of England's nine hundred odd civic societies.[13] Provincial groups sprang up in Liverpool (1877), Birmingham (1880), Glasgow (1882), Edinburgh (1885), Leicester, Bristol, Cheltenham and Nottingham. Later affiliations include the Beautiful Sheffield League and the Beautiful Warrington Society.[14]

However, the Kyrle has often been presented as a rather silly organisation led by well-meaning but deluded middle-class women. The image of distributing fresh flowers or nurturing window boxes in the squalid 'rookeries' of East and South London does indeed seem bizarre, given the deprivations of these areas. Owen comments that the object of the Kyrle, 'to bring beauty into the lives and dwellings of the London poor', seems in retrospect to 'carry more than a whiff of Ruskinian sentimentality… To crass modern eyes some of the Society's projects appear almost whimsically romantic, such as the decorating of walls through the city with elevating sentiments— Octavia proposed Kingsley's words "Do noble deeds" for a wall near Waterloo Station.'[15] But the aims of Octavia and Miranda Hill, the founders of the Kyrle, went far beyond such whimsies.

The cultural context

The Kyrle was central to the New Philanthropy, a movement designed to go beyond ministering to the basic needs of the poor: 'Much has been done in various parishes for their bodily wants, but few people seemed to think that the poor, as well as the rich, needed something more than meat and drink to make their lives complete.'[16] Over and above healthcare and housing, a new generation of philanthropists sought to address the spiritual and cultural needs of the people.[17] The Kyrle was not asking for 'a vital need like medical attendance, or food or shelter… but we are asking you to remember that you yourselves do not… spend *all* your income on necessaries, and rightly you do not. Man ceases to be man if he lives only for creature comforts; there is no one so forlorn and degraded.'[18]

The privileged classes had become all too aware of the plight of the poor through paintings such as Luke Fildes's *Applicants for Admission to A Casual Ward* (1874, Royal Holloway Collection) and documentary accounts including James Greenwood's *A Night in the Workhouse* (1866) and Mearns's *The Bitter Cry of Outcast London* (1883), but it was a novel that aroused direct action: Walter Besant's *All Sorts and Conditions of Men* (1882). This suggested that 'art could close the gap between the classes, improve social conditions, and draw the poor from radical politics'.[19] Besant's heroine shared Octavia's desire to get the poor to join her in 'pleasure and amusement' in a Palace of Arts: 'She was going... to say to them, "Life is full, crammed full, overflowing with all kinds of delights. It is a mistake to suppose that only the rich people can enjoy these things.' The sort of delights Besant had in mind did not include drinking and gambling but a 'knowledge of books... to think in some elemental fashion about Art... a better sense of beauty, and... to cultivate some of the graces of life'.[20] For Besant, art encompassed 'the amusements which made upper-class existence pleasant and which, if practised by East Enders, could bring a bit of joy into their monotonous lives'.[21] His manifesto was 'the necessity of pleasure, the desirableness of pleasure, the beauty of pleasure'.[22] Besant envisioned the poor throwing themselves into dancing, singing, sports, gardening, cookery and all the arts and crafts, till there was no East End house without 'its panels painted by one member of the family, its woodwork carved by another, its furniture designed by a third, its windows planted with flowers by another'.[23]

Besant's People's Palace was actually built on the Mile End Road, while Octavia's Red Cross Hall provided 'rational recreation' south of the river. Reformers attempted 'to make the poor more like the rich', especially in terms of behaviour and habits, and hoped for the evolution of the 'middle-class worker'. Gladstonian Liberalism believed in the prospect of working-class improvement: 'The working class would grow more mobile, more rational, more able to acquire and conserve property; in effect, it would increasingly become like a middle class in working-class dress.'[24] The extension of the vote in 1884 fostered democratic feeling but also the realization that the new electorate needed informing, even 'taming'. There could be no revolution if different sectors of society shared the same values and aspirations. But there were many who opposed the idea of 'democratising' culture, fearing the lower classes would get ideas above their station or that art would itself be degraded.[25] In the context of the 1880s, the mission of the Kyrle was quite daring. Although its objectives, now couched in terms such as 'widening participation' and 'greater inclusion', are institutionalised in bodies such as the Arts Council, the accent today appears to be on 'dumbing-down', while the Kyrle's *modus operandi* was 'elevation'. Although the Kyrle professed its desire to narrow the gap between the rich and poor, it would be accused of condescension and paternalism. Yet the success of the Red Cross Hall and the activities it offered, from flower shows and musical recitals to arts and crafts classes which were eagerly attended, demonstrates that there were plenty of working-class people who aspired to middle-class respectability.

Open spaces

It is as part of the campaign for open spaces that the Kyrle is best known, rasing funds to purchase endangered beauty spots and transforming wasteland into urban gardens, before turning them over to a vestry or other local body. Growing out of the 'condition of England' debates of the 1840s, when cholera and industrial ugliness created widespread apprehension of unchecked urban growth, the open spaces movement argued on the grounds of both moral and physical health for parks and gardens. The struggle to preserve open spaces from building and railways indicates both the continual expansion of the urban population, 'with the retreat of open country beyond convenient walking distance for most', and the growth of the middle classes and their leisure time, which, as noted by Bailey, created a need for respectable society to find justifiable leisure pursuits: 'The public garden promenade was eminently respectable. It enabled the urban middle class to ape a genteel style of life while increasing the property value of surrounding houses.'[26] In the context of the urban poor, space was argued for in terms of 'cleansing'. Cities needed to be opened to purifying sunlight and air, dissipating the airborne contagion, or miasma, that early Victorian bogey blamed for the cholera. Octavia herself played on these fears: 'And... do you really think now, people who live in comfortable houses, that you do or can escape infection by any precautions if small-pox and fever rage in the back-courts of your city ?... Depend on it, your best chance of escape is to make the places inhabited by the poor healthy, to let them have open space where the fresh wind may blow over them and their clothes.'[27] Despite little scientific proof, calls for 'lungs for the city', 'reservoirs of wholesome air' and 'ventilators for the slum' touched a responsive chord.[28]

It was not just contagion, however, that drove activists like Octavia to demand open spaces in the metropolis but also the fear of 'idle hands', which prompted the campaign for 'rational recreation', encouraging the labouring classes to aspire to gentility in all things including leisure. By the 1870s a new world of leisure was opening up for the labouring classes, created by rising wages and the legislative limitation of work hours, including the Bank Holidays Act of 1871. Cheap rail fares enabled the 'vulgar' to invade the leafy glades of the suburban idyll. Many hoped this new-found liberty could be channelled into more improving and disciplined activities than gambling and womanising, preferably in areas 'convenient' to the workers' own residences. Reformers, including Octavia, were preoccupied with opening amenities for deprived East and South Londoners, arguing that existing parks in the more affluent areas of the city were physically beyond their reach. But local amenities had the added advantage of restricting an increasingly mobile and less deferential urban proletariat. Morally, parks and gardens reformed by providing an alternative to the public house and its amusements, providing 'what is in reality a moral, intellectual and physical sanatorium for the ailments that unavoidably attack crowded communities'.[29]

As Octavia loved the countryside and found solace in its beauties, she wanted to instil a love of nature in her tenants. This was initially achieved through excursions, but by 1874 the number of Hill's tenants was so great that to get each family to the country for a day a year required no less than 15 excursions.[30] Ever practical, Octavia reversed her mission, instead bringing the country to the city and thereby enriching the life of the environmentally impoverished Londoner on a more permanent basis.

The Kyrle, the Commons Preservation Society and the Metropolitan Public Gardens Association

Octavia, who was active in the Commons Preservation Society (CPS) from about 1875, justified the Kyrle's existence by stating that, while the CPS would preserve open spaces, the Kyrle would protect and create small public gardens in the cities. Though the CPS was sympathetic, as Malchow points out, 'her concerns were somewhat peripheral to the central work of the Society, which was less an ameliorationist philanthropy than an aggressive protector of the legal rights of (mostly suburban) householders'.[31] But there was a clear overlapping of interests, with Robert Hunter of the CPS on the executive committee of the Kyrle and chairman of the open spaces branch. The latter was established by 1879 at the latest.[32] In 1880, an article in the

Magazine of Art, almost certainly penned by Octavia, details its achievements:

'It was mainly owing to the representations made by the Kyrle Society, and the Commons Preservation Society, that the Corporation of the City of London were induced to purchase Burnham Beeches, and to give the ground for the use of the public forever. The committee are now trying to procure the opening of Lincoln's Inn Fields at stated times to the children of the neighbourhood. Efforts are also in progress to secure the site of the Horsemonger Lane Gaol for a public garden... The Kyrle Society has helped in converting long-disused churchyards, or any other available strips of waste ground, into pretty gardens.'[33]

As a result of lobbying by Octavia and her Kyrle co-workers, the Metropolitan Open Spaces Act was passed in 1881, which 'enabled local authorities to receive and maintain gardens transferred to them by trustees and facilitated the transfer of disused burial grounds directly to local authorities, and empowered them to use public funds to maintain them for use as public gardens'.[34] Malchow comments: 'Hill's parliamentary success in 1881 had been a characteristically personal one, a result of her own dogged persistence and exploitation of contacts', but he goes on to dismiss the Kyrle as ineffective:

'At the time of the passage of the Act of 1881, the advocates of metropolitan amenities were a disparate, loosely associated group of clergymen, spinsters, upper-class philanthropists, and a few radicals who lacked the effective organisation to take advantage of the act, promote further legislation, keep pressure on local authorities, and organise private charity. London philanthropy, though commanding impressive resources as a whole, famously lacked cohesion of purpose and was badly fractured by jealousies and conflicting objectives. The CPS could not provide the kind of focus needed, and the Kyrle was clearly inadequate to this task... As a pressure group, the Kyrle Society had inherent weaknesses both of organisation and of vision. Though some may have wished it to pursue a more aggressive course after a brave beginning, it never succeeded in attracting a very politically aware or activist membership. Many of its projects were diffusely philanthropic, and it typically attracted many middle-class women with time on their hands who appear to have been more interested in individual good works than in aggressive lobbying. It remained in the public eye largely a clubbish group of the well-intentioned, whose social vision was limited to flower boxes and musical concerts for the poor. More serious ameliorationists turned elsewhere, and in 1882 created the Metropolitan Public Gardens Association, a more ambitious, assertive, and effective organisation, able to draw on social prestige and resources which the Kyrle Society could never command.'[35]

According to Malchow, unlike the CPS, the MPGA remained above partisan politics and 'quickly became the most important and representative organisation of the third and last phase of the nineteenth century urban amenities movement'.[36] Malchow's rather inflated opinion of the MPGA stems in part from his sources, which include Mrs Basil Holmes, author of *The London Burial Grounds*,[37] who claimed that the Kyrle had, by the early 1880s, 'made little headway'.[38] Evidently, its funds were small and the work of the open spaces sub-committee limited by the demands of its other sub-committees. But Mrs Basil Holmes, née Isabelle Gladstone, as the secretary of the MPGA, was not likely to offer a fair assessment! The founder of the MPGA was none other than Lord Brabazon, later Lord Meath, who clearly wanted an organisation that reflected his own interests. His book *Social Arrows*, published in 1886, demonstrates not only his commitment to urban spaces but also to physical fitness. Brabazon envisaged his gardens as playgrounds, since fresh air and exercise were vital to the 'health and physique of our city populations… greater facilities for getting into the country have certainly improved the physique of our better-class townsmen. The effeminate shop-clerk, against whom *Punch*, at the time of the Crimean war, used never to be weary of levelling the shafts of his ridicule, has developed into the stalwart volunteer, the oarsman, or the bicyclist.'[39] Brabazon wanted 'places where of an evening a young man can find innocent and wholesome recreation'. He was very keen to promote bodily strength through strenuous physical exercise and gymnastics, as well as using the influence of the MPGA to encourage the construction of baths, wash-houses and swimming-baths.

This ambitious programme was supported by Ernest Hart, Henrietta Barnett's brother-in-law, a co-founder and first vice-chairman of the MPGA, who was willing to merge the open spaces sub-committee of the National Health Society with the new association. The Kyrle, on the other hand, preferred to remain independent, although the society did work closely with the MPGA. In March 1883, for example, a deputation from the MPGA, the Kyrle and the CPS appeared before the trustees of St. James's burial ground to prevent railway encroachment. Interests might overlap, but autonomy was maintained. Brabazon and Hart of the MPGA, George Shaw-Lefevre and Robert Hunter of the CPS and Octavia Hill of the Kyrle were clearly pursuing their own agendas.

Above all, Octavia's open spaces were used to foster 'corporate feeling', evidently 'an ingredient necessary to a truly civilised life'.[40] Her playground at Freshwater Place was used to 'tame' unruly children, who were 'dirty, quarrelsome, violent, and wholly ignorant of games'.[41] They were to be 'educated' to use their leisure more effectively: 'Octavia had been distressed by the sight of children hanging about listlessly doing nothing, or squabbling, gambling, or playing utterly pointless games. That the children must be taught something better, some game that demanded a slight measure of skill, which called for co-ordination of hand and eye, and some power of co-operation among themselves, she had no doubt.'[42] The 'rational recreations' she favoured were to impose order: 'They began to try to play with some regard to the rules and to regard cheating with disfavour.'[43] The children 'flourished' and 'they learned to play with other children, to give and take, in a word, under the cheerful and easy discipline of the playground they became much easier to manage'.[44] May Day celebrations, 'so dear to Ruskin's heart', took place at the playground and 'after the crowning of the little Queen… the children had cakes, biscuits and oranges'. Octavia's mother noted the occasion in 1868, with 'numbers of lovely wreaths, and a throne made of a chair shape' in flowers provided in part by Ruskin. The ceremony began by drawing lots for the queen, and then the children were crowned with their home-crafted wreaths: 'the children looked so pretty—their untidiness only went for picturesqueness. They had cakes, biscuits and oranges; but except one or two boys, the flowers interested them more than the cake.'[45]

Octavia's gardens at Red Cross and Vauxhall were beautiful, with fish ponds, ornamental bridges, sundials and elevating images and texts. The Red Cross garden reflects Octavia's own response to nature, especially her belief in its recuperative powers:

'The space, the quiet, the sight of grass and trees and sky, which are the common inheritance of men in most circumstances… Have you ever thought what the sense of quiet is to the member of a poor family? Many of them have never for years been alone, hardly ever been in silence; crowd, noise, dirt, confusion all round. Your excursion trains and vans only carry noise into the country; let the people stroll from their own homes up the hilly fields, and you may be sure it will do them good.'[46]

Growing up in Finchley, then a country village well north of London, and at Hillside, Highgate, her maternal grandfather's home, did not prepare Octavia for the deprivations of Russell Place, Fitzroy Square, when 'the full weight of London's misery and desolation fell upon me': 'she was plunged into wholly new conditions... from an existence untroubled by knowledge of wealth or want, to one surrounded by evidence of crushing and sordid poverty'.[47] The miseries of urban deprivation could be alleviated by open space, light and fresh air, but Octavia's response was also tinged with nostalgia for those innocent childhood days in Finchley. Under Octavia and her contemporaries, the 'pastoral ideal' was transformed into 'a dynamic purifying force'.[48] While Bailey argues that the founding of the CPS in the 1860s 'is a turning point in a new sensibility to nature', Malchow is nearer the mark, commenting that 'the change is not so much one of general sensibility, but of individuals': 'There was a change in motives and interests which reflected the altered political and social make-up of the preservation movement.'[49]

The Kyrle and its supporters

Malchow's denigration of the Kyrle Society, claiming it lacked a 'politically aware or activist membership', suffered from 'inherent weaknesses both of organisation and vision', which extended only to window boxes, and was essentially a 'clubbish group' of middle-class women with time on their hands, demands a closer analysis. As regards activists and members of high social standing, the Kyrle was well endowed. Octavia's contacts enabled her to assemble an impressive list of patrons. The Kyrle secured royal and aristocratic support, guaranteeing a high profile and press coverage. Princess Louise, Marchioness of Lorne, the most artistic of Queen Victoria's daughters, was vice-president from the Kyrle's inception, with her brother Prince Leopold, Duke of Albany (1853–1884), the Queen's youngest son, installed as president. Following the death of Leopold, at the request of Princess Louise, Alfred, Duke of Edinburgh (1844–1900), Victoria's second son, accepted the position. Upon his death in 1900, Louise herself assumed the presidency. Realising their greater potential for attracting media coverage, Princess Louise ensured that her eldest brother and his wife, the Prince and Princess of Wales, opened Vauxhall Park in 1890.

The General Committee was large, with some 71 members in 1887, dropping to 68 in 1890. Lord Monkwell, as chairman, was accompanied by the Duke of Westminster, Countess Ducie, the Earl of Meath (Lord Brabazon), Lady Wentworth (later Lovelace), Lady Hobhouse, Lord Ronald Gower, Lord Wolmer and Lady Thompson. The Kyrle's subscribers were predominantly professionals, artists and architects. A remarkable number were involved with the arts.[50] Established artists included Walter Crane, Lewis F. Day, Henry Holiday, Robert Hunter, Audley Mackworth, William Morris, Heywood Sumner and G.F. Watts. Crane, Morris and Watts were certainly 'activists'. Morris founded the Society for the Protection of Ancient Buildings in 1877, Crane was the driving force behind the founding of the Arts and Crafts Exhibition Society in 1888, and Watts was a leading force in the Home Arts and Industries Association founded in 1884. If a begging letter were needed, Watts was your man. Other big guns firing for the Kyrle include Edward Burne-Jones, the Earl of Carlisle, Lord Leighton and George Augustus Sala. Moreover, Lord Brabazon, later Meath, the founder of the MPGA, was, alongside his wife, a committed supporter of the Kyrle.

The Society was often wanting in funds, blaming its unobtrusiveness for its lack of support, and made direct appeals in the press, utilising its distinguished supporters. In 1890 George Howard, the Earl of Carlisle (a well-known amateur artist and patron), Burne-Jones, G.F. Watts and Andrew Clark wrote a begging letter to *The Times*:

'May we invoke the valuable aid of your journal in bringing before the notice of the public the present need of the decorative branch of the Kyrle Society, whose work is now almost at a standstill from want of funds ?... at the present moment 22 applications for decorative help have been inquired into and sanctioned by the committee, but not one of these can be put in hand, not from any lack of able artists and architects to draw up schemes or of workers to carry out their designs, but because the committee has absolutely no money to grant for the necessary expenses of materials and fixing...'[51]

Two hundred and fifty pounds was needed to expedite claims that had been under consideration for nearly two years. The decorative branch particularly suffered from a lack of funds. In 1895 Octavia wrote to the press urging readers to donate 'the small sums necessary for materials, fixing or framing' that 'alone are wanting': 'The decorative branch of the society numbers many and most capable artists willing and ready to give their time as volunteers for painting and decoration in the clubs, mission and parish rooms, hospitals, and other institutions for the people from which pressing requests reach them each day....the usefulness of these willing workers is much limited in consequence.'[52] But what the Kyrle really wanted was the volunteer's time and energy:

'... let me plead for that greater gift than any money, the gift of time, which means the gift of oneself. Come among us if you can; let those who paint help to carry out decorative schemes, or give us pictures; those who sing, play, or act, help in our performances; let others help in secretarial work... you will find a glad welcome among your fellow-workers, and believe me, too, you will find it among the poor. Get to known them, to love them, to meet them not with miserable dole of necessaries... but with a gift of flowers... with suggestive or refreshing thought, which ennobles not degrades.'[53]

The Kyrle demanded direct involvement with the 'lower classes' in order to bridge the social gulf; friendship was to be extended rather than doles given, which divided giver from receiver. It was necessary to excite the sympathy of the 'rich' for the 'poor':

'Readiness to give is often checked by the fear that evil rather than good will be done by diminishing the sense of independence in the recipient. No such hesitation need be felt in the present case, for no one can be pauperised... by sitting in a pretty room rather than between four bare walls, by hearing a concert, or by strolling through a garden bright with spring flowers.'[54]

The Kyrle and National Trust

Personal knowledge, the evaluation of individual 'character' or worthiness as a recipient, was the mainstay of Octavia Hill's approach. But if she needed to, Octavia could pull in big sums of money: in just three weeks Octavia raised £8,150 for the Swiss Cottage Fields fund. Octavia raised over £50,000 by public subscription to preserve the privately owned land of East Park and Parliament Hill Fields. It was this project, the extension of Hampstead Heath, that highlighted the restrictions imposed on the CPS, whose remit was curtailed to the preservation of 'common lands'. Increasingly it was privately owned land, over which there had never been any common rights, that was coming under threat. There were proposals for a new conservation body as early as 1884, a land company that could acquire properties, by gift and even compulsory purchase, in the public interest and manage them, but to begin with nothing came of the discussions, as Shaw-Lefevre amongst others feared that it might take support away from the older amenity groups. He rightly forecast the eclipse of the CPS. The Kyrle would also be overshadowed by this new body, the National Trust for Places of Historic Interest or Natural Beauty, which was born under the auspices of Octavia, Hardwicke Rawnsley and Robert Hunter. Given his active role on the Hampstead Heath Extension Committee and his support for the Kyrle, the Duke of Westminster was invited to become President of the National Trust. Octavia foresaw that the Duke's position as a major landowner would inspire confidence in those who might endow the fledgling Trust with land and legacies. The inaugural meeting took place under Westminster's chairmanship in Grosvenor House on Monday 16 July 1894. The Kyrle had served its purpose as a springboard for the National Trust, but its days were numbered. The Kyrle would flounder as Octavia's interests shifted, 'it was essentially a Hill enterprise and had little substance without them'.[55] The Kyrle would outlive Octavia by only five years, ceasing in 1917, but by then much of its remit had been achieved or taken over by institutions more in tune with the thinking of the twentieth century.

Ian Fletcher concludes that 'the Kyrle was a symptom of the old paternalism' and it was to be succeeded by 'a new impersonal paternalism of state benefits that has now, it seems, run its course'.[56] For Fletcher, the Kyrle was 'the best type of private effort'. Politically, the emphasis on voluntarism, promoting humanity without upsetting the social order, appealed to those who, like Octavia, preferred private philanthropy to state intervention: 'There is a blessing on all voluntary work, rich and full.'[57] But as Miss Alice Gruner, the hard-pressed Head Worker of the Women's University Settlement in Southwark, noted, volunteers came and went, often staying for only a few weeks. Permanent paid staff were necessary to provide continuity and also to organise the volunteers. As Octavia's organisations grew, they had to professionalise. Her lady visitors would become social workers requiring academic and practical training. The Kyrle inevitably out-grew itself. The Society did not lack vision, rather it was too ambitious and disparate in its aims, tackling the decoration of public spaces, literature distribution and even 'music for the poor'. The ironic counsel of Bernard Shaw—'never to give the people anything they want; give them something they ought to want and don't'—perhaps best fits the Kyrle.[58]

The Red Cross project

Because of the role played by Octavia and Robert Hunter in the events that led to the formation of the National Trust in 1894, the Kyrle Society tends to be remembered, if it is remembered at all, as an open spaces movement. But the open spaces branch was only one of four: the other three being decorative, musical and literature distribution. From the outset, its mission was to beautify public spaces with murals, mosaics, paintings and prints. However, it is still correct to regard the Kyrle as an early manifestation of the environmental movement, as all of its branches were working to improve the environment of poor people. We can find a perfect example of their interaction on a site on Red Cross Street in Southwark, handed over to Octavia and a board of trustees by the Ecclesiastical Commissioners, which was described by the Earl of Ducie as the most unpromising piece of ground he had ever seen. It would provide Octavia with the opportunity to give physical expression to her ideal in terms of housing and environmental reform. The Red Cross project started in 1886 with a garden, followed by cottages in 1887–88, and a community hall. In 1889 more land was leased for the building of the White Cross cottages to back onto the Red Cross cottages. The Kyrle Society was to lay out the garden and a proposition was put to the Society to decorate the hall with murals commemorating the 'heroic deeds of the poor'.

Both the garden and the hall express Octavia's aspirations for her tenants, her desire to bring them beauty and civilise them. The garden was to be her 'outdoor sitting-room', the hall a 'drawing-room' for 'rational recreation', forming, with the cottages, the Red Cross community or 'village in the city'. Octavia intended this model to be repeated across London. Given the magnitude of the problem of housing the poor, Maltz sees Octavia's rather romantic view of the cottage and the village as an out-dated anachronism: 'surely, the pastoral domesticity Hill envisioned in the small cottage was a fantasy'.[59] Her vision included flower shows, sewing clubs and savings associations, as well as broad tree-lined streets and attractive houses. As Darley comments, Octavia's 'aims were entirely recognisable as those underlying the Garden City and later New Town developments, which were framed in terms suitable to more sophisticated times'.[60]

For Octavia, the 'village in the city' was the setting for a community lifestyle. Management was the key, with order imposed and a community spirit nurtured by the lady rent collectors. Her approach was essentially feudal, dictatorial and dependent on instilling a sense of responsibility and self-respect in her tenants. Octavia's attitude is generally perceived to be one of condescension, as 'surely any working man would question the prerogative of Hill or anyone to urge him to live a *nobler life*',[61] but it seems clear that Octavia's earnestness was also aimed at her own kind, reminding them that they too could lead a *nobler life* in the service of the people.

The Red Cross Hall and its cottages occupied the site of a hop warehouse, a court that had been declared unfit for human habitation and a former paper factory which had burnt down. According to Mrs Russell Barrington:

'Miss Octavia Hill has metamorphosed a desolate space... into a garden well planted with shrubs and flowers, where there are winding paths, a pond spanned over by a bridge, a fountain, a band-stand, a covered playground for the children in wet weather to play in, roofed by a terrace where the more sedate visitors may sit and view the garden... From this garden... you enter a spacious, well-built hall, where entertainments and lectures take place every week; where the cadet corps enrolled by Lord Wolseley in 1888 is drilled, and where gymnastic classes are given. Out of this hall again you pass into a men's club and reading room... [The Hall] is open every Sunday afternoon and many inhabitants of Southwark collect there to spend a quiet hour or two. Newspapers and magazines lie on the tables to be read and to be looked at, while good music is played and sung, and listened to and enjoyed by those that way inclined.'[62]

Although the great days of the Gothic Revival had largely passed, architect Elijah Hoole employed its grandeur for the Red Cross Hall (*see ill.10*). Resembling Westminster Hall or the Great Hall at Christchurch College, Oxford, the hall brought to mind the communal living of the medieval college. Although the final result was humbler than the illustrated drawing, the Hall served its purpose as a meeting place to improve the body and the mind.

The Annual Reports give us a clear indication of its purpose as a communal 'drawing-room', part of the process of gentrifying the working classes:

'The Hall is used every Sunday in winter and forms a large, light, warm and beautiful free drawing-room for the grown up people of the district. Here Mrs Julian Marshall has for many years given on each alternate Sunday the most beautiful concerts, and other friends kindly supply music on the alternate weeks. Here, every Christmas, she arranges a performance of the *Messiah*, when we all meet as at an annual service. Here, every Thursday during the winter, groups of friends are good enough to give entertainments, mainly dramatic, which are much appreciated by the people... Here every Sunday meets the violin class for the people of the neighbourhood. Mrs Marshall supervises it...When the Hall was first opened, Mrs Stephen Winkworth gave a large stereoscope, which has proved a continual source of pleasure on the Sunday afternoons ever since.' [63]

All of the Kyrle Society's areas of interest were on show at the Red Cross Hall: the flower shows, festivals, entertainments and concerts. Recreative activities were essential, setting the boys to fife and drum bands and offering singing lessons to children. Even the children's games had to be competitive, 'with ordered companions, definite object and progressive skill'.[64] Order was imposed on her tenants lives, a 'benevolent despotism'.

There was even a Home Arts Class, which appears to have been initiated in 1887, before the Red Cross Hall was completed. In June that year the Southwark class exhibited, at the Home Arts and Industries Association (HAIA) annual exhibition, examples of 'modelling and carving... showing an improvement in design and workmanship, due in great measure to the course of training which the association has afforded through its voluntary teachers'.[65] The Southwark class was again mentioned in 1889, when George Kimberley won a prize 'for his diapered oak blotting-book cover, carved at the Red Cross class, Southwark'.[66] The Red Cross class submitted an 'overmantel containing a clock', to the HAIA Exhibition of 1891: 'The class at the Red-cross Hall branch have executed an oak clock-case and overmantel for their hall in Southwark. It was designed by Mr Benton Fletcher, with German Renaissance-like foliations [*sic*] in the panel, which are rather thin and wanting in breadth. The cushioned frieze, on the other hand, is heavy looking.'[67] Although this work may have been, to the artistic eye, in some ways deficient, its importance was as a gift from the 'working men who belonged to the carving class'.[68] (1891, p.303.)

The Red Cross Hall class was 'under the skilled superintendence' of

Miss Sewell.[69] In 1898, *The House* noted that 'the nine years Miss Seawell [*sic*] has spent on this labour of love have not been in vain', exhibiting 'a collection of which both workers and teacher were justly proud'.[70] *The House* misspelt the teacher's name, as a Red Cross Hall report credits Miss Sewell, the head worker at the Women's University Settlement in Southwark from 1889 to 1901.[71] The class was obviously a success and in 1901 was still flourishing, when carvings and embroidery were submitted, with a set of bellows illustrated (*see ill. 11*).

The Red Cross cottages

Octavia was a champion of the cottage, stating that 'a third-rate cottage with a small garden, or even a back-yard, is better for a working man than that best tenement that the London County Council can build', even though the new flats would have had indoor toilets.[72] This 'pastoral domesticity' embodied in the small cottage was born out of Octavia's aesthetic tastes and her conviction that the countryside offered a panacea to the conditions of the city. By favouring small cottages over large blocks, Hill ignored the enormous demand for workers' housing. London was growing at a rate of 80,000 people a year. Even William Morris admitted that one would have to build *up*, using 'vertical streets' to ensure green spaces,[73] but Octavia would not go above four storeys. Large-scale state-funded housing was distasteful to her, as Octavia's attention 'was focused on the quality of the immediate environment of the individual family'.[74]

Elijah Hoole designed the Red Cross cottages to Hill's instructions, their irregularly gabled and quaintly ornamented appearance inspired by the homes she had observed on her visits to Germany and the Tyrol (*ills. 2 and 4*). On her trips Octavia noted down the patterns of the windows, which evidently she thought would add to 'the charm of housing in London'.[75] She was particularly struck by the rich external decoration: 'the quaint irregularity of the home-like oriel windows, set on at the corner of the tiny houses in the village streets, with pretty little separate conical roofs, and I seemed to see that this home-like irregularity, this prominence of roof, this simplicity of brick ornament, could be at once applied to our people's houses' (1879, p.121). Octavia claimed that it was Ruskin who had 'taught me to care for permanent decoration, which should endear houses to men, for external decoration which should be a common joy'.[76]

There is a long tradition of 'model villages' in England, stretching back into the eighteenth century, built by philanthropic landowners to improve the lot of their estate workers and enhance the value of their property. The most famous is Blaise Hamlet, near Bristol, designed in 1810 by John Nash and Humphrey Repton for John Scandrett Harford, a banker, merchant and Quaker. Elijah Hoole would have known of Blaise Hamlet and might well have modeled the Red Cross cottages on the *cottage orné*: 'Old fashioned and minute as it is, Blaise Hamlet might remind us of some of the qualities that can help make planned housing estates a pleasure to live in and a joy to visit. Consideration of privacy within a community, identity and security, variety, harmony and daily human needs are involved: articulate relationships between buildings, nature, activity and space can also be as relevant today as in 1810.'[77] These were certainly the concerns of Octavia in the 1880s, by which time the ideal of the model suburb was developing, as seen in London's Bedford Park, begun in the late 1870s.

Moreover, by the 1880s the vernacular revival was in full-swing and she would have seen equally quaint village 'cottages' in Kent and Surrey, both ancient and modern.[78] Pretty brick patterns and tile hanging were a common feature of the vernacular in Surrey and Kent, while fancy plaster-work, or pargeting, was local to the Saffron Walden area. Oriel and dormer windows, irregular roof-lines and massing, were key features of 'Queen Anne', an architectural style that combined vernacular charm with a blend of seventeenth- and eighteenth-century architectural elements, ranging from Christopher Wren to Robert Adam, plus a touch of the Elizabethans. Richard Norman Shaw, Eden Nesfield, Edward Godwin and J.J. Stevenson were pioneers of this English vernacular style, with red brick and white woodwork prevailing in Bedford Park and Hampstead. 'Queen Anne' was the style of the enlightened middle-classes, used for schools, colleges, model villages and alms houses.[79] Hoole was also developing the idiom of the 'Queen Anne' style, as exemplified by Toynbee Hall, Whitechapel, which became the preferred mode for Octavia Hill's cottages.

Octavia longed to see not only the picturesque houses of the Tyrol replicated at home, but the way of life they contained: 'Trees grow among the houses, and children play around them, and clean industrious women knit at their doors.'[80] Octavia's 'desire to recreate a small insular village out of a court'[81] was taken further in the Red Cross project, which can be read as her London village. Indeed Mrs Barrington referred to Octavia as 'the good squiress of the great village'.[82] Octavia's refusal to see 'the city as a whole' was both politically as well as aesthetically motivated: 'If social problems really could be solved on a house-to-house basis, and by voluntary workers, the disturbing thoughts on structural change, or expensive reforms, could be conveniently shelved.'[83] Yet the success of the six Red Cross cottages persuaded the Ecclesiastical Commissioners to grant a lease on more land for a further six—the White Cross cottages, which were let before they had been completed.

The Red Cross garden

Southwark was hardly the Tyrol, but Octavia got to build her pretty gabled and tile-hung cottages, their ornamental windows overlooking the garden, amply planted with bulbs and two plane trees with seats round them. It was further adorned with a bandstand, a goldfish pond and a little bridge, supplied by Robert Hunter, plus ornamental and drinking fountains.[84] There was even a pigeon house.[85] A raised balcony, which gave additional space for those wishing to sit outside, also served as a roof to the children's playground, thus ensuring that they would get fresh air even when it rained: 'the garden forms a valuable outdoor sitting room in summer, where men can smoke, and women do needlework, and children play'.[86] The garden was laid out by the Kyrle at a cost of £1,000, the whole amount being given by the Countess of Ducie.[87] It was beautified with works of art, in true Kyrle tradition:

'A mosaic of the Good Shepherd, executed by Salviati, and presented by Mrs Lynch and Miss Gregg, is fixed on a wall bounding the garden. It has been there since the opening of the garden in 1887, and there is no sign of change of colour or injury from weather, and it is hoped that for many years its refreshing colour may gleam among the Virginian creeper sprays, and bring the message of its story home to many.'[88] (*see ill.3.*)

Miss Minet, who sat on the main committee of the Kyrle, gave another mosaic, the subject of which was 'The Sower' (*see ill.5*). Miss Minet also presented to the garden a beautiful sundial bearing the inscription: 'As hour follows hour, God's mercies on us shower'.[89] Octavia was very fond of 'chiselled messages of virtue and temperance', seeing inscriptions and mosaics as a means of elevating the poor to higher thought and feeling,[90] but she was also mindful of their aesthetic power, as pattern and colour would attract the passer-by's attention. Again the idea came from Ruskin, from the 'The Lamp of Memory', which inspired Octavia with a description of a cottage in Grindelwald that bore a decorative inscription on the façade recording a man's life and his experience and 'thus [raised] the habitation into a kind of monument... into a kind of systematic instructiveness'.[91]

But the Red Cross garden was more than a beautifully decorated space. It was also to be the site, like the Hall, of social events designed to bring the community together. The key fixtures on the calender were the annual tenants' flower show and the May festival for the children: 'On May 25th the Holland Street Board School provided the dances and games which brightened the Maypole festival. Three hundred and forty children from eleven schools were present; kind friends from the country sent beautiful flowers... the teachers took infinite pains to train the little scholars.'[92]

But despite Octavia's success in creating a 'village in the city', there was resistence to middle-class rule. The creation of her first garden at Freshwater Place aroused hostility from the neighbours, 'who resented the clearing up of waste space, which they had been accustomed to use as a place for fighting or loafing or throwing out their rubbish'.[93] These 'unhappy people' hampered the work of creating the garden by stealing bricks, throwing the rubbish back, and interfering with the workers. Octavia appealed to the police but with little effect, as the assailants scattered only to regroup. A watchman was employed to guard the property at night. At the opening ceremony, 'a most happy tea party', complete with 'Maypole, flags, singing and a band from a Boy's Home', hostile neighbours were still heaving 'the occasional stone or brickbat' over the wall.[94] Eventually the local children were given access to the amenity. The Red Cross garden does not appear to have engendered such opposition, but public gardens, with their flowers and ponds, were vandalised by working-class patrons who felt that these amenities were not their own. The MPGA had to employ caretakers and inspectors: 'Maintenance costs were, especially in the East, where refuse dumping and vandalism were common, quite substantial'.[95] Parks and gardens regulated behaviour, whereas the poor appropriated unimproved land to serve their needs, such as growing vegetables, tethering animals and hanging out their laundry: 'Working-class residents understood that the new gardens, with their regulations and surveillance by hired inspectors, were a middle- and upper-class dream of social control come true'.[96] While Octavia spared land for decorative gardens alone, her tenants would probably have preferred allotments to supplement the domestic economy.[97]

The Red Cross Hall murals

At the opening of the Hall and garden on 2 June 1888, the Kyrle Society choir sang and Hardwicke Rawnsley sent one of his poems to commemorate the occasion. But the Hall was in need of beautification, and Mrs Barrington, inspired by G.F.Watts, was keen to commemorate the 'Heroic Deeds of the Poor' in a series of murals.

On 5 September 1887 G.F.Watts had written to *The Times* and the *Spectator* suggesting that the fiftieth anniversary of the Queen's accession might be justly celebrated by a monument raised to 'the unsung heroes of everyday life':

> 'It must surely be a matter of regret when names worthy to be remembered and stories stimulating and instructive are allowed to be forgotten... It is not too much to say that the history of Her Majesty's reign would gain a lustre were the nation to erect a monument, say, here in London, to record the names of these likely-to-be-forgotten heroes... The material prosperity of a nation is not an abiding possession; the deeds of its people are.'[98]

Mrs Barrington seized the moment: 'never has the Kyrle Society had a better opportunity of decorating with art large spaces of wall which would be constantly seen by a public consisting of the poorest classes—those who have the least chance of seeing anything beautiful in their homes'.[99]

Taking up Watts's cause, Mrs Barrington suggested to Octavia that the Red Cross Hall was suitable for 'illustrating the heroism displayed by people', a heroic action being a ' "thing of beauty and a joy for ever" to all, be the hero of it rich or poor; but it is only the well-to-do classes who have the leisure or the means to commemorate the records of heroism'.[100] Mrs Barrington reports that 'Miss Octavia Hill, Lady Wentworth, Mr Walter Crane and the present writer decided they would propose to the Kyrle Society a scheme for decorating the Red Cross Hall with designs by Mr Walter Crane'.[101] This ambitious scheme was beyond the means of the Kyrle, so the money was raised by an appeal in *The Times*.[102]

Walter Crane and heroic deeds of the common people

The Red Cross Hall project would have appealed to Crane on many levels, the design of the building bringing to mind his call for communal living based on the medieval college and linked to the philanthropic cause of providing a 'healthy diet of exercise for mind and body'.[103] Decorated with inspirational mural paintings, this public space would 'restore humanity's shared sense of the past and common goals for the future':

'... in depicting the story of man, and the drama of life, in great public monuments, in commemoration of the past, in the education of the present; in the adorning of domestic and public buildings... we shall find the widest possible field for the exercise for all the capabilities of art... since their foundation will rest upon the welfare of the whole people.'[104]

The design for the scheme, exhibited at the Arts and Crafts Exhibition Society in 1890, comprised panels depicting: 'An Explosion in a Mine'; 'Rescue from drowning by a youth'; 'Rescue from fire: a man holding a ladder while his arms are exposed to a dropping of melted lead'; 'A Sister of Mercy holding back a dog from attacking her school-children'; 'The rescue of a boat's crew from the rocks'. On the facing side, he planned 'Rescue from a well'; 'Alice Ayres'; 'Jamieson'; and 'The Man who took the bull by the horns'.[105] Painted decoration covered the remaining wall space, including allegorical figures such as Fortitude and Vigilance and two maidens bearing the Crown of Noble Deeds; the end of the Hall would be graced by 'England's Emblem', Crane's rendering of St George and the Dragon. The whole scheme, already fully conceived, can be seen in the illustration in *The Builder* (*see ill.10*). 'Alice Ayres' can be seen in the illustration, first panel on the left wall, followed by 'Jamieson' and then 'Rescue from a well'.

For Crane public mural painting represented the ideal: 'the art that is capable of illustrating [the epic spirit] is what is called decorative art... the art which can cover large mural spaces with a people's history and legend in noble and typical forms; the art which can lift our souls with large thoughts, or enchant them with a sense of mystery and romance'.[106] Crane's support of the Red Cross Hall project is clearly his attempt to offer 'the people' serious art, educational and elevating, as well as a beautiful interior, the House Beautiful: 'As the "drawing room" of Southwark, the Red Cross functioned as an open book for moral education, and the murals of Walter Crane depicting the everyday heroic deeds of the worker would provide the lessons.'[107]

The Alice Ayres panel was unveiled in the Red Cross Hall in 1890, 'Jamieson' in 1892 and 'Rescue from a well' in 1894. At that point,

Mrs Barrington's ambitious project petered out.[108] Several explanations have been offered for this. O'Neill suggests Crane fell out with Octavia over the meaning of the murals:

> 'Although united in their understanding of art as a form of moral education, perhaps they disagreed on the lessons these paintings should teach. Possibly Crane's use of a radical political message in the design, however implicit, frustrated their relationship.'[109]

But is unlikely that the people of Southwark read any 'radical political message', and Crane was still on the Council of the Kyrle in 1910, suggesting there was no major falling out.

The problem with the Red Cross murals was one of scale and, most importantly, the subject matter, as Crane seldom attempted scenes from contemporary life. Crane was not comfortable with 'realism', his preferred mode being 'allegory' with symbolic, classically draped, timeless, figures:

> 'When the artist desires to soar a little above the passing moment to suggest the past, to peer into the future; when he looks at human life as a complete whole, and the life of the race as an unbroken chain; when he would deal with the thoughts of man's origins and destiny, of the powers and passions that sway him, of loves, of hope and fear, of the mystery of life and nature, the drama of the seasons, he must use figurative language and seek the beautiful and permanent images of emblematic design.'[110]

But how could Crane transform the story of Alice Ayres into allegory and emblem? Crane wrestled with the problem, especially the difficulty of contemporary working-class dress, and probably concluded that the Cause was best served with personifications and classical drapery.

There was also the question of time and money. The Kyrle did not pay for the services of its artists, as designs were donated, and the labour of executing them was voluntary. The Kyrle boasted that funds were only spent on materials and general expenses. What is remarkable is that Crane was painting the panels himself. It was normal practice in the Kyrle for professional artists to supply designs to be carried out by the amateur female volunteers. It is well documented that Mrs Barrington executed the first panel, with Crane adding the finishing touches. He then decided to take over the project:

'A second panel... I painted in my studio afterwards... A third panel... I also painted, after an interval, and there are now three panels in the Hall. The work had to be largely a labour of love, as very little money was available for such a purpose, and as other work had to be attended to, and the busy years roll on, the scheme is still incomplete.'[111]

Yet Crane did not execute the other projects for the Kyrle Society that utilized his designs. So why did Crane oversee the Red Cross Hall murals so diligently? Probably because he recognised the difficulty of the subject matter and the potential harm to his career if the work was judged to be 'bad art'.

Conclusion

The purpose of the Red Cross murals was to act as a record. This was art 'not only first-rate of its kind, not only educational and inspiring in its motives', but art 'which will be a lasting testimony to the heroism of English men and women, who, in forgetfulness of self-interest, have displayed very typical English virtues—courage, fortitude, and an unquestioning sense of duty'.[112]

But there was also a lesson for the 'well-to-do classes', that the poor were capable of nobility, that the ideal, the 'highest in human nature', was to be found alike in the poor and rich. The murals were to express not just 'the desire to give something to the poor, and share with them the delights of art and culture', but to acknowledge and honour their virtues. The murals were to instill an admiration for the honest working man, 'that condescension on the one hand, and servility on the other, must of necessity cease' in order to 'admit mutual respect and true sympathy' between the classes. Evidently it was not 'poverty, dirt, and untidiness alone which bring about the worst kind of want of self-respect and the lowest depravity in human-nature' but 'a latent sense of injury in the minds of the poor'. It was the callousness of the rich, who lived but a few miles ways in 'unnecessary luxury', which had created this sense of injury: 'It is the feeling that nobody cares for them that makes them care for nobody, and which has made many of the poor grasping and greedy, the clever among them using their brains for cunning and imposture.' [113]

Such images of heroism crossed the divide and reinforced social unity. They were to inspire feelings of 'dignity, strength, noble fire and purity', to 'raise a nation to true greatness', according to Mrs Barrington:

'The great problem that faces any who interest themselves in the question of the amelioration of the condition of the poor is that moral degradation must ensue from squalor, dirt, overcrowding, and ugliness. Are the conditions in which millions of English men, women, and children are *forced* to live, conditions in which it is possible that a "noble fire should burn in their hearts" or "purity chasten their lives"?... the question should not be left to the clergy and the philanthropists alone to struggle with but should be the problem... [of] those who wish to further in a truly *practical* way the right education of the English people.'[114]

The Red Cross murals were the Kyrle Society's *practical* way of addressing the English people.[115]

Notes

1   I would particularly like to thank Helen Meller, Robert Whelan, Diana Maltz and Joseph McBrinn, who have so freely shared information with me.

2   Octavia Hill, 'The Kyrle Society', *Charity Organisation Review*, V, 18, July-Dec, 1905, p.314.

3   For an account of the founding of the Kyrle Society see C. Edmund Maurice (ed.), *A Life of Octavia Hill as Told in Her Letters*, London: Macmillan, 1914, pp.316-17.

4   Samuel Barnett had been vicar of St. Jude's since 1873.

5   There seems to have been some confusion amongst members concerning the date of the Society's formation. Octavia announced its constitution as an independent body, using the name of the Kyrle Society, in the letter for 1876. (In 1875 she had referred to it simply as 'my sister's small society'.) However, Kyrle Society annual reports gave 1877 as the date of foundation on their title pages, until 1909 when it became 1876.

6   Clarissa Campbell Orr, 'Introduction: Women in the Victorian Art World' in Clarissa Campbell Orr (ed.), *Women in the Victorian Art World*, Manchester and New York: Manchester University Press, 1995, p.5.

7   Alexander Pope, 'Moral Essays: Of the Use of Riches', in John Butt (ed.), *The Poems of Alexander Pope*, London: Methuen and Co., 1963, p.582.

8   'Prince Leopold and the Kyrle Society', *The Times*, 28 January 1881, p.10.

9   Joseph McBrinn, 'Decoration should be a common joy: the Kyrle Society and mural painters', *The Acorn*, forthcoming.

10   John Ruskin, 'The Lamp of Beauty', *The Seven Lamps of Architecture*, Orpington and London: George Allen, [1849] 1894 (4th edition), p.187.

11   For many years the Society was run from the Hill family home at 14 Nottingham Place, Marylebone.

12   The literature distribution branch was added in 1886. Books, magazines and periodicals were distributed as loans or gifts to hospitals, infirmaries, workhouses, clubs and libraries. In the 'Summary of Work Accomplished' for 1910 it was noted that 1,372 institutions had received grants, the total number of grants being 3,060, comprising over 82,176 books and 143,625 magazines. The fifth branch, 'The publication of simple and inexpensive pamphlets upon art subjects', was added in 1892, but only a few works were published: No.1 *The Cathedral Church of St Paul* by the Rev. Lewis Gilbertson (1892) and No.2 *Guide to the Italian Pictures at Hampton Court* by Mary Logan (c.1895). Others were planned on Turner and *What to Look for in Pictures* by T.C. Horsfall, an advocate of 'pictures for the people'.

13   Vincent Wait, *Bristol Civic Society: The First Sixty Years*, Bristol, 1966, p.3.

14   Listed in the 1910 *Annual Report.*

15   David Owen, *English Philanthropy 1660–1690,* Cambridge, Mass.: Harvard University Press, 1965, p.496.

16   (Octavia Hill), 'The Kyrle Society', *The Magazine of Art*, London: Cassell, Petter, Galpin and Co.,1880, vol. 3, pp.210-12.

17   For a discussion of how art and culture were used to elevate the poor see Frances Borzello, *Civilising Caliban: The Misuse of Art, 1875–1980,* London: Routledge, Kegan and Paul, 1987.

18   Hill, *Charity Organisation Review,* 1905, p.315.

19   Borzello, *Civilising Caliban,* 1987, p.35.

20   Walter Besant, *All Sorts and Conditions of Men: An Impossible Story,* London: Chatto and Windus, 1888 (new edition), p.125.

21   Borzello, *Civilising Caliban,* 1987, p.36.

22   Besant, *All Sorts and Conditions of Men,* 1888, p.82.

23   Besant, *All Sorts and Conditions of Men,* 1888 p.54. In 1884 Besant would be one of the founder-members of Mrs Jebb's Home Arts and Industries Association. He was clearly inspired by Ruskin but also influenced by Charles Leland, the author of the *Minor Arts* (1880) in the *Art at Home* series, who was a close friend.

24   Gareth Stedman Jones, *Outcast London: A study in the relationship between classes in Victorian society*, Harmondsworth: Penguin, reprint edition 1992, p.9.

25   See Linda Dowling, *The Vulgarisation of Art: The Victorians and Aesthetic Democracy*, Charlottesville and London: University Press of Virginia, 1996.

26   Peter Bailey, *Leisure and Class in Victorian England: Rational Recreation and the Context for Control*, London: Routledge and Kegan Paul, 1978, pp.56-59, quoted in H.L. Malchow, 'Public gardens and social action in late Victorian London', *Victorian Studies*, Vol. 29, No.1, Autumn 1985, p.100.

27   Octavia Hill, 'Open Spaces', *Our Common Land, and Other Short Essays*, London: Macmillan, 1877, pp.136-37.

28   H.L. Malchow, 'Public gardens and social action in late Victorian London', 1985, p.99.

29   C. Goodall, *Illustrated Royal Handbook to Roundhay Park*, 1872, as quoted in John Graham Branston, *The Development of Public Open Spaces in Leeds during the Nineteenth Century*, MA thesis, School of Economic Studies, University of Leeds, 1972, p.40, cited in Malchow, 'Public gardens and social action in late Victorian London', 1985, p.102.

30   Gillian Darley, *Octavia Hill: A Life*, London: Constable, 1990, p.174.

31   Malchow, 'Public gardens and social action in late Victorian London', 1985, p.107.

32   See Darley, *Octavia Hill*, 1990, p.179 and p.365 n.20. The Kyrle Report for 1890 gives Robert Hunter as the branch chairman and W. Derham as the hon. secretary. The committee was composed of J.R. Brooke, F.J. Dryhurst, C.W. Empson, H.A. Foreman, Miss Frankau, Lady Hobhouse, Miss Hogg, Miss Johnson, Miss E. Shaw-Lefevre, H. Marshall, C.E. Maurice, Mrs Maurice, Mrs Shirley Murphy, R.C. Poulter, C. Harrison-Townsend, Miss Vernon and Miss Yorke.

33   *The Magazine of Art*, 1880, pp.211-12.

34   Malchow, 'Public gardens and social action in late Victorian London', 1985, p.108.

35   Malchow, 'Public gardens and social action in late Victorian London', 1985, pp.108-09.

36   Malchow, 'Public gardens and social action in late Victorian London', 1985, p.109.

37   Mrs Basil Holmes, *The London Burial Grounds*, London: T.F. Unwin, 1896.

38   Holmes, *The London Burial Grounds*, p.232, quoted in Malchow, 'Public gardens and social action in late Victorian London', 1985, p.109, n.24.

39   Lord Brabazon, 'Health and physique of our city populations', in *Social Arrows*, London: Longmans, Green and Co., 1886, p.8

40   E. Moberly Bell, *Octavia Hill*, London: Constable, 1942, p.89.

41   Moberly Bell, *Octavia Hill*, 1942, p.95.

42   Moberly Bell, *Octavia Hill*, 1942, p.93.

43   Moberly Bell, *Octavia Hill*, 1942, p.94.

44   Moberly Bell, *Octavia Hill*, 1942, p.96.

45   C. Edmund Maurice (ed.), *Life of Octavia Hill as Told in Her Letters*, London: Macmillan, 1914, p.245.

46   Octavia Hill, 'Colour, Space and Music for the People', *The Nineteenth Century*, vol. 15, May 1884, p.751.

47   Moberly Bell, *Octavia Hill*, 1942, p.19.

48   Malchow, 'Public gardens and social action in late Victorian London', 1985, pp.98-99.

49   Malchow, 'Public gardens and social action in late Victorian London', 1985 p.100 n.10.

50   Ina Bidder, F.M. Cardwell and W.W. Fenn were landscape painters. Mrs Julia Keatinge, W. Savage Cooper and Thomas Ralph Spence are listed as landscape and figure painters. Fred C. Mills was a sculptor. Architects include Basil Champneys, Charles Harrison Townsend, John Dando Sedding, Arthur S. Hayes and C.F.A. Voysey. The exceptions are conspicuously associated with social work: Emily Shaw-Lefevre, Charles and Emily Maurice and Harriot Yorke. My thanks to Diana Maltz for assisting with these identifications.

51   'The Kyrle Society: decorative branch', *The Times*, 12 July 1890, p.4.

52   Octavia Hill, 'A Plea for the Kyrle Society', *The Times*, 5 February 1895. Octavia made further appeals; 'The Kyrle Society', *The Times*, 13 December 1902, p.13 and 'The Kyrle Society', *Charity Organisation Review*, V,18, July-Dec, 1905. In fact the Kyrle appealed regularly for funds in this manner. In 1885 both Octavia and Robert Hunter pressed for financial assistance: 'The Kyrle Society', *The Times*, 19 December 1885.

53   Hill, 'The Kyrle Society', 1905, p.319.

54   Hill, 'The Kyrle Society', *The Times*, 19 December 1885.

55   Darley, *Octavia Hill*, 1990, p.184.

56   Ian Fletcher, 'Some Aspects of Aestheticism' in O.M. Braek Jr (ed.) *Twilight of Dawn: Studies in English Literature in Transition*, Tuscon: University of Arizona, 1987, p.29.

57   Hill, 'The Kyrle Society', 1905, p.319.

58   George Bernard Shaw, 'Socialism for millionaires', *Contemporary Review*, vol. 69, February 1896, p.217, quoted in Owen, *English Philanthropy*, 1965, p.472.

59   Diana Maltz, 'Beauty at Home or Not? Octavia Hill and the Aesthetics of Tenement Reform' in Murray Baumgarten and H.M. Daleski (eds), *Homes and Homelessness in the Victorian Imagination*, New York: AMS Press, 1998 p.198.

60   Darley, *Octavia Hill*, 1990, p.183.

61   Maltz, 'Beauty at Home or Not?, 1998, pp.200-01.

62   Mrs Russell Barrington, 'The Red Cross Hall', *The English Illustrated Magazine*, 117, June 1893, p.611.

63   *Red Cross Hall and Garden, Southwark, Annual Report*, 1907, pp.4-5.

64   Maltz, 'Beauty at Home or Not?',1998, p.201.

65   *The Building News*, 17 June 1887, p.913.

66   'The HAIA at the Albert Hall', *The Building News*, 7 June 1899, p.790.

67   'Works of Industrial Art at the Albert Hall', *The Building News*, 5 June, 1891, p.771.

68   *Red Cross Hall Report*, 1907, p.5.

69   'At The Home Arts and Industries', *The House; its furnishing, decoration, social functions, sanitation, amateur work, cuisine and general comfort*, vol. III, 1898, p.163.

70   'At The Home Arts and Industries', 1898, p.163.

71   The Women's University Settlement in Southwark, opened in 1887, was the first settlement dependent on women volunteers. It developed from a lecture given by Henrietta Barnett at Cambridge, largely to Girton and Newnham girls, but the Oxford women's colleges were invited to join the committee of what was then known as the University Women's Association. The Settlement was initially headed by Miss Alice Gruner who, overwhelmed with work, resigned in March 1889. It was at this point that Octavia joined the committee. With Octavia's backing, her friend Margaret Sewell, who, according to Darley, was a staunch advocate of COS principles, was made head worker (a paid position from July 1889). Margaret Sewell, who worked closely with Octavia in devising a one-year course of training for 'social work', was to hold the post of head worker until she was succeeded by Helen Gladstone in 1901. See Betty Judge, *Octavia Hill and The University Women's Settlement: an Octavia Hill Lecture*, Wisbech: Octavia Hill Society, 1994, p.13.

72   Lionel Curtis, *Octavia Hill and Open Spaces*, London: Association of Women House Property Managers, 1930, p.9.

73   William Morris, 'The Housing of the Poor', *Justice*, 19 July 1884, quoted in Maltz, 'Beauty at Home or Not', 1998, p.198.

74   Martin S. Gaskell, 'Gardens for the Working Class: Victorian Practical Pleasure', *Victorian Studies*, Summer 1980, p.494, quoted in Maltz, 'Beauty at Home or Not?' 1998, p.198.

75   Darley, *Octavia Hill*, 1990, p.207.

76   Maurice, *Life of Octavia Hill*, 1914, p.295.

77   Nigel Temple, *John Nash and the Village Picturesque*, Gloucester: Alan Sutton Publishing, 1979, p.xx.

78   The Red House, Bexley Heath, designed by Philip Webb for William Morris in 1859/60, is said to have precipitated the vernacular revival, with its asymmetric roof line, high gables, tall brick chimneys and white woodwork.

79   Port Sunlight village, in the Wirral, built for Lord Lever's factory workers, is the classic model community. Begun in 1888, it was largely completed by 1914. Half-timbering, tile hanging and incised plaster-work abound. Lever insisted that every worker should have a house with a proper garden and that the social life of the community should be provided for with recreation halls, social clubs, schools and technical college. He had clearly been swayed by Besant's utopia in *All Sorts and Conditions of Men*.

80   Darley, *Octavia Hill*, 1990, pp.206-07.

81   Maltz, 'Beauty at Home or Not?', 1998, p.198.

82   Barrington, 'Red Cross Hall', 1893, p.615.

83   Anne Summers, 'A Home from Home: Women's Philanthropic Work in the Nineteenth Century', in S. Burman (ed.) *Fit Work for Women*, Croom Helm, 1979, p.45.

84   The Red Cross cottages were funded by Lady Jane Dundas. The cost of White

Cross cottages was defrayed by gifts amounting to £690—'about half the money for building them' (1889, p.261), with the remaining capital required borrowed at four per cent. Octavia reminded her supporters that this sum 'could be replaced by donations, should these be forthcoming at a future time' (1890, p.279).

85 Pigeon food crops up as a regular item of expenditure in the Red Cross accounts, offset, from time to time, by income from the sale of these no doubt plump and delicious birds.

86 *Red Cross Hall Report*, 1907, p.4.

87 *Red Cross Hall and Garden, Southwark, Annual Report*, undated c.1896, p.2, gives the cost as £4,000.

88 *Red Cross Hall and Garden, Southwark, Annual Report*, undated c.1896.

89 *Red Cross Hall Report*, 1907, p.4.

90 Maltz, 'Beauty at Home or Not?', 1998, p.200.

91 Ruskin, 'The Lamp of Memory', *The Seven Lamps of Architecture*, 1894, p.332. I would like to thank Joseph McBrinn for drawing this passage to my attention.

92 *Red Cross Hall Report*, 1907, p.6.

93 Moberly Bell, *Octavia Hill*, 1942, p.92.

94 Moberly Bell, *Octavia Hill*, 1942, p.93.

95 Malchow, 'Public gardens and social action in late Victorian London', 1985, p.116

96 Maltz, 'Beauty at Home or Not?', 1998, p.200. See Malchow 'Public gardens and social action in late Victorian London', 1985, p.122.

97 In 'The Future of Our Commons' (*Our Common Land*, 1877, pp.175-206) Octavia makes an overt appeal for public gardens that would be merely ornamental, but she did defend the need for practical outdoor spaces as well.

98 G.F. Watts, 'Another Jubilee Suggestion', *The Times*, 5 September 1887, p.146.

99 Mrs Russell Barrington, 'A suggestion for the Kyrle Society', *The Spectator*, 24 September 1887, p.1280.

100 Barrington, 'A suggestion for the Kyrle Society', 1887, p.1280.

101 Barrington, 'The Red Cross Hall', 1893, p.614. In 1890 Crane was on both the general committee and the decorative branch sub-committee of the Kyrle Society.

102 A letter published in *The Times* on 30 March 1888 put the scheme to the public, who 'responded to it with much practical sympathy'.

103 Greg Smith, 'Developing a Public Language of Art' in Greg Smith and Sarah Hyde (eds) *Walter Crane: Artist, Designer, Socialist*, London: Lund Humphries and the Whitworth Art Gallery, Manchester, 1989, p.23. See Walter Crane, *Ideals in Art*, London: G. Bell & Sons, 1905, p.117.

104 Crane quoted by H.M. Hyndman, *Further Reminiscences*, London: Macmillan

and Co., 1925, p.358, cited in Morna O'Neill, 'Everyday Heroic Deeds: Walter Crane and Octavia Hill at the Red Cross Hall', *The Acorn*, 2003, p.7.

105 O'Neill, 'Everyday heroic deeds', 2003, p.13.

106 Walter Crane, 'The English Revival of Decorative Art', *Fortnightly Review,* vol. 58, 1892, p.823.

107 O'Neill, 'Everyday heroic deeds', 2003, p.11.

108 According to all the sources, including Crane's own *Reminiscences*, the 'Rescue from a Well' was the last panel to be completed, but there is an intriguing entry in the Kyrle Society's Annual Report for 1911: 'Congregational Schools, Victoria Dock Road, Canning Town: By permission of the Trustees of the Red Cross Hall, Southwark, and Mr Walter Crane, one of that artist's designs for the frescoes in the Southwark Hall was enlarged for this Institution. The subject was the rescue of a disabled sailor lying on the sea-washed rocks by a young lad lowered over the cliff in a basket, and is one of the incidents of "Heroism in Modern Life" which are recorded in the Southwark Hall.' This design, highly appropriate for Victoria Dock Road, was illustrated in the *Pall Mall Budget* in 1890, entitled 'Rescued from the sailor's watery grave'. See 'Deeds of Daring: Mr Walter Crane's "Heroic Deeds" at the Red Cross Hall', *Pall Mall Budget*, 9 October 1890, pp.1304-05.

109 O'Neill, 'Everyday heroic deeds', 2003, p.18.

110 Crane, *Ideals in Art*, 1905, p.117.

111 Walter Crane, *An Artists's Reminiscences*, London: Methuen, 1907, p.359.

112 Barrington, 'The Red Cross Hall', p.616.

113 Barrington, 'The Red Cross Hall', p.616.

114 Mrs Russell Barrington, *Leighton and John Kyrle, 'The Man of Ross'*, Edinburgh, p.45.

115 Such notions persisted. St Matthew's, Pell Street, Shadwell was painted by Audley Mackworth with three pictures illustrating heroism in modern life: 'One represents the rescue of a child from a burning house, and the other two incidents of life-saving at sea.' *Kyrle Society Annual Report*, 1905, p.10.

APPENDIX 3

Octavia Hill and the Ecclesiastical Commissioners

IAN GINSBERG[1]

One of Octavia Hill's most important collaborations among her many housing projects was with the Ecclesiastical Commissioners for England, who administered a proportion of the property of the established church. Her association with the Ecclesiastical Commissioners appears to have begun in Southwark in 1884, where she was employed, via their agents, Cluttons, to collect rents in a number of old properties in the borough. Her employment in this capacity represented one facet of the attempt by the Ecclesiastical Commissioners to deal with their increasingly problematic ownership of large areas of 'slum' property in London.

With this association began an expansion of her work beyond all previously recognisable proportions. While most of her work was undertaken in properties rented or purchased piecemeal by friends or supporters, the Ecclesiastical Commissioners represented the only large-scale landowner for whom she worked. While no accurate counts have been made, the Ecclesiastical Commissioners' land, either rented, sold or managed, easily accounted for the major part of all the housing under Octavia's control.[2]

The relationship between the two was not merely important for Octavia's work, however. Almost single-handedly Octavia brought about a massive change in the Commissioners' housing policy, shaping both the principles and practices of housing on church lands, the traces of which can still be seen in Church Commissioners' properties today.

The Ecclesiastical Commissioners

The Ecclesiastical Commissioners were established by Act of Parliament in 1836 to take over responsibility for various aspects of church affairs from Parliament.[3] Initially this included the organisation of diocesan territories, the administration of episcopal revenues and the redistribution of church funds. Following later Ecclesiastical Commissioners Acts,[4] the Commissioners also became involved in the management of church property, and this would eventually form a major part of their work. Between 1840 and 1890, most of the endowment estates of bishoprics, deans, chapters and collegiate churches were gradually vested in the Ecclesiastical Commissioners, as the beneficiaries to the various estates died. It was ownership of these properties, in particular the Archbishopric of Canterbury Estates[5] and the Bishopric of Winchester Estate[6] that were to be the cause of their encounter with Octavia.

Southwark and the church's housing problem

In December 1883 the Commissioners decided to set up a select committee to investigate what action to take with regard to:

'the condition of certain house property of very inferior and dilapidated character situate in Southwark, the leases of which have of late years, more especially in 1881, fallen in, so that the Commissioners have become the landlords in possession of tenements let at weekly rents to occupiers in circumstances of great poverty...'[7]

The Commissioners' Southwark property, comprising two parishes, St. Saviour's and St. Peter's, had been transferred to the Ecclesiastical Commissioners in 1869. Originally an episcopal residence, it had been leased out by the Bishops of Winchester through a system of leases and subleases redeemed against lives. Most of the leases on church land appeared to operate this way. Rather than issuing leases for periods of years, properties were leased for the lifetime of either the lessee or lessor. This system was highly complex, but its central implication was that, until the leases 'fell in', the Commissioners bore little responsibility for the direct management of their estates. The leasing and subleasing was abolished as a result of various Ecclesiastical Commissioners Acts, but the beneficial leases persisted until they fell in between 1861 and

1883. A small number of leases began falling in by 1881 and a considerable number in 1883, so that by 1883 the Commissioners found themselves confronted by the problems of administrating estates across London, a significant portion of which contained very low-grade housing.[8]

The broader context of the committee's establishment was the public furore that had attended the publication of a number of pamphlets and articles, most notably *The Bitter Cry of Outcast London*[9] and *Horrible London*.[10] These exposed the decrepitude of London's slum estates. Without implicating the Commissioners directly, the *Bitter Cry* presented detailed and incendiary accounts of lives of the deserving poor, living in 'pestilential human rookeries', and its author called upon the church to act against 'the terrible flood of sin and misery gaining upon us'. The reports prompted a number of concerned citizens to set up committees to confirm the veracity of the claims, and, if necessary, to push for action. The most significant of these were the Brompton Committee, whose findings were published in *The Times* on 3 and 16 January 1884, and the Homes of the Southwark Poor Committee, established in 1883, who sent a deputation to the Select Committee to intervene on behalf of residents.[11] The significance of these two committees was that both explicitly mentioned the Commissioners as landlords in those areas, associating in the public mind the Ecclesiastical Commissioners as landlords with the poverty over which they governed.[12]

It would be inaccurate to suggest that the Ecclesiastical Commissioners' new-found concern regarding the state of their properties was a direct response to the opprobrious reports of the condition of housing on church land. Certainly the establishment of the select committee could not have been a direct response to the reports of the Brompton or Southwark committees, as initially claimed, for the select committee was brought into being *prior* to the publication of both reports. The report of the select committee instead implied heavily that the Ecclesiastical Commissioners had not sought to deal with the housing problem seriously before 1883 on account of the lease and sublease system, which meant they were unable to exercise any control over their property before then.[13] While this may be true, the Ecclesiastical Commissioners were, however, generally aware of adverse press coverage before establishing a committee to deal with Southwark housing. On 20 July 1883 the Metropolitan Board of Works issued a very public circular to the vestries demanding reports of action being taken under the Artisans' Dwellings Acts,[14] and a letter from Cluttons on 12 December 1883, discussing Red Cross Street and the cottages that had recently come into its possession, is written 'with reference to recent statements made in public'.[15] While it would not be accurate to suggest, therefore, that the Commissioners' intervention in the question of slum housing was simply a nineteenth-century public relations exercise, it is clear that in formulating their response, they were well aware of public opinion, and this may have played some role in moving the committee towards the decision it finally took.

The Ecclesiastical Commissioners' response to the housing situation and the commencement of Octavia's work in Southwark

The committee finally reported in 1884, reaching the conclusion that the best solution to the problems presented to them by ownership of the land would be to lease a large portion of it for the development of labourers' dwellings. While the select committee had been convening, the Commissioners had received a number of offers from benevolent housing societies to erect dwellings for labourers.[16] Having dismissed the possibility of building themselves, the Commissioners finally accepted an application from a syndicate founded to provide improved dwellings on Red Cross Street, between Falcon Court and Adams Place, on 7 February 1884.[17] These eventually became Stanhope and Mowbray buildings, constructed by the Victoria Dwellings Association and the Metropolitan Industrial Dwellings Company, in which Octavia would later collect. They housed 431 families.

In March 1884 Octavia was also invited by the Commissioners to begin collecting rents in some old properties in Southwark.[18] Few people seem to know how Octavia came to the Commissioners' attention. Her biographer, Gillian Darley, can only speculate that it may have been 'someone in her organisation'[19] who contacted the commissioners, and the Commissioners' historian, G.F.A. Best, was similarly unable to trace the connection.[20] However, an intriguing letter discovered in the correspondence of the Archbishop of Canterbury, Archbishop Benson, sheds new light on this. Lucy Tait (the daughter of Archbishop Campbell Tait, the previous Archbishop of Canterbury, who had confirmed Octavia in 1857) wrote to Archbishop Benson on 4 March 1884 introducing Octavia's work and suggesting Octavia be considered for the Commissioners' property.[21]

It is likely then, that Archbishop Benson, via Lucy Tait, was the link between Octavia and the Commissioners. The first mention of her work is in a letter from Cluttons to the Commissioners' secretary Sir George Pringle on 20 March 1884 confirming Octavia's appointment.[22] The conditions of the collection are clear from the letter. Octavia would take a commission of five per cent of the gross rents and spend no more than one-sixth of the gross rents on repairs:

'We beg to report that in compliance with the instructions of the EC, we have seen Miss Octavia Hill and have, subject to the Commissioners' approval, made the following arrangement with her, *viz* Miss Hill is to collect the weekly rents of property comprised in Blocks A and B[23] on the plan attached to the Report of the Special Committee (except that let to M. Pink) being allowed five per cent commission on the gross rents. Miss Hill is to be at liberty to expend in repairs a sum not exceeding one-sixth of the gross rents. In the event of a larger sum being required it is to be the subject of a special report to the CS. Miss Hill is to pay over the money to us from time to time and render an account every half year to enable us to include the amount in our rental account, but for which we are to make no charge.'

It is important to note that the nature of the Commissioners' response represented less a policy commitment to the housing of the poor than an expedient solution to a particular historical problem. The Commissioners' primary commitment as land owners remained to provide a return for the benefit of parishes:

'Your Committee are not forgetful of the fact that, the Commissioners being a body of trustees, and the objects of their trust being specifically defined, they would not be justified in giving up their property for the promotion of other objects, however good those objects may be. The value of the land in question cannot be put entirely out of sight.'[24]

It was on account of the 'very special circumstances' operating in Southwark that the committee felt the Commissioners 'would be justified in not requiring the full market price for the land, if they can thus facilitate the provision of substantial and healthy dwellings for the present tenants'. Their relationship with Octavia in this respect appears to have also been seen as something of an interim arrangement, whereby Octavia would begin collecting in those properties on the estate for which demolition was not imminent. Presumably, therefore, as the old cottages were demolished, so Octavia's work would diminish. This is alluded to in a letter from Octavia addressed to the Secretary of the Ecclesiastical Commissioners:

'The portion of the property handed over to our charge appears to be that most directly doomed to destruction, either by rebuilding by others, or by railways, or owing to its condition or situation.'[25]

Southwark and the expansion of housing work

It is fairly evident that, at least initially, the Commissioners considered their duty regarding housing provision largely discharged with the building of Stanhope and Mowbray Buildings. The report of 1884 states that, having built new dwellings for a greater number of tenants than those dispossessed, the Commissioners had 'no objection to letting for commercial or any other suitable purposes the sites of any premises which it may be thought undesirable to retain as house property'. There were also a number of instances in which later requests for the Commissioners to build more model dwellings were turned down on the basis of the fact that the Commissioners had already accommodated sufficient numbers in Mowbray and Stanhope Buildings.[26]

In spite of this, Octavia's work for the Commissioners developed. In November 1884 Octavia applied to collect rents in more houses in Southwark and was duly granted them by the Commissioners.[27] Moreover, the Commissioners found themselves developing their housing policy in ways explicitly discounted in the original 1884 report. It might appear to be slipping dangerously towards hagiography, but the evidence does appear to suggest that this had much to do with the influence of Octavia herself. She wrote to the Commissioners to complain that they were only giving her the worst properties, due for demolition, in which she had no opportunity to build up the sort of relationship with tenants on which the success of her work depended:[28]

'What is feasible is, first, to give over to our care some of the weekly tenements which are in a more solid state of repair, and which may therefore stand longer as cottages; and to give us these in addition to what we have. So you would extend our work. So you would give us the interest of more permanent work... Second you might give me, or some of my friends, a lease of some of your houses. As you (as Commissioners) do not see your way to keep them under your own direct control, you might lease them to us, though leases are hateful things.'[29]

As suggested by this letter, her ambitions for Southwark were much greater than those of the Commissioners or Cluttons. In November 1886 Octavia met the Commissioners to discuss the Southwark properties. Her meeting had a number of results, but represented a major victory in one particular respect: the Commissioners allowed her to collect on a more permanent basis among the old cottages, proceeding in increments to improve the area. Octavia reports this modestly in her letter of 1886:

'They [the Commissioners] were very kind about seeing me, and we had a long talk, with the result that, I believe, they will, by preference, leave cottages standing, instead of clearing them away, so long as they are not interfering with plans for new streets or rebuilding.'[30]

This encounter was recalled somewhat more colourfully by Bishop Temple in a speech to the Charity Organisation Society some years later:

'When she had talked to us for half an hour we were quite refuted. I never had such a beating in my life! Consequently I feel great respect for her. So fully did she convince us, that we not only did what she asked us to do on that estate, but proceeded to carry out similar plans on other estates.'[31]

Octavia's powers of persuasion over the Commissioners are further emphasised by the abrupt rebuttals received by most other philanthropic societies. At least three other groups[32] received stony replies when they wrote requesting the Commissioners do something to address the condition of labourers' dwellings on their land. The erection of both Stanhope and Mowbray Dwellings was beset too by quibbles over the purchase price.[33] Contrast this with the grovelling response of the Estates Committee, recorded in the minutes of their meeting with Octavia:

'Miss Hill was assured by the Commissioners of their anxiety to co-operate with her in ameliorating the condition of their poor tenants and to avoid all needless interference with her existing management of the property in question and also that the C's best consideration would be given to the possibility of meeting her wishes as now expressed to them.'[34]

Southwark: gardens, leasing, building

The work in Southwark represents, in embryonic form, the concrete ways in which the Commissioners' approach to the whole question of housing and their relationship with Octavia was gradually transformed from a short-term marriage of convenience to a healthy, almost symbiotic relationship following their meeting in 1886. This manifested itself in three important respects. The first was their concession to the establishment of a garden, of dead, uncommercial space, that was to become Red Cross garden, a centrepiece of her work. It was decided that Henry's Place, originally one of Octavia's blocks, would be a suitable site for the creation of the garden. Between November 1886 and March 1888 Octavia negotiated a lease for a piece of ground 124 x 120 feet with the Commissioners, taking personal responsibility for nominating the trustees and drafting the lease[35] under the aegis of the Kyrle Society.[36]

The Red Cross site also saw the first houses built upon land leased from the Commissioners by Octavia's friends for dwellings designed in accordance with her principles.[37] In June 1887 the Ecclesiastical Commissioners provided the land for the six Red Cross cottages and their adjacent Hall, where two properties of which the leases had fallen in in 1881 had formerly stood. They looked out onto the garden. On 2 December 1889 the Commissioners agreed to lease more land for the six White Cross cottages, backing onto Red Cross cottages. The Commissioners continued to lease ground for extended periods to Octavia's friends, including Miss Townsend in 1897 (1897, p.400) and Lady Selborne in 1898 (1898, pp.414-15).

The third main departure for the Commissioners from their original course was to begin building their own housing. They had explicitly ruled this out in 1884, but in June 1893 the Ecclesiastical Commissioners authorised the expenditure of £2,500 for the erection of cottages in Orange Street (now Copperfield Street) and Pepper Street (now Risborough Street). These became 1-9 Winchester cottages. Five more cottages were added in May 1894. These tiny 'two-up, two-down' cottages can still be seen on Copperfield Street in Southwark (*see ill. 15*).

They are no longer in possession of the Commissioners, however, and one property was valued in 2003 at £360,000 on the open market—suggesting that they are no longer occupied by the working poor either. Octavia appears to suggest in the 1893 letter that it was she who also influenced the decision to build:

'Encouraged by the satisfactory result of Red and White Cross cottages and Gable cottages, I suggested to the Ecclesiastical Commissioners that they should themselves build similar cottages on their own ground in Southwark. They met my suggestion most cordially, and, after careful thought, decided to build nine new cottages.' (1893, p.336.)

What redevelopment and rebuilding in Southwark there was seems to have been carried out on an *ad hoc* basis by the Commissioners, either by the leasing or sale of particular blocks, and later by the erection of property themselves. While no exact details have been found in the archive, it appears that, after 1884, property in the possession of the Ecclesiastical Commissioners was put into Octavia's charge without any specific authorisation, perhaps as and when leases fell in.[38] It also appears to be the case that any property built by the Commissioners was put directly into Octavia's hands.[39] Octavia's management of old properties grew simultaneously, its expansion only ever checked by occasional demolitions or compulsory purchase orders. In February 1904 a request was put before the Commissioners to increase expenditure on repairs from one-sixth gross rent to one-fifth. At the same time, Octavia was also given official sanction for those areas in which she was collecting. In Southwark this comprised: Argent Street, Loman Street, Orange Street, Golden Place, Great Suffolk Street, Pepper Street, Suffolk Grove, Victoria Place and Whitecross Street, Union Street tenements and Winchester cottages. It is difficult to estimate accurately the extent of Octavia's work in Southwark, perhaps more so than in other areas, but on the basis of references in the letters, from 1884 to 1912, Octavia collected in over 50 old Ecclesiastical Commissioners house and cottage properties, in around 50 cottages leased to friends, in 24 three-roomed tenements built by the Countess of Selborne, five cottages built by Miss Townsend, the 44 tenements and 14 cottages built by the Commissioners, and the model dwellings, Mowbray and Stanhope Buildings, that housed 431 families. The expansion in Southwark remained *ad hoc*, occurring as and when leases fell in or new buildings were erected, but even before Octavia began working elsewhere in London, Southwark had already become the model for Octavia's future relationship with the Commissioners.

Westminster

Just as Octavia's work in Southwark had begun settling into a promising pattern, she was called into action elsewhere, on their Westminster Chapter Estate. On 10 November 1893 the Commissioners were summoned to a court hearing by Westminster police, at which 26-36 (even) Garden Street were declared unfit for human habitation.[40] Over the course of 1894 London County Council served notices on properties across the Westminster Estate, threatening action with varying degrees of severity. The properties in Garden Street were later deemed unsafe under the Metropolitan Building Acts (1855 and 1869) and the Local Government Act, 1888, and threatened with demolition. Closing orders were issued on other properties[41] and further court action was threatened on properties across the estate if the Commissioners failed to make them sanitary.

Nor did the condition of the properties escape public gaze. An open letter to the Archbishop of Canterbury in the *Daily Chronicle* alleged that: 'No improvements seem to have been made on your initiative except when you benefit yourselves pecuniarily…'.[42] The Archbishop of Canterbury replied in the same organ that, of the land in question, the Commissioners owned only a small portion, but the sort of disingenuousness initially displayed in response to the Southwark problems belied a more rapid and effective reaction in Westminster.

The Commissioners had nineteen cottages built in Garden Street in 1894, at a cost of £6,150, immediately turning them over to Octavia's care. Another 19 were built a year later on the opposite side of the road. After the initial flurry of activity that appears to have been forced by the threats of the LCC, the Commissioners' work in Westminster followed a similar path to that in Southwark; *ad hoc*, geographically disjointed, cottages were erected as and when there was demand, in twos or threes, with occasional bursts of larger scale building. All of this property appears to have been turned over to Octavia almost as soon as it was completed, illustrating the increasing trust placed in her management by the Commissioners. Between 1898 and 1900 the Commissioners set about building what was perhaps their largest investment in new housing for the working classes to date—12 tenement houses (four with shops) on Regency Street, Vincent Place and Hide Place, at a cost of £19,341. The Commissioners built two more cottages in 1902 and then had a larger number of properties built between 1905 and 1907. During this time, older properties were also being placed in Octavia's hands. She mentions the transfer of old cottages in Westminster every year between 1901 and 1905. An undated list of workmen's dwellings in the Commissioners archive gives some idea of the extent of the work by the time of Octavia's death in 1912: between 1895 and 1907 in Westminster they had built 213 separate holdings, and controlled 127 old holdings.

The development of the Westminster Estate throws up some interesting features of both Octavia's and the Commissioners' approach to housing the working poor. The first, and most obvious aspect, is that Westminster, like Southwark, still did not represent a coherent or proactive attempt to deal with housing conditions on church lands. It enjoyed neither coherence of geography nor planning, and many of the Commissioners' decisions to build, or, more accurately, not to build, appear to have been dictated by whether tenants displaced by demolitions had been accommodated or not.[43] Moreover, it is clear from the archives that the Commissioners remained aware of the commercial aspect of landowning in London throughout their association with Octavia. This is hinted at briefly in Octavia's letter of 1903, 'a few of the old [cottages in Westminster] are likely to be sold and pass from us, being rebuilt for other purposes than letting to the poor' (1903, p.503). The intention of the Commissioners to demolish buildings immediately south of Westminster Abbey in 1903 to sell to 'speculators and business for the erection of commercial offices'[44] attracted the ire of the residents and press and was even raised in Parliament. The Society of Antiquaries got up a petition against the redevelopment, which they chose to have presented to the Commissioners through the National Trust, whose secretary, Edward Bond, added a covering letter stating that: 'the National Trust is in sympathy with the views expressed in the petition and would respectfully urge upon the Commissioners the extreme desirability of ensuring the preservation of these streets'. Significantly, as Octavia was one of the founders of the National Trust, she did not sign the petition herself, as she may have felt there was a conflict of interests, but it carried the names of many of the great and the good of the Victorian cultural establishment, including the director of the British Museum and Sir Edward Poynter, President of the Royal Academy and Director of the National Gallery. It also carried the names of the local clergy and residents of the affected streets—Barton Street, Great College Street and Cowley Street.[45] Interestingly, we find Mary Benson, 'widow of Archbishop Benson', living with Lucy Tait ('daughter of Archbishop Tait') in Barton Street.[46] Although there had been earlier campaigns by bodies such as the Society of Antiquaries and the Society for the Protection of Ancient Buildings to save individual buildings of architectural merit, this appears to be the first campaign to preserve an urban environment that could not lay claim to any particularly magnificent structure. It was at least partially successful, because although, as the petitioners admitted, Great College Street had already been substantially rebuilt, 'Cowley Street and Barton Street still retain almost entirely their ancient early Georgian character'. They still do, with exceptions such as the official residence built for the bishop of London in the corner formed by the two streets.

This tension between social goals and the need to show a return on investments remained a source of friction between the Commissioners and external agencies. Letters from the 1930s show the Commissioners rebuffing the Westminster Housing Association on precisely this basis:

> '...the Commissioners cannot undertake to refrain from developing for commercial purposes property, which is plainly suitable for this purpose and which is of such value that it cannot economically be developed for housing purposes...'[47]

Westminster also witnessed hints of the subtle expansion Octavia's influence among the Commissioners. In Southwark she had influenced the Commissioners as much by example and encouragement as by anything else—Red Cross and White Cross cottages were a model of viable low-cost property building that preceded the Commissioners' own building. In Westminster they deferred to her as a matter of course on questions of management,[48] but increasingly they sought her advice on other matters. As they began planning larger projects in Westminster they consulted Octavia on the design and layout of new cottages too (1905, p.539). This increasing involvement in all aspects of church housing is seen more clearly, however, in the larger developments in Lambeth and Walworth.

Lambeth

The story in Lambeth was very similar to Southwark and Westminster. A large number of leases fell in on an area of around seven acres in 1901, leaving the Commissioners in direct possession of a massive slum district. As in Southwark and Westminster, the Commissioners were well aware of the state of the Lambeth property. As early as 1882 the Metropolitan Board of Works had begun compulsory purchase proceedings under the Artisans' and Labourers' Dwellings Acts on Ecclesiastical Commissioners' properties in Lambeth. By 1901, however, the Commissioners were ready to respond. They had plans ready for rebuilding, and had a management system in place for the interim. It appears from Octavia's letters that even she was taken by surprise at the confidence with which the Commissioners stepped into action, and thrust their properties into her hands:

'I knew that they [the EC] proposed rebuilding… on some seven acres there, and would consult me about this. But I had no idea that they meant to ask me to take charge of the old cottages pending the rebuilding.'[49]

The land in Lambeth comprised about seven acres, but it appears that only two-and-a-half-acres were fully developed, on what became known as the New Cut. The leases fell in at Michaelmas 1901, but plans were being made for rebuilding as early as February.[50] These plans were more ambitious than anything considered before. It was not just that the Commissioners planned to build on a far larger scale (they anticipated 36 tenements and 24 new cottages), but also that they sought to take into account tenants' lives beyond simply housing. Geography was incorporated into the scheme—the Commissioners proposed replacing two narrow streets with one broader road, to be built at their expense—and the plans made space for a public library, two mission houses and a recreation ground (a sure sign of Octavia's and the Commissioners' priorities coming into line). Two pubs on the site were suppressed. The proposed cost was £71,000, three times higher than any previous project. Between 1901 and 1904 it appears that 36 tenement blocks and 29 cottages were built, covering an area of 90,000 sq ft, averaging a gross rent of £4,000 per annum, and accommodating 256 families.

The dwellings were more spacious than old style 'model dwellings', cottages had two storeys and yards, tenements were built no higher than three floors, 'the greatest care having been taken to obtain the maximum amount of sunlight and the freest circulation of air having regard to the surroundings'.[51] Cottages were well spaced with their own gardens. The whole development received substantial press notice from its inception, and, refreshingly for the Commissioners, this was largely positive. Contemporary reports all highlight the transformation that the New Cut underwent. What was once a 'byword for filth and congestion'[52] had become a 'Garden City'.[53] The estate was completed in 1904, and the garden was transferred to Lambeth Borough Council a little later, but its impact was eclipsed somewhat by the massive redevelopment that was just beginning in Walworth. Nonetheless, it is clear that Lambeth represented a very public achievement, as Octavia's letter to the secretary of the Ecclesiastical Commissioners suggests:

'It is a really wonderful sight to contrast the area near the New Cut now, with what it was when the leases fell in, the wide streets, the clean airy rooms, the nice yards, the public garden that is to be.'[54]

Walworth

The scheme at Walworth was the last and largest collaboration between Octavia and the Commissioners. At Michaelmas 1903 a lease granted by the dean and chapter of Canterbury in 1804 expired. It covered 22 acres. Initially the Commissioners turned the management over to Octavia and put around 800 families in her hands, but the condition of the properties meant that, if the land were to be retained for housing, some building would be imperative. Whereas the Commissioners had only ever developed parts of the other estates, they decided that in Walworth, for a variety of reasons, they would rebuild the 'greater part' of the estate themselves, filling it with cottages, cottage flats and three-storeyed tenement houses. This was a massive undertaking and dwarfed all that had gone before. The estimated cost was £200,000: all of the building in Southwark, Westminster and Lambeth put together had amounted to only £120,000. The plans involved redesigning streets, suppressing pubs, making space for meeting places and open spaces, and, of course, plotting the gradual erection of housing that responded to the needs of the displaced families.

The Walworth project is thoroughly depicted by Octavia in the letters. It would be superfluous to describe the development of the estate in depth, but one can add some detail and colour to her reports from contemporaneous accounts, and draw out some important features of the housing work exemplified by Walworth. The first point of note is Octavia's central role within the whole process. The letter of 1903 gives a very good idea of the extent to which she and the Commissioners were working in concert. Octavia appears to have become a vanguard for the Commissioners, taking stock of the area, meeting tenants, assessing houses for rents and repairs—in effect establishing the Commissioners' priorities for them. Beyond this, it is clear that Octavia was instrumental in the planning process too:

> 'The whole place was to be rebuilt, and even the streets rearranged and widened, and I had promised the Commissioners I would advise them as to future plans.'[55]

Responsibility for Walworth was not in fact Octavia's, but her friend Miss Lumsden's,[56] whose account, written in 1906, gives an insight into the planning process. Key to the entire development was that it was undertaken gradually, 'so as not to displace the old tenants until some of the new houses were ready for them'.[57] The dwellings were built over the course of about a dozen contracts between 1903 and 1908, Cluttons submitting plans to the Commissioners only after previous dwellings had been let.[58]

A range of sizes and styles of dwelling were planned to accommodate different sized families and pockets, as might be expected, but the plans went beyond merely addressing pecuniary concerns:

> '... the Commissioners have given a large allowance of light and air between the buildings, none are more than three storeys high, and all have yards at the back which serve as a drying-ground for washing, and a space for children to play in... beyond the school is St Peter's churchyard, which nearly reaches Walworth Road, so that we get ventilation almost in the middle of the estate.'[59]

Cottages were given porches with tiled roofs, and the windows dressed in Portland stone. Tenement blocks were given gauged red brick arches and red brick window aprons to distinguish them from the others. The detail of the houses' architecture reveal precisely the amount of consideration given to both the physical and, in a broad sense, spiritual well-being of the tenants:

> 'Considerable variation has been made on the exteriors of the houses so as to prevent precise uniformity in the streets, thus trying to avoid for the people a monotonous environment, which tends so much to stamp out individuality of character.'[60]

Inside the houses, staircases were provided with electric light, gas was supplied and care was taken to provide ample cupboard space.

The yards were concrete, but a strip of earth remained in each to allow tenants to make gardens, and every effort was made in the laying out to preserve any trees or shrubs that the tenants had already grown.

In addition to housing, a site was leased to another of Octavia's friends, Maude Stanley, for a club for working girls, a co-operative store was opened in 1907 and an apprenticeship committee established in 1908.[61] Space was set aside for a recreation ground, Faraday Gardens, and this was turned over to the borough council. Miss Lumsden also convinced the Commissioners to yield up some land for allotments. Overcoming their initial scepticism, the Commissioners consented and an account from 1919 reports that Sir Alfred de Bock Porter visited and sampled the potatoes and peas to everybody's general satisfaction.[62]

The life of the Walworth Estate grew under Miss Lumsden's leadership, coming to resemble, on an even larger scale, Red Cross Hall and gardens, with its flower shows,[63] sewing clubs and savings associations. In many ways the Walworth Estate had become the clearest expression of Octavia's vision: the streets were laid out with light and space; the houses offered privacy, independence, light and air, and were pleasing to the eye; management (always the key) was retained in the hands of lady collectors and a community was nurtured among the houses. From Octavia's account of the opening ceremony for the garden, one can perhaps surmise that the Walworth Estate was also considered a very public success. The report of 1919 records various bodies and individuals interested in housing and reconstruction visiting Walworth after the war. The report gave the last word to one such visitor, illustrating both the extent to which Octavia Hill and the Ecclesiastical Commissioners had become synonymous and Walworth's place as the jewel in the Commissioners' crown:

'Miss Octavia Hill has shown what can be done by a more friendly system of rent collecting by women who take an interest in the welfare of the tenants... A visit to the Walworth Estate of the Ecclesiastical Commissioners will convince anyone of the value of the system.'[64]

The end of the affair: the conclusion of Octavia's work, her legacy and the Commissioners today

On 9 March 1912 (the year of Octavia's death) she resigned her charge of the Ecclesiastical Commissioners' properties in Westminster to Ada Covington; on 22 April she recommended Miss Mitchell for Southwark; and on 17 July she proposed Joan Sunderland to take over the work in Lambeth. She received a thankful if hardly effusive response:

'The Commissioners desired me to express their regret that your long association with their working-class dwellings scheme and with the management of the properties erected in pursuance thereof should now come to be terminated and again to express their acknowledgment of the valuable aid that association has been to them in the establishment of those schemes and in their successful administration.'[65]

Following Octavia's death, the work did not cease. The Commissioners continued to employ her successors long after—there are records of such work well into the 1940s—and in many instances this work expanded. While no projects on the scale of Walworth were undertaken, the theatre of operations moved elsewhere, spreading to properties in Vauxhall, Woolwich, Stoke Newington and Paddington. In 1938 Dibdin House in Maida Vale, housing 230 families, and seven blocks on Union Street, housing 89, were opened. In 1939 the Archbishop of Canterbury opened 214 flats in Ethelm Street in Lambeth.[66]

It is worth reconsidering here precisely what legacy Octavia left the Commissioners. When first confronted with the problem of slum housing they had sought to wash their hands of it, letting land at preferential rates to companies producing 'model dwellings'. The rest of the land they were happy to sell off for commercial use. Now they had become philanthropic landlords in their own right, building themselves, and demanding no more than four to five per cent returns, happy to spurn the siren call of the open market. Their properties included cottages and tenements with no more than three storeys, with gardens and light and air. Their estates contained open spaces and commons. Most importantly, they were convinced of the need for the system of management pioneered by Octavia Hill on all of their estates. From being an inert, reluctant slum landlord, they had become proactive, efficient and careful overseers. Not that this ever entirely dealt with housing problems on their estates. In the 1930s Joan Sunderland complained to the Commissioners about the housing situation in Lambeth, but it is revealing that in asking for help, she felt bold enough to ask the Commissioners to act as pioneers in this matter, 'which is as urgent now as it was 60 years ago'.[67]

This healthy inheritance was gradually diminished, however, through a variety of circumstances. Most of the housing was inauspiciously located to survive two world wars. Increasingly stringent building regulations meant that the Commissioners' properties would have to be substantially improved, flats and tenements made self-contained, plumbing and heating modernised. In fact the Commissioners dealt with these two circumstances fairly well, taking advantage of post-war reconstruction to improve large swathes of their properties at the same time. Nonetheless, other circumstances outside their control conspired to diminish the work. Much of the property south of the river was lost to public building projects: the extension of County Hall on York Road, the rebuilding of Waterloo Bridge, the Festival of Britain and the expansion of St Thomas' Hospital all swallowed up housing in Southwark and Lambeth. For a period of several decades in the early part of the twentieth century, vast swathes of the Commissioners' property were under threat of compulsory purchase for these and other schemes, such as a new bridge over the Thames at Charing Cross (which never happened), making it more difficult to plan sensibly for the maintenance and development of the estates.[68] Nor should the impact of the gradual passing of Octavia's lieutenants be underestimated. Ada Covington died in 1921, Mary Lumsden in 1931, Joan Sunderland was killed along with her sister Ruth, then a manager in Lambeth, in a bombing raid in 1940. Not only did this affect the collective memory of Octavia's workers—the 'message' of Octavia becoming weaker—but these were powerful personalities in their own right, whose deaths were publicly noted and lamented in the communities in which they had worked.

The Commissioners were also affected by broader cultural shifts over the course of the twentieth century. The growth in municipal housing[69]—against which Octavia had railed in her own lifetime—the increasing unfashionability of the notion of the collector matriarch, and, on some level, the gradual improvement in the condition of working-class housing, all chipped away at the Commissioners' system. A number of properties were sold to housing associations and other bodies over the years.

Nor did they ever totally escape controversies associated with their ownership of working-class properties. In 1920 the Lambeth Labour Party raised again the allegation from the 1880s in a letter to *The Times*:

'The Ecclesiastical Commissioners... are the largest individual owners of ground property in Lambeth, on which stands some of the filthiest property to be found in the British Isles.'[70]

This provoked, first, an alarmed letter from the Commissioners to Miss Lumsden checking the veracity of the claims, and then an angry reaction challenging the author to provide evidence of the allegations.[71] Similar controversies were generated throughout the 1930s with the publication of pamphlets, petitions and reports of varying accuracy that implicated the Commissioners in some of the worst practices of landlords of the urban poor.

As the extent of the Commissioners' rented property-holdings diminished, the protests became less frequent and less noisy, if never quite disappearing. The latest controversy to face the Commissioners, now the Church Commissioners, results from their proposal in 2000 to raise rents on some of their properties to market levels as existing tenants move out. The remainder of the properties are to be let to public and community employees at affordable rents. This provoked a protest by residents, outcry in local and national media and angry questions in the House of Commons. The Commissioners were accused of abandoning their century-old commitment to providing housing for the working poor 'in the Octavia Hill tradition'.[72] The response of the Commissioners was that their role was never primarily to provide low-cost housing but to provide a return on their assets to augment the income of the church. This argument has a familiar ring to it, having been made in 1884 (see p.739). However, to debate as to whether the Church Commissioners or their critics are being true to the spirit of Octavia Hill is now beside the point. The landscape of social housing has been so radically altered that Octavia would have difficulty in getting her bearings, if she were to return today. Perhaps the more fundamental issue is whether Octavia's vision, of private landlords providing good quality affordable housing and still earning a return, can be realised in contemporary Britain. Many other philanthropic and commercial bodies have already withdrawn from low-cost housing. It is perhaps a tribute to the power of Octavia's legacy that the church remains active in the field.

Notes

1   Thanks are due to Gavin Tucker for his extensive research into the history of the Ecclesiastical Commissioners' estates in Westminster and Lambeth, which has been incorporated into this essay.

2   By the time of her death, the Commissioners had built 1,266 properties (3,852 rooms), all of which were under her control. This figure does not include the old properties in which she also worked nor the properties leased or sold to third parties.

3   The Ecclesiastical Commissioners merged with the Governors of Queen Anne's Bounty in 1948 and became the Church Commissioners. They were and remain subject to parliamentary scrutiny, and the Second Estates Commissioner is traditionally an MP of the governing party, who answers questions addressed to the Church Commissioners in the House of Commons.

4   Ecclesiastical Commissioners Act, 1840 (3&4 Vict. Ch.113).

5   The Lambeth properties, transferred to the Commissioners, 6 September 1862.

6   The Southwark properties, transferred to the Commissioners, 11 November 1869.

7   Minute of Board of Ecclesiastical Commissioners, 13 December 1883, EC file 65065.

8   Report of Select Committee for Southwark House Property, 13 March 1884, EC file ECE/SEC/EST/MAN/1.

9   *The Bitter Cry of Outcast London: An Inquiry into the Condition of the Abject Poor*, pamphlet, 1883. Published anonymously, the pamphlet appears to have been written by Rev. Andrew Mearns, a Congregational minister. Some scholars believe it was written by William Preston, another Congregational minister, on the basis of information supplied by Mearns. (Himmelfarb, 1991, p.59.)

10   This is mentioned in the Brompton Report, 30 January 1884, but is recorded as being printed in 1889.

11   See the letter from John Berry to the EC, 21 December 1883, EC file 65065.

12   However, particularly in the case of the Brompton report, the attribution of particular streets to the Commissioners was factually incorrect. Only Red Cross Street, among the streets mentioned as belonging to the Commissioners, did actually belong to them.

13   This, they argued, meant they were not responsible for the condition of London slum properties, and criticism was therefore unfair. One might argue that a moral rather than a legal responsibility might have driven them to act sooner, but this is fairly academic. Best makes the point, however, that before the properties were transferred to the Commissioners, who shouldered most blame, they still belonged to the church's bishops, deans and canons. See G.F.A. Best, *Temporal Pillars*, Cambridge: Cambridge University Press, 1964, pp.480-81.

14   Circular of Secretary of State to District Board of Works to Vestries of Metropolis, 20 July 1883, EC file 65065.

15   Cluttons to the EC, 12 December 1883, EC file 65065.

16   EC file 65065, *passim.*

17   Minute of Board of Ecclesiastical Commissioners, 7 February1884, EC file 65065.

18   See 1884/5, p.187.

19   Gillian Darley, *Octavia Hill: A Life*, London: Constable, 1990, p.261.

20   'Just how she came into contact with them, whether Ralph Clutton and the archbishop were speaking the literal truth when they said she had "volunteered her services as collector" [Clutton's evidence to the Working Classes Housing Commission, 25 April, Q.6453, and Archbishop Benson in the Lords, 24 March 1884, Hansard, 3/ CCLXXXVI, 558], and who it was (there must have been someone) who ascertained for her that her offer would be well received, the evidence does not suffice to show.' Best, *Temporal Pillars*, 1964, pp.490-91.

21   Papers of Archbishop Benson, vol. 16, folios 124-27, Lambeth Palace Library Archive. Curiously, the letter from Lucy Tait was written on Lambeth Palace stationery, but addressed from 14 Nottingham Place, Octavia's house. This has, to my knowledge, never been published, so here it is in full:

14 Nottingham Place, W.

March 4 1884

My Dear Lord,

I am writing to you for Miss Octavia Hill, as I think that you may kindly be able to bring before the EC a subject in which she is interested.

I believe that the Commissioners own some old houses in the South of London. If this is the case, I think that they might be glad to know of an arrangement that Miss Octavia Hill is just making with a gentleman who owns houses in Deptford, and also that, if they wished it, she would gladly do the same for them. She is practically undertaking to act as Agent for this gentleman. She takes full charge of the collection of rents and of the repairs in his houses, and is paid by him five per cent on all sums collected.

She renders to him, either quarterly or half-yearly—as he wishes—a full account, with vouchers of all that has been received from or spent on the property. He gives her a fixed allowance for repairs, the expenditure of which is left entirely in her hands. This is necessary as she finds it very helpful to be able to spend it on different houses in proportion as the tenants are willing to co-operate with her by taking care of any improvements that are made. She renders, however, to the landlord a full account, with vouchers, of the way in which the money has been spent.

I believe that if the EC own house property inhabited by the very poor, they would find it a very great help to place it in this way in Miss Octavia Hill's hands, even if the houses are not likely to be left standing more than a few years.

You will readily see the difference, in the effect on the people, of this work when it is undertaken as a means of educating them and giving them a training, as it were, preparatory to the time when it may perhaps be necessary to rebuild, and of such work simply undertaken as a profession.

Miss Octavia Hill thinks it better to charge five per cent on the rent collected, tho' the work is chiefly done by volunteers, as it puts the whole transaction on a business footing, and also because she charges a certain amount to any property she manages, that she may employ a paid worker when necessary.

She has, looking at it from a business point of view, been more successful than is generally the case in that class of houses in getting the gross rental.

If you are able kindly to bring the subject before the EC, I shall be very grateful.

Believe me to be
My dear Lord
yours most truly,
Lucy Tait

22   Cluttons to the EC, 20 March1884, EC file 65065.

23   A and B are Parvey Place, Union Court, Worcester Place, a block south from Adams Place and Henry's Place (hand-written note on plan). These were most likely demolished in the first waves of rebuilding.

24   Report of Select Committee for Southwark House Property, 13 March1884, EC file ECE/SEC/EST/MAN/1.

25   Letter printed in C. Edmund Maurice, (ed.) *Life of Octavia Hill as Told in Her Letters*, London: Macmillan 1914, pp.474-76. There is some doubt as to the actual addressee and the date given of March 1887 appears to be wrong (see Best, *Temporal Pillars*).

26   Letters to St Saviour's District Board, May 1892, London County Council, 30 June 1892 and Reverend Thompson, 10 January 1902.

27   See 1884/5, p.187. These were 20-22 Essex St; 1-9 Farnham Place; 1-15 Thornton Grove; 23-31 Gravel Lane; 8-34 Dyers buildings; 2-9 Williams Place. (Letter from Cluttons to the EC, 12 January 1885.)

28   In her brother-in-law, Edmund Maurice's, collection of letters this is dated March 1887, but must have been written earlier.

29   Maurice, *Life of Octavia Hill*, 1914, pp.474-76.

30   1886, p.203.

31   Reported in a letter from Miranda Hill to Ellen Chase (24 February, 1889) in Maurice, *Life of Octavia Hill*, 1914, p.486.

32   Including St Saviour's District Board and the LCC, EC file 65065.

33   *Ibid.*

34   Minute of Meeting of Estates Committee, 25 November 1886, EC file 65065.

35   On 6 March 1888 a deed was submitted to the Trustees, including, among other conditions, a covenant that ensured the gates on the roadside would be painted brown, and those between properties would be painted pink and brown. The reason for this remains a mystery.

36   The lease for the garden was for 999 years (1886, p.204), but the land for the Red Cross Hall and Cottages was held on a shorter lease until 1893, when the Ecclesciastical Commissioners brought them into line by offering 999 years (1893, p.340).

37 This was the first lease to one of Octavia's associates for new building, but not for taking old properties off their hands. Miss Janet Johnson had already leased 41 old houses in Southwark from the Commissioners, in order to collect there. (1884/5, p.188).

38 It is possible that this may have been on the basis of arrangements made directly between Octavia and Cluttons, without reference to the Commissioners, hence the absence of archive material.

39 1893, p.336; 1894, p.353; and 1895, p.372.

40 Letter from Cluttons to the EC, 11 November 1894.

41 6 Galston cottages, Regency Street (Report from Miles, Jennings, White & Foster to the EC, 5 January 1895).

42 Letter from Mr J. Hunter Watts of the Social Democratic Federation to the Archbishop of Canterbury, *Daily Chronicle*, 19 February 1894.

43 'The commissioners felt justified in pulling down, partly because the cottages were worn out, partly because they had provided numerous and excellent dwellings for people working in the immediate neighbourhood'. (1901, p.466.)

44 *St James's Gazette*, 1 August 1903.

45 Although this is now a very expensive area, it could best be described as 'bohemian' at the time of the petition. The list of residents includes a smattering of MPs and clergy—to be expected from the proximity to parliament and Westminster Abbey— and some artists like Alfred Munns and Ernest Shepherd. However, the publisher Grant Richards recalled in his autobiography that when he had lived in Barton Street in the early part of the 1890s he had been kept awake for hours at a time by 'the appalling rows that the dwellers in the neighbouring Tufton Street made in the hours that followed midnight. Murder seemed on the point of happening two or three times a week; sudden death must have been very common indeed, judging by the hideous shrieks and cries.' Richards believed that the area's rise on the social scale was partly the result of the campaign to save the buildings, as a result of which 'it began to be visited by people who had never before heard of the district's charm'. (Grant Richards, *Memories of a Misspent Youth*, London: Heinemann, 1932, p.218.)

46 According to an unusually revealing memoir of his mother written by E.F. Benson, the homosexual novelist and creator of the Mapp and Lucia series, Mary Benson, after a nervous breakdown that effectively ended her marriage, 'like all very intellectual women, formed a strong emotional attachment to her own sex... Lucy slept with my mother in the vast Victorian bed where her six children had been born.' (E.F. Benson, *Mother*, 1925, quoted in A.N. Wilson, *The Victorians*, London: Hutchinson, 2002, p.568.) It was Lucy Tait who had originally introduced Octavia to the Ecclesiastical Commissioners (see p.738).

47 Letter from the EC to Westminster Housing Association, 30 May 1930.

48 Petitions from residents complaining about the size and appointment of the new tenements were dismissed, largely on her advice. (1900, p.447, n.1.)

49 1901, p.468.

50 Letter from Cluttons to the EC, 13 February 1901.

51   Metropolitan estates, 'Provision of Dwellings for the Working Classes', Report of the Estates Committee, 21 January 1904.

52   *The Times*, 29 February 1904.

53   *Daily Telegraph*, 31 March 1902.

54   Octavia Hill to Alfred de Bock Porter, 19 December 1903.

55   1903, p.500.

56   Octavia was keen to place the work on an independent footing, so asked for it to be transferred to Miss Lumsden's care.

57   *The Ecclesiastical Commissioners' Housing of the Working Classes. London Estates, 1906.*

58   See, for example, the letter from Cluttons to the EC, 24 August 1905.

59   *The Ecclesiastical Commissioners' Housing of the Working Classes*, 1906.

60   *The Ecclesiastical Commissioners' Housing of the Working Classes*, 1906.

61   1906, p.558.

62   'Account of the Ecclesiastical Commissioners' Walworth Estate, 1903—1919.'

63   The first show was held in 1912 and was organised mainly by the tenants themselves.

64   'Infant and Child Welfare', the Medical Officer of Health in Sheffield. Quoted in 'Account of the Ecclesiastical Commissioners' Walworth Estate, 1903—1919.

65   S.E. Downing (EC secretary) to Octavia Hill, 30 July 1912.

66   Best, *Temporal Pillars*, 1964, p.495.

67   Letter from Joan Sunderland to S.E. Downing, 26 July 1932.

68   The London County Council (General Powers) Bill 1935 conferred on the LCC the power to purchase much of the EC's Lambeth Estate. The Commissioners were unhappy with several aspects of the scheme, particularly as the Bill gave the LCC authority to take over only those parts of the site easiest to develop, with the option of taking on the rest later. The EC pointed out that for more than 20 years they had been prevented from developing the estate because of sporadic proposals concerning the Charing Cross Bridge scheme and that this would exacerbate a difficult situation. The LCC agreed to shorten its option to purchase, the EC withdrew its opposition, and a price of £875,000 was agreed for all of the land required by the LCC for its schemes. (EC document, 3 April 1935.) The sale was confirmed in December 1935, but was not completed because of the outbreak of the Second World War. In 1949 the scheme was resurrected and extended, with the LCC purchasing parts of Westminster Bridge Road, Lambeth Palace Road and Stangate Street as part of their preparations for the Festival of Britain in 1951. (Minutes of the Estates and Finance Committee, 2 March 1949.) The council augmented this purchase with parts of York Road and Addington Crescent. The total cost of these additional purchases came to £31,000. (Cluttons document, 21 March 1949.) St Thomas' Hospital then purchased property on Boniface Street, Carlisle Lane, Royal Street, Stangate Street, Finck Street, Upper

Marsh, Waxwell Terrace and Westminster Bridge Road for £90,000. (Letters from Cluttons to what was by now the Church Commissioners, 26 January 1950.)

69   In 1914, 88 per cent of all households were in the private rented sector (The Private Rented Housing Sector, House of Commons Environment Committee, HC40, London: HMSO, July 1982, vol. II, p.170). By 2002 it was ten per cent (Office of National Statistics, *Social Trends 33*, London: The Stationery Office, 2003). This decline has been attributed to two main factors. The first is regulation, the second is the competition offered to private landlords by municipal housing at subsidised rents. The first rent control legislation was introduced in 1915 as an emergency measure, to last for the duration of the war and for six months afterwards. Instead of being lifted, it was confirmed by further legislation controlling rents and giving security of tenure to tenants. The increasing municipal subsidies made it impossible for private landlords to provide housing for low-income tenants at a profit. In so far as the private rented sector still exists, it accommodates middle-class tenants who can afford high rents and large deposits.

70   Letter from W. Lockyear, Chairman of the Lambeth Labour Party, *The Times*, 18 June 1920.

71   The fact that the Commissioners had been prevented, for more than 20 years by that time, from being able to plan the development of their Lambeth estate by the sporadic outbursts of the abortive Charing Cross Bridge scheme, was not appreciated.

72   Resolution of Board for Church and Society, 8 May 2001.

Select Bibliography

Alexander, Alan (1985) *Borough Government and Politics: Reading 1835–1985*, London: George Allen & Unwin.

Ashbee, Felicity (2002) *Janet Ashbee: Love, Marriage and the Arts and Crafts Movement*, New York: Syracuse University Press.

Barker, Felix, and Jackson, Peter (1990) *The History of London in Maps*, London: Barrie and Jenkins.

Barnett, Henrietta (1918) *Canon Barnett: His Life, Work and Friends*, London: John Murray, 2 vols.

Barrington, Mrs Russell (1893) 'The Red Cross Hall', *The English Illustrated Magazine*, June.

Blunt, Wilfrid (1975) *England's Michelangelo: A Biography of George Frederic Watts*, London: Columbus Books.

Brabazon, Lord (1886) *Social Arrows*, London: Longmans, Green & Co.

Cecil, Evelyn, *London Parks and Gardens*, Constable: London, 1907.

Chase, Ellen (1929) *Tenant Friends in Old Deptford*, London: Williams and Norgate.

Crane, Walter (1907) *An Artists's Reminiscences*, London: Methuen and Co.

Crawford, Elizabeth (2002) *Enterprising Women: The Garretts and their circle*, London: Francis Boutle.

Darley, Gillian (1990) *Octavia Hill: A Life*, London: Constable.

Denny, Barbara (1993) *Notting Hill and Holland Park Past: A Visual History*, London: Historical Publications.

Dormer, Ernest (1911) *Erleigh Court and its Owners*, Reading: G.A. Poynder.

Harris, José (1989) 'The Webbs, the Charity Organisation Society and the Ratan Tata Foundation: social policy from the perspective of 1912' in Bulmer *et al.* (eds) *The Goals of Social Policy*, London: Unwin Hyman.

Higham, Florence (1955) *Southwark Story*, London: Hodder and Stoughton.

Hill, William Thomson (1956), *Octavia Hill: pioneer of the National Trust and housing reformer*, London: Hutchinson.

Hilton, Tim (1985) *John Ruskin: The Early Years*, New Haven and London: Yale University Press.

Hilton, Tim (2000) *John Ruskin: The Later Years*, New Haven and London: Yale University Press.

Himmelfarb, Gertrude (1991) *Poverty and Compassion: The Moral Imagination of the Late Victorians*, New York: Knopf.

Hyndman, H.M. (1925) *Further Reminiscences*, London: Macmillan and Co.

Judge, Betty (1994) *Octavia Hill and the Women's University Settlement*, Wisbech: Octavia Hill Society.

Kirkman Gray, B. (1908) *Philanthopy and the State, or Social Politics*, London: P.S. King. Published posthumously.

Lees-Milne, James (1945) *The National Trust: A Record of Fifty Years' Achievement*, London: Batsford.

Legg, Rodney (1994) *The National Trust Centenary: Common Roots of 1895*, Wincanton: The Wincanton Press.

Leighton, Baldwyn (1872) *Letters and Other Writings of the late Edward Denison, MP for Newark*, London: Richard Bentley and Son.

Loch, C.S. (1912) 'In Memoriam: Miss Octavia Hill', *Charity Organisation Review*, September pp.158-161 and October pp.213-222.

Lockhart, J.G. (1949) *Cosmo Gordon Lang*, London: Hodder and Stoughton.

Lovelace, Lady Mary (November 1928) *The Architect's Journal*, Rural England Number, 14.

Malpass, Peter (1998) *The Work of the Century: The Origins and Growth of the Octavia Hill Housing Trust in Notting Hill*, London: Octavia Hill Housing Trust.

Marsh, Arnold (1962) 'Octavia Hill and Clean Air: A Smoke Abatement Pioneer', in The Society of Housing Managers' *Quarterly Journal*, vol.V, no.8, pp.21-23.

Maurice, C. Edmund (ed.) (1914) *Life of Octavia Hill as Told in Her Letters*, London: Macmillan.

Maurice, Emily (1928) *Octavia Hill: Early Ideals*, London: George Allen and Unwin.

Moberly Bell, Enid (1942) *Octavia Hill: A biography*, London: Constable.

Murphy, Graham (1987) *Founders of the National Trust*, London: Christopher Helm.

Nettlefold, John Sutton (1905) *A Housing Policy*, Cornish Brothers.

Nettlefold, John Sutton (1908) *Birmingham Municipal Affairs: A Message to the Citizens*, pamphlet.

Nettlefold, John Sutton (1909) 'No Room To Live', *The Open Review*, vol.1, no.3, July, pp.193-202.

Nettlefold, John Sutton (1910) *Slum Reform and Town Planning: The Garden City Idea Applied to Existing Cities and Their Suburbs*, pamphlet.

Nevinson, Henry (1923) *Changes and Chances*, London: Nisbet.

Norwich, John Julius (2003) *Paradise of Cities: Venice and its Nineteenth-Century Visitors*, London: Viking.

O'Neill, Morna (2003) 'Everyday Heroic Deeds: Walter Crane and Octavia Hill at the Red Cross Hall', *The Acorn*, vol.2.

Ouvry, Elinor Southwood (1933) *Extracts from Octavia Hill's 'Letters to Fellow-Workers', 1864 to 1911*, London: The Adelphi Bookshop.

Owen, David (1965) *English Philanthropy 1660–1960*, Cambridge, Mass.: Harvard University Press.

Pevsner, Nikolaus, and Cherry, Bridget (1983) *London 2: South*, The Buildings of England, Harmondsworth: Penguin Books.

Prochaska, Frank (1980) *Women and Philanthropy in 19th Century England*, Oxford: Clarendon Press.

Ranlett, John (1981) 'The Smoke Abatement Exhibition of 1881', *History Today*, November.

Rawnsley, Eleanor (1923) *Canon Rawnsley: An Account of His Life*, Glasgow: MacLehose, Jackson.

Rawnsley, Hardwicke (1914) 'A National Benefactor: Sir Robert Hunter', *Cornhill Magazine*, vol.36, 1914.

Rooff, Madeleine (1972) *A Hundred Years of Family Welfare: A study of the Family Welfare*

Association (formerly Charity Organisation Society) 1869–1969, London: Michael Joseph.

Sexby, J.J., (1898) *The Municipal Parks, Gardens and Open Spaces of London*, London: Elliott Stock.

Smith, Greg (1989) 'Developing a Public Language of Art', in Smith, Greg, and Hyde, Sarah (eds) *Walter Crane: Artist, Designer, Socialist*, London: Lund Humphries and Whitworth Art Gallery, Manchester, 1989.

Sturge, Elizabeth (1928) *Reminiscences of My Life*, printed for private circulation.

Sunderland, E.S.S. (1995) *Dibdin and the English Establishment: The Public Life of Sir Lewis Dibdin, Dean of the Arches, 1903–1934*, Durham: The Pentland Press.

Tarn, John (1973) *Five Per Cent Philanthropy: An Account of Housing in Urban Areas Between 1840 and 1914*, London: Cambridge University Press.

Vincent, A.W. (1999) 'The Poor Law Reports of 1909 and the Social Theory of the Charity Organisation Society', in Gladstone, David (ed.) *Before Beveridge: Welfare Before the Welfare State*, London: Institute of Economic Affairs.

Waterson, Merlin (1994) *The National Trust: The First Hundred Years*, London: National Trust Enterprises and BCC Books.

Weinreb, Ben, and Hibbert, Christopher, *The London Encyclopaedia*, London: Macmillan, 1983.

Whelan, Robert (ed.) (1998) *Octavia Hill and the Social Housing Debate: Essays and Letters by Octavia Hill*, London: Institute of Economic Affairs.

Whelan, Robert (2001) *Helping the Poor: Friendly visiting, dole charities and dole queues*, London: Civitas.

Whetlor, Sharon (1998) *The Story of Notting Dale: From Potteries and Piggeries to Present Times*, London: Kensington and Chelsea Community History Group.

Wilson, A.N. (2002) *The Victorians*, London: Hutchinson.

763

Bibliography
of Octavia Hill's
writings

COLLECTIONS OF OCTAVIA HILL'S WRITINGS

Hill, Octavia (1875) *Homes of the London Poor*, London: Macmillan. Includes: 'Cottage Property in London'(*Fortnightly Review*, November 1866); 'Four Years' Management of a London Court'(*Macmillan's Magazine*, July 1869 under the title 'Organised Work Among the Poor. Suggestions Founded on Four Years' Management of a London Court'); 'Landlords and Tenants in London'(*Macmillan's Magazine*, October 1871 under the title 'Blank Court; or Landlords and Tenants'); 'The Work of Volunteers in the Organisation of Charity'(*Macmillan's Magazine*, October 1872); 'Co-operation of Volunteers and Poor Law Officials'(Report to the Local Government Board, January 1874); 'Why the Artisans' Dwellings Bill Was Wanted'(*Macmillan's Magazine*, June 1874); 'Space for the People' (*Macmillan's Magazine*, August 1875).

(1877) *Our Common Land*, London: Macmillan. Includes: 'Our Common Land'(*Macmillan's Magazine*, 33, April 1876, 539, but not acknowledged in the book); 'District Visiting' (talk, 4 May 1876); 'A Few Words to Volunteer Workers Among the Poor'(talk, 23 June 1876); 'A More Excellent Way of Charity' (talk, July 1876, published in *Macmillan's Magazine*, 35, 126-31, but not acknowledged in the book); 'A Word on Good Citizenship'; 'Open Spaces' (talk, 9 May 1877); 'Effectual Charity'(talk, 18 June 1877); 'The Future of Our Commons'.

(1970) *The Homes of the London Poor* by Octavia Hill reprintd with *The Bitter Cry of Outcast London* by Andrew Mearns, Frank Cass and Co.

Jeffery, M.M., and Neville, Edith (eds) (1921) *House Property and its Management: Some Papers on the Methods of Management Introduced by Miss Octavia Hill and Adapted to Modern Conditions*, Introduction by I.G. Gibson, Ministry of Health, London: George Allen & Unwin. Chapter I: 'Management of houses for the poor' is from *Charity Organisation Review*, 1899 (see below); Chapter II: 'Cottage property in London' is shortened from *Fortnightly Review*, November 1866 (see below); Chapter III: 'Blank Court' is shortened from *Macmillan's Magazine*, October 1871 (see below); Chapter IV: 'Influence of model dwellings upon character' is shortened from Booth, Charles (ed.) *Life and Labour of the People in London*, vol.III, 1892 (see below); Chapter V: 'Small houses in London', source unknown; Chapter VI: 'Small houses in London' is a brief extract from the Letter to Fellow-Workers for 1886; Chapter VII: 'Women managers – a Crown estate' is from *Housing*, the official journal of the Ministry of Health, 27 September 1919, and is signed E.A.C. (E.A.Charlesworth); Chapter VII: 'Letters to Fellow-Workers' contains a selection of brief extracts from LFW between 1875 and 1903; Chapter VIII: 'Management of municipal houses in Amsterdam' is from *Housing*, 19 July 1920, signed E.A.C.; Chapter IX: 'Report on house property management' is the report of a sub-committee set up in October 1920 by the Women's Section of the Garden Cities and Town Planning Association to consider 'the methods and practice of house property management, especially with regard to what is generally called working-class property and management by women'.

Maurice, Elinor Southwood (ed.) (1933) *Extracts from Octavia Hill's Letters to Fellow-Workers*, Foreword by Neville Chamberlain MP, London.

Payne, James L. (ed.) (1997) *The Befriending Leader: Social Assistance Without Dependency, Essays by Octavia Hill*, Sandpoint, Idaho: Lytton Publishing company.

Whelan, Robert (ed.) (1998) *Octavia Hill and the Social Housing Debate: Essays and Letters by Octavia Hill*, Institute of Economic Affairs Health and Welfare Unit.

ARTICLES AND PAMPHLETS BY OCTAVIA HILL

Hill, Octavia (1866) 'Cottage Property in London', *Fortnightly Review*, November, 6, 681-87, reprinted in *Homes of the London Poor*, q.v. (1867) 'Poor Play-grounds', *All The Year Round*, 4 May, 17, pp.446-49.

(1869) 'Organised Work Among the Poor. Suggestions Founded on Four Years' Management of a London Court', *Macmillan's Magazine*, July, vol.20, reprinted in *Homes of the London Poor*, q.v.

(1870) 'The Importance of Aiding the Poor Without Almsgiving'. In *Transactions of the National Association for the Promotion of Social Science*, ed. Edwin Pears, London: Longmans, Green, Reader and Dyer. (Speech given in Bristol in 1869 to the Social Science Association.)

(1871) 'Employment or Almsgiving? Being an account of the plan of relief now adopted in a district of Marylebone', London: James Martin, printer.

(1871) 'Blank Court; or Landlords and Tenants', *Macmillan's Magazine*, 24, pp.456-65, October, reprinted in *Homes of the London Poor*, q.v.

(1872) 'The Work of Volunteers in the Organisation of Charity', *Macmillan's Magazine*, vol.24, October, reprinted in *Homes of the London Poor*, q.v.

(1872) 'Further Account of the Walmer Street Industrial Experiment', London: George Pulman, printer.

(1874) 'The Elberfield System in London', *Charity Organisation Reporter*, pp.317-21.

(1874) 'Co-operation of Volunteers and Poor-Law Officials', Report to Local Government board, January, reprinted in *Homes of the London Poor*, q.v.

(1874) 'Why the Artisans' Dwellings Bill Was Wanted', *Macmillan's Magazine*, June, reprinted in *Homes of the London Poor*, q.v.

(1875) 'Space for the People', *Macmillan's Magazine*, August, reprinted in *Homes of the London Poor*, q.v.

(?1876) 'A Word on Good Citizenship', *Fortnightly Review* n.s. 20, pp.321-25, reprinted in *Our Common Land*, q.v.

(1876) 'District Visiting', *Good Words*, 17, pp.488-93, reprinted as a pamphlet by Longmans, Green and Co and the Charity Organisation Society, 15 Buckingham Street, Adelphi, W.C., price 3d. Reprinted in *Our Common Land*, q.v.

(1876) 'Our Common Land', *Macmillan's Magazine*, April, 33, p.539, reprinted in *Our Common Land*, q.v.

(1876) 'A More Excellent Way of Charity', *Macmillan's Magazine*, December, 35, pp.126-31, reprinted in *Our Common Land*, q.v.

(1877) 'A Few Words to Volunteer Visitors Among the Poor', Occasional Paper No. 28 of the Charity Organisation Society (read at Westminster 23 June 1876), reprinted in *Our Common Land*, q.v.

(1880) 'The Kyrle Society', *The Magazine of Art*.

(1883) 'Improvements Now Practicable', *The Nineteenth Century*, December, vol.14, pp.925-33, as part of a symposium of working-class housing that appeared under the heading 'Common Sense and the Dwellings of the Poor', reprinted in *Octavia Hill and the Social Housing Debate*, q.v.

(1884) 'Colour, Space and Music for the People', *The Nineteenth Century*, May, 15, pp.741-52, reprinted in *Nineteenth-Century Opinion: an Anthology of Extracts from the First Fifty volumes of The Nineteenth Century, 1877–1901*, London 1951. Published by Kegan Paul, Trench as a 12-page pamphlet at 3*d*.

(1888) 'More Air For London', *The Nineteenth Century*, February, vol.23, no.132, pp.181-88.

(1889) 'The Charity Organisation Society', Occasional Paper No. 15, first series, London: Charity Organisation Society. 'A paper read at a meeting of the Fulham and Hammersmith Charity Organisation Committee on February 1 [1889] at Fulham Palace.' Reprinted in R. Whelan (2001) *Helping the Poor*, London: Civitas, pp.164-65.

(1889) 'A Few Words to Fresh Workers', *The Nineteenth Century*, September, vol.26, pp.452-61. 'Read at the summer meeting of University Extension students at Oxford, August 1889.'

(1891) 'The Charity Organisation Society', Occasional Paper No. 20, London: Charity Organisation Society. 'An Address Delivered at the Annual General Meeting of the London Charity Organisation Society, on April 23, 1891'.

(1891) 'Our Dealings With The Poor', *The Nineteenth Century*, August, vol.30, no.174, pp.61-70.

(1892) 'The Influence of Blocks of Flats on Character', in Booth, Charles (ed.) *Life and Labour of the People in London*, vol.III, 'Blocks of buildings, schools and immigration', London: Macmillan.

(1893) 'Trained Workers For The Poor', *The Nineteenth Century*, January, vol.33, pp.36-43. Reprinted in *Signs of the Times: Extracts from The Nineteenth Century*, London: Henry S. King, 1893.

(1898) 'The Need of Thoroughness in Charitable Work', *Charity Organisation Review*, November.

(1899) 'Management of Houses For The Poor', *Charity Organisation Review*, January, No. 25, New Series.

(1899) 'Open Spaces of the Future', *The Nineteenth Century*, July, vol.46, pp.26-35.

(?1904) 'Housing Difficulties: Management versus Re-Construction', *The Daily Chronicle*, republished in pamphlet form in 1904. Reproduced in *Octavia Hill and the Social Housing Debate*, q.v.

(1905) 'The Kyrle Society', *Charity Organisation Review*, V, 18, July-December, pp.314-19.

(1905) 'Natural beauty as a national asset', *Nineteenth Century and After*, December, vol.58, pp.935-41.

(1907) 'Management of Houses for the Poor', *Occasional Papers of the C.O.S.*, second series no.7, London: Charity Organisation Society.

ARTICLES, CHAPTERS, PAMPHLETS AND BOOKS EITHER WHOLLY OR PARTLY ABOUT OCTAVIA HILL

Best, Richard (undated) *Octavia Hill and Housing Today*, The Octavia Hill Society Inaugural Lecture 1993, Wisbech: Octavia Hill Society.

Brion, Marion (1995) Chapter 2: 'Octavia Hill', in *Women in the Housing Service*, London: Routledge.

Brion, Marion, and Tinker, Anthea (1980) Chapter 6: Looking Back – Octavia Hill and the Beginning of Housing Work for Women' in *Women in Housing: Access and Influence*, London: Housing Centre Trust.

Clayton, Peter (1993) *Octavia Hill: born in Wisbech*, Wisbech: The Wisbech Society.

Jeffery, M.M. (1929) 'House Property and Estate Management on Octavia Hill Lines',

Occasional paper no.12, fifth series, London: Charity Organisation Society.

Judge, Betty (1994) *Octavia Hill and the Women's University Settlement,* Wisbech: Octavia Hill Society.

Lee, Amice (September 1936) 'Recollections of Octavia Hill', *Cornhill Magazine,* London.

Lewis, Jane (1991) Chapter 1: 'Octavia Hill', in *Women and Social Action in Victorian and Edwardian England,* Aldershot: Edward Elgar.

Loch, C.S. (October 1912) 'In Memoriam: Miss Octavia Hill', *Charity Organisation Review,* vol.32, new series.

Lumsden, Mary (April 1913) 'Octavia Hill and the Housing Problem', *Edinburgh Review.*

Macadam, Elizabeth (1934) 'Housing and Voluntary Social Service', Chapter Six in *The New Philanthropy: A Study of the Relations Between the Statutory and Voluntary Social Services,* London: George Allen and Unwin. Not exclusively about Octavia Hill, but contains an interesting assessment of her work from an inter-war perspective.

Maltz, Diana (1998) 'Beauty at home or not? Octavia Hill and the aesthetics of tenement reform', in M. Baumgarten, and H.M. Daleski, (eds) *Homes and Homelessness in the Victorian Imagination,* New York: AMS Press.

Morell, Caroline (1996) Chapter 4: 'Octavia Hill and Women's Networks in Housing', in Anne Digby and John Stewart (eds.), *Gender, Health and Welfare,* London: Routledge.

Rooff, Madeline (1972) *A Hundred Years of Family Welfare: A Study of the Family Welfare Association (Formerly Charity Organisation Society) 1869—1969,* London: Michael Joseph. Contains references to the great value of Octavia's experience in housing management in developing the COS method of 'visiting'.

Society of Housing Managers (1962) *Quarterly Journal: Octavia Hill 1838–1912,* October, vol.V, no.8.

Wohl, Anthony S. (1977) 'Benevolent Despotism', chapter seven in *The Eternal Slum: Housing and Social Policy in Victorian London,* London: Edward Arnold.

BIOGRAPHIES

Bell, E. Moberly (1942) *Octavia Hill,* London: Constable.

Boyd, Nancy (1982) *Three Victorian Women Who Changed Their World: Josephine Butler, Octavia Hill, Florence Nightingale,* Oxford: Oxford University Press.

Darley, Gillian (1990) *Octavia Hill: A Life,* London: Constable.

Hill, William Thomson (1956) *Octavia Hill: Pioneer of the National Trust and housing reformer,* London: Hutchinson.

Maurice, C. Edmund (ed.) (1914) *Life of Octavia Hill, as Told in Her Letters,* London: Macmillan. This was the first biography, written by the son of Rev. F.D. Maurice, who had married Octavia's sister Emily. It consists of large numbers of letters from Octavia, together with some letters to and about her from her mother, sisters and John Ruskin, strung together with a brief text by Maurice putting them into context. The book has been invaluable to subsequent biographers, as most of the letters no longer exist.

Maurice, Emily Southwood (1928) *Octavia Hill: Early Ideals,* London: George Allen & Unwin. Emily Southwood Maurice was Octavia's sister and the wife of Edmund Maurice (see above). This consists of letters from Octavia Hill to Mary Harris, and from John Ruskin to Octavia Hill. It lacks the biographical passages that link the letters in her husband's book, but it is included in this section because it was conceived of as a sequel to that.

Tabor, Margaret E. (1927) *Octavia Hill,* London: The Sheldon Press. This pamphlet is number seven in a series of eight 'Pioneer Women'. The other subjects included Elizabeth Fry, Florence Nightingale and Hannah More. They were also published in two collected editions of four pioneer women each.

List of Donors

This list includes all individuals who contributed to the donation fund, work-room fund, playground fund, fund for improving houses, Red Cross fund, Mariner's Hill appeal (1908) and the industrial experiment (1870 and 1871). Occasionally, people contributed more than once in a year: they may have made several contributions to the donation fund, or contributed to the donation fund and another fund like the Red Cross fund. Donations 'per' an individual are listed, unless they are 'per' Octavia Hill, in which case we have no idea where they came from. Payments for the next year or the previous year are listed under the year for which they were intended, rather than that in which they were made. Whilst every attempt has been made to group all payments made by an individual together, this has sometimes been impossible where several donors share the same surname, and are not always distinguished by initials, for example the Misses Harris. In these cases a separate category has been introduced for the unattributable donations. Typographical errors and obvious mis-spellings of names have been corrected wherever possible. Multiple spellings are given where it has not been possible to do this with any certainty, for example Mrs Westbury Milton/Westbury Mitton/Welbury Mitton who, making every allowance for bad handwriting, may also have been Mrs Melbury Mitton.

A.J., 1877
A.M.P., 1891
A.S., 1887
Abercromby, Lady, 1871
Aitken, Miss, 1878
Alford, Rev. B.H., 1891, 1892, 1893, 1895
Allen, Mrs, 1874, 1875, 1876, 1877, 1886
Allen, A.C., 1887, 1890, 1891, 1892, 1893, 1894, 1895, 1896, 1897, 1898, 1899, 1900, 1901, 1902, 1903, 1904, 1905, 1906, 1907, 1908, 1909, 1910, 1911
Amphlett, Baron, 1876
Anderson, Patrick, 1876
Andrewes, (Dr and) Mrs F.W., 1902, 1903, 1904
Andrewes, (Mr and) Mrs Herbert, 1898, 1903, 1905, 1906, 1907, 1908, 1909, 1910, 1911
Arkwright, Henry, 1873

Arkwright, Miss M., 1887, 1889
Armitage, Miss, 1875
Ashe, Miss, 1908
Ashe, Mrs, 1902
Ashmead, Mr F.A., 1897
Astley, Miss, 1882, 1883, 1908
Astley, Mrs, 1881
Atkinson, Mrs, 1871, 1879-80
Atkinson, C.T., 1911
Austin, Miss, 1893, 1895, 1896, 1897, 1898, 1899, 1900, 1901, 1902, 1903, 1904, 1905, 1906, 1907, 1908, 1909, 1910, 1911

B., 1887
B.S., 1901, 1902, 1909
Bailey, John, 1901, 1902, 1904, 1905, 1906, 1907, 1908, 1909, 1910
Bailey, Mrs John, 1911

Bainbridge, E.P., 1902
Bainbrigge, Colonel, 1902, 1908
Baiss, Miss, 1886
Baldwin, Miss F., 1874, 1875, 1876, 1877
Ball, Miss M., 1883, 1885, 1886, 1888
Bannerman, Mrs, 1902, 1903, 1904, 1905, 1906, 1907, 1908, 1909, 1910, 1911
Bannerman, Miss Lilias, 1896, 1897, 1898, 1899, 1900, 1901
Barclay, Mrs, 1909, 1910
Baring, Hon. F.H., 1908
Barker, Miss, 1871, 1873
Barnes, Miss A.M., 1894, 1895
Barnett, Rev. S. and Mrs, 1874
Barnett, W.H., 1905
Barrett, Miss, 1879
Barrington, Miss, 1871
Barrington, Mrs, 1888
Barrington, Hon. Augusta, 1874, 1875
Bartlett, Miss C., 1903
Bartlett, Miss Hannah, 1894, 1896, 1897, 1898, 1899, 1900, 1901, 1902, 1903, 1904, 1905, 1906
Bates, Mrs, 1879-80
Baumgartner, Miss, 1895, 1899
Bayley, Mr E., 1908, 1909, 1910, 1911
Bayley, Mr G.F., 1907
Bayne, Mr and Mrs P., 1870
Baynes, Mrs, 1892
Beaumont, Somerset (MP), 1870, 1871, 1891, 1897, 1900, 1904, 1907
Beckwith, Edward L., 1897, 1901, 1904, 1906, 1907, 1908, 1909
Behrens, Miss, 1874
Bell, Miss, 1871, 1872, 1875, 1887
Bell, Mrs, 1871
Benecke, Miss, 1881
Bennett, Major, 1907
Berridge, Miss, 1908
Berry, Miss Maud, 1882
Berry, Rev. W., 1871
Bevan, Mrs, 1887
Biggs, Mrs W.R., 1889
Bigland, Percy, 1876
Bird, Mrs, 1886
Bird, Miss Laura, 1887, 1888
Black, General, 1873
Black, Miss, 1892
Blair, Mrs H., 1874
Bland, Miss, 1908
Blandford, Miss, 1887
Blandy, Mrs, 1908
Bleckley, Mrs, 1887, 1890, 1897
Blundell, Mr and Mrs J.W., 1876
Blyth, Patrick L., 1895, 1896, 1900, 1901, 1902, 1903, 1904, 1905, 1906, 1907,

1908, 1909, 1910, 1911
Bond, Mrs, 1875, 1878, 1879-80, 1882
Bond, Edward, 1873, 1874, 1875, 1876, 1877
Bond, Rev. John, 1876
Bonham Carter, Miss, 1870, 1887, 1889
Bonsor, H. Cosmo, 1907, 1908, 1909, 1910, 1911
Booth, Charles, 1894, 1895, 1898
Booth, Mrs Charles, 1901, 1903
Bosanquet, C.B.P., 1874, 1877, 1879, 1902
Boulter, A.E., 1904
Bousfield, W., 1876
Bowan, Mrs, 1908
Boyle, Rev. R., 1872, 1908
Braby, Miss, 1888
Braby, Mr F., 1888, 1889
Bradley, Miss Meta, 1882
Bragg, Miss, 1876
Bragington, Miss, 1908
Brand, Miss, 1884
Brander, Mrs, 1888, 1891, 1908, 1909, 1910
Bridgeman, Colonel, 1897
Bridgeman, Charles, 1891, 1893, 1894, 1896, 1898, 1899, 1900, 1901, 1902, 1903, 1904, 1905, 1906, 1907, 1909, 1911
Bridgeman, Mrs Charles, 1889, 1891, 1892, 1893, 1894, 1895, 1896, 1897, 1900, 1901, 1902, 1903, 1904, 1905, 1907, 1909, 1911
Bridgett, Miss, 1907, 1908, 1909, 1910, 1911
Brightwen, George, 1876
Brinton, Miss M., 1909, 1910, 1911
Britten, Miss, 1887
Brock, K., 1875, 1876, 1878, 1879-80
Brogentin, Miss, 1910
Brooke, Mrs Stopford, 1871, 1872, 1873
Brooke, Rev. W. Ingham, 1889, 1907
Brooks, Miss, 1895, 1897, 1898, 1900, 1901, 1902, 1903, 1904
Brown, A., 1908
Brown, Mrs M.R., 1887
Brown, S., 1870
Browne, Mrs, 1878, 1908
Browne, W.S., 1879-80
Bruce, Mrs Robert, 1875
Buchanan, Miss, 1876
Buckin, Miss, 1886
Bulkeley, Rev. H., 1884, 1889
Burdett-Coutts, Baroness, 1887
Burgess, Miss S., 1890, 1900
Burnaby, Miss, 1875, 1877
Burrage, Miss, 1888, 1903, 1904, 1905, 1907, 1908, 1909, 1910

Bush, Miss E.M., 1878
Buxton, Mrs Charles, 1885, 1887

C., Mrs, 1877
C.K.W., 1874
C.L., 1883
Cadogan, Lady, 1879
Campbell, Miss, 1878
Camperdown, Countess of, 1872, 1874, 1875
Caritas, 1884
Carpenter, Rev. (and Mrs) Estlin, 1879–80, 1881, 1882
Causton, Rt Hon. R.K.M., 1905, 1908, 1909
Cave Brown, Miss, 1876, 1879–80
Chalmers, Miss, 1878
Chamberlain, Miss, 1877
Chamberlain, Mr W., 1908
Channing, Rev. W.H., 1873
Charteris, Lady Caroline, 1871, 1872, 1874
Chase, Miss Ellen, 1887, 1888, 1889, 1890, 1893, 1894, 1902, 1904, 1907, 1908
Christian, Miss G. Eleanor, 1906, 1908
Chute, J.L., 1908
Clark, G.T., 1887
Clark, Mrs S.E., 1878, 1881
Clarke, Mrs, 1888
Cleveland, Duchess of, 1893, 1894, 1895, 1896, 1897, 1898, 1899, 1900, 1901
Clover, Miss, 1873
Clutton, Ralph, 1907
Coates, Miss, 1875
Cobbett, W.W., 1891, 1892, 1894
Cock, Miss, 1872
Cockerell, Mrs G.R., 1888
Cockerell, Miss Olive, 1909
Cockerell, Sydney C., 1895, 1897, 1899, 1900, 1901, 1902, 1903, 1904, 1905, 1906, 1907, 1908, 1909, 1910, 1911
Cockerell, S.J., 1876
Cockerill, Miss, 1904, 1907, 1908
Cocks, Miss, 1908, 1909
Cohen, Mrs Arthur, 1877
Collum, Rev., 1883
Colquhoun, Rev. J.C. Campbell, 1908
Cook, Mrs, 1883
Cookson, Mrs, 1875
Cornish, Rev. J.F. (or T.F.), 1887, 1898
Cornwall, Mrs, 1875
Cortauld, Mrs, 1873
Courtenay, Miss, 1887
Covington, Mr Stenton, 1903
Covington, Mrs Stenton, 1902, 1904, 1906, 1907, 1908, 1909, 1910, 1911
Cowper, Henry F., 1887

Coxhead, Mrs, 1886
Critchett, C., 1875, 1877
Cropper, James, 1873, 1875, 1876, 1882
Crowder, A.G., 1871, 1874, 1875, 1876, 1877, 1879, 1879–80, 1881, 1882, 1883, 1884, 1886, 1887
Cruikshank, Miss, 1887
Cruikshank, D., 1885
Cudworth, Mrs, 1902, 1903, 1904, 1905, 1906, 1907
Curry, Misses M. and E., 1909, 1910, 1911
Curteis, Miss, 1908, 1909, 1910, 1911
Curtis-Hayward, Miss, 1876
Curzon, N.C., 1876, 1878

Dakin, Miss E., 1907, 1908, 1909, 1910, 1911
Darwin, Miss, 1888
Darwin, Mrs, 1891
Davenport Hill, the Misses, 1895
Davenport Hill, Miss Florence, 1889
Dawbarn, Miss, 1871
Dawson, Miss, 1872, 1901, 1904, 1905, 1907, 1908, 1909, 1910
Dawson, Mrs, 1899, 1902, 1903
Deane, Mrs, 1887
Debenham, William, 1891
Denison, Miss L., 1879–80
de Rothschild, Baroness Meyer, 1874
de Rougement, C.J., 1908
Dewick, Rev. E.S., 1887
Dibdin, Lady, 1911
Dilke, Lady, 1872
Dixon, Miss L.M., 1888
Dodgson, Campbell, 1908
Dodswell, C., 1885
Dowling, Mrs, 1876, 1888, 1889, 1890
Dowson, Felix N., 1906, 1907, 1908, 1909, 1910, 1911
D'Oyly, Miss, 1887
Drew, Mr W.F., 1889
Dubois, the Misses, 1887
Ducie, Countess of, 1875, 1893, 1894
Ducie, Earl of, 1901, 1902, 1903, 1904, 1905, 1906, 1907, 1908, 1909, 1910, 1911
Duckworth, Miss, 1896
Duckworth, Mrs Herbert (*see also* Stephen, Mrs Leslie), 1871, 1872, 1873, 1874, 1875, 1876, 1877, 1878
Duer, Miss M., 1879–80
Duer, Miss S.K., 1879–80
Duff, Miss, 1908
Duff, Miss Gordon, 1908
Dundas, Lady Jane, 1890, 1891, 1893, 1894, 1895

Dunn, Sir William, 1910, 1911
Dunsany, Lord, 1876, 1878
Durrant, Mrs, 1877, 1878
Dutton, Hon. Julia, 1870

E.F.J., 1891, 1899
E.R.B., 1909
Earl, Mr E.A., 1908
Eastlake, Lady, 1871
Edwards, Miss, 1875
Edwards, Colonel H., 1910
Edwards, W., 1876
Eiloart, Mrs, 1876
Elliman, Mrs, 1902
Elliott, G.E., 1886
Ellis, Mrs G.H., 1890
Ellis, Mrs R.H., 1887
Elm, 1876
Erle, Miss Eleanor M., 1876, 1887, 1888,
    1889, 1890, 1891, 1893, 1894, 1895,
    1896, 1897, 1898, 1899, 1900, 1901,
    1903, 1904, 1905, 1907, 1908, 1909,
    1910, 1911
Evans, Miss, 1887
Evans, Mrs, 1887, 1888
Evans, Mr Richardson, 1896, 1897, 1898,
    1899, 1901
Evans, Mrs Richardson, 1900, 1902, 1903,
    1904, 1905, 1906, 1907, 1908, 1909,
    1910, 1911
Eve, Miss M.M., 1889, 1890, 1894
Ewart, Miss, 1894, 1908
Ewing, Dr, 1908

F., Miss, 1879-80
F.B.E., 1887
F.D.D., 1911
F.P., 1903
F.T., 1879-80, 1881
Farrer, Mr H.R., 1897
Farrer, Mr T.C., 1893
Faunthorpe, Mrs, 1878, 1887
Fawcett, Mrs, 1879-80
Field, Mr Rogers, 1887, 1897, 1898
Fiertz, Miss, 1903, 1907
Fisher, Mrs, 1909
Fisher, Miss Edith S., 1884, 1885, 1886,
    1887, 1888, 1889, 1891, 1892, 1901,
    1902
Fitch, Mrs, 1875
Fleming, Owen (and Mrs), 1901, 1903,
    1908
Fletcher, A.P., 1879-80
Fletcher, Miss Alice, 1875, 1876, 1877,
    1878, 1879, 1879-80
Fletcher, John, 1876

Fletcher, Lionel, 1874
Flower, Charles E., 1879-80, 1881, 1882,
    1883, 1884, 1885, 1886, 1887, 1890,
    1892
Flowers, Mrs, 1876
Ford, W., 1876
Fordyce, Miss, 1908, 1909, 1910, 1911
Forman, H.A., 1875, 1893
Forman, Miss J., 1875, 1879-80, 1881,
    1882, 1883, 1884, 1885, 1886, 1887,
    1888, 1890, 1891, 1892, 1894, 1895,
    1896, 1897, 1898, 1899, 1900, 1901,
    1903, 1904, 1905, 1906, 1907, 1908,
    1909, 1910, 1911
Fortescue, Earl, 1904
Fortescue, Hon. Dudley, 1908
Fothergill, 1883
Fowler, Miss O., 1892, 1893, 1896
Fox, Francis, 1872
Frankau, Miss, 1886, 1887, 1888, 1889,
    1890, 1891, 1892, 1893, 1894, 1895,
    1896, 1897, 1898, 1899, 1900, 1901,
    1902, 1903, 1904, 1905, 1906, 1907,
    1908, 1909, 1910, 1911
Fry, John, 1908, 1909, 1910, 1911
Fry, Lewis, 1908
Fullager, Miss, 1885

G., 1873
G.G., 1887
Gandar, Mrs, 1887
Gander, Miss, 1879-80
Gardiner, Mrs, 1901
Gardiner, General Lynedoch, 1884, 1895
Gascoigne, Mrs, 1874, 1875
Gibson, Miss, 1876
Gillson, (Mr and) Mrs, 1870, 1872, 1873,
    1874, 1875, 1876, 1877, 1879, 1881,
    1883, 1884, 1885, 1886, 1887, 1888,
    1889, 1890, 1891, 1892, 1893, 1894,
    1895, 1897, 1898, 1900, 1902, 1907,
    1909
Gimson, Miss, 1908, 1909
Gladstone, Miss, 1903, 1904, 1905, 1907,
    1908, 1909, 1910, 1911
Gladstone, Rev. H., 1908
Glanville, Miss, 1884, 1886
Gloucester and Bristol, Bishop of, 1876
Glover, G., 1874
Goldsmid, Lady, 1886, 1887
Goodenough, Miss, 1887
Goodlake, Mrs Gerald, 1870
Gordon, Mr Evans, 1888
Gosling, L.D., 1908
Gosset, Miss, 1883, 1884, 1885, 1886,
    1887, 1888, 1889, 1890, 1892, 1893, 1895

Hutton, Miss, 1908
Hutton, Mrs John, 1902, 1903, 1904, 1905, 1906, 1907, 1908, 1909

Inglefield, Miss, 1907

J.H., 1907
J.K., 1879-80
Jackson, Miss, 1877, 1879-80,1908
James, C., 1881
James, Rev. C.L., 1884, 1887
James, H.(MP), 1873
Janson, Percy, 1908
Jardine, Miss, 1908
Jekyll, Miss, 1878, 1879
Johns, Miss, 1897
Johnson, Miss, 1884, 1885, 1886,1890, 1907
Johnson, Miss Amy, 1886
Johnston, Miss(es), 1879-80, 1888, 1890, 1892, 1894, 1895, 1896, 1897, 1898, 1899, 1900, 1901, 1902, 1903, 1904, 1905
Johnstone, Edith, 1886
Jones, Miss Meyrick, 1890
Joshua, Mrs, 1876
Jukes, Mr E., 1890

K.L., 1898
Kaufmann, Mr L.H., 1908
Kay-Shuttleworth, Sir U., 1879-80
Keightly, Mrs, 1881
Kennedy, the Misses, 1878
Kincaid, Mrs, 1872
Kinder, Miss, 1874
King, Miss, 1878
Kirby, Miss, 1893, 1906, 1907, 1909

L., 1903
L.B., 1904, 1905, 1907, 1908, 1909, 1911
L.L., 1887
L.W.B., 1908
Lakin, Miss, 1877
Lambert, Rev. Brooke, 1874
Langenbach, Mrs, 1892, 1893, 1894, 1895, 1896, 1898, 1899, 1901, 1902, 1903
Lawford, Mrs, 1871
Lawrance, Miss, 1887
Laycock, Mrs, 1889, 1891
Lazenby, Mrs, 1908
Lees, Mr H., 1907
Lee-Warner, Miss, 1895, 1897, 1900, 1901, 1903
Legge, Rev. Augustus, 1875
Leighton, Sir Baldwyn, 1871
Leith, Miss, 1894

Leon, Dr John, 1901, 1902
Lewes, (Mr and) Mrs, 1872, 1879, 1885, 1905
Lewes, Miss M., 1903
Lewis, Miss, 1893
Lewis, Mr and Mrs, 1870
Liddle, Mrs, 1875
Lidgett, Miss, 1877
Lindesay, Mrs, 1870, 1871, 1872, 1873, 1875, 1876
Lipscombe, Mrs, 1875
Litchfield, R.B., 1877, 1889, 1895
Littledale, Rev. Dr, 1884, 1885, 1886, 1887
Llangattock, Lady, 1907 , 1909
Llangattock, Lord, 1908, 1910, 1911
Llewellyn, Mrs, 1876, 1877
Lloyd, Mr E.H., 1897
Loch, Mr and Mrs Charles Stewart, 1908
Longstaff, Dr,1908
Lovegrove, Miss, 1871
Lowater, Mrs, 1908
Lowndes, Miss K., 1899, 1900, 1901, 1903, 1904, 1905, 1906, 1908, 1909, 1910, 1911
Lucas, Sir Thomas, 1897
Luker, Miss, 1907
Lukin, Miss, 1872
Lukor, Mrs, 1901
Lumsden, Miss, 1909
Lushington, Miss, 1884
Luxmoore, Mr H.E., 1888, 1891, 1892, 1899, 1901, 1902, 1904, 1909, 1910, 1911
Lyell, Miss, 1872, 1878, 1879
Lyell, Mrs, 1877, 1879, 1879-80, 1888
Lynch, Mrs, 1883, 1893, 1900

M.E.J., 1893
M.E.R., 1871
M.G.G., 1887
M.R., 1887
Macaulay, Mrs, 1870, 1871, 1872, 1874, 1875, 1879-80, 1881, 1882, 1883, 1884, 1885, 1886, 1887, 1892, 1893, 1894, 1895, 1896, 1897, 1898, 1899, 1900, 1901, 1902, 1903, 1904, 1905, 1907, 1908, 1909, 1910, 1911
McCrea, Mrs Gower, 1884
Macdonald, Miss, 1908
MacDonald, Mrs, 1874
MacDonald, Dr and Mrs George, 1892
Macdonell, Mrs George P., 1908, 1909
Macdonell, Mrs James, 1884, 1890, 1891, 1892, 1893, 1895, 1898, 1899, 1902
Macfie, Miss, 1910
Macfie, Mrs, 1904, 1908

Perkins, Mrs, 1907

Peto, Miss, 1893

Phillips, Mr, 1875

Phillips, Mrs, 1894, 1895

Phillips, Sir George, 1872, 1873, 1874, 1875, 1876

Pilcher, Mrs, 1887

Pipe, Miss, 1871, 1872, 1873, 1874, 1882, 1883, 1884

Plummer, Mrs, 1888

Plummer, Rev. Charles, 1884, 1885, 1887, 1889, 1890, 1891, 1892, 1893, 1894, 1895, 1896, 1897, 1898, 1899, 1900, 1901, 1902, 1904, 1905, 1906, 1907, 1908, 1909, 1910, 1911

Pollard, Mrs, 1874, 1875, 1876, 1877

Pollock, Lady, 1903, 1910

Pollock, Sir Frederick (and Lady), 1887, 1888, 1892, 1893, 1894, 1895, 1897, 1898, 1899, 1900, 1901, 1903, 1904, 1907, 1908

Pomeroy, Hon. Esther, 1872

Pooley, Mr and Mrs, 1875, 1878, 1879, 1879-80, 1881, 1882, 1883, 1884

Powell, Miss, 1908

Powell, (Dr and) Mrs Douglas, 1890, 1891, 1892, 1894

Powell, Sir Richard Douglas, 1898

Poynter, Ambrose, 1902, 1903, 1904

Praed, C., 1907

Praed, Mr then Sir Herbert B.,1888, 1897, 1908, 1909, 1910, 1911

Prance, Miss, 1887

Price, Miss C.R., 1910

Pryor, Mrs,1883

Punch, Miss Catherine, 1887

Pyne, Miss, 1872

Ralli, Mrs Stephen, 1871, 1872, 1873, 1875, 1879-80, 1883, 1887

Ravenscroft, Miss, 1892

Rawlinson, Mrs, 1877,1878

Reiss, Mrs, 1876, 1877

Reiss, Mr C.A., 1888

Richardson, Miss, 1893

Richardson, Mrs, 1887

Rickett, F., 1888

Ridley, Miss, 1871

Robarts, Miss, 1875

Robarts, Mrs, 1888

Roberts, Mrs, 1900, 1901, 1902, 1903, 1905, 1908, 1909

Robins, Mr E, 1889

Robinson, Miss J., 1908

Robinson, Mr W.F., 1888

Roe, Mrs Ramsden, 1889, 1890, 1891, 1896

Roget, Miss, 1888

Roleston, Miss, 1876

Rolfe, Mrs, 1887, 1896, 1903

Rotch, Miss, 1909

Rothschild, Miss, 1874

Rowland, Miss Henrietta, 1871

Rucker, Miss, 1889

Ruskin, John, 1870, 1877, 1878

Russell, Miss,1871

Ryan, Sir Edward, 1873

S.B., 1872, 1877, 1902

S.C., 1896

S.R.D., 1879-80

Salisbury, Marchioness of, 1883

Sargant, Mrs, 1882

Sargant, Miss Alice, 1891

Scaramanga, Mrs, 1870, 1871, 1872, 1873, 1874, 1875, 1876, 1877, 1878

Schmitz, Miss, 1902

Schuster, Miss, 1902, 1904, 1908

Schuster, (Mr and) Mrs, 1895, 1898, 1899, 1901, 1902, 1903, 1904, 1906, 1907, 1908, 1909, 1910, 1911

Schuyler, Miss, 1875

Scorer, F.K., 1908

Scott, Miss, 1871, 1874

Scott, Mrs, 1884, 1908, 1909

Scott, Arthur L., 1892

Scott, Lindsay, 1893

Scrase-Dickins, General, 1907

Scrase-Dickins, Mrs, 1888, 1890, 1891, 1892, 1893

Scully, Mrs, 1897

Selborne, Countess of, 1897

Sellar, Miss, 1875

Seton-Kerr, W.S., 1875, 1876, 1888

Sewell, Miss, 1907, 1908, 1909, 1910, 1911

Shaen, Miss A.E., 1891

Shaen, Miss Lily A., 1887, 1888, 1889

Shaen, Mrs William,1874, 1875, 1876, 1878, 1879, 1881, 1882, 1884, 1885, 1887

Shaen, William, 1877, 1879, 1883

Sharp, Miss Jane, 1892, 1893

Shaw, Mrs, 1870

Sheard, Miss, 1901

Sheffield, Mrs F., 1887

Sheffield Neave, Mrs, 1870, 1871, 1872, 1874

Shiels, Miss, 1871

Shuttleworth, Miss A., 1879-80

Siemens, Mrs, 1891, 1892

Sim, Miss, 1908

Simpson, Mrs (and Miss), 1887, 1905

Urlin, Mrs Denny, 1887, 1889

Vaughan, Mr A., 1893
Vaughan, Charles, 1887
Vaughan, E.L., 1896
Vaughan, Miss F.O., 1894
Vidal, Rev. R.W., 1876

W.M., 1871
Waggett, Miss, 1871, 1872
Wagner, Henry, 1906, 1907, 1908, 1909, 1910, 1911
Walker, Mrs, 1886
Walker, Miss M.A., 1904, 1905, 1906, 1907, 1908, 1909, 1910, 1911
Wallace, Sir Richard, 1873
Wansey, Miss, 1884
Warburg, Miss Agnes, 1908
Ward, 1907
Warner, Miss Lee, 1890, 1907, 1908, 1909, 1910, 1911
Waterhouse, Mrs Leonard, 1887
Waters, the Misses, 1884
Watson, Mrs, 1872, 1887
Watts, G.F., 1875
Weardale, Lord, 1908
Webb, Miss, 1884
Webb, Mrs Randall, 1889, 1894, 1895, 1898, 1901, 1902, 1903, 1904, 1905, 1907, 1909, 1910, 1911
Wedgwood, Miss, 1907, 1908
Wells, Miss Jane, 1885, 1887, 1891
Wells, Miss Mary, 1875, 1877, 1879-80, 1881, 1884, 1885, 1886, 1887, 1888, 1890, 1891, 1892, 1893, 1894, 1895, 1896, 1897, 1898, 1899, 1900, 1901, 1902, 1903, 1904, 1905, 1906, 1907, 1908, 1909, 1910, 1911
Westbury-Milton/Westbury-Mitton/ Welbury Mitton, Mrs, 1904, 1906, 1907, 1910, 1911
Western, Mrs, 1873
Westgarth, Mr W., 1888
Westmorland, Colonel, 1894
Whately, (Mr and) Mrs Arthur, 1871, 1872, 1874, 1875, 1876, 1877, 1879, 1879-80
Whelpdale, Mrs, 1891, 1892, 1893, 1894, 1901, 1907, 1908

White, Miss C., 1872, 1876, 1879-80
White, Miss M., 1879-80
Whittaker, the late Mrs, 1871
Whittaker, Mrs, 1872, 1873, 1874
Wickenden, Miss, 1872
Wickens, Mr J., 1870, 1872
Wigan, Sir F., 1905
Wilcox, Miss, 1907
Willcox, W.H., 1905, 1908, 1909, 1910, 1911
Wilde, Miss, 1888
Wilde, Mrs, 1886
Wilkins, Mrs, 1874, 1875
Williams, Mrs, 1902
Williams, Miss C., 1876
Willington, Miss, 1878
Willink, Mr H.G., 1906
Wilson, Miss, 1874, 1879
Wilson, R.D., 1874, 1875, 1876, 1877
Wing, Miss, 1879-80
Winkworth, Stephen, 1879, 1879-80, 1881, 1882, 1883, 1884, 1885
Winkworth, Mrs Stephen, 1876, 1877, 1878, 1879, 1879-80, 1881, 1883, 1884, 1885, 1886, 1887, 1888, 1889, 1890, 1891, 1892, 1893, 1894, 1896, 1897, 1898, 1904, 1905, 1906, 1907
Winterton, Percy C., 1898
Wise, Mrs, 1887
Wood, Miss Daisy, 1908, 1909, 1910, 1911
Wood, Mr W.R., 1907, 1908, 1909
Wolmer, Lord and Lady, 1886
Wolmer, Lady Maud, 1887, 1888
Wood, Rev. Basil K., 1875, 1876
Wordsworth, Miss, 1885
Wright, Mrs Caleb, 1875, 1876, 1877, 1878, 1879, 1879-80, 1881, 1882, 1883, 1884, 1885, 1886, 1887, 1888, 1889, 1903, 1904
Wright, J. Hornsby, 1870, 1871, 1872, 1873, 1874, 1875, 1876, 1879, 1882
Wynyard, William, 1879-80

Yatman, Mrs Hamilton, 1887
Yarborough Anderson, 1908
Yorke, Miss Harriot, 1877, 1879, 1879-80, 1881, 1882, 1883, 1884, 1885, 1889, 1891, 1895, 1897, 1902, 1907, 1908, 1909

Index

This index includes references to people, places and events in the editor's introduction, the letters and the appendices. It includes significant references in the footnotes and endnotes. It does not include references in other editorial matter or in the accounts.

Abel, Frederick, 133
Agar, Miss, 595, 637, 658
Alexander, Francesca, 575
Alfred, Prince, Duke of Edinburgh, 286, 712
Alice of Hesse-Darmstadt, Princess, 87, 378-9
Allen, A.C., lvi
Allen, Mrs, lvi, 285
Anderson, Elizabeth Garrett, 65
Artisans' and Labourers' Dwellings Improvement Act (the Cross Act), 66-7, 88, 161, 737, 747
Artisans', Labourers' and General Dwellings Company, 543
Astley, Miss, 244
Ayres, Alice, 281-2, 344, 724-5

Bainbrigge, Colonel, 466, 555
Bank Holidays Act (1871) 708
Bannerman, Mrs, lvi, 472
Bannerman, Lilias, 472
Barnardo, Thomas, xxxii
Barnett, Henrietta (*née* Rowland), xxviii, liv, lv,7-8, 20, 65, 87, 132, 219, 223, 265, 664
Barnett, Samuel, xxviii, liv, lv, 7-8, 20, 23, 87, 223, 246,507, 664
Barrington, Mrs Russell, 281-2, 320, 344, 356, 717, 720, 723-7
Barter, Miss G., 285
Bedford, Duchess of, 417
Bell, Mr, 596, 622
Bennett, Cyril, 508
Benson, Edward White (Archbishop of Canterbury 1883-1896), xliv, 243, 259, 264, 738, 744, 746
Benson, Mary, 745-6
Beresford, Colonel, 659
Besant, Walter, 706

Beveridge, William, 598
Bitter Cry of Outcast London, The, xxx, 706, 737, 754 n.9
Blackwell, Elizabeth, 132
Blyth, Patrick, 317, 339, 371, 385, 399
Blyth, William, 317
Bond, Edward, lv, 745
Boord, Miss Eva, 454, 555
Booth, Charles, xxx, lvi, 502
Booth, Mary, 421
Booth, William, xxxii, 305
Brabazon, Lord, Earl of Meath, 133, 228, 710-11, 713
British Medical Association, 85
Brock, Mr and Mrs Clutton, 524, 546, 577
Brooke, Miss, 344
Brooke, Mrs Stopford, 3, 17, 85
Brooke, William Ingham, 246-7
Browning, Elizabeth Barrett, 68, 156
Browning, Robert, 68, 371-2, 499, 536-7, 601
Burdett-Coutts, Baroness, lv, 189, 362
Butler, Josephine, xxvii
Buxton, Edward North, 509

cadet corps, liv, 246-7, 262-3, 283-5, 303-4, 455, 576, 578, 596, 622-3, 638, 642
    club in Union Street, 505-8, 524;
        formation of corps in Notting Dale, 659
Canterbury, Archbishop of, *see* Benson, Edward White and Tait, Archibald Campbell
Carrick, Rev. R.M., 556
Carter, Mr and Mrs, 658
Cash, Mrs, 264, 304
Cassells, publishers, 245, 263, 356, 438, 505, 562
Casson, Elizabeth, 636, 658